THE ART
OF BEING HUMAN

Laurent de La Hire, *The Allegory of Music*, 1649 (The Metropolitan Museum of Art, Charles B. Curtis Fund, 1950)

Third Edition

THE ART
OF BEING HUMAN

THE HUMANITIES
AS A TECHNIQUE
FOR LIVING

Richard Paul Janaro
New World School of the Arts

Thelma C. Altshuler
Miami Dade Community College

1817 **HARPER & ROW, PUBLISHERS, New York**
Cambridge, Philadelphia, St. Louis, San Francisco,
London, Singapore, Sydney, Tokyo

Sponsoring Editor: Barbara Cinquegrani
Project Coordination: R. David Newcomer Associates
Interior and Cover Design: Carrington Design
Cover Art: Claude Monet's *Sunrise,* Courtesy Musée Marmottan, Paris
Photo Research: Mira Schachne
Production Manager: Jeanie Berke
Production Assistant: Paula Rappolo
Compositor: G & S Typesetters, Inc.
Printer and Binder: R. R. Donnelley & Sons Company
Cover Printer: Lehigh Press Lithographers

The Art of Being Human: The Humanities as a Technique for Living, Third Edition

Library of Congress Cataloging-in-Publication Data

Janaro, Richard Paul.
   The art of being human.

   Includes index.
   1. Conduct of life.   2. Humanities.   I. Altshuler,
Thelma C.   II. Title.
BJ1581.2.J36   1989   170'.44   88-32839
ISBN 0-06-043252-7

88 89 90 91   9 8 7 6 5 4 3 2 1

*To the memory of a
great scholar and humanitarian
whose mark is everywhere in
these pages*
DONALD M. EARLY

CONTENTS

PREFACE

This third edition to *The Art of Being Human* is, like its predecessors, an introduction to the humanities. Keeping the best features of previous editions, it is reorganized and almost completely rewritten. The focus has not changed. It is not about Western culture alone, for the humanities concern all people; nor is it a history of great names and accomplishments, which nonspecialists may find remote or threatening. The emphasis is still on what the humanities do for those who express and those who appreciate; on the interaction between the arts, religion, and philosophy; and on the humanities as an unending source of personal joy.

We have changed the structure of the book. The first half emphasizes the practitioners—the artists, musicians, writers, and philosophers who have made major contributions. The second half presents major themes in the humanities, real problems that we all know about. Aristotle, for instance, pondered the theme of happiness; Nietzsche the balance between planned order and spontaneous action; Cervantes the attraction of the ideal; other great thinkers have used their imagination to contemplate love, justice, purpose. These topics do not remain in the past but continue to affect us today.

The book urges a recognition of this continuity in the human enterprise. But matters of immediate concern—machines and film, for example—have been thought significant enough to warrant chapters of their own. In addition the tools to recognize contributions both past and present are introduced by expanding the section on critical thinking into two chapters. As in previous editions, critical thinking in everyday life is given a chapter of its own, with familiar examples showing the importance of withholding hasty judgments, of recognizing context, rejecting aimless digression. The ability to think (and to listen) critically assists students in all their classes. A separate use of critical thinking, applied to the arts, is useful particularly in humanities courses.

Toward these ends, we have added apparatus: Glossaries with key words at the end of each chapter; a very explicit overview at the beginning, outlining what is to be covered; updated examples and allusions to illustrate definitions; and an increase in the number of illustrations and reproductions found throughout the book.

The response to the first two editions has been gratifying. There have been tributes from students who claim that the textbook is "readable" and from teachers who have been pleased to find contemporary examples to illustrate important concepts. We have tried to keep the readability and the freshness without stooping to ill-advised juxtapositions in an effort to achieve "relevance." At the same time we have acted upon the suggestions of readers who have offered detailed explanations about how this or that chapter might be strengthened or which figures should be included in a new edition.

Whatever the changes, our original purpose is still here: to show the humanities as the collective expression of all who sing and share the song with us, and the collective possession of all who take time to listen. If we choose not to, our lives, alas, are that much less than they could be.

We would like to acknowledge the letters we have received and the reviews written by those who saw the manuscript in various stages of preparation: Milt Ford, Grand Valley State College; E. B. Hannen, University of Southern Alabama; David Levee, Broome Community College; Ken Marisseau, Mt. Wachusett Community College; Larry Short, Austin Community College; and Mary Ellen Young, Lakewood Community College. We would like to acknowledge three people who worked above and beyond the call of duty in the interest of obtaining art for this book: Palmira Carretero Melero, who braved the traffic in Madrid for a personal visit to The Prado, and Barbara Cinquegrani and John Callahan of Harper & Row, who had to cope with New York. Without their heroic efforts at sidestepping bureaucratic red tape and without their loving care many deadlines would have been missed. We would also like to thank Professor Joan Cronin of Miami-Dade Community College for her work on the study guide that accompanies this book. We hope the final result in some way justifies the amount of time they have so graciously given to the enterprise.

Richard Paul Janaro
Thelma C. Altshuler

CHRONOLOGICAL LIST OF NAMES

The names of those who appear in this book recur in connection with their contributions to human thought and accomplishment. We furnish the following chronological list as a helpful reminder of the order in which they were born.

Homer	9th century B.C.
Thales	640–546 B.C.
Anaximander	611–547 B.C.
Gautama	563–483 B.C.

Sophocles	496−406 B.C.
Euripides	480−460 B.C.
Socrates	469−399 B.C.
Aristophanes	448−380 B.C.
Aristippus	435−356 B.C.
Plato	427−347 B.C.
Aristotle	384−322 B.C.
Epicurus	342−270 B.C.
Augustine, St.	354−430
Epictetus	1st−2nd centuries, A.D.
Anselm, St.	1033−1109
Aquinas, St. Thomas	1225−1274
Dante Aligheri	1265−1321
Giotto de Bondone	1266−1337
Van Dyck, Jan	1370−1440
Joan of Arc	1412−1431
Leonardo da Vinci	1452−1519
Machiavelli, Niccolo	1469−1527
Copernicus, Nicholas	1473−1543
Michelangelo Buonarroti	1475−1564
Calvin, John	1509−1564
Cervantes Saavedra, Miguel de	1547−1616
Galileo Galilei	1564−1642
Shakespeare, William	1564−1616
Descartes, Rene	1596−1650
Milton, John	1608−1674
Racine, Jean	1639−1699
Newton, Sir Isaac	1642−1727
Moliere (Jean-Baptiste Poquelin)	1662−1673
Swift, Jonathan	1667−1745
Congreve, William	1670−1729
Pope, Alexander	1688−1744
Voltaire (Francois Marie Arouet)	1694−1778
Hume, David	1711−1776
Rousseau, Jean Jacques	1712−1778
Smith, Adam	1723−1790
Kant, Immanuel	1724−1804

Goya, Francisco	1746–1828
Bentham, Jeremy	1748–1832
Sheridan, Richard B.	1751–1816
Blake, William	1757–1827
Beethoven, Ludwig van	1770–1827
Hegel, Georg Wilhelm Friedrich	1770–1831
Paine, Thomas	1771–1809
Byron, George Gordon, Lord	1788–1824
Schopenhauer, Arthur	1788–1860
Shelley, Percy B.	1792–1822
Keats, John	1795–1821
Shelley, Mary Wolstonecraft Godwin	1797–1851
Emerson, Ralph Waldo	1803–1882
Hawthorne, Nathaniel	1804–1864
Mill, John Stuart	1806–1873
Darwin, Charles	1809–1882
Dickens, Charles	1812–1870
Kierkegaard, Soren	1813–1855
Thoreau, Henry David	1817–1862
Bronte, Emily	1818–1848
Marx, Karl	1818–1883
Melville, Herman	1819–1891
Queen Victoria	1819–1901
Ibsen, Henrik	1828–1906
Dickinson, Emily	1830–1886
Manet, Edouard	1832–1883
Twain, Mark (Samuel Langhorne Clemens)	1835–1910
Whistler, James McNeill	1834–1903
Peirce, Charles	1839–1914
James, William	1842–1910
Nietzsche, Friedrich	1844–1900
Edison, Thomas Alva	1847–1931
Gogh, Vincent van	1853–1890
Shaw, George Bernard	1856–1950
Veblen, Thorstein	1857–1929
Dewey, John	1859–1952
Housman, A. E.	1859–1936

Barrie, James   1860–1937
Robinson, Edwin Arlington   1869–1935
Gandhi, Mohandas K.   1869–1948
Lenin, V. I.   1870–1924
Norris, Frank   1870–
Russell, Bertrand   1872–1970
Mondrian, Piet   1872–1944
Jung, Carl   1875–1961
Frost, Robert   1875–1963
Griffith, D. W.   1875–1948
Ravel, Maurice   1875–1937
Einstein, Albert   1879–1955
Spengler, Oswald   1880–1936
Teilhard de Chardin   1881–1955
Picasso, Pablo   1881–1973
Joyce, James   1882–1941
Modigliani, Amedeo   1884–1920
Sennett, Mack   1884–1960
Lawrence, D. H.   1885–1930
Anderson, Maxwell   1888–1959
O'Neill, Eugene   1888–1953
Hitchcock, Alfred   1889–1980
Prokofiev, Serge   1891–1953
Huxley, Aldous   1894–1963
Wilder, Thornton   1897–1975
Gershwin, George   1898–1937
Hemingway, Ernest   1898–1961
Welles, Orson   1915–1985

THE ART
OF BEING HUMAN

Mary Cassatt, "Peasant Mother and Child"

INTRODUCTION: TO BE HUMAN

The humanities include the creative expressions and the creative experiences of everyone who belongs to the human species. It is, of course, possible to be human without writing a song or singing to yourself as you walk through the woods, but people who avoid creativity, either as generators or appreciators, derive less from their span of time upon this earth. That is the whole premise behind this book. One can be casually, even *randomly*, human—living, behaving, doing what has to be done day after day, earning enough to survive or earning more than one might ever really need, but never expressing, never hearing or seeing what does not *have* to be there to be seen or heard;

1

or one can decide one's life will be a work of art. The choice is there, whether one comes from a privileged background or has to struggle to make ends meet. The humanities do not exist to be appreciated just by the privileged few.

The humanities are what humankind does with its "leftover" humanness. After the wheel has been invented and the subatomic particles made to release their awesome energy (for good or ill); after we have learned to build shelters and bridges and mountain tunnels and we know how to pay the rent, we eventually have to come home and, dinner having been eaten, think about what else we are here for. Some never do that, and maybe they are a little bored with their lives without quite knowing why.

The Man with No Time for Beauty

Once there lived a man about whom no one could find much to complain. He had been a devoted husband for 40 years, had sired two sons who grew up to be modestly rich and successful, paid off his mortgage, and had never received a traffic ticket. In short, not one breath of scandal ever came near this man—a neighbor all could wish for, exemplary in every respect. Except one. His life was essentially dull. It never caught fire.

By the time this man—call him Woodrow Tatlock—got around to facing the dullness of his life, he had long since become frozen in his ways. His political views had not changed substantially in years. He lacked all capacity for opening himself up to new experiences, even to making new friends. Whenever he traveled, he returned as absolutely the same man, or perhaps a trifle more apt to agree with Ralph Waldo Emerson that traveling is a fool's paradise. He spent his declining years without his wife, who was not "supposed" to die before him; all he did was fish, but even this activity was carried on without zest. He made regular visits to his physician, out of habit, and took whatever pills were prescribed, without being able to say just why it was important for him to be alive.

Mr. Tatlock, of course, had no motivation for changing. He lived among people who could not define what was missing from their lives, if indeed the need to do so ever crossed their minds. He lived among people who accepted the fact that on Sunday afternoons, after the football season was over, one was supposed to sit around and wonder *what* to do; they hadn't opened a book in years, or attended a concert or art gallery, and couldn't even start an interesting conversation with each other.

There is no official name for what might be, after all, the most important skill anyone can acquire. But we all know what it is—we talk about it all the time. Sometimes we just call it living. We may say of a person, "He has a great deal of money, but does he really know how to live?" or "She died without ever having lived."

We can say, "He (or she) doesn't know how to live," of just about everyone, even a president of the United States, an actress whose permanent address is Paris, or the person who scoops out ice cream at a corner stand. We can say the opposite of someone who never earned an enormous salary, or of someone who did. To have life—to breathe, to have a heartbeat, to have operating senses, to possess motor skills—is not what constitutes living; nor is living a matter of having wealth, fame, or good fortune. Living is more than a skill: it is an art. It is not inborn, but the art is not necessarily taught, either. At some point it is acquired.

At some point you know that you are living more effectively or less effectively. No amount of rationalizing, no amount of taking inventory of your possessions, degrees, powers, and friends can convince you that you are living effectively if inwardly you do not believe it. Mr. Tatlock was never defensive about his life. He never defended his way of being in the world any more than he consciously sought to make it better. He never knew that something was wrong. Only someone who had once had more and then was deprived of it could have known that something was wrong.

Though this nation possesses many fine symphony orchestras, museums, playhouses, and galleries, and though the United States has contributed its share of writers, poets, and artists to the mainstream of Western civilization, ours is not a society in which the humanities are paid special homage. Only a very small portion of our gross national product goes to the humanities. Traditionally, we have discouraged those who pursue a career in the humanities. "You want to be a *what?*" is the usual question exploded at the artist-to-be, followed by the inevitable "How do you expect to make a living?" Any use of the term *living* that does not specifically include a means of livelihood and a ballpark *amount* of livelihood is incomprehensible.

Like his neighbors, Mr. Tatlock was accustomed to the strictly economic sense of the word *living.* He was conditioned to think of the verb *do* as something one was paid for. If we were to ask what Mr. Tatlock did in terms of being in the world, he would probably not even have answered, "I like to fish." Prior to his farewell lunch, after 37 years in the hardware company, he would surely have said, "I am an assistant manager." After the luncheon, he would just as surely have replied, "I *was* an assistant manager," and refer often to his former occupation even in conversations about other topics. His title was his identity. Now that he was retired, it seemed sad to say, "I don't do anything anymore."

To be able to fill leisure intelligently is the last product of civilization.

Arnold Toynbee

Like so many others, Mr. Tatlock cast a wistful eye back to his days of employment but retained also a secret and nagging feeling of insecurity about himself and his relative lack of accomplishment. That is why Mr. Tatlock admired the people who "made good." Stories of poor people who struck it rich in the state lottery filled him with as much awe as a lover of the humanities feels in the actual presence of Michelangelo's *David.* Mr. Tatlock was in awe of success, and the only way he knew of measuring success was an economic one. What he wished was not that he had taken time to fill his life with beauty, but that he could boast of having made a higher salary.

In our culture we say of men and women: "What are they worth?" This is a fiscal question. So is "What have they done with their lives?" From the moment we are born we accumulate *equity,* and woe to the wretch who attains the age of 65 and has *nothing*—meaning bank accounts, property, stocks, and a respectable collection of durable goods.

We live in an economic context. This in itself is not disastrous—we have to live somewhere, we have to eat, we need clothes. We also see no reason not to hope for certain luxuries. Few set out in life with the deliberate goal of just barely getting by. On all sides we are urged to consume. You can't be a consumer unless you have money with which to purchase goods.

The trouble is that we spend a great deal of time thinking about how we are going to get *enough* money. There never seems to be enough no matter how wealthy we become. Because money buys goods and everyone tries to make as much money as possible, there aren't enough goods to go around. In fact, if this were going to be a book about economics, we would begin by saying that the law of life—that is, our economic life—is scarcity. Our material wants are insatiable, but the resources to satisfy those wants are limited. Consequently, most people never have as much as they would like. Like Mr. Tatlock, they go around secretly feeling their *un*worth.

If only Mr. Tatlock had learned the truth! He assumed that only a scarce resource can matter; but the humanities have a far different story to tell. The economics of humanities is based on the principle that the resources of art, music, drama, dance, opera, architecture, philosophy, and religion—not to mention science itself as a representative example of what the searching human mind can discover—that these resources are infinite and inexhaustible, like the energy which drives the very universe we inhabit. Unlike the desire for durable and consumable goods, however, the creative wants of the average person are less insatiable than they have to be. In fact, if the situation were reversed, if the average person couldn't have enough theater or visits to art galleries but was quickly bored with new cars and clothes and delicious but unnecessary foods, the entire economic network of society would soon collapse.

The premise behind this book is hardly that our material wants are unimportant and should remain unsatisfied. It is, rather, that other options are open to us. Suppose that someone had every possible luxury money could buy and had no further need to earn a living. What then? What if that person were like Mr. Tatlock and had no use for all that leisure? Would the long upward struggle seem to have been worth it? How would that person measure "success"?

A few years ago, while Mrs. Tatlock was still alive, her husband was lying in bed one night, eyes wide open, perspiration glistening on his forehead. In soothing tones she tried to make him relax, but alas, all he could do was mutter a litany of the tasks he had to complete the next day at the store. "Forget it, my dear," she whispered. "Think of something else." He stared at her for a few moments, and then finally whispered back: "I have no other thoughts."

THE HUMANITIES— AN ETERNAL QUEST FOR FORM

If we had to find one word that best links all of the humanities, one word that unites those who create and those who enjoy their creations, one word that truly distinguishes humankind from all other species—at least as far as we know—that word would be *form*. Humanity is a form-seeking, form-making species.

At heart, nature may have form as its ultimate secret. Certainly, much evidence exists in both theoretical and laboratory science to suggest that nature aspires to uniformity and simplicity in the operation of its laws. It may well be that the human quest for form is a working out in human terms of what is going on way down where the tiniest particles break apart and make new combinations. On the other hand, we have yet to prove that there is a principle of complete uniformity in nature—what physicists call the *Grand Unification Theory*. There may be more chaos than we want to find. What matters to the study of the humanities, however, is that human beings have the *need* to discover uniformity, organization, *togetherness* in the world out there and the world inside. "Getting it together" has become the anthem of our time.

Form, in one sense, exists in the rest of the animal kingdom. We know about ant hills and beehives—models of organization, of time and motion efficiency. But the difference between ants and people is that ants appear limited to formal principles that are instinctive, that are passed down from one generation to another, changing only very slowly, with adaptive processes directing the show. Human beings are capable of colossal disorder, because *they are always try-*

ing out new forms. Sometimes the new ones work, sometimes they don't. Humankind can be characterized by its staggering capacity to make mistakes. No other species could foul up so many things, so royally, and survive for so long.

Indeed, we get a clue to what it's all about from the fact that most of the world's great dramas are tragedies: that is, plays about human blindness, stupidity, and crashing error. Many of the rest are great comedies, again dealing with human blindness, stupidity, and error. There would *be* no drama if we were as efficient as the bees. If we had not developed the potential to put ourselves out of existence, *we would probably not have achieved as much as we have.* There appears to be no ant version of Shakespeare. When would they have time?

To create form out of formlessness—to destroy forms that hinder change and create new formlessness, out of which emerge new forms—that is the human process. The humanities are, above all else, a record of that process.

There is indeed a structure of order in the universe, far more magnificent than any structure that could be built of stone or glass and steel, and our civilization has discovered ways of codifying this structure. These human codes, these ways of making sense out of the seeming chaos of existence, must stand among the noblest accomplishments of the human race. Take, for example, the periodic table of the elements, which gives a strict and beautiful order to all matter, arranging the chemical elements in octaves similar to those of music.

George Leonard

What *is* form? To understand the phenomenon—indeed, to understand the rest of this book—we need a very broad definition. Obviously, *form* means more than a shape of some kind. A sculpture has a definite three-dimensional shape, but the form in Michelangelo's *David* is not the shape of the statue. It is the way Michelangelo has arranged all of his elements—marble, height, width, his craft, and his own *feelings* about his subject—into a whole that would not have existed if he had not brought it into being. But now, all arrangements of elements possess form in this sense. Form—artistic form—is *the rightness of an arrangement,* perceivable not to the eye of the beholder, as the popular if confusing saying would have it, but to an inner, sometimes called *esthetic,* sense.

Defining this sense and explaining where it comes from are difficult tasks. (Some philosophers have spent their lives trying to uncover the secret.) Analogies help us to come close. What is there inside that tells us we have regained our health after a long illness? What is it that happens when the depression we haven't been able to explain suddenly lifts like predawn fog? Or when we have forgiven ourselves for some long-forgotten transgression and see the world in a very different way: there is a tiny bird perched on the windowsill; the sun is warm and friendly; from down the street comes the reassuring purr of somebody's lawn mower. Who does not know what it is like to sink back into the pillow and just lie there, feeling good?

Inner rightness is by definition extremely personal. No one can tell you to feel good about life if you don't, nor has the cynic any right to insist that you be depressed about life if you don't choose to be. The issue becomes complicated, however, when Woodrow Tatlock visits the Academy in Florence and announces that *David* is an overrated piece of stone.

The recognition of astonishing form in *David* is so widespread that it can be deemed fundamental or traditional in our culture. If Woodrow's put-down is allowed to pass unchallenged, then we are really saying that artistic standards are meaningless. Few people with wide exposure to works in the humanities would be willing to go this far.

We are not discussing verdicts about music, paintings, novels, or buildings that vary from age to age. Antonio Salieri, now considered a minor Italian composer of the late eighteenth century, was in his time held in higher esteem than Mozart, his contemporary. Melville died believing his novel *Moby-Dick* had been a colossal failure; but now it has taken its place among the great novels of the world. Critical reexamination of the past goes on all the time in an effort to maintain, but not destroy, artistic standards.

True, the esthetic values of one culture may appear strange to another. Westerners who have never seen Japanese Kabuki players may shake their heads at the stilted movements, the unrealistic pitch of voices, and the monotonous twanging of unfamiliar musical instruments. But the Kabuki is dramatic form of the highest order to Japanese theatergoers of taste and discernment.

There are whole traditions of form in art which constitute the heritage of a given culture. Critical agreements about these forms exist in African culture as well as in Hindu or European cultures. Their artistic forms give each people a continuity, a hold on the earth. People have learned to establish formal standards even as they have developed technology.

If *form* is defined as the rightness of an arrangement, the motive behind our quest for form is *our need for completeness.* Without our forms we would be inhabitants of a lonely wasteland, with only nature's forms for companions. Nature can be very beautiful indeed, but nature is not art. This is not an insult to nature, nor is it an insult to humanity to say that people could never have created the Grand Canyon. We are talking about two separate realms. Nature is never finished. The artist reaches the end of something—a sequence of musical notes or a play. Maybe the urge to completeness has something to do with the fact that we as part of nature are never finished changing. Our treasured forms are things that can stay put. The painter just knows when the last brush stroke has been applied.

Much of esthetic tradition is concerned with forms that can be repeated. That seems to be their point. An obvious example is the folk song which is so familiar that everyone immediately begins to sing without conscious effort. Is the pleasure of singing "Fee fi fiddley ei o" to be found in the deeply meaningful, poetic words, or the group togetherness the song engenders? Human relationships are hardly models of completeness, but they can be temporarily so when people sing as one.

For most of us in the West, having tea or coffee with friends is a casual amenity. We seldom think about the beverage or the act of drinking it. In Japan, however, being invited for tea means being invited for a total ritual. It is the same as if *we* were to invite a Japanese friend to a concert or ballet. Dressing up, going to the theater, mingling in the lobby, experiencing the performance—all the components are important.

Everything about the tea ceremony—from the initial sound of water boiling to the removal of the tea service—is performed with style and grace and, above all, in relative silence. Communication is limited to making known minimal needs and, when possible, is carried on through brief gestures. The participants become acutely conscious of the look and feel of the cups, the sound made by the tea's being poured, the color of it and its pungent aroma. There is almost always a floral arrangement in the center of the table, representing yet another Japanese art of a very high order.

The Japanese tea ceremony is a beautiful example of how some humans like to put form even in places where none seems the least bit necessary.

In Japan, as in other Asian countries, all human relationships aspire to the level of form. There are prescribed ways of greeting strangers, friends, and family members. The word *honorable* is added to commonly employed terms like *dinner, company* and *grandfather.* The suffix *san* is added to all proper names and, though usually translated as *Mr.* or *Ms.,* it is a verbal symbol of respect for which the West has no real equivalent. Western visitors returning from Japan remark on the politeness of the people. But the formalism of Japanese everyday customs goes beyond politeness. It is the art of being human, practiced daily.

Human artistic forms, then, can occur in everyday social customs; but most of the time we are dealing with forms created by human beings we call artists out of their inner need to do something that seems complete. Once it is created, the work of art is *its own reason for being.* If it is a novel or a play, it may have what we like to call *meaning* or *significance.* It may even bring about some important social change. *Uncle Tom's Cabin* contributed mightily to a national awareness of slavery and its evils. Its meaningfulness has no doubt given the novel a place in our literary history. But meaning alone is seldom enough. Literary historians give credit to *Uncle Tom's Cabin* for its moral intentions, but few regard the book as one of our literary masterpieces. Michelangelo's *David* has also been "interpreted." The Biblical David was a small boy compared to the giant Goliath, even as Michelangelo's Florence was tiny in power and prestige when compared to Rome, the world center of art and culture, not to mention the mighty empire of Catholicism. Was Michelangelo prophesying that the underdog would eventually triumph? We do not know, nor does any affirmative answer to the question explain what is great about the statue.

Human beings create lines of continuity using their artistic forms. We call these *cultures.* To say of people that they lack culture is to say that they have managed to remain outside the continuity to which they are entitled. It is sad but true that many wish to be only of their time. They grow up listening to certain musical styles. They adapt their esthetic needs to these styles and see no reason to discover any others. What they are doing is paradoxical. They want to immerse themselves in the present in order to live to the fullest, yet by denying themselves the unlimited resources of the humanities, they derive so much less from life than they might.

Another paradox is that many people resist the humanities because they like themselves the way they are and resent efforts at change. This fundamental conservatism is itself an expression of the human need for completeness and permanence which is responsible for human art in the first place. The difference is that completeness won at the expense of exploring new possibilities of form represents a tragic waste of human potential.

The great artists reach moments of completeness only after much restlessness and, as we said earlier, discontent. Never to be discontented with your life is to miss out on those exhilarating times which come after struggle. Always to stay secure in the knowledge that you are right is to miss out on a possible victory. You cannot win if you don't enter the game. Contemporary artists are both artists and contemporaries because the arrangements of the past do not satisfy them. They see other forms in their minds. In a sense they are doing nature's work on the human level: moving forward, changing, tearing down, building up. The study of the humanities does not teach us to kneel reverentially before the past and look with despair upon the present. It shows us the dance of forms and invites us to join in.

The art of being human is the art of finding within oneself the capacity to love and cherish the forms that are there for us as our cultural heritage; to applaud and seek to understand the new forms that aspire to become part of that heritage; and to explore the unending possibilities of joy that we can experience when we step beyond the safe limits of the familiar and wander through the forms that stand on distant shores, created by persons different from ourselves except in the one important respect that all of us are human beings.

The art of being human is to live many times over by entering the minds and hearts of others through holding in our hands the forms they have made for us, and perhaps even determining to say thanks by one day giving back the forms we ourselves create.

GLOSSARY

artist: The human being who is able to create forms that discerning persons perceive as esthetically right. This perception does not always coincide with the creation. It may not even occur during the artist's lifetime. Sometimes critical acclaim is strong during that lifetime but diminishes during the reevaluation of later periods.

culture: The cumulative customs, traditions, and forms of art cherished by a group of people united by common ethnic background or geography. The term is also, but not advisedly, used to mean the sophistication some people develop after long exposure to the arts.

form: (A key term throughout this book.) The quality which distinguishes a work of art from other attempts to achieve the status of art. The arrangement whose elements become a totality that strikes the esthetic sense as being right. Often most understood by its absence.

humanities: The cumulative artistic and intellectual achievements of humanity, as well as the experience of those who appreciate but do not create. In a secondary sense, a study of those achievements and the critical process by which they can best be appreciated. In other words, a body of work *and* an academic discipline devoted to an appreciation of it.

philosopher: The human being who pursues complex thoughts when there is no direct or practical need to do so. The cumulative body of philosophical ideas is sometimes referred to, generically, as *wisdom,* but this term can be confusing if it excludes scientific thought. The dividing line between the philosopher and the scientist is often thin indeed. The latter is not always concerned with laboratory proofs, while the former may consider that the questions he or she asks—such as "What is everything made of?" asked by early Greek thinkers—are quite scientific. Intellectual inquiry is philosophical when no possibility of *immediate* verification exists or when verification is beside the point, such as in asking the question "What is the good life?"

The reader may wonder why philosophy belongs in the humanities or what relationship the philosopher has to the artist. Philosophical arguments possess form when conclusions spring rightfully from an integrated sequence of thinking *whether we accept those conclusions or not.* The test of a great philosopher is not whether his or her ideas are "true" or even how many people are in some way affected by them, but whether they represent the marvelous workings of a great mind. In this sense the great philosophical systems are beautiful in precisely the way that Michelangelo's *David* is beautiful.

Our ultimate reward in studying the arts and philosophy is that we become adept at *sharing* the great esthetic and intellectual experiences. We learn to use the human-ness which is our birthright. We thus become more powerful representatives of our species, putting to much better use the time we have on this earth.

A more practical reason is that immersing ourselves in the humanities means we not only develop an appreciation of form, but inevitably introduce form into the conduct of our own lives. We think more clearly, and we are in closer touch with our feelings. We know better who we are. To do this is to make of living a day-by-day work of art.

Pablo Picasso, "Guernica"
(Prado Museum. Giraudon, Art Resource)

1

THE WAY OF THE ARTIST

I have wanted to give the impression of a way of life quite different from that of us civilized people. Therefore I am not at all anxious for everyone to like it or to admire it at once.

Vincent van Gogh, to his brother, Theo,
in reference to The Potato Eaters

Do you think I know what art is? Do you think I'd think anybody knew, even if they said they did? Do you think I'd care what anybody thought? Now if you ask me what we're trying to do that's a different thing.

Georgia O'Keeffe

Learn by heart the forms to be found in nature, so that
you can use them like the notes in a musical composition.
That is what these forms are for. Nature is a marvellous
chaos, and it is our job and our duty to bring order into
that chaos and—to perfect it.

Max Beckmann

Art is what the artist does.

Robert Thiele

Overview

The people quoted above are all artists, and their sentiments allow for
a wide range of definitions on the subject of art. Note, however, that
only one—the last artist cited—makes a direct definition *statement;*
and note that this statement seems deliberately, almost coyly, to be
begging the question. But that, we might as well recognize, is the right
of artists, who take it anyway, so why resist? They are never going to
come clean and tell us what *really* goes on in their minds—why one
artist insists on stretching an enormous curtain from one mountain to
another in Colorado and audaciously calling it art; why another spends
months working on a sculpture he calls *Giant Ice Bag,* which looks
like nothing else but a—giant ice bag!

The most precise and memorable definitions of art usually
come from those who teach but do not create art. This pattern is
hardly unique; we seldom find composers clearly defining music or
poets stating categorically that "a poem is . . ." Most creators—not
just those in the visual arts—seem to shy away from analysis, interpretation, and in some extreme cases, even praise. Artists either know
(like Michelangelo) that they are titans and will be remembered for all
time, or else they find (like van Gogh) that the question of fame is a
matter of indifference to them. Artists who have completely revolu-
tionized the form and scope of art (like Picasso) may nod politely in
the direction of public taste, but in their hearts they know the public
is going to have to catch up with what they are doing—and will
someday be able to appreciate their work, however critics choose to
define it.

The reader who prefers precise definitions of art can find
them in any number of excellent sources, sources that present a
chronological survey of the visual arts in their historical contexts.
Since the present text aims at offering insights into the utilization of

the humanities as a means of enhancing the quality of life, we are less concerned with defining what art *is* (for to do that would indeed require a vast historical approach that is beyond our scope and intent) than with suggesting by way of representative examples what art is capable of *doing.* In this context Leonardo da Vinci and Georgia O'Keeffe are not so far from each other. The former is Renaissance, the latter contemporary, true; but both will survive, both will still be around a century from now—not because they fit certain definitions, but because what they left behind is still functioning to make human existence a happier thing.

Regrettably, many people avoid museums and galleries because they remember sterile classroom environments, stale memorized lists, and boring true-false tests. If the visual arts are to be living and vital components of our personal worlds, then we must first establish a true link between ourselves and the artists. What aspect of humanness do we and the artists share? Each of us must ask: What is there in *me* that can best relate to what is hanging over there on that wall or towering above me on the Sistine Chapel ceiling? If we do not begin here, we shall go through life with the uneasy feeling that the people who sign their names in the lower right-hand corner are just plain different from us: strangers as silent as the marble halls of the museums.

Many people avoid museums and galleries because they remember sterile classroom environments, memorized lists, and true-false tests.

IMITATION:
THE UNDERLYING FACTOR

Long ago Aristotle attempted to analyze the nature and purpose of almost every phenomenon he considered crucial to human existence. For all we know, he may have commented on all of the arts practiced in his time; but his observations on drama at least have survived. In fact, he has given us a definition which ranks among the most influential of all definitions, one with which nearly every college student in liberal arts has become familiar. The opening words are what interest us in this chapter: "Drama is the imitation of an action." These words can be puzzling when related to the Greek theater of Aristotle's time, in which actors walked on stilts, wore masks, and spoke in unnatural, declamatory tones. The classical Greek tragedies are all about violent deaths, yet the deaths are only talked about, never shown on stage. What, we might ask, were the Greeks imitating?

Aristotle's exact word was *mimesis,* which resembles our words *mime* and *pantomime.* We can better understand what the philosopher meant by imitation if we think of mimes we have seen:

Honoré Daumier, "The Fifth Act in the 'Gaité'," 1848
(The Granger Collection)

faces whitened with clown-white makeup; eyes made larger and more expressive with eye liner; their pretending to walk great distances while actually walking in place; their pretending to lean against an invisible mantle or pressing their hands against a wall that is not there. Mimes make us laugh because we believe they are really in danger of falling from a high wire, even though their feet are planted solidly on the floor. Mimes identify familiar actions, otherwise most of the time we would not know what they are doing; but occasionally we really have to watch closely because they get *inside* human behavior instead of showing it from the *outside*. Nevertheless, they are still imitating.

    Our visual artists are also imitators, even though they sometimes show us things we have not seen before. It is possible for artists to imitate what they have seen in their imaginations.

The Act of Imitating
Can Be an End in Itself

The question asked most often in galleries that display contemporary, nonrealistic art is, of course, "What does it mean?" Almost no one voices that question about a landscape painting, even if it is a faithful drawing of an ant hill. One might ask, "Why would anyone draw that?" but never wonder what is *meant.* The precise replication of an object or face is always, we understand, its own meaning, though the artist may have intended that we draw some inferences from what has been imitated. Turn to page 440 and look at the painting of "The Lackawanna Valley" by the American landscape artist George Inness (1825–1894). One may simply accept the work as it is, enjoying the lines, the sense of perspective, and the evocation of a simpler time when only one or two factories marred an otherwise lovely area. Or one may suppose the artist was making an environmental statement, one that has steadily gained in relevance to us. Or one may agree with critics of Inness, who point out that he was an artist who had no trouble accepting a natural world that was being reshaped by human hands. The point is that, to enjoy the work, one doesn't have to think any of the above thoughts.

If Aristotle is correct when he says that the "instinct of imitation is implanted" in us from childhood and that "through imitation" we learn our "earliest lessons," then we must conclude that the need to imitate is like the need to learn the name of everything. It may be even *more* fundamental. Youngsters blabber all day long before they have any idea of what they can use their voices for. They are imitating the noises made by the big people who are always picking them up and making gurgling sounds. Walt Whitman once captured the universal experience of the small child:

> *There was a child went forth every day,*
> *And the first object he look'd upon, that object he became,*
> *And that object became part of him for the day or a certain*
>   *part of the day,*
> *Or for many years or stretching cycles of years.*

Like all artists, children love to mimic, either directly from their surroundings or from their busy interior worlds, which are made up of new things composed of little bits of old things.

Aristotle added that imitation is pleasurable to us:

> Objects which in themselves we view with pain, we delight to contemplate when reproduced with minute fidelity: such as forms of the most ignoble animals and of dead bodies.

Perhaps when we are all children *and* artists, we also enjoy the sense of control over our surroundings—especially the scary parts—that *mimesis* makes possible. After all, to the child the world outside is enormous and hovering. And what should we say of the crazy, noisy, kaleidoscopic inside world? May not the act of imitating those worlds be said to enhance the feeling we so desperately need that we exist on equal terms with them?

As the visual artist matures, he or she probably never loses the child's love of imitation, of recreating things seen or imagined: colors vividly felt, shapes that excite, the look on a face that probably no one else noticed. And because our artists have the ability to capture, to *freeze* moments that the rest of us may have overlooked, they have cumulatively built a world of shapes and colors every bit as real as the so-called "natural" world, one that—even better—does not deteriorate with age.

It Begins with Seeing

The act of imitating involves, as we have said, exaggeration, reformulation, even reproducing what is inside our heads, unseen by anybody else. But the most universal form of *mimesis* in the visual arts is the instinct to draw what is there before us. Even at a very early age some people seem to be able to do just that with little effort. They look at a face, and before you know it, they have transferred it to a flat surface. Most of us recall, however, what happened when our kindergarten teachers asked us to draw our houses. We made the generic drawn house, just as we made a stick figure to represent a person. We made the *symbol* of a house, because it was easier to do that than to try to reproduce the actual thing. We made the symbol of a face, the symbol of a person. Most of us don't imitate anymore because we don't see. The artist paints a sun that has radiance, depth, and color shadings. The rest of us paint something like this:

which could just as easily be a porcupine peeking from behind a fence.

In recent years there has arisen a totally new school of thinking about artistic talent. This new way of thinking is an offshoot of medical research into what is called *hemispheric asymmetry.* As everyone knows, just like a globe of the earth, the brain is divided into two hemispheres. The brain's hemispheres, which are separated as well as connected by an intricate network of nerve fibers, the *corpus callosum,* really make up two complete brains, right and left, one acting as a backup to the other, in the same way that a commercial aircraft has a chief and a backup pilot. In the case of a severe cerebral accident to either brain, the other can get the whole job done, given sufficient rehabilitation time. Rehabilitation in this case means the transference of functions from one brain to the other. Patients who do not recover all of their functions after a stroke, for example, have suffered damage to both sides.

But now the question is: What does a normal person do with two brains? The new research hypothesizes that, over the thousands of years during which the human brain has been developing, the two hemispheres have each come up with their own individual specialties. In other words, while either one can be the entire brain, if necessary, both hemispheres in the normal person work together, each contributing something the other lacks. Thus the phrase *hemispheric asymmetry* means having two halves that are *not* the same.

The left hemisphere seems to handle abstractions, concepts, and all forms of symbolism, including language. The right hemisphere seems to specialize in intuition and creativity—whatever cannot be verbalized.

Exponents of this new school of thinking point out that we have developed into a left-brain–dominated society. The dominant hemisphere controls the reverse side of the body. Thus most of us are right-handed and use our right foot to start walking or running. There are also the unfavorable connotations of the word *left,* going back to the origin of the word *sinister* from the Latin word for *left side.* Also, *right* sounds *correct* or true.

Betty Edwards, a California art teacher, has produced some extraordinary results after convincing beginning students that anyone can draw who can see. She has detailed these in a book called *Drawing on the Right Side of the Brain.*[1] Edwards believes that those who say they have no artistic ability do so because they *see* with their left brains. They abstract from their familiar surroundings. Hence, if asked to draw a quick picture of a man driving a car, invariably they produce a stick figure. Is this *all* they can do? Edwards's answer is that stick figures are symbolic of human beings and therefore controlled by the left brain.

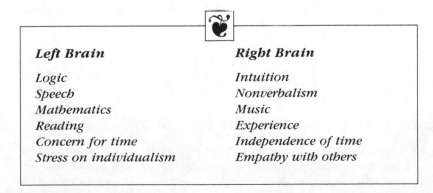

Left Brain	Right Brain
Logic	Intuition
Speech	Nonverbalism
Mathematics	Music
Reading	Experience
Concern for time	Independence of time
Stress on individualism	Empathy with others

When, however, the left brain is not allowed to interfere, the nonverbal right brain—or what Edwards has labeled the "R-mode of consciousness"—takes over. But how to block off the interference? We can alter the stimuli to which the left brain responds with its customary abstraction. For example, if we wish to imitate a painting or photograph done by someone else, we might turn it upside down and draw what we see. The new stimulus will be strange and unfamiliar, forcing us to see rather than to abstract. If we cannot readily identify the stimulus, we must reproduce it completely rather than symbolically. Symbolic seeing involves the exclusion of details, a cumulative process which separates us further and further from reality the older we become.

Another trick is to draw—that is, imitate—*negative space,* the space which surrounds an object, which gives it spatial identity. Normally we don't see negative space. In concentrating on negative space, rather than on the object it surrounds, we are again responding to an unfamiliar stimulus. Portrait painters sometimes squint in the direction of their models, placing them in noncustomary spatial surroundings: that is, *isolating* them, in order to break up the dense reality we *think* we are looking at. This technique is the opposite of focusing on negative space. But both approaches represent the R-mode of seeing.

> Now open your eyes and focus on whatever you observed before—that plant or leaf or dandelion. Look it in the eye, until you feel it looking back at you. Feel that you are alone with it on Earth! That it is the most important thing in the universe, that it contains all the riddles of life and death. It does! You are no longer looking, you are seeing.
>
> Frederick Franck

Just as in music we must learn to like silence and solitude before we can appreciate musical sound, so in art we must take the time to walk in silence and look at whatever is there to be seen—without preconception; turning off the left brain with its symbols; looking without prior knowledge of the subject or a prior commitment to accept, reject, or be indifferent. Perhaps then, the urge to imitate—often called artistic ability—will manifest itself.

Earliest Art—A Need for Imitation?

We have known for a long time about art and the cave dwellers, and it has been assumed that the Michelangelos of 17,000 years ago believed in the magical properties of their peculiar skills. Drawing an animal on

Female Bison and Head of Black Bull (?), cave drawing at Altamira, Spain (Courtesy Department Library Services, American Museum of Natural History)

the wall of the cave made one more successful in the hunt. Cave artists, it was believed, thought their drawings could manipulate reality. Speculators could not imagine that cave people were anything but pragmatic, down to earth, interested only in survival.

In 1940 a group of young boys in southwestern France accidentally fell into what is now known as the great cave at Lascaux. Since then archeologists and art historians have declared the spot to be an astonishing museum of Paleolithic art. As we might expect, there are wall paintings of many animals, including deer, horses, and cattle. Recent findings also include animal bones, enabling excavators to determine the kind of meat actually consumed by these early people. A surprising discovery sheds much light not only on Paleolithic art, but on the nature of the basic imitative impulse. Analysis of bone suggests that the artists of Lascaux were partial to the meat of young reindeer, but this may have been less a matter of gastronomic preference than of what game was available. It is of interest in this connection to note that only one of the animal paintings at Lascaux depicts a reindeer.[1] Facts such as this help to emphasize the hazards facing those who seek to speculate about the "why" of Paleolithic painting.

Further explorations of the cave have uncovered more than 15,000 engravings on almost every conceivable wall surface—surely an indication that the cave artists were concerned about the art of imitation itself, though they may have lacked the terminology or philosophy of their craft. (On the other hand, we should not *assume,* from our lofty, "civilized" vantage point, that they did!)

The explosion of the artistic urge at Lascaux seems almost certain proof that the desire, the *need,* to imitate what is seen, pre-

The explosion of the artistic urge at Lascaux seems almost a certain proof that the desire, the need, to imitate what is seen predates the emergence of formal language

dates the emergence of formal language. It may be associated with the desire to belong more solidly, to gain a secure foothold wherever one may be. Or maybe, even at that far distant time, artists were showing their feelings about things by drawing them. The ancient need also appears to tell us that direct imitation from nature was the first trend in art. That these early engravings are not realistic, in the same way that a Dutch landscape painting of the seventeenth century is realistic, may only indicate that early artists lacked the technique of direct imitation, not that they were *trying* for symbolism.

Perspective: The Coming of Realism

Greek and Roman artists specialized in sculpture—both the three-dimensional kind, standing free on all sides, and *bas-reliefs* (figures that project slightly from their background, as on the façades of their great buildings). Many of the figures they produced from stone were meant to represent the gods. Since no artists, as far as we know, ever saw one of the inhabitants of Mount Olympus, they imitated the human body in idealized form. They did the same when their subjects

Giotto, "Meeting at the Golden Gate"
(Courtesy of Museo Civico de Padova)

Raphael, "The Alba Madonna," 1510
(Courtesy of the National Gallery of Art, Andrew W. Mellon Collection)

were ordinary mortals. That is, the stone figures look too perfect to have represented actual people. When one studies classical art, one keeps running into terms like *ideal* and *idealized.* You will not find the term *realistic.*

The Greeks and Romans were not naturalists either. They did not believe in letting the world remain as they found it. They can be called the inventors of *civilization* as we understand the term. They preferred theaters to trees, debate to conservation. They were in awe of the human mind, not the rainbow. Small wonder that their *mimesis* was not direct imitation of nature. In a sense, Greek and Roman artists must have believed they were improving on nature. Show me a dog, said the Greek artist, and I will recreate him in stone; I will immortalize him. Stone lasts forever. Nothing in nature does.

During the Middle Ages artists attempted flat-surface, or two-dimensional, art. Its purpose was to help the devout visualize the holy figures: God, Christ, the Virgin Mary, the saints, and the angels. Unlike classical artists, however, those of the medieval period did not start from nature and idealize it. They created from their imaginations. But early medieval two-dimensional art is almost childlike in appearance. The Madonna's face is too small, a golden halo stuck to rather than floating over her head. The child in her arms usually has a man's face, and no part of the body has the right proportion. Nothing moves or breathes in early medieval painting. Colors are bold and distinct, figures sharply separated from each other, as they are definitely not in reality. By the fifteenth century we are coming into the Renaissance, which is often taught as being the time when Western civilization rediscovered the earth and its wonders and when artists wanted to paint what they saw as *exactly,* as faithfully as possible.

We are sometimes told that medieval artists were "otherworld"-oriented and thus had no reason to reproduce earthly appearances. But even if their aim were solely to imitate what they imagined holy figures to look like, why would they not desire them to appear three-dimensional? The explanation is probably that they lacked a sophisticated technique for making a flat surface look as if it had depth. In other words, there is no reason to believe medieval artists did not wish to be convincing, even in their imaginative flights. There is no reason to believe all of the artists imagined identically flat, childlike images. The world of two-dimensional art needed a new method that would tolerate the imitative impulse.

The sense of perspective lacking in flat-surface art became an exciting new technique for Italian artists in the early Renaissance. It is one thing to paint or draw real-looking figures, but quite another to correctly size them relative to each other and to a background which approximates what the eye sees when it looks at the real world. The artist who pioneered in creating the sense of depth is Giotto (1266–1337), a Florentine who made the two-dimensional medium look like three when he started placing foreground figures at the bottom of the painting—at eye level with the viewer—and putting background figures and objects in diminishing sizes at the top of the painting.

After Giotto, artists kept improving the technique, largely through the painstaking care with which they were able to make background objects smaller, thus getting greater depth. They introduced a brand new element into the medium: the *central vanishing point,* a spot in the center of the flat surface at which the background literally disappears, as it does for the naked eye. They also introduced *chiaroscuro,* a technique of having some figures in light and some in darkness and obscuring the distinctions between them, for artists realized that the eye does not view all figures under the same light conditions or as sharply defined forms.

No doubt the triumphant Renaissance painting is Leonardo's *The Last Supper,* a mural for which the artist was commissioned by the church of Santa Maria del Grazie in Milan, in 1495. It was to occupy the entire far wall of the refectory, and, though the paint is fading and the entire work has become fragile, visitors continue to be astonished when they enter the refectory today and experience the illusion that the room extends into the painting and continues on to the wall behind Christ and the disciples!

But perspective is only one of the work's extraordinary features. Leonardo also used chiaroscuro to heighten the realism of the scene. The interplay of light and shadow is haunting to behold, as are the faces of the twelve disciples, who have just heard Christ's words: "One of you will betray me."

Each disciple can be studied separately as a psychological portrait, and dominating the entire scene is the figure of Christ himself, with a face that defies precise verbal description. Certainly Leonardo has put sadness into it, but also resignation and a transcendent beauty. In fact, with this work and the equally famous *Mona Lisa,* the artist used his art to capture and crystallize the mysterious complexity of the human face. Art has gone beyond realism. It has become a way of looking into the soul. Leonardo makes us see what we normally miss when we look at people, *because we do not look long enough or closely enough.*

One other artist was to do equally as well by the human face, and that was Rembrandt (1606–1669), who especially found beauty in the careworn lines of aged subjects and who refined the technique of chiaroscuro to such an extent that it became the single most identifying element in his work. To look at a Rembrandt painting is to see such a contrast between light and dark that we are tempted to believe the source of light must be external to the painting. One marvels that paint applied to a flat surface could have created such intensity of light and such profundity of shadows. In the massive *Night Watch,* a canvas of more than 168 square feet, the artist has painted an entire military company in full regalia as well as the onlookers, creating a unity of light, shadow, and faces that can occupy the attention of visitors to Amsterdam's Rijksmuseum for hours.

With the flowering of European art throughout the seventeenth and eighteenth centuries, portrait and landscape painting reached near perfection. The subtleties of human vision were thoroughly explored, as was a greater range of color. Artists found special blends of colors that seemed to suit their needs, to express their particular vision of the world. Some "did" skies better than others; some, trees; some, water; and so on. In truth, there seemed little challenge left in the medium. Some art historians say the Dutch masters, including Rembrandt, carried realism—or representationalism—as far as it could go. With the mastery of perspective, light, and color shading, artists were ready to imitate the creative process itself—to bring into existence what was not there before: to imitate what the mind (the right brain?) sees only in dreams and fantasies.

Rembrandt, "Self-Portrait"
(Courtesy of The Metropolitan Museum of Art, Bequest of Benjamin Altman, 1913)

Imitation as Alteration

The imitation of reality is only one of the things art can do.

When the viewer who is not accustomed to seeing modern art comes into contact with the unfamiliar, an initial reaction is likely to be: *But why doesn't it look like anything?* Of course, it *does!* What the viewer means is that it doesn't look like the good old trustworthy, everyday world. What it looks like is nothing more or less than itself. The artist is imitating the image found in the mind. Why should *that* not have the right to be projected into space and become part of the everyday world? Artistic imitation becomes alteration of the environment, the artist assisting in nature's own work.

At an exhibition of the works of Vasili Kandinsky (1866–1944), an abstractionist whose work still has the power to alarm or intimidate the unprepared, a young woman was overheard asking what a certain painting was "supposed to be." After studying the work intently for several minutes, the woman's friend suddenly cried: "Why, it's two electric light bulbs!" The previously baffled viewer smiled, nodded, and voiced high-level approval of the painting. For many museum visitors the idea is that "It's good if you know what it is and bad if you don't"—as if the artist must be forever committed to the same motivation that underlies the work of many artists in the past.

Most contemporary artists in cultures with a broad tolerance for divergent thinkers—those who want to imitate themselves, not others—have experienced the satisfaction of changing the world in ways even they may not always understand. Art becomes *behavior* rather than a body of work which has to fit into a tradition. Artists speak of what they *do,* not what they show or mean. Often they appall those who insist upon a certain definition of art. Edward Kienholz (b. 1927), for example, has dazzled some and befuddled others. Here is an account of *Still Live—1974,* one of his more controversial— what is the word?—achievements? audacities?

> Inside a barricaded space an armchair sits in front of "a black Box mechanism containing a live cartridge and a random timer triggered to fire once within the next 100 years." After eight years, it still hasn't gone off. Viewers

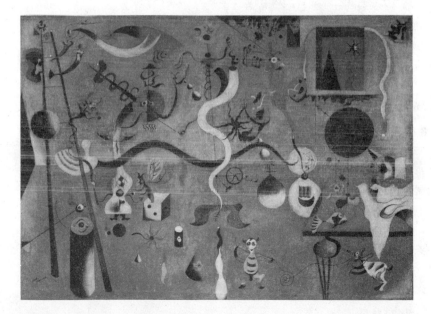

Joan Miró, "Carnival of Harlequin," 1924–25
(Courtesy of Albright-Knox Art Gallery, Buffalo, New York, Room of Contemporary Art Fund, 1940)

Constantin Brancusi, "Adam and Eve," 1916—21
(Courtesy of the Solomon R. Guggenheim Museum, photo by Robert E. Mates)

foolish enough to want to sit in this "hot seat" must sign a waiver. Kienholz told me, with some scorn and disbelief, that at the opening almost a dozen people did.[3]

What entitles *Still Live* to be considered art? When the live cartridge finally goes off and the work no longer justifies its name, will it still be art? An even more intense question: If someone were sitting in the hot seat when the cartridge fired and the mechanism became a death machine, would it still belong to the world of art? Or does it not belong to that world even now because of what it is? And finally: What indeed *is* it?

No doubt a great many people might dismiss the last question as irrelevant because *Still Live,* being a potential instrument of destruction, cannot be considered beautiful. But it may be risky anyway to insist upon beauty as the deciding characteristic a would-be work of art must possess. Philosophers and art critics alike have debated for centuries over the meaning of beauty, particularly over the crucial question of whether something *has* beauty in the same sense that a plant has flowers, or whether it is only *perceived* as having beauty. If the latter is the case, then no universal standards can exist to determine the beautiful, and Kienholz's armchair and black box might well be beautiful to some. Still others would argue that a work of art doesn't *have* to be beautiful, no matter how we define the word.

Kienholz's armchair and black box might well be beautiful to some. Still others would argue that a work of art doesn't have to be beautiful.

ART IN SOCIETY

All of us, as we have said, have imitated what we see outside or in the private worlds of our imagination. Some of us are lazy, or else suppose that we have no "artistic ability," remaining content with stick-figure people and porcupines peering out from behind fences. Others are more adventurous; they keep working on their imitations. When the need to draw, paint, or sculpt becomes an obsession, relegating other activities to positions of secondary importance, then, of course, we are talking about a serious artist. Such an individual more often than not wants others to see and admire the work that is produced. One doubts that the artists who put more than 15,000 engravings on the cave walls at Lascaux were content solely with the inner satisfaction of a job well done. Perhaps there were exhibitions even then.

Generally speaking, the visual arts are social. Unlike drama, they *can* exist alone. If no one had ever looked upon van Gogh's *Starry Night,* it would be no less a masterpiece. If *Hamlet* could not be staged, the world would have a great poem, but not a great play. Van Gogh, however, is atypical of the artist. His letters indicate he cared more about what he was doing in art than about receiving any critical acclaim or money for his efforts. Most artists like to see themselves projected into space and know that others are aware of their presence. To have one's visions, captured in oils, prominently displayed before admiring eyes . . . this is the dream.

The Artist as Cultural Champion

One of the oldest and most enduring functions of art in society is to represent the cultural group which has nurtured the artist: to embody its values, mores, standards of beauty, and mythology. Often the embodiment is conscious and well rewarded by the group.

Michelangelo's *David,* often cited as the most nearly perfect example of statuary art ever produced by a human being, is often pre-

Michelangelo, "David"

The cultural group has a collective need for art that parallels the individual's need for horizontal exten-sion—evidence that one is "out there."

sented by art historians as a mighty symbol of the city which fostered its creation, a symbol of Florentine pride and independence. Just as the biblical David conquered the giant Goliath with a mere slingshot, so too was Florence of the early sixteenth century, with its newborn liberal humanism, standing up against the colossus of the Vatican, seat of the powerful Christian empire. The artist himself picked the subject and did so because he felt there was an analogy between David and Florence, but the statue also embodies Michelangelo's vision of ideal youth and manly beauty. It is 13½ feet high, from the top of the ped-estal. Michelangelo himself was small in stature and by his own admis-sion not physically beautiful.

The point is that works of art can be both personal and cul-tural, and both cultural and universal. The greater the work, the more it is likely to embody many meanings and to exist on many levels. The Florentines who looked on with open mouths as the gigantic statue was wheeled into the city must have responded with a rush of civic pride to its cultural meanings, just as Americans respond to the Statue of Liberty. The *David* may have told them who they were and what they stood for. Once the statue was ensconced in the large open-air piazza, the citizens did in fact rally around it, and, even though the destructive effects of climate forced it indoors, the *David* remains to-day the pride of Florence, as well as one of the world's major symbolic expressions of human strength and endurance.

The culture has a collective need for art that parallels the individual's need for what we might call *horizontal extension*—evidence that I or *we* are "out there." Much cultural art, like the Greek Parthenon, provides beautiful places for specified group activities: religious rituals, conversation and debate, theater- and concert-going, the viewing of art itself within an ambience which enhances the experience. All of this is part of that fundamental human instinct for imitation. As nature creates suitable environments for its many forms of life, so do cultures provide for needs that are esthetic; cultures tend to require more than is absolutely essential for survival (though regrettably there are many individuals who settle for much less than they have to).

Like responsible parents, cultures nurture and develop the artists in their midst, especially during their own periods of development, before they occupy confident places in the sun for themselves.

Edmonia Lewis, "Hagar," 1875
(Courtesy of the National Museum of American Art, Smithsonian Institution. Transfer from the National Museum of African Art. Gift of Delta Sigma Theta Sorority, Inc.)

The artist as cultural champion is as necessary as the hunter or the warrior or the diplomat. The less secure the culture, the more intense the nurturing.

Sometimes artists are a minority within a dominant culture, and, in order to win approval, they offer an allegiance which may spring from necessity more than conviction. In our century, totalitarian cultures like those in Soviet-bloc countries have had difficulty with artists who will not work under a rigid set of rules governing what they may and may not express. The minority artist can operate on a personal as well as social level. The avant-garde movement among Polish artists in the early 1980s offers a prime example of dual-purpose art.

When a culture emerges into full sunlight, its artists are usually leading the way. For several decades now, black artists in America have been preoccupied with expressing the feelings and pride of their ethnicity—a complex of mind and heart growing out of what it means to be a repressed minority. Some few have thought of themselves as artists first, concerned with problems integral to *being* an artist, problems of shape, color, composition, balance, and so on. But for the most part, the tensions inherent in black existence have far outweighed other considerations.

Black art is as likely to be found on the outside wall of a condemned building as it is in a museum, now more than ever by choice rather than necessity. And when it *is* showcased, black art takes viewers outside the hushed enclosure, reminding them that repression, suffering, and bitterness must be reckoned with, no longer ignored or passively tolerated. Black art, above all, expresses pride of heritage, something seldom found in cultures that have long since stopped insisting on their greatness. The descendants of white European culture are not what's new in the New World.

Obviously, times have changed. The black artist of the last century could be a cultural champion only indirectly. Recognition came, if at all, from a display of excellence within a framework established by the dominant white Anglo-Saxon culture.

The first black American sculptor to gain notoriety, for example, was Edmonia Lewis (1844–?), who faced the added challenge of trying to achieve renown as a female in the male-dominated art world. Her career began unpromisingly enough. Enrolled at Oberlin College, where she learned to paint and draw, she was accused of nearly killing two of her friends with a poisoned drink, dragged off by an angry mob, brutally beaten, and left to die. She was, naturally enough, reluctant to continue her academic studies; instead she moved to Boston, determined to vindicate herself by achieving fame in an arena that had been shut tight against minorities. She quickly found she had a genuine talent for realistic sculpture, scoring a mild sensation with a bust of Robert Gould Shaw, an eminent Bostonian and

Civil War hero. Soon she had earned enough money from her work to follow in the footsteps of many other American artists: moving to Europe and becoming an expatriate. She opened a studio in Rome, which eventually became the fashionable place for visiting Americans who desired to commission expensive family portrait busts.

In 1868 Lewis did a bust of the poet Henry Wadsworth Longfellow, and from that association she became a great admirer of Longfellow's *Song of Hiawatha.* Her own mother had, in fact, been a Chippewa, and so the artist felt deep empathy for that other long-repressed minority—the Native American. She fashioned two complex works—*The Marriage of Hiawatha* and *The Old Arrow-Maker and His Daughter*—based on themes and incidents from the poem. At this point in her career Lewis became a symbolist. There is little doubt that she saw parallels between Longfellow's poem and what was happening in America. Hiawatha and Minnehaha were lovers from two feuding tribes, and to Lewis their eventual union represented her hope that the deep scars left by the recent Civil War would heal and that a new nation, strong and free, would emerge, a nation of diverse cultures living side by side in peace and harmony. From here it was only a short step to the theme that she felt most deeply: suffering and alienation of black people. In what is considered her masterpiece, the statue of Hagar, who in the Bible was chosen by Abraham to be the mother of his children, then was cast out by the tribe after Sarah, Abraham's wife, became fertile, Lewis created a symbol of a black American wandering through an alien land, and also perhaps of women in general, denied their God-given rights in a male-dominated society.

Finally, in *Forever Free,* Lewis decided she no longer had to conceal her message behind symbols. This work depicts a male and female, both newly emancipated slaves, breaking through their chains. We have few facts about the life of the artist after completing *Forever Free,* except that she continued to work in Rome. Her fame, however, was short-lived, possibly because the popularity of decorative sculpture began to dwindle or possibly because America was not ready for a champion of this cultural minority. America was still looking for its own secure place in the sun, something it would not achieve until after its victory in World War I.[4]

By the middle of the twentieth century, contemporary black artists were able to assert themselves as both cultural champions and important forces in the metropolitan art scene. "Black is beautiful" became the resounding cry, and there were plenty of artists to capture for all of us new visions of beauty in the Afro hairstyle, the high cheekbone, the flared nostril. Black artists led the way in a revival of brilliant colors in clothing, not seen since the days of Gauguin, colors that suggested proud African roots.

But also—and just as important—in expressing a sense of fierce independence, a sense of I-will-do-it-my-way, of alienation from

Lewis's work was much in demand during the heyday of the "literary" sculptors. Her studio, listed in the best guidebooks, was a fashionable stop for Americans on the grand tour.

Marilyn Richardson

mainstream American culture, black artists have become as much a part of the modern art scene as any of their peers. Most contemporary American artists (as well as their colleagues abroad) are nothing if not alienated from the values and life-styles of the middle class, from dull conformism. They do *not* want their work to be traditional or realistic, or to be used for interior decoration, to match the carpet and drapes. They want the viewer to come to *them.* Though they may shake their heads at what is happening to our country, in an unusual way the majority of modern American artists are all becoming champions of a vanishing American culture—the America of the lone and free spirit.

Michelangelo: Conquering the Medium

Visual artists express themselves through materials: canvas, paint, stone, clay, wire, string, old washboards. Whatever emerges and however it is evaluated, art comes into existence as an interaction between the artist (eyes, hands, inner feelings) and some kind of material—that which we call the artist's *medium.* To look past the medium itself, going directly to the content, is to miss a great deal of what creativity is actually about.

What we must grasp essentially is that there exists an ancient rivalry between the artist and the medium. The medium does not surrender willingly to the hands of the artist. This much is true no matter what kind of art we're speaking of. The blank paper in the typewriter stares up at the novelist, daring her to find—somehow, somewhere— just the right words in just the right order. The sonnet's structure hangs there in the memory of the poet, daring him to fill it with new images and new sounds that seem miraculously to require just 14 lines. The legs of human beings were never meant to do what the ballet dancer commands them to do. Ivory keys coldly reflect overhead stage lights—so still, and offering no help to the pianist.

The paradox of art, however, is that the achievement often seems effortless. Olympic ice-dancing champions glide in perfect balance across the silver-blue ice—he lifting, she perfectly still and weightless. The dancer-swan extends from the fingertips of the prince and pirouettes faster and faster until she becomes a white blur, then stops instantly. Not a motion wasted.

Visit St. Peter's Basilica in Rome and spend an hour just looking at the *Pietà* of Michelangelo. Look at the hands and feet of Christ, Joseph's robe; look deeply into Mary's face. You will soon forget you are staring at marble. You will see human love, human sorrow—pain frozen for all time in a soft peace that seems as far away from marble as anything can be. Sometimes we say to ourselves: Art means pretending there is no artist. Yet let us not deceive ourselves. A vital function of the artist in society is to keep alive the myth that well-nigh impossible things are within human range. Marble doesn't want to look soft.

Michelangelo took it from the quarries of Carrara and forced it to do his bidding.

Michelangelo Buonarroti (1475–1564) is to his media what Shakespeare is to the English language and Beethoven is to sound. He came upon the scene in Florence as a young boy, knowing that sculpture was considered by many to be a trade rather than an art; and when he was finished, when he had given the world the towering *David* and the awesome *Moses,* in addition to the Vatican *Pietà,* he had put sculpture up among the stars.

Michelangelo is known to have said time and again that the forms were always waiting, locked inside the marble. But the Florentines who were there for the unveiling of the *David* knew otherwise. They knew the statue had been carved out of a 17-foot block considered flawed and inferior. Leonardo himself, originally offered the chance to do the tallest sculpture ever executed, had rejected the very notion. Michelangelo, a lesser choice, regretted at first the commitment he had made. Who could do anything with a huge piece of flawed marble? But he himself did not fully know then.

Michelangelo was driven by a passion that seems to prey on genius. It is a glorious, immortal, and incurable virus that brings terrible suffering to great souls. The vast majority of us are not inflicted with the malady, but, though it has caused genius unending misery and even led to suicide (as in the case of van Gogh), it can be a thrilling experience for *us* to see (or hear or read or touch) the things it drives genius to accomplish.

Achieving almost instantaneous success as a sculptor, Michelangelo was driven to attempt one superhuman task after another; and each one seemed more impossible than the one before. The media—paint as well as stone—seemed to grow more, not less, resistant to his will. Why? The reason is that *the will demanded more and more of the artist.* What do you do to top near-perfection? (Except that genius, of course, believes its work is not and never will be perfect!) Michelangelo knew he must conquer the marble over and over and make paint do all that Leonardo and Raphael had achieved— and more.

An undreamed-of challenge arose when Pope Julius II, who had already commissioned Michelangelo to carve figures for his own tomb (a tomb that was never to be completed), asked the artist to paint the ceiling of the Sistine Chapel inside the Vatican. Michelangelo's imagination was immediately stirred. There was the location itself, as close to heaven as one might be. There was the huge expanse of the ceiling, allowing for a series of paintings on religious themes that would at the same time present to the viewer a totally unified effect. But most of all, perhaps, Michelangelo recognized the challenge of *fresco,* a technique of painting in watercolors on wet plaster that when dry combines with the paints to form a wholly new kind

Dancing is a sweat job. . . . You may go days getting nothing but exhaustion. This search for what you want is like tracking something that doesn't want to be tracked.

> *Fred Astaire*

But we see only the finished product, the flawless pas de deux.

> *Ellen Goodman on Astaire*

. . . we must recognize the emergence of Michelangelo as one of the great events in the history of western man.

> *Kenneth Clark*

of material, one whose texture creates a vivid sense of immediacy. To create such immediacy in so sublime a place—and to do it while lying on his back, high in the air! Did an artist's medium ever resist so mightily?

It took Michelangelo four years to finish the ceiling. Though millions of visitors have passed below it, gazing up in awe at the incredible number of human and divine figures, dominated by the central piece, "The Creation of Adam," the viewer wonders whether the artist himself ever experienced a true sense of profound satisfaction. The sheer physical beating which the medium gave the artist has been re-created in a biographical novel:

> drawn up tight against his belly for balance, his eyes a few inches from the ceiling, until the unpadded bones of his buttocks became so bruised and sore he could no longer endure the agony. Then he lay flat on his back, his knees in the air, doubled over as tightly as possible against his chest to steady his painting arm. Since he no longer bothered to shave, his beard became an excellent catchall for the constant drip of paint and water. No matter which way he leaned, crouched, lay or knelt, on his feet, knees or back, it was always in strain.[5]

A commitment to fresco is a drastic thing under even ideal conditions, since the paint must be applied before the plaster dries. But under the extremes of physical pain Michelangelo endured, the commitment would have taxed the dedication of all but one who could not live with himself if he failed to accept this supreme challenge.

He lived to be 89 and continued working virtually up until the moment of death. Why shouldn't he have? He had already destroyed, or nearly so, many of his later works, including the *Pietà Rondanini,* an old man's version of the agony of the Holy Family, except that this time the emphasis is on Christ's face, no longer the youthful, serene, almost feminine Christ of the Vatican *Pietà* but a man who has, like the figure's creator, suffered greatly. In his declining years he worked feverishly on the plans for Saint Peter's. A brief remark written in a 1557 letter is most illuminating: ". . . neither do I wish to fail the fabric of St. Peter's here, nor do I wish to fail myself."

In many of his letters and in his poetry the artist continually expressed the conviction that his work was not for the multitude, not for the critics, but for God Himself. There is little reason to doubt Michelangelo believed this implicitly, that he attempted to judge his work as though to determine its worthiness for God. One suspects the artist knew why his media resisted him so mightily. He was asking them to do tasks meant for an ultimate critical approval.

When the medium is so evidently unyielding—like marble—and when the artist's conquest of it is so clear, humanity takes another step forward. But, of course, much time has passed since the 17-foot block succumbed to a superior, a *human* force. In today's art world there exist, there are accepted, many media that classical artists would not have recognized. At contemporary exhibits one finds butcher's wrapping paper, broken bits of glass, sand glued to canvas, plastic, tar, coat hangers, nails, tin cans, rusty used mufflers, and so on. Today's artists and sculptors are not trying to equal or improve on Michelangelo. They seek to leave their own signatures upon the world—in language they understand.

A critic recently commented that where anything is possible, nothing matters. Some would contend that, when the range of media is extended to include everything, then the domain of art becomes weakened. Are we too permissive when we allow the artist to say, "Art is what the artist does"? Are we entitled to ask who decides who is an artist? Defining something has meant placing certain limits around it. Michelangelo is a supreme example of someone who worked within excruciating limits. Many believe the tension produced by the struggle between the passion and the limits is indeed the true, the secret ingredient of *all* art.

When Limitations Become Too Limiting

Michelangelo sought, among other things, to make his materials radiate forth an illusion of life. As he and other Renaissance artists gained mastery over perspective and other techniques of an emerging realism, as the seventeenth-century Dutch and Flemish masters created canvases that invite the viewer to step inside and hold a conversation with the figures depicted, eighteenth-century landscape and portrait painters served notice that through art humanity could leave behind a permanent and accurate record of itself, we might have thought the flat-surface medium had been conquered once and for all. Yet, as we have already seen, direct imitation from life, no matter how challenging the task, is not the extent of the visual artist's ambitions. Artists also like to give objective existence to interior phantom figures and those shadowy landscapes we fleetingly recall at the moment of waking, when we inhabit a dimension of reality for which we have no words. Artists may also look at the very same world out there that you and I are observing, but they "see" much that we don't.

Above all, the visual artist—like counterparts in other disciplines—may not enjoy being limited by those very constraints which once engendered masterpieces like the *David.* The great pioneers conquer the medium, open the way for others to explore, create standards of glory to which others must aspire. Sooner or later the great innovators become the artistic, the *classic* establishment. By the eighteenth century, techniques for the imitation of the external world were so finely tuned that society, which had to wait another century for the invention of photography, probably did not suffer one whit from the absence of such imitation. Individual and group portraiture was a thriving profession. Landscape painters made every corner of the known world visually accessible to those who could not travel.

As a result, new generations of innovators began to seek out unfamiliar pathways. Among them was Spain's major artist of the late eighteenth century: Francisco Goya (1746–1828). His early works are realistic—landscapes depicting the natural beauty of the Aragon countryside in which he was nurtured, and portraits of astonishing vitality, with finely detailed photographic likenesses of his subjects. Though Goya was little known when he came to Madrid, the cultural center of Spain, he soon grew in popularity among the aristocrats, largely because of his skill in portraiture. But after a time, he risked his fame and fortune in the name of a far more compelling drive: his own needs as an artist.

In Goya's time realistic painting was not only a profession, but it could turn into downright hack work, luring many of the potentially great because of the money that could be made from it. An artist had only to study the established techniques carefully, spend a few years

Francisco Goya, "The Family of Charles IV"
(Courtesy of Prado Museum Giraudon)

in apprenticeship, copying the style of a master, and then develop a sophisticated, professional style of his own. Little of the self needed to go into the work. After a while, professionalism in this sense failed to suffice for Goya. His eyes turned inward, and he felt a burning need to paint what he saw and felt as a unique human being. Goya introduced the element of personal psychology into his art.

The person he discovered through his paints was essentially a cynic. Goya found himself out of tune with the life of polite society— the superficial manners, the idle conversation, and, worse, the continual intrigues of people driven by the need for power and position— and he was unable to keep his cynicism out of his works. His "portrait" of royalty, *The Family of Charles IV,* completed in 1800, best illustrates Goya's mood at the time when his motivation as an artist was beginning to change.

The family is shown standing in a gallery: the king, the queen, and young aristocrats of varying ages and sizes. In Rembrandtian style, there is light coming into the gallery from some undefined source beyond the canvas. There is just enough light to illuminate the faces. Certainly they do not represent the idealization of royalty that artists were normally paid to create. Goya showed the family not at its best, but at its worst. The youngest children have bizarre, almost paranoiac expressions. Perhaps for the very first time an artist has captured the less-than-enviable life-style of children who are not so much spoiled and pampered as enslaved to certain behaviors. The queen seems insensitive to them, indeed to just about everything. She is posing foolishly, as though she were not very bright and has a naive conception of what regal bearing is all about. The king is equally silly-looking, and there is also a trace of sadness in his face, a sense of now-unremembered, occasional happy times in a youth he never really had. We know that the children will grow up and be very much like their father.

The fact that the royal family must have been pleased with the portrait   after all, they did accept it and did not throw the artist out of the palace—remains one of the ironies in art history. Were the king and queen so vain or so blind to reality that they never noticed Goya's insulting approach? If so, then the artist was probably right in his assessment of the court of Madrid. His style became even darker, more pessimistic.

The invasion of Spain by Napoleon during the first decade of the nineteenth century did not help Goya's disposition much. The ravages of war, the inhumanities human beings were capable of inflicting on each other, depressed him further. In two of his masterpieces, *The Second of May* and *The Third of May,* Goya dramatized the theme of war's cruelty. In the latter painting we see the execution of several Spaniards by Napoleon's firing squad. Realistic detail has been minimized. There is pure fear on the faces of the condemned men, and those who are about to fire the guns are lacking in any expression.

Salvador Dali, "Inventions of the Monsters," 1937
(© 1988 The Art Institute of Chicago, Joseph Winterbotham Collection. All rights reserved.)

Nothing in the painting detracts from the overwhelming presence of fear. It would be hard for many viewers to ascribe beauty to the work.

Because of Goya's originality and innovative artistic techniques and the total range of his work, his significance in the history of art is assured. However, his later paintings, especially *Saturn Devouring His Son,* seem unpleasant, if not hideous, to many viewers. They raise even now, as they surely did then, questions of the legitimacy of art that seems less than beautiful, that affects the viewer—but often negatively, provoking feelings of outrage and horror.

Contemporary art which intentionally disturbs the viewer is so commonplace that many of Goya's descendants would consider us impertinent if not foolish to ask whether art always has to be beautiful. They would contend that art by virtue of its artistry *is* beautiful, no matter what its subject matter or technique; that it is a beautiful experience to observe the creative personality in the act of self-assertion. Above all, if art is conquering the medium, is breaking through limitations, then what, one might further ask, is not beautiful about the astonishing feat of capturing on canvas those elusive passions which also define our humanness?

After the Camera

With the coming of the camera in the mid-nineteenth century, realistic painting became less fashionable and a good deal less profitable. In France, Edouard Manet (1832–1883) was the first to provide a comprehensive, antiphotographic rationale for art. A painting, he said, should not be a direct imitation of reality, but instead something to experience totally for itself; it is an *event,* something unprecedented, the creative result of the way the artist sees and feels things. It is not to be judged in relation to the things themselves—as, for example, a good photograph must have been in those early days. Manet and some of his colleagues began working in a new style, which for a number of years had no name. Their goal was to project onto the canvas new ways of experiencing color and form—or, more precisely, to break down altogether the distinctions between color and form, between shadow and light. To them reality as experienced was a continuum of these elements.

This new style at last found a name when Claude Monet (1840–1926) exhibited his painting entitled *Impression: Sunrise.* The subjective visions which became the content for the *Impressionists* affected the viewer with the emotion felt by the artist. Color burst upon canvas in a profusion never before known. Artists experimented feverishly with new combinations of colors and new brushstroke techniques. The race was on to see who could approximate most closely the subtleties of visual consciousness. The new challenge posed by the medium required the blending of innumerable colors and shadings into a unified emotional effect.

The latter half of the nineteenth century was dominated by similar revolutions in all of the French arts. The Impressionism of Monet, Manet, Renoir, Degas, and Pissarro had a musical counterpart in the 12-tone scale, the indeterminant rhythms, and unfamiliar harmonies of Claude Debussy; a literary counterpart in the psychological prose-poetry of Marcel Proust, the sensuous, subjective novels of André Gide, and the haunting verse of Baudelaire, Mallarmé, and Rimbaud, who found words for inner states never acknowledged before, let alone articulated. This emphasis on subjectivity seemed to some critics an overindulgence in the self and a too easy surrender to sensuality as the dominant concern of personal experience. Others hailed it as a breakthrough, as a freeing of the artist from the rigid formalism of artistic media. Painting need not tell a realistic story; poetry could open new vistas to the imagination; music could introduce new and strange sounds; the novel could be something other than a narrative of cause and effect in the external world. Those who shook their heads and said that standards in the arts were disappearing often called the revolution "decadent."

What *really* happened is that artists were imposing their will upon their medium and altering the medium; but, in so doing, they were setting up new barriers, new challenges for themselves. The foremost American Impressionist was James McNeill Whistler (1834–1903), who painted the famous portrait of his mother in 1871. Though the work is universally admired for the subject matter, though

All human experience of
visual reality, to which art
ultimately appeals, has
been gained through eyes
which move continually in
all directions, located in a
head which constantly
changes its height above
ground and its angle of tilt.

Philip Rawson

reproductions have sold in the millions and are probably as omni-present as "Home Sweet Home" embroidery samplers, most people are unaware that the painting's full title is *Arrangement in Black and Gray: The Artist's Mother.* Whistler used his mother as a subject—a woman in a particular setting, in a complex of color, form, light, and shadow—to be experienced as a total event. The point is that the artist was not satisfied merely with doing justice to his mother's image, or even her personality, but, rather, sought to convey each and every segment of a certain moment in time, when a particular human being sat in a particular way, in a visual context that the artist captures.

Similarly, the work of another American, Mary Cassatt (1845–1926), illustrates the artist's concern with totality—not in depicting the isolated subject against a background, or in forcing the viewer's eye to come to rest at a central point. *The Bath,* for example, shows a woman bathing a young girl, but the subject of the piece is not as important as the total orchestration of color and form. The artist even chose a vantage point *above* the scene in order, perhaps, to disengage the viewer from the normal way of looking. From an elevated perspective, background and foreground attain an equality. The wall behind the woman and the child, the pitcher of water, the rug—each is as meaningful as the human figures. So are the stripes and texture of the woman's outfit. The new artists thus liberated viewers from having to ask the traditional questions like "Does she really look like that?" and "What is the artist trying to tell us about this person (or this place)?" The appropriate questions now became: "What happens on the canvas?" or better still, "What is the effect and how does the artist achieve it?"

Impressionism and related movements in the arts took hold so strongly on both sides of the Atlantic that, as we might expect, the altered medium soon became as authoritative as the traditions it replaced. Newer artists emerged who began to resist slavish imitation and go their own ways. The label *Post-Impressionism* has been coined by art historians as a convenient way of referring to the work of van Gogh and others; but we must remember that the label does not identify a specific group with common characteristics. The Post-Impressionists shared only the need to use their medium to define themselves. Of this group Vincent van Gogh (1853–1890) was surely the most original and the most intense.

Van Gogh's lines and bright
colors virtually scream
from the canvas. His art
comes as close to sound as
is possible in a silent
medium.

Van Gogh remains the prototype of the artist who creates entirely for himself. His style was so strange in its time that the few critics who ever took notice of his work were generally baffled, having nothing with which to compare it. He lived most of his life in abject poverty, supported in part by his brother, Theo, who believed in van Gogh's genius and stood by him even when his work was denounced and ridiculed. Only one of the artist's paintings was ever sold dur-

Vincent van Gogh, "First Steps"
(Courtesy of The Metropolitan Museum of Art, gift of George N. and Helen M.
Richard, 1964)

ing his lifetime. Tragically, he committed suicide before his fortieth birthday.

In fact, van Gogh is the prototype of the artist for whom art becomes the last outpost of being itself. Totally alienated in this world, totally misunderstood by almost everyone except his brother, rejected twice as a suitor (once with a vehement cry of "No, never, never!"), hovering much of the time on the thin border between functional rationality and insanity (eventually to cross the border, never to return), he survived as long as he did mainly because of his work. Small wonder that the viewer of his paintings becomes enveloped in a completely altered version of reality. What obligation did the artist feel toward an everyday world through which he passed as a stranger?

In works such as *Sunflowers, Wheatfield with Crows,* and *Starry Night,* which have become priceless since van Gogh's death, the viewer witnesses a brushstroke method that has become utterly identified with its creator: a short, stabbing technique, as opposed to the flowing line, that makes the entire canvas appear to be throbbing with energy. His rational mind seldom under control, van Gogh abandoned himself to the sensuous impact of life's forms and colors, absorbing them fully and converting them into a heightened reality—an explosion of pure feeling transferred to color, shapes, and paint textures. The one critic who within van Gogh's lifetime found the work praiseworthy used a singularly appropriate term to describe it: insolent. Van Gogh's lines and bright colors virtually scream from the canvas. His art comes as close to sound as is possible in a silent medium.

That van Gogh achieved no fame or recognition in his lifetime does not mean the artist deliberately withdrew into himself, deliberately flaunted artistic tradition. Strange as his behavior may have been at times, he can also be described as an innocent. At an early stage of his development he remarked to his brother that he enjoyed making "childish drawings" to pass the time (and, one suspects, as a refuge from the world of social relationships in which he was ill at ease). The child in van Gogh never left him. What art historians now describe as a bold and revolutionary technique was presumably the only technique he knew. In lucid moments his innocence manifested itself in a wide-eyed confidence that someday his works would do very well in the marketplace.[6]

As we move into the current century, however, we find artists blatantly insisting on refashioning art to suit themselves, demanding that society follow *them*.

Picasso

If you were to ask the leading intellectual lights of our day to name two or three people of the twentieth century who more than any others changed the direction of human development, the name of Pablo Picasso (1881–1974) would no doubt appear frequently. What great poets did for human language, great composers for sound, scientists for the conquest of disease and the knowledge of our universe, Picasso did for the range of human visual experience. Picasso has given us totally new ways of seeing, and, in capturing on canvas what he himself saw, added new forms and colors to our human environment. Easily on a par with Leonardo and Michelangelo, Picasso was a genius of sublime proportions who has influenced not only the direction of art and sculpture, but architecture, drama, and literature as well. It is not too much to say that, had Picasso never existed, the modern world would neither look nor "feel" quite as it does.

We have already said that imitation, the driving force behind all visual art, includes altering; but no amount of verbal explanation can help the reader fully comprehend what "altering" means in Picasso's work. One needs to experience as much Picasso as possible. If originals are not readily accessible, there are many, many art history books to look through, as well as magnificent coffee-table volumes devoted exclusively to the artist.

Looking at a work typical of Picasso's Cubist period, one is likely to see recognizable shapes, but only in the sense that we "recog-

Pablo Picasso, "Three Musicians," 1921
(Courtesy of The Museum of Modern Art, Mrs. Simon Guggenheim Fund)

nize" stick figures as being intended to stand for human figures. A Picasso man or woman might have an angularly shaped head with one eye here, another there; a nose like an arc; or, as in his famous *Three Musicians* (1921), a mouth in the shape of an hour glass. When *Cubism* burst upon the art scene in the early twentieth century, some critics and art lovers thought it was intended to be funny. What else could be the point of doing paintings and sculptures that were not totally abstract—that is, comprised of shapes, colors, and lines that looked like nothing but themselves—but, rather, were depictions of people and things that at the same time looked like no people or things ever seen before?

An important influence on the development of Cubism may have been the explorations of optical science into the true nature of the eye and the way we see. It began to be understood that our *minds,* not our eyes, see things as whole and distinct entities. If vision alone could be separated from the entire complex of the experience we call seeing, if we could stop for a fleeting instant and catch just what the eyes are looking at, then the world would look something like the disembodied, often floating shapes that we find on the canvases of Picasso.

Picasso and fellow Cubists discovered that we actually see objects as *events* extending over a given period of time, no matter how rapid. The eye, moreover, is in continual motion and observes a thing from continually shifting viewpoints. From where we sit or stand we *think* we are looking from one particular and fixed vantage point. Both realistic paintings and photographs foster the misconception that such a thing exists as a fixed observer with a stable field of vision. As one critic said:

> [The Cubist] wished to present the total essential reality of forms in space, and since objects appear not only as they are seen from one viewpoint at one time, it became necessary to introduce multiple angles of vision and simultaneous presentation of discontinuous planes. This of course shatters the old continuity of composition imposed by the Renaissance single viewpoint.[7]

What the critic means by "simultaneous presentation of discontinuous planes" can be easily understood from a careful study of *Guernica,* a mural painted in 1937 for the Spanish pavilion at the Paris World's Fair and now widely considered Picasso's masterpiece as well as one of the great art works of all time.

Picasso's *Guernica* presents the essence of one of the most inhumane events of this century: the German air force's so-called "saturation" bombing of Guernica, the cultural center of the Basque region in northern Spain and a stronghold of the Loyalist troops during the Spanish Civil War. The destruction of the town was accomplished in a few minutes by the most massive air strike ever mustered by one nation against another, and during which not only Loyalist soldiers but hundreds of civilian men, women, and children were massacred. Picasso, up to that time an artist with no political leanings, wanted the mural, for which he had been commissioned, to make a universal statement about man's inhumanity to man and the true horror of war. Without Cubism, a style that can present simultaneously things that happen over a period of time, how could he have shown the world the total scene of devastation? What would a realist have done facing such a challenge?

In *Guernica* we can feel the tremendous impact that Picasso has had upon not only art but our entire civilization. In addition to giving us new viewing experiences, he has made events accessible to the imagination that might otherwise have remained abstract to anyone not at the scene to experience them as they occurred. Advanced motion picture technology has made possible a work such as Oliver

Stone's *Platoon* (1986), the heightened realism of which brings viewers into direct confrontation with modern infantry war as it actually is. But viewers always have the recourse with movie realism to divorce themselves from what they are seeing, or, we might say, to recognize that the blood and gore they are witnessing in such massive amounts is not after all *really* real. The style of *Guernica,* as well as the eloquent silence that is art, makes us less likely to turn away from what it shows. That is, by not pretending to photographic realism, it achieves truth rather than reality, as that is normally understood to be. Picasso's enduring greatness lies in the fact that he found a new pathway to truth, even as Freud was doing with the inner world and Einstein was doing with the physical universe.

Alteration as Abstraction

Picasso as alterer sought ways of coming closer to the optical truth of events as well as making possible the telescoping of many events in one canvas, as he demonstrated so epically in *Guernica.* At the same time—that is, the early twentieth century—there were artists whose major concern was to get back to what they considered the primary essence of visual art: the formal design that is the work itself. There were artists who rebelled decidedly and especially against the Impressionists and Post-Impressionists, claiming they were using the canvas as an outlet for their personal emotions; and doubtless many shook their heads at the "propagandistic" aspects of a work like *Guernica.* Art, so said more than a few, is not intended to make a statement of any kind. It is meant to add beauty to the world.

An example of this kind of art is a painting called *Composition,* by the modern Dutch artist Piet Mondrian (1872–1944), a work of absolute and austere simplicity, one in which all dynamic motion is absent, a work in which colors, shapes, and lines are there not to move or excite us, but to have the placid effect which the beautiful may also evoke. Mondrian was a pioneer on the road to a school of art which is popular today. Known as *Minimalism,* this movement decries subjectivism in art, demanding that the discipline be used in and for itself and that artists be thoroughly versed in the formal requirements of their craft. Minimalism is perhaps the purest form of abstraction in art, because it reduces the event to a very simple juxtaposition of design elements. And this Mondrian certainly does, though he really comes too early to be classified as a bona fide member of this school.

At any rate, *like* the Minimalists of more recent times, Mondrian gives us paintings in which content, in the ordinary sense of that word, is missing. He is not imitating optical events of the external world, as Picasso very definitely was. His imitation is of the geometric shapes emanating from his own mind. But since no artist can conceive of a shape that does not first exist somewhere else in *some* fashion, we can say that abstractionism in visual art occurs when the artist's mind rearranges prior shapes to a point at which an entirely new *thing* emerges. In Mondrian's case, rearrangement also means perfecting geometrically, since the artist deals in forms that require rulers and planes, not free brush strokes.

Another pioneer in early-twentieth-century art and another artist whose work begins to suggest what the Minimalists would do is the American Georgia O'Keeffe (1887–1986). The total body of her work, which spans nearly a whole century, definitely belongs to the abstractionists style of contemporary art, but it differs radically from that of Mondrian. The latter gives us geometric perfection that does not exist in the natural world, unless by improbable accident. O'Keeffe *begins* from the natural and, to her, wondrous forms of the external world, and then reduces them to what we could call a minimal essence of shape and color. One work, *White Canadian Barn, No. 2* (see page 53), quintessential O'Keeffe, is in a style that, fully developed, would become the artist's lifelong signature.

First there is the obvious fact that as an abstractionist the artist is not concerned with the subject per se. There is nothing grand or even meaningful about a barn. Who would even notice such a thing? No one. No one, that is, except an abstractionist who sees design where the rest of us probably would not. Of course, we *do* see it after the alteration process has taken place and the artist's canvas has raised the "naturally insignificant" to the level of artistic beauty.

O'Keeffe's technique is suggestive of Oriental art in the impression it gives of being quite rapid. A Zen painting is accomplished in one or two brush strokes. *White Canadian Barn* does not appear to have required many brush strokes. One is not aware of painstaking intricacy of execution, of the subtle shading found in a realistic landscape, for example. Of course, as we have said before (and it bears much repeating): Great art often seems effortless. Simplicity requires genius. Or, to put the matter in another way: One of the functions of genius is to afford us glimpses of simplicity. Our lives, after all, are generally complex enough without our needing to seek out additional complexity in the world of art. One of O'Keeffe's major goals as an artist was to help the viewer to see the world as "simply" as she did.

O'Keeffe's way of seeing— her deep appreciation of nature synthesized in works of art—is unique. She pursued her vision when she was unknown, when she was the only American-educated woman in the select group of European-educated male artists exhibited by Alfred Stieglitz in the twenties, and when she found her home in the American Southwest.

Jan Garden Castro

ART VERSUS SOCIETY

We began the preceding section by considering the value of the artist as cultural champion, and we concluded it by considering the importance of artists who present us with an extremely altered reality. Do not imagine for a moment, however, that every artist is recognized by society or that every artist is conscious of playing an important social role. When we use expressions like "we are able to see" or "the artist shows us what we would normally miss," we are talking about *possibilities,* not necessarily actualities. Sometimes there is bitter hostility between the artist and society. Sometimes what the artist expresses is alienation itself, a sense of loneliness that springs from being cut off from the mainstream of life. Alienation is especially characteristic of contemporary artists (in every discipline). One reason is a feeling that, as society grows fatter and people become increasingly preoccupied with material possessions and pleasure, the true value of the artist is less and less apparent.

Art as Social Commentary

What often happens is that artists in affluent societies such as ours, societies which hold dominant positions in world affairs, become critics rather than cultural champions. Unlike Georgia O'Keeffe, for example, who noticed shapes and colors that others did not, some contemporary artists see injustice, discrimination, the effects of loneliness and poverty in a fast moving, money pursuing society in which not every one can be successful; they see vanishing appreciation for the artist, as

José Clemente Orozco, "Zapatistas," 1931
(Courtesy of The Museum of Modern Art)

well as the appalling waste of human potential in a society that is over-fed, undereducated, insensitive, and violent.

When art is consciously projected as social commentary, it is likely to be either hyperrealistic or bitingly satiric, influenced by the cartoonists and such daily comic strips as Garry Trudeau's *Doonesbury*, which are meant to do much more than entertain us.

During the boom times of the 1920s in the United States, that flapper era of sudden riches and soaring stock prices, the tone of American art—not to mention literature, drama, and music—was curiously melancholy. Our creative minds were picking up the sad strains faintly heard in alleyways and the rooms of sleazy hotels, strains of the lonely, the disenchanted, and the poor. Our artists knew that beneath the glitz lay many broken hearts. Edward Hopper (1882–1967) is perhaps the most enduring of these "artists of alienation." His work, almost photographically realistic and scrupulous in its detail, has left behind for us a stirring pictorial record of the underside of the 1920s, as well as the mainstream of city life during the depression of the 1930s. His paintings show cheap hotel rooms, late-night diners, and desolate gas stations sparsely peopled by forlorn figures, hunched over cold coffee and soggy cigarettes, resigned to their bitter fate. Hopper paints not for the beauty of form and colors, but for the sad beauty that can be found in feeling a kinship with the oppressed. Such an artist, cut off from the life of fashionable society as he is, provides a valuable service for those whose conscience demands that they remain in close touch with social realities that are not always pleasant.

A newcomer to the international art scene, a sculptor whose work is seldom described as either pleasant or beautiful in the usual sense of those words, is Duane Hanson (b. 1925). In the late 1960s Hanson taught art in a community college while he worked secretly in an old garage-turned-studio, turning out a series of sculptures that would once have scandalized the art world. Perhaps indirectly influenced—and amused—by the frightening realism of Disneyland blood-less robots, who smile toward you and deliver life-affirming platitudes, Hanson decided to take sculptural realism one step further. In those early days he created figures more lifelike than anything you can find at Madame Tussaud's Wax Museum, and often far more terrifying: teenagers dead in a motorcycle wreck; soldiers slaughtered on a Vietnamese battlefield; a girl raped and then stabbed repeatedly with numerous pairs of scissors, her lifeless eyes still wide open in the horror of her final moments.

Achieving sudden and wholly unexpected fame as art critics, looking for the new, happened upon his garage, Hanson added to his rogue's gallery a succession of less violent but more subtle and delicious subjects, such as the *Supermarket Lady* pictured below. You will observe not only the artist's extraordinary technique, but his sly yet not uncompassionate humor. This person is a recognizable social type, a victim—though she does not know it—of the social structure and the value system that makes our middle class what it is. We might try hard to express in words the nature, direction, and purpose (or lack of it) of middle-class life in contemporary America; but does not this figure say it all for us? It is reminiscent of Goya's portrait of King Charles IV and his family: same sly humor, same social criticism. In Goya's case the subjects of the painting may or may not have gotten the joke. In Hanson's case the satire is deliberately planned, the workmanship meticulous so that the artist cannot fail to achieve his purpose.

True enough, the charges by some art lovers that Hanson's work, at least in this early phase of his career, is hardly the work one

Duane Hanson, "Supermarket Lady"
(Courtesy of Duane Hanson)

would purchase and show off proudly in one's living room! But the decorative function of art is not always important. Despite the abstractionists and Minimalists, who maintain that art should not be an outlet for personal expression, there are many, like Duane Hanson, who have much to say and use their talents to make us listen, even if they must sometimes shock our sensibilities.

Women in Art

We have had occasion throughout this chapter to single out a number of artists who happened to be women—Edmonia Lewis, Mary Cassatt, and Georgia O'Keeffe. We say "happened" because what they produced appears to have had nothing whatever to do with gender. If, however, we are looking long and hard at the interaction between the artist and society, we would be remiss if we did not pay some attention to a glaring fact of history: *Most of the major artists have been men.* Are we to assume that women are by nature lacking in some mysterious combination of genes or hormones which impart to men the intrinsic ability to reproduce on canvas or in marble what they see or feel? Or, even more, are we to assume that women, who have been on the whole outnumbered in *all* of the arts throughout history, are somehow less artistically oriented?

The participation of women in the arts has nothing to do with hormones and everything to do with social institutions and customs.

We find ourselves in total agreement with Linda Nochlin, a contemporary art historian, who points out that the participation of women in the arts has nothing to do with hormones and *everything* to do with social institutions and customs. Women have, for example, been very much in the foreground in both dance and singing:

> Where there is a need there is a way, institutionally speaking: once the public, authors, and composers demanded more realism and range than boys in drag or piping castrati could offer, a way was found to include women in the performing arts.[8]

Women's Liberation, when applied to artists, seems to me to be a naïve concept. It raises issues which in this context are quite absurd. At this point in time, artists who happen to be women need this particular form of hysteria like they need a hole in the head.

Bridget Riley

While the nineteenth century produced some major women novelists, like the Brontë sisters, George Eliot, and George Sand, they all were published because they pretended to be men. A woman could have been, in other words, a "closet" writer. But a woman would have had a difficult time indeed learning the skills necessary to practice a visual art. Those women who were given an education of some sort were still not allowed to be present in life-drawing classes, to look upon nudes of either sex. How else were women, then, to acquire an adequate knowledge of anatomy? The days were over when a burgeoning artist would dare, as Michelangelo had dared, to steal cadavers from cemeteries.

Georgia O'Keeffe, "White Canadian Barn, No. 2"
(Courtesy of The Metropolitan Museum of Art, The Alfred Stieglitz Collection, 1949)

Times have certainly changed, and women everywhere are making their presence felt strongly in the art world. If such a thing exists as specifically *feminist* art, this is only to say that some women have much to say about the struggle for sexual equality that is still not won. Men artists have been making statements for a long time. *Guernica* shows clearly that a work can be both formally magnificent and personally meaningful to the artist. But feminist art as such is probably a passing trend. Social conditions "permitting," female Michelangelos and van Goghs will eventually be adorning the walls of the great museums.

Skeptics assume that no artist—feminist or not—can resist the pressure to depoliticize their work once it travels in exalted economic circles.

Elizabeth Hess

The Artist and the Bill-payers

In a vintage British film called *The Horse's Mouth,* a band of artists, all social outcasts, move themselves into several palatial apartments while their owners are away. No one has invited them. They simply break and enter. One artist, with an obsession for feet, proceeds to cover each wall in "his" apartment with murals depicting feet of every size and shape. Another carves a giant pair of marble buttocks. When it is time for the owners to return, the artists simply move out, leaving the horrified residents to clean up the mess.

Though a bit exaggerated, the film focuses our attention on an ongoing conflict: the attempt of artists to change the environment as *they* see fit versus the avowed rights of those who say they do not want *that kind of change.* A large international airport in the United States was recently the scene of such a battle. A duly appointed Art in Public Places committee was given a certain sum to spend and de-

Diego Rivera, "Man at the Crossroads," 1932
(Courtesy of The Museum of Modern Art)

cided to buy, among other projects, an extremely large painting by a prominent artist, which featured a huge slab of bacon floating in outer space. The proposed exhibit spot for the painting was a main concourse with a large daily traffic volume. The president of a major airline fought the committee tenaciously, condemning the work as trivial and unworthy of the label "art." The conflict had a characteristic outcome: no "difficult" art in the concourse.

Centuries ago Michelangelo was having his own problems. Summoned to Rome from his native Florence by the Church, he was required to perform such Herculean feats as painting the Sistine Chapel ceiling or doing statues for the proposed tomb of Pope Julius II without ever being able to satisfy his patrons. The pope finally canceled the order for his tomb, setting off an art scandal that had Italian tongues wagging for nearly ten years and causing the artist to regard himself as a secular failure, though he never doubted he possessed divine gifts. But it was his painting *The Last Judgment* that created the most explosive controversy. Michelangelo's vision of the final moments on earth is so graphic, with the naked bodies of sinners writhing in pain, that the Church condemned it as blasphemy and demanded that the offensive nakedness be covered. The issue is clear: Those who pay the bills believe they are entitled to be the arbiters of taste; artists frequently believe otherwise.

When we visit great cities like Paris, Florence, and Athens, we cannot help admiring the art work which surrounds us. But may we not be tempted to wonder how many artists were kept from public display because they failed to meet certain criteria? There have always been municipal committees designated to pass judgment on statues and murals intended to adorn public places, and they have always claimed the right to make final decisions.

During the 1930s a bitter conflict ensued when Nelson, grandson of John D. Rockefeller, commissioned the Mexican muralist Diego Rivera to paint a mural for the lobby of the newly constructed Rockefeller Center on New York City's Fifth Avenue, a monumental architectural feat in its time and surely a soaring expression of capitalist power. The Rockefeller family had long been patrons of the arts, a source of countless millions of dollars for artists and their projects. Though Rivera was an avowed Communist, Rockefeller recognized his preeminence in mural art, leaving both subject and treatment to what he believed would be the artist's sensitive discretion.

The result was a mural of staggering proportions, depicting highlights of the Russian Revolution, with the figure of Lenin boldly claiming center stage. This on capitalist home ground! Rockefeller was horrified, ordered that the mural be erased, demanded an apology, and refused to pay for the work. Rivera countered that a bargain is a bargain and that the intentions of the artist are beyond question. Nonetheless, the mural isn't there.

The poet E. B. White captured the essence of the dispute:

"It's not good taste in a man like me,"
Said John D.'s grandson Nelson,
"To question an artist's integrity
"Or mention a practical thing like a fee,
"But I know what I like to a large degree
"Though art I hate to hamper,
"For twenty-one thousand conservative bucks
"You painted a radical. I say shucks,
"I never could rent the offices—
"The capitalistic offices.

"For this, as you know, is a public hall
"And people want doves, or a tree in fall,
"And though your art I dislike to hamper,
"I owe a little to God and Gramper.
"And after all,
"It's my wall."
"We'll see if it is," said Rivera.[9]

There are two interpretations of this final line that seem reasonable. One is rather obvious: The political Rivera is warning the capitalist Rockefeller that, when the Revolution is complete, there will be no private ownership of such an imposing edifice. But a secondary meaning is that art belongs to the people as a whole, not to a single individual, no matter who pays the bills. The issue has never been resolved, and one can only expect the debate to grow more intense as the entire question of what constitutes art in the first place grows even more nebulous.

GLOSSARY

chiaroscuro: The alternation of light and shadow in painting—a technique developed during the Renaissance to produce greater depth and realism.

Cubism: A contemporary movement in art (epitomized in Picasso's *Guernica*) in which figures become geometric designs.

fresco: A mural created by applying paint to freshly spread, moist plaster.

Impressionism: A mid-nineteenth-century movement in art; to some extent, a response to the invention of photography, whereby the attempt to be realistic is completely abandoned and, instead, artists project onto canvas a subjective experience of the world as color and form.

medium: In this chapter, the characteristic material used by an artist (e.g., marble, bronze, watercolors, oils, etc.).

Minimalism: A contemporary school of art which stresses design elements and disapproves of the artist's use of the medium to express subjective feelings. (See also Chapter 2.)

perspective: The technique of rendering, on a plane or curved surface, objects as they appear to the eye; developed and refined during the early Renaissance.

Post-Impressionism: A broad term for a variety of painting styles developed by such artists as Cezanne, van Gogh, and Gauguin, who started out as Impressionists but eventually refused to be bound by the limitations of any particular "school" of art.

Renaissance: Perhaps the most important single era in the history of Western civilization. It began in northern Italy during the fourteenth century as a movement in the arts reflecting a resurgent faith in human values and life here on earth. Gradually it became a political and social movement as well, marking the end of the medieval, Church-dominated world and the emergence of the modern, science-dominated world.

NOTES

1. Betty Edwards, *Drawing on the Right Side of the Brain* (Los Angeles: J. P. Tarcher, 1979).

2. Arlette Loroi-Gourhan, "The Archeology of Lascaux Cave," *Scientific American* (June 1982), p. 108.

3. John Perreault, "Forging Ahead: A Sculpture Conference Diary," *Village Voice* (September 21, 1982), p. 84.

4. Marilyn Richardson, *VITA: Edmonia Lewis, Harvard Magazine* (March/April, 1986), p. 40.

5. Irving Stone, *The Agony and the Ecstasy,* pp. 529–530. Copyright © 1961 by

Doubleday & Company, Inc. Reprinted by permission of the publisher.

6. Van Gogh must have been clairvoyant, for in 1987 his painting *Sunflowers* sold at auction for $38.5 million.

7. Gardner's *Art through the Ages,* 7th ed., revised by Horst de la Croix and Richard G. Tansey (New York: Harcourt Brace Jovanovich, 1980), p. 819.

8. Thomas B. Hess and Elizabeth C. Baker, eds., *Art and Sexual Politics* (New York: Collier Books, 1973), p. 6.

9. E. B. White, "I Paint What I See," *Poems and Sketches of E. B. White* (New York: Harper & Row, 1933). Copyright 1933 by E. B. White. Originally appeared in *The New Yorker* and reprinted by permission of Harper & Row, Publishers, Inc.

Paul Klee, "Twittering Machine," 1922
(Courtesy of The Museum of Modern Art)

MUSIC: SOUND AND SILENCE

2

Overview

Music is controlled sound. Musicians tell us music is essential, not only because it is a treat, a pleasant way to spend time, or even a beautiful enrichment of life. Of course, music is all these things; but most of all life would be less without it. Music is almost as necessary for survival as food or language. In a sense, music is both, translated into sound.

Human beings live in the midst of an *unplanned audio environment.* No one knows just when a jet will streak overhead or brakes will squeal or a screaming mob will turn the corner. The dawn of human time may have been a bit quieter, but hostile mammoths were probably sending forth horrendous bellows when it occurred.

I have often regretted my speech, never my silence.

Publius Syrus

59

Anyway, the past scarcely matters in this regard. Today the majority of the world's population exists at the mercy of unwanted sound, audio pollution as damaging to mental health as air and water pollution are damaging to physical health.

As art has altered our visual surroundings, adding forms and colors that were not there before, so too has music altered our audio surroundings. We have options: the sound of a stick being dragged along a wrought-iron fence, the wraparound rhythms of a supermarket amplifier, a Beethoven symphony, a rock band.

The gift which music appears to offer us as one of our most treasured resources for living is *variety*—a wealth of sounds and forms, making possible a wide range of experiences. Limiting ourselves to one specific *kind* of music is as detrimental to growth as not experiencing variety in all of the other arts. Or indeed in life itself.

Music as an art is made up of a number of separate elements. It can be produced by instruments, each with its own sound, or by the human voice. It cannot be produced by nature, though some musical sound imitates nature. Flutes can sound like birds. The string section of an orchestra, playing a certain part of Jean Sibelius's *Tapiola,* sounds almost exactly like wind in a deep forest.

The sounds of music can be loud and soft. They can be heard by themselves or in combinations. In music of any age of culture, sounds must be experienced in a sequence, usually with underlying rhythmic patterns. Instrumental notes and human voices can accompany each other, or work together to constitute a sound unity new to nature.

People who won't allow themselves to experience the variety that music has to offer usually have never taken the time and trouble to listen—*really listen*—perhaps because they are not sure what to listen *for.* This chapter will first separate the musical experience into its component parts; then it will provide some insight into a number of contrasting forms that experience can assume.

Poor Wordsworth. Poor Thoreau. What would such seekers of isolated streams and wildflowers say today?

Skip Lowery

Too often we stay with what is comfortable and familiar, unwilling to stray into alien territories.

MUSICAL ELEMENTS

The human control over unplanned noise probably came with the discovery of musical *tones,* single sounds that are either low or high in pitch and are produced either by the human voice or by instrument. Tones are caused by vibrations of sound waves. Whether they are low or high in pitch is determined by the frequency of these vibrations. Not unexpectedly, as pitches go from low to high, frequencies increase.

Single sounds—primitive words or shouts—no doubt have existed since there have been creatures with any sort of communicative strategies. One can also imagine early people banging sound-producing elements together for any of a variety of reasons. But there was no such thing as music itself until they banged away in something like *rhythm* and until it was discovered that a sequence of sounds was possible: tones separated from each other by definite *intervals.* The arrangement of tones most familiar to all of us is an eight-tone scale: do re mi fa so la ti do. (Most often we refer to these sounds as musical *notes,* but musicians prefer to call the sound itself a tone, and the sign or symbol for it a note.)

Beginnings of the Scale

No one can be sure just what instrument first produced tones in a definite sequence from low to high. However, we *do* know that the Greeks either invented or made abundant use of the *monochord,* probably a very remote ancestor of the guitar and mandolin. The monochord was a simple, rectangular wooden box with an opening on top and with a single string tightly stretched across the opening. A movable bridge, probably made of wood, could be pressed down at certain points along the string, dividing it so that one side was held taut while the other could vibrate. It had been discovered that whether the produced sounds were low or high depended on the rapidity of the vibrations. An early form of the simple scale was probably the result. It would be hard to imagine that the Greeks, with their passion for order and form, did not create a musical system of tones spaced at regular intervals. Many cultural historians attribute to the Greeks, in fact, the formalization of musical art. The word *music* itself, not surprisingly, derives from the Greek *mousike,* which means "the art of the muse."

One prominent theory is that the art of *mousike* came into being as a means of perfecting the art of poetry. A melodic accompaniment to the epic chanting (or possibly singing) of heroic poetry was probably very popular. Perhaps the desired effect on the listener was the illusion that the Muse herself was performing. We know that Plato was so charmed by this art that in his *Republic* he rated music as the very highest kind of education he would want in an ideal state. He maintained that experience in listening to music would liberate the spirit of pure reason within the soul, since music offered an ideal arrangement of meaningful words. To inhabit a realm of pure musical beauty was the same thing as inhabiting a realm of pure thought.

Rhythm

We have, of course, no surviving authentic Greek musical manuscripts and therefore can only speculate on what their music might have sounded like. But we *can* hazard the guess that music reached high levels of sophistication during the "Golden Age," which spanned the fifth and fourth centuries B.C. Music was used for almost every sort of ceremonial occasion: sports events, tragic theater, the honoring of heroes, and, of course, the wild dancing orgies held in connection with the worship of the god Dionysus. There are written accounts of some of this music, as well as the moral distinctions that were made. Certain rhythms were held to be appropriate for inspirational ceremonies because of their uplifting effect on the soul, while other rhythms—most certainly those of the orgies—were deemed immoral, conducive to wild, licentious behavior.

There is little doubt that *rhythm*—the alternation between stress and unstress—is older than musical sounds produced by even a simple instrument like the monochord. Most likely, a rat-a-tat rhythm with sticks and stones could be singled out as a major transition in human development. Very young children left to their own devices can be observed rat-a-tatting with blocks, the beat becoming more pronounced and regular as the child matures. Dances must have preceded the discovery of distinct musical tones. Perhaps rhythm was always there, waiting for the right someone to make the connection—to put rhythm and tones together.

Chapter 14 analyzes two contrasting aspects of human culture and human personality called Apollonian and Dionysian, after the Greek gods whose characteristics inspired the philosopher Friedrich Nietzsche to use these two terms as psychological labels. The *Apollonian* half of us, as we shall see, enjoys order; the *Dionysian* half can exult in disorder and frenzy. Neither side is sufficient by itself. A person who is always orderly, precise, and logical sometimes needs to let go, be impulsive, behave unpredictably. But a person who is always spontaneous, always intuitive, never planning anything in advance can prove unreliable, may never carry a project to completion.

Rhythm has the same contrasting extremes. Apollonian dances, such as the waltz, the minuet, and even the time-honored fox-trot, tend to slow people down, bring their sensibilities into line. They produce a feeling of calm well-being. Apollonian rhythm is also necessary for all stately occasions: graduations, presidential inaugurals, and, of course, funerals. Apollonian rhythm clears the brain. Our impulses are held in check. It is hard to go emotionally off the deep end with a steady beat sounding in your ear.

Music has a *beat* when its rhythmic pattern is regular, as in the waltz, in which the pattern of long/short/short is continually repeated. Of course, composers and songwriters sometimes change the beat in any particular piece, but they seldom do so incessantly. In a classical symphony an alteration in the beat is a major event, usually a very exciting one. The dependability of the rhythmic underpinning is generally what holds music together.

When a piece by a composer like the Impressionist Claude Debussy strikes the untrained ear as lacking rhythm, the reality is that the pattern is there, but the beat is not as pronounced as in, for example, *The Bolero,* a well-known work by fellow Impressionist Maurice Ravel.

Few composers attempt to be totally arhythmic, though irregular beats are not uncommon in contemporary concert music. Very steady beats are often associated, as we have said, with Apollonian order; and one of the ways in which a contemporary composer can empathically rebel against the establishment is by refusing to follow its time-honored rhythm patterns.

Students of cultural history cannot ignore the insights afforded by the predominant rhythms of particular eras. Victorian manners were reflected in the Apollonian waltz and ragtime tempos leading up to World War I. In the United States, newly arrived immigrants were eager to assimilate into the prevailing culture, and, while they preserved the dances of their native countries, they also acquired the elegant rhythm of those who had been here longer.

Students of cultural history cannot ignore the insights afforded by the predominant rhythms of particular eras.

The acknowledged master of ragtime was Scott Joplin (1868–1917), who came not from the music salons of major eastern cities but from their back rooms and brothels, where talented black musicians and composers were forced to remain. We might expect his music to throb with the beat of anger, or to anticipate the blues, or to imitate the moans of field workers barely able to lift the last bale of cotton. But such was not the case. The goal of turn-of-the-century popular music was Apollonian. Joplin wanted to perform before white audiences—elegant ones. And so was born ragtime, which is slow (he always insisted on that) and stately, close in tempo to the French square dance known as the quadrille. Ragtime was Joplin's way of winning acceptance by the Apollonian majority, and for a time at least the composer was fashionable, performing in elegant supper clubs, performing a style of music which charmed white patrons and which they immediately made their own.

From the decade of the 1920s right up to the present time, popular music in America has been marked by alternations of Apollonian and Dionysian beats. The decade of the speakeasy and bathtub gin the 1920s—had its Charleston and other lively dances in which the emphasis was on jumping around and looking much less elegant than one's parents. The late 1930s and early 1940s brought forth "swing," which can be described as a partial return to elegance without sacrificing Dionysian looseness. The big-band rhythms of Glenn Miller, Harry James, and Benny Goodman were intricate and sprightly, suitable enough for chandeliered ballrooms but not too slow for soldiers and sailors on a two-day pass, who could not afford long silences in which to think about battle zones and casualty reports.

Our age is, without question, the age of rock; and while rock has its quiet side, its overwhelming appeal lies in its incessant rhythms—the crashing cymbals, the amplified sounds of bass guitars, and the screaming voices, chanting words that must be heard over and over before they are understood. Even then, they are usually understood only by an in-group audience from whose ranks Apollonians are forever barred.

This is not to say that rock music cannot be enjoyed by those who "swung and swayed" in the chandeliered ballrooms to Glenn Miller's muted brass. The rhythms of rock can be therapy for those trapped in the stress of Apollonian responsibilities.

On the other hand, what if rock were the only rhythm to which we were able to respond? Dionysian release is important, is *necessary* if we are caught in an Apollonian freeze. There are times when we could do far worse than be swept up in a frenzy of percussion and lose ourselves in a gyrating mass. Those who consider themselves "purists," who close their ears (and hearts) to the sounds and messages of rock, need not boast that they alone possess "culture." Yet the continual craving for those sounds bears scrutiny. The distinguishing rhythmic feature of rock is generally its nonstop pulsations, which may be adrenalin to those who need the contrast, but numbing to those who hear little else in their musical lives.

Silence

The reader may be surprised to find silence listed as a musical element, for how can that which sends forth no sound be considered a component of the art of music? Yet silence—when you think about it—*is* the unpublicized "ingredient" that makes music possible in the same way that the empty space around a sculpture makes the sculpture possible, or the judicious use of wall space can make or break an art exhibit. Just imagine 25 original van Goghs crammed together: "Where is *Starry Night*? Oh, there it is. We almost missed it. Funny, but somehow it's just not as exciting as I thought it would be."

Ever hear a symphony on tape at accelerated speed? The sound is ludicrous, definitely unmusical, but not just because the tones are not being played at the proper cadence. The acceleration has erased the silences, which are as significant as the tones themselves. *Music is the shaped sound between silences.*

If we would deepen our appreciation of music, we must learn to hear and to enjoy silence itself. The pauses in the second movement, the "Funeral March," of Beethoven's *Third Symphony* are as famous as the themes which precede and follow them. The effect is like that of someone trying valiantly to hold back tears. The main theme of the movement, a dirgelike melody appropriate for a funeral procession, comes in a halting, irregular rhythm, the silences between the tones enlarged. Think of the last time you were in the presence of someone struggling for self-control while obviously overcome by a powerful surge of emotion. Were not the silences full of meaning? Great composers handle silences in the same way that great artists since

One of the first things a visitor to a London park notices, for example, . . . is the sign at the entrance which prohibits transistor radios from the area.

Skip Lowery

Music is the shaped sounds between silences.

Leonardo have known how to handle shadows. Great stage actors owe something of their greatness to the mastery they have achieved over the words in a play which they do *not* speak.

The hush that comes either before or after the great moments in the arts is often responsible for those moments' greatness, though people are not always aware of the fact. Perhaps the most famous solo theme for French horn occurs soon after the opening of the fourth movement of Brahms' *First Symphony.* The moment is heralded by a tympani roll and then a pause, which dramatically intensifies the significance of what follows. No one could listen to the sequence without experiencing a sudden heightened awareness. The French horn enters like an actor making at long last a delayed appearance for which the audience has been eagerly waiting.

Perhaps the most well-known moment in all of theater history is that in which Hamlet, believing himself to be alone on stage, begins the most celebrated soliloquy ever written for an actor. It has become traditional for the performer to pause, *not* to launch at once into "To be or not to be . . ."; or else to allow a long pause between phrases: "To be . . . or not to be."

What ultimately distinguishes one aspiring musician from another in a music conservatory is not the ability to play the notes as written and at the proper tempo, but the musical *intuition* which manifests itself. One way in which the professional ear can detect the presence of this intuition (or "feeling for the music" as it is sometimes called) is to listen to how the performer manipulates the silences which surround the tones. Three world-class pianists might record Beethoven's *Pathetique Sonata,* and though each plays exactly the same notes, giving proper attention to the pace and the mood indicated by the composer, the interpretation by each will have subtle touches unique to that musician. In almost every instance the telling factor is the handling of silence. Here a pause is elongated; there, foreshortened. As with the space surrounding a sculpture, silence in music helps to define, to single out, to create individuality.

In any group, the person who interests us, who seems to demand our careful attention is the person with silences. Who is likely to warrant a second look? The one who calmly sits there with a faint smile, saying nothing? or the one who comes bursting into the room, breathlessly reeling off a torrent of words? Of course, the impression made by the silent person will be greater on a silent observer. People with silences appreciate each other.

Our age, however, is the age of the transistor, the Walkman, and the cordless headset. People run, exercise, and ride their bikes encased in a secret world of ear-splitting noise. One would think that in urban areas, already noisy enough without electronic assistance, everyone would gladly seek moments of quiet, of solitude, to escape the throbbing of the marketplace, moments to breathe deep and re-

Heard melodies are sweet, but those unheard Are sweeter.

John Keats

Ours is the age of the transistor, the Walkman, and the cordless headset. People run, exercise, and ride their bikes encased in a secret world of ear-splitting noise.

If we would deepen our appreciation of music, we must learn to hear and to enjoy silence itself. The pauses in the second movement of Beethoven's Third Symphony are as famous as the themes which precede and follow them.

examine one's thoughts and emotions and sort them out like newly washed clothes. Is it perhaps that our addiction to noise is an excuse *not* to look into ourselves for fear of the disorder we might glimpse? The absence of silence in daily life as well as in music may be neither good nor bad, but it certainly is significant, affording us some insights into what we and our world have become. Perhaps we are a frightened generation, and loud noise is like the night-light our parents used to leave on when they went away.

Melody

No musical element is subject to as many definitions and evaluations as melody. No musical element comes with as many preordained expectations. The casual concertgoer in the presence of a contemporary work by a young, adventurous composer, hearing only a baffle of noise, demands to know what "happened" to the melody.

Melody can be defined as the sequence of lead tones in a piece, as opposed to the supporting tones which are used for harmony and what would be the bass tones on the piano or the lower-register orchestral sounds that come from cellos, basses, and percussion. (Of course, in any given work the melodic lines can proceed from *any* instrument, even a drum.)

Many people, however, do not define melody so much as impose requirements upon it. That is, they wait for a sequence of sounds they are willing to label melody; or, failing to hear one, they denounce a work as not having melody, or being unmelodious. Seldom does one even hear that "the major melody of the piece is unfamiliar or unpleasant." Rather, the detected presence of a melody indicates that at least "some" portion of a work is beautiful. In other words, for many, a melody is a procession of sounds which fall pleasantly upon the ear. A melody has to sound beautiful. But even a scant historical perspective in the humanities will tell you that, while Plato may have believed in the existence of absolute beauty, standards by which society determines what is beautiful are continually changing. What casual concertgoers define as a beautiful sound sequence is never going to be the unfamiliar.

Though the era of Romantic music was the nineteenth century, people still tend to apply Romantic standards for the beautiful and therefore the melodious. Consider a popular piece in the concert repertoire: Tchaikovsky's *Romeo and Juliet.* Ask the casual listener to whistle or hum the "melody," and you are sure to hear the first few bars of the song "Our Love," which was adapted years ago from the "main melody" of the work. When "Our Love" was topping the charts in the 1940s, many came to know the name Peter Ilyich Tchaikovsky for the first time. Many became Tchaikovsky enthusiasts, even attending symphony concerts which included *Romeo and Juliet* in the program. Some found they could enjoy the entire work, while others sat patiently through the dull sections, awaiting the familiar strains of the "melody."

Melody in the Romantic sense has several distinguishing characteristics. First and foremost, it constitutes a sequence of tones which *must* be repeated. In musical vocabulary this is called a *theme*. Second, the sequence has a sensuous quality about it, in contrast to other segments of the score which somehow or other do not. That which is ordinarily called sensuous is gratifying or appealing to one or more of the senses. Examples are a rich profusion of colors in a sunset and a sumptuous buffet table awaiting the hungry guest. Sensuous musical lines can evoke remembrances of sunsets, or water lilies floating quietly on a pond, thunderstorms (as in Beethoven's *Sixth,* or *Pastoral, Symphony*), ocean waves crashing (as in Debussy's *La Mer*), a lovely face half glimpsed through a curtain (as in Debussy's *The Maid with Flaxen Hair*). Romantic composers, such as Beethoven, Schubert, Brahms, Mahler, and Strauss, express inner feelings through melodic lines; and since most feelings are associated with memories, it is only natural that, when we listen to those melodies, we form our own associations. Each of us has a Romantic side, and the more music—especially of the nineteenth century— that we come to know, the more themes we enjoy hearing over and over. The familiar Romantic melodies serve as an external anchor for our emotions. Thus do we sometimes reject the bizarre and unfamiliar, the unmelodious, so to speak, when the listening experience does not allow for us to indulge in our emotional past.

A third characteristic of Romantic melody is its appeal to the Western emphasis on individualism. To stand out, to be isolated from our surroundings and our time, has been a major goal in Western society. There is very likely a connection between the development of the literary novel, with its heroes and heroines—unique, larger-than-life individuals—and the development of theme dominated music.

The theme, or major melodic line, of a piece is ordinarily developed by the Romantic composers through one or more sets of *variations*—tone sequences that are similar enough to the original to evoke similar associations but changed sufficiently to move us ahead into new experiences.

The nineteenth century also witnessed the emergence of the *idée fixe,* or fixed idea—a melodic line that represents a character or a statement about life which the composer wishes to make. Hector Berlioz's *Harold in Italy,* first performed in 1834, is at once a viola concerto and a musical narrative, based on episodes of Byron's *Childe Harold's Pilgrimage*. The viola in this work is the Byronic hero translated into musical sound and deliberately made by the composer to stand out in brilliant relief from the rest of the orchestra, its themes also boldly separated from the rest of the score. The major melodic

When "Our Love" was topping the charts in the 1940s, many came to know the name Peter Ilyich Tchaikovsky for the first time.

line of *Harold in Italy* is both sensuous and unforgettable. Berlioz describes his use of the viola:

> I conceived the idea of writing a series of scenes for orchestra, in which the viola should find itself mixed up, like a person more or less in action, always preserving his individuality.

Works involving the idée fixe have greatly contributed to the ongoing tradition of what is generally accepted as melody, at least in Western music.

Readers who have heard much Japanese music, on the other hand, will immediately reflect on how that music differs from our notions of what is acceptably melodious. Japanese composers do not usually isolate certain themes from the rest of the music. To most Western ears each tone in a Japanese piece is equal to every other tone. Few Westerners find themselves listening in rapt attention. Indeed, most would not go out of their way to hear a concert of music which seems to wander on and on forever, never "getting anywhere," by which they, of course, mean never reaching the statement of a "definite" theme.

Much contemporary concert music is the work of *Minimalist* composers, who, analogous to the Minimalists in the visual arts, reject the idea that music ought to be the expression of one's inner emotional states or that it exists to produce such states in the listener. They want to create "pure" music—tones, harmonies, and rhythms, which, like color and design in art, reflect the creator's mastery of her or his chosen discipline. In particular do the new composers limit the definition of melody, as they fear their potential listeners have done.

Listening to a new work that does not intend to evoke sensuous memories can be a strange and baffling experience. How can we "enjoy" ourselves when what we are hearing lacks "warmth" or "soul"? But we must remember this: Like other arts, music is what it can and will be. We have the right to turn away, as, of course, we can turn away from strangers. However, we also possess the freedom to make friends.

Harmony

In Eastern music, tones are normally played by themselves, that is, without *harmony,* the simultaneous production of tones by voices or instruments other than those which produce the dominant or lead melodic line. So accustomed are we to hearing such simultaneous production that we tend to take harmony for granted. But like the Romantic conception of melody, harmony in music has historical as well as cultural roots. Early Greek music very probably did not include harmony either. The Greeks, who gave the world philosophy, theater, law, and democracy, were strong on individualism, not group togetherness. They honored heroes, poets, winners of athletic contests, *not* teams of people accomplishing great things through a united effort. One can easily suppose their music to have consisted of solitary, clear tones, a musical counterpart to their heroes.

During the Middle Ages, so far as we know, music was confined mainly to the churches and the monasteries, a complement to the act of worship. Perhaps the strong influence of Plato on medieval Catholicism helps explain the importance placed on song as a means of communicating with God. Plato, as we have said, believed music to be the ideal arrangement of words—the way the soul would sound if it had a voice. Medieval music is therefore *sung prayer*. It was not intended to be a sensuous, appealing element in the mass, though many would argue that church music in all denominations has evolved into just that.

The sung prayer is also known as *plainsong*. As much as Greek music probably suggested the importance of the individual, plainsong was probably intended to have exactly the opposite effect. Medieval Catholicism discouraged a stress on worldly desires and accomplishments, and thus would have had no room for extolling singular personalities or achievements. The plainsong or chant was (still is) sung by any number of voices, but with the purpose of sounding like one voice asking God for mercy and forgiveness. Plainsong is saying that humanity is completely unified in being sinful and undeserving of salvation except through God's love for God's fallen children.

A dominant aspect of the Renaissance was that it veered away from medieval values. It represented a resurgence of the belief in human worth, in the glories of life on earth, and the infinite possibilities of the individual. Royal castles were no longer austere, uncomfortable, and drafty, but places of colorful, extravagant, and pleasurable banquets and parties. Music had a key place in the new pleasure-oriented scheme of things. The Renaissance emphasized enjoyment during one's brief stay on earth, and music could fill leisure hours with many joys. The royal courts all had musicians on hand continually. Scarcely an hour of the day went by without the sounds of lute, recorder, or oboe, playing sometimes alone but increasingly in small consorts, as Renaissance composers explored the harmonious interweaving of different instruments and voices, as if to say that music should be the contribution of a *number* of individuals, each adding to the pleasure, each with a statement to make.

As music evolved in Western society, composers utilized harmonic effects to make unity out of complexity, and this phenomenon remains one of the essential musical experiences. The reader who has not sat in a concert hall and listened to a major symphony orchestra will have to take our word for it that there is a rare excitement in watching a hundred musicians, each concentrating on the score propped up on his or her own music stand and on the capacity of his or her own instrument to send forth a unique sound; yet at the same time hearing a totality that is more than the sum of its parts.

The symphony orchestra, which grew in size and dimension throughout the nineteenth century as musical technology added more and more complex instruments and as composers eagerly sought to experiment with the new sounds, has become a model of human society at its most ideal. It requires every musician to pull together for one common purpose. No one sound can be any more important than another. The melody is no more beautiful than the harmony and rhythm which support it. The lifetime achievements of each player are as nothing if the whole entity does not create an experience for the listener that is intense, focused, and charged with electricity. At the same time, the ultimate product is a testimony to the genius of the individual. If one tone is flat, the entire enterprise collapses.

Learning to listen to the interweaving of great sounds can also shed much light on oneself, on one's closeness to the varied musical strands. Is there perhaps a single melodic line? "That's the way I am, the way I've always been, and the way I intend to stay!" Or can one accommodate different moods, intentions—is there a willingness to strike out on new and untried paths? And if such variety exists, is it under control like an orchestra? Or are we forever tuning up?

MUSICAL FORMS

Music does not depict scenes or describe objects or tell stories, but it mysteriously embodies the continuous motion and emotion that we experience at the sight of objects and scenes and events.

Jacques Barzun

As the art of music developed, the elements of music, some of which we have been considering, became organized into given patterns to serve specific purposes. These patterns are called *musical forms.* When you sing your favorite popular song in the shower, you are practicing music but not necessarily a form. A bunch of old friends, arm-locked around a piano, constitutes a good time, not a cantata.

Musical forms include the symphony, the concerto, chamber music (pieces for a small ensemble), opera, jazz, and so on. Over the years musical forms have acquired specific rules and guidelines by which they can be judged, though these change continually. At any given time there are conflicts behind the scenes over whether this or that piece can really be called music. As in the history of the visual arts, the history of music is filled with the names of great people who never lived to know that one day they would be considered great.

The Song

For many readers, their earliest musical experience will have been a song, a musical form that, like the sonnet in literature, is usually restricted in length. The standard pop "tune" is comprised of 32 measures (a *measure* is the basic musical unit). The standard rhythm is what we call quarter time, or 4/4 time. This means that a measure contains four rhythmic beats. If each tone in a measure is equally stressed, then the measure will contain four notes, called quarter notes. If there are eight tones (eight notes) in the measure, then the eight counts have to be accomplished in the length of time it takes to beat out four quarter notes. You undoubtedly know that 1-2-3-4 repeated over and over constitutes the rhythmic underpinning of a great many songs and dances. You will not find many songs with 32 measures each containing just four notes, but the typical song has a total of 128 beats.

We are certain the Greeks had songs, but assuredly those songs were not limited to 32 measures. We do not even know that the Greeks had any units such as the measure. Very probably there were minstrels who sang the heroic poems like *The Iliad* and *The Odyssey.* In the Greek plays the action was interrupted by odes sung and danced to by a chorus. As we have said, the earliest Western music may well have been sung words. Such a phenomenon would not have been surprising for the Greeks, who venerated rational discourse above all else. The musical accompaniment was perhaps intended to heighten the effect of words, not to be a source of enjoyment in and of itself.

Lyrics to songs (except for the rock tunes of our noise-dominated age, whose words are not always meant to be heard) are as important as the melodies. There are the nursery songs which constitute our first musical experiences; the popular songs of our adolescent years, many of which we forever associate with the happy times before responsibility set in and which preserve our memories of first loves and faraway friends; and songs which remain in our minds to mark the milestones of our existence. "What were they playing the night I fell in love? the night our first child was born? the day the family moved into the new house?"

But whether we're talking about a personal repertoire of meaningful songs or a song recital or a musical comedy we attended, there are *always* lyrics to draw from us a response: "That's *exactly* how I felt when I became aware that I had met just the right someone!" or "when I knew for certain that the right someone was all wrong!" or "when I learned that the love I felt was not returned!"

Song lyrics seem immune to time and change. Elizabethan composers set to music the plaintive words of lovesick swains who had sensibilities remarkably similar to those of young people today. When Madame Butterfly, blind to the obvious implications of her American husband's three-year absence from her and their child, sings with a smile that "one fine day" he will return, we are listening to a grand-opera version of the very same emotions we can find in countless popular songs expressing self-imposed illusions necessary for survival. Don José's final condemnation of the faithless Carmen is different in style, not in feeling, from countless lyrics expressing the love-filled hatred of the betrayed.

Why do we listen over and over to lyrics that tell us nothing we do not know? When the great French entertainer Edith Piaf stood there in a solitary spotlight, her huge eyes moist with tears, and sang of "La Vie en Rose"—that life *must* be seen through rose-colored glasses—she was not conveying any startling new insights to her audience. (And how often must the loyal Piaf fans have begged and screamed for that same number?)

The power of song—often the simpler, the better—lies in the enormous importance to human beings of *network*—a reaching out of hands and hearts, a touching of souls. Just knowing that others feel what we feel brings a comfort, a reassurance, that is one of life's distinct pleasures. The songs we collect as our personal treasures—from the most soaring aria to the earthiest of blues—make us feel part of a warm circle of human beings whose lives have very much in common. Without songs to bind us together, each of us would feel more loneliness than we might be able to bear.

Song is an established musical form and thus can be evaluated esthetically, even as a new symphony or opera must be. Unfortunately, today's standard for popular songs is the Top 40. A song that fails to sell is considered a flop. By this yardstick just about every song written by Franz Schubert would have had to be placed in the reject file.

At its most effective, a song is a unified blend of music and words that makes a simple restatement of a very universal experience (as in Leonard Bernstein's "Lonely Town"); that finds a new way to express an old feeling (as in Stephen Sondheim's remarkable "Send in the Clowns," the very title of which says much about the absurdity of a love relationship); or that suddenly opens a new door and reveals something about ourselves we hadn't thought about or at least expected to find in a song (as in Don McLean's "Vincent," which reminds us of how often we fail to listen and how little we see). What distinguishes song from other experiences in life is the fact that the experience—the insight, the feeling—is there every time the song is heard. A great song is thus one that has been around for quite awhile, or that we are sure *will* be.

Folk Music

Folk songs are likely to be exceptions to the esthetic "rules" we have mentioned. A wry lecturer on the college circuit once observed that the reason folk music is so bad is that it is written by the folks. One presumes the speaker was not able to take folk songs seriously as a significant form of human expression. Often the dedicated concert-goer considers folk music altogether too haphazard in its origins and careless in its execution to warrant serious consideration. But folk songs do indeed fulfill a major requirement of art: *They have endured.*

Folk music is not intended as a concert experience. It is a participant's art. It has strong sociological functions. It is an external anchor not so much for one's personal self, but for one's group or ethnic identity.

Folk music is likely to be nonsensical in subject matter. The pop tune of a few years back "I'm Looking over a Four-Leaf Clover" was no doubt jeered at by musical purists. Yet if only one person in a group starts to sing it, most assuredly everyone will join in. Or let a fiddler introduce the first two notes of "Turkey in the Straw" and almost immediately people are clapping their hands or dancing. Something has to be said for music that can so dramatically alter group behavior.

The history of folk music includes *commemorative songs,* which derive from times before people had written records of important events. During the Middle Ages, for example, troubadours kept people informed of battles and skirmishes. Maritime lore abounds with songs commemorating events that took place at sea, such as atrocities committed by a pirate captain or the sinking of a ship to its lonely, watery grave.

Of particular interest is that the narrators of commemorative songs seldom if ever identify themselves. The song's opening words are likely to be something like: "My name is nothing extra / So that I will not tell." One song winds up in this self-effacing manner: "Now to conclude and finish, too far my lines have run." The focus is clearly the event itself, and the obscurity of the balladiers makes possible an easy transfer to the group. It is always *our* song, never *their* song.

The *work song* is highly durable, for it is hard to imagine a time when work will not be central to most people's lives. In some cases the work song reflects great hardship and a state of tension between management and labor. Often, however, the music is jolly and the words are full of bounce and nonsense:

> *I've been workin' on the railroad*
> *All the livelong day;*
> *I've been workin' on the railroad*
> *Just to pass the time away.*

The nineteenth-century folk ballad "John Henry" reflects the conflict between worker and machine at a time when the steam drill was about to replace human arms and hammers. John Henry became a folk hero, the prototype of the superhuman individual who is stronger and smarter than a machine.

The *accumulation* song is deliberately never-ending. Songs like "The Twelve Days of Christmas" and "Old MacDonald" start off with one detail (one gift, one animal) and then add more, always repeating the list from the very beginning. Accumulation songs exist to keep the group together and prolong the high spirits of the night.

The *scoundrel* song celebrates the Dionysian personality— the perennial favorite of our hidden selves—the lawless, irresponsible, but endlessly charming rogue you couldn't trust or marry or put in charge of an important operation but who is always fun. An Irish favorite is "The Wild Rover," which upholds a life of drinking, gambling, carousing, and avoiding work. The hero proudly announces that "them that don't like me can leave me alone," and who can argue with that premise? He intends to

> . . . *drink when I'm dry,*
> *And if moonshine don't kill me,*
> *I'll live till I die.*

To be sure, society would perish if it depended upon wild rovers, but at the same time, nobody ever composed a folk song about a law-abiding accountant or a pious minister or a faithful husband.

During the 1960s, a period of wholesale fragmentation and alienation in the United States, a significant revival of folk music took place. Young people, often far from home, got together for the night around a campfire and became instant—if temporary—friends through the common bond of singing.

Sophisticated performers like Bob Dylan, Joan Baez, Phil Ochs, and Judy Collins sang new folk songs, using the familiar structures of the past, to make statements against war, pollution, and the corrupt establishment; and, if their listeners did not always sing along, the words of the songs usually reflected the audience's own feelings. But often—with such songs as "We Shall Overcome" and "Amazing Grace"—the solo performer might be joined by as many as 10,000 voices.

This Renaissance of the folk song brought back into our national consciousness forms like the *spiritual,* which had had its special beginnings in the black need for a cosmic identity. Taken—stolen—away from their homeland, blacks in the United States of the last century, with no future except slavery, pain, and death, concentrated on their relationship with God and an ultimate reward in a paradise where everyone was free. The socially aware generation of the 1960s recognized that such pain was not a thing of the past, that the need behind the songs was still, tragically, there.

In spirituals there is much emphasis on God's personal concern for each person, however obscure God may be in the eyes of other mortals. For instance:

> *I sing because I'm happy,*
> *I sing because I'm free,*
> *For His eye is on the sparrow,*
> *And I know He watches me.*

If all music does not have to express or appeal to the emotions, the spiritual is one kind that exists to make emotional release possible. We cannot imagine what life would have been like for slaves, or what it could be like today in the fetid air of inner cities, without this profound music of earthly sorrow and religious hope. That such music came into being hardly excuses those responsible for the suffering, nor is the music ample compensation for the conditions which produced it. We can only be in awe of its passionate majesty.

A persistent feature of the spiritual is the elongation of syllables, as in the famous opening line: "Swing low, sweet chariot." Feelings, to be liberated, need space, breathing room, even though the singer had none.

In *gospel* songs, liberation is even more pronounced. The singer soon leaves the stated theme and takes flight, allowing the melodic line to serve as guide, to keep the emotions of the singer from overwhelming him. Nonetheless, gospel allows a profound catharsis of the emotions, perhaps more than any other musical form. It is, of course, the wellspring of contemporary soul music.

A Bach Fugue

"Yes," you may say, "I completely understand why 'We Go Together' from the musical *Grease* will always be dear to me, reminding me of my first high-school sweetheart. But I also know that, if I were suddenly asked to focus my attention on a fugue by Bach, a composer totally alien to my time and personality, I might be confused, if not resentful. What has Bach to offer me?"

Johann Sebastian Bach (1685–1750) was born in a Germany that did not consider music an art form; that did not in fact recognize what music could do for humanity's spirit; that viewed music as court entertainment, composed and performed for upper-class amusement by hirelings paid to do a job, or else as an adjunct to religious services. The music with which Bach is associated, which indeed he came to epitomize, grew out of religion but went beyond religion in its impact and influence on the future of music as an art. It was the music we call *baroque,* belonging to a period in Western humanities ranging from the late sixteenth century to (for historians' convenience) the year in which Bach died.

The baroque period was characterized by an architectural grandeur and an excessive use of color and ornamentation. Civic buildings, such as those which still line the Ringstrasse in Vienna, were adorned with gilt, statuary, and other forms of embellishment, none of which was intended to be purely functional. Baroque buildings were to be enjoyed as objects of vision, not simply as places in which certain tasks were accomplished.

The baroque church offered perhaps the most characteristic architectural style of the period. In sharp contrast to the austere churches of the Protestant Reformation, which wanted to "purify" religion of its Catholic sensuousness, the baroque houses of worship reintroduced marble, brilliant colors, and statues, perhaps as an effort to reinvest religion with an appeal both to the spirit and the senses. Throughout Germany, Austria, and Poland there are churches, dating from the seventeenth century, with flying angels suspended from brightly painted ceilings and smiling gold cherubs peeking out from behind the tops of marble columns. These churches, many of which are Catholic, were for their time the last word in opulence, and offered dramatic and esthetic appeal without apology.

Catholicism found in baroque splendor one means of bringing defectors back to the fold. But the impetus toward elaborate ornamentation also touched many Protestants as well as secular artists. As the era progressed, composers, especially in Italy, sought to outdo one another in the intricacy of their compositions. A unique feature they used was *counterpoint,* playing one melodic line against another, both melodic lines being given equal value and dominance. *Harmony,* of course, was already standard in music. But counterpoint carried complexity a step further.

It is a rediscovery of the world of which I have the joy of being a part. It fills me with awareness of the wonder of life, with a feeling of the incredible marvel of being a human being. The music is never the same for me, never! Each day it is something new, fantastic and unbelievable. That is Bach, like nature, a miracle!

Pablo Casals

Baroque counterpoint at first sounded strange to the ears of Bach's congregation in Arnstadt, where he was employed as church organist, a workman who happened to compose his own pieces and whose appetite for experimenting with organ sound was insatiable. Seeking to expand his musical horizons, Bach went to Sweden in 1705 to study with the famous organist Buxtehude; he returned to Arnstadt with new works of such intricacy and virtuosity that the church choir often could not sing them. Bach achieved some notoriety throughout Germany as word spread of the new music. Eventually he became musical director and choirmaster at St. Thomas's Church in Leipzig, where he remained for the better part of his productive life, scarcely traveling more than a few miles in any direction. His notoriety began to fade as he grew older, though the complexity of his work deepened. He became known as an eccentric; and though music itself in Germany was attaining stature as an art form, the great repertoire of Bach—the cantatas, the oratorios, and the magnificent displays of counterpoints known as fugues—were considered dated even before they were ever really discovered. Bach's music would have to wait a full century before it would take its place among the acknowledged masterworks of humankind.

Confined both geographically and professionally, Bach found liberation in exploring the possibilities of musical language. The baroque style called for long, highly fluid melodies and countermelodies, but also for *improvisation*—a spontaneous variation or set of variations on a given theme. Through improvisation Bach could take wings and soar into the endless skies of inner space.

Bach lived in an era when music's only purpose was to be an adjunct to something else, such as public or religious ceremonies. Few would have understood if a composer had stated unequivocally a belief that music should express the composer's own personality or inner feelings. While Bach's music is frequently labeled "intellectual" and is today preferred by many mathematicians to that of all other composers, there is a very fine distinction between the mathematical complexity of the work and what others might call "a trip." Surely there is an emotional side to mathematics. One need only read some of the letters that pass back and forth between physicists—those, for instance, who are hunting for a mathematical formula that would unify all of the known natural forces—to understand how intoxicating can be the excursions into those unfamiliar regions of the mind where intellectual connections take place. Listening intently to Bach's great *Toccata and Fugue* in D Minor, we are drawn into a vortex of sensations which are all but indescribable. The ear discerns the many melodic strands which play against each other, and the inner eye translates the sounds into patterns of light and lines that criss-cross, engulf each other, and continually change into shapes never before seen or imagined.

In the great animated film *Fantasia* (1940), the Disney artists did indeed convert the counterpoint of Bach's *Toccata and Fugue* in D Minor into a stunning visual sequence that can be called nonemotional only because the viewer/listener is taken on a journey so strange that immediate personal identification is difficult. But that millions of people have been touched by the sequence in the intervening half-century indicates that, long ago, Bach himself touched a universal but mysterious inner force that operates whether we are waking or sleeping and connects words or images or sounds—a force we can call simply "intelligence" or mystically "the human spark." Bach, sitting at the organ in his church, allowed his mind and the keys to become one, and thus he allowed glimpses of the way the mind works, many centuries before biofeedback.

A *toccata* is a free-style musical form designed to allow the performer of Bach's day to display virtuosity and is frequently, as in the case of the D Minor work, followed by a *fugue,* which is more strictly controlled by established musical laws. In the *toccata* the composer or performer may improvise on the stated themes, taking them in virtually any direction. This practice has definite counterparts in jazz. It is no coincidence that jazz players often acknowledge a strong debt to Bach, particularly for his genius at improvisation, and often include variations on Bach melodies in their repertoire. The *fugue* allows for the simultaneous hearing of different melodies; it is a usually rapid form, which is stabilized by the laws of counterpoint. That is, the melodic lines heard simultaneously must complement, not conflict with, each other. Since the Bach fugue was written to be performed by one musician and since the melodies are played by the left and right hands of the performer, the body's own limits of coordination really keep the lines in contact with each other.

You need only listen to the D Minor work to be astounded that one pair of hands could engage in so difficult a task. The idea behind the fugue is to demonstrate that what should not be a coordinated effort (that is, what for the average person would be an impossibility) is indeed well within the capabilities of the performer. Thus the Bach fugue in particular satisfies (harmonizes) two of our needs which at first seem to be in conflict—the need for total freedom (or the lack of coordination) and the need for some principle of control. It offers an experience continually on the brink of getting beyond control, but which always stays within its form.

In baroque music we experience the complexities little by little, point by point.

The music of Bach also parallels in sound the richness of the entire baroque period. We sometimes suspect that music, rather than art or architecture, serves as the ideal expression of baroque taste, because its linear (sequential) form allows us to experience its complexities little by little, point by point, rather than have them overwhelm the vision as many baroque interiors do.

Jazz: An American Musical Form

Jazz is so popular throughout the world that one might suppose every country claims to have been its originator. But jazz is American in the way that a folk song like "John Henry" is American. It has much to do with the *insistence upon freedom.* It evolved, as much American art has evolved, from the everyday life of the people—far from music conservatories, institutions of higher culture, or the great tradition of the concert repertoire.

It evolved from many strains of folk and popular music, arising out of churches and fields, brothels and bars—all of them, but mainly the brothels, the houses of prostitution where, in the early years of this century, black musicians could get work and were free to weave whatever musical spells suited them so long as the paying customers stayed happy.

Accounts of how jazz got started sometimes give the impression that the performers were all untrained musicians who just "happened" to come up with something that had style and grace. In truth, we don't know much about the pioneers; but as the decades of the twentieth century rolled by, the form did attract a range of musical geniuses, some who taught themselves, some who had been classically trained. They had—and continue to have—one thing in common: They know how to maintain a balance between control and the need for soaring release.

As we pointed out, jazz instrumentalists and composers admire Bach because he more or less invented improvisation, the art of taking flight from a set theme. A typical jazz piece follows a disciplined pattern. The group, or the soloist backed by the group, will play the main theme once through, sometimes a well-known song, sometimes an original tune composed for the group. Then one instrument after another performs a variation of the theme. Original jazz works have deliberately offbeat titles, like "Take the A Train," "Red Clay," and "Maui-Waui." The common philosophy behind such titles is that jazz must be its own thing. Jazz shapes and defines the "cool scene"—a late-night urban version of cowboys around a campfire exchanging tall tales and nonsense songs.

In the early decades of this century, great jazz soloists like Charlie Parker and Louis Armstrong became famous for going off on lengthy variations, often improvising for 10 or 15 minutes before returning to the theme. The literary novel *Young Man with a Horn* was inspired by the tragically interrupted life of Bix Beiderbeck, a cornet player known for his extraordinary improvisatory flights. The book deals with a musician's unsuccessful quest for a perfect note, beyond the known range of his instrument. Fortunately we can still listen to the recorded improvisations of Beiderbeck as he strained his cornet to the limit—and further.

Musical histories that deal with jazz as a serious and major art form give preeminence to Edward Kennedy—known universally as Duke Ellington (1889–1974), the person who did the most to bridge the gap between the concert hall and the cabaret. A bandleader who had Manhattan society driving to the Cotton Club in Harlem during the late 1920s, Ellington sought to expand the range of jazz through continual experimentation

Music historians who deal with jazz as a serious and major art form give preeminence to Edward Kennedy—known universally as Duke Ellington.

> with what he called his "jungle effects." When the sounds of "growling" trumpets and trombones, sinuous clarinets and eerie percussion were recorded, the originality of the orchestration was immediately grasped internationally by music critics and record buyers. . . . As a jazz arranger his great gift was in balancing orchestration and improvisation.[1]

Ellington brought jazz to Carnegie Hall, where it could be played and evaluated "up there" with the great names in music. In so doing, he wrote out elaborate and complex orchestrations—something no one had done before him. He did leave room for solo flights (or else it would not have been jazz), but his own compositions and his arrangements display a classic sense of discipline and musicianship.

Ellington's achievements lend insight not only to what constitutes jazz at its finest, but to the enduring appeal of Bach to jazz musicians. The key word is *control,* without which the freedom sought by the improviser is impossible. In both jazz and Bach, tension is created between the need for soaring and the requirements of the music. In this tension lies the beckoning magic found in all art. It is one of the profoundest secrets of human creativity. *Where anything is possible, there is little to intrigue us.* We become fascinated—or "hooked" if you prefer—when we feel that the artist's soul is straining to free itself from the bondage of "the rules." But the rules themselves are the secret ingredient. The rules make disobedience possible, but not reckless or random disobedience. The price the artist pays can be called form or order. The struggle between the rules and disobedience gives a work a sense of urgency, or of mattering very much to our consciousness. At its greatest, jazz illustrates the struggle, the form, and the mattering.

A Beethoven Symphony

In the baroque musical tradition, which Bach epitomized, composers worked in a limited range of musical forms to find their own way through the music. Bach achieved greatness by making the forms accommodate his tremendous intellect and his need to explore inner space. Ludwig van Beethoven (1770–1827) may well have outdone Bach—in fact, every other composer—by exploring his own needs and inventing new musical forms to fulfill them. In so doing, Beethoven earned his place as the greatest composer. Music would never be the same again.

Whereas Bach was primarily a church composer/performer, hired to do a very specific job writing lucrative religious music, Beethoven composed for church, concert hall, small salons, private performances, royal chambers, but, above all else, for himself. When he completely lost his hearing during the peak of his musical career, Beethoven turned inward, and out of his complex and anguished soul came sounds no one had yet heard. Even today, more than a century and a half after the composer's death, when every note written by him has been played and interpreted by thousands upon thousands of musicians and heard by millions of listeners, new listeners can find in the music some as yet undisclosed aspect of Beethoven's personality as well as some unexplored region of their own inner space.

Of course, Beethoven did not emerge from a vacuum. He was building upon the new expansive tradition in German music established before him by Franz Joseph Haydn (1732–1809) and Wolfgang Amadeus Mozart (1756–1791). This tradition combined secular, reli-

If we were a people much given to revealing secrets, we might raise monuments and sacrifice to the memories of our poets, but slavery cured us of that weakness. It may be enough, however, to have it said that we survive in exact relationship to the dedication of our poets (include preachers, musicians and blues singers).

Maya Angelou

Nobody has proposed that Beethoven leads all the rest solely because of his rhythm, or his melody, or his harmony. It's the combination.

Leonard Bernstein

gious, and nationalistic trends all into one. It declared that the music of northern Europe was every bit the equal of Italian music—indeed would become supreme in all the world.

One can trace the evolution of the symphony, that major musical form, in the work of these three composers. Haydn wrote 104 symphonies, Mozart 41, and Beethoven "just" 9. (Later, Johannes Brahms, intimidated by the majestic symphonic creations of Beethoven, would spend 20 years working on his first symphony and would leave the world "just" four!)

In 1804, Beethoven, after having given the world two symphonies in the tradition of Mozart, who had already stretched the limits of the form beyond anything yet known, came forth with his *Third,* or *E-Flat Major, Symphony,* later to be called *Eroica.* The premiere proved to be an occasion for which the music world was not completely prepared. Mozart's *Forty-first* and last *Symphony,* the titanic *Jupiter,* was massive in its conception and was thought to have said quite the last word as far as symphonic works were concerned. After all, a symphony was originally intended to be a 15- or 20-minute concert diversion, consisting of four movements: the first moderately paced, the second slow and lyrical, the third rapid and light hearted, and the fourth rousing and climactic. The four movements were related only in terms of the composer's characteristic style, but taken together, they were not expected to make a unified statement of any kind. The *Jupiter* changed all that and by all rights should have remained the symphonic achievement of the centuries.

Yet now emerges the *Eroica*—twice the length of Mozart's masterpiece—a work so huge in conception, so complex in execution, and so overwhelming to experience that by all rights it should have invited immediate comparison with Michelangelo's *David* or the Sistine Chapel ceiling. Unfortunately, many of the first listeners could not accommodate themselves to the work's heroic dimensions or to its daring innovations, particularly Beethoven's heavy use of seventh chords, up to that time a musical taboo, considered barbarically dissonant, unfit for civilized ears.

In the opinion of music historians, the most astonishing aspect of the *Eroica* is that it is not the work of a musical adventurer, creating bigness for its own sake. One critic sums up the matter:

> We are used to the scale of the *Eroica,* but what is forever new is a musical substance which requires every second of the vast time expanse which Beethoven organized to contain it. In its size it is wholly efficient, as fine an example of economy of structure as any four-minute Bach fugue.[2]

We have a great work of art when the magnitude of the artist's message so fits the vehicle which carries it that we never lose sight of it, never let go of the communication. In contrast, Tchaikovsky's *1812 Overture,* with its thousand musicians and its exploding cannons, is too big for its own good, and, like a huge space probe that has cleared the tower, soon leaves the onlooker far below.

In the *Eroica,* the four movements not only constitute a unity, but each succeeding movement sounds like a perfect complement to the one before it. It is clear that Beethoven did not finish one movement and then tack on another as though the preceding one had not existed. The first movement of the *Eroica* is on as grand a scale as Western music has ever reached, and it has given to the symphony its name. The story is that Beethoven had been inspired by the heroic image of Napoleon and created in this opening movement a music that paralleled his feelings. The work was originally dedicated to the man Beethoven perceived as the heroic savior of the free world. When word reached the composer that his hero had demanded to be crowned Emperor, Beethoven rescinded the dedication.

One is tempted to hear in the second movement a musical parallel to Beethoven's profound disillusionment. Profound sorrow is certainly there, as indicated by the tempo notation: *marcia funebre* (funeral march). It is the slowest of all slow movements, dirgelike and heartbroken. We have already spoken of it in the section on silence as a musical element. Whether Napoleon was the direct cause of the sorrow or whether Beethoven, having exhausted the range of noble emotions, found himself exploring the depths of sadness, we cannot know; but we *can* say that the first two movements of the *Eroica* strongly suggest an experience common to nearly everyone: the passage from heroic, idealistic youth to tragic maturity.

The third movement, by contrast, almost shocks us with its galloping pace and precise horns, all of it sounding like nothing so much as a hunting party. Out of place? Surely not. If you listen carefully to every note of the funeral march, you'll find there is only so much emotional "wrenching" you can take. Life must go on. The depressed spirit must pull itself up from despair.

The finale begins with a graceful, dancelike melody suggestive of polite society: civilization restored, so to speak. This leads through an intricate development back into the same heroic mood which opened the symphony. We have passed from romantic illusion to the depths of tragedy and, through struggle, upward again to a more mature, sober, and deliberate affirmation. The *Eroica* is Beethoven's *Divine Comedy* and *Paradise Lost*—one of the very few times an artist has captured the human soul in full range. It would not mark Beethoven's last glimpse of paradise.

Beethoven's *Ninth* and final *Symphony* was composed around 1818, when he had become totally deaf. It is easily four times the length of a late Mozart symphony, and double that of the *Eroica.* Not the journey of a young man's soul coping with the sobering realities of life; the *Ninth Symphony* is rather the final statement of a gigantic mentality that has struggled for years with both physical and creative suffering—of a person who has labored to find and capture it all, as Michelangelo, two centuries earlier, had sought perfection in marble, and as Einstein, a century later, would seek the ultimate equation for unifying all interactions among all parts of the universe.

During the first three movements of the *Ninth,* Beethoven gives us one haunting melody after another, complex rhythms, intricate harmonies, and shattering dissonance. He seems to be striving for nothing more or less than to find a musical equivalent to every feeling that can be experienced. By the fourth movement he appears to have concluded that the orchestra alone was not enough to express the sounds he must have heard in the far recesses of his silent world. Other composers before him had written large choral works: Bach's *Passion According to St. Matthew,* Haydn's *Creation,* and Mozart's *Requiem,* to name three supreme examples. But Beethoven pushes the human voice farther than many believed—and many *still* believe—possible.

There remains considerable controversy about the final movement of the *Ninth.* Some critics have said it takes us as close to the gates of heaven as we can get in this earthly lifetime. Some have called it a musical embarrassment, totally unsingable. One soprano, after attempting it, vehemently declared that Beethoven had no respect whatever for the female voice. Anyone hearing the movement for the first time is likely to be swept away by its incredible momentum and may be hearing not human voices at all, but dazzling combinations of sounds there is no time to identify. In an interview with the authors, a tenor described what being in the huge chorus is like:

> I keep my mouth open and manage to hit about every third or fourth note. The pace is frantic and the notes, the conclusion of the work, are beyond my reach. I think they are really beyond the reach of most voices. Nonetheless, a curious exuberance is created which compensates for the straining of vocal chords. The singers' struggles are concealed by the crashing of the orchestra, and the entire work, perilously close to disaster, miraculously escapes and achieves a glory most people experience only a few times in their lives, if they are lucky to do even that.

The poet Theodore Spencer, in calling Shakespeare's *King Lear* "the greatest single work of mankind," hastily added that Beethoven's *Ninth* is its closest rival for the honor.

By far, the majority opinion about the work is that it transcends its own "unsingability" and any breach of musical taste it may commit. Something so vast is its own awesome self—like a dinosaur

At the moment when the theme of joy appears for the first time, the orchestra stops abruptly, thus giving a sudden unexpected character to the entrance of the song. And this is a true touch; the theme is rightly divine. Joy descends from heaven enveloped in a supernatural calm.

Romain Rolland

that stands framed against the horizon, shaking the surrounding earth with its unearthly sounds. Asking whether one "likes it" or not seems beside the point. One can only feel humbled by its majesty. Listening to Beethoven's *Ninth Symphony* is discovering what human creativity *really* means.

EPILOG

We cannot deal in a single chapter with all possible musical experiences. But we have explored some; that is the important thing. The more we listen, the more variety we will develop in our musical tastes and the stronger will become our identity with sound. To limit ourselves to only one form of music is to know only part of our personality.

There are hundreds of composers today no longer satisfied with what Beethoven did, seeking to expand the limits of musical form and musical sound in ways that are meaningful to *them*. There are composers working with electronic instruments and composers who say that anything (even a washboard) can be a musical instrument. You can hear sounds today that would have scandalized Beethoven himself, who in turn had shocked his own generation with dissonance which some critics said ought never to have been inflicted upon the human ear.

The willingness to open one's ears is fundamental to the entire humanizing process.

As Beethoven won his case and set new standards, so will much of today's new music eventually have its day and win acceptance. The smart listener is the one who takes chances, is open to new sounds, is among the first to applaud. If you are that person—and even if time proves you wrong—what have you lost except time spent on an unusual experience? What is it to be human artfully except to seek out experience, to be aware of it, to savor it, to ponder it, to wonder at it? But first, of course, take the time to listen, really listen, to the sounds which have already graced the audio environment, to the important sounds we have identified in this chapter. Then spend part of a day with your silences.

GLOSSARY

Apollonian music: Music with a regular beat, such as waltzes, minuets, ragtime, fox trots. Usually with a predictable rhythm. Offers certainty, sometimes a calming effect.

arhythmic: Sounds played against irregular beats.

Dionysian music: Music, such as rock, which stimulates, shocks, and deliberately uses noise as well as incomprehensible words. Antidote for excessive Apollonianism.

dissonance: A principle in music whereby two or more uncongenial notes are sounded or sung at the same time, producing an unfamiliar and usually unpleasant effect. The effect is almost always deliberate; the reasons for it, quite varied. Often, however, the composer or arranger is attempting to avoid overused harmonic patterns that fall pleasantly but unexcitingly on the ear.

fugue: A musical composition, or section within a larger composition, in which two or more melodic lines play against each other. The form, popular during the baroque period, was given its most memorable embodiment by J. S. Bach.

harmony: A principle in music whereby two or more notes, congenial or otherwise, are sounded or sung at the same time. Harmony includes both dissonant and nondissonant effects.

improvisation: A spontaneous variation, or set of variations, on a stated musical theme.

Minimalists: Contemporary composers who reject the idea that music ought to be the expression of inner emotional states or that it exists to produce such states in the listener.

melody: Either any arrangement of notes in a flowing sequence, or a significant sequence of musical notes which form a unity and are usually meant to be distinguished from what comes before and what follows.

plainsong: The major musical form of the late Middle Ages; a continuously flowing melodic line, intended to be sung, without harmony, by an indeterminate number of voices so that the effect is as of one person singing.

rhythm: The alternation of stress and unstress in music, usually created by a percussion instrument. Its effect is to unify the sounds. When rhythm is very pronounced, one is almost compelled to move the body, as in dancing. So basic is the "rhythmic urge" that a reasonable argument could be made for the possibility that all music began as pure rhythm for human rites.

symphony: The major orchestral musical form from the late eighteenth century to the present, consisting of four movements of contrasting tempi. Originally no unity of style or feeling was intended, but as the form developed, composers increasingly insisted upon such unity. In symphonies from the latter half of the nineteenth century to the present, one will even hear the same themes recurring in different movements.

toccata: A more or less unstructured musical form, popular in Bach's time, usually composed for organ or harpsichord and allowing for an overpowering display of musical virtuosity by the performer.

variations: Melodic sequences based on previously heard themes, similar enough to them to evoke associations but changed sufficiently to allow the listener to move ahead to new experiences.

NOTES

1. Alan Bullock and R. B. Woodings, eds., *20th-Century Culture* (New York: Harper & Row, 1983), p. 212.

2. Abraham Veinus, Syracuse University (quoted on the jacket to the Vanguard recording).

Oskar Kokoschka, "Kokoschka, Drama-Komoedie," 1907
(Courtesy of The Museum of Modern Art)

3

THEATER: TWO MASKS

Overview

Greek amphitheaters were so vast that stage makeup—even if the Greeks had such—would not have sufficed. Instead, actors wore large masks with greatly exaggerated expressions. The actors could not very well change masks every time their characters changed emotion. So the sorrowful mask of tragedy was worn for that kind of play in which the outcome was catastrophic, and the grinning mask of comedy was worn for light-hearted plays with happy endings. Thus began the separation between the tragic and the comic.

Life, however, is neither wholly tragic nor wholly comic; instead, it is made up of events which we interpret as happy or sad—or as somewhere in between—to the extent that they conform or fail to conform to our individual hopes. Pure tragedy and pure comedy exist only in the art of theater, and not always even there. For instance, the famous graveyard scene in Shakespeare's tragedy *Hamlet,* in which the hero is to discover that a grave being dug is for the drowned body of his beloved Ophelia, opens on two men who are not only the grave-diggers but clowns exchanging puns. In Shakespeare's *Antony and Cleopatra,* Cleopatra, just before her suicide, indulges in comic banter with the clown who is delivering the deadly snake which is to be the instrument of her death. Another example: As the great silent-screen comic Charlie Chaplin developed his art, his character became less foolish and more humanly pathetic.

Theater art has come to recognize that a subtle blending of the tragic and the comic brings the drama closer to reality, even though classic and contemporary works in which the clear separation is maintained are still produced. In this chapter we shall examine differences between the "two masks," similarities between them, and, finally, how both comedy and tragedy can serve as resources for living.

Laughing Matters

The Greeks invented the art of stage comedy because they wanted to send their audiences home in a happy state of mind after they had sat through three (count them—THREE!) full-length tragedies in the course of a single day. The apparent theory behind comedy was that it helped confirm the audience's notion of what was normal and rational by displaying abnormal and irrational behavior that could be laughed at. The Greeks discovered that laughter was a healthy release of tensions, especially when thousands of people were engaging in it all at the same time. We know that laughing alone is seldom as satisfying as laughing with the rest of an audience.

Comedy helps confirm the audience's notion of what is normal and rational by displaying abnormal and irrational behavior that can be laughed at.

Comedy can be divided into three basic types. The first emphasizes situation and two-dimensional characters and is called *farce;* the second deals with more well-rounded characters, and we designate it as the *comedy of character;* and the third, intended to make us think, has two subcategories: *satire* and *the comedy of ideas.*

Farce: Its Character Types and Situations

In a *farce,* characters are deliberately two-dimensional, easily described in a word or two. Once the character types have been identified through costume, speech, and mannerisms, little more will be revealed than what appears to first glance. At the end of the play, no one will have changed much. There will be no greater understanding, no earth-shaking revelations. Because the characters are deliberately superficial, audiences are not expected to identify with anyone or to dig beneath the surface. After all, surface is all there is. Comic types are like dolls, and indeed some of them were once puppet characters in traveling shows. As a result they are very close to not being people at all, and when they are abused physically or emotionally there are no lasting effects. They are like the animals in modern-day cartoons who reappear whole in a scene after they have exploded or been kicked off a cliff. Consider a few examples:

> the stingy old man who sees everything in terms of money
> the sex kitten
> the bragging coward
> the health nut
> the clumsy, unpolished social climber
> the spoiled, destructive brat
> the totally self-absorbed actor (or beauty queen)
> the dumb athlete
> the fast-talking wise guy
> the shrill, overbearing, unsympathetic wife
> the innocent fellow from the country

You can probably add to this list of comic characters. Audiences who laugh at their antics tend not to feel cruel, although some of these types, if presented in a "close-up" rather than the usual mechanical way, might make good candidates for the psychiatrist's couch and our compassion. We need never worry that someone will probe motives and say, for instance, "Tell me, Mr. Miser, when did money begin to be so important to you? How has the love of money interfered with other pleasures in life? Do you want to change?" Such questions would spoil our fun. The comic type is ridiculous, and audiences can enjoy ridicule without feeling cruel, for the comic type is not a total human being.

Once the character types have been selected, the playwright must put them into combinations which will make up the scenes of a play. For instance, what if . . . a very proper social dowager enormously concerned with etiquette were to be wooed by a crude fortune hunter? Make the setting a very formal one, such as opening night at the opera, with the lady a prominent benefactor; have the fortune hunter sitting at her side in a box. His silk hat falls, is handed to him by one of the operagoers in a nearby seat. He tips the man a quarter. Meanwhile, his uncouth companions in ill-fitting clothes are selling peanuts and popcorn while the orchestra turns the pages of the overture to *Il Trovatore* and plays the score of "Take Me Out to the Ballgame," which the clowns have stuck to the musicians' pages with chewing gum. . . . And so on.

Farce emphasizes physical action, comic types, and an ending filled with wild coincidences.

It took the inventiveness of the Marx Brothers and the authors of the 1935 film *A Night at the Opera* to make the above formula work well, but farce always includes the interplay of unlike types. Later in that same scene, the villainous tenor (we know he's a villain because he loses his temper at the innocent Harpo, will sing only for money, and makes insulting remarks about the purity of the heroine, Rosa) tries to sing while the scenery behind him keeps changing. Harpo is running around backstage, climbing the ropes and pulling one backdrop down and another up. The tenor continues singing his Italian aria, first in front of a battleship, then before a fruit stand, then at a railroad station—one inappropriate backdrop after another.

The tenor is exhibiting one of the prime attributes of comedy: *single-mindedness*—a comic flaw leading to the undoing of its possessor. Nothing will stop the tenor's pretentious ambition, and, of course, the orchestra goes along, playing as if nothing were wrong. The audience goes along, too, enjoying the mechanical behavior of both. No one expects plausibility in this kind of comedy—called *farce* because it emphasizes physical action, comic types, and an ending filled with wild coincidences.

The writer of another sort of comedy begins with the following premise: What if a fanatically neat man were to share an apartment with a complete slob? The answer is found in Neil Simon's hilarious *The Odd Couple* (1966). An enduring question of ancient comedies is: What if twin brothers separated from birth are both in the same town but neither knows the other is there? The notion of mistaken identity has fascinated writers, going all the way back to classical Greece and Rome. Shakespeare adapted these old plots for *A Comedy of Errors* (1591), *Twelfth Night* (1600), and *Two Gentlemen of Verona* (1592). The confusion potential in the phenomenon of twins delights audiences, perhaps because personal identity is so important in our culture and the mixing up of that identity, normally a reason for serious concern, we laugh at willingly. The universal constant in laughter is its reaffirmation of normalcy, when chaotic misunderstandings are not supposed to happen.

While the comedies of the Greeks and Romans exerted tremendous influence on later theater, of equal impact was the *commedia dell'arte,* an Italian theater movement originating in the middle of the sixteenth century. Given its name because its performers were highly skilled professionals rather than amateur actors, the *commedia* was equally at home in a royal court or in the streets, attracting huge crowds and dispensing the healing medicine of laughter wherever it played. Many of the stock character types still found, especially in television comedy, derive from *commedia* traditions.

The "plays" had scenarios that wcre little more than a rough outline of the action, which always concerned the interaction of two young lovers trying to get together, the miserly father of one lover, a pedantic old bore who thinks himself a suitable mate of the girl, and a bragging soldier who is exposed as a coward. All the actors wore exaggerated masks except the young lovers, who were never considered funny and served only to give the plot some direction. The *commedia* comic types were the ancestors of the buffoons and clowns of subsequent periods, winning our laughter from the physical abuse and pratfalls they continually suffer. The Marx Brothers, Laurel and Hardy, the Three Stooges, Jerry Lewis, and Lucille Ball—all great performers adept at bodily contortions—are descendants of the Italian legacy. Above all, the comedies of Molière (to be discussed presently) would not have been possible without it.

Television sitcoms have their share of farcical, two-dimensional types, notably the lecherous Jack Tripper in *Three's Company,* pretending to be gay so that he can share an apartment with two beautiful women; Ethel and Fred Mertz, the nagging wife and tight-fisted husband in *I Love Lucy;* the continually frustrated wife and her morose, sexually inactive husband of *The Ropers;* and the man-hungry Major Margaret Houlihan of *M*A*S*H,* who conceals her desires behind an obsession for maintaining military discipline.

Like the *commedia* masks, farcical names are usually a tip-off to the particular kind of absurdity the actor represents. For instance, Jack Tripper hardly suggests someone who is "cool" and in control of his own destiny. The seventeenth and eighteenth centuries specialized in the identification of the comic trait through names. Without knowing anything about the plays in which they are found, consider what you can already guess about characters called Sneerwell, Waitwell, Fidget, Quack, Squeamish, Lady Wishfort, Sir Fopling Flutter, and a scoundrel named Horner. In those days, if you held up two fingers behind the head of an unsuspecting husband, people would know what you meant: The unfortunate man had been the victim of *cuckoldry* (the act of infidelity performed by his wife and a lover). The two fingers symbolized horns, and horns became the symbol of a deceived husband. Audiences of the day, looking at the cast of characters in the program, knew at once the sort of rogue whose intrigues would be celebrated in the play, and they looked forward to it immensely.

The Rogue Hero

The knave, or rogue, is not funny in the way the pedantic bore of the *commedia dell'arte* is funny. He is not derided by the audience for single-mindedness or clumsiness. Instead, he is witty and clever, and if he resorts to less than honest (or moral) means of getting what he wants, he is usually seen as less blameworthy than the corrupt or stupid people he deceives. The rogue hero has been popular for centuries

I learned from reading George Bernard Shaw years ago that you can get away with murder as long as you make people laugh.

Saul Bellow

and still is very much with us. He does the underhanded things we all fantasize doing, and thus he provides a useful escape from the tensions created by our conformity.

Rogue heroes are "con" men: making false claims for shoddy merchandise—like the Pardoner in Chaucer's *Canterbury Tales* (1387–1400) pretending to have supernatural powers; or like the hero of Richard Nash's *The Rainmaker* (1953), who deludes an entire drought-ridden town into believing he can cause rain, for a price; or like the stranger in Meredith Willson's *The Music Man* (1958) who sells band uniforms to another gullible town, on the promise that he has a miraculous method for teaching music overnight. Rogue heroes have charm and far more personality than most of the people we deal with in everyday life—people who walk the straight and narrow but nevertheless are *dull.*

During the seventeeth century, in both England and France, moral codes became more liberal than they had been, but behind closed doors. On the surface, aristocratic society was bound by rigid codes of behavior, and the rogue hero flourished on the stages of London and Paris. Even a final-act exposure of the culprit was never intended to be taken very seriously or to cloud the memory of the hero's magnificent naughtiness.

One of the most notable such creations is the very same Mr. Horner mentioned in the preceding section. The central character of William Wycherley's *The Country Wife,* a scandalous success of 1675, Horner has deliberately spread the false rumor that he is sexually impotent and that therefore London husbands are safe in allowing their wives to see him. Among his willing "victims" is Lady Fidget, delighted to be unfaithful to her marriage vows so long as she can maintain the illusion of social respectability. In the famous "china scene," Horner has been locked in a back room with Lady Fidget, ostensibly helping her choose a piece of china from his valuable china collection. After a long time, Lady Fidget returns to the front room, where her husband and friends have been waiting. The scene is full of *double entendre,* or double meaning, a favorite source of humor, especially when the "second" possible meaning is unacceptable to polite society. Here's the dialog:

Lady Fidget:	And I have been toiling and moiling for the prettiest piece of china, my dear.
Horner:	Nay, she has been too hard for me, do what I could.
Mrs. Squeamish:	O Lord, I'll have some china, too. Good Mr. Horner, don't think to give other people china and me none; come in with me, too.
Horner:	Upon my honor, I have none left now.

Mrs. Squeamish:	Nay, nay, I have known you deny your china before now, but you shan't put me off so, Come.
Horner:	This lady had the last there.
Lady Fidget:	Yes, indeed, madam, to my certain knowledge, he has no more left.
Mrs. Squeamish:	Oh, but it may be he may have some you could not find.
Lady Fidget:	What, d'ye think if he had had any left, I would not have had it too? for we women of quality never think we have china enough.

London upper-class audiences were delighted by the clever Mr. Horner, his lustful female companions, and their foolish husbands. The hero might have been a pleasant fantasy for women trapped in an unexciting marriage and to men who secretly recognized their lack of sexual aggressiveness.

On the other side of the English Channel, one of the greatest playwrights of all time, Jean-Baptiste Poquelin, who called himself Molière (1622–1673), filled the stage with comically blind, incessantly self-deluded creatures and, in one glorious instance, with one of the greatest rogues of all time: the title character of *Tartuffe* (1664), who claims to be more pious than anyone else. Tartuffe has gained the confidence of a wealthy man and been invited to move in with the family. Though the other characters talk of him from the beginning, he doesn't actually appear until almost halfway through the piece, when he calls to his manservant: "Hang up my hair-shirt, put my scourge in place." He then whips out a handkerchief and demands that the maid cover her bosom with it, an action he is willing to perform himself. Before long he has attempted to seduce Elmire, the wife of his benefactor ("I may be pious, but I'm human too"), and has promised to keep their affair a secret if she should agree to let him worship her beauty in an intimate way. While directing his lust toward the attractive Elmire, he directs his greed toward the fortune of her husband, and nearly succeeds in escaping with all of it.

The rogue hero, perhaps more than any other comic tradition, has an enduring record of popularity. He has never gone out of style, though he flourishes more richly in certain periods than in others. It's a good bet he is more appealing in times of tighter social mores than in times of rampant permissiveness. Earlier in this century, when Victorian morality was dominant, we had W. C. Fields and his rogues' gallery of delightful con artists, forever cheating at cards, forever making wry antiestablishment comments out of the sides of their mouths. We had Groucho Marx, with the ever-present grin and the long cigar, flicking his ashes on the carpets of polite society. We had Mae West, flaunt-

Famous rogue heroes: Mr. Horner, Tartuffe, Mack the Knife, Hawkeye Pierce. The rogue hero does the underhanded things we think about doing in our fantasy life, and is thus a useful escape from the tensions created by our conformity.

ing her sexuality at the prim and proper, wiggling her hips and finding no reason to believe immorality does not pay. "Goodness!" cries a middle-class housewife, staring at Mae West's expensive mink. The reply: "Goodness had nothin' to do with it."

The German music-drama *The Threepenny Opera* (1928) has a totally amoral hero, Mack the Knife, who bribes the police, cuts throats, lies to women—and gets away with his crimes thanks to a thoroughly implausible pardon from Queen Victoria at the end of the play. The rogue hero's outwitting of the system constitutes a cynical attack on the idiocy and corruption of a society in which such a person can flourish.

The 1960s would seem to have been a period when the rogue hero was replaced by the rebellious loner, a character openly flouting the establishment rather than cleverly pretending to be part of it and undermining it from within. The "hippie hero" was not meant to be a comic figure, nor did he reflect mainstream values, which were still basically conservative. The term "Moral Majority" was gladly applied by the mainstream to itself. Its disapproval of activists and draft-dodgers intensified the more the resistance movement grew. Yet the Moral Majority was bound to elicit a comic response, and it came in 1970 in the person of Hawkeye Pierce, rogue hero of the film and later of the classic television series *M*A*S*H.*

Hawkeye is a brilliant surgeon, drafted into the army and sent to the front lines in Korea to serve in the 4077 Mobile Army Surgical Hospital, where he and his weary colleagues toil, sometimes for 20 hours straight and in primitive facilities, to sew a glimmer of life back into terrified soldiers so they can be sent back into action to face death once more. Hawkeye is not like rogue heroes of the past, however. His underhanded attempts to thwart a rigid military establishment are carried on in the name of rationality and human decency, *not* out of self-interest. Hawkeye totally disregards Army rank, is almost never in uniform (preferring to wear Hawaiian shirts, much to the annoyance of visiting brass), steals when he thinks human need warrants it, always looks out for the underdog, and is especially helpful to Army misfits (with whom he easily identifies). He became a spokesperson for all those who deplored the Vietnam War, and the continued popularity of *M*A*S*H* in reruns strongly suggests that he remains the spokesperson for those millions who work in some way against militarism.

More recently, the rigid, rule-bound police establishment has helped make a star of Eddie Murphy, who specializes in rogue heroes. In *Beverly Hills Cop* (1984) Murphy's character easily outwits the system. Replacing the seventeenth-century wit and elegance of Horner with street-smart "cool," he nonetheless makes himself at home in formal society, which is never a match for him. Like Hawkeye, Murphy's character will break the laws if necessary; but both characters have their hearts in the right place. Unlike earlier rogues, *they* break the law in a higher cause. The idea behind their characters is a simple one: Society is a shambles, but *somebody* has to save it!

The Comic Fool

As we observed, the rogue hero is not someone we laugh at, but someone we laugh *with.* He is so much smarter than the society around him that we cannot help siding with him, no matter how unethical his tactics may be. The main body of comedy, however, is made up of fools, characters we willingly laugh at, characters who, like the comic types in farce, are single-mindedly obsessed with something and evoke almost merciless laughter from us. Often they are duped by the rogues, but their stupidity (often coupled with arrogance) prevents us from feeling pity toward them. We know they deserve what they get.

Some philosophical analyses of comedy call comic fools antisocial and potentially dangerous persons. Their single-mindedness is a rigid barrier against growth and change, and society cannot function unless the majority of its members are rational and willing to alter their behavior when they realize it is harmful to the well-being of others. Fools are interested only in their own petty problems and never see what is done to others. Laughter is society's revenge. Laughing at fools helps us confirm our own sanity.

Amost every comedy with a rogue hero has a fool he can deceive. In the case of Tartuffe, the fool is Orgon, a man single-mindedly driven by his desire for holiness. In becoming the slave of the hypocritical Tartuffe, Orgon believes he is living a good life. As usual in a Molière play, the fool is also blind to his family's real needs and tries to force his daughter to marry a man she despises, in this case Tartuffe himself. The old man never hears the daughter when she entreats him to spare her. Even when he hears the very words of an indecent proposal made by Tartuffe to Orgon's wife, he denies the evidence and instead believes Tartuffe's absurd explanation.

Molière specializes in fools. He remains the master of comedy as Shakespeare is the master of tragedy, because his fools include universally and timelessly antisocial types. There is never a danger that an audience will find them unfunny. His roster of fools includes

> a man overly concerned with his health, who wants his
> daughter to marry a doctor
> a man overly concerned with social status, who wants
> his daughter to marry a man with a title, whoever he
> might be
> a man overly concerned with money, who wants his daugh-
> ter to marry any man who will take her without a dowry

a man overly concerned with the innocence of his bride, to the extent that he whisks his chosen one away from the temptations of Paris to be properly supervised in an isolated country house

Molière's contributions to the art of comedy are so rich and varied that we must never believe he limited himself to a single-minded fool or a rogue hero in any given play. *The Would-Be Gentleman,* for example, has for its central character the man, listed above, who expects his daughter to marry the titled aristocrat of his, not her, choosing. But the play generously offers other fools as well. Monsieur Jourdain, who has no intelligence, grace, or social charm, hires tutors in music, dancing, fencing, and philosophy. Not only are his own pitiful efforts deliciously funny, but the tutors themselves are single-minded mockeries of what their professions should represent. Each tutor is so immersed in his own specialty that he refuses to acknowledge the importance of the others'. Without *his,* the world could not exist. The dance "master" claims, for example, that studying dance brings about a world of peace, for, after all, "war begins with a false step." The philosopher, calmly explaining to the others that philosophy teaches moderation, suddenly bursts into irrational violence when his opinion is challenged.

The Comedy of Character

What would happen if poor bumbling Monsieur Jourdain, the would-be gentleman, were allowed by his creator to exhibit a degree of sensitivity? What if he recognized, even only a little, that his tutors were laughing at the hopelessness of turning him into an aristocrat? Or if he were the victim of a cruel and inhuman joke—as indeed he is in the final act—but suspected that others were taking advantage of his stupidity? The answer to these questions is that we would soon find him less funny. As the art of comedy developed and became more and more sophisticated, dramatists took more chances, tried new kinds of plots, often veering away from the traditional comic types, especially the bumbling fools, replacing them with characters who begin to approach true human beings. In real life people are not as single-minded, as blind to their own inadequacies, as the comic fools. *In real life, nobody is continually funny.*

The comedy of character, which is what we call the sort of play in which people who are funny also acquire more complex human characteristics, existed well before Molière carried fools and rogues to new heights of comic greatness. Shakespeare has also given us well-rounded comic as well as tragic figures, but none more comic than Sir John Falstaff, the heavy-set, hard-drinking, roguish companion to young Prince Hal in *Henry IV,* Parts 1 and 2 (1597 and 1598).

As a voter I never take anyone seriously who takes himself seriously. I have to believe most people are like that. They trust people with a sense of humor because that's what humor is— truth—with a little exaggeration and self-effacement thrown in to make it palatable.

Erma Bombeck

Since these were history plays intended to be serious chronicles of the early years of the British empire, Shakespeare—practical man of the theater that he was—probably introduced Falstaff and the prince's other barroom cronies to add a bit of variety and to give the plays a welcome change of pace. As so often happens, the comic relief steals the show.

Falstaff, who is far more than either a rogue or a single-minded fool, is the great philosopher of fun and corruption. Nothing is sacred, nothing is to be taken too seriously in this all-too-brief existence. Knowing that Hal will one day become Henry V and assume the awful responsibilities of the monarch, heavy burdens that will eventually wear him down, Falstaff encourages the prince to eat, drink, and be merry, and in so doing, becomes the world's spokesperson for the carefree, irresponsible, but irresistible life.

Falstaff is a consummate rogue. Faced with the task of arming a group of men for war, he spends the allotment on himself instead of on uniforms. He is also a consummate—and unashamed—coward. Faced with the chance to meet a member of the opposing force in hand-to-hand combat and cover himself with glory, he rolls over and plays dead, after first delivering a speech on the dubious value of honor in which he decides that the people who have attained honor are dead:

> Can honour set to a leg? No. Or an arm? No. Or take away the grief of a wound? Honour hath no skill in surgery, then? No. What is honour? Air; a trim reckoning! Who hath it? He that died o' Wednesday. Doth he feel it? No. Doth he hear it? No. 'Tis insensible, then. Yea, to the dead. But will it not live with the living? No. Why? Detraction will not suffer it.[1]

Falstaff amuses us because what he stands for is not what we are taught to admire; but we *like* him in the way that we cannot really like Molière's Monsieur Jourdain. What is the difference? Falstaff is honest, and Jourdain is not. Falstaff knows who is he and what his limitations are; Jourdain does not. There are things about Falstaff that are scandalously admirable.

In *Henry IV,* Part 2, there occurs a scene in which Hal rejects Falstaff, and laughter stops. We can never be sure of every Shakespearean dramaturgical motive, but in this case we find it safe to conjecture that, when it came to the moment of Prince Hal's coronation as Henry V (who, by the way, was to defeat the French at the Battle of Agincourt and thus become the most revered of all English monarchs before Queen Elizabeth I), the dramatist could not afford to offend the Queen by having it believed that her ancestor kept a ne'er-do-well as a lifelong friend. Even in *Henry IV,* Part 1, Hal delivers a soliloquy in which he tells the audience that he is only acting the role of a playboy, but when the proper time comes, he will step forth in the shining light of his true royal self.

Outside Westminster Abbey, Falstaff and his drinking buddies await the arrival of the man, now King, whom they believe to be one of their own. The overjoyed Falstaff attempts to approach, calling the King "my sweet boy!" Outraged, King Henry pushes him aside:

> *I know thee not, old man: fall to thy prayers;*
> *How ill white hairs become a fool and jester!*
> *So surfeit-swell'd, so old and so profane;*
> *But, being awaked, I do despise my dream.*
> *Make less thy body hence, and more thy grade;*
> *Leave gormandizing; know the grave doth gape*
> *For thee thrice wide than for other men.*[2]

In Shakespeare's defense for what readers and viewers have often regarded as an unforgivable crime against their favorite character, King Henry *does* add that, should Falstaff reform his roustabout ways, he will be taken care of for life. On the other hand, most of us secretly hope the old man will not take the bribe. In our fantasies we still see him in the tavern at Eastcheap, pinching a buxom waitress and pleading for one last pint.

Whatever the Queen's private feelings about the image of her ancestor may have been, we know that Falstaff was far from horrifying her. In fact, so enamored did she become of this glittering creation that she requested Shakespeare to do another play in which the same scoundrel would be the central character, and his amorous adventures the central theme. The result was *The Merry Wives of Windsor* (1600). And today Falstaff is still very much around: on the label of a popular beer named for him; and in performances at New York's Metropolitan Opera House, as the hero of the great Verdi comic opera named for him.

Like any great character in drama, Falstaff transcends all circumstances of all the plots in which he has been involved. He has become a prototype by which we can evaluate people in real life whose behavior (and also the excuses for it) reminds us of his.

Sentiment and Psychology

If King Henry's rejection of the old man is attributable to the policies of monarchy, it can be said that the coming of the so-called "common man" movement in the eighteenth and nineteenth centuries brought about a change in the way some comic characters were treated on the stage. We must remember that Shakespeare's audiences, accustomed to the right of monarchs to show no feelings toward a person, would not have blamed the King for the rejection. In fact, throughout the seventeeth century, which was also the period of Molière, audiences would have considered a playwright's display of emotion toward his characters extremely vulgar. Well-bred people simply did not publicly show or express their feelings. For this reason, Monsieur Jourdain and Molière's other fools could have expected no mercy either.

After the revolutions on both sides of the Atlantic, however, the adventures of ordinary people became fit subjects for literature and drama. The great English comic novel *Tom Jones* by Henry Fielding (1749) exemplifies the new trend. It has its share of farcical types left over from the previous century: self-deceiving tutors; sexually frustrated aggressive women who hypocritically maintain an aristocratic air of detachment; and so on. Its hero, Tom, a foundling, should by all rights be classified as a comic country bumpkin with no urban finesse whatever. Tom can be amusing, yes, in his sexual naïveté, and in his innocence, which allows him to be used and deceived by a good many cleverer people. But Tom has feelings, and these are respected by the author. Indeed, why else would a bumpkin be made the hero and not just a figure in comic subplot? Fielding may have been infected with an early dose of an emerging philosophy called *primitivism,* which held that the natural wisdom and goodness of simple, untutored people was worth more than the learned traditions of past intellectual greats. Primitivism held that feelings were healthy and good, and one should not be ashamed of having them. Nor should one laugh at others because they might lack social graces.

As a matter of fact, by the late eighteenth century important new comedies were absent from the theater. Between Richard Brinsley Sheridan, the outstanding comic dramatist of the 1770s, and the emergence of Oscar Wilde and George Bernard Shaw in the late 1800s, the English theater could boast of no major writer of *any* kind. The reason appears to be the enduring popularity of sentimental, or "feeling," plays at which audiences were allowed to weep copiously but to neither laugh nor think. The emphasis on excessive feeling led, as we would expect, to sheer melodrama, or what Hollywood used to call the *tear-jerker.* The plots for nearly all Italian operas came out of this kind of theater, and if you have read a synopsis of any opera plot, you know what real melodrama can be like. Farcical types—those unbelievable buffoons from the past—are replaced by tragic types—not funny, of course, yet no more believable. *One cannot have major comedy in times which do not allow for intelligent audiences to laugh at human folly. One cannot have major comedy in times which do not encourage the belief that rationality is more important than indiscriminate emotionalism.*

What is the case in our time? Is important comedy being written today? Already-mentioned contemporary works like *M*A*S*H* indicate that it is. Is *M*A*S*H* closer in spirit to, say, the work of Molière or to that of novelist Henry Fielding with his mixture of humor and sentiment? The answer is a very complex one.

Hawkeye Pierce, as we stated, is a rogue hero, but he is not one in the sense that Tartuffe is. He is well-rounded, sensitive, humanized. He has feelings for others, and we feel for *him*. Like Falstaff many centuries before him, he transcends his material and becomes a real person for us.

We are not living in a period of neoprimitivism or neosentimentalism. The "common man" movement is supposedly a thing of the past, to be taken for granted by now. But there *is* something central to our time, something that was not there in the late eighteenth century when the comedy of character was replacing the theater of rogues and fools, and that something is psychology. How can one laugh at, let alone judge, anyone whom one understands? Understanding replaces the indiscriminate feelings of the earlier period. Indiscriminate laughter seems cruel as one draws close enough to sense hurt feelings, shyness, embarrassment. The clumsy boob of an earlier time would now seem to be someone who wants to be graceful and doesn't know how, *but should not be ridiculed for it.*

Whom then do we laugh at? People we *don't* understand? How does one pick and choose? Or do we laugh at people who should be understanding but are not? People whose educational background and social advantages should make them well-rounded, caring human beings but who are so absorbed in their own ambitions they blind themselves to the reality about them? Such people are still fair game. In *M*A*S*H*, whom does Hawkeye try to outwit? Pompous army brass. Hypocrites with rank but no human feeling. People he considers stupid but who, considering their advantages, have no right to be stupid.

Nowadays we also have the barbed wit of the political satirist Mark Russell, especially poisonous during presidential election years. Are politicians fair game in this era of "understanding"? The answer again is yes. The premise appears to be that those who aspire to be the world's major leaders should not have the ordinary human weaknesses we can excuse psychologically in others. Or, if they do, these weaknesses need to be exposed, not graciously ignored.

Psychology has helped spawn a kind of comedy that is peculiar to our time: the art (and often we are generous in using such a label) of the stand-up comics. Often using scandalously obscene language, they remind us that perhaps all of us think these things but are afraid to say them aloud. Their alleged purpose is to help us shed our outer covering of social convention and be comfortable being who we are. The problem is that not all of us may be who they say we are supposed to be. True stand-up artists like Robin Williams specialize in the right to be themselves, however we may or may not identify with them, and serve as a role model for the off-center personality, an en-

One cannot have major comedy in times which do not allow for intelligent audiences to laugh at human folly. One cannot have major comedy in times which do not encourage the belief that rationality is more important than indiscriminate emotionalism.

couragement to the rest of us to honor, not be ashamed, of our own differences.

Also peculiar to our time is the comedy of self-criticism. Comics like Woody Allen and the *early* Joan Rivers allow us to laugh at the merciless exposure of their own weaknesses, hang-ups, hidden fears, and guilt complexes. They help us understand the universality of the neurotic personality by directing the laughter at themselves and away from us, and in so doing they invite us to face ourselves without defense mechanisms.

That so much of contemporary comedy is of the performance rather than the literary variety has much to do with the decline of language. Wit and double entendre flourished on seventeeth-century comic stages, when audiences not only tolerated but eagerly sought intellectual exercise by straining to catch verbal subtleties. About all we have left nowadays are outrageous one-liners like those Hawkeye tosses off from the side of his mouth.

To Make Us Think While We Laugh

We have just mentioned Mark Russell, the political satirist whose popularity rises every four years. Even so, his popularity is limited to those who faithfully watch public television stations. The average television viewer has never heard of him. One reason is that satire is very serious business, not intended as casual entertainment, *never* intended to help us escape from our troubles.

We could say, in fact, that every comedy, except, of course, for the wildest kind of pie-in-the-face burlesque, has a dominant idea, a rational point of departure in terms of which what we are seeing is supposed to amuse us. Some comedies, on the other hand, put the idea first, not the laughter. Their intention is to have some effect on the thinking of the audience. *Satire* is perhaps more urgent. It wants action, usually social or political reforms. The works of George Bernard Shaw (see later) are true comedies of ideas. They can be called comedies only in the broadest definition of the word. They contain wit and humor; they have some characters whose outrageous behavior evokes chuckles. But mainly, the viewer's critical intellect smiles inwardly as it recognizes Shaw's subtle ironies.

Earlier in this chapter we pointed out that the Greeks invented the art of comedy as a means of ending their all-day festival of tragedy on an "up" note. The final piece of the day was called the *satyr* play, because that mythological creature, which was half man and half goat and traditionally a central figure in very off-color folk tales, was its star attraction. We have only hints of what satyr plays were like— from scattered historical records—but we do know that each tragic dramatist who entered the competition for best work of the festival was required to present three tragedies on a related theme and one comic afterpiece. Presumably, the satyr play poked fun at the tragedies the audience had just witnessed. Since each tragedy consisted of a few main actors and a unified chorus of some kind—citizens of Thebes or women of Troy, say—which commented on the action, the comic afterpiece used a chorus of satyrs, which must in itself have been howlingly funny. From satyr play, then, derived the word *satire,* which is the art of poking fun.

Aristophanes (445–385 B.C.) is, to our knowledge, the world's first entirely satiric playwright, writing no tragedies at all. Since this was the case, we should not be surprised that he developed the art, used a varied assortment of choruses—frogs and birds, for example— and made fun not only of tragedies but of existing wrongs in the city-state of Athens. Aristophanes is thus the first known dramatist to use the stage as a forum for ideas he hoped would lead to change. He was an angry young man, aware that the noble experiment in democracy, shaped earlier in the fifth century, of Pericles, was beginning to come apart.

For years, young Athenians had been sent off to die in extremely unpopular wars, first against Persia, then against Sparta (a war Athens finally lost). The culture of Athens had very definitely been peace-oriented. After the victory over Persia—a wholly unexpected one—Athens became complacent, refused to maintain a standing army, thought itself invincible, and finally became a sitting duck for the disciplined and militaristic Spartans. During the time of uneasy peace, the state became riddled with corrupt government officials. There was moral decay in society and esthetic deterioration of the arts, including that of the theater itself. The time, in short, was just right for the emergence of Aristophanic satire.

The art of satire is a devastating weapon, causing us to laugh even at things we normally respect. It does this by taking something which is true to some extent and then exaggerating it until it becomes so ludicrous we can never quite respect it again. The television series *M*A*S*H,* which has been given much praise in this chapter, belongs to the Aristophanic tradition of satire. Despite much to praise in the way our military operates, *M*A*S*H* is far more aware of the absurdities of bureaucracy, petty egos, and false priorities.

Thousands of years ago, the very idea of war as a means of solving human problems struck Aristophanes also as absurd. In *Lysistrata,* perhaps his most enduring work, he created a plot in which women of both Athens and Sparta call a sex strike, refusing to consort with husbands or lovers until all hostilities ceased. Like any great satire, *Lysistrata* hits at more than one target. Not only is war a target of ridicule, but so is human weakness, as some of the strikers find abstinence a high price to pay.

War has probably been the most common satiric theme over the centuries. Terry Southern's film *Dr. Strangelove: Or, How I Learned to Stop Worrying and Love the Bomb,* a 1964 work we shall mention again in Chapter 13, concerns the dropping of a nuclear bomb on the Soviet Union and the Soviet retaliation in the form of a Doomsday Machine designed to rid the planet of any life for the next 99 years. As politicians and military strategists on both sides prepare to take shelter deep underground, they look forward to the time when their descendants will be able to continue the hostilities, once the earth has breathable air again.

Another popular target for the satirist is an idea or a philosophy that is popular with a great many people but, in the satirist's opinion, does not deserve to be. The philosophy is ridiculed in a way that would make it difficult for any rational person ever again to take it seriously. A classic example is *Candide* (1759), by the glitteringly cynical French novelist, philosopher, and social critic François Marie Arouet, who wrote under the more familiar pen name of Voltaire (1694–1778). In the novel Voltaire attacks a popular optimistic philosophy of the day, associated with a German thinker named Leibniz, that this is the best of all possible worlds. Looking at the world around him, which a benevolent God had supposedly created, Voltaire decided somebody must be crazy, but it was not he.

The hero of *Candide,* whose name reflects his innocence, is raised by a tutor, Dr. Pangloss, and taught the philosophy of Leibniz. Candide, Pangloss, and his lady fair Cunegonde are then separated by a series of catastrophes, including the Lisbon earthquake. They are captured by all manner of barbarians, sold into slavery, beaten almost to the point of death, and sentenced to hang. All the while, Candide continues to believe that everything must be happening for the best in this best of all possible worlds. Following the earthquake, while Candide is repeating the maxim (which is bringing less and less comfort to him) he is overheard by a high-ranking official of the *Inquisition* (an austere Catholic court of no appeal that tried and sentenced—often to the stake— those found guilty of heresy against established Church doctrine). The official is appalled and charges Candide on the spot with heresy on the grounds that, if everything happens for the best, it must happen according to a predetermined plan, thus ruling out the possibility of free will, thus challenging official Church dogma. In an absolute mockery of the Inquisition hearings, Voltaire shows us how the Grand Inquisitor hands out sentences according to the whim of the moment and with no relation to the seriousness of the charge: a hanging here, a burning there, and, in the case of Candide, a "ritual flogging" for the crime of "listening to a philosopher."

After much suffering the now-broken hero is willing to say that "if this is the best of all possible worlds, I would hate to see the others." He and the once-fair but now ugly Cunegonde are finally re-united—somehow—and decide they will spend the rest of their lives tending to their own garden and expecting nothing from God or from other people.

One of the bitterest of all satiric works had already appeared in 1729, exactly 30 years before the publication of *Candide,* and that was a relatively brief pamphlet called "A Modest Proposal for Preventing the Children of the Poor People in Ireland from Being a Burthen to Their Parents or Country, and for Making Them Beneficial to the Public." The author was Jonathan Swift (1667–1745) (see Chapter 9 for further discussion), an Irish-born Episcopal clergyman who became Dean of St. Patrick's Cathedral in Dublin but never once sacrificed his brilliant and deadly satiric pen for his religious duties. In 1726 he had brought forth *Gulliver's Travels,* which most of us knew in our early childhood as an exciting adventure tale but which in reality is a devastating satire on every institution ever established by humanity, a species Swift absolutely despised.

Though born in Dublin, Swift hated the Irish about as much as he hated everyone else, except for the British (who did not accept him socially because he was Irish). But though he would not live among them, Swift believed the Irish did not deserve the cruel and inhuman treatment inflicted upon them by their close neighbors across the Irish Sea. His heart ached when he thought of the filth and disease in which the children of the Irish poor were raised while English aristocrats stuffed themselves in their country manors. He gave vent to his anger in "A Modest Proposal," and in so doing, invented a new satiric technique we still call *Swiftian irony,* by which technique the satirist pretends to be the very sort of person he is denouncing and to espouse the very cause he finds despicable. Writing in a matter-of-fact and perfectly rational way, Swift proposes the breeding of Irish babies as potential gourmet entrées for London dinner parties:

> I have been assured by a very knowing American of my acquaintance in London, that a young healthy child well nursed is at a year old a most delicious, nourishing, and wholesome food, whether stewed, roasted, baked, or boiled, and I make no doubt that it will equally serve in a fricasse or a ragout.

Swift was in such control of his prose that his horrible suggestion sounds increasingly plausible as he continues. He goes into elaborate detail about the fees to be paid the mother, the best method of growing this "livestock," delivery procedures, and the appeal of this novelty menu to bored hostesses.

To the obvious question "But how can you suggest such a barbaric thing?" the satirist could have responded: "Why in the world

Satire he used as a weapon to "mend the world," to lash ignorance and corruption, in the belief that men were open to correction, not irretrievably lost.

Harold Williams on Swift

not?" "Because," you retort, "it's not what you do to human beings!" "True," says the satirist, "But what do you call what the English are doing to the Irish?"

Satire *must* have a point. The satirist must know what is wrong and what ought to take its place. For instance, in 1965 Tony Richardson's film *The Loved One,* based on Evelyn Waugh's novel of the same name, went beyond its source in making savage fun of the funeral business in the United States and the generally unrealistic attitude toward death held by many Americans. The setting of the film is a Disneyland kind of mortuary-cemetery in Hollywood, which instantly reminds us of Forest Lawn, the real-life, expensive, Los Angeles resting place of many former stars. In the film, the mortuary is filled with garish, often nude statues of angels and other heavenly creatures, has canned music blaring over loudspeakers day and night, and includes segregated areas where "like-minded" corpses and their loved ones lie together in plush, moisture-proof, silk-lined caskets. The film makes fun of hysterically grieving but hypocritical survivors, motivated by greed, and money-grubbing funeral directors out to seize their share of "the take." It offended many people, and it intended to do just that. The film also led to an investigation of the price structures of many funeral institutions.

The nonsatiric, fundamentally serious comedy of ideas, as we pointed out, is easily associated with the towering figure of George Bernard Shaw (1856–1950), who began writing for the theater during the late nineteenth century, when the new realism of Henrik Ibsen in Norway was beginning to make a stir (see Chapter 12 for a discussion of Ibsen's *A Doll's House*). Shaw, a great supporter of Ibsen, whose works were having a difficult time finding audiences, also believed the time had come for the theater to do more than casually entertain. Shaw, however, is not plodding and heavy-handed, but uses scintillating wit and an ability of Shakespearean proportions to create fully rounded human beings in order to drive his ideas home. His plays deal with the impoverishment of British education, foolish romanticism, war profiteering, hypocrisy, capitalism—almost any subject a serious dramatist might treat.

The moving force behind Shaw's work is what we might call *Shavian irony.* Shaw's ironic technique is to present a given situation or set of relationships toward which we are encouraged to develop a particular attitude, and then at the end to pull the rug out from under us by showing that the opposite attitude is really the more intelligent of the two. A good example is *Major Barbara* (1905), a play which remarkably anticipates the so-called generation-gap idea of the 1960s and the rebellion of idealistic young people against their establishment parents. Barbara is the daughter of Undershaft, a munitions manufacturer. She has been raised in luxury but then denounces her background, becomes a street marcher (and Major) in the Salvation Army, and engages in idealistic debates with her father over his profession. The audience is at first totally on her side. But Undershaft makes a deal: He will visit the Salvation Army headquarters and observe the "good" that Barbara claims is being done there, if she in turn will agree to visit his munitions plant. The girl willingly agrees, certain that there will be no contest.

The visit to the Salvation Army is not what we expect. The well-meaning volunteers, who are all from genteel backgrounds, cannot cope with the angry street people, for whom a piece of bread and a badly sung hymn are scant recompense for a lifetime of poverty and governmental neglect. The munitions plant, on the other hand, is modern, well-equipped, clean, disciplined, and peopled by happy, well-fed, well-paid workers. To Barbara's objection that their salaries are possible because somebody plans to blow up society, Undershaft responds that every so often society *has* to be blown up! Barbara's idealism is shattered, and the audience leaves with a very different idea from the one originally entertained.

Shaw was a socialist and believed England could not survive in monarchy and with rigid class barriers. While he made that point quite clearly in *Major Barbara,* his greatness lies in the fact that he did not belabor the same point in every other play. Each work of Shaw's tackles a complex new idea with subtlety and the author's piercing intellect. No other playwright in history has been able to make intellectual dialog, the exchange of really intricate thoughts, so engaging and absorbing. Shaw lifted comedy to heights it may never reach again. He is to comedy what Shakespeare is to its counterpart, tragedy.

The Experience of Tragedy

Traditionally, dramatists aspire to create important tragedies, feeling that, as a result, their audiences will be moved as profoundly as theater has power to do and their place in the history of drama will be assured. A popular movie of the early 1940s was *No Time for Comedy,* dealing with a playwright whose successful light comedies had made him rich and famous but who deliberately turned aside from his winning formula to try his hand at lofty tragedy. The disaster that befell his attempt was worse than the one he was writing about. He had learned his lesson. Nevertheless, dramatists continue to seek recognition through "heavy" plays. Why?

Tragedy as the Purgation of Emotion

Aristotle believed the whole point of tragedy was the purgation of feeling.

Twenty-five hundred years ago Aristotle became the first theater critic when he wrote his *Poetics,* which has survived only partially. Fortunately, we have intact his essay on tragedy, with its remarkable psychological slant (remarkable considering that Greeks knew nothing of a formal science called psychology). The emphasis is on what tragedy *does* to and for its audience:

> Tragedy, then, is the imitation of an action that is serious, complete, and of a certain magnitude; in the form of action, not narrative, through pity and fear bringing about the proper purgation of those emotions.

Since for Aristotle the ideal human being was the person of reason and virtue, we may conclude that the great philosopher regarded pity and fear as debilitating emotions, barriers to the calm practice of rational faculties. Whether we can single out pity and fear as the dominant feelings every tragedy inspires, we will agree that tragedy, which always ends in catastrophe, is a fierce assault upon the emotions. We emerge from the theater totally drained and incapable of feeling anything more, at least for a while. The aftermath of seeing a tragedy is similar to what happens to us when we have grieved over the loss of a loved one. We have the "formal feeling" of which the poet Emily Dickinson speaks in this famous poem:

> *After great pain a formal feeling comes—*
> *The nerves sit ceremonious like tombs;*
> *The stiff Heart questions—was it He that bore?*
> *And yesterday—or centuries before?*
>
> *The feet mechanical*
> *Go round a wooden way*
> *Of ground or air or Ought, regardless grown,*
> *A quartz contentment like a stone.*
>
> *This is the hour of lead*
> *Remembered if outlived,*
> *As freezing persons recollect the snow—*
> *First chill, then stupor, then the letting go.*

The difference is that the aftermath is tragic purgation, or *catharsis,* not a letting go. By identifying with great suffering, by empathizing with great people overwhelmed by great odds *in a fictitious context,* we can leave our emotions behind in the theater. Our sense of reason returns, sharper than ever. We have the strength to confront real disaster if unfortunately it should strike.

The academic attitude toward tragic literature in this century has been that we shall never again have a Sophocles or a Shakespeare. No new play will ever stir an audience the way *Oedipus Rex* or *King Lear* does, because modern characters in the context of ordinary life are not important enough to devastate our emotions. Whether this is true or not is highly debatable.

The fashion of contemporary theater is to imitate the way people actually speak instead of the way they ought to speak.

It is also said that most of the major languages of the world have been shorn of elegance and power in the gradual shift toward a more democratic view of communication. Where once the king's way of speaking was the standard to emulate, now, so the claim goes, the line between the grammatical and the illiterate is thin to nonexistent. And the fashion of contemporary theater is to imitate the way people actually speak instead of the way they ought to speak. Consequently, the soaring poetry which once helped the dramatist to assault our emotion is sadly lacking. We leave the theater unsatisfied because too much has been left unsaid.

The Importance of Plot in Tragedy

Aristotle did not sit down one day and decide there should be an art form called tragedy which should affect us in certain ways. Actually, he wrote his critical analysis of theater in the century following the time of the great Greek tragic dramatists: Aeschylus, Sophocles, and Euripides. By observing their work and its effects on audiences, Aristotle developed his critical principles.

In addition to defining tragedy, Aristotle divided it into its main components: plot, character, thought, diction, spectacle, and song. The last two he considered important theatrical decorations, but not the soul of tragedy. The first four were the means by which a work caused the purgation of our emotions. Of prime importance was *plot*.

Many confuse plot with story. In a play or novel the story is an abstract summary of the major events and characters. When we retell the story, we usually begin with something like, "It's about a woman who . . ." The plot, on the other hand, is the way the events of the story are arranged; and the writer's skill is usually demonstrated by the ingenuity of the arrangement. Two writers of very different abilities could take the very same story and create either an exciting or a dull product.

In tragedy, irony is frequently the device which determines a workable plot arrangement; and there are two major kinds of tragic plot irony. One involves the arrangement of events so as to develop very early within the audience a sense that a certain disaster is inevitable. In other words, the audience knows long before the main character what his or her fate must be, and knows that nothing can be done about it. The emotional assault is from the mounting terror of anticipation. Such an arrangement is often called *Sophoclean irony,* after the Greek tragic playwright who used it to great advantage. In fact, Sophoclean irony is the one structural principle of *Oedipus Rex,* which may be the greatest single play ever written. The other major ironic structural principle is called *Euripidean irony,* after another Greek dramatist, one who enjoyed twisting a knife in the back of his audience. In Euripides, we are sometimes led to expect—or at least strongly hope for—a happy resolution, only to be dealt a severe blow when the situation takes a decided turn for the worse. Thus the two dominant forms of tragic irony are at completely opposite poles in terms of how they work upon our emotions. With Sophoclean irony we know what is coming; we brace ourselves for it—like the feeling we have when slowly climbing the initial incline of a roller coaster. The long build-up always intensifies the emotional release we feel when the expected outcome finally happens. With Euripidean irony we know that a certain disastrous outcome is a distinct possibility; we keep telling ourselves that the writer could not be so cruel. But it comes about anyway. The assault on the emotions can be even more powerful under these circumstances.

Sophocles (496?–406 B.C.) wrote *Oedipus* when he was an old man, after having achieved considerable success as a tragedian. His long experience must have led him toward this sublime achievement of plot, a miracle of simplicity and the unrelieved battering of audience emotions. Not one word of this play is wasted. Not one moment exists which does not bring us closer to the inevitable doom of the main character. The advantage Sophocles possessed over his modern counterparts was that Greek tragedies were always based on mythical tales passed down from one generation to another and therefore well known to the entire audience before it ever arrived at the theater. From the moment that King Oedipus steps onto the stage and asks the assembled chorus of Theban citizens what they desire of him, speaking his name in the process, the audience would have flashed ahead in their imaginations to his catastrophe.

Oedipus is married to Jocasta, a woman considerably older than he and the mother of his four children. At the outset what neither realizes, but the audience *does,* is that the queen and king of Thebes are really mother and son, having lived together for many years in an incestuous bond.

As the myth goes, Jocasta and her former husband, Laius, bring a male heir into the world, only to be told by a prophet that the child will one day grow up to kill his father and marry his mother. Anxious to evade the prophecy, the royal couple bid a servant take the child, tie his feet together, and leave it in a desolate place far from the palace. But, unable to commit so horrendous a crime, the servant gives the child to a herdsman in a neighboring kingdom, who in turn gives the baby to his own childless king and queen.

Grown to young manhood, Oedipus (so named because his feet had become swollen by the leather ties) is dismayed when he is told by a soothsayer that he will one day kill his father and marry his mother. Wishing, like his real parents before him, to cheat the prophecy, he leaves his homeland. While on the road to the kingdom of Thebes, he has a hostile encounter with Laius and slays him, little dreaming that he has murdered his natural father. Ultimately he is

For by the cartload they are annually burned. Sometimes from out the folded paper the pale clerk takes a ring—the finger it was meant for, perhaps, moulders in the grave; a bank-note sent in swiftest charity—he whom it would relieve, nor eats nor hungers any more; pardon for those who died despairing; hope for those who died unhoping; good tidings for those who died stifled by unrelieved calamities. On errands of life, these letters speed to death.

Herman Melville on the Dead Letter Office

united in marriage with the now-widowed queen of Thebes, Jocasta, and the ancient prophecy is fulfilled.

Sophocles's tragedy begins with a devastating plague which has fallen upon the city of Thebes. Eager to aid his subjects, Oedipus seeks advice from the oracle, who informs him that the plague will destroy the city unless the murderer of its former king is found and properly punished. In a passionate speech that must have terrified the audience, Oedipus vows to bring down his full fury upon the head of the killer, who is, of course, himself!

The play is the essence of starkness, as the king's investigations lead him closer and closer to the dreadful truth. What makes the plot work, of course, is the fact that the deeds and the consequences the hero cannot hope to elude—the murder and the incestuous marriage—have already happened. So the suspense, unlike that in most plots, consists of our awaiting the hero's recognition. Having vowed to his people that he will destroy the murderer, Oedipus has sealed his fate.

Playwrights since Sophocles have recognized the tremendous power of *Oedipus* and perhaps have tried to be as effective. The use of Sophoclean irony is, however, severely limited. It is a precious commodity, like a magnificent flower that blooms only once in a century. The reason is that the Greek playwrights had a rich mythological heritage upon which to draw. Without books, television, and movies, they relied on story-telling and story-listening. Of course, in our culture today we have a few commonly shared events, like the assassination of Lincoln and the sinking of the *Titanic;* but our writers cannot keep going back to them. Perhaps the scarcity of such material helps explain why so many writers have used and continue to use the Euripidean plot structure, which has been likened to one in which the hero is himself suddenly murdered and there is no one left to save the day and expose the killer.

Euripidean irony depends upon our thinking we know the outcome, expecting a happy ending, only to be "tricked"—horrifyingly.

Sophoclean irony depends upon our knowing the protagonist's fate in advance— and then waiting in horror for the inevitable disaster.

Euripides (c. 480–460 B.C.) uses the structural principle in *The Trojan Women* and, like Sophocles in *Oedipus,* focuses intensely on a single situation. It is just after the fall of Troy. The heirs to the throne of Troy are all dead except for one young boy. The women of the title gather around to mourn the dead and to protect the boy. A Greek soldier arrives, anguished because he is to carry out the boy's sentence: death by being hurled from the mountain.

The simplest possible treatment of this situation would, of course, be tragic enough. There would be the soldier's sorrow, the mother's vain pleadings, the charm and innocence of the boy, and the inevitable moment of unbearable pathos when the boy's body is carried onstage by the wretched solder. But Euripides deepens the character of the soldier. He also introduces a short scene in which the boy is shown playing with stones on the ground. The soldier kneels down and helps the boy at play. This humanizes the whole event so much that the viewer cannot believe the soldier would actually complete the horrible mission on which he has been sent. *Yet he does.*

In Shakespeare's *King Lear* (1605) there occurs a most appalling moment, which also illustrates Euripidean irony. The old monarch is in his eighties and has been on the throne for so long that he cannot imagine what it is like not to be in power. His vanity knows no bounds. Having decided to retire, he summons his three daughters around him and promises to leave the largest share of the kingdom to the one who loves him the most. Goneril and Regan, the two evil schemers, outdo each other in protesting hypocritical affections for the old man. But Cordelia—young, innocent, and truthful—quietly observes that the kind of love promised by her sisters to their father is suitable only for a wife to give to her husband. Since she herself is to be married, she intends to love her father as much as is appropriate, but certainly no more and not as intensely as her sisters proclaim. King Lear is furious, denouncing Cordelia and dividing the kingdom equally between Goneril and Regan.

The skull of life suddenly showed through its smile.

Dorothy Canfield Fisher

Euripidean Irony in Shakespeare:

Juliet is given a potion to make her sleep so soundly it will appear that she is dead. When Romeo sees her lying in the tomb, he believes she is dead and stabs himself. Juliet awakens too late.

Soon Lear realizes his mistake, but the recognition comes far too late. Goneril and Regan are engaged in a vicious struggle against each other, one which sees Lear reduced to the status of a prisoner without money or power. Cordelia's husband, the king of France, raises an invading army to save the old king, but during the battle, Cordelia is captured and sentenced to death along with her father. As soon as the tide of battle is turned, the king of France sends a messenger to stop the executions.

King Lear then enters, carrying the body of Cordelia. The stay of execution has arrived soon enough for him, too late for her. He cries,

> . . . *No, no, no life!*
> *Why should a dog, a horse, a rat, have life,*
> *And thou no breath at all? Thou'lt come*
> *No more, never, never, never, never,*
> *Never!*[3]

Whenever there is a premature loss—the death of a child, a young spouse, an artist just beginning what promises to be a great career—

one feels a hollowness, not unlike what Lear felt, at the recognition of the apparent injustice at the heart of things. One contemporary author has referred to it as the "rotten streak in life's nature."

Euripidean irony suggests the watchful eye of the playful, even malevolent, gods. Everyone remembers the O. Henry story "Gift of the Magi," in which the wife trims and sells her hair to buy her husband a watch fob, while he is selling his watch to buy combs for her beautiful long hair. Then there is Stephen Crane's story "The Open Boat," about four men adrift at sea in a frail craft, three of whom survive the fury of the waves, and one of whom, the physically strongest, perishes.

Both Sophoclean and Euripidean ironies can be more than methods of plotting. They can constitute a profoundly tragic vision of life held by the playwright. Greek dramatists, for example, must have been influenced in their thinking by the fatalistic strain in their common cultural heritage. Their myths show human beings caught up in a titanic battle against the gods, whom they try to emulate; and for their sins they are doomed, as the gods display their superior powers. Small wonder that Greek tragedies are plays in which we watch helplessly as fate overcomes the protagonists.

Some of the plays of Euripides have contrived happy endings in which an actor representing a god comes down from the "sky" and resolves everyone's fortunes for the better. Such contrivances in no way minimize the tragic impact, for we are still being shown a universe in which the destinies of people are determined by whimsy and chance, in which the reward for goodness can be death or suffering, or a sudden happy turn that is in no way morally connected with good deeds. Indeed, the happy endings of Euripides are in some respects even more tragic. In the distance we hear the laughter of the gods.

The Tragic Protagonist

The plot structure of a tragedy contributes in large measure to the emotional wrenching we go through in order to achieve a sense of purgation. But plot alone is not enough. There are many plays and films, called *melodramas,* that are entertaining pieces which involve us emotionally *up to a point* but do not leave us feeling that we have just undergone an unforgettable experience; pieces in which people die or are abandoned or confront each other with raw emotions, but which do not demand our full emotional commitment.

Aristotle recognized that *character* was of crucial significance in determining how deeply tragedy can affect us, and he placed it second in importance to plot. Many dramatists of our time—a time when the theater has reflected the influence of psychology—believe that character is first in importance, and they are writing plays about human beings and their complex relationships with each other and with themselves, plays in which there is not much overt action and little that we could traditionally label plot.

In the *Poetics,* Aristotle looked back, as we said, at the golden age of Greek theater, and, in considering the works he felt were most effective, he analyzed the characteristics of their major protagonists. The tragic hero, as Aristotle summed it up, is a person of noble birth who occupies a powerful enough position to make choices which involve great numbers of people, decisions which can bring catastrophe to an entire kingdom. In other words, the protagonists with tragic potential are the ones whose actions *matter* a great deal.

In addition, the tragic protagonist must be primarily good. He cannot be perfect, because the suffering and fall of such a person would offend the moral sensibilities of the audience. Nor must he be totally evil, because audiences would not be able to identify with a depraved character. He must be virtuous enough for us to care about what happens to him, but possess a tragic flaw of character so that we are not witnessing the unacceptable suffering of an innocent being.

Aristotle noted that the flaw which all of the major tragic protagonists displayed was pride, or *hubris.* This particular trait, when we think about the matter, is inevitable if one is to meet two of Aristotle's primary requirements: being of noble birth, and being in a position so powerful that one's choices affect the destiny of many others. Pride makes one blind to possible consequences, and of all tragic flaws, it is the one with which we easily identify. Few are those human beings who can remain completely objective about themselves, who can put aside their egos. One need not have the power of an Oedipus to share the trait of hubris.

Aristotle's analysis of the tragic hero appears to assume free will. Can the consequence of a bad choice be tragic if the choice could not have been averted? Can our emotions be totally assaulted when there never is a possibility of a better fate, a happier ending? Yet, as we have already said, the Greek mythology upon which the tragedies are based was fatalistic, and the idea of unavoidable doom is one of the *meanings* of tragic theater.

One way of looking at this dilemma is to ask ourselves whether *any* tragic protagonist can ever be said to have a totally free will. If there is a flaw of character, then does not that flaw itself control the choice? Hubris *itself* is fate. We do not need the gods at all. In contemporary theater, the gods are absent, but our major tragic characters— Willy Loman in Arthur Miller's *Death of a Salesman,* Blanche DuBois in Tennessee Williams' *Streetcar Named Desire,* the four members of the Tyrone family in Eugene O'Neill's *Long Day's Journey into Night*—are all doomed by one form of tragic blindness or other, not necessarily hubris, but a blindness that prevents them from saving themselves.

Remember: Aristotle said merely that the protagonist must have a flaw of character, otherwise his doom would be unbearable to watch. Again, the tragedy of Oedipus illustrates the point. The whole story in the myth involves an ancient curse on the house of Cadmus

The tragic hero usually has a final moment of painful self-awareness. The comic fool often remains blind.

(the doomed household was a very popular theme), an ancestor of Oedipus, whose incestuous marriage following the murder of his father was the working out of the curse in a particular generation.

But the *Oedipus Rex* of Sophocles is not the tragedy of a man who does terrible things. Rather, it is the tragedy of a man whose pride blinds him to the reality of what he has done, whose pride will not accept the cards fate has dealt him, who insists reality is what *he* says it is, and who therefore has absolutely no strength with which to face the truth when it finally and cruelly stares him in the face. It is the tragedy of a man who fights against fate, and this makes his final doom overwhelming to our emotions. Perhaps, we could even say, Oedipus *did* have a choice of whether to believe the truth of his deeds—and he chose not to. In all of theater there is no better example of hubris, the tragic pride that blinds. One strong reason for the enduring popularity of this work is the timelessness of that tragic flaw. Most of us can identify with it because we know what it is to resist the truth, even when there is no place to hide.

In a tragedy about the later life of the same doomed family, *Antigone,* Sophocles created another powerful embodiment of pride. Creon, king of Thebes after Oedipus, has always tried to be a good and just ruler. But his fairness is tested after the two sons of Oedipus, the previous king, slay each other in battle. One son has been the rebellious leader of an enemy force, bent on capturing the kingdom. As a punishment to the young man's soul, Creon orders his body left unburied, thus preventing his soul from finding peace in the next world.

Antigone, daughter of Oedipus, defies Creon's order and performs the burial rites for her brother. She too has her pride and puts family honor above the law of the land. But Creon has announced that *any* violation will be punished, no matter who the criminal may be. Despite pleas from his son, Haemon, who loves Antigone, Creon sentences the girl to death by being walled up in a cave. In condemning someone who was only carrying out the will of the gods, Creon has acted as if he were greater than the gods.

But now occurs what we may call the *scene of false hope.* Learning that Haemon has remained inside the cave to die with his beloved, the heartbroken father acts to undo the wrong and to free the lovers—unfortunately, too late, as you may have guessed. In an extraordinary exchange of ironies, Sophocles borrows the plot technique of his younger contemporary, Euripides. Creon sees the body of Antigone and witnesses the suicide of his son.

The deaths of the two and the news of the Queen's death are followed by a *speech of recognition,* which is absolutely essential to the fullness of the tragic experience:

> Lead me away. I have been rash and foolish. I have killed
> my son and my wife. I look for comfort; my comfort lies

> here dead. Whatever my hands have touched has come
> to nothing. Fate has brought all my pride to a thought
> of dust.

In a similar speech, Oedipus consigns himself to exile, away from
friends and comforts, to spend the remainder of his life as a blind
wanderer.

Third in importance on Aristotle's list of tragedy's main components is *thought,* by which he meant an overview of the moral significance of the events that take place. Much of the thought is supplied
by the onstage presence of a *Chorus,* a group of actors representing
the common people, who are fortunately free of the tragic flaws of
their superiors and who therefore can see what the protagonist cannot. But the speech of recognition is very much a part of classical and,
later, Shakespearean tragedy. The purgation of the emotions is complete when we hear from the protagonist Creon's own lips that his
blindness has brought him to this pass. If that recognition does not
come (as it does not in many modern tragedies for reasons we shall
investigate), we leave the theater still frustrated, no matter how powerful the overall experience may have been, for there is the implication
that the protagonist has been a mere victim, not the driving force of
the tragedy. Even if the life of Creon has been the working out of a
curse or some other kind of fate, that flaw of character belongs to *him;*
he can blame nothing else for what happens. He would not wish to
renounce the last vestige of human greatness: to *accept responsibility.*

In Shakespeare's greatest tragedies, with the exception of
Hamlet (which works as a tragedy for reasons that no one quite understands), the death of the hero is preceded by a recognition speech of
surpassingly beautiful and passionate language. The hero not only accepts responsibility for the doom brought on by his flaw, but *reminds*
us of his greatness. In Shakespeare, hubris is at once a blindness and a
super-strength. But Shakespeare (1564–1616) wrote during the Renaissance, an age which placed great stress on soaring individualism,
on the human being as the equal of all the ancient and outmoded gods.

Shakespeare appears to have possessed a double vision. On
the one hand, he was the product of his times. Language extolling human greatness poured from his pen. On the other hand, the tragedian
in him saw the dangers of greatness: power devouring itself by its
own excesses; overriding ambition that becomes evil and must be destroyed; egos flattened beyond all reasonable bounds so that they lose
touch with reality. In *Othello* (1604) we have a nearly perfect tragic
work: a simple plot structure governed by the principle of Sophoclean irony; a protagonist whose blindness is a profound jealousy that
eats up this once-virtuous leader's capacity for reason and compassion;
and, Shakespeare's trademark, glorious poetry that gives the actor
abundant language with which to express the most searing emotion.

Othello is a Moor, a prince in his own land, and now a general in the Venetian army. He is married to a highborn Venetian woman, Desdemona, with whom he is as deeply in love as it is possible to be. But the man's heroic stature and the favor he enjoys on all sides—not to mention his possession of Desdemona—inspire a treacherous soldier named Iago to a profound hatred. In the hundreds of years that actors have been performing Iago, this archvillain's complex personality has been subjected to innumerable interpretations, including the modern one which presents him as a man overcome by unreasoning racism.

Villain though Iago may be, Shakespeare has not written a melodrama, a play which resembles tragedy but the characters of which are two-dimensional stick figures. The plot turns on Iago's carefully executed scheme to destroy Othello by planting and then nurturing in his mind the belief that Desdemona, his beautiful wife, is unfaithful. Sophoclean irony drives the plot forward. In scene after scene Iago's hold becomes stronger; the Moor's clear-headed good sense vanishes. We know that nothing will prevent the doom that engulfs Othello and Desdemona. We know that he must kill her.

But none of this is happening to an ordinary man. Othello is a great general who is being deceived, a man whose vast mental powers we have seen at the beginning of the play; and it is with horror that we soon discover a capacity for irrational jealousy we could not have expected in one so noble. Never has tragic blindness been so clear. Othello is capable of far better things. Othello should see right through Iago. But for some complex reason, which every actor who plays the role must determine for himself, there is that flaw.

After he has suffocated Desdemona with her own pillow, the truth—as usual in tragedy—comes to light; but it is too late, and Shakespeare gives us *this* recognition speech:

> *Soft you; a word or two before you go.*
> *I have done the state some service and they know't.*
> *No more of that. I pray you, in your letters,*
> *When you shall these unlucky deeds relate,*
> *Speak of me as I am; nothing extenuate,*
> *Nor set down aught in malice. Then must you speak*
> *Of one that lov'd not wisely but too well;*
> *Of one not easily jealous, but being wrought,*
> *Perplex'd in the extreme; of one whose hand,*
> *Like the base Indian, threw a pearl away*
> *Richer than all his tribe; of one whose subdu'd eyes,*
> *Albeit unused to the melting mood,*
> *Drop tears as fast as the Arabian trees*
> *Their medicinal gum. Set you down this.*
> *And say besides, that in Aleppo once,*

Where a malignant and a turban'd Turk
Beat a Venetian and traduced the state,
I took by the throat the circumcised dog,
And smote him, thus.

(He produces a concealed weapon and stabs himself,
falling beside the body of Desdemona.)

I kiss'd thee ere I kill'd thee: no way but this,
Killing myself, to die upon a kiss.

(Falls on the bed, and dies.)[4]

In Shakespeare's universe there appears to be a moral order,
though we may question whether there is a God to administer it. The
great tragic heroes violate that order, and dire consequences follow,
with the innocent as well as the guilty suffering. But in nearly every
instance, the hero ultimately affirms the moral order by word and, usually, deed. The audience has been emotionally devastated, but both the
state and the cosmos are set to right and function once again as they
are supposed to. The Shakespearean hero is like diseased tissue that is
finally discarded by a body so that it may regain its health.

In Greek tragedies the Chorus generally tells us that moral
order has been restored. In Shakespeare the greatness of the protagonist reasserts itself and says: I have violated; now I shall make whole
once again, that order.

In our own time dramatists continue to strive for the heights
of tragedy, but two questions arise: (1) Are there great people anymore? and (2) Is there a moral order in terms of which a deep flaw of
character is tragic?

In Shakespeare's universe
there appears to be a moral
order, though we may ques-
tion whether there is a God
to administer it.

Contemporary Tragedy

Before we tackle these two big questions, let us consider one obstacle
that, according to many critics, prevents our ever being able to rival
the Greeks and Shakespeare; and that is *language.* Aristotle placed language fourth among the main components of tragedy, but only after
plot, character, and thought. For Shakespeare, however, language, character, and thought are too intertwined to separate. Theater historians
bemoan the demise of great language on our stages.

In some cases music substitutes for poetry; but with some
rare exceptions, blank verse is gone. Democracy may be the key reason. Not even the nobility in Shakespeare's time ever spoke so beautifully offstage, but the convention of poetic dialog for aristocratic
people was accepted. Today the fashion in theater is naturalism, not
the creation of a stage reality that is appropriate for tragedy. Our dramatists are probably at their best when they dispense with words al-

The tragic protagonist—
whether classical or mod-
ern—must have a flaw of
character which causes the
catastrophe.

together and give us pulsing moments of silence. Ours is a theater of moments, but seldom of works that can combine plot, character, thought, and language into an experience that sweeps over us and carries us toward total purgation of the emotions.

Democracy has also made us less willing to accept one particular person as a great leader, a noble individual whose decisions affect the destiny of many. Of course, attempts have been made to find such figures. Earlier in this century the playwright Maxwell Anderson wrote *Elizabeth the Queen* and *Mary of Scotland,* dipping into history to justify the use of aristocratic persons and blank verse. The result was interesting historical drama, but hardly tragedy with which audiences of today could identify. In the 1930s, the same dramatist, seeking a formula for modernizing the tragic experience, wrote *Winterset,* a play in which the inhabitants of New York tenement houses speak imitation Shakespearean verse, and not very convincingly.

A most ambitious attempt at modern tragedy has been Arthur Miller's *Death of a Salesman* (1949), in which even the title encourages us to accept the ennoblement of a common man. Willy Loman—a "low man," not a king or prince—has reached the age at which he is no longer successful at selling and has been reduced to the humiliating position of having to beg for even an office job that will guarantee him $60 a week. There is no question about audience identification in our understanding of Willy's total acceptance of the American dream or a success that has escaped him all his life.

Now that he is old and must accept charity from the boss, he will not see how he has given up his whole life in the pursuit of something never within his grasp. Instead, he does what so many do in Willy's situation: He transfers the dream to his children. He looks upon his son Biff, once a football hero and now a "buck-an-hour" drifter, as a prince who will yet bring importance to the family. Willy's flaw is similar to that of Oedipus: blindness to reality. The man's ardent belief that his son "is going to be magnificent" leads him to a suicidal death in a traffic accident so that Biff will have the insurance money to make a new start in life.

Warnings by his wife, Linda, that Willy is contemplating suicide do indeed introduce a decided note of Sophoclean irony into the play. Doom, symbolized by the towering landscape of New York City that dwarfs Willy's little house, stares at us from the curtain rise until the final "Requiem" scene at Willy's grave, in which Linda whispers to her dead husband the news that the house is finally paid for and "we're free!"

There is no recognition speech, a convention lacking, for one reason or other, in every modern tragedy. For one thing, the American dream of success, which has motivated the entire plot, is not the same as the moral order of ancient times. Willy does not violate the dream—quite the contrary. Miller, a decidedly political writer in the decade of

Some critics say that modern life prevents us from developing a character important enough to be tragic.

the '40s, wishes to show that the dream is a fundamental evil in a business society which destroys everyone in its path. To that extent Willy Loman is a victim, as Oedipus and Othello are not. Whether the victimized "low man" can ever attain the stature of the great tragic heroes is still being debated.

A reason often given for the absence of recognition speeches is modern psychology, which has shown that true self-knowledge is rare. If writers are to strive for realism, they know that people driven to the depths of despair, whether by a tragic flaw or by an economic system over which they have no control, are not rational enough to recognize what is happening to them.

Yet, if we lack the stirring recognition speeches of old, we have impressive substitutes, such as the final scene of Tennessee Williams' *A Streetcar Named Desire* (1947), in which the protagonist Blanche DeBois, driven to madness by a brutal sexual assault as well as her neurotic unwillingness to accept the unpleasant truth of her own behavior, timidly greets the people who have come to take her to an institution, putting herself in their hands with the pitiable statement that she has always depended on "the kindness of strangers."

Both Williams and Miller seem to be asking: Is this the best we can do for human beings? In theater the very best we can do may well be to create shattering plays about losers, not kings. After all, if we remove the mask of nobility or the old belief in a moral order that governs the universe, what we have left may be the losers. Perhaps life at its most tragic *is* a slow and agonizing process of losing.

Losers are ultimately shown not to be responsible for their fate. We would thus say that the American dream, not Willy's tragic flaw, causes his tragedy; and Blanche's deeply neurotic loss of touch with her personal identity causes hers. It appears that the old myth of nobility gave to people like Oedipus and Othello the aura of being entitled to better things because of their innate dignity and rationality. Our tragedies *at their best* offer terrifying glimpses into the disordered lives of people destroyed by *the flaws of existence itself.* If this is the case, then we may say that Willy and Blanche *never* could have led happier, more fulfilled lives.

It has been said that tragedy at its greatest appalls us with the waste of human potential. Perhaps it is this sense of waste that is most conspicuously lacking in present-day theater. But we cannot blame the dramatists. The price of democracy may be that no one person is considered indispensable; so in what respect is the destruction of any life a waste? The price of psychological insight may be that disaster and rationality are seldom believed to go hand in hand; so we cannot expect to have tragic protagonists who really know what is happening to them. Pity may be the strongest emotion our theater can evoke.

On the other hand, Aristotle, long ago, said that a tragedy pulls from us the emotions of pity and fear. Whatever has led to a tragic

Masterpieces of the past are good for the past: they are not good for us. We have the right to say what has been said and even what has not been said in a way that belongs to us.

Antonin Artaud

downfall, we humanly pity those who suffer, and we fear that the same thing could happen to us. Democratic tragedy, after all, may not be too far from Aristotle in this all-important, this *human* respect.

GLOSSARY

catharsis: The release, or purgation, of the emotions which ideally takes place at the conclusion of a powerful tragedy. Aristotle, the first known critic of the drama, held catharsis to be the purpose of the art form, for having undergone emotional purgation, the viewer is able to reestablish a rational balance without which, Aristotle believed, the proper conduct of life was impossible.

comedy: A form of drama which displays some violation of the audience's rational expectations regarding human behavior and human relationships. The gap between the norm and the situation creates an inner tension which is eased through laughter. Thus it is said that a sense of humor is an invaluable asset to the restoration of sanity.

commedia dell'arte: Originally, an Italian theater movement of the mid-sixteenth century; an improvisatory theater in which highly skilled professionals created comedies on the spot, using stock characters, such as the foolish old man pursuing a very young girl.

double entendre: A comic device, popular for centuries, in which lines have a double meaning, the second of which is usually unacceptable to polite society.

Euripidean irony: In a tragedy, a perverse twist of fate leading to an ending that is usually more appalling than expected. Often, as in the final act of *King Lear,* the possibility of a happy outcome is raised, only to have the playwright dash our hopes to the ground.

farce: A highly exaggerated comic play using two-dimensional, stock characters, unbelievable situations, and improbable resolutions.

hubris: A Greek term for "pride"—the usual failing of character which drives the protagonist in Greek (and other) tragedy to his or her doom.

primitivism: An eighteenth-century philosophy which holds that people living the simple life, close to nature, are nobler than their educated, city-bred counterparts.

satire: A form of literature which greatly exaggerates a situation the humorist finds intolerable. By inducing others to laugh at the situation, the humorist hopes to bring about a change for the better. Satire is the most moral of the comic arts.

satyr play: The comic afterpiece to a three-part tragedy performed in ancient Greece, probably to make fun of what had gone before and send the audience home in a brighter frame of mind. Origin of our word "satire."

Shavian irony: A technique used frequently by playwright George Bernard Shaw whereby the play turns out to mean something quite different from what we at first thought.

single-mindedness: The most universal flaw in comic characters—an irrational tendency to respond to whatever happens in terms of one overriding passion.

Sophoclean irony: A structural technique in drama, especially tragedy, whereby the audience knows what fate has in store for the main character, although the main character does not.

Swiftian irony: A satiric method, named after Jonathan Swift and in which this creator of *Gulliver's Travels* excelled, whereby the humorist pretends to espouse the very thing he is against (though in an exaggerated and distorted version) in order to point up its outrageous failings. Swift's "A Modest Proposal" contains one of the purest examples of this technique.

tragedy: A form of drama in which the audience is carried to a purgation of the emotions through an intense involvement with the downfall of a sympathetic protagonist, generally one who deserves a better fate.

NOTES

1. *Henry IV,* Pt. 1, V: i: 12–21.
2. *Henry IV,* Pt. 2, V: v, 51–58.

3. *King Lear,* V: iii, 807–810.
4. *Othello,* V: ii, 338–360.

Vivien Leigh as Scarlett O'Hara in Victor Fleming's "Gone With the Wind," 1939
(Courtesy of The Museum of Modern Art/Film Stills Archive)

4

THE
MOTION PICTURE:
ART AND
INDUSTRY

Overview

The motion picture is indeed a vehicle of creative expression, and no study of the humanities is complete without considering it. Some of its practitioners have been and are touched by genius. But of all the outlets for human creativity since the very first esthetic impulse breathed through our remote ancestors, film (along with its companion medium, television) has proved to be the most profitable. It has become a mega-industry. Take it away, and the whole economic picture of the world changes drastically. A study of film cannot ignore its potential for making people rich very quickly. Sometimes art is created using

Before the advent of cinema, it took the best of poetry, prose, and drama—the combined effort of litera-ture through centuries of time—to make clear to us that when we discover the balance, the fusion of mind and spirit we view as order and civilization, which causes human life to be-come productive and liv-able, that life, that order will always express the high-est aspiration of our poets, our philosophers, our proph-ets, and through them our hopes for mankind.

So do the screenplay and cinema at their best.

Sam Thomas

the very formulas that guarantee wealth. Sometimes one has to choose between art and commercial considerations.

A clue to the art-versus-commerce problem was present right at the outset of movie-making. No other medium ever progressed so far so fast. There is a span of only 26 years from the first official motion picture, in 1889 (which lasted a matter of seconds), to the appearance in 1915 of the first motion picture epic, *The Birth of a Nation* (which lasted nearly 3 hours!). What are 26 years compared to the length of time humanity has had to develop the visual arts, music, drama, and philosophy? Think of the stir the movies created in the early days. On both sides of the Atlantic the infant art was like a new technological toy, and entrepreneurs were quick indeed to realize and exploit the financial possibilities.

An artist's need to create and the human desire for wealth are not necessarily warring opposites. True, some creators have shown little concern for anything *except* their work. But the majority of the people whose achievements we celebrate throughout this book were not averse to the good things money can buy. Discovering that one's art can bring financial rewards need not lead to creative impotence.

Nonetheless, the film industry was and continues to be domi-nated by people who seek to do far more than break even. Sometimes legitimate works of motion picture art manage to get themselves born, though no one is aiming specifically at art. With *Casablanca*, art devel-oped quite unexpectedly from an *entirely* commercial enterprise. With *Citizen Kane*, genius insisted upon being served whether the mass public was ready for it or not and no matter what the producers thought.

In this chapter we shall look very briefly at milestone events in the relatively brief history of the motion picture. We shall single out a few notable achievements which illustrate the peculiar strengths of this art, indicating along the way some artists of film who are likely to take their place in the history of the humanities. We shall focus on those motion pictures which have held their critical reputations over a span of years and which may justifiably be regarded as classics.

EARLY MILESTONES

Some say the motion picture got its start as far back as 1824, when a seemingly minor event occurred that would have a direct bearing on the development of a new kind of art. In that year, in France, Peter Mark Roget, creator of the popular *Thesaurus,* formulated a theory which he labeled "The Persistence of Vision with Regard to Moving Objects." Roget gave some thought to something we all do thousands of times every day, yet never consciously: *blinking the eyes.* When we blink our eyes, should not our vision be continually interrupted by intervals of blackness, however brief? In fact, we see as if we never blinked at all. The reason, according to Roget's theory, is the eye's ability to retain an image for a split second after the stimulus is removed, that is, during the time it takes for the eyelid to close and reopen (like a camera shutter). Though the eyes keep blinking, the images retained keep overlapping each other, producing the *illusion* of continuous vision.

An early proof came with the discovery of a "trick" that is well known to all of us: A series of drawings was made of a figure in successive stages of motion, then stacked up and held firm so that a thumb could easily flip through it. The result, as you can predict, is that the figure actually appeared to move! We know, of course, that it was the papers that moved, not the figure, just as we know it is celluloid film inside a projector that is moving, not our favorite actors up there on the screen. It is Roget's theory which explains the trick. If our eyes could not retain the images for those split seconds, we would "catch" the still photographs as they were being projected onto the screen.

During the mid-nineteenth century people were charmed by this "trick" and tried to exploit it by any means possible. The development of photography gave further impetus, for pictures of actual people could replace drawings. In a sense, animation came first, quickly to be followed by "real" (photographed) subjects. Inventors on both sides of the Atlantic went to work to develop mechanisms to move the pictures faster and create an ever better illusion of actual motion. One mechanism was a circular drum with slits through which the eye peered. Inside the drum one could fasten still images, and when the contraption spun around, the eye saw fluid motion.

The origin of motion pictures can be traced to the theory of Roget—the The-saurus *man—that the eye retains an image for a split second after the stimulus is removed.*

Flickering Images

Thomas Edison, who is usually given credit for having invented the motion picture camera and projector, certainly knew about the excitement moving pictures were creating. He was, however, more concerned with trying to invent the phonograph. But his faithful assistant William Dickson took up the challenge. On October 6, 1889, Dickson gave his employer a private premiere of a movie. Running about ten seconds, the movie starred Dickson himself, who both moved and spoke.

Image technology was, however, far in advance of sound technology. The race was on to see who could build a better projector. Aided, of course, by electricity, inventors were obsessed with the goal of providing large enough pictures for a group of people to watch at the same time, of replacing the peep shows, which could accommodate only one person at a time. Think of how much more profit could be made! By 1896, people were going to the movies to watch ex-

Mack Sennett's Keystone Cops
(Courtesy of The Museum of Modern Art/Film Stills Archive)

tremely brief films, each of which presented one unified action, such as a person swimming or running or even going through the agonizing phases of a sneeze.

The early public was childlike in its acceptance of the toy. Almost anything was entertaining *as long as there was plenty of action.* Nearly a century later, regardless of the psychological subtleties which sound and editing have made possible, physical action remains the primary ingredient of popular films. From the car chases of the Keystone Cops to the car chases of today's private-eye films, box-office receipts clearly show that audiences like their movies to *move.*

The first filmmaker to add a true plot to the action was another Frenchman, George Méliès. In 1900 he created *Cinderella,* albeit a much shortened version of the fairy tale but with plot ingredients intact and, even more significant in the history of the motion picture as art, with special effects. Méliès realized that a unique quality of film was its ability to seem real to the viewer no matter what camera tricks the director might pull. People could appear and disappear, like Cinderella's Fairy Godmother, for example. One could introduce monsters, demons, or spirits; as a matter of fact, audiences were paying good money to be terrified and baffled. They *wanted* to be deluded.

Despite these rapid advances, films were not big business at first. While audiences were delighted by them, movies were at best only a few minutes long, shown at neighborhood vaudeville houses as novelty "acts." The peep show, which was Edison's personal contribution, proved to be a bigger financial boom at the turn of the century. The machines, simple ones requiring little maintenance, were turned out by the thousands as the Penny Arcade industry catered to the great demand. The peep shows were the video games of their time. And the mastermind of the Penny Arcade was an exfurrier with a decided preference for the entertainment business by the name of Marcus Loew, soon to become the first of the Hollywood moguls. Loew, who would launch Metro-Goldwyn-Mayer and the era of the great studios as well as establish the theater chain that still bears his name, opened the Royal Theatre in 1907, the first showplace devoted to films.

Porter and the Cut

The reason the time had come for Loew's move had much to do with the rousing success in 1903 of Edwin S. Porter's *The Great Train Robbery,* a film that actually ran for eight minutes, told a sustained story, and, most important of all, introduced the *cut,* a technique that would revolutionize the motion picture industry. The demands of the narrative led Porter to the realization that the fixed camera, photographing action as it happened with or without special effects, was an extremely limiting device. For his story involving both the holdup itself and the subsequent capture of the bandits, parallel lines of action were required. Early in the film the station attendant is tied up by the bandits so that he cannot telegraph for help. Then the bandits are shown stopping and boarding the train. But how to let the audience know that the culprits are not going to succeed? Porter's answer is to cut back to the station to show the attendant being untied by his daughter. Porter thus also introduced to the movies *simultaneous action.* This first and still famous cut was to be employed in hundreds of cowboy-and-Indian movies, with audiences cheering the predictable flashes of the cavalry riding to the rescue, as cameras cut back and forth from the rescuers to the heroes about to be burned at the stake.

The cut was by no means the only innovation of Edwin S. Porter. He took his casts on location for greater authenticity. He introduced the camera angle and the close-up to heighten dramatic tension and make viewing easier for the audience, and, in so doing, he found that the emotions of audience members could be manipulated. They could be made to experience whatever reality the director wanted them to have. In short, Porter did away with the linear approach early movies had borrowed from the stage. He saw that a motion picture scene could, like a patchwork quilt, be a whole composed of many different pieces. A part that looked good could be salvaged, while others could be reshot and fit into place later, perhaps days later.

Porter recognized that the true language of the screen was made up of what the camera could do *plus* the cutting and pasting that took place in the editing room. The director could say things with this language, and in ways not possible in any other medium. For example, in his film *The Kleptomaniac* he used the cut as *ironic juxtaposition:*

Contributions of Edwin S. Porter to Cinema Art

The cut
Location shooting
Camera angles
Close-ups
Ironic juxtaposition

showing simultaneous action that also makes a bitter social comment. He cuts from a scene in which a poor shoplifter is given an outrageously stiff sentence by a cruel judge to one in which a rich shoplifter receives a light sentence for almost the same offense.

D. W. Griffith

In 1915, the year in which the elegant and huge Strand Theatre opened on Broadway, D. W. Griffith gave *The Birth of a Nation*—all three hours of it—to an adoring and dazzled public. This was the same year in which Metro Pictures Corporation, with Louis B. Mayer at the helm, came into being, a company which Loew would acquire in 1920. In that brief span from 1889 to 1915, movies had indeed arrived as highly skilled entertainment, crafted by people, like Griffith, who knew exactly what they were doing.

Griffith's grand *The Birth of a Nation* is epic in scope, following the course of the Civl War and the period of Reconstruction in the South. It was the film that unquestionably established the movies as a mass medium. Alternately praised as art and denounced as backlash racist propaganda, inciting audiences both to cheers and indignant taunts, the film had everyone talking in a way that had probably never happened before. The more intense the controversy, the longer the lines at the movie houses. Up until the present era of high admission

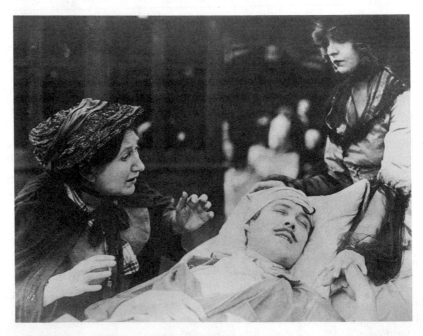

D. W. Griffith's "The Birth of a Nation," 1915
(Courtesy of The Museum of Modern Art/Film Stills Archive)

prices and residuals from TV showings and videotape rentals, only *Gone with the Wind* has earned more money at the box office.

The Birth of a Nation is treated with appropriate respect because it was the first film to exhibit a definite directing *style,* one which Griffith did not happen upon by accident but which seems to have been carefully planned. There are distinct ways in which Griffith's camera moves in for a close-up at a climactic moment, then cuts to a scene that moves at a very different tempo. Griffith's work is the first to be labeled *rhythmic,* because of the manner in which editing is used not simply to tell a story, but to control the pace at which the story is experienced by the audience.

Extraordinarily ahead of its time was the lingering take, which Griffith employs—sparsely, it is true, but always unexpectedly and therefore effectively. A *lingering take* is a shot which remains on the screen for a longer time than mere plot demands require. Directors since Griffith, especially those making mystery or horror films, have put this technique to abundant use right up to the present time. Who has not seen a film in which a handful of characters, having engaged in a conversation of some sort, all make their exit, leaving behind an empty room? Instead of cutting to an exterior scene to follow the characters' further progress, the camera remains behind, brooding mysteriously on the emptiness and raising tantalizing questions: Is there some unseen presence in this room? Will something tragic happen here later? Is there some clue to the murder staring us in the face?

During one famous moment in *The Birth of a Nation* a young Confederate soldier, rushing across a battlefield, stops at the sight of a corpse lying on the ground. It is that of a Union counterpart who, it turns out, was the boy's close friend before the war. The soldier's grief is short-lived, for he is suddenly pierced by a bullet and falls across his friend's body. Griffith does not cut to the next scene but allows his camera to hold the moment. There they are: two close friends, both dead in a cause neither is old enough to comprehend. If the film were being made today, one cannot imagine a director's improving on what Griffith did. Would the scene not end silently? Would the camera not linger? At least one hopes we could match the power of Griffith's scene.

Contributions of D. W. Griffith to Cinema Art
Directing style
Rhythm
Lingering take

Silent Comedy

Filmgoers of today sometimes think of the era of silent films as "prehistoric," with silent movies being what people had to endure because they were unfortunate enough to be living at a time before sound. This attitude stems from the uninformed arrogance of those who view time as a carefully developed, ever-improving sequence—a working out of a vast cosmic plan for the human race. Nonetheless, as some literary critic once put the matter, the ancients never knew they were ancient.

Audiences who waited in line to see *The Birth of a Nation* or who roared with laughter at Charlie Chaplin as they tried to forget the grim reality of war in 1917 included college professors, other actors and actresses, famous writers, and political figures. These were not silly, naive people who "didn't know any better"; they had discriminating taste and knew that some movies were better than others. The very best films were those which were totally visual, communicating through imagery, the proper language of the screen. The less successful were those which had to stop every few seconds and insert a word card so the audience could tell what the actors were saying. The imagery of screen was especially suited for comedy.

The silent films brought into preeminence two major comic artists: Mack Sennett (1884–1960) and Charlie Chaplin (1889–1977). Sennett's name is associated with movie slapstick—a brand of rapid and violent farce in which people lose their human dignity completely, get struck in the face with pies, crash their cars into each other, and wind up getting doused with water. Sennett's world is one of total chaos, kept in disorder by a band of idiotic, incompetent, bungling lawmen known as the Keystone Cops.

From our lofty, all-knowing historical perspective, we tend to think that the speeded-up jerky movements of the Sennett films were the results of inferior technology. Nothing could be further from the

Charlie Chaplin in "City Lights"
(Courtesy of The Museum of Modern Art/Film Stills Archive)

truth! Sennett became obsessed with the "sight gag" and with the potentially unlimited resources of film to provide it. One obvious thing a director could do was control the speed at which motion was viewed on the screen. Sennett photographed action at an average of 10 frames per second, but ran the film through the projector at an average of 18 frames per second—almost twice as fast as it really happened. The effect of the difference was to dehumanize all of his characters so that the violent catastrophes—his stock in trade—could not be taken seriously.

While working for Sennett, Charlie Chaplin happened to put together a comic costume for himself for a crowd scene in which a certain amount of improvisation was allowed. In baggy trousers and shoes much too big for him Chaplin became a tramp, a social misfit, but this persona was lost amid the usual Sennett confusion.

Chaplin's developing interest in using character, not sight gags, as the principal source of comedy led him to leave Sennett and strike out on his own. The result: Charlie Chaplin became the most famous and popular figure the screen world has ever had, the first truly big and international *star.* His comic creation, the Little Tramp, waddling ducklike through an incredible number of films, remains one of the great artistic achievements of motion pictures. The Little Tramp's characteristic appearance is beautifully summarized by film critic Bosley Crowther:

> At first glance, the Little Tramp looks foolish, a callow and nondescript grotesque, too ludicrously put together to be anything more than a caricature. His large head set on narrow shoulders and topped by an antique bowler hat that requires frantic clutching to prevent it spinning off into space; his diminutive, pencil-thin body packed into a too tight coat, usually an old-fashioned jacket buttoned up to a bat-wing collar and tie; his oversized, baggy trousers; his obviously much too big shoes; his moustache; his bamboo cane—they shape up into an image that is outlandish and absurd.[1]

What are the ingredients of this persona that made this such an endearing figure for the audience? First and most obvious, the Little Tramp is an *incongruity*—a being that is always out of place wherever he is—and people can laugh at incongruities. Second, while laughable, he is not so ridiculous that he ceases to have humanity, as Sennett's outrageous Cops do. What humanizes the Little Tramp is the attempt at dignity, implicit in both the costume and the face; and people can identify with someone who refuses to see himself as a loser. Third, the Tramp *is* a survivor. The world is harsh and cruel, but he manages to summon up the know-how to get by, even if this means an occasional

Charlie Chaplin's Little Tramp, one of the great comic creations of all time, is laughable but never ceases to have humanity. He is also a survivor.

lapse into cheating or stealing. Fourth, though the Tramp is thin and weak-looking, the villains and bullies who threaten him are always naive and trappable. The ongoing myth in such Chaplin films is the eternal triumph of the underdog, which is funny because we know what the world is *really* like and that underdogs do *not* succeed as much as we might like, but which is also uplifting to the spirit.

Among Chaplin's silent masterpieces is *The Gold Rush* (1925). Like many major comedies, its plot contains elements of tragedy. The Little Tramp comes to Alaska with hundreds of others, lured by the dream of sudden riches. But in this struggle for survival, he is no match for the cruel environment or the continual threats from physically stronger bullies. Like Don Quixote he is an idealist and falls in Platonic love with a woman who seems to him the embodiment of the most wholesome beauty. She, however, a street-wise dance-hall hostess, finds him absurd, and rejects him.

In this film Chaplin reached the summit of his creative powers. There are laughs galore: The Little Tramp gets desperately hungry, so he cooks his shoes and eats the laces like spaghetti. His tiny cabin is blown to the edge of a cliff during a blizzard, and he unknowingly exits through the door—nearly to his doom.

But we become deeply involved, even through the laughter, because of the Tramp's human fragility. We care even as we laugh, an extraordinary feat which no other film artist has ever been able precisely to duplicate. Suddenly we realize why it is that this unique blending of the serious and the comic *works* so well. Chaplin's Tramp is so likeable, so in need of our protection, that without the softening edge of comedy we would be unable to tolerate the disasters which befall him. Thus it is that the film gives us the kind of happy ending for which Hollywood has become famous: Charlie stikes gold, becomes wildly rich, and does indeed marry his heart's desire.

There is little doubt that Chaplin is knowingly perpetuating a myth. He is far too wise to think life works out for the best, and perhaps his happy endings also have a bit of the funny and sad intertwined. Many of his films end with the Tramp waddling away down the street, twirling his cane confidently as he becomes smaller and smaller in the distance. Wherever the plot has taken him, he will, we know, remain the outsider.

Eisenstein

Some people think movies started in New York, then moved to California. In truth, *American* movies did just that. But other countries had audiences just as anxious to be entertained by the new art. For instance, motion pictures were especially welcomed in Russia, where Soviet directors, fresh from the Bolshevik Revolution of 1917, seized upon this obviously mass medium as a golden means to the true pur-

pose of all art: the celebration of the working class. No less an imposing figure than Lenin himself made the comment that of all the arts, the
cinema was the most important.

In the early years following the Revolution the Russians had
to rely mainly on imported films, but they quickly evolved skills of film
editing in order to make sure these films had the correct message for
the Russian people. In fact, they became so enthralled with the craft of
snipping and pasting to achieve a desired effect that they were really
the first to devise an elaborate theory of the medium. They were the
first "intellectuals" of the new art. Their editing was clever enough to
make good acting almost superfluous.

The Russian director who first looked through the camera
with the eyes of an editor was Sergei Eisenstein, as great an artist in his
own right as Griffith or Chaplin. His *Potemkin,* released in 1925, the
same year as *The Gold Rush,* is still required viewing in all film
schools; and it contains one scene in particular which has set the standard for editing techniques ever since: the depiction of a massacre by
Cossack troops on a long flight of steps in the city of Odessa.

Before the making of *Potemkin* Eisenstein had immersed himself in the study of films, and the study rapidly became an obsession.
Even more than Griffith he was concerned with the rhythm or flow of
a film, and he coined the term *montage,* meaning the way the director
arranges the shots so as to assault the emotions of the viewer. Though
Eisenstein was a loyal party member and was committed to the Soviet
doctrine of art as anticapitalist instruction for the masses, he used film
in an artistic way which went beyond mere propaganda. The artist in
Eisenstein saw in films a challenge no other form of communication
could equal.

The most famous innovation for which Eisenstein is credited
might be called the *elongated moment.* If, Eisenstein reasoned, the
wonder of film is that the director is not limited to the fixed perspective of the theater and is thus able to cut from place to place and time
to time, why not take a similar liberty for a given location and a given
time?

Let us suppose that the action of a film covers a number of
years, during which time the main characters, through artfully applied
makeup, age from 20 to 50. The audience will accept this convention,
though they have been sitting in the theater for under two hours. By
the same token they will accept the fact that an action which in real
life could take place in a minute or two requires a longer period of
time in this film. Eisenstein was the first director to dissect time and
show it in its complexity, revealing what would normally be missed.

Potemkin celebrates a bloody period in Soviet history, one
that in 1925 was still fresh in Russian memory: the unsuccessful uprising against the Czar which took place in 1905. A key episode in this
war was the mutiny of the sailors on the battleship *Potemkin* and the

sympathy strike by the dockworkers in the port of Odessa. Eisenstein's original plan called for brief shots of the Cossack troops riding through the city and killing people indiscriminately. Like Griffith, however, he wanted to shoot on location for absolute authenticity, and there in Odessa he saw the great steps on which part of the massacre had taken place. His directing instincts seized the opportunity, and the result was a $6\frac{3}{4}$-minute sequence depicting a minute or two of real time and requiring the splicing together of 157 different shots in all. The result: a microcosm of inhumanity.

The sequence begins with 57 separate shots that show an assortment of happy and unconcerned Odessa townspeople on the steps just before the massacre. Carefully, Eisenstein introduces key figures to whom he will return again and again while the atrocities are being committed. But most significant of all, the director chooses a young mother wheeling her baby in a carriage—the very symbol of innocence about to be destroyed.

Then the troops come thundering to the top of the steps, splattering carnage as they ride. Eisenstein cuts from one of his key figures to another for $6\frac{3}{4}$ minutes of unrelieved terror. The massacre is experienced by the audience over and over. Now it is a little boy separated from his mother and crushed to death in the stampede. Now it is the mother, having found her son's body, lifting him up as an appeal to the soldiers, who respond by gunning her down. Back to the baby carriage sequence. We see the mother being mangled by Cossack sabers. Now a close-up of the abandoned carriage rocking back and forth dangerously at the edge of the steps, pushed ironically over the brink as the mother, bleeding to death, falls against it for support. A close-up of the innocent child inside the careening vehicle, which is hurtling down the steps over and around hundreds of corpses.

Another character whom Eisenstein involves is an apparently cultured woman wearing fragile reading glasses. From the moment we first see her, we can tell she has never been subjected to any cruelty. We feel protective toward her, as we do toward the baby. Throughout the massacre the director returns to her, and each time she is more splattered with blood. Finally we see a Cossack rider slashing out at something out of our view, followed by a rapid cut to the woman's face. She has been mortally struck in the eye. As one noted film editor says of this moment:

> It never occurs to us that we did not actually see the saber strike her. (Any more than we are aware, while watching Alfred Hitchcock's terrifying adaptation of this technique in *Psycho,* of the absence of direct knife hits during the shower sequence.)[2]

We are living at a time when filmmakers are like guests at a buffet table filled with a wide array of special screen effects. Their ap-

Film is strongest when it makes greatest use of what is peculiarly its own—the ability to record time and space, slice them up into fragments, and glue them together in a new relationship.

John Bigby

Sergei Eisenstein's "Potemkin," 1925
(Courtesy of The Museum of Modern Art/Film Stills Archive)

petite for blood and violence is especially insatiable. One would think they would realize by now that true terror—a very legitimate experience for motion pictures to attempt—has never been accomplished through direct graphic means. Audiences have always shuddered at the dark hallway, not the ghost itself.

We might say that Eisenstein was led to art through necessity. Using the cinema for the purpose of stirring up antiroyalist sentiments in the Soviet audience, he found the most effective means of doing just that. He did not overstate his case. The artist within him prevailed.

Others in the new filmmaking industry were not as scrupulous as Eisenstein. Their god was money, not art. At about the same time that Eisenstein was planning his directing strategies for *Potemkin,* a film version appeared of Thomas Hardy's tragic novel *Tess of the d'Urbervilles.* Louis B. Mayer, the producer and one of Hollywood's legendary titans, objected to Hardy's ending, in which the heroine, having killed the man who seduced and deserted her, is sent to the gallows without mercy. Though this denouement is a bitter pill for the reader to swallow, literary critics have always recognized that it is consistent with Hardy's pessimistic view of human existence, in which the world is seen as a savage place where good seldom triumphs, or else does so strictly by accident. Mayer decreed the film be given a happy ending in which Tess's basic virtue is ultimately rewarded. In England, Thomas Hardy—unhappy at what Hollywood had done to his work—

I am an old man and have no defense against this sort of thing.

> Thomas Hardy on
> Hollywood

Contributions of Sergei Eisenstein to Cinema Art
Montage
Elongated moment
Use of film editing to convey a message

sadly observed, "I am an old man and have no defense against this sort of thing."[3]

This would not be the only time that Hollywood would use the cinema to uphold popular moral attitudes and reaffirm the myths that people seemed to need in order to live.

AN ARTISTIC ERUPTION

No one knows exactly why, but the history of human art abounds with certain spectacular eras in which hosts of geniuses appear all at the same time. It is almost as though the gods every so often decide to smile favorably on the human enterprise and endow it richly, while at other times they seem to forget that art exists. The movies had been a going concern for about half a century when the audience for art was forced to admit that a new form had indeed arrived and had to be taken as seriously as great music or painting or drama.

Certainly the signposts were there almost from the outset. Chaplin and Eisenstein were not only "pioneers," they were significant artists in their own right. Each took the silent film about as far as the medium would allow. But, as we know from our vantage point, sound is now a major component of cinematic language. By the late 1930s and the 1940s, cinema artists were putting all of the components together: the cut, the lingering take, the elongated moment, the montage, color as well as artful advances in black-and-white cinematography, and ever more realistic sound as well as its significant opposite, silence.

Sound, introduced in 1927 for the Al Jolson musical drama *The Jazz Singer,* had originally been nothing more than a novelty aimed at bringing more money to the box office. People paid to see anything that made noise. But an artist like Chaplin disdained the new technology until well into the '30s. Since films could talk all they wanted, early sound movies were often imitations of talky stage plays. For a time, stilted dialog replaced action and the sophisticated editing techniques à la Eisenstein.

Yet, again in an astonishingly short period of time, artistic advances came about in the use of sound. Not only did the technology itself improve drastically, but so did the quality of the dialog. The 1930s, in fact, saw the heyday of a genre that the motion pictures both invented and perfected: the screwball comedy.

Screwball Comedy

The screwball comedy was named for the well-known baseball pitch that doesn't come straight at the batter but takes an erratic course. The plots of these films did just that, using short scenes, frequent cuts, and

Screen writers had to invent dialogue that was at once rich and colorful, pungent and amusing, but also stripped of inessentials. They had to learn not only what to say, but also how much could be left unsaid—how much could be left to the camera and the actor and the director to put on the screen through action and gesture or by implication.

Arthur Knight

fast-moving, witty dialog to lift audiences on a magic-carpet ride through an escapist world of rich, sophisticated, but thoroughly disorganized people: the perfect antidote for a Depression-weary country headed for another war. The characters—usually a husband and a wife who basically love each other—become enmeshed in a ridiculous disarray of circumstances that very nearly but not quite terminates the marriage. One or the other meets someone else. Infidelity is suspected. People hide in closets or under beds. Husband and wife hurl abuses at each other in clever dialog, as neither takes the time to listen to the facts.

In many of these films women attained a somewhat elevated status. Stars like Claudette Colbert, Myrna Loy, Katharine Hepburn, and Irene Dunne brought intelligence, glamor, and elegance to the screen. They played wives who refused to accept the traditionally subservient roles society had ordained for them. In the popular *Thin Man* series—sterling examples of the detective movie genre—Myrna Loy and William Powell played a married investigative team for whom the solving of murders was almost incidental to the verbal banter they exchanged. Naturally it was she who apprehended the killer, not through the logical methods employed by her husband but through a mysterious kind of intuition that clearly only a woman could possess.

On the whole, the screwball comedy did not consciously strive to be screen art. Its formula required that it take place amid affluent surroundings and that its plot revolve around the doings of upper-class, hence educated people. Therefore its stress on witty interchange between civilized men and women, and *this* helped to change the screen image of female characters, who had been very often the drooping violets of the silent film. But, as frequently happens with movies, art develops when least expected.

Frank Capra's *It Happened One Night* (1934) stands quite apart from all other screwball comedies. It belongs to the genre mainly because of its rapidly moving plot line, but it is a film that is at once witty, entertaining, believable, and truthful.

Claudette Colbert, a major star of screwball comedy, plays Ellie, a rich, bored, and, on the surface, brainless young woman engaged to marry an equally wealthy and brainless, but also arrogant and instantly unlikable, man named King Westley. Unable to bear the thought, she runs away from home, determined to make it on her own with no idea of what she is doing (so far, very formula screwball). With very little money, she takes a bus, on which there is riding a young, handsome, and more than slightly sexist reporter played by Clark Gable. Discovering who she is, Gable pretends to be interested in her, hoping to write the exclusive story on the runaway heiress and strike it big in the newspaper world.

What Capra does with the formula is to humanize it. The reporter is the culturally acceptable macho hero, who changes as a result of a real connection with the girl. Ellie, in turn, is a "dizzy" and

Clark Gable and Claudette Colbert in Frank Capra's "It Happened One Night," 1934 (Courtesy of The Museum of Modern Art/Film Stills Archive)

irresponsible rich girl because her upbringing has demanded that she play this role in life. But experiences on the road bring to the surface a toughness, an instinct for survival, lurking inside. In the beginning she doesn't even know how to dunk doughnuts. Soon she is able to steal fruit and vegetables from a farm and to hitchhike by showing her leg to a passing motorist—something her macho companion is unable to do! When at length she returns to her wealthy home and her waiting groom, she stuns the wedding guests by refusing to say "I do" and jilting the brainless suitor at the altar.

The final message is typical of the screwball genre: love is more important than money. But the difference here is that the choice is a real one, made by a three-dimensional human being. She has actually given up a fortune—something that never happens in the other comedies, in which rich characters talk about the priority they will give to love, while remaining rich at the same time. Moreover, the chemistry between the two main characters goes beyond the witty interchanges audiences came to expect. It develops out of the adventures they have shared, becoming integral to both of them. Each changes in ways that are consistent with their experiences: she becoming a high-spirited, strong-willed, independent woman with a very definite idea of the man she wants; he becoming less chauvinistic and attracted in the end to an assertive woman who neither needs nor wants to be sheltered.

The screwball comedy has all but disappeared from the Hollywood repertoire, not because movies have downgraded women but because the cinema, like the stage, seems to be afraid that people will not listen to language. As cinema technology has grown during the past three decades, stunning visual effects and wraparound stereophonic sound batter our senses. There is very little time for wit and very little likelihood that anyone could hear it if it were there.

There is a distinct possibility that the reason motion pictures erupted as a major art form during the late '30s and into the '40s is the existence of *just enough*—but not too much—technology.

Gone with the Wind (1939)

The literary novel *Gone with the Wind,* which was published in 1936, was the work of an unknown Southern writer named Margaret Mitchell, who had researched the Civil War and then told the story from the Southern point of view. She created an enormous panorama of antebellum Georgia, the war itself, and the chaotic Reconstruction period that followed. The book, running more than one thousand pages, caused a national sensation that has never been precisely equaled.

The novel seemed to be just what escape-oriented Americans needed in 1936. The detailed recreation of the homes, landscapes, and battles of the period enthralled the readers. But most of all, Margaret Mitchell had created a hero and a heroine so real that people everywhere discussed their stormy relationship as if it had actually happened. Scarlett O'Hara and Rhett Butler are, in fact, still alive today in the imaginations of millions, because they were born at a time when screen art was waiting to embody them.

The movie of *Gone with the Wind* announced to the world the real potential of films, for its stars Vivien Leigh and Clark Gable were full artistic collaborators with the author of the novel. Clark Gable *was* Rhett Butler, somehow jumping into the author's typewriter and entering her world. With *Gone with the Wind* the cinema played an unprecedented role in turning a myth into reality, one that is now always available, because the film continues to be shown, giving to the characters an immortality far more immediate than we can find between the pages of the novel. Not necessarily *better,* but definitely more immediate and accessible.

Free-flow discussion is built into the nature of the film medium. Wrapped in "the narcotic shadow" of the film, viewers normally are swept along by the pace of the film. During the screening there is no time for critical reflection. Each new image and sequence stimulates immediate emotional responses. Unless the projector breaks down, you can't call time out.
    Reverend John M. Culkin, S.J.

Gone with the Wind spared audiences nothing. In the chaos of war, the good as well as the wicked suffer. Neither side is idealized. The genteel Southerners, though idealistic, are not really fit for battle. The North wins, but follows up the victory by allowing a ruthless exploitation of the South by the carpetbaggers. Out of the wreckage the titanic figures of Scarlett and Rhett survive and marry, as befits a myth, for there is no one else the equal of either one. But they do not live happily ever after. Their child, who was to save their marriage, is thrown from a horse and killed. Scarlett, with the rich blood of fictional ancestors like Huck Finn in her veins, shares with them the curse of restlessness. Rhett Butler is wealthy; yet despite Scarlett's possessing every material comfort she ever thought she wanted, she is still in love with Ashley Wilkes, the romantic idol of her youth. Scarlett will always be in love with people not available to her, and she will always cast her eyes on the distant horizon. Such is the burden of being an American heroine.

The typical happy ending upon which audiences were supposed to thrive just did not materialize. Rhett Butler, fed up with Scarlett's instability, decides his own future is more important than hers, and so he packs his bags. As he stands at the door, listening to her repertoire of "defenseless female" tricks, audiences waited with hearts loudly beating to hear whether the movie would allow Rhett to give the novel's final answer to Scarlett's final question "If you leave me, where will I go? What will I do?" As everyone gasped, he *did!* "Frankly, my dear, I don't *give* a damn."

Down on her luck once again as she was when, after the fall of Atlanta, she had returned to Tara, her home, to find the place in ruins, Scarlett has to pick up the pieces and begin again. Just as the great American novels *Huckleberry Finn* and *Moby-Dick* "end" with their respective heroes starting life over after a series of disasters, both the novel and film conclude with Scarlett's renewed surge of optimism: "Tomorrow is another day." Hers is the will to survive often found in the great works.

Gone with the Wind, for all its excessive length and unnecessary scenes, is a masterwork of screen art, not only because it retains the integrity of the novel, but because it found an eloquent screen language of its own. Color, for example, was still very new to Hollywood in 1939. Lacking were the sophisticated processes of today. Instead of the sharp and vibrant hues we are accustomed to, audiences of the '30s saw lighter, more delicate color, often resembling the pale pastels of the French Impressionist painters. Some of the visual images in *Gone with the Wind,* such as the famous shot of Scarlett and her father standing under a tree, silhouetted against a Georgia sunset, have museum-worthy artistry.

Building on the innovative camera techniques of people like Griffith, the director, Victor Fleming, pushed available technology as far as it could go. The burning of Atlanta remains one of the most awesome sequences in film history. No trickery was involved. Atlanta was not a small-scale model, set ablaze with a cigarette lighter and photographed at close range. The director actually burned down old studio sets. This meant the shooting had to be perfect the first time around, and *that* meant weeks of planning. Hundreds of shots were to be used.

As in Eisenstein's Odessa steps sequence, cameras elongate the time span by cutting from burning buildings to fleeing people to frightened horses stampeding. In the center of this carefully designed confusion are Rhett and Scarlett driving a rig out of the doomed town as screaming people try to climb on. The horse, blindfolded to keep him from panicking, nearly trampled hundreds of extras to death. The effect comes close to matching Eisenstein's power.

Then there is the famous scene at the railway station. Scarlett's close friend Melanie is in labor with her first child. Scarlett rushes wildly into the street to find the family doctor, who is desperately trying to save lives at the train depot, now become not a hospital but a cemetery of unburied corpses. Blundering onto the scene and, in her dazed condition, unaware at first of where she is, Scarlett slowly perceives she is in the midst of death on an unbelievable scale. The camera very gradually backs away from her horrified face as the scene "opens" for us wider and wider, and keeps on opening as if it were never going to stop. One cannot think of a passage in literature in which words express the horrors of war with more eloquence than does this scene from *Gone with the Wind.* In the final analysis the true measure of screen art is the same as that of a great poem: One must be convinced that there is no other way of saying something.

Citizen Kane (1941)

Two years later, in 1941, appeared *Citizen Kane,* a film produced, directed, and coauthored by an amazing 26-year-old named Orson Welles. Several years before, when he was barely old enough to buy a drink, he had done a radio adaptation of H. G. Wells's *The War of the Worlds,* about a Martian invasion of the earth, performed as a news bulletin "alert" and executed so realistically that people tuning in after the opening credits actually believed the invasion was really happening. After the national panic and subsequent notoriety for Welles, Hollywood came clamoring, seeing in this exciting talent a potentially bankable star. *Citizen Kane* was not a box-office sensation; its techniques were too unfamiliar for too many viewers. But its reputation as screen art has grown steadily with each passing decade. Orson Welles acquired a deep respect from many who normally denounced movies as being not art but a business interested only in profit. From 1941 until his death in 1984 Orson Welles was known as Hollywood's

Citizen Kane was not a box-office sensation; its techniques were too unfamiliar for too many viewers.

Orson Welles in "Citizen Kane," 1941
(Courtesy of The Museum of Modern Art/Film Stills Archive)

fiercely individual artist/director, a man who did what his taste compelled him to do, whether it made money or not.

In *Citizen Kane* the myth is once again the American dream, and it is, of course, as much a part of our folklore as Scarlett's survival instinct. The film is based on the actual success story of William Randolph Hearst, who in the early years of our century rose from obscurity to become owner and ruler of a newspaper empire. But Welles had no intention of romanticizing the truth. His film ultimately reveals the hollowness behind the dream and the tragedy of those whose only concerns are money and power.

Audiences were startled by the use which theater-trained Welles made of lighting. His sets—enormous ones to embody the bigness of the theme—are perpetually underlighted. Whether we are in Kane's mansion *Xanadu* or in the vaults of the public library, everywhere we look are corners hidden in deep shadow, as if Welles were searching for a visual equivalent to the shadowy regions of Kane's mind.

Despite the man's wealth there is a melancholy deep inside him which we do not at first understand. In fact, the entire movie represents a young reporter's search for a clue to the tragedy that has haunted the great man up until his death. The famous opening sequence, in which the camera travels from the imposing fortress-like gates of Xanadu through corridors filled with the costly and useless trappings of success into the huge bedroom where Kane lies dying, culminates with a shot, taken at floor level, of Kane's face. On his lips, as the very last breath escapes them, is one single word: "Rosebud!"

Unlike *Gone with the Wind, Citizen Kane* was written directly *for* the screen, in screen language—the language of external imagery. Knowing that the camera cannot photograph what is inside a human being and that in reality we can only guess at what lies hidden in each of us, Welles makes the investigating reporter the central character. The camera becomes his (and our) eyes. Together we must try to solve the mystery of "Rosebud," a seemingly trivial thing in comparison with the might of Kane's fortune.

Welles works indirectly, moving always *around* his subject, as his camera moves around and under objects, seldom shooting a scene head-on. The reporter interviews everyone who knew Kane and also goes into the cavernous vaults of the public library in an attempt to recreate every incident of a life which begins for us with Kane as a little boy playing happily in the snow just before he is told that he has inherited a great deal of money and must leave home to claim his fortune. As the reporter begins to piece together the fragments, we follow the success of Kane's first newspaper venture, the opening of his chain of papers, his increasingly gaudy life-style, his developing monomania—the total self-absorption of someone who seems to have everything but is never satisfied. Kane wants to be governor, then perhaps president, to be a world figure, a legend with a firm place in history. America is a democracy, but with enough money and power one can become *royal.*

In one famous sequence Welles demonstrates not only Kane's power-madness but the blindness it creates. He also demonstrates that film can do in a very brief time what novelists do—and perhaps less memorably—in many words. We find ourselves on stage at a great opera house, where Kane's second wife is making her debut. He has literally bought her way into the company. She is dull-witted and has almost no singing ability, but Kane's sense of his power makes him believe he can accomplish any feat with money. As the lady drones on and on in uninspired cadences, the camera slowly ascends from stage level, up through the massive riggings which raise and lower the backdrops, finally coming to rest on a grid-walk which seems to be hundreds of feet from the appalling desecration below being witnessed by a formally attired crowd of opening first-nighters and critics. On this walk are two stagehands, old-timers who, we know, have heard many legendary voices. As one stagehand looks on in amusement, the other pinches his nose with two fingers to signify that the great debut is giving off a distinct odor. What words could have the same effect?

Similarly, words could never carry the impact of the scene in which Kane and his socially prominent first wife are shown breakfasting at either end of a very long table. He has married her for the prestige she will give him; she has married him for his wealth. There has been little communication between them ever; both are reading newspapers. From the smile on Kane's face we assume he is reading one of his own papers, but the camera reveals that Mrs. Kane is absorbed in a rival paper. It would take many, many prose paragraphs to give us the details of a failed marriage. It took Orson Welles just a minute.

The final scene of Citizen Kane *reverses the technique used in the Atlanta railroad station scene in* Gone with the Wind. *The camera starts wide, without focus, then zooms in on a trivial object—Kane's sled.*

In the very final sequence, all of the deceased millionaire's expensive but meaningless art treasures are shown boxed and labeled in the Egyptian-tomb-like cellar underneath Xanadu. The scene opens with the epic image of thousands upon thousands of boxes, reminding us of the thousands of dying soldiers lying outside the Atlanta railway station in *Gone with the Wind.* Only, Welles *reverses* Victor Fleming's technique. If you recall, the Fleming sequence begins with a close-up of Scarlett's anguished face, then opens up wider and wider until the full horror of the scene is revealed. Welles's camera allows us to see the full might of Kane's material empire, then slowly begins to move in toward a flickering light seen in the distance. As we draw close, we see that it comes from a furnace into which a workman is tossing the "junk" nobody wants. At length, this motion picture of incredible scope reaches its final shot, in so relatively confined a space: the interior of this furnace, where, about to be consumed in flames, is the sled which, we remember, the young Kane was playing with in the snow just before he was informed of his inheritance and taken away from his simple and, we suppose, happy childhood existence. Was this insignificant object the thing that has haunted him all his life? Is it a symbol of the ordinary pleasures money cannot buy? The film definitely raises more questions than it answers, but the rich imagery of Welles gives us much to think about long after the film has ended.

Often throughout his career Orson Welles remained on the fringe of Hollywood—recognized as a cinematic genius, but gaining a definite reputation as a high box-office risk. He never compromised. Though not every venture was the artistic equal of *Citizen Kane,* he always allowed himself to be governed by his taste as an artist, not his ambition as a producer.

Casablanca (1942)

Casablanca illustrates how film art can suddenly appear in the midst of commercial considerations. The producer, who understood the Hollywood success formula, made sure he had all the right ingredients for a slick adventure film. For director he chose Michael Curtiz, who had gained a reputation for making fast-moving action movies, a man who knew how to get the most from the script, knew about pacing, how to build suspense, and how to pare dialog down to its bare essentials. For leading lady he chose Ingrid Bergman, an actress recently im-

*Humphrey Bogart and Ingrid Bergman in Michael Curtiz's "Casablanca," 1942
(Courtesy of The Museum of Modern Art/Film Stills Archive)*

ported from Sweden in a Hollywood attempt to capitalize on the respect critics were beginning to give foreign actors. But by far the major coup—*how* major they could not have predicted—was to cast Humphrey Bogart as the leading man.

In *Casablanca* we have perhaps the finest example of screen art achieved through a *persona* adopted by a particular star. In the context of motion pictures, the term *persona* refers to a character type that suits the abilities of a given actor. What generally happens is that an actor plays a certain role so well, is so believable to the public, that producers begin looking around for other scripts which involve a similar character or that can be rewritten to include one. If the actor succeeds a second time, he or she finds that material is being tailor-made for the persona. After a time the public so identifies actors with their personae that it becomes all but impossible for them to create any other kind of character. Gary Cooper, for example, was such a "specialty" performer. Whether playing a sheriff or a homeless drifter, he was always a man of few but wise words, quiet intensity, impeccable integrity, and unflinching bravery. The public naturally assumed that Cooper in real life was exactly the same person as Cooper on the screen.

At its best, the tradition of the screen persona has the powerful effect of true art. The characters are so real to us that, if their value system, if their general manner of behaving in this world, is impressive

The Bogart Archetype
*Kills when he has to.
Is antisocial but not psychotic, because he is always a superrealist.
Often operates on the wrong side of the law but is never lacking in ethics or integrity.*

and admirable, then they have contributed a standard by which we can measure our own actions, our own values. Sometimes a persona is so convincingly cruel and callous as to be the very definition of evil—another sort of standard by which we tend to get our bearings. The psychologist/philosopher Carl Jung (see Chapter 10) speaks of the *archetypes*—the heroes, villains, themes, and symbols—found in the world's major myths, which help to shape our belief systems and our visions of reality. The great screen personae are examples of mythic archetypes.

The Bogart persona had not yet been fully realized prior to *Casablanca*. Somehow there occurred an almost miraculous blending of the plot circumstances and the actor's own growing awareness of the person he was becoming. The character overwhelmed the public, and the studio front office, traditionally conservative, obliged by bringing him back again and again, but never with the same impact.

Who is this character? And why has he held his reality for nearly half a century? To comprehend the phenomenon, we need to see how he evolved. Bogart made his stage debut in 1930 in a drawing-room comedy as a spoiled, pleasure-loving young man of leisure who actually spoke the famous line "Tennis anyone?" He was genteel and thoroughly innocuous, but when he got to Hollywood, somebody thought he could play a gangster.

Throughout the '30s Bogart developed a specialized approach to the gangster persona, and the persona of *Casablanca* would use some of those traits. He is ruthless, to be sure, but not in the totally unfeeling, sometimes sadistic manner of others. Without question he is menacing, because you always know he will shoot to kill *when he has to*. He always seems to be a gangster—because the times require it, not because the profession is necessarily his number one choice. He is not shown as the victim of a bad environment, hence, in his own way, an underdog. The Bogart gangster is a super-realist whose code is "It's either you or me, and it sure isn't going to be me!" Such a character is dangerous but not illogical, antisocial but not psychotic. Such a character had a peculiar kind of integrity that fascinated audiences.

In 1941 John Huston, an artistic and perceptive director, found a script in which both he and Bogart could explore and deepen the character. Instead of portraying a gangster, the actor would play a "private eye," for the novelist Dashiell Hammett had in *The Maltese Falcon* created a seemingly cold-hearted realist of a detective that exactly suited Bogart's screen style and personality. True, he would be on *this* side of the law, but just barely.

Sam Spade, the private investigator, lives and works in San Francisco, a meeting place for the cleverest, most sophisticated of international crooks. His partner has been murdered, and, though tracking the killer should be the work of the police, Sam the realist knows that, if he wants results, he must take the law into his own hands. "When your partner is killed," he comments without emotion, "you're supposed to do something about it." The dictates of reality are the constant Bogart guidelines.

As Bogart and Huston worked on the film and the persona evolved, the character of Sam Spade deepened. The super-realist with the tough exterior developed vulnerability. In fact, he falls in love with a woman who turns out to have been his partner's killer. The Bogart trademark was born. Spade hides his feelings of both love and disillusionment. In a world like this, you cannot afford to take a false step, cannot afford to let emotion cloud your vision. He turns the woman over to the police, commenting soberly that, if she escapes hanging, he'll be waiting for her. If not, "I'll always remember you." The Bogart persona would be the tough, unflinching man of steel with a susceptible heart and an uncanny ability to survive both danger and heartbreak.

In *Casablanca,* Sam is now Rick Blaine, operator of a cafe which is also an illegal gambling casino. Casablanca, the capital of French Morocco, is theoretically neutral territory, and to it come hundreds of desperate people trying to escape the Nazis and get to the free world. But freedom really means having enough money to buy an exit visa from the corrupt French police. In an effort to raise the needed money, these people gamble at Rick's place. As we would expect, Bogart's Rick is an unemotional realist, at heart concerned about these people, but never willing to become involved in their lives. He cannot afford to. He needs the blessing of the French chief of police in order to keep his place running.

Despite the general state of the world in this time between the fall of Paris in 1940 and the American invasion of Normandy in 1944, despite the dangerous intrigue that surrounds him, Rick is peculiarly content in his well-ordered, unemotional life. But all of this changes abruptly and his role of the detached observer is put to a severe test when the Laszlos come into the cafe.

Victor Laszlo is the world's number-one Nazi-fighter and therefore the Nazis' number-one target for extermination. He has come to Casablanca to buy his way to freedom. The problem for Rick, however, is that Laszlo's wife (Ingrid Bergman) had been Rick's lover in Paris but had disappeared mysteriously after promising to run away with him. Now he understands the reason—her earlier marriage. Yet this proof of loyalty to her dedicated husband does not lessen the bitterness of the experience for Rick. The lady had committed a sin against honesty, and because she had, Rick has become more than ever confirmed as a hard-shelled realist.

Still, the chemistry is there. Hidden beneath the hard exterior are the tenderness and vulnerability Bogart showed in *The Maltese Falcon.* He agrees to aid the Laszlos in their dangerous mission, knowing that, to be successful, he must outfox the French chief of police.

The plot reaches its crisis when, having obtained not only visas but two tickets on the Lisbon plane, Rick must decide whether to use them for himself and Laszlo's wife, an outcome she seems to want very much.

The final scene, the scene no one in the cast even knew about until the day of filming (such was the creative confusion out of which this work was born), has become famous in film history. Pursued to the airport by a frenzied Nazi official, Rick is forced to kill the man. But presumably Rick is now someone who will do anything for love. With Mrs. Laszlo waiting for him outside the plane, whose engines are throbbing in the fog-engulfed night, Rick tells her that Laszlo is already on the plane and she must go with him. She seems not to comprehend his reasons, nor perhaps does he—completely; and it is here that the full complexity of the Bogart persona is glimpsed.

Is the hard-shelled realist what the chief of police accuses him of being: a sentimentalist at heart? Is he someone who, for all his apparent amorality, cannot desecrate the sanctity of a marriage, especially when the wronged husband is a noble individual? Or is he perhaps thinking that their love would probably not last? After all, what does? Or is the whole truth an irreducible combination of motives? The realist survives, however, even as the sentimentalist takes one last look at the woman's beautiful face, and, knowing that beautiful moments are inevitably pushed aside by the onward surge of time, he says simply: "Here's looking at you, kid."

To seem real and three-dimensional, and to be lasting, a character need not, *should* not, be transparent and easily understood. The fact that audiences continue to watch *Casablanca* and wonder, through their tears, why Rick did not board the plane, is ample evidence of the character's durability. Characters whose motivations are transparent soon become uninteresting to us. In real life we seldom "know" each other any better than we "know" ourselves.

Casablanca is legitimate screen art like *Citizen Kane* and for the same primary reasons. Both films employ dialog sparingly. Neither central character reveals his personality and his motives through words. Both films use the screen medium to create a complex reality which we must interpret, even as we do in real life. Neither one makes a direct, easily phrased statement about people or existence. The great works never do!

Yet *Casablanca* and *Citizen Kane* each achieved their status as art through very different means. *Citizen Kane* was consciously designed to be a quality film from the very beginning. The youthful director had no ties with Hollywood and was more or less allowed to go his own brooding way. In short, the studio took a chance on him and hoped for the best. *Casablanca* grew to be what it is in what can only be described as hit-or-miss fashion. Paying Bogart and Bergman very high salaries, the producers had to make sure they would get their money back and therefore kept tinkering with the film. The chaos surrounding the making of the film is now legendary. Bergman reported in an interview that she was convinced the movie would be a disaster. How Bogart was able to maintain the integrity of Rick Blaine is an unanswerable question: Scenes were shot, reshot, and often replaced as the plot line sputtered, came to a halt, and then—somehow—chugged itself back to life. Cast and crew eased their tensions by making fun of the whole enterprise. Art, one must assume, is continually creating itself by some means not always known even to the artist.

A final note of some interest: Several years back, during a revival of *Casablanca* at the Harvard Square Theatre in Cambridge, the sound track broke down for a few minutes. Not at all disconcerted, the audience chanted the missing dialog until the spoken words were restored.

Auteurs of the Films

People go to a movie because (1) a star of some magnitude is in it, (2) critics have been "raving," (3) their friends said they enjoyed it, or (4) from the ads it looks funny, sexy, violent, or scary. Nine out of ten box-office bonanzas of this year will have been forgotten by next. How can one decide which films will last, which ones deserve to be called art?

Auteurism

In literary criticism a writer's lasting reputation is ordinarily based on a significant *body* of work. In film, *auteurs* are the directors who can be said to have a vision of movies as art, bringing to each script an imagination and style that are trademarks of their work. They have their favorite shots, camera angles, and kinds of montage. They look for stories and characters that suit their method of work. In some cases, they insist on the scripts they direct.

Over the years a number of directors— not very many compared to the total number of people making films—have developed reputations for possessing a recognizable and effective film style and/ or communicating certain attitudes toward life. Out of the ongoing critical debate over who should be considered the artist if film *is* art, the consensus is that in most cases the primary artist is the director with a controlling vision. Motion pictures are, to be sure, a collaborative art. A work like *Gone with the Wind* owes its greatness to Margaret Mitchell's novel, Victor Fleming's direction, the technicolor artistry of Natalie Kalmus, the music of Max Steiner, and the performances of Clark Gable and Vivien Leigh and others. In *Citizen Kane,* however, the master hand of Orson Welles dominates at each moment.

Auteurism *maintains that the film director is to the film what the author is to the novel or the play.*

When he is not on the screen as Charles Kane, we know that he is behind the camera overseeing every detail.

Andrew Sarris, a film critic for the *Village Voice,* and Jean-Luc Godard, a French director, have applied the term *auteur,* which of course means author, to such visionary directors. They are the authors of their films, and like novelists or poets they can be studied and analyzed very seriously. What they do with camera, sound, color, and lighting, as well as with the script, is all part of the *literature* of, the tradition of, motion pictures.

Alfred Hitchcock

Even before his death in 1980, Alfred Hitchcock (1889–1980) had been singled out as a film auteur. Yet, unlike Orson Welles, who arrived in Hollywood with the artist mystique and the determination to create a work of film art, Hitchcock only *gradually* acquired a reputation as a director whose work should be taken quite seriously.

Known at first as a man who made thrillers about spies and murders among highly civilized British people, by the late 1930s Hitchcock had been dubbed the "master of suspense." The plots in his films were filled with unexpected twists, and always there was a breathtaking finale with an always new and ingenious kind of danger, as in *Saboteur,* when hero and villain meet for a fight to the death on the torch of the Statue of Liberty. But Hitchcock soon tired of exploiting in obvious ways the audience's love of being terrified. In the '40s his works acquired greater subtlety, especially in the handling of the spies, killers, and other assorted evildoers. As we look back now on the body of his work, we see that his criminals were not merely the stick figures required in the thriller genre. They were suave, sophisticated beings who had learned how to assume the trappings of the civilized but who were, underneath, inhuman, disordered, and dangerously antisocial.

Hitchcock brought to the movies an altogether new version of the menace: not a monster or a mad scientist, but someone who seemed perfectly normal, someone you'd really like to know. If evil could come in so human and smiling in appearance, *who* could be safe? The master of suspense was also becoming a philosopher with a genuine vision of evil. "Evil," he once observed during a television interview, "is complete disorder." Most of us know how things ought to be, how people ought to behave, and what right and wrong are; but there are people walking among us who have everything except basic human reason. They break the social code without feeling guilty. Hitchcock began to create frightening portraits of *indifference,* more chilling than Frankenstein's monster. That they are overcome in the end, that the decent people, especially those who are young and in love, manage to survive is the price Hitchcock had to pay to Holly-

Hitchcock is obsessed with a common theme: that evil is the result of disorder, in nature, in society, within the human heart.

wood's moral code. The man himself believed we live in a fundamentally amoral universe in which good triumphs, if at all, only by
accident.

Among Hitchcock's masterworks are *Psycho* (1960) and *The
Birds* (1963). In *Psycho,* evil assumes the form of an apparently sweet,
shy, and lonely young man who needs love and understanding, a boy
who craves his mother to the point of exchanging identities with her
and committing brutal acts without knowing what he is doing. Apparently what appalled Hitchcock was the loss of rational control, the
frightening possibility that the world really *belongs* to the irrational.
Coming as he did from a conservative and civilized environment, he
sensed that civilization was a mere façade. His demonic killers are not
wrongdoers who deserve punishment—that would be too rational,
too predictable. His killers are primordial savages in familiar depart-
ment-store clothes.

In *The Birds* we have two possible visions of disorder. This
frightening fable about the siege of a northern California coastal community by thousands of birds, destroying human beings for no apparent reason, might be showing us what could happen if the natural
order suddenly goes out of control. Or it might be warning us of what
could happen as a result of what humanity has *done* to that order. In
either event, the residents of Bodega Bay go about their peaceful
everyday routines when, without warning, the birds begin attacking
them—at first a solitary gull swooping down on a woman in a boat;
then a whole flock suddenly wreaking havoc at a children's birthday
party. As the suspense builds, so too do the numbers of hostile birds.

*Tippi Hedren in Alfred Hitchcock's "The Birds," 1963
(Courtesy of The Museum of Modern Art/Film Stills Archive)*

In one of the screen's most memorable moments, as well as Hitchcock's most identifying sequences, a woman sits outside an elementary school waiting for the school day to be over. She is smoking a cigarette, lost in her personal problems, totally unmindful of the grim scene taking shape behind her, where hundreds of black birds are massing on the metal jungle gym in the play yard. Are we seeing human indifference to nature? Or the vanity of human beings who fail to realize how insignificant they are compared to nature's awesome forces, which they will never understand or control? Film geniuses like Hitchcock can make one image say many things, free from the limitations of words. To underscore the horrible irony he is creating in the schoolyard scene, Hitchcock adds the sound of the children innocently singing a monotonous rhyme, with its continually repeated, rhythmic refrain: "Nickity nackity noo noo noo." The rhythm could be civilization's attempts at order, while the birds watch and wait in chilling silence, tolerating the proceedings, but not for long. Soon the screen erupts in Hitchcock's version of Eisenstein's elongated moment at the Odessa steps. The children and the woman are running down a steep hill holding up their arms to shield themselves from the shrieking onslaught. Hitchcock cuts from one fleeing person to another in a montage too rapid for us to see the full horror of an eye torn from a socket or a head bashed to a pulp. The technique had already been perfected in the shower murder scene from *Psycho,* which lasts 45 seconds and is made up of 78 distinct shots. In Hitchcock we "see" more than we *see.* The real irony, of course, is that here was a screen *auteur* who believed that evil was disorder, yet who communicated that disorder to us in a very planned, meticulous way, with the intricate details of every shot put down in writing before the cameras were ever turned on.

Ingmar Bergman

Other countries also have film histories and tradition. Sweden, in particular, is rich in screen art and could easily have been the focus of this chapter. During the 1940s, Swedish director Ingmar Bergman (b. 1918) began to practice his craft and did it so well that he has become one of the great *auteurs* of this century. Bergman did not come to the movies because of their glamor and the promise of quick wealth and stardom. Like Orson Welles he was a serious theater director very much intent on creating art, and he saw in films a challenging medium which could afford him a greater freedom than the stage to explore his subjects. For a decade he studied the technique of cinema, and then by the mid-1950s he had made Sweden very nearly the film art capital of the world.

In the span of two years, 1956–1957, Bergman gave the world two masterworks, *The Seventh Seal* and *Wild Strawberries,* in-

*Scene from Ingmar Bergman's "Wild Strawberries," 1957
(Courtesy of The Museum of Modern Art/Film Stills Archive)*

dicative of a creative intensity probably no other director will ever match. Bergman was, and is, a philosopher/filmmaker, and in the '50s he was wrestling with ultimate questions about the human place in existence. We are fortunate that the craftsman and the philosopher came together at just the right moment.

In the years following the end of World War II, Sweden, like much of Europe, was caught up in a philosophical movement known as *existentialism.* (For a fuller discussion, see Chapter 6.) The central assertion behind this movement is that we can be certain only of the *fact* of our existence; that is, ideas about the *purpose* and *destiny* of humanity all rest on assumptions that we derive from religions, other philosophers, and mythology. How do we know that we are made in the image of a divine nature? How do we know that there *is* a divine nature? Since we are human, how can we even comprehend such a thing? All philosophies must begin with the simple fact of existence and work up from there.

The films of Ingmar Bergman ask why we create rigid norms of civilized behavior and impossibly high intellectual standards which imprison the multidimensional human being within each of us.

Yet many people can go no further. Without a sense of God, without the belief that they are in this world for some reason, they feel themselves alienated, cut off, mere meaningless entities walking around on the earth for a few years then vanishing into an endless night as though they had never been at all. We shouldn't be surprised that such was the mood of a devastated Europe during the 1940s.

The Seventh Seal is a medieval fable about a young knight who has just returned from the Crusades and ironically finds Death awaiting him, though he has up to now escaped the grasp of this black-robed figure carrying a scythe. Feeling he has nothing to lose, he challenges Death to a game of chess, the contract being that he can stay alive until Death holds him in check. The knight's purpose is to delay the inevitable until he is satisfied that his life has had some meaning. So, while the fantasy game is proceeding, the knight is also journeying about the countryside in search of something—a person, a cause, a religion—that will convince him existence has not been an absurd waste of time. The plot is ideal for the existentialist as film director, for it forces him to reach some conclusions about life in order to provide an ending for the film. (Bergman also wrote or collaborated on all of his screen plays.)

In the great tradition of the mythic journey (see Chapter 10) the knight has many adventures and interacts with many people along the way. The least satisfying encounters are with the Church. Organized religion gives humanity a sense of sin and guilt, but does not make existence seem valuable. The knight discovers that life is rich and full only when he meets a young married couple (named Joseph and Mary) and their child. Only in the loving warmth of the family circle, where people support and nurture each other, does life seem to make sense. Not to have lived is not to have known love and joy. Bergman's message is simple but not simplistic. He finds it only after struggling with utter *nihilism* (the belief that all comes to nothing in the end). With the knight's help the young family escapes Death. Though the *knight* will die, his is a joyous vision, and the film ends with a dance led by the figure of Death, with a parade of people all celebrating the bliss of simply *being*.

But, of course, that was the Middle Ages. Bergman was not ready to shape the identical vision in contemporary terms. *Wild Strawberries* is the story of a 78-year-old doctor facing death, not in allegorical terms, but in very real, biological terms. As in *The Seventh Seal,* Bergman finds an ingenious and simple situation and uses a journey as his plot structure. The old man must travel to a great university in order to receive an award for distinguished life achievement. The journey gives him an opportunity to look closely at his life and ask himself whether it has *really* amounted to something.

The Seventh Seal mixes fantasy and reality. *Wild Strawberries* blends reality, dreams, and memories of the past with such sophisticated editing techniques that one cannot believe it was made decades ago. Using the story-telling economy that film makes possible, Bergman shows us the present state of the doctor's relationships with his mother, his wife, his son, and his daughter-in-law. All are strained and lacking in either warmth or spontaneity. Clearly, neither they nor he derive any value from the fact that they are members of the same family.

Picking up some hitchhikers, including two young men and a girl who are casually dressed, unconventional, and utterly lacking in the awe that the university and the award ought to inspire, the old man finds that it is still possible for him to enjoy the company of people just because they are human. He has no intellectual rapport with them, but they help to free him from the emotional repression that has destroyed his family relationships. Gradually he slips into daydreams of summers in the country when he was a free-spirited boy, long before he became a victim of the codified adult, university world; when he could be as spontaneous as the delicious fruit that gives the film its title.

Again Bergman's message is simple. If this present existence is all we know for certain, why then do we ruin it for ourselves? Why do we create rigid norms of civilized behavior and impossibly high intellectual standards which imprison the multidimensional human being within each of us? *Wild Strawberries* is an ageless and poetic plea for humanity to hold fast to youth, to love, to caring.

POSTSCRIPT

We have barely scratched the surface of film art. There are other *auteurs,* surely, who might have been mentioned: François Truffaut and Jean-Luc Godard of France; Federico Fellini and Vittorio da Sica of Italy; Akira Kurosawa of Japan; Satyajit Ray of India. There are Americans that many will argue have already attained the stature of the *auteur*—notably, Stanley Kubrick, who took the genre of science fiction and in 1968 gave us *2001: A Space Odyssey,* a massive work about space travel and astronauts that also incorporates very complicated ideas from the new science about the origins of the universe and the evolution of the human race.

Recently there has emerged Woody Allen, once a stand-up comic, now a writer-director-actor, with an undeniable vision of life and a deep compassion for lonely, unfulfilled, sensitive people, fragile souls dwarfed by the towering structures of Manhattan, a city Allen both adores and fears. Allen the actor has immortalized the persona of the pallid, underweight, neurotic Jewish kid, plagued by feelings of guilt and sexual inadequacy. Allen the writer has captured the tragic and comic rhythms of the big city. Allen the director has learned from Bergman, his idol, how to use the art of the motion picture to suggest, to provoke, to open the mind of the viewer by indirection.

On the other hand, some may argue that we have paid too much attention to an art form that is still relatively young. When compared to human outpourings that extend back to the cave era, movies

The world is full of people who are quick to tell you what films you should be doing and what to cut out and what to put in. There is an old proverb: "He can't think, but he knows all about it."

Woody Allen

are definitely the new kid on the block. But they had technology going for them and were from the outset big business; and even though the lure of money often got in the way of art, it also helped to induce a lot of creative people to see what they could do with a camera. The extraordinary advances films have made in "just" a century are, after all, humanity at work and are reason enough to earn them a place in our study.

GLOSSARY

archetype: Term used by philosopher/psychologist Carl Jung to denote characterizations found in the world's major myths and other works that aspire to myth status, which help to shape our interpretations and expectations of reality. Classic archetypes are heroes and villains, the good guys and the bad guys. Hollywood has been a rich source of contemporary archetypes, including the famous Bogart persona, discussed in this chapter.

auteur: French term for "author"; used in this chapter to refer to certain film directors who develop a reputation as artists, whose imprint is to be found in every film they make, and who have recognizable camera styles, rhythms, themes, and symbols. Ingmar Bergman, the Swedish director, is a consummate example of the film auteur.

cross-cut: A specialized form of cut whereby the director takes us back and forth from one scene to another, usually to create an ironic effect, such as showing the contrast between rich people at a banquet and poor people in a soup line.

cut: A cinematic technique whereby the flow of a scene is interrupted and the audience finds itself in another scene or looking at the same one from a different point of view.

directional cut: Means of changing scenes in a film by using motion transition, e.g.,

an actor in a dark suit walking into a camera, followed at once by another actor in a dark suit walking away from the camera to open another scene before we are aware there has been a change.

elongated moment: A technique invented by Sergei Eisenstein and imitated by many directors, such as Alfred Hitchcock (in *The Birds*), in which an action is broken down into many component parts shown in linear succession so the entire scene takes far longer than it would in reality.

existentialism: A modern philosophical movement, popular in Europe following World War II, which holds that we can be sure of nothing except the basic fact that we exist. We do not know for certain why—or whether we even have the right to ask such a question. But we *are* indeed free to define our existence, provided we take the responsibility for what we make of ourselves.

formal cut: A technique of changing scenes by using a symbolic form of transition, e.g., cutting from an audience wildly applauding to a shot of a roaring waterfall, the sound of which reminds us of applause.

genre: French term meaning type or category; used mainly in literary or film analysis as a convenient means of communicating some general characteristics of a work without having to go into a lot of detail. For example, if we know that something is a tough detective story, we already know quite a bit about it.

persona: In this chapter, a characterization used by a screen star in more than one film, and one which becomes closely associated with him or her, often to the point at which the public comes to believe the star is very much like the character.

NOTES

1. *The Great Films* (New York: Putnam's, 1967), p. 49.

2. Ralph Rosenblum and Robert Karen, *When the Shooting Stops . . . the Cutting Begins* (New York: Viking Press, 1979), p. 55. Rosenblum, incidentally, has been the favorite editor of Woody Allen for a number of years.

3. Bosley, Crowther, *The Lion's Share* (New York: Dutton, 1957), p. 87.

František Kupka, "The First Step," painting dated 1909
(Courtesy of The Museum of Modern Art, Hillman Periodicals Fund)

5

THE PHILOSOPHERS

Overview

Philosophers do not attract much popular attention. They write, if indeed at all, quite a bit less than do authors of best-sellers, whose readers number in the millions. Since the invention of printing in the late fifteenth century, Plato's *Republic,* held by many to be the single greatest work of the philosophical mind ever penned, has sold fewer copies than revelations of a reformed drug user or a ruthless tycoon unable to find true love. Countless people go through life and do quite well for themselves, thank you, never having heard of Descartes, Hume, Kant, Schopenhauer, James, Kierkegaard, Russell, or Dewey. Philosophy courses usually enroll fewer students than do practical subjects like accounting and physical fitness.

The philosopher is just not very visible, gliding phantomlike through the commerce of everyday life, appreciated by perhaps a few friends who listen. Extraordinary fame almost never comes to a philosopher. Socrates, the West's first major philosopher (as far as we know), did achieve a measure of renown for his teaching and his supposedly anarchistic pronouncements. But what he got for his fame was a trial, conviction, and execution—not a very exciting model to attract the uninitiated.

Philosophers are people who become disturbed by either of two conditions: (1) widespread acceptance of an invalid belief by other reputable intellectuals, or (2) persistent, unanswered questions. When philosophers think the existence of a belief has been accepted as valid by too many others of respectable intellectual stature, who should know better, they try to set things right, to clear the air, to make a strong rational case for an opposing view. Possibly the most famous example of this philosophical repair service occurred several thousand years ago, in the fifth century B.C.

Protagoras, a dominant personality in Athens, led a professional sect called the *Sophists.* Together they operated what amounted to the world's first law school. That is, for a specified fee they would teach the rhetorical and dramatic skills needed to win a case in court. Their business irritated Socrates no end, primarily because it was predicated on the assumption that no such thing as absolute justice existed. If you won, justice apparently triumphed. If you lost, justice miscarried. Looking deeper into their philosophy, Socrates discovered they were cynics who believed in no absolute truths whatever.

Though Socrates himself wrote no works—at least none that have survived—his best student, Plato, *did,* giving the world, among other incredibly great books, the *Republic,* in which the cynical idea of justice propounded by the Sophists is to Plato's satisfaction corrected once and for all. Written as a series of dialogs, with Socrates as the principal character, the *Republic* sets out to prove it an error of thought to maintain that justice can be one thing here and another thing there. A character in the *Republic* who frequently challenges Socrates is Thrasymachus, who is made to sound exactly like a Sophist. At one point Thrasymachus defines justice as whatever is in the best interest of the ruling party: in short, might makes right. Socrates quickly pounces on this, asking Thrasymachus whether in his opinion it would ever be possible for the ruling party to make a mistake—to pass a bad law that would *not* turn out to be in their best interest. Of course it would, replies the unsuspecting Sophist, who is then forced to confront the embarrassing implication that the ruling party could

Philosophers love to show us the intellectual traps into which humanity is likely to fall, and, if possible, to rescue us from them.

theoretically be in the position of requiring obedience to a law that does harm to them. Would they not, therefore, consider the requirement "unjust" and seek to do something about it? Plato's position is that the recognition of justice is the same for everyone.

Our legal system is still based on Plato's belief, even though we have widespread disagreements about how to interpret a law and whether it applies equally to all. In other words, we can continually recognize *in*justice, a fact which means that its opposite must be a reality to all of us. To contend that there are no standards, no universal values, would be to throw the whole system into chaos. The contribution of philosophy to the future of humanity is here quite impressively shown.

The other condition which can disturb the philosopher, even as it does the scientist, is the persistence of unanswered questions, unsolved problems. While to the faithful there is never a need to ask whether God exists or how this existence can be known, many philosophers throughout the centuries have been considering the question. Immanuel Kant, for example, dismissed all previous philosophical attempts to prove God's existence by reminding us that they began with the assumption that "God is something which necessarily exists." That is, I cannot prove whether an all-powerful being exists without assuming that that being is indeed all-powerful. And that being cannot be such without existing to begin with.

Philosophers love to show us the intellectual traps into which humanity is likely to fall, and, if possible, to rescue us from them. The value of philosophers to us is not so much that they change our thinking by the direct influence of their own thoughts (though this may well happen), but that they inspire in us the habit of thinking *when it is not absolutely necessary to think.* In this respect we know we belong to a unique species—one that thinks because something is there to be thought, not because a *practical* problem is waiting to be solved. Philosophical thinking is not very different from the critical thinking we talk about in Chapter 9. (The professional philosopher, however, is more specialized than the critic, more apt to employ a particular and intricate *method.*)

In this chapter we shall focus on three big ideas that have occupied the philosophical mind for centuries: the idea of mind, the idea of God, and the idea of reality. In the authors' opinion, these ideas are worth spending time on for their own sake. But more than that, understanding how various philosophers have approached the problems generated by these ideas gives us a very special insight into how the adventurous mind thinks boldly for itself. If we do not learn how to do this—in no matter how slight a way—we may one day discover that someone else has been doing our thinking for us.

MIND

▌ What is mind? No matter. What is matter? Never mind.

Bertrand Russell

In the above lines the modern philosopher Bertrand Russell is passing along to us one of philosophy's perennial and favorite jokes. As in the best witticisms, however, there is an extremely serious subtext. Philosophers have argued the issue for centuries, but the final words have yet to be said or written on the subject of *mind.*

No one doubts that human beings *have* such a thing as a mind. It has a legal identity, if not a definite philosophical one. Murderers have escaped severe punishment on the grounds that they were legally insane, or not in their "right mind." We speak about mind all the time as if it were a thing in its own right, despite the fact that no one has ever seen it. Sometimes it appears to be a place, as when we say we have "ransacked our minds" or "gone over every inch of our minds" in an effort to remember something.

Since, whatever it is, mind *appears* to be immaterial—at least *not* the sum of material parts (blood, cells, nerves, etc.)—some people have claimed that mind is not part of our bodily makeup. Thus it never could have been "born" when we were, and, consequently, cannot "die" when we do. Many cling steadfastly to a belief in life after death on these, rather than religious, grounds.

The classical view of mind (that is, the one held by the ancient Greeks and Romans and the medieval Christian world) is that of a nonmaterial entity, one that distinguishes humanity from the animal species. Classical humanism is predicated on the assumption that humanity is superior to everything else on this planet by virtue of its possession of mind.

So accustomed are we to using the term *mind* that we usually fail to remind ourselves that it has *yet* to be licensed for universal applicability. The argument goes on. At the heart of the argument is the question of whether we know because we have experienced and have thus learned from what we have experienced, or whether we can learn because we *know how to know.* If mind is part of our body and develops after birth like organs and muscles, how does mind develop unless there is something we might call intellect present from the beginning to "make sure" we learn? What we learn is not necessarily the same thing as the process of learning!

But if mind is something that precedes our experiences, is it with us from birth? Where is it located? Where did it come from? Why are not all minds the same? Or do they merely fail to develop equally their potential? If the latter is the case, what after all *is* such potential?

Plato's Theory of the Forms

Plato thought about the above questions, but if he encountered some difficulties along the way, his ultimate contribution to the issue was quite certain and unwavering. The inquiry led him to one of the truly giant conceptualizations ever to come from our species: the theory of the Forms. If few believe the theory implicitly today, few also will deny the impact it has had over the centuries or the issues it can still raise. The foremost value Plato's theory of the Forms has for future generations of thinkers is probably its beauty as a myth that, if accepted, explains almost anything that might puzzle us about mind. Plato's theory establishes the ghostly presence of mind inside each of us— an invisible organ without which none of us could function.

Many centuries after Plato, other philosophers would come along and try their hand at thinking through the problem of how to define and explain mind, and many of them would contend that mind is nothing but the sum total of ideas we derive from experience. Each would wind up in a maze of complexities, because none could satisfactorily explain how we learn from experience without having something that does the learning for us.

For Plato, mind is in us at birth. It contains the knowledge of what he called universals, or *Forms,* or what we would call abstractions. A very simple example is the knowledge each of us possesses of a *tree.* Suppose you move into a neighborhood that at present is devoid of vegetation. You meet the couple next door and engage in a wish-filled conversation about what you intend to plant. "And, of course," you conclude, "I'll have about five trees on the front lawn." Although you do not specify what *kinds* of trees, your neighbors have no trouble understanding what you are saying. They do not have to visualize a certain tree. Both you and they can converse, in the abstract, about trees, and those abstractions are communal truths, possessing reality in their own right, even though no one has ever planted a tree in the abstract.

Where does the knowledge of such trees come from? Most of us would say the *abstraction process,* an activity of which our "minds" are capable. After having directly experienced *x* number of specific trees in our past history, we have—without quite knowing it— retained the awareness of characteristics they share. But here the issue becomes a little cloudy. Does each have a trunk? Does each have leaves? What about date palms? (Palms have fronds.) Trees grow above the ground, but so do a lot of other things we *don't* call trees. Some trees change colors in the fall; some are green all year round. Some, but not all, give shade. Nevertheless, we probably know enough to call a particular tree a tree even if we have never seen it before and no one has told us it belongs to the tree "family."

For Plato, mind is in us at birth. It contains the knowledge of what he called universals *or* Forms, *or what we would call* abstractions.

Plato believed we are born with the knowledge of generic classifications as well as of other abstractions like justice, truth, honor, virtue.

Plato believed we are born with the knowledge of generic classifications as well as of other abstractions, like justice, truth, honor, and virtue. Otherwise, how could we understand when two vastly different specific examples are said to belong to the same family? Plato reached this conclusion by force of sheer reason, because he could not account for such knowledge in any other way.

Since he could not believe that knowledge came from direct sense experience, he was led, further, to ignore the senses, at least as being the explanation for human intelligence. In other words, one does not know that a tree is a tree just from having seen a tree and having been told what it is. Does this mean that, if one were never to have experienced a single entity—a single instance of tree*ness*—one could still understand what others were talking about when the subject of trees arose? Apparently *yes!* And here we have the aspect of Plato's theory that most philosophers today find unacceptable.

If abstractions—or Forms—are with us from the beginning (since we could have "gotten" them no other way), we are naturally curious to know where they come from. Plato's answer is that minds—like what Christians were centuries later to call souls—are immaterial entities that can neither come into or pass out of existence. They move—or migrate—from body to body. Mind therefore has nothing to do with your particular personality, your characteristics as this person rather than that one, your idiosyncrasies. All minds are equal in the sense that one cannot say one abstraction is different from (clearer than, *truer* than) another. Thus Plato's theory requires us to accept the conclusion that abstractions like justice and virtue are also the same for everyone.

While one is easily tempted at first to smile condescendingly at the notion that all abstractions are the same to everyone, Plato's defense of it is quite powerful indeed. It occurs in *Meno,* the dialog named for its principal character, a wealthy nobleman of Thessaly who challenges Socrates (Plato's spokesperson, and the central figure in all of the dialogs) to explain how the abstraction of virtue can be taught to anyone who has not experienced many deeds which have been called virtuous and thus developed a general knowledge of virtue in the process. Socrates makes an analogy with the general knowledge of color. We understand when we are told the specific color of a certain object because we already possess the general concept of color. If we did not, what we are told would not make any sense to us whatever. Then Socrates makes the famous declaration that "learning is remembering." Meno, unconvinced, demands to see an example of such "remembering" at work. He challenges Socrates to produce universal knowledge from an untutored subject, and invites one of the slave boys in the household to join them. Supremely confident, Socrates asks the boy to explain some complicated axioms of geometry. At first confused, the boy—seemingly mesmerized by the gentle prodding of

In the dialogue Meno *there is the famous incident in which Socrates, by asking the right questions, shows that a slave boy possesses an inborn understanding of geometry.*

the master—begins to display an accurate grasp of mathematical principles. Where did the boy come by such wisdom? Did someone teach him? "You are sure to know that," Socrates smiles at Meno, "since he was born and brought up in your house."

Education, then, is the activity by which young people are patiently guided, not forward but *backward*—back to the knowledge they already have. When the teacher, recognizing that a certain point has been understood, cries out in undeserved triumph, "You've got it!" the actuality is that the pupil has remembered, even as one might recall a song title. The pupil has threaded the way through a morass of sense impressions, which are not the source of knowledge, and has come at last to a truth. Both teacher and student know when this has happened, for both possess the same truth.

If all minds are the same, what accounts for obvious differences in what we call intelligence? What accounts for what passes widely in the academic profession as "learning disability"? Can anyone really be stupid? Can anyone be forever barred from "scaling the heights of intelligence"? Or is "it" all there, just waiting for a patient Socrates-like teacher to come along? Despite the widespread criticism of Plato's theory, we should not be so quick to label anyone stupid. There are too many absolutely astonishing success stories on record: people diagnosed as retarded who suddenly display acute insights into complicated subjects like trigonometry; people who escape a predicted future on welfare rolls and become genuine leaders.

Those in the academic world know that Plato's theory is still quite viable, is in fact at the very heart of a current educational controversy over whether values should be and *can* be taught. If justice, truth, honesty, right, and wrong are indeed universals, as Plato believed, then they are the same for everybody, and "teaching" them means only reminding students of what they ought to know. Those who oppose values education do so, of course, on the arguable grounds that values are relative to time, place, and culture. For them Plato is in error.

An apparently defensible position is one that accepts Plato's belief that abstractions are universal without having to say also that they are born with us. The contemporary philosopher Mortimer J. Adler (b. 1902), for example, agrees with Plato that there are some objects in the mind which are purely sensible (particular dogs, trees, cows, and so on) and some which he calls "purely intelligible." Among these he lists liberty, infinity, and God—abstractions which are public by nature, not private, even though they are not objects which we can see in the material world. They are public because two people can have a conversation about them without confusion. One person can say he does not believe in God, and the other that she indeed does, without either of them misunderstanding the issue. Adler believes not in mind as a ghostly entity in us from birth, but in intellect, a process peculiar to the human species, which enables us to abstract classifications of things and general principles from experience with particulars.

Giving careful consideration to Adler's revision of Plato's theory, we might be tempted to ask those who insist that all values are relative whether they really mean this, or whether they are saying only that one can always argue over the application of a given universal to a given particular. If a serial killer is given ten years in a mental institution and then released after three, one might well contend that justice has not been done, but not that justice *itself* has no existence.

"I Think, Therefore I Am"

This statement is perhaps the most famous contribution given by philosophy to human vocabulary. It represents at once a milestone achievement in thought, however simplistic it may at first sound, and the beginning of a philosophical nightmare Descartes, its author, did not intend.

Rene Descartes (1596–1650), alternately called the first major modern philosopher and the man who nearly killed philosophy altogether, was a fervent Catholic who'd been taught to accept the teachings of the Church on faith alone. He was also caught up in the wave of scientific fervor that was sweeping Europe during the emergence of scientific methodology, fueled by such things as Galileo's development of the telescope and the audacious announcement by Polish astronomer Copernicus a century earlier that the Church had been wrong in teaching about an earth-centered universe.

Descartes had no intention of upsetting the centuries-old traditions of Christian thought in which he was thoroughly trained. But he was a man of his times, and he thought it was possible for the human mind, utilizing scientific method, to achieve certainty in all matters. He even used philosophy to "prove" the existence of God, though the Church had so often and so vigorously denied that such proof was necessary. His idea was to make the certainty of God's existence compatible with science. There was a God, no matter whether you came to this conclusion through faith *or* through science. Unfortunately, his intellectual adventures did not have quite the results he anticipated.

Following scientific method, Descartes made an initial assumption: We cannot assume the truth of things to be already present in the mind, as Plato had long ago maintained. In fact, one cannot assume *anything.* One starts out as though there had never been a philosophical tradition. One starts out, in short, as though one knew nothing whatever. Then, to make sure he was in the proper state of "mindlessness," Descartes proposed to doubt everything he thought he knew, and to keep on doubting until he arrived (if indeed he *could* arrive) at a position, a certainty, that defied further doubt. Not only did he doubt the familiar truths which were supposedly his human heritage—the Platonic abstractions of virtue, love, justice, liberty, and so on—but he also doubted the evidence of his senses:

> Accordingly, seeing that our senses sometimes deceive us, I was willing to suppose that there existed nothing really such as they lead us to imagine. . . . [W]hen I considered that the very same thoughts which we have when awake may also come when we are asleep, while there is at that time not one of them true, I supposed that all the objects that had ever entered my mind when awake, had in them no more truth than the illusions of my dreams.[1]

So when you doubt that there is any world at all "out there" and that the image of yourself you think you see in the mirror is actual, you would seem to be at an impasse. Everything can be doubted, and thus there can be no certainty *anywhere*. Right? Descartes' answer was a very stirring "Wrong!"

Pretend you are experimenting with the method of doubt, absolutely committed to doubting everything you can. You doubt there is a world at all. You doubt there is a you in that world that isn't there to begin with. In a passing jest you wonder why—if there is nothing—you *imagine* you see and hear things. Then you even toy with the idea that instead of God there is a Grand Deceiver somewhere up there who thoroughly enjoys weaving illusions for us. Then you are forced to doubt even *that*. Then you ask yourself (pretending there is a you, of course) whether you can even doubt that you are doubting. Why not? You've successfully doubted everything else. Is it possible to go on doubting to infinity? To doubt that you doubt that you doubt that you doubt . .?

Descartes said: I cannot doubt that I doubt. If I were to do this, if I were to go on doubting into infinity, I would still be confirming something: namely, that I am doubting.

Now comes that little point of truth that Descartes was seeking, one of those ingenious, incredible flashes of insight that seem so absurdly simple—that, in fact, *are* absurdly simple yet have the distinction of being solely and completely one's own, in this case Descartes'. He said: *I cannot doubt that I doubt*. If I were to do this, if I were to go on doubting into infinity, I would still be confirming something, namely, that I am doubting. If one doubts that one doubts, one must admit one is doubting; otherwise the act could not be accomplished. Or, if one adopts the opposite view—not to doubt that one is doubting—one is affirming the act all the same. Either way, one is doubting!

For Descartes, confirming the doubt also means confirming his own existence, for there could be no doubt without a *doubter*—someone who engaged in the doubting process, which is also a thinking process. Thus was he led to declare "*Cogito ergo sum*" (I think, therefore I am). Presumably Descartes could as easily have said, "I doubt, therefore I am."

> I observed that I could suppose that I had no body, and
> that there was no world nor any place in which I might
> be; but that I could not therefore suppose that I was not;
> and that, on the contrary, from the very circumstance that
> I thought to doubt of the truth of other things, it most
> clearly and certainly followed that I was.[2]

Having reached a certainty that satisfies the criteria he has set forth—that is, having reasoned his way to something that is beyond doubt—Descartes now finds himself forced to accept a way of defining what that self is which he knows to exist beyond all doubt. He first asks the question "But what am I?" The answer can be nothing except "I am a thing which thinks." The confirmed self is a thinking device *assuredly* nothing more:

> I thence concluded that I was a substance whose whole
> essence of nature consists only in thinking, and which,
> that it may exist, has no need of place, nor is dependent
> on any material thing.[3]

Later generations of intellectual historians have referred to Descartes' discovery as a colossal blunder. He has been charged over and over with having painted his way into a philosophical corner from which there is no escape. For, once you have confirmed your existence as a thinking thing by the act of doubting everything else, you are unable to grant to that "thing" a license *ever* to be anything except a "thing which thinks"—not a three-dimensional person inhabiting a real world, but only a "thing which thinks," only a *mind.*

Critics of Descartes, while acknowledging his importance for opening up a very complicated issue, have insisted that he ended up proving nothing at all, nothing about the world, about existence, about reality. Who cares that there's a disembodied mind hovering in a sea of nothingness? Another contemporary philosopher Gilbert Ryle (b. 1900) has referred to the "thing which thinks" as "the ghost in the machine." If there is a body—and Descartes eventually "proves," with a rather unconvincing argument, that there is—it must necessarily be completely distinct from the mind, since the act of proving the mind does not guarantee the body. They are therefore two distinct substances. The mind goes its way, and the body runs by entirely mechanical principles utterly unknown to the mind.

Descartes' way of getting out of the dilemma is to say that the mind enables us to make a very clear and obvious distinction between objects perceived by the mind and those perceived by the imagination. We remember that he has successfully doubted the existence of the material world. Now, however, he revisits the original doubt. Is it possible that, if his mind is all that exists, his mind is just imagining the world? His answer is no, and the reason is that, while one can easily by an act of will conjure up all kinds of things in the imagination, one cannot will the appearance and disappearance of things in the world "out there." You can look at your arm, for example, and wonder whether it exists, but you cannot force it not to be there, as you could "see" or not "see" a unicorn with your eyes closed. Your arm is always going to be there whether you want it to or not, and the same must be true for everything else you perceive to exist "out there."

Critics have been disturbed by the Cartesian separation of mind and matter and the implication that knowledge of mind comes first. If Descartes has to prove through reason alone that there is a world, then what is the role of the senses? We are back to the old question of whether we learn from experience or whether we experience because we know how to. As with Plato, for Descartes the mind is simply *there*; and for many critics this is a myth that has been around far too long.

Significantly, Catholicism long ago adopted Plato's theory eagerly, saying Plato was really talking about the soul. Descartes, of course, was a Catholic, and in Gilbert Ryle's opinion was simply taking the ancient faith in the soul and passing it off as a revolution in thought.

Maybe Descartes' reasoning was not the revolution he hoped it would be, but it *did* raise the question of mind in the context that was supposed to be scientific not religious. To condemn Descartes for being "secretly" religious is not to dismiss the question. Saying there is no such thing as an immaterial soul—as many now do—is still not proving there is no such thing as a mind that distinguishes humanity from all other species, a mind—or faculty of reason—that is *more* than the sum of material parts.

A tantalizing and persistent philosophical question is whether we learn from experience or we experience because we know how to.

Let us suppose for the sake of argument that one *is* born without a preexistent mind, without a "ghost in the machine." Let us then suppose that the images we retain from the operation of our senses are the basis upon which we develop that inner being, or inner consciousness, which has gone by the name "mental life." Can we then conclude that abstractions like God and justice can have no meaning because they cannot be experienced by the senses?

Thus, the importance of the Cartesian argument is no longer that Descartes appears to have made an unacceptable separation of mind and matter, but that he forces us to confront over and over the age-old, unsolved problem: How do we reason if not through mind? Adler tells us we are being absurd if we argue that we do not reason or that universal truths do not exist.

A less famous but perhaps far more significant moment in the writings of Descartes occurs when Descartes tries to prove that we experience things not because of our senses but because of the understanding we possess, an inner process we cannot explain but must accept. He asks us to consider that we are holding a ball of wax in our hand. It's easy enough to say we know it is wax because someone once pointed to wax and named it for us. But now suppose we place the wax in a dish and set fire to it. The substance undergoes changes in color, odor, and, above all, consistency. It becomes liquid. *Here is the crucial question:* Did someone have to tell us that strange things can happen to wax but it remains wax? Or did we observe the changes and, through our reasoning faculty, decide that wax must be a substance capable of change when set on fire? Chances are very good that nobody ever had the time *or* the need to explain the phenomenon to us.

Descartes is still valuable to us, if only because we may need to have our rational selves reaffirmed every so often. If indeed we are rational beings, if we are capable of mastering our own destiny through the application of reason, then we ought to get on with the business of our humanness, lest we waste time denouncing it and thereby defeat ourselves!

GOD

Back in the 1940s there was a religious movie that began with a comment to the audience: "For those who believe in God, no explanation is necessary; for those who do not believe in God, no explanation is possible." Throughout the history of philosophy, however, explanations for God and the rational defense of believing in God have been alternately considered necessary, possible, and impossible. Many philosophers have chosen to ignore the subject, but an equal number have found the issue of God to be the single most important question anyone can ever ask.

In the Beginning

Since almost the earliest days of human history there has been a belief, an assumption, that the things we see around us (and whatever it is we are) did not create themselves. Belief in supernatural intervention in human affairs can well be figured into the anthropological theories of human emergence, along with the discovery of fire, the earliest use of weapons, the invention of the wheel, and so on. In fact, someone was probably sacrificing to the gods long before transportation was even thought of.

An interesting book called *The Origins of Consciousness in the Decline of the Bicameral Mind*[4] sets forth the theory that early peoples believed in gods because they heard voices inside themselves and assumed these must be coming from afar. The author maintains that these voices were really only the right hemisphere of the brain communicating with the left. Whatever the reasons—and there are probably many—early peoples could not get along without an awareness of God.

Meanwhile, the urge to philosophize, which originally had nothing to do with God awareness, developed on its own. Socrates speaks of God without defining or analyzing God as a concept. Aristotle, who inherited the wisdom and rational methods of Socrates and Plato, is the first philosopher to use God as an intellectual necessity.

Aristotle could not solve the following crucial problem without asserting God as the answer. In its vulgarized form the problem is well known to all of us: Which came first—the chicken or the egg? Aristotle does not, however, phrase it this way. Instead he takes up the question of *motion*. There is nothing already in motion, he argues, which was not set in motion by something else. Believing that the sun and the stars are heavenly bodies moving about the earth on fixed wheels, he concludes that they too must be moved by another force. No doubt beyond the entire spectacle of the moving heavens is an outer wheel, a First Mover, so to speak. But could this outer wheel have *always* been in motion? Or, even more repugnant to reason, could it somehow have started up by itself?

Like many thinkers to follow, Aristotle immediately rejected the idea of the perpetual, uncaused existence of anything. He preferred instead to postulate what he called an Unmoved Mover, and this is the first philosophical argument for the necessary existence of a force—or phenomenon or indefinable entity—which must be exempt from all known laws but is responsible for all the others. In Aristotle's version, God has no personality, no human qualities. It is not a "he" or a being of any kind. Reason dictates that it can be neither explained nor imagined. We cannot possibly comprehend what an Unmoved Mover is like—a causeless causer. Philosophy simply requires the prior existence of—to be vulgar again—an egg that always was and therefore never came from a chicken.

With the coming of Judaism and then Christianity we have a completely different chapter in the history of god awareness. God became very personal to each believer, and no proof was needed except an inner feeling. What is usually and somewhat misleadingly termed The Old Testament, however, comes close to a philosophical statement in *The Book of Job*. Job, the old patriarch, visited by devastatingly bad fortune sent by God to test his faith, nearly gives up and is ready to renounce God. God's angry voice comes crashing down out

Early Christian philosophers found themselves confronting very puzzling questions when they tried to think logically about the revealed truths of their religion. For example: Could God have had any purpose in creating the world? Can an all-powerful God have a purpose? Purpose implies a need.

of a whirlwind and tells Job humanity has no right to *expect* anything from God. Humanity neither created nor supervises the world. Everything exists at the whim of God, who exacts love and obedience in return. *Job* is tough talk, but the position it takes is ultimately grounded in reason, not sentiment.

Early Christianity, on the other hand, offered promises predicated less on reason than on the doctrine that God was capable of endless love and forgiveness, no matter how unworthy God's children. Vain, materialistic, godless tyrants would come to grief as the poor inherited the earth—*provided* strict moral precepts were carefully observed. Christianity and Judaism both stressed moral behavior—in particular, the caring for others. Judaism promised an earthly reward in the form of a land flowing with milk and honey where the Hebraic tribes could live in peace and plenty. Christianity promised heaven as a reward for a humble, pious, and moral existence.

As both traditions grew, they defined wisdom as the knowledge of the holy books, not free speculation that might lead the thinker in *any* direction. Nonetheless, Christianity produced some philosophers in the first few centuries after the death of Christ. (Not surprising when one considers that the tradition developed in the very backyard of Greek and Roman learning: Plato and Aristotle were still very much alive.) These early Christian philosophers found themselves confronting very puzzling questions when they tried to think logically about the revealed truths of their religion. Some instances follow.

Can this world be the extent of God's creation?   If the ability to create matter *ex nihilo* (from nothing) is intrinsic to God, then why must we believe that He stopped with this one achievement? At the same time, the thought that God might go on endlessly creating worlds staggers the mind.

Could God have had any purpose in creating the world?   Revealed religion maintains that God created this world for humanity, and this fact alone places an obligation on human sinners: to worship and adore God for His kindness. Yet how may an all-powerful God be so limited as to have had a purpose? Purpose implies an existing need. But if God had a need, how then could He be all-powerful?

Does God think?   Human beings engage in the act of thought in order to know something that was not known before. If God is all-knowing as well as all-powerful, what can He have to think about?

If God does not think, how can He then respond to human need?   What is the use of praying to a God Who, because He does not think, cannot be concerned about us? Is it not futile to believe that God will intervene in human affairs?

If God is able to intervene in human affairs, does this not mean He can change His mind?   Let us assume that God's being all-knowing means that He must think, or at least that He has a mind which contains all possible knowledge. How then may He change that mind in response to human prayer? How could an all-knowing mind become less or more all-knowing? Surely the contents of one all-knowing mind cannot be equivalent to those of "another" all-knowing mind.

As the centuries rolled on, the concepts "all-powerful" and "all-knowing" became at once impossibilities for human thought and intellectual necessities within that thought. The first of the great Christian philosophers, who was ultimately to say that philosophy cannot take Christians where they need to go, was Saint Augustine (A.D. 354–430); but before he came to this conclusion, he wrestled with some other agonizing questions.

How to Explain Evil

If God is good—an assumption as necessary for believers as that God is all-knowing—how do we account for the terrible things that happen in this world? How do we account for both natural and human evil? for devastating storms and earthquakes that wipe away millions of innocent people? for ruthless dictators who give orders to maim and kill and often seem to flourish anyway? These questions are with us now, and they were there very early, too.

Like Paul, who preceded him by several centuries, Augustine became a convert during his mature lifetime. In his case the catalyst was a Christian mother who had despaired over his wanton ways and kept urging him to reform, to acknowledge and confess his sins in prayer to a loving and forgiving God, and to devote the rest of his life to God's work. Though Augustine eventually renounced his life of sin and entered the Christian fold, he did not do so easily.

Augustine's *Confession,* one of the most personal and candid works ever written by a philosopher, deals with the intellectual difficulties facing him upon his conversion. One of his first concerns was intellect itself: Why was he given such a thing by God when it was inadequate to comprehend the divine scheme? The *creatio ex nihilo,* the necessary belief that God, the divine substance, both preceded material substance and created it from nothing, was at first repugnant to his reason, as shown by the following excerpt:

Faith—an illogical belief in the occurrence of the improbable.

H. L. Mencken

> Nor in the whole world didst Thou make the whole world; because there was no place where to make it before it was made, that it might be. Nor didst Thou hold anything in Thy hand, whereof to make heaven and earth. For whence shouldest Thou have this, which Thou hadst not made, thereof to make anything? For what is, but because Thou art? Therefore Thou spakest, and they were made, and in Thy Word Thou madest them. But how didst Thou speak?

Augustine considered the existence of evil—or the *apparent* existence of evil—both physical and moral, to be an even graver problem. If God created the world, it follows that the world must be an ideal, a perfect order. How might a perfect God make a mistake and bring into being something less than perfect? Yet it is clear that things are far from ideal. From physical disasters to moral depravity, the human race is continually plagued by monstrous deviations from perfection. How do we reconcile the existence of evil with the belief that God, being perfect, is all-good?

Evil, Augustine concluded, cannot be a "thing," cannot exist in the way that material substance exists, for if it were a material substance, would evil not be—as is all matter—the creation of God?

> That evil then which I sought, whence it is, is not any substance: for were it a substance, it should be good. . . . I perceived therefore . . . that Thou madest all things good, nor is there any substance at all, which Thou madest not.

The problem posed by Augustine stipulated that nothing made by God can be evil, but yet evil exists. Or does it? Augustine answered the problem by defining evil as *the absence of good,* comparing it to a disease which temporarily attacks the body:

> In the bodies of animals, disease and wounds mean nothing but the absence of health; for when a cure is effected, that does not mean that the evils which were present . . . go away from the body and dwell elsewhere: they altogether cease to exist; for the wound or disease is not a substance, but a defect in the fleshy substance—the flesh itself being a substance, and therefore something good.

Augustine's analogy raises many questions—more indeed, many critics have said, than it answers. First, is disease necessarily evil? One may believe that material substance is by its very nature subject to decay and ultimately death. Why raise the question of evil at all? But

At first Augustine had to wrestle with many Christian truths that seemed repugnant to reason, among them the idea that God created the world from nothing.

Faith—an illogical belief in the occurrence of the improbable.

H. L. Mencken

not raising the question in one connection does not mean it should not be raised in another. Is moral evil the absence of good? If so, where did the good *go?* Can goodness appear and disappear? If it can, does not God, being all-powerful, control its behavior?

This last question was not ignored by Augustine. It is, after all, the question at the very heart of Christianity: the question of *sin.* Let us ignore for now the problem of where goodness goes when it is absent. We have been told often enough that moral evil is the result of human sinfulness, of *human beings deliberately disobeying the will of God.* Should not this explanation be the end of the problem? It creates, however, another altogether *awesome* problem.

If humanity can sin, as the Church taught, humanity is then answerable to God for violating His commandments. Such accountability implies the option of choosing between right and wrong. But if God is all-knowing, He must be aware *in advance* of what choices will be made. If such is the case, we must conclude that human destiny is already mapped out. Before one is even born, God must know whether one's actions will be good or evil. Is one then responsible for them? The answer is yes, even though reason cannot comprehend why.

Augustine finally accepted the idea of *predestination,* for nothing else was compatible with the necessary idea of God's perfection. Predestination and human responsibility appeared to cancel each other out, yet one could not be a Christian without accepting them both. The answer had to be that human reason, being a quality of material substance, cannot understand divine substance; otherwise it would be equal to it. Why must we reach all conclusions through reason then?

In His infinite mercy, said Augustine, God has given us *faith,* which is the faculty of believing without understanding. What seems paradoxical to the human mind must not be so for God. And if God understands, we know *the issue is understandable!* Why does it have to be understood by *us?*

> *Absence of evidence is not evidence of absence.*
>
> Carl Sagan

> *Augustine at length concluded that God has given us the gift of faith, which allows us to accept many things that seem to violate reason.*

Faith Is Not Enough

The certainty which transcended human analytical thinking began to lose its hold on Christian intellectuals at about the time that the great universities of Europe were being founded. Oxford, the University of Paris, Bologna, to name a few, opened their doors to young men studying for holy orders. But the growing need for disciplined training of the mind as well as the spirit set in motion an inevitable intellectual movement. A university by its very nature brings together students and teachers engaged in the common purpose of learning and teaching a body of doctrine, and exchanges of ideas and debates surely must take place. Little by little the university movement, also called *Scho-*

> *The university movement, called* Scholasticism, *created a new approach to religion that attempted to reconcile faith and reason.*

lasticism, created a new approach to religion, one which attempted to reconcile faith and reason.

An important personality in the very early history of the new movement was not a scholar but rather the Archbishop of Canterbury: Saint Anselm (1033–1109). Anselm's work in philosophy clearly paved the way for later developments in Christian thought, which were to result in a new approach to religion aimed at agnostics and atheists, one still used to convince those who cannot accept Christian belief on faith alone.

Anselm did not see himself as a rationalist but rather as a mystic. His mission, as far as he was concerned, was to protect the faith against those who assailed it. He lived at a time when, in the inevitable course of things, established truth was being questioned. The questioners used reason as their weapon and scoffed at religion on the grounds that it would not dare—would not know how—to counter the attacks with the same weapon. Anselm's reply was that Christians had the same right to use reason as anyone else and, though rational proof of God's existence was not necessary for the devout believer, such proof was possible.

Anselm's most famous contribution to early Scholasticism was the so-called *ontological argument.* Ontology is that branch of philosophy which deals with the phenomenon of being. An ontological argument for God's existence seeks to prove that it is illogical and absurd to suppose God has no being. Though Anselm's argument is complicated in its wording, in outline it goes as follows:

> We must assume that nothing greater than God can be conceived (for if there were something greater than God, that something would have to be called God). In other words, God, by definition, is the ultimate.
>
> There are two ways to conceive of something. It can be an idea that exists only in the mind, or it can be an objective reality of which the mind can become aware.
>
> Whatever exists in objective reality is necessarily greater than an idea that exists in the mind alone.
>
> Since nothing greater than God can be conceived, it follows that God necessarily exists, independent of the mind.

The most ambitious effort to prove God's existence through analytical means came from Saint Thomas Aquinas (1225–1274), who many believe epitomizes the Scholastic movement. Educated originally by Benedictine monks, he then entered the University of Naples, became a Dominican, and later moved to Paris, which was already a major intellectual center. Here Aquinas came into contact with the

According to St. Anselm, rational proof is not necessary for the devout believer, but such proof is possible.

Anselm's most famous contribution to early Scholasticism was the so-called ontological argument.

analytical method of Aristotle and achieved his major fame as a philosopher by applying logic to every phase of Christian doctrine. More than any other person, Aquinas was responsible for making the philosophical approach to religion both fashionable and acceptable after many centuries dominated by mysticism and faith. Even today, students in Catholic seminaries are thoroughly trained in Thomism, the name given to St. Thomas Aquinas's logical method of teaching Christian doctrine.

Aquinas developed the famous Five Proofs of God's existence, which are briefly summarized below.

Aquinas attempted to prove logically what Augustine had accepted through faith alone.

Argument from Motion

Some things in the universe are in motion. It is clear that what is in motion must be set in motion by something else. But it is impossible to trace motion back infinitely. There has to be a first mover, which is itself unmoved. Only God can be the first mover.

Argument from Causation

There is no known case of something's having been the cause of itself. Everything is caused by something before it. But as with motion, it is impossible to trace causation back infinitely. There has to be a First Cause, which is itself uncaused, and this can only be God.

Argument from Being (an ontological argument)

Though we have only to look around to see that things are, it is indeed possible to imagine that they should not be. That is, the possibility of there never having been existence can and does occur to reason. On the other hand, though it is possible for nothing to be, it is clear that there is existence. Hence there must be a necessary being from which all other being derives, and this can only be God. (This third proof is generally regarded as the strongest.)

Argument from Gradation

Wherever we look we see greater or lesser amounts. We do not conceive of "better" unless it is also possible to imagine "best." Everything we know of points to the existence of an ultimate—a best in everything—and this can only be God.

Argument from Design

Since there is evidence of order and design in the universe, there must exist a designer, a super-intelligence responsible for this order, and this can only be God.

In this "enlightened" age, it is easy to scoff at some or all of these proofs, to say—as indeed many have said—that Aquinas always begs the question. But whether we are prepared to accept logical arguments for God's existence or not, we should give due respect to the ingenuity of Aquinas. If, for example, you counter with, "Why should the super-intelligence be God?" the Thomist can come right back with, "Call it by any name you wish, as long as you grant that there is a super-intelligence." If you persist, saying, "How can we know there is order?" the Thomist can come back with, "Show me how life is founded on the assumption that there is chaos in the universe."

Of course, the question of order can be countered by the observation that assuming there is order does not mean that that assumption is indeed a fact. Some of today's particle physicists believe they are going to discover that nature *is* orderly, but they will hasten to add a disclaimer that it all depends on what you mean by *orderly.* In any case, no particle physicist would argue that the kind of order which might be revealed is ample proof of *both* a design and a designer.

A large blow against Thomism was struck by Immanuel Kant (1724–1804), who vigorously asserted that logical proofs for God's existence were foolish and trivial, because they were true only by definition. To Kant both Aristotle and Aquinas were saying, in regard to the argument from motion, that God is *defined* as the only possible Unmoved Mover, and, further, that an Unmoved Mover is defined as that which causes all other motion. Thus they believed that since there obviously *is* motion, there is also, and just as obviously, God.

Descartes, whom we met in the preceding section on mind, also contributed his own ontological argument, stating that, since God must be a perfect being, we cannot conceive of a perfect being's *not* existing. But again, in the Kantian objection, we can see that Descartes is defining God in such a way that the conclusion is inevitable.

Thomism survives, though it does not constitute the only way to reach God through philosophical means. The American philosopher William James (1842–1910), for example, came out in favor of a variety of ways in which belief was possible. Belief in God could be a viable option for people who find no good reason to disbelieve. Belief in God could be *psychologically* true without having to be subjected to proof. Kant himself had spoken of a "practical philosophy," which included the belief in God, accepted by millions of people who required neither logical nor scientific evidence. As one might expect,

In the eighteenth century, Kant was saying that logical arguments to prove God's existence are fallacious since they only prove what is already implied in the definition of what they are trying to prove. For example, he said that most arguments for God's existence begin with the assumption that God is that which necessarily exists.

there are philosophers who tell us we must confront the theory that, philosophically, we *cannot* meaningfully entertain any such belief.

The Negative Argument

Atheism is not an evil plot against the human race, but a philosophy that tries to present rational proof that God does not and cannot exist. It is not a science any more than Thomism is a science, and it has whatever credibility one is willing to give it. It is, however, a legitimate aspect of philosophical thought.

By far the most commonly employed method used by the atheist is what in philosophical circles is called *reductio ad absurdum,* by which is meant that a particular statement—e.g., God does not exist—is held to be true because its exact opposite—in this case, God does exist—is an absurdity. Another simple case in point: We must accept the truth of the proposition "Two and two are four" because it is absurd to say that two and two are not four. Atheists often put their shoes on the other foot, so to speak, arguing from negativity rather than the other way around. Their argument can be readily summed up: Since there is no good reason for a belief in God, we shall not entertain such a belief.

American philosopher Charles Sanders Peirce (1839–1914) was a leading exponent of atheism, not because he deliberately set out to undermine the faith of millions but because he wanted philosophy to serve humanity by turning on the light of sanity in the darkness of muddled thinking. Religious beliefs are among many types of thought he considered muddled. According to Peirce, religious beliefs are also among those held because they soothe "the irritation of doubt." One takes comfort in the thought that God exists and is watching over us; but comfort is surely not the basis for accepting something as true.

Religious beliefs are also not disprovable by any known scientific method. In a famous passage Peirce talks about belief in an afterlife:

> Thus, if it be true that death is annihilation, then the man who believes that he will certainly go straight to heaven when he dies, provided he has fulfilled certain simple observances in this life, has a cheap pleasure which will not be followed by the least disappointment.[5]

If the afterlife is not provable or disprovable through actual experience, however, there is at least one doctrine in Christianity which *can* be subjected to experiential testing, and that is *transubstantiation,* or the act by which the Communion wafer, which is a bread, is believed to turn into the body of Christ, and the Commu-

Atheism is not a terrible plot woven by evil people against the human race, but a philosophy that offers to present rational proof that God does not and cannot exist.

nion wine, into the blood of Christ. Peirce attacks the second part of the doctrine, the suggestion that wine is wine one minute and blood the next:

> We can mean nothing by wine but what has certain effects, direct or indirect, upon our senses; and to talk of something as having all the sensible characters of wine, yet being in reality blood, is senseless jargon.[6]

Thus Peirce maintains that the only good reason to accept something as true is that it is predictable. It is always the consequence of certain repeated actions. A scientist who performs an experiment over and over and always with the same results is in a position to state a scientific law, a truth that is true whether the nonexperimenter wants to accept it or not.

Now, one *can* argue that the belief in God has beneficial results for the believer and can be accepted as truth on those grounds alone. But even then, can we not foresee a time when this belief would *not* bring comfort? What might happen to the faith of the young bridegroom who watches his wife die after an accident that could have been avoided? But postulating God's existence because of an inner sense—even if it *were* always the same—is not a reliable avenue to truth. After all, how may it be said that everyone has the same inner sense? Clearly such a statement is not in the same category as the scientist's announcement that such and such an experiment has yielded the same results 500 times, forcing us to conclude that anyone would get those results if he duplicated conditions of it.

Since there are no good universal grounds for stating that God exists, one is justified in accepting the negative side of the statement: God does not exist. No more rational proof is necessary than to point out the absurdity of the statement's opposite. It is absurd, in Peirce's logic, because it contradicts the conditions which the philosopher lays down as being required of *any* truth—namely, that it be the consequence of repeated actions. Actions are actions. They are out there in the open for all the world to see.

On the other hand, Peirce's logic can be perilous, too. Following it, one is led to deny existence to justice, morality, goodness, rightness, wrongness, and so on. Wine is wine because we have had experience with particulars. But justice is something that is universal and has no particulars. True, a given action can be just or not just; but a given action is not the same thing as justice.

It could be argued, further, that universals like justice and goodness are related to human experience in a way that God is not. If an airplane crashes, the observation "It was the will of God" represents a very personal interpretation of an event. However, the observation, after a trial, that "justice was done" has the advantage of being something that two people could meaningfully discuss even if they disagreed on the application of "justice" to a particular situation. Neither could say: "I have no idea what justice is." People *do* say this, of course, but what they really mean is that they cannot say for certain whether a given situation illustrates justice.

As the reader may already suspect, the argument against God's existence is far from being the last word on the subject, though the thinking person should not be afraid to confront it or indeed any other argument that rational beings have developed.

THE FIRST SUBSTANCE

As commonly employed, the word *substance* refers to anything that has a material nature so that it can be weighed, measured, combined with other things, and altered when acted upon by other things. We think of substances therefore as material entities. When we call an argument substantial, we imply that it has a certain body, a certain amount of depth.

In ancient philosophy the term *substance* used to have a more specialized meaning: that which existed independent of the will or each person's private awareness. This definition would, of course, cover what we normally think of as the familiar world, the world of everyday, or "commonsense," reality. But it also could cover immaterial possibilities like mind, soul, God, and the universal abstractions we considered in relation to Plato's theory of Forms. There used to be huge debates over (1) whether both material and immaterial substances can be real; (2) whether one came before the other (as in the Christian belief that God, an immaterial substance, created matter out of nothing); or (3) whether all that appears real to us might not have developed from some yet to-be-discovered First Substance, material or otherwise.

The early difficulty lay in the apparent fact that cause and effect together combined to form a universal law. Everything had to be *caused* by something else. Thus the problem of how to say that the ultimately real is the everyday world without also saying how this came into being. Ancient philosophers busied themselves with proving through reason that whatever was the cause of everything else deserves the honor of being called the First Substance, hence the one, the true ultimately real thing.

That no consensus was reached on the subject shows us how tricky the enterprise was—and still is. The chicken-and-egg dilemma was there from the outset. Reason might, for one thinker, strongly point to this or that answer; but it was easy for another thinker to carry

The philosophical search for the ultimate reality goes back at least as far as the sixth century B.C. and is still a hot issue.

the possibilities back even further. We can also appreciate the attraction offered by the notion of a nonmaterial First Substance. This at least had the advantage of not needing to be accounted for through the law of cause and effect that seemed to govern the material world.

Early Answers

Before Aristotle's Unmoved Mover, and many, many centuries before Thomas Aquinas spoke of God as necessary being, there were philosophers arguing about the subject of ultimate reality. We are talking here about philosophers who actually looked around at the world they saw and asked, "Yes, but is reality just these separate things we see—these mountains, this ocean, these trees, other people—or are all these things only *apparently* separate?" This was truly an amazing question to have been asked six centuries before the birth of Christ and well over 2000 years before the birth of modern science.

The early philosophers who pondered the nature of reality during the sixth century B.C. all lived in cities bordering the Aegean Sea, which separates the peninsula we now call Greece from what used to be called Asia Minor and is now Turkey. This area has often been designated—rightly or wrongly—as the cradle of our civilization. In any case, it did produce some minds that were pretty advanced for their particular time. In Miletus, on the west coast of Asia Minor, in the year 585 B.C., an astronomer and mathematician named Thales predicted an eclipse of the sun, and, according to all historical records, quite accurately. Perhaps his success helped induce the conviction that the world was understandable, that things about nature were discoverable, that with its intellect humanity possessed the power to know it all.

Thales eventually asked the question we hold to be the first known philosophical inquiry: What is the world made of? He probably was not aware that he was dabbling in philosophy. If the choice had been his to make, he would probably have called himself a scientist. He was a seeker of truth, a claim made by philosophers and scientists alike. But Thales lacked technology. He could not *prove* his answer, and so philosophy rightfully claims him as a distant pioneer. Lacking instruments, Thales had to seek an answer through his reason. What he came up with is recorded for us in Aristotle's *Metaphysics,* which credits Thales with having been the discoverer of "first principles," the fundamental one being that *water* is

> the original source of all existing things, perhaps taking
> this supposition from seeing the nurture of all things to
> be moist, and the warm itself coming-to-be from this and
> living by this (that from which they came-to-be being the
> principle of all things)—taking the supposition both from

this and from the seeds of all things having a moist nature, water being the natural principle of moist things.[7]

Thales had no idea of the controversy he was about to create. He was being, he believed, eminently logical. But, of course, he side-stepped the whole question of whether, if water were indeed the "natural principle" of things, it was also the prior reality which existed before anything else.

Anaximander, a pupil of Thales and 14 years his junior, noting that there were four known basic elements—earth, air, fire, and water—saw no reason to believe that water should be singled out as being prior to the others. Instead he set forth the theory that the four elements came from something he called the *apeiron,* the Indefinite. Since water was indefinite, it could also be infinite and at the same time causeless. Anaximander believed water contained within itself— and apparently without beginning—the seeds of the four elements, which in turn were the direct causes of the world we see.

The philosopher Heraclitus, born around 540 B.C. in Ephesus, also on the western coast of Asia Minor but somewhat to the north of Miletus, made his contribution to the controversy by wondering why there had to be a substance other than the separate things we see around us. Since these things are forever changing, perhaps we could say that *change itself was reality.* "You cannot," he once said, "step twice into the same river."

Yet even this "commonsense" approach has its difficulties. Heraclitus, knowing that the notion that whatever is out there is what's real could not tell the whole story, said reality was the *principle* by which all things change. But even if we argue that the principle is "bound up" in material things and need not be considered apart from them, we still have to show where it came from. Can a principle by itself be the one and only reality? Of singular interest is the fact that these early philosophers had quite convinced each other of one all-important requirement: *the ultimately real was one thing.* Even if the changing things that Heraclitus spoke of each had their own identity, the parent of them all was a principle—one principle— the principle of change.

Parmenides, from the city of Elea in what is now southern Italy, most emphatically denied that the principle of change could be the ultimate reality. He proved—at least to his satisfaction—that change could not even exist at all, that nothing really *can* change. For a thing—or a person—to change implies that it becomes something else, something other than it was before. But how can *becoming* be real? Reason requires that there be either being *or* becoming, not both. If something is, it is. We cannot speak of what it shall become, because that has no existence. If this is true, then how does "what it shall become" ever have an existence? What is true always is that something *is.* Certainly we can say that things can *appear* to change, can look different. But the principle which governs the world is not a principle of change; it is an eternal law of being. It is a law of *necessary* being, otherwise nothing would be at all.

The debate between Heraclitus and Parmenides is by no means confined to the ancient world. It continues today. Mortimer Adler in *Ten Philosophical Mistakes* (1985), for example, cites many great harms that have been caused by the notion that nothing has an unchanging being. What about moral responsibility, for example? And legal responsibility? How can you be asked to pay for a crime which "you" committed five years ago when "you" are now a different person? Adler's solution to the problem is to accept both being and becoming as possessing *different kinds* of reality. Change is something that happens to an enduring thing.

If Adler's view is accurate, then we may be permitted to apply it to the question of a First Substance. If indeed something came before everything else, can we say that that something had to obey the principle of eternal or necessary being, and then everything else, everything that came later, was subject to the principle of change? In a sense this is implicit in the view of Parmenides. But it does not explain why the original thing was not "content" to just be what it was without giving rise to everything else.

In the fifth century B.C., Democritus and Leucippus decided there was no good reason for believing that a First Substance was not material, for what evidence was there that anything except the material world really existed? They invented the philosophy of *materialism* and said that reality was ultimately reducible to little bits of matter they called *atoms,* which in Greek means "things that cannot be cut or divided." They were convinced there was an underlying world people could not see, and that the world that seemed to be "out there" was made up of these elementary building blocks. Further, they believed atoms always existed and were therefore exempt from the law of cause and effect.

Duly impressed by this first atomic theory, the Roman poet Lucretius, in the first century B.C., drew a picture of what the world was like eons ago, before there were oceans and trees and mountains and people. At that primeval time there was nothing but a *rain of atoms*—little particles just falling endlessly through a great void—until something caused them to start knocking into each other. (This is perhaps an ancient Roman version of what today we call the theory of the Big Bang, the huge explosion that started the whole thing.) The cosmic collisions led to mounds of atoms, some of which solidified to become the familiar world around us.

With the advent of Christianity and its hold on the thinking of much of the world, materialism took a back seat to the accepted belief

The first known atomic theory was advanced by Democritus and Leucippus in the fifth century B.C.

that there were two kinds of substance—God and matter—and that matter was brought into being by God and was whatever He wanted it to be. There was no need to ask *how* it came to be. Insignificant humanity was never meant to comprehend such things.

We Are Asking the Old Questions Again

For a long time—centuries, as a matter of fact—the question of whether there was a First Substance was dropped from the repertoire of the philosophers. The impact of the Judeo-Christian religious tradition had been such that, if one were a believer, one had no doubt that a divine substance had come before everything else and was the cause of material substance. As the Middle Ages began to fade and the early light of modern science began to appear on the horizon, nonbelievers were kept quite busy trying to keep up with scientific discoveries about this material world without worrying about chickens and eggs.

Far from resolving the question of a First Substance, scientific method even had a negative impact on philosophy in some quarters. Never mind asking about ultimate reality, said some, when there is probably *nothing* that can ever be known for sure. Scientists, after all, are cautious beings. For a thing to be labeled a certainty, it had to pass muster in a laboratory, and there was always the possibility that somebody somewhere else would eventually disprove what a given scientist offered as a truth. If scientists were hesitant, how could philosophers be less so? How foolish to speculate on First Substances. Who could see them? Who could put them under a microscope?

Beliefs about immaterial and divine substances remained, to be sure. The separation between God and this world, His creation, was still accepted by millions as religious dogma. Indeed, as we have seen, the existence of God often helped philosophy out of a quandry, as when Descartes concluded there had to be a material world as well as a mental one because God would not delude His children. In the pioneer days science was the rebellious child, religion the stern parent. Whatever could be supposedly "proved" in the laboratory had best not contradict established teachings. In the seventeenth century the Church put on an awesome show of strength when it forced Galileo to deny his earlier statement that Copernicus had been right when he said that the earth moved around the sun. Galileo retracted his views despite the fact that he had with the telescope produced the technology which showed many things *not* taught by the Church.

The denial did nothing, however, to slow down the progress of science. Galileo became a symbol of the new age, the new spirit of inquiry—scientific, not philosophical. With Isaac Newton and his declaration of the immutable laws of nature—such as those governing motion and gravity—there seemed to be a definite promise that

It seems to me fascinating to reflect that today . . . men are seeking to wrest solutions from problems posed by the Greek philosophers more than two thousand years ago.

Werner Heisenberg

through science the day would come when everything real would be known.

Philosophy, however, continued on its course of denying that anything could be known for sure. A significant philosophical development of the eighteenth century was associated with David Hume (1711–1776), a Scottish thinker who labeled his philosophy *skepticism*. Definitely influenced by the cautious method of the scientists, skepticism said what we call truth was a matter of habit, that's all. If something always seemed to come about because of something else, people got into the habit of expecting it to happen. But habit is not certainty. There are no certain truths.

Alarmed by skepticism, Immanuel Kant in Germany tried to determine whether anything could be known for sure through the power of reason itself, apart from the methods of science. Kant's answer was that what we call knowledge—scientific as well as philosophical—comes from the way the mind is structured, not from any direct contact with reality. Reality itself, said Kant, is unknown and unknowable, including any reality one chose to believe in. If one believes in God, for example, one does so out of what we might call psychological necessity, not because one can justify faith rationally.

Even so, if religion held on tenaciously as the last outpost of a belief in a divine First Substance, but if faith were to keep itself separated from scientific pursuits, a colossal battle was inevitable. The skeptical philosophers more or less aided the cause of science by saying that the method used by the scientists was the only one that made any sense, even if it did not lead to a perception of ultimate truth. A new kind of philosophy, sometimes called *positivism,* developed in the nineteenth century. Positivism reduced the sphere of philosophy to whatever could be scientifically proved. It made philosophy, in short, a spokesperson for science, and it laughed at anyone who tried to believe in anything else.

Darwin's theory of evolution, first presented in *On the Origin of Species* (1859), dealt perhaps the most devastating blow to established religious truths. How could it be said that material substance was what religion had taught when the behavior of that substance was beginning to be shown in a very different light? How could God have created the world out of nothing in six days when evolutionary theory claimed the process to have been extremely gradual?

In some quarters, believers tried to reconcile evolution and biblical teaching. Soon after the new science of geology had become a legitimate arm of university research, a book dealing with the age of the earth appeared. The first three words of its extremely long title tell the whole story of what it attempted to do: *Vestiges of Creation.* Here was proclaimed a new way to show that God truly existed: make a scientific study of how the divine plan for the world had shown itself.

Other reconcilers tried to prove that evolution itself was God's method of creating humanity. Some said that, because the Hebrew word for "day" also means "age," the Bible really means six *ages* when it speaks of the six days of creation. Earlier in the twentieth century, religious philosopher Teilhard de Chardin (1881–1955) applied evolution to divine substance itself, postulating that the divine was in the process of becoming. Eventually the Super Christ, as he called it, would make an appearance in the world.

With all the claims made *for* science—but not necessarily *by* it—science seemed to many people of a century ago the way to arrive at all final answers. How could science not discover ultimate reality? Ultimate reality had not been discovered earlier because the technology had not been there. Now humanity had both the brains and the machines to do it. As we climb aboard the twentieth-century express, we find philosophers caucusing in small compartments, talking about what their new domain will be now that science is about to define and explain reality once and for all.

What has "really" happened, however, is twofold. First, science—especially physics—has gone, is *still* going, much further than even Albert Einstein ever dreamed. It has created machines—first, atom-smashers, and now, particle-accelerators—that the majority of people do not know much about, and whose dimensions are staggering. It has expended mega-sums of money, probably as much as the national debt if the truth were known, often without significant payoffs. It is getting closer and closer to rewriting the biblical *Book of Genesis*, but this time with mathematical equations involving numerical values that go into inconceivable, unpronounceable figures. (A *jillion* would be small potatoes!) It can trace the origin of the universe back to a thousandth of a second after the Big Bang, and it is now beginning to speculate on what was there *before* the Big Bang. If *that* is ever determined, how much closer to ultimate reality do you think humanity could get?

On the other hand, the physicists' speculations about ultimate reality are running far ahead of the technology, impressive as much of it has been. If physics had its way and all the money it could ever want, experimental proof of the latest theories might be in the offing. Here is an example of what is currently needed:

> the construction of a gigantic new accelerator called the Superconducting Supercollider, a machine some sixty miles in circumference to be constructed somewhere, anywhere, in the empty American prairie. If built, the multibillion-dollar ring would collide protons together at energies that have not been reached since the first fractions of an instant after the Big Bang.[8]

Nothing will be changed if God does not exist. We shall find ourselves with the same norms of honesty, progress, and humanism, and we shall have made of God an outdated hypothesis which will peacefully die off by itself.

Jean-Paul Sartre

Such a supermachine is needed so physicists can study the results of high-speed particle collisions, in the effort to simulate experimentally the conditions that prevailed when our universe came into being. A 60-mile-long machine? Instead, here is what more often takes place:

> The Berkeley laboratory where Lawrence worked had no money, no professional engineers, no tools more complicated than a lathe. Accelerator parts were scavenged from radios, bought second-hand, or made on-site. Nothing worked exactly the way it was supposed to. . . . Sometimes the flammable hydrogen leaked into the accelerator, where it blew up. If the machine was on when physicists descended into the bowels of the enormous magnet, it created electric currents in their brains—a form of self-induced shock therapy.[9]

Even so, theoretical physics is on a sure track. No one asks anymore whether there is a First Substance. They wonder, instead, which of the many, many tiny particles it will be.

Democritus' and Leucippus' 2500-year-old atomic theory was a fantastic advance, but now we know, of course, that the atom, far from being unsplittable, far from being the smallest unit of matter, is actually a relatively large system, a miniuniverse, if you will, containing not just a nucleus and an electron, but, within the nucleus, great numbers of particles that collide, interact, and form other particles that in turn contain other particles, and so on and on a very long way.

Right now the Big Bang is generally accepted as more than a theory. It was indeed an explosion of unimaginable magnitude that took place billions of years ago. The burning issues (pun intended) are what caused it and what it was that exploded. These are not precisely philosophical issues in the traditional sense, because scientific answers are on the way—if not imminently through experimental proof, then certainly through mathematical equations upon which a consensus will be reached among the prominent physicists. The philosophical part of it all resides in the "leftover" questions that are already beginning to intrigue those philosophers who keep up with the latest developments.

The reason the Big Bang is more than a theory is that everything known about the universe appears to confirm the idea that all the suns and planets and moons in their orbits, as well as conditions on our own earth, represent the aftermath of a giant explosion whose "debris" is still cooling down even as it keeps flying outward, as always happens to the parts of something that has blown up: flying outward from the central point where the Big Bang occurred.

A current prediction is that at some time in the future— maybe a billion years or so from now—the expansion of our universe

It is even harder to realize that this present universe has evolved from an unspeakably unfamiliar early condition, and faces a future extinction of endless cold or intolerable heat. The more the universe seems comprehensible, the more it also seems pointless.

Steven Weinberg

will have reached its limits, and contraction will begin. One theory—and this is *just* a theory—sees the force of gravity pulling the "debris" back from where it started: a black hole.

A black hole would be the result of the compression of the entire material universe into such a density that nothing, not even light, could escape. It would parallel the nothingness—or void—that Judeo-Christian belief says preceded the creation of the world. For those who reject such a belief, a black hole has the advantage of not *being* a void. Accepting the black hole theory frees the doubter from having to explain how everything got started if indeed God is not the cause.

Of course, the theory does not take care of the most puzzling question of all: If there was always densely compressed matter, which exploded into our universe, how did *it* get there? No one has yet stepped forward to suggest that maybe God put it there, because no known religion has a god who is said to play around with black holes and huge explosions.

Both physics and philosophy hate voids as much as they hate anything. There is another, and extraordinary, theory that glimpses the disturbing yet *possible* idea of a preexisting nothing that was fundamentally unstable, fundamentally unable to *remain* nothing. A void that wasn't exactly a void, in other words:

> Just as there is a tiny chance that virtual particles will pop into existence in the midst of subatomic space, so there may have been a tiny chance that the nothingness would suddenly be convulsed by the presence of a something.
>
> This something was an inconceivably small, inconceivably violent explosion, hotter than the hottest supernova and smaller than the smallest quark[10], which contained the stuff of everything we see around us. The Universe consisted of only one type of particle—maybe only one particle—that interacted with itself in that tiny, terrifying space. Detonating outward, it may have doubled in size every 10–14 seconds or so, taking but an instant to reach literally cosmic proportions.[11]

A nothingness too unstable to remain nothing, so it exploded into a single particle which "interacted with itself." And then in less time than it takes your eyes to blink, this single particle expanded to become the universe, and has been expanding for billions of years!

A century or so back, when intellectuals knew far less than science knows now, it was fashionable to pooh-pooh the old idea that nature was a beautiful set of laws operating in perfect harmony. American historian Henry Adams once said that chaos is the law of nature. In

But even if the black-hole theory is valid, we are still faced with the puzzling task of explaining where such densely packed matter came from to start with.

certain quarters, philosophers were betting their whole future this was true. Now they are not so sure.

There was a time when the notion that the whole universe started as just one particle would have been as hard to swallow as Aristotle's Unmoved Mover became for a good many of his critics. Now it is starting to be a good bet that the original particle "interacted with itself" because it was activated by a force—the one, the original force—which very quickly (in an instant of time) split up into the four forces known to us today: gravity, electromagnetism (which keeps electrons circulating around the nucleus), a strong force (which holds the nucleus together), and the recently discovered weak force (which causes some particles to release energy and become lighter as a result of colliding with other particles).

As science steers an increasingly unwavering course toward the final definition of reality, it continues to raise huge questions that probably still belong in the domain of philosophy, even though many scientists will be unable to resist trying their hands at solutions, questions such as the following.

Why just one force in the beginning?   Einstein also believed that all the known universal forces probably sprang from one unifying force, though he died without being able to produce the master equation that would have proved him right. Einstein admitted to becoming increasingly "religious" in his later years, though not, of course, in the traditional sense of the word. He found the behavior of the universe awe-inspiring.

Why just four forces since the beginning, and no more?
One might think that a particle with enough power to expand to become the universe in just a blink of the eye would keep on generating force after force. Nonetheless, the whole enterprise appears to have stopped at four. Philosophers will want to ask themselves: What is the principle that limits the possibilities of this universe?

Are we back to Aquinas' ontological argument?   If you remember, Aquinas' third argument, called ontological and believed to be the strongest, required that there be a principle of necessary being in order to explain why there is something instead of nothing. Aquinas called this principle God. Even if one does not wish to go this far, is it possible that this necessary being is the same as the "something" which "convulsed" the original nothing and brought everything else into existence?

There are many scientists who allow their thinking to go back to that same eye blink *after* the Big Bang, but not before. Perhaps there is something frightening about trying to understand an original particle and a single force that apparently sprang into existence from

Unlike Candide, who lived in the best of all possible worlds, we might live in the only possible world.

Robert P. Crease and
Charles C. Mann

We see the universe the way it is because if it were different we would not be here to observe it.

Stephen Hawking

an unstable vacuum. Frightening, because at the moment the image is beyond the proof of science: No one can prove the one-particle theory—yet. Maybe no one ever will.

But the excitement will always be there, beckoning the adventurous thinker. Perhaps the most exciting part of all is that the mental powers which enable us to think about such enormous possibilities may themselves have come spiraling out of that strange explosion.

With philosophy around, one need never be bored in this life. The challenges of philosophy continue to interest people who know how to think and who are willing to follow through even to uncertain conclusions, even to still-unimagined places.

No one can prove the one-particle theory—yet. Maybe no one ever will. But the excitement will always be there, beckoning the adventurous thinker.

GLOSSARY

creatio ex nihilo: Latin, meaning, literally, "creation from nothing." A long-standing belief in both the Hebrew and Christian religions that God both preceded material substance and brought it into being from nothing.

faith: A technical term in Christian thought, used by Saint Augustine to refer to God's gift to humanity of the ability to accept without question many things which appear to violate the laws of human reason (such as *creatio ex nihilo*).

Forms: In the specialized use of the word associated with Plato: universal ideas—such as beauty, honor, and justice—which exist independent of the individual and can never change. Also, value. Plato's theory is still very much with us and is still cited by those who insist that fundamental human values are universal and not subject to individual interpretation.

mind: The subject of much philosophical debate: Is it material, like blood, cells, nerves? Or is it an immaterial substance (and there is disagreement over just what that means)? Is it born with the body? Or is it separate from the brain? Does it exist at all? Plato believed mind is separate from sense experience and that it exists eternally in one body or another.

ontological argument: A logical proof of God's existence, advanced by both Saint Anselm and Saint Thomas Aquinas, which holds that there must be a necessary being from which all other beings derive.

positivism: Late nineteenth-century school of philosophy which holds that truth is limited to what can be scientifically proved.

reductio ad absurdum: A technique used by some logicians by which a proposition is proved true by showing that its opposite would be absurd.

Scholasticism: Late medieval school of Christian thought, associated with Aquinas, which attempts to reconcile faith and reason, to prove logically those doctrines which were said earlier not to require proof.

skepticism: Philosophy, associated with David Hume, which holds that nothing can be known for certain.

Sophists: Group of Athenian philosophers, contemporary with Socrates, who would teach for a fee rhetorical devices to assist in winning an argument on any side of an issue.

substance: In ancient philosophy, that which exists objectively, independent of the will or private awareness. A major issue has been whether there is one substance, divine or material, or two substances totally distinct from each other. Christian and Jewish thought has traditionally held the latter view.

Thomism: The logical system of thought devised by Aquinas to prove the truths of religion. Almost interchangeable with the term *Scholasticism.*

Unmoved Mover: According to Aristotle, a causeless causer, the force which set everything else in motion but which is itself exempt from all known laws and is responsible for the beginnings of the universe. This force is not the same as the Biblical God, for it makes no rules for humanity and has no interest in human affairs.

NOTES

1. Rene Descartes, *Discourse on Method,* trans. Stuart Hampshire.

2. Ibid.

3. Ibid.

4. Julian Jaynes, *The Origins of Consciousness in the Decline of the Bicameral Mind* (Boston: Houghton Mifflin, 1976).

5. From "The Fixation of Belief."

6. From "How to Make Our Ideas Clear."

7. G. S. Kirk and J. E. Raven, *The Pre-Socratic Philosophers* (New York: Cambridge University Press, 1963), p. 87.

8. Robert P. Crease and Charles C. Mano, *The Second Creation* (New York: Macmillan, 1986), p. 255.

9. Ibid., p. 257.

10. A *quark* is the whimsical but still serious name given to a tiny particle within the nucleus of the atom. No quark, of course, has ever been seen, but equations in contemporary physics demand its existence.

11. Crease and Mano, op. cit., p. 405.

Jacques Louis David, "The Death of Socrates," 1787
(Courtesy of The Metropolitan Museum of Art, Wolfe Fund, 1931, Catherine Lorillard Wolfe Collection)

THE MORAL ISSUE

6

OVERVIEW

Popular and philosophical approaches to morality differ. In popular usage, the word *morality* has underlying assumptions that are rarely examined. Sometimes *morality* is spoken of as a corrective to an irritating situation, whether it be inappropriate clothing, low productivity, or teenage pregnancy. It becomes a cure to be applied by one part of the population to prevent the pleasures of another. In popular belief, too, moralists are accused of limiting freedom, of not practicing what they preach, and of being unable to agree among themselves. Moralists respond to such accusations by pointing out that rules are all that protect civilization from base human nature. The accusations fly, and the talk goes on: "injustice," "corruption," "irresponsibility." Every time people call something "unfair," they are talking about morality, at least vaguely so.

Talk without thought, however, is a random exchange of passionate opinion, heat without light. Philosophers move beyond opinion to attempt to associate morality with its broadest implications: the search for the good life through a clear examination of the nature of good and evil. This examination includes fundamental human concerns: whether or not humankind is free; whether or not there are universals like justice and virtue; whether ideals ever take precedence over self-interest; how we can know the source of right behavior; how right behavior can be enforced; and how (or if) we can apply general rules to particular problems, large and small.

One major source of such rules has been human reason. Philosophers who ponder the nature of the good life maintain that there must be a rational way to describe how people *should* behave toward each other. What would make sense? What would provide the best social and political environment? How may human beings avoid the obvious evils of war and other forms of cruelty? Philosophers with a belief in reason seek universal rules, principles which they say must surely be apparent to anyone willing to think about the best way to live.

Religious spokespeople are still likely to argue that moral principles need not be rationally defended, since they are, after all, the teachings of God. The so-called Golden Rule is perhaps the best known of such principles, but it can also be cited by nonreligious thinkers as the most sensible way to order a society. Doesn't it make sense, they ask, to keep a promise? Would you want to live in a society in which you could not depend on other people's promises? It logically follows therefore that we should require of ourselves what we require of others.

In recent years the psychologist has often replaced both the theologian and the philosopher. The psychologist who explores human nature as a kind of social science avoids *should*s and *should not*s in favor of descriptive (rather than prescriptive) terms. Certain activities encourage "mental health." Others are clinically "antisocial." Human beings have different needs, based on parental training, societal taboos. What appears to be individual choice really is not, but can be traced to either genetic or external influences. In any case, they say, all moral choices are based on the individual desire for pleasure and contentment. People who transgress social codes are to be understood, not censured.

Once pleasure becomes a measurement, so worry some philosophers, there is a less firm basis for inhibiting certain behavior such as stealing. Without either divine commandments or a belief in reason, one might agree with Ernest Hemingway that "What is moral is what you feel good after." Other, more popular, sayings emphasize individual pleasure: "Do your own thing"; "Look out for Number One." Neither statement takes into account the feelings of others. Even the seemingly benign recommendation "Live and let live," with its unlimited tolerance, offers no suggestion of what this really means. The rule then becomes *No Rules,* except that in return for your neighbor's expecting nothing of you, you supposedly expect nothing of him.

We can only outline the extent of the problem. This chapter will examine how a number of prominent philosophies examine specific cases involving moral choice, whether based on principle or consequences. It will span the centuries and include a variety of opinions drawn from a variety of regions, political structures, and philosophical climates. It will refer, where appropriate, to the moral observations of literary figures and economists as well as the more traditional philosophers. Included will be references to Socrates and Plato, to the Bible, to Machiavelli, to Immanuel Kant, Jeremy Bentham, Adam Smith, and Henry David Thoreau, and to a sampling of contemporary beliefs about moral behavior. It is hoped that enough interest will be provoked to invite continued reading, as the wisdom of these varied and provocative thinkers are explored in greater depth in a lifelong search for answers to some of our most vital questions.

We begin with the assumption that there is free choice, whether the issue is large or small, and therefore that moral issues are meaningful.

THE SOURCES OF MORAL VALUES

Any debate over moral values invariably deals with human nature, with whether people are naturally able to reason, to govern themselves, to seek justice as an end in itself. Debates begun 2000 years ago continue today, for these concerns may hold not only the nature of the human species but the fate of the planet itself.

Moral philosophers agree on one point: namely, that freedom is basic to moral decision. Without freedom—if destiny has planned every significant event in our lives—we cannot be held responsible for our actions. We begin therefore with the assumption that there is free choice, whether the issue is large or small, and therefore that moral issues are meaningful. At the end of this chapter, to illustrate the fact that moral philosophy remains vital to all of us, the reader will be invited to apply the views of the various philosophies to a list of contemporary problems, many of them of great significance.

Let the following small anecdote serve as the basis for our deliberations. It is chosen for its very size, to emphasize the fact that while major decisions are being made about war, euthanasia, test-tube babies, pollution, terrorism, and a host of other items from the nightly news, most of us live with daily moral decisions on the order of this:

> A woman has lunch in a restaurant, and when she looks at the check she realizes the waiter has failed to charge her for an item she ordered and ate. The total should be $3 higher than the amount shown on the check. As she pays the bill, should she remind the waiter of the oversight? Should she tell either the cashier or the restaurant owner?

If the woman decides to pay voluntarily, should she congratulate herself on her honesty, deriving satisfaction from having done the right thing? Or, if she is short of cash, will she find ways to justify this passive kind of good fortune, telling herself that she may embarrass the waiter, cause trouble, or that she even "deserves" the lower bill as compensation for previous meals which were unsatisfactory and therefore excessive in price?

The woman's dilemma is indeed a microcosm of the moral issue, though many, alas, would probably find the questions trivial. We assure you: *they are not!*

Fear of Getting Caught

In the *Republic,* a series of dialogs between Socrates and various young men, the main subject is justice, by which Plato meant the rational order of humanity, society, and the universe. Plato maintained that moral values are universal and unchanging. When faced with a moral choice, according to Plato, we select the rational action, not necessarily the one which promotes our own interest. Socrates, representing Plato's views, is always on the side of reason. At one point in the *Republic,* a debate arises over the motives from which people usually behave morally. Is it indeed for the sake of reason, or for another purpose?

Taking the other side is Glaucon, one of several young men questioning Socrates and debating with him, who argues that people are just because the laws require them to be so and because they fear possible punishments for breaking these laws. Doing wrong, he maintains, is far more basic to human nature; he contends it is even very pleasant. But because punishment is so *un*pleasant, the person with the power to do wrong is held in check by these laws. If, however, all restrictions were suddenly removed, justice too would disappear.

In the "Ring of Gyges" dialog, Glaucon maintains that people avoid committing wrongs for fear of being caught.

To illustrate his point Glaucon tells the story of two men who possessed magic rings. Whoever wore them had the power to become invisible at will. One man, Gyges, a shepherd, was totally unjust; the other, totally just. Gyges used his power to take whatever he wanted without fear of being caught. He stole, raped, murdered—all with impunity. Above all, his invisibility protected his reputation, his good name in the community.

Glaucon maintains that the just man who discovered that he had godlike powers would do no better:

> No one, it is commonly believed, would have such iron strength of mind as to stand fast in doing right or keep his hands off other men's goods, when he could go to the market-place and fearlessly help himself to anything he wanted, enter houses and sleep with any woman he chose, set prisoners free and kill men at his pleasure. . . . Surely this would be strong proof that men do right only under compulsion; no individual thinks of it as good for him personally, since he does wrong whenever he finds he has the power.[1]

Socrates argues that a just man values the just act for its own sake, that reward and punishment are not guides for everyone. But Glaucon suggests that the just man is driven by the same motive as the unjust man, namely, his good name in the community. He scorns unjust actions, allegedly out of respect for virtue. But if, Glaucon adds, everything were to be taken away from him *except* virtue, if he has a reputation for wrongdoing even though he has done no wrong, would he continue to find satisfaction in the exercise of virtue? Suppose he were thrown into prison for crimes of which he was innocent? Would his innocence comfort him then?

By the same token, Glaucon asks us to imagine the unjust man who nonetheless has the reputation of being just, who can go merrily along, reaping rewards because of his good name.

> With his reputation of virtue, he will hold offices of state, ally himself by marriage to any family he may choose, become a partner in any business, and, having no scruples about being dishonest, turn all of these advantages to profit.[2]

Socrates believed that the good and just person behaves morally whether others know it or not.

Society does not even *expect* virtue to be anything more than an appearance, argues Glaucon. Society is content so long as appearances are maintained and fundamental selfishness and deceit are hidden.

The issue is not, Glaucon concludes, whether justice is superior to injustice, or right superior to wrong. Everyone acknowledges the goodness of justice. The issue is whether morality is the result of pressure brought to bear upon each of us by society or whether morality is the result of the human capacity for reason.

Plato's Socrates is unwilling to accept Glaucon's pragmatic view, and, if history can be believed, the real Socrates lived those beliefs, in a sense paying for them with his life. The rational man, Socrates

Plato's Glaucon is the eternal spokesperson for the practical approach to morality. People are honest because they fear public opinion were they otherwise, and society does not expect anything else.

One may go wrong in many different directions, but right in only one.

Aristotle

The Socratic view is that the rational man lives according to the law, even if the law in a particular case were harmful to him.

maintains again and again, would live according to the law, even if the law in a particular case were harmful to him. When an Athenian jury called for the execution of Socrates, he went willingly to his death, refusing the alternatives of exile or escape through the bribery of his jailer. In insisting upon adherence to the principle of law, he continued teaching his followers until his death and has since been considered a martyr to an ideal—in diametric opposition to Glaucon's self-serving Gyges. Of course, we must realize that the jury which convicted Socrates was made up of all the vote-casting citizens of Athens, who, if reason had prevailed, should have acknowledged Socrates as a virtuous and honorable man. But Socrates was known to have had dealings with Alcibiades, considered an enemy to the state, and therefore politics—as often happens—took precedence over reason. Where, one wonders, was Socrates' rational man when the old mentor needed him?

In the *Republic* Plato ultimately admits that the majority of the people will always be governed by self-interest. For this reason he advanced the belief that the ideal state is governed by a philosopher-king, the most enlightened human being that can be found. Most citizens, lacking the capacity to allow reason to be their guide, would be assigned tasks not requiring intricate decision making.

In our times Plato's state is often considered totalitarian, operating against the principles of human rights. This may be the case. On the other hand, since there has never to our knowledge existed a philosopher-king, since no one has ever reported the operations of a political entity guided by pure reason, we cannot, and probably never will, know how limiting or liberating Plato's Republic would be.

Rational Arguments for Self-Interest

During the more than 2000 years since Socrates lived, great books of fiction and philosophy have dealt with the issues of good and evil, reward and punishment, and the temptations of corrupt power. Among philosophers, human motivation has often been described in terms that Glaucon would have understood, with emphasis on rational distrust and practicality rather than the belief in a rational ideal of virtue. Perhaps the most famous rational argument for self-interest as the springboard for morality belongs to Niccolò Machiavelli (1469–1527), a Florentine statesman and political writer. For him it would be illogical to expect the woman in the restaurant not to keep the $3.

Machiavelli's major work is for leaders. *The Prince* (1513) argues that the best rulers must assume their subjects are guided by self-interest. No effective leader, argues Machiavelli, can make laws which assume that people will ever seek justice inconvenient to themselves. He therefore urges the leader to demand respect and obedience through fear rather than love, to dress well, to be surrounded by the trappings of power—magnificent carriages, a large retinue of impressive-looking followers. It might be good, he adds, to be loved as well as feared, but if there must be a choice, fear on the part of the subjects is superior to affection. To reinforce what he considered his practical guidelines, he remarked that most people would rather lose a parent than the inheritance from that parent!

His views evoked distaste and a sense of moral superiority in others. In *Les Misérables,* Victor Hugo, writing three centuries after *The Prince,* pointed out that Machiavelli in the sixteenth century "seems hideous, and he is so, in the presence of the nineteenth."

Every century has not necessarily viewed Machiavelli in this way, however. Today the term *Machiavellian* may actually imply approval for a clever leader who has managed to deceive and outwit his rivals and even his followers. The Machiavellian, through concentration on the human desire for self-interest (including one's own), will never be accused of naive trust in the inborn goodness of anyone, and there are many who applaud what they regard as a realistic view. One could probably find heirs who claimed they were too busy or poor to attend a parent's sickbed but who managed to find both time and money to contest the disposition of funds provided in a will.

Machiavelli viewed humanity as selfish and prone to corruption, and therefore he maintained that the ruler is justified in using strong measures to maintain order in society.

In the beginning of the nineteenth century Jeremy Bentham expounded the moral philosophy of *utilitarianism.* Like Machiavelli, Bentham believed that people were selfish and pleasure-loving, but, unlike others who sighed over the fact, he did not turn to cynicism or despair. Instead, he formulated a scheme called a *hedonic calculus,* which was designed to make moral judgment numerical through an accounting system which gave a specific value (plus or minus) to actions relative to the pleasure or pain caused by each. Assuming that the search for pleasure was the universal motivation therefore determined numerically that the most moral action was that which promoted the "greatest good for the greatest number."

Utilitarians also viewed humanity as being driven by self-interest, but they saw this as natural and therefore good.

For the individual, the hedonic calculus, according to Bentham, would be the guide in all decisions about marriage, travel, care for family members, even leisure time. In public life, decisions made by officeholders and the electorate would take into account the pluses and minuses of a new tax, a zoning ordinance, a law limiting the rights of one group of citizens against the rights of another. All is done by numbers, and the majority rules.

Some philosophical implications arise out of utilitarianism. In practice it may be difficult to administer, since there will always be disagreement about the number of minus points assigned to those made unhappy by a given choice; there may well be a temptation to adjust the computations to coincide with a decision arrived at by other than mathematical means. In addition, there is the question of whether, even in a society in which all people may be *politically* equal, their pleasures are also equal. What will be the effect (what *is* the effect?) of having majority rule in matters of public taste? Won't a kind of Gresham's law allow easy, cheap, distasteful literature to drive out that which can be enjoyed by the relatively few who have been educated to respect the more demanding? One contemporary effect of majority rule can easily be seen by a glance at television ratings; but more than the arts are involved here. What of the moral impact of some practice enjoyed by the many but still harmful to the few? A startling example is provided by Robert Paul Wolff in a discussion of utilitarianism:

> Suppose that the Americans, like the ancient Romans, positively enjoyed watching people being tortured. . . . Now Bentham will obviously believe that torture is an evil to the person who suffers it, for torture is painful and pain is evil. But the pleasure that a group of sadists get from watching the torture is good, for pleasure, says Bentham, is good. So for a utilitarian, torture can be justified when the total pleasure produced outweighs the total pain produced. . . . We shall therefore institute a new TV show called "Torture of the Week." This is a live show in which real victims really do get tortured. . . . According to utilitarians, if there are enough viewers who are ecstatic at the sight of this torture, then their pleasure might outweigh the pain suffered by the victim. And if no other show on television has anything resembling its high ratings, then we can assume that putting on the torture show is not only justified, but positively morally obligatory.[3]

For Machiavelli, there just isn't enough of the good life to go around; hence it is better for the privileged few to have it in abundance than for anarchy to reign and for nobody to enjoy it.

In writing *The Prince,* Machiavelli was at least admitting that self-interest was adequate motivation for the leader. By ostentatiously parading his power and setting aside all notions of honest affection or humility, the Prince was an ideal Renaissance man, unencumbered by the restraints of a Christlike existence. For the utilitarians, however, self-interest is not limited to the leader, but is seen as the driving force of the entire populace. Rather than decry it as did Victor Hugo, the utilitarians *recommend* self-interest for all personal and public decisions.

Adam Smith's theory of laissez-faire, *which is the eighteenth-century basis of capitalism, maintains that the key to a sound economy is to allow each person the freedom to advance his or her own interest, for in this way everyone profits.*

In the eighteenth century, the economist Adam Smith (1723–1790) said that self-interest worked for the benefit of everyone. The business person is the indirect benefactor whose enterprise provides jobs for everyone else. Naturally the businessperson desires a profit, but in choosing a product to manufacture, market, and distribute, he or she is providing employment for all those who help. No one needs to think in terms other than personal profit. What holds an entire society together therefore is *mutual benefit.* Certainly it is not in anyone's interest to continue to make a product which does not sell.

Smith believed in the free market system—allowing all people to do what is best for themselves without interference from government. Smith's doctrine, which he called *laissez-faire*—meaning, literally, "allow to do"—remains the classic basis for capitalism. With perfect trust in the workings of the free market, each person can know she or he is part of a system working for the benefit of everyone. This market is self-correcting. If one entrepreneur becomes too greedy, seeks too much profit, she or he is automatically priced out of the market.

Smith's theory helped to raise the businessperson to new respectability. When aristocracy was in power and when craftspeople, servants, and others lower in the hierarchy were expected to know their place, the merchant was somehow excluded from the traditional categories. In both town and country, wealth or poverty had a fixed place: the gentry, the clergy, the farmers, the artisans—each did their job, relatively content with their assigned lot in life. Only merchants seemed not to fit, as they traveled to new lands, bringing back strange new products and making fortunes which ordinary people were not supposed to have. Merchants had previously been welcomed for their goods but had not been assigned an honored place in society.

Smith's idea—that business was at the heart of society, that it was responsible for making everything work and prosper—gave new dignity to the people who provided it. No longer was an ancient name the only standard for rank in society. Now *money* could provide entry to previously closed doors.

How realistic was Smith's theory? Has capitalism turned out to be the system which best accords with Smith's view of human nature? Are we driven solely by self-interest, by the desire to "get ahead"? Is turning a neat personal profit really at the heart of all our actions? What of Smith's certainty that it is right and good for each of us to try to fare better than anyone else, that competitiveness is healthy and aggressiveness the law of life? Smith was convinced that human economic aggression *always* corrected itself, like the market. The famous law of supply and demand would see to it that wealth could never rise to the top like cream. That self-interest underlies *many* of our actions would seem undeniable. That it is the only way to understand humanity may be open to serious debate.

Even more debatable is Smith's faith in the existence of what he called an "invisible hand" which binds together all people, even though they are engaged in competition with each other, a hand which maintains a balance of economic forces. Classical communism, based on the teachings of Karl Marx (see Chapter 16), also believes in the invisible hand, but not one born of the free market system. Marx's hand is the one which inevitably strikes down the moneyed classes when they become too fat and brings into being a classless society in which all property is publicly owned. Marx thought this would hap-

Smith believed the free market would always correct itself according to the law of supply and demand, but reality has not been equivalent to his vision. Producers of goods will often cut production when they are dissatisfied with the price structure. Competitors can also get together to "fix" prices.

Marx disagreed with Smith. For the public good the pursuit of self-interest must be curbed.

pen automatically, without blood or violence. Lenin, the philosophical architect of the Russian Revolution of 1917, added that the classless society needed a little help in the form of guns and sabers. Since then, the maintenance of a classless society in the USSR has required a strong totalitarian government, which does not appear to be classless at all.

But there are also questions about capitalism in its classic sense, in Adam Smith's sense. Political conservatives tend to be people who continue to long for laissez-faire, who believe that the free market system can and does work as long as the government keeps out of its affairs. Political liberals aren't so sure. They distrust the market and do not believe in its being self-correcting.

At the other end of the spectrum from Smith was John Maynard Keynes (1883–1946), an English economist, who more than any other economist influenced Franklin D. Roosevelt's "New Deal" economic policies, who maintained that an unmanaged free market system would never lead to society's goal of full employment. For one thing, Smith never took into account the principle of "collusion," by which entrepreneurs making the same goods could (and did) band together and set their own prices. Or what about cartels—huge corporations which could become the sole providers of certain goods and dictate what their price should be? Keynes believed the government's role in a free society was to interfere and exert controls over such tactics.

The so-called law of supply and demand has also not worked out exactly as Smith supposed it would. True, there are abundant examples which appear to support Smith's theory of a self-correcting market. Electronics goods like microwave ovens, video cassette recorders, compact disc players, and home computers all seem to cost less each year. One is tempted to say that prices come down as increasing demand makes entrepreneurs more willing to supply the market. Yet even in Smith's theory things are not supposed to work quite that way. Prices may well have come down because of a *glut:* The demand was there, and so everyone rushed to satisfy it.

As many economists see the matter, there are really two laws, the law of supply and the law of demand. The first can be stated thusly: Entrepreneurs are more likely to manufacture a good at the highest possible price. The second, thusly: Consumers are more likely to purchase a good at the lowest possible price. If these laws are accurate, then the market is not necessarily self-correcting. Smith did not foresee the possibility that *entrepreneurs might decide to cut production if they were dissatisfied with price structures.*

One can still argue that, with all its problems, the capitalist market system is still sound and the only system predicated on the truth of human nature: self-interest. In our society consumers for the most part seem to have what they want. If they can't afford it, they can go into debt (though heaven knows what the outcome of our indebtedness is going to be). But does the "law" of self-interest automatically ensure that people really want what they think they want? Or are we sometimes pressured into wanting things we don't need? To pay for our so-called self-interest many of us work at jobs which deaden the mind and seem to remove from life all of the pleasure, which is what self-interest is supposed to promote to begin with. Can the free market, in the long run, be expected to care about hazards to health and the quality of the human environment? How much pollution was there in Adam Smith's Scotland?

In the short run the self-interest of Bentham seems to work. Add up the pleasure, subtract the pain. In the short run the self-interest of Smith continues to be the driving force which sends most of us to college and determines what our "major" will be as well as the barometer by which we measure whether our classmates "made it" or not.

The Universal Sense of Ought

Despite the many believers in self-interest as motivating force, Immanuel Kant (1724–1804) is one philosopher who believed that people know and want to do what is right. In attempting to find universal laws for morality he too used mathematics. Just as laws of mathematics and logic work throughout time and space, he thought, so too there must be laws for moral behavior, truths which would be just as universally applicable to the actions of all human beings. He believed we are born with categories of truth into which we fit experience. One of them was what he called the Categorical Imperative, or Universal Sense of Ought, which was uncompromising and unconditional.

Kant based his ethics on the belief that people are to be treated as ends in themselves, not as means to an end.

Everyone does not do the right thing, but, for Kant, everyone knows what it is. To prove this point, Kant suggested that a person contemplating an action should will that it be universally required, since each of us knows intuitively what is universally right. If we planned to commit robbery, we should say: "It is right and just that all people steal." If as potential thieves we could *not* do this—and the Categorical Imperative, Kant was convinced, would prevent us from doing so—we would then have to regard ourselves as the single exception to a universal law. Everyone would agree on the absurdity of such a position. To put the matter a different way: Wrongdoers understand and accept the moral decency of most people. In fact, they *count* on it; otherwise they could never surprise their victims. Hence they are indirectly affirming the universality of the good and just.

Another rule had to do with human dignity: Treat people as an end in themselves rather than as a means to an end. That is, no one was to be cultivated as a friend in order to achieve future profit. (In today's world, this would prohibit us from making lists of "prospects" or business "contacts" from which an eventual sale or signing of a contract is our actual goal, while pretend-friendship is our means of achieving it.) People were not to be degraded. The logical argument might go this way:

Major Premise: All persons have dignity and are worthy of respect.
Minor Premise: X is a person.
Conclusion: Therefore, X has dignity and is worthy of respect.

When we recognize that Kant died before the abolition of slavery, prostitution, and the abuse of workers, we can see how revolutionary were his ideas of universal laws for the treatment of people as people rather than for personal gain.

Kant was also concerned with the motive behind a good action. Not satisfied with just the end result, or "bottom line," he insisted that actions should be based on principle. To give reluctantly or because an act of charity would increase one's reputation was to destroy the goodness in the act of giving.

Many historians of philosophy view Kant as, in fact, the last major thinker to bring to philosophy a total vision of rational and moral order. Since Kant, philosophy has become either poetic declamation about the rights of the individual or, in our century, the art of minutely analyzing meanings—the art of getting the question right even if no answer appears on the horizon. In the opinion of these analytical philosophers, moral issues do not exist, since the terminology used to formulate them has no clear meaning. There remain, however, a few philosophers who decry the waning interest in morality as a crucial subject of inquiry.

The State and the Moral Life

Those who say self-interest is the source of moral values are also saying that the moral life is the good life. Machiavelli believed that it was good, and therefore moral, for the ruler to use almost any means available to keep his subjects in line. Utilitarians believed that it was good, and therefore moral, for both individuals and society to satisfy the greatest possible number of their wants.

The role played by the state relative to the good life has always been a concern to moralists. For Machiavelli, both the state and the individual cannot enjoy the good life equally. People are greedy and selfish and thus cannot be left to their own devices. A clever and manipulative ruler deprives them of what we might consider their rights, but presumably for their own good. There just isn't enough of

There is no such thing as Society. There are individual men and women and there are families.

Margaret Thatcher

the good life to go around; hence it is better for the privileged few to have it in abundance than for anarchy to reign and for *nobody* to enjoy it. The common person will have to be satisfied with the little favors that may trickle down.

The utilitarians took just the opposite approach: An individual trying to realize the fulfillment of desires must be granted the maximum amount of freedom. The state is there to see to it that conditions remain favorable for the pursuit of happiness, which the utilitarians defined as pleasure. Utilitarian philosophers created a political party whose major platform issue was civil rights.

Over 2000 years before the utilitarians came into being, Aristotle had formulated a clear-cut philosophy of both the good life and the role of the state, radically different from the utilitarians' in its basic assumption—a philosophy which we would do well to revisit, because it may give us some insight into some of our basic problems.

Aristotle shared two things with the utilitarians. He agreed (or would have if he had known about them) that the goal of life is the happiness of the individual and that the function of the state is to promote that goal. Why then do we call his philosophy radically different? The answer should be obvious. *He did not define happiness as they did.*

In Chapter 12, which deals with various theories of happiness, the reader will find a fuller discussion of the Aristotelian view, which is one of the major ideas contributed to humanity by any philosopher. What we need to know here is that happiness—or the good life—meant for Aristotle the satisfaction of every possible human *need*, not want! The utilitarians made no such distinction. If you wanted something, they assumed, you needed it. The logic of their position leads us inevitably, for instance, to the conclusion that for alcoholics access to the greatest possible amount of alcohol constitutes the good life, and that, moreover, it is morally wrong to deprive them of what they "need."

Aristotle believed there were universal human needs, such as those for shelter, food, love, wealth (by which he meant only sufficient means, not all the money you could ever hope to have), knowledge, and, above all, virtue (by which he meant the recognition that one's life is a stable, balanced one, emphasizing satisfaction in moderation rather than excess). To pursue one need—say, for food—to the exclusion of another—say, for knowledge—would be to fail in one's goal of fulfilling all needs. Achieving this goal of fulfilling all needs is achieving happiness. Thus happiness is not equated with the attainment of all possible pleasures.

We can see clearly that the utilitarian concern for human rights was predicated on a pleasure-seeking, not need-fulfilling, principle. Since nobody knows how many pleasures are "enough" or if indeed one can even speak meaningfully of "enough pleasures," the state has what could amount to an impossible job ahead of it: ensuring the right of each person to an infinite number of pleasures. If, however, we are talking about the moderate satisfaction of universal needs, then the state has a chance not only to fulfill its mission, but to be the only agency that can "spread the moderation around," so to speak. The state becomes involved in the proper distribution of wealth and all the natural resources people need in order to live, as well as guaranteeing the right of each person to the best possible education.

An American philosopher who also believed people had a right to fulfill their needs was Henry David Thoreau (1817–1862), but he was no Aristotelian as far as his views on the state were concerned. In fact, he began his famous essay *Civil Disobedience* with these strident words:

> I heartily accept the motto,—"That government is best which governs least"; and I should like to see it acted up to more rapidly and systematically. Carried out, it finally amounts to this, which I also believe,—"That government is best which governs not at all."

Thoreau would probably have agreed with the utilitarians that the state had no right to interfere with the right of the individual to pursue the maximum amount of happiness possible, but he would certainly not have accepted their equation of happiness with pleasure. Indeed, the objective of *Walden, or Life in the Woods* (1854), his most famous work, was to persuade the reader that true happiness consists of simplifying one's desires, ridding oneself of the greed for material possessions, and learning to live in close harmony with nature.

Thoreau believed the world was meant to be inhabited by natural people in natural surroundings, not institutionalized people in bureaucratic surroundings.

As the most famous loner in American letters, Thoreau believed emphatically that the world was meant to be inhabited by natural people in natural surroundings, not institutionalized people in bureaucratic surroundings. He believed that nature, having been "in business" far longer than the human race, knew best what was good for each species, including humanity. If one would detach oneself from the unnatural structures of society, retreat (as he did) to the solitude of the woods, and listen to the inner voices whispering the dictates of nature, one would lead a sane, balanced, and serene existence, free from the desire for unnecessary pleasures.

Since to live naturally often collided with governmental restrictions, Thoreau became an activist, vigorously opposing certain government policies, including the administration's willingness to pursue fugitive slaves and return them to their "owners." He personally assisted runaway slaves but did not join the abolition movements, because he was by nature not a joiner. He also refused to pay a Massachusetts poll tax because the revenue was being used to support the war against Mexico, cheerfully electing to go to jail, a place he recommended for all people of conscience. Overload the jails, he advocated, in order to demonstrate opposition to oppressive policies.

Aristotle and Thoreau would, however, have come together on one crucial issue: *Moral values begin with individual need.* They differed in their philosophy of state. Aristotle wanted the state to assume a dominant role in maintaining a well-ordered society; Thoreau believed a strong government was an unnatural, hence evil, institution, desirous of feeding its own hunger, not concerned for the welfare of the citizen. Since the dream of neither philosopher has ever been remotely realized, we can perhaps never know which direction yields the better results. Aristotle's state might well become corrupt by virtue of its own power; Thoreau's governmentless state might well see anarchy run wild in the streets. May *every* natural instinct be trusted?

Moral Values and Religious Authority

O Lord, thou hast searched me, and known me.
Thou knowest my downsitting and mine uprising,
thou understandest my thought afar off.
Thou compassest my path and my lying down, and
art acquainted with all my ways.
For there is not a word in my tongue, but lo,
Lord, thou knowest it altogether.

The above words begin Psalm 139 (King James Version of the Bible). They could not have been part of the Greek religious belief because they refer to God's ability to see into the thoughts of the Psalmist. The Greek gods were powerful, able to cause trouble, often unpredictable and difficult to please. But Greek writers did not refer to their gods' ability to search or know or be acquainted with the unspoken words of the believer.

There is therefore no place to hide, and for the Jew, Christian, or Moslem who believes in an omniscient God, Glaucon's ring of invisibility provides no protection against a Deity who knows all. The young lady who was pondering whether to pay the missed charge on her restaurant bill would have no problem if she were religious, because she would not be limited to the social restraints described by Glaucon. Nor does her reputation with the surrounding public matter: Her conscience would remind her that God knows what she is feeling and thinking; she must be honest and do what she has been taught is right because she is always being watched. God's knowledge is all-pervasive. His laws are immutable and not to be questioned.

What is called the Old Testament, or the Hebrew Bible, contains detailed commandments on property, sacrifice, charity, punishment of crime, treatment of strangers, behavior toward servants, and

The Old Testament gave us an absolute morality built upon laws handed down by God.

the preservation of customs. A case could be made that the Old Testament is the cornerstone of much of civilized behavior, the basis of our fundamental moral laws, though some Biblical historians would insist that the laws of the Old Testament cover mainly overt actions and are therefore civil rather than moral in the strictest sense. Harold H. Watts, in *The Modern Reader's Guide to the Bible,* urges us, however, not to make superficial contrasts, as if the Old Testament recommends only the

> law of retaliation which allows for taking an eye for an eye and a tooth for a tooth. We may judge, superficially, that this atttitude was chiefly superseded by the willingness to turn the other cheek taught by Christ . . . [but] to dwell exclusively on the defects of the legalistic approach to the problems of behavior is to underestimate the need for law. It is to miss the significance, in the history of man, of the appearance of any code of law, whether Babylonian, Hebrew, or the Byzantine one promulgated by Justinian (483–565 A.D.). Though to later stages of human development a code of law may seem to offer many barriers to freedom and spontaneity, at the time of its invention or compilation it was a very great support to mankind; it held him up and allowed him to gather together the strength to step forward toward the later attitudes that we say are superior because they are inward and place emphasis on intention rather than deed.[4]

There were, of course, laws as such before the emergence of the Hebrew Bible. There had to have been. Yet we may assume they were arbitrary things designed to keep subjugated people under control. The Bible law is universal, binding on all people, not because a ruler says so, but because God says so. The much-cited "eye for an eye" code was perhaps necessary at the time for the preservation of the Hebraic tribes, but it is hardly the only law we find in the Bible. The Ten Commandments prohibit murder, theft, the desecration of marriage, not to mention the decision to go off and find another god whose laws may be less demanding. The Sermon on the Mount, recorded in Matthew: 5, adds prohibitions against evil intent but in no way invalidates the laws already set down in the Bible. How could it? God the Father is the same being in both books.

The important point is that Biblical law covers both personal and social morality. It preserves the tribe, the group, the city, the state, the nation; but it is not a social contract that can be broken if enough people decide to do so or a legislated bill that can be repealed. It does not serve the private needs of the ruler. Commoner and king share in common the ability to sin against the law, and both, if they do, incur the risk of punishment by God, which has remained for centuries a more powerful deterrent than society's punishments.

In the Bible punishment is physical, taking place here on earth. Adam and Eve are forced to leave the Garden of Eden. Job is given a severe tongue-lashing by God for his sins of self-pity and resentment toward his maker. And, of course, in the time of Noah everybody except for one family is wiped out in the flood. The morality of the Bible is intended to govern behavior in this world and is on the whole *group* oriented, setting forth rules for the family, the tribe, a society.

What is called the New Testament tends to focus on the individual. It says that, since God can see into your heart, sins of thought as well as deed will be dealt with at the proper time.

> Ye have heard that it was said by them of old time: Thou shall not kill, and whosoever shall kill shall be in danger of the judgment. But I say unto you, That whosoever is angry with his brother without a cause shall be in danger of the judgment.

One may presume that Jesus is here referring to the traditional concept of judgment as a penalty to be paid in this life for earthly wrongdoing. There are Biblical scholars, however, who believe that Jesus was talking about inner retribution—the judgment of one's own conscience.

As the centuries rolled on, beliefs in heaven and hell became the basis for ideas of rewards or punishments as further underpinnings of moral values. Dante popularized heaven and hell in *The Divine Comedy* (c. 1380). The personal inner hell suffered by the sinner is powerfully dramatized for us in the novel *Crime and Punishment* (1866) of Fyodor Dostoevsky. Today, emphasis in religion is likely to be more than ever upon psychological guilt and torment, something already there in Persian poet and philosopher Omar Khayyám's famous work *The Rubáiyát*, written sometime in the twelfth century:

> *I sent my Soul through the Invisible,*
> *Some letter of that After-life to spell:*
> *And by and by my Soul returned to me,*
> *And answered "I Myself am Heav'n and Hell":*

One cannot imagine where any of us would be in our consciousness of human behavior without the powerful influences of Biblical morality, with or without a professed belief in God. Biblical morality is seldom absent from the pages of the daily newspaper, though it continues to undergo reinterpretations. Think of the many versions "Thou shalt not kill" has been given in debates about abortion, contraception, euthanasia, and war.

Zealots

Truly devout believers, perceiving a daily struggle with Satan, often take it as their responsibility to assist others along the path of righteousness. Early Puritan church leaders rudely awakened those who slept during long church services. Even the Salem witch trials ostensibly had salvation as the underlying justification for persecuting and then hanging those found guilty of traffic with Satan.

The Puritans lived in tight communities. Everyone knew everyone else's business. Puritan morality instantly became the community morality. In the witch hunts the Puritans were linking themselves to an ancient tradition, stretching back to long before the Judeo-Christian era—a tradition in which the community possessed one mind when it came to right and wrong. Evildoers had to be driven out, or else the entire community would suffer the vengeance of some deity.

In modern communities some of the same tradition survives. Certainly we note lingering reminders of the Puritan public moral conscience in the advice people give to others on how to live their lives and how to raise their children. Whether conscious of it or not, the advice-givers serve as guardians of the dominant, mainstream morality, which has had both religious and communal sanctions for so long that no one dreams of questioning it. Instant guilt often accrues to the parent who is told by a neighbor: "Far be it from me to tell you what to do about your own children, but if that were my daughter, I'd want to know who she's with until all hours of the night."

If such moral advice is acceptable to those who receive it, if it does indeed create guilt, then the public conscience is not necessarily a bad thing or an invasion of privacy. Some parents probably do not know what to do with their children. Often the children themselves sense the confusion of their parents and secretly wish someone would exert strong moral authority over them. The public conscience, which exists in every community in the world, acts as a check upon flagrantly antisocial behavior.

Sometimes, however, a relatively small group of true believers claims to represent the public conscience and sees its mission as changing the behavior of others. We have all encountered such true believers, the zealots of the world. A *zealot* is someone with so much enthusiasm to effect change that he or she may be called a fanatic. Zealots are motivated by either religious fervor or secular zeal. Religious zealots are so certain of salvation that they want to convert everyone to the true faith. Zealots carry their message to the public in a variety of forms. Some stand on street corners and urge passersby to accept a pamphlet; some go door to door, determined to talk to people in their homes; some are on television, sharing their religious stories with a nationwide audience; and some are in the next seat on a bus or airplane, or even among the strangers one meets at a party.

No matter what the topic, the zealot will usually find a way to turn the conversation to the overriding topic on her or his mind: religious salvation and the benefits of a particular approach. Frequently a contrast is made between life before and after the zealot was saved. In the past, life was empty, sin and temptation were easily followed, but there was no permanent joy. But after the experience described by the zealot, everything changed. Now life has meaning, activities are tied to the church, anyone who has not joined is missing what is most worth living for.

Sincerity is not the issue, though certainly some orators seem to equate conversion with donation. The television evangelists are zealots when they promise that in return for money the new member will find solutions to earthly problems. Testimonials seek new converts: "Listen to the story of a young woman without a job, unable to sell her car, feeling lost . . . until she sent in her pledge and on that same day was offered a job, found a buyer for her car . . ." What is at issue is the insistence on converting others. To those who object, the zealot responds with an example: "If you found something good in clothing or a restaurant wouldn't you want to share it with your friends? Well, my religion is good and I want to share it with you." The zealot's fervor may even reach such a pitch that it becomes impossible for the zealot to be friends with anyone of another faith, or of no faith.

There also exists a kind of human being we might label a *secular zealot.* This is a person who sees very clearly what other people must do and the values they must hold—a missionary. To the secular zealot, morality is never a private matter. It is *what needs to prevail if the world is to be saved.* While such persons can and often do do much good for society, they can easily go to extremes and become single-minded, obsessed to a fanatical degree with particular causes, unwilling to see other sides of an issue. The secular zealot sees public issues always as potential reform movements. Causes vary from one decade to another, but they usually have certain things in common: (1) they are formulated without specific examples; (2) they include the words *should* or *ought* somewhere in their lexicon; and (3) they cite a secular authority such as a survey or study of social conditions, or the opinions of a prominent journalist.

To secular zealots others are immoral when they fail to participate loudly and clearly in efforts to change untenable conditions and unjust laws. Though fanaticism is usually not fruitful under any circumstances, we cannot afford to turn away from issues such as the need for AIDS research, conservation efforts, a redefinition of national energy policies, a closer look at government spending priorities, and a change of attitudes toward traditional sex roles. Even if one disagrees with a zealot's cause, the raising of the question at all is beneficial for society. We need periodically to consider just where we stand on matters like capital punishment, mental illness, censorship, educational standards, and right to life.

If zealots represent only a portion of the public moral conscience, it is usually a highly audible portion. They stir up more often than they stabilize, but one might well argue that the price of stability is all too often the suppression of healthy dissent.

History records the memory of important zealots who have contributed mightily to the preservation of human dignity, who have become fortresses against the public moral conscience when that has meant majority rule right or wrong. During the last century the great libertarian John Stuart Mill (1806–1873) wrote a pivotal essay entitled "The Tyranny of the Majority." In it he asserts that all people must be allowed to do what they like—up to a point. The majority may not justify restraint on the grounds that it is in the best interest of those whose rights are denied:

> The object of this essay is to assert one very simple principle, as entitled to govern absolutely the dealings of society with the individual in the way of compulsion and control, whether the means used be physical force in the form of legal penalties, or the moral coercion of public opinion. That principle is, that the sole end for which mankind are warranted, individually or collectively, in interfering with the liberty of action of any of their number, is self-protection. That is the only purpose for which power can be rightfully exercised over any member of a civilized community, against his will, is to prevent harm to others. His own good, either physical or moral, is not a sufficient warrant.

Still, Mill's position does not take care of all matters. Who decides what constitutes or truly threatens the "self-protection" of the majority? What constitutes harm to oneself as opposed to others? Are people who abuse their bodies through use of alcohol or narcotics really harming only themselves? And what about people who smoke in public places without bothering to ask permission from those around them? If such people become ill from practices which harm "only" themselves, are they entitled to the support of family and public institutions such as county hospitals? If "self-protection" does indeed warrant interfering with someone's liberty, who decides which methods of protection are justified? For some, even violence against the transgressor would be nothing more than the efforts of a civilized community to preserve its standards.

A champion of human rights, John Stuart Mill believed the only excuse for exercising power over an individual against her or his will was to prevent harm to others.

What is morality in any given time or place? It is what the majority then and there happen to like and immorality is what they dislike.

Alfred North Whitehead

"Of Course"

An awareness of right and wrong begins for most of us in childhood, with the acclaim or disapproval of the parents who observe our actions. In the earliest years, comments directed toward the child are almost always moral, are matters of "yes" and "no." There is praise for learning to drink from a cup or climbing stairs without help, and anger for touching hot stoves, being rude to grandma, or crossing the street in traffic. Originally, childhood morality centers on survival. Later on it branches out and becomes the socialization process.

Disgust may greet a child who breaks things, gets dirty, refuses to share a toy. Almost invariably, parental disapproval comes to equal "bad," perhaps for a lifetime. Being required to kiss grandparents, whether one wants to or not, teaches family attitudes toward the elderly and puts a restraint on preoccupation with self.

Among the rules learned are some not directly pointed out to the child. Children observe and listen to adults fighting with and praising each other, and discussing the behavior of other people. From these observations come many of the automatic assumptions of later life, assumptions which become rules of courtesy, order, or concern for the opinion of others. Children who often hear, "What will the neighbors say?" may for the rest of their lives have difficulty getting over the feeling that someone is watching and that somehow apologies are always in order.

Parental moral authority is sharp, direct, and to the point. Often a sudden blow is the stinging reminder that the authority is over five feet tall and has very powerful eyes—and hands. In school, the teacher and to some extent the other students also exert an authority which helps to form the unexamined assumptions of later life. People sometimes go through their entire lives thinking that such learned behavior is "natural," to be taken for granted. Unexamined assumptions underlie statements prefaced by "Of course . . ."

Subtle, pervasive, and hard to pin down, the authoritarianism of the "Of course" moral code grows in intensity as we approach adulthood and often stays with us for a long time, if not forever:

> "Of course, there is no excuse for being late."
> "Of course, you may not stay out until midnight."
> "Of course, you may not date someone of a different
> religion."
> "Of course, you must take required subjects. Why else
> would they be required?"
> "This is your very first year to vote, darling. Of course, you
> will vote for the family's party."

The family circle "of course" is a swift and direct way of dealing with violations, ranging from corporal punishment in the early years to the steady application of guilt in adolescence. Passing one's majority does not guarantee safety from family justice. Who does not know of close kin who haven't exchanged a word in 40 years because of some now-forgotten breach of family ethics?

School is even swifter in inculcating morality. Posted signs everywhere inform us of what will "of course" be done and who may do it. Report cards and honors assemblies reinforce, reward, or depress. Less obvious is classroom structure, with a standing leader watching the suspect people while a favored group is approvingly called upon to read or go to the chalkboard to demonstrate expertise before the disgraced and the envious. Children know, without being directly told, who are expected to achieve. At an early age they learn to admire or envy achievement, to size themselves up on the achievement scale: *Hey, what did you get?* And often they carry into life these initial attitudes toward themselves as worthy or unworthy beings. The sense that the world is ready to approve or disapprove or that we at last no longer care about approval underlies many of our moral choices in later life.

"Fortunate" are those whose early and later years are so much the same that they never have to adjust. Even more fortunate are those who in later life recognize all the early, unquestioned assumptions—all the "of course" statements they once wore like summer clothing—to discard or retain them in the light of mature reflection.

Popular Slogans

When moral philosophy is taught, sloganism is seldom mentioned as an important source of values. Yet the *moral aphorism*—a concisely phrased, eminently quotable axiom—is so much a part of our daily lives that we can ill afford not to give it consideration. Professional philosophers probably assume they themselves are beyond the influence of slogans. But the rest of us need to be reminded of how deeply rooted are the ramifications of the homespun ethics anyone can turn to when a situation involving moral choice arises.

Still with us—but of declining impact—are some basic slogans deriving from the Calvinist beginnings of our country. There are aphorisms which extol not only the dignity but the Christian reputability of hard work: *Idle hands are the devil's workshop.* Others, including *A stitch in time saves nine,* discourage laziness and advocate careful planning. In the days before rampant inflation, we had *A penny saved is a penny earned,* but now we are more likely either to want information about smart investments or to spend the penny before it decreases in value even more.

If, as the sociologist Max Weber (1864–1920) believed, there is a documentable relationship between the Protestant work ethic and the rise of capitalism, then the numerous slogans encouraging self-interest as an acceptable motive for actions are also legacies of our Puritan past, even as they seem especially applicable to present society.

Looking out for Number One is a modernized version of a fundamental capitalist tenet, which holds that it is not only acceptable but right and just that people act so as to advance their own cause. The father of economics, Adam Smith (1723–1790), indicated that, in serving themselves, people really benefited all of society. This attitude has never met serious challenge from the vast majority.

Charity begins at home has been around for centuries and is still going strong, especially in these days of reaction against continual pleas from nonprofit organizations for "tax-deductible" (Number One implied here as well) contributions. The time-tested aphorism is always appropriate to justify turning a deaf ear to sometimes desperate appeals for support.

The idea that if we find money or some other valuable possession we are not obliged to return it to the owner, or even undertake a reasonable search for the owner, is adequately covered by the enduringly popular *Finders keepers, losers weepers,* an axiom which also has rhyme, hence literary tradition, going for it.

As either the rate of inflation or unemployment figures accelerate, as jobs become harder to get and hold, we note a rise in overt cynicism about the importance of altruism. In a game of economic musical chairs, when some must in the course of events wind up on the floor, there are whimsical-seeming but deadly earnest perversions of axioms which once advocated concern for others. Thus the Golden Rule becomes *Do unto others before they do unto you.*

Should we doubt for a moment the morality of self-interest, there are aphorisms to justify a life dedicated to materialistic pursuits, such as the ever-present *Eat, drink, and be merry, for tomorrow we die* and the insistent *Nothing succeeds like success.* In our society we cannot readily abandon the quest for fame and fortune without experiencing pangs of guilt.

Human-growth-and-development specialists, appalled that people dislike examining their actions too closely, causing them to resist change, offer substitutes for what they consider dangerous slogans such as "I like you just the way you are." In recent years they have given us *This is the first day of the rest of your life,* an aphorism immediately countered by the famous poster of the forlorn dog telling us, "If this is the first day of the rest of my life, I'm in trouble." Rather than support the idea of change and growth, popular morality prefers *Hang in there!* not to mention the classic denial of growth: *The more things change, the more they remain the same.*

Finally, despite the consciousness-raising efforts of those who herald a new dawn of sexual equality, the slogans continue to support chauvinism, and women who object haven't gotten new ones on the charts yet. Perhaps we hear less of *It's a wise father who knows his*

We are living at a time when the principle of looking after No. 1 is widely proclaimed as a respectable principle of personal and public morality.

Bishop of Birmingham, England

own child, but there seems no let-up from *Isn't that just like a woman?* or the more subtle, but no less sexist, *Leave it to a woman!* This slogan extols the virtue of intuition, without directly confronting the notion of the "supremacy" of male rationalism. We can only hope that the future will bring new slogans that do not rely on old stereotypes. But none of us may live to hear that *A man's place is in the home.*

Work

Preoccupation with work is so central to our culture it crops up everywhere. We hear of the millionaire businessman who doesn't know how to play and who falls victim to stress; we have denigrating terms for those who don't work: lazy, bum, loafer; and there are the resentments of those who do work directed against those who don't (or won't). Work is certainly crucial to an understanding of contemporary morality. The power of the concept is found everywhere.

One of the most poignant reminders of work's fierce hold on us is contained in this passage from a novel by Isabel Allende, *Of Love and Shadows* (1987). Looking at the body of his brother Javier, Francisco, the hero, tries to understand what would have led the man to kill himself. Javier has been unable to find work after the military authorities blacklist him. Then Francisco finds a connection between the family work ethic and his brother's sense of worth:

> He remembered his father's lesson: work as a source of pride. Idleness was foreign to the family. In the Leal household, holidays and even vacations were spent in some worthwhile undertaking. The family had had its difficult moments, but they had never dreamed of accepting charity, even from those they had previously helped.[5]

Javier, a biologist, tries to find any kind of work, but the authorities block his efforts. Hours of waiting and rejection result in humiliation and sleeplessness:

> Without a job, he gradually lost his identity. He would have accepted any offers, however mean the pay, because he desperately needed to feel useful. As a man without employment, he was an outsider, anonymous, ignored by all because he was no longer productive, and that was the measure of a man in the world he lived in. . . . The day his youngest son put on the kitchen table the few coins he had earned walking rich men's dogs, Javier cringed like a cornered animal. Since that moment he never looked anyone in the eyes; he sank into total despair.[6]

One need not be as desperate as Javier to sense the importance of work. It affects our attitudes toward time, ambition, respectability, appearance, marriage, and satisfaction with ourselves. Even retired people boast of being exhausted from their many activities, as if leisure time must be "spent" as actively as paid employment. Time must not be "wasted," as it would be if one were to sit around "just" thinking. The worker who is satisfied with a job may be questioned about the future—"Where do you go from here?"—as if one must continue to climb. Parents boast of children's occupations with high earning potential and worry about an announced intention to do something fulfilling in other ways. Many never examine even the *benefit* of the work they do, whether it is making cigarettes or assisting in the operating room; work, no matter what kind, is done for the paycheck rather than the consequences.

Literature is full of scenes recording the importance of work, ambition, and the appearance of success. In Shakespeare's *Hamlet,* Polonius tells his son Laertes to dress well, to look good: "Costly thy habit as thy purse can bear. But not expressed in fancy—rich, not gaudy. For the apparel oft proclaims the man." This long speech is filled with one parental reminder after another and concludes "To thine own self be true," a difficult goal if Laertes has memorized all the other advice about choosing friends, avoiding quarrels, and lending money.

Polonius was not meant to be one of Shakespeare's heroes. Throughout the play he is presented as a windy fellow, and it is probable that Shakespeare had other measurements besides clothing for judging the worth of a man. But today, national magazines urge that we not only have the qualities of a good worker, but that we seriously "dress for success."

In 1941 Budd Schulberg wrote what he thought was a warning in *What Makes Sammy Run?,* a satiric portrait of a hustling little man with more nerve than creativity who was able to make a fortune by exploiting his friends, lying his way to the top, and winning everything but true affection. The author thought at the time that he was writing a morality tale by showing readers what an awful life his main character was living. Now when Schulberg meets college seniors, he says, they *thank* him for providing them with a role model for success!

In our democratic society we do not yet introduce people by their (or their husband's) title, as some cultures have done: "May I present Lawyer So and So, Mrs. Engineer Such and Such." At the same time, one's work is apt to be mentioned soon after one's name, and today that work is often elevated to the title of "profession," once granted only after years of study and dedication. Today, we hear about the "profession of realtor" or "professional hairdresser," with the term *professional* perhaps meaning "dedicated to something outside the making of money," as a remnant from the old days when kinds of work were set apart from ordinary business and understood to be an identity rather than a means of gainful employment. We are therefore disappointed to hear about doctors unwilling to put in extra time when patient care requires it, or unwilling to testify against another doctor accused of wrongdoing. We hold them to a higher standard than the clock-watching clerk. We would like the professions to be morally upstanding and we are therefore far more outraged when a lawyer dips into a trust fund or a professor claims credit for another scholar's effort than we are when we read about a holdup in a local store.

We may also be disappointed at our own jobs. Somehow, despite all the importance society places on work, we may find ourselves one more replaceable part in a large machine, our name barely recognized by the receptionist, even after we have put in years of service. The gulf widens between "us," the workers, and "them," the managers. Conspiracies abound: hints of plotting to reduce costs in a way that will adversely affect the product or service (deferred maintenance on commercial aircraft, for example); workers retaliating by using up sick leave, taking longer coffee breaks, making too many personal phone calls, failing to work hard unless directly supervised, petty theft of paper clips as well as time.

A reason often cited for the double standard when it comes to the morality of work is the growing separation of workers from the products of their labor. Can the assembly-line worker who fastens engine bolts into place all day long ever point to a particular automobile and think, "I have a share in that beauty"? Computer experts may take pride in having figured out a way to save the company millions of dollars, but there is no actual thing standing there to represent their creativity—nothing except the computer itself, which somebody else, or some corporation, has created. We are fast becoming a nation specializing in services not products. Information-gathering is an end in itself rather than a means of communicating about splendid new inventions like a better mousetrap or a sturdier log cabin. For the most part we are engaged in endless comings and goings: receiving a piece of paper at the end of the week, depositing it in a bank, and writing out pieces of paper to send to others. The tangible product of our labors is often a monthly bank statement.

On Making Moral Judgments

After reviewing the various sources of moral values, we should be able to make a moral judgment in a particular instance. However, there is a very wide gap between knowing what moral philosophies there are and being able to evaluate an action with a high degree of certainty. Why then do we bother looking at moral philosophies at all? The answer is that they provide a basis for making meaningful choices by which we morally judge ourselves as well as others. We are going to make moral judgments anyway, so why not do so within a clear context which we can defend? Moral confusion about our judgments surely leads to moral confusion about our actions, and we find ourselves in the unfortunate situation of trying to defend what we imperfectly understand.

Nonetheless, there will always be grounds for much debate. Let us look at a hypothetical situation which clearly involves an action that can be morally judged. Suppose there is a college professor who, having been at his post for many years, is a typical example of what we call "burnout." He regularly assigns homework but never talks about the material, never tests his students to find out whether they have read their assignments or what they have gleaned from the reading. He asks for writing but never returns it. No syllabus exists for the course. He spends most of the period making jokes, and leaves early.

His easy-going, jaunty behavior is a cover-up for a deep fear that he isn't really getting away with anything, that his students are biding their time before they visit the dean or even the president. To forestall their protest he announces his grading policy: A for those who attend regularly and B for those who attend sometimes. He has followed this policy for a number of years and has received no complaints.

Some colleagues, however, believe there is a profound moral issue involved. They discuss it from the point of view of three well-known moral philosophies:

> *Self-interest.*   In the short run the professor is morally
>   blameless. He has managed to survive, and he is not
>   harming the students, because he gives good grades.
> *Kant.*   He has violated the universal sense of ought. Can
>   he will that his policy be universal? That all grades
>   should be based on attendance? He would hardly say so.
>   Would he or anyone else wish to patronize the graduates
>   of a medical school that conferred degrees based on at-
>   tendance only?
> *Religion.*   God is watching the professor and knows his
>   intentions, knows that his grading policy is only a ma-
>   neuver to save his job. He is morally wrong and will suf-
>   fer in one way or another.

We could add Plato's Glaucon to the debate. No doubt considering himself strictly a realist, Glaucon would say that the professor, having artfully concealed his motives, has become invisible, like Gyges. Having discovered—as so many have—a way to be invisible without a magic ring, he cannot be expected to have any moral integrity. The latter does not exist anyway.

Others might argue that, since each of us is entitled to life, liberty, and the pursuit of happiness, the good grades will contribute toward scholarships and better jobs for the students, who, after all, were not guilty of anything. What would you have them do—go to the dean and refuse to accept grades they hadn't earned?

Meanwhile, back at the restaurant, the woman with the cheap lunch check is aware (1) that reason decrees she pay the missing $3; (2) that self-interest tells her to pay the actual check and slip away "invisibly"; (3) that years of working for low pay and an insensitive company justify anything she can get away with. Her old Sunday school teacher might remind her that God is watching. But doesn't He, for heaven's sake, have more to do than worry about this little matter of $3?

MORALITY IN ACTION

The complexity of making moral judgments in the matter of both the professor and the lunch lady offers one reason among many which could be cited for the shift some moral philosophers have made—a shift from a value-centered system of thought which is supposed to apply to any situation, to one which revolves around the examination of the three major components in a moral issue: *the value, the action, and the consequences.*

The professor's behavior, unknown to administration and students, is immoral if his personal values are the sole issue. But what happens when we consider the consequences of giving someone high grades? True, these may help some students in the short run, but will not reality finally catch up with others in the long run? If so, are we not making a moral judgment based on the outcome rather than the principle? If we decide the outcome is more important, then do we say that, in the case of a really good student who receives an A for the wrong reasons, the professor is to be praised, not blamed?

There are those with an action-centered morality who say that some universal moral standards are still possible, and those who say that moral judgments are pretty much confined to time, place, and circumstance and will thus change continually.

The Lifeboat

Socrates believed that moral values are eternal and unchanging no matter what the situation. In our time, however, a new breed of moralist has come forth with the contention that the specific situation changes the weight of the value. The *situationalist* believes that moral choice has to be examined in relation to circumstances, motivation, consequences, and the numbers of people who can benefit from or be harmed by it.

There is a famous legal case involving the aftermath of the sinking of a great ocean liner. A high-ranking ship's officer found himself on a lifeboat which could accommodate no more than 25 persons. Amid the panic and desperation many more than 25 people attempted to climb on board. The officer instructed several crew members to throw the "extras" into the sea to ensure the survival of those already on the lifeboat. In a few instances those who resisted were shot. Later the officer was tried for murder, found guilty, but subsequently pardoned. The case attracted widespread attention. Some observers pointed out that the issue was not whether the murders were justified, but whether the method of selecting those who remained on the lifeboat was fair. The officer, as a matter of fact, had tried to restrict the deaths to men only, but the suggestion was made that straws should have been drawn for the "honor" of leaving the lifeboat.

In another famous case, two men and a young boy were marooned at sea on a life raft. Recognizing that the child was clearly weakened and near death, the men decided to end his life so that he could be eaten and thus ensure *their* survival. They too were found guilty but were pardoned.

The situationalist is fond of citing such cases, for they are the stuff of which real life is made. Can we say that murder is always wrong? Or that cannibalism is never justified under any circumstances? Does the need to survive take precedence over any other need?

What of the man whose wife was ill with cancer and in great pain, who had exhausted almost all of his funds and could no longer afford the price of a certain drug the wife needed in order to ease her pain? What of the additional fact that the druggist, knowing her need, decided to take advantage of the situation and charge an exorbitant amount for the medication? Suppose the desperate husband broke into the store and stole the drug. Suppose he were caught in the act, arrested, and brought to trial. Ought the judge to take the husband's motivation into account? The unfairness of the price? Or is stealing always stealing?

The situationalist knows that decisions of this sort are not easy. To say that murder or stealing in one instance is not the same as murder or stealing in another gives the judge an awesome responsibility. Yet to argue the reverse—that murder and stealing are never justified and are never to be condoned—can lead to miscarriages of justice.

The advantage of situationalism, say its advocates, is that each problem is examined on its own merits and not in terms of an abstract moral code devised long ago to fit a very different world. The disadvantages, say its critics, are that situations can be interpreted to some-

The situationalist *says that moral choice depends upon circumstances, motivations, consequences, and the numbers of people who can benefit or be harmed.*

one's private advantage and that unfortunate precedents are always being created. If it was morally permissible for the two men to eat the young boy, what would prevent some future survivors on a raft from taking a life long before it was evident that that life was nearly over?

How the Existentialist Views Morality

Morality can be, as we have seen, a matter of law, supported by the authority of God; a product of unexamined assumptions from our early years; a result of society's attitudes; an attempt to follow a slogan derived from a variety of sources; an effort to calculate pleasure and pain mathematically; or a rational conclusion about what constitutes universal righteous behavior. Some philosophers have insisted that human beings are naturally inclined to do the right thing, while others have claimed that humans are naturally selfish, even ruthless, unless carefully watched. The second of these positions was the one taken long ago by Glaucon.

We now come to the contemporary moral philosophy which builds on the assertion that there is no such thing as human nature and that a person cannot be described in terms of purpose in the way that we can define, say, a paper cutter. Without a nature and without any apparent reason for existing, human beings cannot be expected to perform actions "appropriate" to the species. Instead, each action is performed on the basis of the conviction, clear or confused, at the moment of choice. No book or person can give advice on particular instances. At the moment of choice each of us is alone.

During the last century a Danish philosopher named Søren Kierkegaard (1813–1855) acquired the distinction of being the founder of this new school of thought. Called by him *existentialism,* the new philosophy was really not a philosophy in the traditional sense of the word, for it held that existence could be comprehended only through the concrete realities of living it, not in terms of abstract intellectual concepts. It held that human reason was incapable of discovering, with absolute certainty, a vast cosmic scheme and that consequently reality must always be a subjective matter.

Existential morality grows out of the concrete realities of living, not abstract concepts.

Kierkegaard began as a pious Christian, went through phases of agonizing doubt and feelings of abandonment, and finally reaffirmed his Christianity on radically new grounds. To Kierkegaard, religion was a psychological need, not a philosophical truth, and had to be dealt with on that level. When one reached the point of absolute despair and felt ready to turn to God, one could take a "leap of faith." One chose the path of faith because one was compelled to, not because the choice could be justified in terms of an intellectual system.

In that leap, however, lay undeniable anxieties. The leap had to be made over many counterarguments, especially scientific evidence which seriously questioned religious beliefs. On one's knees in the darkness of the church, one might feel one's prayers soaring heavenwards and have an almost mystic sense of union with God; but one could not know for sure that God was listening—or was even there at all. To have faith in the existential (that is, to have faith in the concrete existence of something, even something cosmic, such as God) meant exactly that; it did not mean to know, to be sure; it meant to *believe without knowing.*

To dramatize the existential plight of the believer, Kierkegaard recounted the Biblical tale of Abraham and Isaac. An angel appears to Abraham and tells him God demands the sacrifice of his son Isaac. Abraham is no doubt appalled, but what can he do? If God wants the sacrifice and if he is God's servant, he must obey. But in that leap of faith, in that raising of the knife, must not Abraham experience unutterable anguish? Faith is faith, but Isaac is also Isaac. And suppose the angel was not really from God—what then? This anguish of Abraham represented for Kierkegaard the very heart of the existential dilemma of humankind.

Contemporary existentialism has developed since World War II. The tradition begun by Kierkegaard is usually referred to as Christian existentialism, and it has its supporters. But the most influential strain of existential thought is undoubtedly that associated with the French philosophers Jean-Paul Sartre, Albert Camus, and Simone de Beauvoir, all of whom represent an atheistic approach. Existence, they say, is absurd in that it cannot be shown to serve any purpose. Species simply are whatever they are, *including* humanity. Since God cannot be shown to exist, there can be no such thing as a divine master plan for humanity, no such thing as humanity's basic "nature." If humankind has no mission, has nothing to prove worthy of, has no sins to atone for and no paradise to attain someday, the brutal fact must be faced that each of us is alone in an absurd situation. None of us makes any sense to begin with.

Who can go on living with such an idea? Yet once we recognize the fundamental absurdity of our existence, we also recognize the basic premise of existentialism: People are completely free to define themselves as they wish, free to create their own reason for being.

> If man, as the existentialist conceives him, in indefinable, it is because at first he is nothing. Only afterward will he be something, and he himself will have made what he will be. Thus, there is no human nature, since there is no God to conceive it. Not only is man what he conceives himself to be, but he is also what he wills himself to be after this thrust toward existence.[7]

A person, says Sartre (1905–1980), has two and only two choices. We may accept the existential challenge, defining our own nature, creating our own identity, and taking responsibility for it; or else we may decline the challenge, remaining undefined, uncreated, unauthentic, hence irresponsible. We may remain a thing, instead of becoming a fully human being. In other words, to be human is to be authentic, to announce to all the world who and what we are and to be consistent with the identity we have developed. It must be added that as Sartre grew older, he became increasingly pessimistic about the willingness of the average person to accept the challenge. People, he believed, do not want to define their own natures because they do not want responsibility.

If we do attempt to become authentic, however, we run into the same problem as Kierkegaard's Christian existentialist; that is, we can never be completely sure of choosing rightly, or of choosing well. It is one thing to be free and responsible; another, to have choices proven wise. But what can we do? We can only act from the full integrity of our defined being and hope for the best.

For this reason, existential choice is filled with anguish for the chooser. An existentialist ship's officer, faced with the awful decision of having to kill people or risk sinking the lifeboat (see preceding section), might eventually shoot desperate people in cold blood. But he would not be able to argue later that he had been a victim of circumstances. He would have to admit responsibility for his actions.

Existentialism Revisited

Existentialism swept over the philosophical world in the 1940s like a cyclone. It had been around since Kierkegaard in the nineteenth century, and possibly long before that. Some have even claimed Socrates was the first existentialist, arguing that the Greek philosopher was, after all, talking about personal integrity and bearing responsibility for one's actions—the same message Sartre was delivering to the World War II generation. The European philosophical world was, however, ready in the 1940s for a system of thought that was rooted in the self—something almost buried in the debris of bombed-out cities—and in the idea of freedom—something Europe had nearly lost. Both sides of the Atlantic were ready for a system of thought which seemed to promise that people of vision and integrity could, if they chose, create a new and brighter future.

Can one who creates his own values do anything at all that is morally wrong?

Dagfinn Follesdal

Moral philosophers, however, have tended to be wary of existentialism, though a new, solid basis for morality was exactly what the philosophy promised. The crucial question has been: How may one resolve the apparent conflict between saying that all of us are responsible for our actions and rooting all values in the private world of each person? In terms of what values do we assume responsibility for a deed? May I not argue that, according to my freely chosen set of values, I have done nothing wrong when *you* accuse me of, say, a breach of good faith in having reneged on a verbal agreement?

In the world of human relationships, existentialism seems to have fallen down on the job. Sartre himself was hardly a model individual. His biographies show us a man who could use people rather ruthlessly, who permitted no criticism of himself or his work, and who often rushed into print about other people without carefully checking his facts. Yet, say his critics, a profound moral philosophy is supposed to assist one in handling relationships with integrity, with *authenticity*.

Sartre does talk a great deal about the "other"—the non-me with a different set of values—and the difficulty this creates. But his critics are now asking how we can possibly have a world of "others" in which everyone is both free and responsible. In Sartre's most famous play, *No Exit* (1944), occurs the ringing line "Hell is other people," a line that recognizes the agony of trying to keep oneself pure and whole in the midst of conflicting egos. What is one to do? Retreat to a desert island and have no relationships of any kind?

Sartre believed that the shame and guilt each of us experienced from having treated someone else badly would act as a check against the danger of unbridled freedom. This resembles the Judeo-Christian idea of conscience, with one important difference: In Sartre there is no God to take note of what we have done. It is up to the individual to decide whether his or her actions have truly hurt another, and so one can always decide that the hurt did not really take place. As Dagfinn Follesdal, Norwegian philosopher and critic of Sartre, puts the matter, "Can one who creates his own values do anything at all that is morally wrong?"[8]

> *If we're all free, why can't we handle our relationships better than Sartre says we can?*
>
> Carlin Romano

A Return to Universals?

In *The Closing of the American Mind* (1987) the American thinker Allan Bloom finds that philosophies (like existentialism), rooted in extreme subjectivity, have undermined clear thought and universal values to such an extent that there may be no turning back from a head-on collision with total chaos. People now believe moral values are either unimportant altogether or can be reinvented every morning. Education in particular is called on the carpet by Bloom for having devoted far too much time to the myth that all values are "up to the individual"—a theme that also became an obsession in popular nonfiction of the 1970s. By now, Bloom says, a kind of arrogant stupidity has spread like a cancer throughout this nation. No one really works toward the attainment of moral integrity. Never mind conscience. If your actions harm others, blame circumstances, blame oppression, blame "the times." Above all, remain ignorant of history and the human intellectual tradition. The less you know about anything, the easier it will be to scream out your own value "system."

Hannah Arendt (1906–1975), another contemporary thinker, is a primarily political philosopher who won international acclaim with her assessment of the Nazi war criminal Adolf Eichmann during

> *For us in the financial services industry—for society as a whole—there is no field of inquiry more critical than that of ethics.*
>
> Louis V. Gersther, President of American Express

the time he was on trial in Jerusalem. Surveying the full extent of the atrocities Eichmann both committed and allowed to happen, Arendt sought an answer to the question that has haunted civilization for nearly half a century: "How could such things have come to pass?" She found the answer both simple and complex: simple, because one could say that neither Eichmann nor the whole Nazi enterprise obviously know right from wrong; but complex—frighteningly so—because Eichmann, like all Nazi power figures, continually argued that hc was only following ordcrs, and in a sense this was true.

Michael Denneny, in his essay "The Privilege of Ourselves: Hannah Arendt on Judgment," paraphrases Arendt and points out that Eichmann's crime was not defying the rules by being *bound* by rules:

> He never looked at the particular case in front of him and tried to judge it without a rule. And the rules society gave him to work with were criminal. . . . [I]n court Eichmann said he recognized then that what he had participated in was perhaps one of the greatest crimes in history, but, he insisted, if he had not done so his conscience would have bothered him at the time.[9]

What better argument for a return to universal moral principles than the knowledge of what can happen when moral relativism becomes institutionalized with the might of a super-totalitarian state behind it? The Nazi devastation and the holocaust resulted from a slogan ("My country right or wrong!") gone totally mad.

EPILOG

What if a survey revealed that one woman in a thousand claimed she would tell the restaurant owner of the mistake on her check? What would that make her— courageous? ridiculous? nothing special—just an honest person?

The woman with the lunch check may not have seemed very significant when the reader first opened this chapter, but her dilemma—if indeed she is fortunate enough to be experiencing one—may have acquired more and more meaning as we surveyed the various schools of moral philosophy. She might well be telling herself that looking out for Number One is the only rational code in a society where nobody cares about anyone else and personal survival is all that matters.

A final note is worth turning over in one's mind. What would happen if the person in question, having decided that a crime against a large and obviously rich restaurant chain is an act of self-assertion (and having read a dozen books on that subject), is mugged upon stepping out into the street and has *all* her money taken? One possibility is that she would suddenly become Socratic or Kantian and denounce the mugger on the grounds that stealing is universally contemptible.

GLOSSARY

absolute: An eternal, unchanging truth or value which supposedly holds for all people in all cultures and in all periods of time.

Categorical Imperative: An inborn condition of the mind which Kant believed determined everyone's knowledge of right and wrong.

existentialism: A philosophy which stresses both the necessity and the anguish of choice as well as the need to assume full responsibility for the consequences of choice. The freedom to choose is both the glory and the burden of the human race.

hedonic calculus: Jeremy Bentham's application of strict mathematical values to actions giving either pleasure or pain. By using it, the state, he believed, could determine "the greatest good for the greatest number."

moral: Referring to a choice among significant options, the outcome of which will either benefit or harm others. Thus, a moral *problem* precedes a significant

choice, and a moral *dilemma* occurs when one is caught between equally desirable (or undesirable) alternatives.

morality: A set of values (whether derived from reason, religion, family, peer group, education, the state, or some other source) which serves as the philosophical basis for making important choices.

situationalist: One who believes that all actions are to be evaluated in relation to motivation and consequences and that the validity of choice in one situation may not apply in another.

utilitarianism: A nineteenth-century school of philosophy which holds that the pursuit of pleasure is the natural goal of human life, but that since no one can have unlimited pleasure without interfering with the rights of others, some system of curbs is absolutely necessary. Utilitarians were early proponents of civil rights in their belief that no government should interfere with a person's promotion of legal means to achieve a good life.

NOTES

1. *The Republic of Plato*, trans. Francis Macdonald Cornford (London: Oxford University Press, 1971), p. 43.

2. Ibid., p. 45.

3. Robert Paul Wolff, *About Philosophy*, 3rd ed. (Englewood Cliffs, N.J.: Prentice-Hall, 1986), pp. 66–67.

4. Harold H. Watts, *The Modern Reader's Guide to the Bible* (New York: Harper and Brothers, 1959), pp. 101–102.

5. Isabel Allende, *Of Love and Shadows*, trans. Margaret Sayers Peden (New York: Knopf, 1987), p. 115.

6. Ibid., p. 116.

7. Jean-Paul Sartre, *Existentialism and Human Emotions*. trans. Bernard Frechtman (New York. Philosophical Library, 1947), p. 15.

8. Dagfinn Follesdal, "Sartre Imitates Life," *The Village Voice Literary Supplement* (November 1987), p. 15.

9. Hannah Arendt: *The Recovery of the Public World*, ed. Melvyn A. Hill (New York: St. Martin's Press, 1979), p. 255.

Utagawa Kuniyoshi, "River Between High Banks in the Rain," Japanese, 19th century
(Courtesy of The Metropolitan Museum of Art, purchase, Rogers Fund, 1936)

7

WESTERN TERRITORY, EASTERN SPACE

OVERVIEW

In the preceding two chapters we examined the role of the philosopher and looked at some key philosophical questions, particularly those which involve the moral life. Since the discussion moved about a good deal in time, we assume that by now the reader recognizes the importance of historical context; recognizes that, while some of the issues dealt with have remained viable over many centuries, focus and conclusions differ from one historical period to another. A good example of such a difference is the matter of moral relativism versus universal, timeless moral principles.

In the famous debate over the ring of Gyges, the young Glaucon challenges the moral absolutism of his mentor Socrates with what was at the time a shocking and startling suggestion: People behave morally to protect their reputations, not out of any sense of universal standards. Plato used Glaucon in order to attack what we might very well call *situational morality,* which was then an upstart—and, for Plato, absurd—notion. But as indicated by the question mark in the last section of Chapter 6—titled "A Return to Universals?"—those who believe in universal moral standards are now probably in the minority.

Beliefs and issues must be placed in *geographical* as well as time contexts, especially the two major geographical contexts of "East" and "West." The ideas, assumptions, and value systems with which we have been thus far concerned can be called "Western," if only because they belong to philosophical traditions that can be traced from major centers in the United States and Western Europe back to origins in the Greek and Roman worlds.

Despite the changes in emphasis that historical context discloses, there are several assumptions which run through time in the West. One is *the importance of the individual,* in which *the individual* often means in philosophy the soul, the self, the mind, the intellect. Even the generic term *reason* is usually rooted in an individual's rational processes used to reach some conclusions. We also think about the personal soul, self, mind, or intellect as a definite entity inside us with the same tangible reality as, say, the heart or the lungs. Psychoanalysis, for example, is a distinctly Western invention. The psychoanalyst diagnoses the ills of an individual's *psyche* (Greek for "soul") as the physician diagnoses the ailments of the body.

A second, and intricately related, assumption in the West is that, since the mind is a solid entity, its products, which we may call thoughts, ideas, concepts, principles, and so on, also have a certain kind of solidity. In short, *ideas are real.*

Some Typically "Western" Beliefs

The importance of the individual
The reality of ideas
The desirability of owning things

Despite the centuries-old tradition of Judeo-Christian thought, focused, of course, on God, and despite the obvious importance of God to countless millions, the fact remains that Western values are generally rooted in the material world and in the importance of understanding, shaping, and owning that world. After all, if we have no part in divine substance, if it is unknowable to us in this life at least, how can we be realistically concerned about it?

Central to the lives of most Westerners is the importance of possessing material objects—farms, animals, other people, coins, jewels, machines, etc.—and, by inevitable association, the reputation which goes along with having things. The possessors are admired and respected, not merely for the powers they display, but for the things their success makes possible.

None of what we have just said is to imply that people in the East do not care about possessions or that they do not believe in the self or the reality of thoughts. We live, as Marshall McLuhan informed us several decades ago, in a "global village," that is, on a planet where distances keep shrinking and where not only people but now computers can interact in a matter of milliseconds.

Does the fact of our living in a global village therefore obliterate the importance of geographical context? The answer is no. Do "East" and "West" still have meaning as points of reference? The answer is decidedly yes. We can see the differences in so simple and straightforward a case as an automobile factory in Japan, where so-called "quality control" is maintained by making the ultimate product more important than the worker's "self." The product, further, is admired for its overall excellence and esthetic beauty, though created also to be exported to the West in order to satisfy someone's need for ownership.

Fortunately, the reduction in our world's size gives us options in the ways we can live our lives. Tokyo has made so much money from Western obsessions that it is beginning to look more like New York than the cherry-blossomed set for the Puccini opera *Madam Butterfly.* Conversely, if you have the money, you can find an architect to design a house with teakwood furniture, rice-paper sliding doors, and a lily pond. In some areas of the United States—notably northern California and Colorado—serious interest in Oriental religions, customs, and values is growing.

The impact of the East here on our shores has been greatest from two particular branches of Buddhist thought, to which the designations "Tibetan" and "Zen" are appropriate.

WHAT IS BUDDHISM?

There is not just *one* school of Eastern thought or religion to which the label *Buddhism* is applied; there are different *kinds* of Buddhism. But there is a common basis, a foundation shared by the various kinds.

In its most pervasive use, the term *Buddhism* connotes a religion practiced by millions of people, principally in Asia, including Japan and the Republic of Formosa but not those countries currently under Communist rule. It is a religion in the sense that it involves certain rituals practiced in places appropriately designated and held sacred and has an ancient tradition of belief which unifies those people born into it or choosing to follow its teachings.

It differs from Islamic, Jewish, and Christian religions in that it does not have a principle of godhead. Its dominant ritual—meditation, or the act of sitting quietly without any particular project—appears to resemble prayer, but it is not prayer. Buddhist meditation is a technique for tuning in to the subtleties of the present moment, for understanding the patterns of sensations, thoughts, and emotions that make

Buddhists believe that all unethical behavior is motivated by self-interest.

up human experience, and for cultivating a wakeful state of mind. Buddhists make no attempt to communicate with a transcendent god figure. Meditation is thus central to the life-style of the Buddhist. Unfortunately it is often misunderstood by people in the West who wish to cultivate the practice of meditation as a means of attaining inner peace, of "getting themselves together."

It is precisely because there is no self that needs to be defended, enhanced, improved, or even made more moral, that the realization of that truth releases us into action that is free from the burdens of selfhood.

Joanna Macy

Buddhist meditation—or sitting—helps to detach one from a sense of self. It has no object. It does not involve concentration on anything. What it does is give one a panoramic and intense awareness of one's surroundings without the interference of thoughts and emotions. If one acquires the discipline of sitting for long enough stretches of time, one gradually loses the sense of being solid, separate, isolated individuals. To the Buddhist, self is an illusion. What we are is sensations, thoughts, and feelings which drift in and out of consciousness. There is no bounded entity inside each of us, except one that we pretend is there if we accept the myth of the self.

Of course, there might be nothing wrong with believing in a continuous self, with believing each of us has a personal identity that is clearly distinct and more important than all others, *if* such a belief made us happy and responsible. Fundamental to Buddhism is the conviction that the myth of self is responsible for most of our suffering and for our unethical behavior.

The recognition of the ego as an illusion is in dramatic conflict with Western value systems.

While Buddhists do not talk about a god figure, Buddhism *is* nonetheless profoundly ethical. All unethical behavior is motivated by self-interest. Whether acts of violence are physical or more subtle and psychological, they always spring from intense desire or intense fear and a sense of the self as isolated, vulnerable, and needy. Buddhists claim that, as people see more clearly and realize that the sense of separation is illusory, they uncover a tremendous warmth and resourcefulness within themselves which allows actions to be spontaneously appropriate to situations as they arise. Buddhist morality is not dependent on a transcendent god who lays down rules and punishes people for breaking them. It is instead dependent on freeing oneself from the idea of existing as a separate being, on discovering one's own *egolessness.* The recognition of egolessness as the natural state and of ego as an illusion is often in dramatic conflict with Western value systems which take the reality of the self for granted.

The Buddha

For most Westerners unfamiliar with Buddhist lore, Buddha (without the article *the*) appears to be a god. They know that throughout the Orient one finds temples with many statues of "Buddha," who is often depicted as a very fat man sitting in the lotus position with his eyes closed and an expression of great peace on his face. Documentaries about Eastern religion often show thousands of people, assumed to be devout worshippers, engaged in what looks like prayer in front of what seems to be an altar or shrine.

Meditation practiced in a temple before a shrine which contains a statue or painting of *the* Buddha is, in fact, a centuries-old ritual intended to free the self as well as to pay homage to the timeless wisdom (or enlightenment) which, it is believed, was attained by an actual person, a prince named Siddhartha Gautama, who lived in India around 500 B.C., roughly a hundred years before the death of Socrates. Reaching enlightenment made Siddhartha worthy of the title of "The Buddha," which in Sanskrit means "one who is awake."

According to many historians, Siddhartha was a prince of the Brahmin caste, the very highest social class in the Hindu system of rigidly separated castes. He had immeasurable wealth, a beautiful wife, a handsome son, and many servants who cared for the family in a resplendent palace. He was in short the epitome of what we in the West regard as a successful man, measuring success, of course, by the number of expensive objects he owned.

Siddhartha was educated in the tradition of Hindu thought, but there was one Hindu belief which gradually came to make less and less sense to him: reincarnation. According to that doctrine, when people passed from this present life, their accumulated *karma*, or moral debts, made it necessary for them to be reborn in a different body; and in that next go-round they would have the opportunity to pay off those debts—in short, to live a better, more ethical life. If one's karma were excessive, one would be reborn into a lower social class than the one one had left. If one's moral debts were light, one would move up the ladder. The lowest social class was inhabited by the diseased, wretched homeless people known as "the untouchables." The highest caste belonged to the Brahmins, the aristocratic order of people who were considered holy because they were closest to enlightenment. If one died a morally pure Brahmin, one was then eligible to enter the state known as *nirvana*, which was not a heaven (though many Hindus probably did and still do regard it as such) but a condition of eternal oneness with the soul of the universe, a condition of unending bliss, free of all pain and unfulfilled desires, a state of never having to be reborn.

What troubled Siddhartha was the paradox of his own life. If he were a Brahmin and presumably one step away from nirvana, why was he so unhappy? Why did his pleasure-filled existence seem such a waste of time? How could he have lived before in a *worse* state than he was in now? And if a prince with unlimited wealth and a beautiful wife was restless and bored, who indeed was happy? What was bliss, after all? Should he not be able to have at least a glimpse of what was in store for him?

Siddhartha was caught up in samsara, *which means the general futility of a life lived for the satisfaction of momentary desires.*

Perhaps his discontent indicated that he was not yet ready to take the next step. If so, he might have to be reborn into a lower class and thus prolong his dreary, unhappy lot. He was familiar with the belief that some people take thousands of years to attain nirvana. The only ray of hope—and it was a slim one—was the Hindu scriptural prophecy of the Buddha: Every eon—or roughly 25,000 years—there would be born a perfect individual who would reach nirvana after only one lifetime. This was the Buddha: He who is awake, who fully and profoundly realizes the full potential of being human.

Unable to find peace and happiness at home, Siddhartha left his wife and son and embarked on a long search, without knowing what he was looking for or what he might find. At first, he tried the life of a hermit, eating, so legend has it, one sesame seed a day, spending his hours in intense thought. All he found was further confusion. He grew thin, emaciated, and weak and very far from bliss.

At length he resolved to seek a middle way between the two extremes of total materialism, his former life, and total asceticism, his present life. After restoring himself to health, he continued his wandering, still sick at heart, still confused, seeking a fulfillment for which he had no name. The explanation given by Buddhists for Siddhartha's unhappy state at this time is that the Prince was experiencing the profound despair of having been caught up in *samsara,* Sanskrit for the general futility of a life lived for the satisfaction of momentary desires, a life guaranteed to be hollow and frustrating. But where was another kind of life? And how could one find it?

One day, so the story goes, Siddhartha sat to rest under a rose-apple, or Bodhi, tree. After a while he became increasingly and vividly conscious of his surroundings. Little by little the torment he was feeling inside began to slip away. As his ego awareness vanished, his awareness of reality—*everything exactly as it was*—became sharper and a deep peace came over him. Some say he sat there, totally wakeful, for 40 days and nights.

Now, Hindu tradition taught that the coming of a Buddha—a totally enlightened human being—had been foretold for thousands of years, in the same way, for example, that the Old Testament foretold the coming of a Messiah. Siddhartha had been destined for his transformation from birth, though he became aware of it only during his meditation under the Bodhi tree. While he sat there, wondrous things supposedly took place:

> Mandarava flowers and lotus blossoms, and also water
> lilies made of gold and beryl, fell from the sky onto the
> ground near the Shakya sage,[1] so that it looked like a place
> in the world of the gods. At that moment no one any-
> where was angry, ill, or sad; no one was evil, none was

proud; the world became quite quiet, as though it had reached full perfection.[2]

The reference to "the gods" is wrapped up in Buddhist folklore; they are a throwback to Hindu mythology. *Buddhism,* the philosophy which grew out of the teachings of Siddhartha, has no central god figure, but it does have symbolic deities which symbolize states of mind. The anonymous author of the above passage knew no other way to describe the phenomenon of the enlightenment.

Other stories indicate that evil demons attempted to distract the Buddha during the long sitting, to prevent the enlightenment from taking place. In any event, it *did* happen. The prince saw that all notions of self were beside the point and very far away. Thoroughly immersed in the world as it really was, he realized that self and separateness were illusions. Without the barrier of inner thoughts and emotions, he became part of all he saw around him. He experienced the unity of all being. He had, in short, attained nirvana, and as the prophesied Buddha, he had accomplished this feat in one lifetime.

When Siddhartha finally arose from his long meditation, he did so because he had decided not to remain in nirvana, which he could have claimed as his right, but to go out into the world to share with others what he had discovered: the path to enlightenment. And so began Buddhism: the philosophy of the path. The very first way in which it was to differ from Hinduism was in its teaching that the nearly endless cycle of death and reincarnation was not essential, that one could, like Siddhartha, find peace at virtually any time. Above all, it taught that Buddha-hood was not a condition reserved for only one special person every 25,000 years.

According to legend, the Buddha could have entered the blissful state of nirvana and stayed there forever. But he chose not to; he chose to go among the people and show them the path to bliss.

The Dharma

Like Jesus after him, the Buddha went among the people and taught them how to live. What he told them constitutes the *Dharma,* or the Way. Central to his teachings is the denial of an absolute self or personhood.

Egolessness, as Buddhists call the condition of being nonseparate, is neither self-sacrifice nor loving one's neighbor as oneself. It is the belief that nobody is a "me" enduring through time as an unchanging central core. A contemporary Buddhist philosopher explains:

> A man does not have a core or a soul which he can consider to be his true self. A man exists, but he cannot grasp his real being—he cannot discover his own core, because the existence of a man is nothing but an "existence depending on a series of causations." Everything that exists

> is there because of causations; it will disappear when the
> effects of the causations cease.
>
> The waves on the water's surface certainly exist, but can
> it be said that a wave has its own self? Waves exist only
> while there is wind or current. Each wave has its own
> characteristics according to the combination of causa-
> tions—the intensity of the winds and currents and their
> directions, etc. But when the effects of the causations
> cease, the waves are no more. Similarly, there cannot be a
> self which exists independent of causations.
>
> As long as a man is an existent depending on a series of
> causations, it is unreasonable for him to try to hold on
> to himself and to regard all things around him from the
> self-centered point of view. All men ought to deny their
> own selves and endeavor to help each other and to look
> for co-existence, because no man can ever be truly
> independent.[3]

The Buddha recognized that what is usually called the "inner self" is made up solely of thoughts and feelings that come and go. Take away the causation, and the self disappears. By extending this logic, we see that, if we are not chained to causations, we will not be chained to an idea of self. What is then taking place within? Where is that "self"? The self can be known only when these thought processes—these re-actions to causations—are happening. But if the thoughts themselves become transparent, so does the self.

One of our thoughts concerns this very impermanence. Fun-damentally we recognize how fleeting and how unstable the self can be. It is discontinuous, and in the gaps "we" disappear. To resist such discontinuousness, the illusion known as ego is created. It too is a thought, an idea; it is a reaction to a causation, namely, the fear of non-existence. To sustain the illusion, thoughts keep generating them-selves. Buddhists call this "mind chatter." We are afraid to let it stop, for then the sense of self fades.

To most of us in the West the very idea of letting go of the sense of self, of relegating that sense to a position of utter insignifi-cance, is unthinkable, even insane. If we think of the pain and torment we experience when, say, an all-consuming love has fizzled out, we say that pain is happening to an "us." The Buddhist truth of the matter is, however, that the "us" is the very *reason* for the pain to begin with!

Pain, resulting from the myth of ego, became for the Buddha the fundamental roadblock to nirvana. Thus did he teach what he called the *Four Noble Truths:*

Life is filled with pain.
Pain is caused by the need to possess.

There is a way out of pain.
The way to nirvana is the Eightfold Path.

The *Eightfold Path* is the Middle Way the Buddha had sought for so long a time. It is divided into the fundamental segments of anyone's life, which need to be approached without ego. These segments are:

Right Views	Right Livelihood
Right Intentions	Right Effort
Right Speech	Right Mindfulness
Right Conduct	Right Concentration

If one were pragmatically able to sit (or meditate) continuously, there would be no need for the Eightfold Path, or indeed for the Four Noble Truths. The problem of pain begins when one rises from the Bodhi tree, so to speak, and becomes immersed once more in the commerce of everyday life, when one reenters the world of samsara. Then does the cycle of cause and effect start all over. One reinvents the myth of ego, acts and reacts as if the self were real, becomes defensive, aggressive, and covetous.

One cannot avoid samsara. One can, however, carry the sitting attitude into the cycle of human affairs. That is the meaning of the Eightfold Path. "Right" means "intelligent"—doing all things with the understanding that self is not a sacred, indivisible entity. The last component of the Path is "concentration," which refers to the sitting attitude, and is by far the most important element. To retain the sitting attitude is to be not a self existing continuously, but intelligence operating appropriately.

Because of the illusion of ego, say the Buddhists, we face the world with illusory expectations. Most of the time the events we experience are not what we want to happen according to the false picture of the world we nourish inside. Instead of allowing impersonal intelligence to observe what is actually the case, we attempt to manipulate reality so that it agrees with our false picture.

Intelligence sees that ego always acts out of self interest. It decries such actions, for, since the self is an illusion, there can be no such thing as self-interest. It is insane to behave out of illusory motives. No sane result can take place. This, the Buddhists tell us, explains why the world is always in a state of chaos. *There are simply too many conflicting illusions serving as the basis for what people do.*

According to *Buddha-Dharma* (or the Way of the Awakened), seeing through the illusions of ego will reveal compassion as a fundamental fact of existence. This does not mean feeling sorry for others. Pity is very often a subtle action of ego; it bolsters our illusion of a positive self to believe that others are going to pieces. The nature

The present world atmosphere is not healthy. Things are decided by force, guns and money.

The Dalai Lama

of *compassion* is described by one American Buddhist practitioner as follows:

> It's not really a question of the need for compassion, but in fact when there's no demand, only then can real compassion take place. Actual compassion is based on a person's ability first of all to be clear about what's going on in a situation: what's going on with his own energy, his own desires, his own uncertainties as well as those of other people. When he sees those things clearly, then spontaneously he does what is appropriate to the situation. This is the real meaning of compassion.[4]

As we meditate and understand the patterns of the mind, we become more and more even-handed, about not only our own processes but those of other people as well. We recognize with ever-deepening insight what drives others to say or do certain things. It is not a matter of forgiving and forgetting, nor of turning the other cheek. We merely withhold judgment and respond intelligently.

The foregoing represents an interpretation of Buddha-Dharma by many contemporary practitioners of Buddhism, particularly those psychologists who believe Siddhartha Gautama, the Buddha, was able to reach a state of total mental health, resulting from a total contact with reality, unobstructed by the barrier of self.

The Eightfold Path, taught by the Buddha, leads not to riches, happiness, or personal satisfaction. In the contemporary psychological view of Buddhism, these goals cause continual frustration. When we move toward total contact with reality, we are also moving beyond personal goals. Buddhists do not see that life is *supposed* to yield dividends. Life is simply what it is—to be taken as it unfolds.

If, however, we insist upon a reward, we could say that, in overcoming self-preoccupation, in developing the sense of compassion, we are spared the suffering caused by the conflict between reality and the desires of self. But contemporary Buddhists caution us not to suppose that theirs is a dry retreat from the world. They insist that what is gained is a continual delight in experiencing the dance of life, a profound appreciation for whatever arises.

TIBETAN AND ZEN BUDDHISM

Since its founding 25 centuries ago, Buddhism has split into many sects. They all share a fundamental acceptance of the Eightfold Path, but they differ with respect to ritual and practice. Two of the most prominent sects in the United States are Tibetan Buddhism and Zen Buddhism.

The Tibetan Tradition

Tibetan Buddhism has emphasized the Buddha's decision not to enter nirvana but to remain in the world to guide others. It is based on the concept of the living, ongoing Buddha-mind, as opposed to centralizing an homage to the historical Buddha. Siddhartha Gautama was, we might say, a role model of the totally aware human being. In this respect, the Tibetan school appears most congenial to the concerns of psychology.

In Buddhism a sense of delight accompanies the experience of life.

This school also places great importance on and devoutly honors the transmission of wisdom from one generation to another through the lineage of enlightened beings. In Tibetan Buddhism one seeks a teacher who either belongs to this lineage or who has been trained by someone who does; the teacher becomes a lifelong friend and confidant. One identifies with the mind of the teacher and is perpetually guided by it along the path of life.

Tibetan Buddhism can be considered somewhat more democratic than the mainstream Buddhism of Asia, in which homage to the historical founder gives to the practice features in common with other world religions, such as Judaism, Islam, and Christianity. Mainstream Buddhism may well have lost sight of the promise in ancient Hindu scriptures that at the end of each eon of time a new Buddha would appear. Siddhartha Gautama was, in this sense, the "most recent" Buddha.

Buddhism is not a dry retreat from the world.

In the view of Tibetan Buddhism there will continue to be more Buddhas, just as there are now on earth many *Bodhisattvas* (those who are destined for enlightenment). Each generation, as a matter of fact, produces a hierarchy of Bodhisattvas, beginning with the recognized Dalai Lama. The term *Dalai* means "the sea—measureless and profound."

The Dalai Lama's position is not inherited; it is not passed down from generation to generation in the same family. The incarnation of the Dalai Lama for each age must be discovered by means of an elaborate ritual:

> The first step is to find out from the State Oracle the locality in which the Dalai Lama has reincarnated. As soon as this important fact is known, search parties, which have been selected by lot or by the State Oracle, are sent out. On the basis of their reports the government draws up a list of possible candidates. In the meantime, the Regent of Tibet visits the sacred lake believed to be the abode of the Goddess Kali—for she appeared to the first Dalai Lama and solemnly vowed to watch over all his successors—and there he sees in the depths of the lake a vision indicating the location of the Dalai Lama's new birthplace.[5]

But the Dalai Lama is not the only Bodhisattva in each age. In Tibetan belief there can be a number of others, some totally unrecognized, living in humble circumstances, dedicating their lives, as the Buddha did his own, to guiding others along the spiritual path to enlightenment.

The Bodhisattvas are regarded as potential Buddhas at the middle stage of the way to enlightenment. But even having reached a middle stage in the progress toward spiritual perfection is awe-inspiring; thus the Bodhisattvas earn the highest possible praise and respect from their followers.

Implicit in Tibetan Buddhism is a hierarchy of persons, arranged according to their proximity to the ultimate goal, which is the full incarnation of Buddha-hood. A lama is a Bodhisattva, and he is also a *guru,* or holy teacher. There are many gurus, and not all of them become lamas. But even so, the guru is a very special, very fundamental unit in Tibetan Buddhism.

The Tibetan tradition stresses the *sangha,* or community (though all Buddhist strains recognize the importance of the fellowship of meditators). Without a home base, so to speak, without the community, meditators run the risk of being overwhelmed by space long before coming close to their goal.

Legendary Origins of Zen

Zen Buddhism is that strain of the parent religion which has come to be most closely associated with Japan. It originated in India at the same time as Buddhism itself. In the beginning it was that aspect of Buddhism intensively concerned with the meditation practice and the techniques one must acquire to master it. Its name stems from the Chinese word for meditation: *Ch'an.*

Zen meditation is very long and sometimes very painful. In a very real sense Zen intelligence begins in the buttocks and works its way slowly upwards.

The founding of the Zen tradition as a specific school of Buddhism with its own rituals, methods of sitting, and folklore is attributed to an Indian monk named Bodhidharma. A thousand years after the enlightenment, Bodhidharma traveled to China with the missionary zeal to win converts to the Buddha's teachings. Zen legend sometimes adds the awesome story of how Bodhidharma sat so still for a full nine years that his legs fell off, thus demonstrating in somewhat hyperbolic terms the tremendous importance of the sitting practice in the Zen tradition:

Obeying the instruction of Prajnatara, his teacher, Bodhidharma started for the East and arrived in China in 520 A.D. The Emperor Wu-ti invited him to Nanking for an audience. The Emperor said: "Since my enthronement, I have built many monasteries, copied many holy writings and invested many priests and nuns. How great is the merit due to me?" "No merit at all," was the answer. "What is the

> Noble Truth in its highest sense?" "It is empty, no nobility
> whatever." "Who is it then that is facing me?" "I do not
> know, Sire." The Emperor could not understand him.
> Bodhidharma went away, crossed the Yangtze River and
> reached the capital, Loyang, of Northern Wei. After a so-
> journ there he went to Mount Wu-t'ai and resided in the
> Shao-lin Temple where he remained and for nine years,
> facing a cliff behind the edifice, meditated in silence.[6]

This anecdote also demonstrates the traditional Zen delight in
indirection, whimsy, and cryptic utterances. Of all the schools in Buddhism, Zen has become the most systematically devoted to the tran-
scendence of not only ego but the rational process as well. It views
pure intelligence as something greater than rational knowledge. It is
arrived at through the intuition that comes only after years and years
of steadfast, disciplined sitting meditation. In a very real sense Zen intelligence begins in the buttocks and works its way slowly upwards.

Zen Today

Complex historical currents carried the Zen school from China to
Japan, where it eventually found a lasting home. To explain how and
why this happened would require a detailed analysis of the Japanese
character and way of life, both of which have found in Zen a most congenial practice.

Everyone knows, however, that the Japanese have traditionally exhibited a strong feeling for the beautiful, especially the delicately, exquisitely beautiful. Graceful movement and hand gestures in
drama, dance, and puppetry are prime examples of the Japanese esthetic bent. The Japanese delight in taking that which can be clumsy
and graceless and making it fluid and rhythmic. They delight in fine
craftwork—in the tiny brush strokes of the painter's art or the intricacies of the carver's art. In short, the Japanese prize all artistic expression which can be achieved only after long years of often painful discipline. Discipline and form are quintessential to the Japanese, and of all
the schools of Buddhism, Zen is probably the most formal and the
most disciplined.

*The traditional Japanese sense of the beautiful as well as the profound si-
lences of Zen meditation must now compete with the modern Japan of auto assembly lines, the lucrative electronics industries, and the fastest-moving mass
transportation system in the world.*

Of course, the traditional Japanese sense of the beautiful as
well as the profound silences of Zen meditation must now compete
with the modern Japan of auto assembly lines, lucrative electronics
industries, and the fastest-moving, most crowded mass transportation
system in the world. It is well known that, amid these hectic surroundings (ever watch the daily proceedings at the Tokyo Stock Exchange?),
ancient Japanese customs sometimes gasp for air.

Still, the centuries-old influence of Zen has not totally disappeared. There are the martial arts: judo, karate, and aikido, for example. They teach one—through long and painful discipline—to pro-

tect the body when necessary but not to be aggressive. Like all forms of life, the body is sacred; ego is not. Not surprisingly, martial arts are enjoying a vogue in the United States. which has seized upon their competitive possibilities. The original meaning of *karate* is, however, "open palm," a meaning not inconsistent with the open position of the hands during meditation and one which can suggest nonaggressiveness.

Family honor remains central in Japanese thinking, motivating such acts as suicide, resorted to by many who fail to be accepted to a prestigious university or who cannot stand the pressure of rigorous studies and are asked to leave or who, having graduated, fall short of the mark in the business world. Suicide has long been accepted by Japanese society as the dignified way to save a family the embarrassment of having a failure in its midst.

The stress on family, the overwhelming importance of family, give evidence that ego and personal reputation are generally not as important to the Japanese as they are to Americans. Indeed, one cannot imagine a less gratifying prospect to the ego than the admission of failure, owning up to the fact that one is entirely responsible for a disastrous state of affairs and will do the expected thing for the sake *not* of oneself but of others. In this sense, family honor is analogous to the handed-down wisdom—the lineage—in Buddhist traditions. The Japanese regard for family is also similar to the Tibetan Buddhist regard for sangha, or community. In all cases, the personal self is dwarfed by much larger considerations.

Zen masters can be very rough indeed. An overseer who catches someone beginning to doze during meditation may take a long stick and strike the nodder soundly on the shoulders.

The full and devoted practice of Zen is, however, accomplished by the individual, who, whether in solitude or in community, must learn through long months and years of sitting to become detached from what seems increasingly to be the foolishness of the everyday world, of samsara. The practitioner also becomes detached from the self. Zen masters are the sternest of all gurus, believing that other Buddhist sects are too free with the word "enlightenment." Sitting for as long as 12 hours at a time without stretching the legs or taking in sustenance of any kind is not an uncommon practice in a Zen monastery or in the *zendo,* a community of persons voluntarily living under the same roof, practicing meditation, and sharing chores.

Zen masters can be very rough indeed. There is always an overseer to the *zazen,* or sitting period; and an overseer who catches someone beginning to doze may take a long stick and strike the nodder soundly on the shoulders.

The position of the Zen master is that the battle against ego is hard won, if at all, and that too many persons deceive themselves into supposing they are well on the way to nirvana when in fact they are proud as peacocks over their accomplishments, thus having come, in reality, not one step along the way.

Sitting in Zen is not intended to be exhilarating or relaxing or a positive spiritual experience of any kind, though many beginners, both here and in the Orient, probably hope it will be just that. The point of sitting for hours at a time is not to transcend the pain and the boredom until a state of euphoria is reached, but to confront that pain and boredom directly—to discover the Void which underlies all existence, the Void which ego insists on covering up. Zen masters know that beginners entertain themselves with mind chatter and so must keep sitting until they grow weary of entertaining themselves and are able to see the Void for what it is. Only then have they begun to understand and free themselves from ego:

> The Zen tradition in Japan creates a definite style of boredom in its monasteries. Sit, cook, eat. Sit zazen and do your walking meditation and so on. . . . The black cushion is supposed to suggest no color, complete boredom.[7]

While Zen has become popular in certain parts of the United States, especially California, one of the most difficult tasks facing Americans who submit themselves to the rigorous discipline is the attainment of a passive willingness to do anything required, no matter how lowly and demeaning to a sense of personal dignity, which is difficult to renounce. In Zen, it must be absolutely all the same to the practitioner, whether asked to sweep the floor or carve a statue. Zen people cannot say, "But that's not my job" or "Do you know who I am?" An oft-repeated Zen maxim is "Wash your rice bowl," given as a terse reply to any objection based on self-interest.

Because of the emphasis on the destruction of ego, Zen masters can be biting and satiric, seizing every opportunity to deride, revile, and humiliate. They enjoy making students aware of their mind confusions, especially the absurdities and nonsequiturs in their conversation. On one occasion a group of American filmmakers visited a Zen master for the purpose of filming an interview. Tea and cakes were being served. One of the visitors bit into his cake and commented: "It doesn't have any sugar in it." The statement just hung there in the room with nowhere to go, but a colleague came to the rescue: "Mine doesn't have any sugar either." The master, with a twinkle in his eye, bit into his own cake and said that it too was free of sugar, adding: "Why don't we go around the room and find out if anybody has a cake *with* sugar?" Nobody said anything. Nobody dared!

Zen has been called antirational, but this is not the case at all. It works against the chaos that passes for logical discourse. It would empty the mind and allow the light of pure intellect to take over, intellect devoid of personal concerns.

Zen is not much on language. It views language as a barrier between the intellect and reality. What really *is,* simply *is*—it has no name. Zen teachings are full of paradoxes and riddles, all of which

Zen teaching often takes the form of riddles and paradoxes. Its point is to empty the mind of false and limiting logic and allow the light of pure intellect to take over.

stress the fact that the real truth is always staring people in the face but that they are too caught up in their own mind chatter to see it. For instance:

> Kassan had a monk who went round all the Zen temples but found nothing to suit him anywhere. The name of Kassan, however, was often mentioned to him from far and near as a great master, so he came back and interviewed Kassan, and said, "You have an especial understanding of Zen. How is it you didn't reveal this to me?" Kassan said, "When you boiled rice, didn't I light the fire? When you passed around the food, didn't I offer my bowl to you? When did I betray your expectations?" The monk was enlightened.[8]

But what is that truth, that stark reality? The Zen answer, typically cryptic, is: *If you have to ask, you will never understand it.* And yet the "truth which has no name" is also absurdly simple, perhaps best summed up in this simple line by the old Chinese sage Lao-Tzu: "Everything is what it is." There is just what happens—the flow of things—nothing more. It is to be observed with neither joy nor sorrow—without judgment, without analysis.

Japanese practitioners will tell you that Zen is as foreign to vast numbers in Japan as it is to the majority of Americans. Even those who are familiar with Zen teachings often argue that both the philosophy and the practice are too passive: The solitary monk will simply let things happen and put up little resistance. Zen has little to offer energetic, young, up-and-coming businesspeople with an eye to shaping the world of the future, to making the world a better place for everyone. What, they ask, has Zen to do with improving the lot of humanity? We suspect that a typical Zen reply would be this: If you could attain serenity, why would you wish to improve upon it?

THE EAST IN THE WEST

To many Westerners the East probably remains remote and mysterious, a place unlikely to be visited, populated by beings difficult to comprehend. They may have acquired a few bits of information; but, likely as not, they cannot imagine themselves in any way involved in Eastern issues. As far as they are concerned, human existence begins and ends in their own backyard.

For others, however, Eastern modes of living hold genuine options. The Buddhist East is beginning to effect a radical change, in particular, in the way some Americans live, in the way they think and perceive. There are American Buddhists—people born in Kansas as well as New York or California—gainfully employed and eminently functional in American society, commuting to work just like everybody else, doing their weekend shopping at local supermarkets, going to malls for dinner or a movie; but in their homes they have meditation rooms, lit by candlelight, where they sit in the lotus position for long periods (instead of watching television), and they confront the stillness of things as they are. American Buddhists take strong issue with some Western values they find no longer acceptable.

Success and Failure

Prominent among these values is the polarization of success and failure, of "making it" and "blowing it." It is the either/or proposition that has blighted many worthy lives for a very long time. For all too many, the perception of their worth can take place only within the parameters that in our society are preordained. Evaluating oneself as being close to or far from "success" becomes ultimately a life-long obsession.

What is worse, the definition of "success" keeps changing as we advance even closer to what we suppose is "the goal." One must keep getting ahead, moving always upwards from one plateau to another, never really believing one has "arrived," always assuming somebody else *has*. It is difficult, therefore, to be egoless, to become detached from self-preoccupation, when one must always worry about one's standing in the imaginary hierarchy of successful people.

Buddhism, on the other hand, is opposed to the evaluation *at all* of events, people, achievements. Things happen; things change; people come and go; life is a continual flow, an unending *moving on*. It is not a ladder to a gold-paved land over the rainbow.

Buddhists regard success and failure as imaginary opposites, distorting the perception of events as they really happen. A man loses his job after 20 years. He and his wife start bickering over finances until at length she leaves him. Unable to stand the thought of living in the same house without her, he moves to New York. He cannot find a job. He is either too old or overqualified, and the good-paying jobs are held by people of his own age who have moved steadily up the ranks. In a short time he has exhausted all his funds. It is late autumn. As he walks along the cold and windy streets, he looks at the city as a cruel, heartless place and upon himself as a total failure.

In Buddhist philosophy the feelings you have about yourself are *only* feelings. You may harbor them if you wish. You may project them out into the world, as our jobless man did, and imagine that the world is an embodiment of them: You are a failure; the windy day *looks* like failure. Or else the world—a sunlit clear day—mocks you: Although the day is bursting with success, we alone do not measure up, do not deserve such a day.

Western

You have lost your job; you walk along the cold and windy streets of a big city, which you regard as a cruel and heartless place; and you see yourself as a total failure.

Eastern

The feelings you have about yourself are only feelings; you may project them out into the world if you wish; but feelings have no objective existence.

Western

Territory is everything— your possessions, your thoughts and feelings, your supposedly continuous identity.

Eastern

Forget self, forget possessions, develop an expansive, panoramic sense of total reality.

In Buddhism everything you feel about yourself is entirely up to you. Feelings have no objective existence. Nor do evaluations. "Successful" people may speak of themselves as such and manipulate you into believing them, but you have the option of believing nothing whatever about them. The recognition that success and failure are of one's own making has proved for some Americans a welcome antidote to the poison gushing forth from a wounded ego.

Territory and Space

Siddhartha finally understood that the need to possess things and people was a sickness of the soul. This became the second of his Noble Truths. One can never possess enough; therefore one is forever dissatisfied, frustrated, miserable. Or else one fears that one cannot *keep* what one has accumulated. For the possessive and the covetous, life is an endless succession of worries, paranoid obsessions, even guilt-shattered sleep, for if we have indeed amassed a goodly number of possessions, perhaps we secretly have not earned them.

Humans, says Robert Ardrey in *The Territorial Imperative,* are property-oriented, sharing this characteristic with all other animals. The instinct to find, protect, and preserve a nesting place, a point of continual return, is basic to all animals. Behavioral psychologists, however, say human beings do *not* have instincts, that all their tendencies and actions are the result of conditioning.

Buddhism agrees in this instance with the behaviorists. The obsession to accumulate territory is bred into us by the culture in which we live. In the early years of this century young American boys were encouraged to read the books of Horatio Alger, all of which were variations on one plot line: the inexorable rise in the business world of a handsome, virtuous, ethical, hard-working product of respectable parents and a Christian upbringing. The relationship between the accumulation of wealth and property and Christianity has been noted by intellectual historians, including Max Weber, whose principal work *The Protestant Ethic and the Spirit of Capitalism* (1930) has been mentioned in Chapter 6. According to Weber, the Protestant belief that success in business ventures is a sure sign of God's favor has permeated our cultural unconscious to the point that even nonbelievers generally accept the notion that exhibiting the tangible evidence of one's business know-how is the number-one priority. According to an earlier observer, Thorstein Veblen, an economist whose study of Western consumerism *The Theory of the Leisure Class* appeared in 1901, we are less interested in the work ethic which leads to success than we are in the conspicuous display of money and possessions. In fact, conspicuous consumption, as he calls it, is our total obsession: *One must be perceived as owning many things.* In today's vortex of plastic credit cards we could add that our obsession is to be thought to own things even if they are not paid for.

Buddhism, on its part, believes that, since such "territorialism" is cultural rather than instinctive, we have the option of rejecting the urge to own. Most of the songs and stories which arose from the attempted cultural revolution of the 1960s focused on the jobs of the open road, communal living with loving strangers, and dropping out of the so-called "establishment." Not to have a permanent home or job— to own nothing, in fact, except the backpack one carried—was regarded as the highest good. This is very definitely an Eastern value, and, not surprisingly, American interest in Eastern modes of living and thinking quickened during the '60s.

Buddhism in America is not evangelical. It likes to share its vision of ultimate happiness with those who are seeking an alternative to conditions which do not satisfy them, but it has no illusion that it will ever bring peace to a well-fed population with every possible convenience except joy. It believes its secret to be that joy and territory are irreconcilable opposites.

More subtle perhaps but no less dominant in the Western scheme of things is the need for *inner* territory, what the Buddhists call the myth of ego, the sense we cultivate of being a solid self, a conscious whole of attitudes and personality which is always there and which is indelibly stamped with our trademark. In Western circles, it is meaningful to say that someone has behaved in a most "uncharacteristic" manner. If one departs too radically from society's perception of allowable behavior, one is labeled mentally ill. Buddhism, as we have seen, does not believe that we exist continuously and therefore always in a characteristic way. Buddhism believes the law of life is that of continual change. How can there be an unchanging inner self?

Buddhists in America know that sitting in meditation discourages clinging to thoughts and the sense of self and encourages the individual to be open to what Chögyam Trungpa, Rinpoche, has called the "fluid intelligent quality of space":

> The fear of the absence of self, of the egoless state, is a constant threat to us. "Suppose it is true, what then? I am afraid to look." We want to maintain some solidity but the only material available with which to work is space, the absence of ego, so we try to solidify or freeze that experience of space.[9]

Thus there is a Western fear of physical space—that is, being without territorial possessions—as well as a Western fear of inner space— having outer-directed consciousness without a solid inner orientation, being panoramically aware of everything out there without being trapped in the prison of thoughts and feelings the Buddhists call mind chatter. The Western intellectual life, in particular, has had as its goal the achievement of a focused rational mind inside each of us which accurately views and processes events as they take place. The vast uncharted land of inner space has traditionally been regarded in the West as a place of hazard, far too dangerous to wander in. The underlying premise of psychoanalysis is that one must bring all of one's thoughts and feelings under the conscious control of the ego. To operate spontaneously, to operate from the unconscious, is to be neurotic, even perhaps psychotic.

Many Americans hold important jobs and then go home to practice meditation at night. East and West are not incompatible ways of living.

Buddhism in America does not blind itself to the reality of mental illness caused by a fragmentation of consciousness, a person's being driven by drives and impulses of which she or he is unaware. Indeed, it sees mental illness as one of the gravest problems in our society, and it attributes its prevalence to our immersion in samsara, the continual round of acting and reacting without ever detaching ourselves from the process to see objectively what is going on. Buddhism advocates sitting meditation as an alternative to both the illness itself and the hours of therapy often required. If one would sit, says the Buddhists, mind chatter would begin to fade away; one would see one's behavior from the detached vantage point of an uninvolved observer.

Instead of the conscious, controlling ego of Western therapists, Buddhism speaks of wisdom or enlightenment, both of which are terms for the perception of all things exactly as they are. This perception has nothing to do with individual personality. One person is not wiser or "smarter" than another. One has either opened oneself to enlightenment or one has not. There is no in-between.

In a very real sense, the Western tradition of philosophy began on a note that was much closer in spirit to the East than we are now. Plato and Aristotle, when dealing with what they called reason, were indeed talking about something eternal, something universal, something that was not the exclusive property of a particular great mind. In Plato's dialog *Meno,* mentioned in Chapter 5, Socrates contends that, if given proper time and attention, a slave boy would be able to handle exceedingly complex mathematical problems. Why? Because all persons are born with identical wisdom. They differ, as Aristotle was later to make clear, in terms of *the degree to which they actualize their potential.*

In Aristotelian language we could say that the guru, the Bodhisattva, and the Buddha all represent a hierarchy of actualization. Each is closer to the condition of total wisdom. Plato shows actualization taking place not through sitting meditation but through stimulating interchange with a teacher—in his case, Socrates. But the way Socrates prods and challenges his students, reported for us in *The Republic,* is similar to what happens between the Zen master and the Zen novice, except that the latter relationship is filled with derision, sarcasm, even physical punishment.

Since the Renaissance, however, the West has undeniably shifted toward the idea of great minds—great individual minds—who, because of their special insights, are able to bring about significant changes in the world, changes that benefit lesser minds. There is no scientific and technological tradition in the East to match what has been called "Western progress." True, the East, particularly Japan, is catching up. In electronic and computer technology there is frequently no contest anymore, with Western centers like Silicon Valley in California regularly importing Japanese know-how. Could we not say that this state of affairs represents the West moving into the East, even as the springing up of meditation centers represents an opposite trend?

Buddhism is not, we underscore, an alternative to progress, to scientific brilliance; or to educational systems or creative endeavors. Many American Buddhists attend or have been graduated from the most prestigious universities in America. Many no doubt hold key positions in Silicon Valley or along Route 128 in Massachusetts, which has more computer companies than Las Vegas has casinos. Buddhism believes that long years of sitting meditation can so enlarge one's perspective that one is both enlightened and able to deal with complex problems that would defeat someone else whose life is fragmented by concerns. Buddhism believes that the enlightened practitioner is more valuable in the world of commerce than the neurotic "go-getter."

Some American Buddhists have done very well in business but have given up lucrative jobs and the promise of financial security in order to join a sangha and devote most of their time to sitting. A 9-to-5 job does not give them this time. They do not believe they are wasting their lives because they are not "making a name for themselves." They want no part of what they regard as a vicious circle of challenge and response which leaves them confused, exhausted, and always unfulfilled.

Critics of Buddhism in America argue that the sitting practice is less effective in our upwardly directed society and more effective in less-developed countries, where individuals count for less than they do in the United States. It works best, they say, for people whose lives tend to be without hope and are so monotonous that the boredom of continual meditation is easily accepted. Americans, on the other hand, are raised to be continually mobile, continually "on the go." The passiveness of sitting is foreign to their nature.

For their part, American Buddhists are not likely to be swayed by criticism, even that lodged by families who despair over a son's or a daughter's lack of initiative or selling out to a lazy, unproductive way of life. The decision is often painful, however. What will happen to the family business if the heir prefers a zendo to an executive office? But then, we need not suppose Siddhartha failed to experience a few tugs of remorse as he waved goodbye to his wife and son.

The art of being human is the art of recognizing options. There is always a price for the choice. If the marketplace has taught us anything, it is surely that we need to weigh the price against the joy we may receive from a purchase.

GLOSSARY

Bodhisattva: In ancient Hindu belief, the name given to the incarnation in each lifetime of the next Buddha—the "Buddha on the way," so to speak. In Tibetan Buddhism, a Bodhisattva is one who is recognized as being on the road to full enlightenment and whose teachings are therefore worth heeding. There can be more than one Bodhisattva alive in any period.

Buddhism: Considered a world religion because of beliefs, practices, and rituals which are shared by millions. It is also a philosophy and a systematic manner of living one's life without ego or aggressiveness. Buddhism is based on the teaching of Siddhartha Gautama, who maintained that, contrary to Hindu scripture, anyone could achieve nirvana within the space of a single lifetime. The central practice of Buddhism is that of sitting meditation, through which one achieves the totally wakeful state and is able to see the reality of the immediate moment exactly as it is without the barrier of thought or emotion.

compassion: In Buddhism, the capacity for recognizing the motivation and goals of others. Through meditation one becomes detached from one's own inner processes, in the sense that one sees them objectively. And when this happens, one begins to observe the processes of others from the same detached viewpoint. (Note, however, that "detached" in Buddhism does not mean "unconcerned," but rather "without emotional confusion.")

Dharma: In Buddhism, the structure of moral and social obligations underlying all existence. Unlike the moral law of Judeo-Christian belief, the Dharma was not imposed from a deity, but is implicit in the nature of existence.

egolessness: According to Buddhism, the fundamental condition in which we live. The conscious awareness at any given moment is an intersection of cause and effect. That is, either one is reacting to a previous cause or one's action is about to have an effect. There is no such thing as a constant, unwavering self that endures through successive instants in time. There *is,* however, an illusion of such a thing, and we call it *ego.*

Hinduism: The most ancient of the world's major religions. It is still practiced today in India and elsewhere by millions of people, who believe as their ancestors did that one must live through many cycles of birth and rebirth before one is blessed with the gift of nirvana. In Hindu scriptures the Buddha is the one exception, a being who, having actualized his Buddha nature, attains nirvana without ever having to be reborn. In Buddhism, however, anyone who follows the Buddha's path may do the same thing, though the way is admittedly difficult.

karma: Sanskrit term, of central importance in Hindu religion, meaning the moral debt each of us accumulates in a lifetime that must be paid off during the next lifetime.

nirvana: In Hinduism, the final emancipation from the pain of birth and rebirth, and ultimate reunion with Brahman, the universal soul; in Buddhism, a release from suffering brought about through intense meditation and the renunciation of ego.

samsara: A Sanskrit term, found in both Buddhism and Hinduism, meaning the seemingly endless round of give and take in which we become involved when we plunge into the daily business of life without the detachment and separation from ego necessary to achieve inner peace.

Zen: Originally the most austere and monastic form of Buddhism, it means today the highly disciplined practice of meditation and egolessness in which one aspires to nearly total detachment from worldly concerns. It is also a systematic method of transcending the rational activity of the mind, which Buddhists believe prevents us from seeing things as they are.

NOTES

1. Some say Gautama was born a member of the Shakyas, a warrior tribe living near the foothills of the Himalayas. He is thus referred to as the Buddha Shakyamuni (or "Sage of the Shakyas").

2. *Buddhist Scriptures,* trans. Edward Conze (London: Penguin, 1959), p. 51.

3. Junjiro Takakusu, *The Essentials of Buddhist Philosophy* (Delhi: Motilal Banarsidass, 1975), p. 17.

4. From an interview with David Rome, executive secretary of Vajradhatu, the central administration of Tibetan Buddhist meditation centers in North America, conducted July 21, 1977, in Boulder, Colorado.

5. Lobsang Phuntsok Lhalungpa, "Buddhism in Tibet," in *The Path of the Buddha,* ed. Kenneth W. Morgan (New York: Ronald Press, 1956), p. 231. Reprinted by permission of John Wiley and Sons, Inc.

6. Takakusu, *The Essentials of Buddhist Philosophy,* p. 167.

7. Chögyam Trungpa, Rinpoche, *The Myth of Freedom* (Boulder, Colorado: Shambhala Publications, 1976), p. 25.

8. R. H. Blyth, *Zen and Zen Classics,* Vols. 1–5 (Tokyo: Hokuseido Press, 1960–1970).

9. Trungpa, *The Myth of Freedom,* p. 21.

Alberto Giacometti, "The Palace at 4 a.m.," 1932–33
(Courtesy of The Museum of Modern Art)

8

ON BEING
A CRITICAL
THINKER

OVERVIEW

Toward the end of William Wharton's novel *Dad,* the main character, en route to his father's funeral, gets a glimpse of his own aging and eventual death:

> I'll become a bore to others, a drag in conversation, repeat myself, be slow at comprehension, quick at misunderstanding, have lapses in conceptual sequence. All this will probably be invisible to me. I won't even be aware of my own decline.[1]

What he fears is the loss of a highly treasured human trait, the power of thought. At the time he makes the prediction he is able to see things whole—his own place in the progression of generations. He is clearly a man who has enjoyed the use of his critical faculties, and while they may eventually fail him, his life will have been richer because of their use. He is only one of many who have paid tribute to the importance of that unique human skill, the ability to think critically.

Of all the creatures on earth, from the smallest to the largest, apparently only human beings can understand concepts. Other creatures have instincts. They seek food and shelter and cleverly achieve these ends; they have families and nurture their young; they fight, run, even play. But they don't plan or read or make word jokes or find similarities in apparently unlike objects. They lack the power to contemplate, to speculate, to make valid inferences and to laugh at foolish inconsistencies. So do computers—those amazingly quick, astonishing storehouses of memories. Computers possess skills which are limited only by the creative imaginations of those who manage their circuits and prepare their software. Human beings are not only creative, they are the only creatures capable of the joy of thinking.

The man who said he feared the loss of comprehension has at least been able thus far in his life to enjoy thorough use of his brain. What can be said of those much younger who refuse to take advantage of what they have? What would make people reluctant to use that frequently unused human faculty, the mind? Do we think only during school examinations and then escape to leisure-time activities which require as little thinking as possible? And why does that special form of thinking called "critical" have such a bad reputation?

Criticism is not limited to finding faults.

We will begin by rejecting one definition of critical thinking. A critic is not necessarily the person who enjoys finding fault, who tears down rather than builds up. Criticism may involve praise of the highest order or the withholding of judgment until all the returns are in. Criticism is analysis leading to an evaluation. It is the condition, the state of mind which should precede choices and actions. Though capable of both spontaneity and intuition, the critical thinker depends less on them than on careful observations and reasoned conclusions.

Critical thinking is the ongoing process of criticism. It is the disposition of the mind to define, describe, and analyze as accurately as possible. It is a lifelong commitment.

Criticism, then, is an activity of the mind which carefully defines, describes, and analyzes something—a movie, an event, a presidential decision, a daughter's desire to move into her own apartment. It probably should be, but often is not, the mental activity which people enjoy engaging in more than any other. Opposed to critical thinking are: constant complaining; the suspicion that the troubles of the world derive from plots and conspiracies; skill in claiming to be right at all times; the tendency to form conclusions at once, refusing to be led astray by facts; and the tendency to fall immediately into line with another person's viewpoint.

Critical thinking is also the ongoing process of criticism. It is the disposition of the mind to behave in a certain way, that is, to define, describe, and analyze as accurately, as fairly, as dispassionately, as possible. It is a lifelong commitment.

Critical thinkers quickly become known, become identified as people whose opinions can be trusted. Many times over they have demonstrated a knack for hitting a situation squarely between the eyes, commenting clearly on what is taking place, assessing a matter reasonably, and making a memorable pronouncement on a subject.

It is not at all difficult to distinguish critical from noncritical thinkers. The latter take things literally and fail to move on quickly to the next step. They have a hard time figuring out why people say what they say. They are not aware of what we might call the shape of experience. The morning after a party, noncritical thinkers cannot put it into perspective. Critical thinkers, on the other hand, will tell you concisely just what happened and what it felt like to be there.

Critical thinking is not an exact science. But it has identifiable characteristics. It has goals. There are certain ways of achieving it, ways that can be articulated. The purpose of this chapter is to systematize these ways as much as possible.

THINKING ABOUT THINKING

The first step in becoming a critical thinker is to develop some idea of what is meant by thinking. For centuries, speculations about the mind belonged exclusively to philosophy. It was believed by many that the mind was a spiritual, or at least nonmaterial, entity, floating somehow within but not connected to the body. Today psychology believes that all functions of mind, from dreams to the most complex series of interwoven ideas, are localized in the brain. Take away the brain, and the mind disappears. For all practical purposes, the brain *is* mind.

Old Brains, New Brains

By making plaster casts of primitive brains on indentations found inside ancient skulls, California anthropologist Ralph Holloway has constructed a theory that the brain has gradually grown larger. Carl Sagan (in *The Dragons of Eden*) describes a three-part division of the brain, the bottom and middle sections being the survivors of millions of years of evolution. These are the old brains. The topmost section is most advanced in Homo sapiens—humanity in its present form.

The oldest, or *reptilian,* brain once belonged to early inhabitants of planet Earth. These creatures needed a brain to process information delivered by the sense of sight as they foraged about for food and shelter. They needed to be alert to danger, to the possibility of encountering creatures larger than they. Hence this brain developed survival techniques, including aggression ("Get them before they get you"); what Robert Ardrey has called the "territorial imperative"

Characteristics of the Reptilian Brain
aggression
territory
chain of command
ritual
resistance to change

and

Characteristics of the Mammalian Brain
insights
intuitions
shelter
family

("This area is mine, so keep off!"); and an insistence upon and respect for hierarchy, or chain of command ("You'd better take orders from me, or I'll kill you").

As time went on and mammals began to evolve, a new kind of brain was needed to process information passed on from the sense of hearing, developed out of the necessity for recognizing threatening sounds from a considerable distance. The mammals, traveling at night when the reptiles were sleeping, developed a brain with insights and intuitions of both danger and safety. This brain came to value all those things associated with shelter, including the family instinct, love, charity, and self-sacrifice. As leadership of Earth passed into the keeping of mammals, brains, not brawn, assumed priority. The reptiles that remained became smaller, and the mammals grew larger. Today whales and especially dolphins exhibit versions of this middle brain. Examples of their intelligence as well as their "tender" qualities have been documented.

Bottom-Brain Thoughts

What shall we have for supper tonight?
Can we afford to pay the rent?
I was here first.
I'll get to the top if its takes me ten years.
How much does he earn?
Who does she think she is?
Who's in charge here?
I am in charge here.
Now that I'm the manager, I'll need a larger house.

Middle-Brain Thoughts

Be home by ten.
Don't go out with him; he's not for you.
Married ten years and only one child?
She's old and helpless; we have to take her in.
I don't quite trust him; he has shifty eyes.
I'll get a job if you promise to stay in college.

The topmost brain in Sagan's theory is, of course, "ours." But "ours" may be too sweeping a term. Does everyone share the brain power of an Einstein? Courses in the humanities are likely to tell you that, by virtue of being *born* human, we have a glorious heritage. The brilliant achievements of our species are proof that to be human is automatically a reason to marvel at oneself. But potentiality is not actuality. Aristotle pointed that out 2500 years ago, though he stressed that the potential is always there for the development if one is so inclined.

Courses in the humanities sometimes suggest that we have a historical right to wear laurels. Reading a book about human giants of the past and passing a test about them links us to the human "tradition." But alas! We don't always belong to the tradition. Consider what humanity is doing to its own environment and to its prospects for survival on this planet. Have we not been told that the present generation is the first to wonder whether it will be the last? Make a list of the inhumanities and one of the humanities; see which is longer!

The future of humanity—assuming we can keep from blowing one another up—could be one in which brain levels exist in a tall and ascending hierarchy. At the top will be those who have powers of analysis and synthesis far beyond anything known today. But how many of these superbrains will there be? How many will live at the bottom? And, more important and more frightening, how much freedom will they enjoy?

As our understanding of the human mind increases, old ideas about the brain's span of usefulness are changing. Traditional notions about aging are being put aside. Loss of the rational faculties and loss of short-term memory (senility), for example, are less and less thought to be inevitable by-products of age. Recent intelligence testing of people as they grow older is revealing that those who continually use their brains, who accept more and more difficult mental challenges, grow *more,* not less, intelligent with age. In his early nineties, Bertrand Russell was still writing, lecturing, and working on complex philosophical puzzles that would have baffled much younger people. George Bernard Shaw lived to be almost a hundred, showing little if any diminution of his mental powers, especially his legendary wit. And George Abbott, to celebrate his own centennial year, opened a play on Broadway. On the other hand, tests indicate that those who spend their lives in nonmental pursuits, who never use their analytical faculties, display brain loss at an age when their mentally agile contemporaries are still engaged in productive intellectual labors.

There is yet another belief still current about the brain: Some people are "just born smart," while others "just don't have it." Quite possibly some parents themselves are responsible for encouraging in their children attitudes of resignation that can remain with them for life. Or quite possibly some people find it easier to accept themselves as mentally inferior, thereby wriggling free from the hook of others' expectations ("I'm dumb, so I don't ever have to prove anything!").

It is important to recognize that the brain needs exercise just as much as do legs and arms. An exercised brain will reward you even more than other parts of the body. Physical well-being is gratifying, but the exhilaration that comes from having completed a taxing bit of mental work—reading a difficult book, writing a complicated paper, solving a tricky puzzle, say—is incomparable.

When the brain is left to flounder and grow flabby from nonuse, the capacity for sustained logical discourse may not be there when the need arises. Ever try proving your innocence under cross-examination with a skillful prosecutor hammering away at every statement you make?

Behind Closed Doors

I do not feel obliged to believe that the same God who has endowed us with sense, reason, and intellect has intended us to forego their use.

Galileo

The belief that critical thinking is confined to a small part of the populace is shared by those who have it and those who don't. Those who think critically may want to retain the skill which sets them apart from others, to maintain their superiority. If the ability to think is not teachable, then well-paid and prestigious work remains out of reach for the majority, even those willing to work hard. Critical thinking is something you have to be born with, like an aristocratic title. Education serves only to develop the intellectual pedigree one already has.

In his satirical anti-utopian novel *Brave New World,* Aldous Huxley created a well-run society in which the brainy people are the ones in power. The Alphas make all the decisions because they have literally been *bred* in test tubes to have the intelligence required for governing the rest. Other groups, conditioned to be pleased with their own special, but lower, qualities, do not expect to improve their ability to think. In the real world, critical thinking is often considered beyond the range of all but a small segment of the people. Corporate bureaucracy is based on the assumption that managing directors and chief executive officers have to make the tough, intricate decisions, or the company will fall into chaos.

But those with power are not the only ones who claim that critical thought is a special gift. People with poor self-concepts tend to agree. Sure that they won't be able to do the job, they give up without really trying. Each penalty for poor performance leads them to the certainty that the next failure is preordained. After a time, it is.

The Feeling Level

Those who work outside the closed doors of the critical decision makers often maintain that people who *feel* more than they think are somehow more trustworthy and charitable than their highly paid, less emotional "superiors." The ability to express emotion—even uncontrolled anger—has a good press in our thought-suspicious times. "Feeling" people tend to attract our sympathies. They sometimes see themselves as martyrs, perennial victims of injustice at the hands of the callous and calculating. Conversely, those "unable to feel" are often urged to let themselves go and be "human." But there is no reason to equate humanness with feeling, or critical thinking with lack of humanness. The emotional approach to life can be a whole lot easier and a whole lot less effective than trying to analyze what is really happening and coming up with a workable solution to genuine problems.

Thus a lack of perceived compassion for the weakness of others is deplored, while illogical thinking either goes undetected altogether or is dismissed as insignificant. Even when there is little evidence to indicate that nonthinkers are automatically warm and tender, they are often thought to be. Since many people avoid what they believe will be the "pain of thought," they display an easy tolerance for mental lapses in everyone else. The "difficult" subjects in school are always those requiring the closest reading and the most intense concentration; and low grades in such subjects tend to be laughed off by many, who may also find drunkenness an amusing and harmless trait.

Each of us is able to operate on three different levels of consciousness. The first we might call "casual." In everyday conversations with friends and family or in just letting the mind ramble on in its usual, undisciplined way, we are hit-or-miss in our thinking. Sometimes some of us carry a thought process in a direct line for a minute or more. Mostly we can't. The level of critical thinking—which is the third level of consciousness and involves sustained, careful maneuvers of the mind through the shoals of irrelevance—requires time, solitude, and silence but seldom competes successfully with the second, or feeling, level, which is even less difficult, at least for some, than casual conversation. Frustration, anger, resentment, or concern, warmth, and passion . . . all can be summoned front and center without needing our concentration.

> We allow our ideas to take their own course, and this course is determined by our hopes and fears, our spontaneous desires, their fulfillment or frustration; by our likes and dislikes, our loves and hates and resentments. There is nothing else anything like so interesting to ourselves as ourselves.
>
> James Harvey Robinson

The time has come to seek a balance among the three levels of consciousness. We want sometimes to chit-chat with our friends (or ourselves), to let our mind amble along at its own pace and go wherever it will. If we have tenderness or anger to communicate, we want the right to do so. But without the critical level, we can run the risk of becoming permanently displaced in a world of never seeing very clearly what we and others are about, and of not being able to transcend events, observing issues and principles at work.

EXERCISING THE CRITICAL FACULTIES

If we believe there is an immediate survival reason for every human skill developed since our species first evolved, we could argue in favor of letting the brain work only when necessary. If we are not trapped in a burning building, lost in a dense forest, adrift in a remote sea with a dead outboard engine, or struggling to remember an obscure date on the Graduate Record Examination, we may safely ease out of the girdle of tight thought and "let our minds go." We may also conclude that, if we have no present need of muscle power—for instance, if we have not fallen down a well and therefore have no need to hoist ourselves up along a slender rope—the body may safely be allowed to flop into an easy chair directly after dinner. But not exercising the body could mean not having what it takes to accomplish a physical task when the need arrives. Ever try to push a heavy car off the road single-handedly? By the same token, when the brain is left to flounder and grow flabby from nonuse, the capacity for sustained logical discourse may just not be there when the need arises. Ever try proving your innocence under cross-examination with a skillful, trained prosecutor hammering away at every statement you made?

In this section we look at a few examples of how the critical faculties can be exercised on a daily basis. After all, even great dancers still report to the studio each morning for their barre exercises.

Beyond Chit-Chat

As pointed out in the preceding section, we spend a great deal of time on casual thinking, which is not sustained and nearly always lacks transitions from point to point; and on casual conversation, which is even less organized. Long, rambling conversation seems harmless enough, in the same way that junk food, with its heavy concentration of starch, sugar, and salt, seems safe enough "now and then"—that is, for lunch every day but never for dinner. But chit-chat's cumulative effect on the mind can be every bit as dangerous as the cumulative effect of French fries.

Social conversation can be turned into an exercise in critical thought. Avid fans of a sport can spend highly enjoyable time in serious analysis of the coach's strategy. Monday-morning quarterbacks can play their own critical game of "If . . . then . . . and that would have provided the opportunity to . . ." Between games there is talk of player contract and front-office decisions about management. When talk is knowledgeable, not merely the recitation of statistics or preferences, it is *critical* talk.

There need be no immediate outcome of critical conversation, of course. Someone remarks, for instance: "I suppose I should root for one of the teams in the playoff." A friend answers, "It makes it more interesting. But I can't find any reason to care about the teams that are left. Neither is from a city I've ever lived in, and there's no one player I care about." Another says, "I usually wait till one team has lost two games in a three-out-of-five series, and then root for the underdog." Yet another pipes in, "Or the team with a lot of older players. It's their last chance to make it." The environmentalist adds, "Or from the standpoint of fuel conservation, teams that are close to each other . . ." Infuriating to a passionate fan, this conversation is critical in that it rises above—or outside of—unexamined "rooting" and makes tentative remarks about the reasons behind a choice. People are making statements and noting their reasons for doing so. At least some kind of thinking is taking place as they talk.

If we always make choices without analyzing them, then we will fail to develop the capacity for making crucial choices when we *really* must. We may "naturally"—for reasons obscure to ourselves— root for *any* underdog, a basis for choice which may not be appropriate or make sense if we think about it.

Solving Problems

The problems of everyday life offer the most obvious chance for most of us to tune the critical faculties. "That no-good, no-account brother" who always needs money exists in some guise in nearly every family closet. The typical solution, which is to ignore the problem and hope it will go away forever, is not the critical approach. The attitude of "It's easier to pay the money than to have the hassle" may well avoid a painful thought, but not a painful scene further down the line.

The first step in solving a problem is to determine whether there is one at all. Whether to place an aging relative in a nursing home or provide home care yourself may not be a problem if no legitimate choice exists. Should money not be an issue, one obvious question suggests itself: "Do I want to assume the responsibility of caring for grandma?" If the answer is no, then the "problem" disappears, unless the original question can be replaced by yet another: "Will I be able to handle the guilt I may feel after I've signed the papers?" However, guilt versus responsibility may be an unbalanced set of alternatives. Is nursing-facility care better suited to your grandmother? Or is she still well enough and alert enough to experience a harmful feeling of rejection? In the first instance, the logic of choosing the nursing home should make guilt unnecessary. In the second, the alternatives seem equally compelling: no, for the good of your relative; yes, for your own good. So you may conclude that you definitely have a problem.

The second step is usually to determine who owns the problem, or, in the case of the nursing-home dilemma, whether you are the sole owner. Are there others in the family who could share the need to choose? Often we make ourselves miserable by supposing that we are not, or ought not to be, sole owners. "Why me?" is a frequent, if rhetorical, question people ask. If there is no answer, then the question is foolish but psychologically damaging. It's necessary to be hard-nosed—that is, brutally realistic—about deciding the question of ownership. To be so saves time and emotional wear and tear. If your

The first step in solving a problem is to determine whether there is one at all. Whether to place an aging relative in a nursing home or provide home care yourself may not be a problem if no choice exists.

no-good, no-account brother is the only other possibility, then he can be readily forgotten and ownership of the problem accepted with resignation. Recognizing that we seldom receive rewards for good deeds puts us well on the way to not expecting any. The business of living can be much easier without fantasies.

Challenging Assumptions

A good exercise for the critical faculties is to pay close attention to what people say and, just for fun, to freeze the action and examine the statement. If the cost of hurting people's feelings is too high a price, then examining assumptions in the privacy of one's thoughts is free.

Suppose, for example, you hear someone say, after reading a front-page horror story: "They shouldn't let those people out of mental hospitals and turn them loose to hurt innocent people." Immediately you might list a number of assumptions being made:

1. Everyone in a mental hospital deserves to be there.
2. All people admitted to mental hospitals are both incurable and violent.
3. Those in charge of mental hospitals are in no position to make accurate judgments about the future behavior of any patient released.
4. Confinement to a mental hospital should be permanent.

Having listed the assumptions, you are now in a position to question them.

> The word "criminal" is not only on a much higher level of abstraction than "the man who spent three years in the penitentiary," but it is . . . a judgment, with the implication "He has committed a crime in the past and will probably commit more crimes in the future." The result is that when John Doe applies for a job and is forced to state that he has spent three years in the penitentiary, prospective employers . . . may say to him, "You can't expect me to give jobs to criminals!"[4]
>
> S. I. Hayakawa

The noncritical person in a debate is likely to be unable to stay with the subject and will become personal as well as shrill. For instance: "You never come up with any good ideas . . . just like your brother. I once knew someone who was in a mental hospital . . . at least I think so. Or was he just visiting? Anyway, all psychiatrists are crooks." Assumptions, such as the latter statement, come to the surface suddenly, like whales, then dive below just as rapidly. Personal fears, old prejudices, and unresolved guilt mix with illogical thinking to produce a pandemonium of wild talk that can absolutely stagger you once you set about to really listen.

> *A good exercise for the critical faculties is to pay close attention to what people say and, just for fun, to freeze the action and examine the statement.*

The highly emotional assumption maker may be too far gone to benefit from the critical thinker's relatively calm analysis of the assumer's argument. But where rational confrontation is possible, critical thinkers advance their own cause and that of the assumer by assisting in the process of recognition. The challenge should, however, be gentle, never officious or self-righteous, for to be such is to throw around a few untested assumptions of your own.

School Examinations

Educators may disagree on principles and strategies, but there is general agreement on the value of critical thinking in school. In order for students to answer critically, they must go beyond the recall level, which consists of factual answers to factual questions. The authorship of *Don Quixote,* the temperature at which water boils, the nationality of Kierkegaard, and the definition of "Manifest Destiny" are facts worth a few points on objective tests.

The best essay questions are valuable critical exercises, though even straight recall helps tune the brain. If the lecturer has described the court of King Louis XIV and the Palace of Versailles and has then played music of the mid-seventeenth century, the student who can recall what the lecturer said about the history of the time and the way the arts reflect that history is still on the level of recall. An essay question about the relationship between the music and the formal gardens of Versailles forces the student to make a connection on his own. Making responsible connections is at the heart of critical thinking.

Or, having given an overview lecture on the neo-Classical age, with Versailles as a prime example, the instructor may ask the students to provide their own overview about an entirely different period. The essay question then might read: "In what way did the arts of the Renaissance indicate a belief in the greatness of humankind?" A wealth of "evidence" awaits the student—Michelangelo's statue of David, the paintings of Leonardo, the great heroes of Shakespeare, and so on. The essay would require the student to match concrete examples with general principles about the Renaissance as a whole, about ways in which implicit belief is exemplified in art.

Here are some other critical topics:

1. Explore the possible audience of a local radio station by listening to the vocabulary of the announcers and making inferences about

the prospective users of products advertised. What part of the population seems to be the target? How do you know?

2. Examine the "signals" being transmitted by the environment in two different parts of the city. Observe carefully the manner of dress, types of stores, and lettering on signs which alert visitors would notice.

3. (Name of play) has been called tragedy. Read or see the play and, without resorting to quotes from authorities, tell how you think it does or does not match classical principles of tragedy.

4. Describe an incident you have experienced or observed which offers a clear moral choice. Demonstrate your knowledge of two ethical ideas by describing two courses of action and the implications of each.

5. Using all the information you have about a historical event (the French Revolution, for example), tell under what circumstances it might have been avoided.

Note that some of these suggested assignments combine recall information with other kinds of knowledge. The critical thinker knows the basis definition (of tragedy, for example) and is familiar with the plot of the play, but is not willing to be content with mere summary. It is in the matching of plot with definition that the higher order of thinking occurs.

The question "Did you like it?" is basically not a critical one at all.

Not included in the exercise on tragedy is the question "Did you like it?" or "Is it great?" The former question is subjective, often valid, but not basically critical; the latter is evaluative, requiring the ability to describe and compare before the pronouncement that a work of art may be called "great" has any meaning beyond empty words.

For national examinations such as the Scholastic Aptitude Test and the Graduate Record Examination, as well as tests to determine eligibility for law school, critical thinking is apt to be required. Because there is so much variation in the curricula of school systems throughout the country, the test questions must seek evidence of critical thinking rather than the memorizing of specific information. A law school candidate may be asked, for example, to match a general principle with a specific situation involving the ability to recognize the difference between bribery, extortion, and theft, except that instead of writing definitions, the would-be lawyer must be able to relate the proper charge to the real issue. Doing this requires practice in careful, systematic thinking.

Or one may be asked questions about the meaning of particular lines or words of a poem. In "Loveliest of Trees" by A. E. Housman, for example, there appears the line "Now, of my threescore years and ten, twenty will not come again." The examination asks, "How old is he?" The distracted or impatient test taker translates "three score years and ten" and gives "seventy" as the answer. The more careful test taker answers correctly, "Twenty."

At the end of that same poem are the following lines:

And since to look at things in bloom
Fifty springs are little room,
About the woodlands I will go
To see the cherry hung with snow.[2]

The critical reader, noticing "in bloom," knows at once that the season mentioned is spring. Asked to identify an image in the poem, the critical reader remembers that a poetic image is indirect, figurative, and allusive and answers that "snow" is an image referring to the blossoms rather than to a phenomenon of winter.

How does one develop the critical skills required to score well on examinations? Taking critical ability seriously and resolving to concentrate on the matter at hand are always the inside track. The absolutely wrong approach is to use the chit-chat model, whereby you begin writing without the slightest awareness of what will come forth. Taking the essay test should not mean, as it frequently does, starting to write without surveying the situation, gaining a perspective on the question, formulating precisely in your mind what is being asked, then determining the best available strategy for answering. The skillful essay is clearly introduced and summarized, not long and rambling with no center of gravity.

Looking for Principles

In listening to the statements of others, we sometimes fail to hear principles—or, at all events, the ones that are *actually* there. A principle is a particular kind of assumption—a moral or ethical judgment that is held to be universally applicable. The confusion of principles is one of our commonest errors.

According to the philosopher Kant, to test the moral validity of a proposed act we should will that it be universally binding on all people. For example, the thief who justifies robbing a grocery store agrees that everyone who has been unfairly treated by society should steal from others. The "others" would, of course, have to include the thief. But a thief who is robbed on the way home from committing a robbery is unlikely to approve the action of the second thief. Therefore the thief's "thinking" prior to the stealing has to be revised: "Robbery is not acceptable, except when I do it."

You are waiting for a bus, and you hear a bystander remark: "Mother's Day came and went, without even a lousy card from my son." As a critical thinker, you entertain yourself by seeking out the principle from which the remark springs. How about starting with "Evidence of love is a greeting card arriving by a certain day." You can push the analysis further: "Even" suggests that a card is minimally acceptable, that an expensive gift would be a stronger sign of love. Turning the assumption into a principle, you have: "Children ought to show their love for their parents by giving them expensive presents by a particular deadline." A moment's reflection should tell us that this is a very weak application of a universal principle.

Here is a statement reported in a newspaper account of a trial in which a former professional football player was charged with selling drugs: The athlete's attorney quipped, "So this is the thanks he gets for all the pleasure he has given the public!" To turn that remark into a universal principle, try starting out with "People who play football professionally . . ." or "As long as someone is engaged in an activity which entertains the public, that person may . . ." Even more: "In such cases, the public's duty is to . . ." At the very least the attorney was saying "Outstanding athletes should be judged by different standards from other people." Having "straightened out" the statement, we are then in a position to analyze it. We may well begin by questioning the phrase "has given the public." Since the man was a highly paid player, "given" seems inappropriate. In light of the hero worship of young fans, we may be tempted to ask why an outstanding athlete should not be held to an even higher standard of behavior than those not in a position to become role models.

Here's another statement, also reported in a newspaper: "It is just as dangerous to allow poisoned literature into the school library as to allow poisoned food into the school cafeteria." The principle seems clear: "We may safely base moral judgments on analogies." But is a valid comparison really being made here? The critical thinker notes differences. The logic of the analogy centers on the equal applicability of "dangerous" in both school areas. Laboratory analysis can tell us what is poison in food and what is not. But what device will detect poison in literature as objectively?

All of us, surely, would like to believe we are persons "of principles." Most of us would like to believe that we operate according to clear and approved principles. Some of us, however, become very confused when we attempt to match a concrete example with an appropriate principle.

LITERALISTS AND FIGURATISTS

Because people do not easily fall into categories, it is not fair to insist upon hard-and-fast distinctions. Critical thinkers are not always critical. They are capable of being impulsive, overemotional, and childish.

They are inconsistent, too, being hurt on some days by remarks that on other days they would have overlooked or laughed at. Sometimes they become discouraged by the inability to solve a problem, when the brain seems to let them down.

But people who make up their minds to adopt the critical approach to living do acquire certain definite characteristics, and so do those who choose not to. In this section we are concerned with the way in which critical thinkers respond to and talk about experience. Critical thinkers tend to be figurative rather than always literal in their speech and their understanding of things.

On Being Literal

The literal person, or *literalist,* avoids or does not see the general principle but concentrates on specific examples. The literalist changes the subject and is preoccupied with self. There are times and places for being specific rather than general, for being concrete rather than abstract, but the following conversation shows what happens when the literalist responds without really hearing what is being said:

> *A:* I wish life would provide experts. I'd love to have someone whom I could ask important questions: where to live, whether to change jobs, what school is best, what suntan lotion to use.
>
> *B:* My dermatologist gave me the name of a good suntan lotion. Just a minute. I have the name written down.

A is making a rueful observation that there is no certainty, that in a philosophical sense we are all alone. This is the general principle behind the observation. B hears only the examples, but not the random nature of them. B, who is not accustomed to hearing or discussing principles, is unaware that A is uninterested in suntan lotion no matter what the actual words may have been.

Consider still another imaginary conversation:

> *Mother:* I find the only safe topic with my teenage son is something noncontroversial. I can't talk about his car, expenses, girlfriends, or his plans for school and a career. I know he's interested in baseball, so this morning I mentioned how well the Dodgers are doing. I told him they were six games ahead, and he corrected me. Ten games! It gave him a chance to explain something to me, and it worked. At least we didn't fight this morning.

> *Friend A:*   I know. The only safe topic in our house these days is the new television lineup.
>
> *Friend B:*   The Dodgers are twelve games ahead.

The literalist reacts to random stimuli—parts, never wholes.

The secret of figuratism is knowing what is appropriate to think and say about a given phenomenon.

Which friend is the literalist? More important, by what process did either reply come to be what it is? Friend A listened to what was being said by Mother. Friend A heard the general principle: Since it is difficult to communicate with the younger generation on our own terms, we must find terms that will work. Knowing the point of the observations, Friend A replied in kind. Friend B, on the other hand, is probably not in the habit of listening very carefully to begin with. Literalists see object by object, hear sound by sound, but are unaware of wholes. Their conversation tends to be tedious, except perhaps to other literalists, because they themselves do not speak to significant issues or principles. The literalist back from a trip can give endless details about gas mileage, every morsel of food eaten at each stop, the cost of items purchased or passed up. Even a pause now and then to sum up—"It wasn't worth it!" or "Travel is a pain, but you have to get away sometimes"—would break the total concentration on pointless detail.

Literalists often change the subject without realizing they have done so. Since they have not grasped the original subject, they will often hang on to the very last thing that has been said and take it in a direction that is totally away from the point. Consider the following observation:

> *A:*   The problem of capital punishment torments me. I see no easy solution. On one hand, the planned and deliberate taking of a human life disturbs me, but on the other, I object to the tax dollars it takes to support a murderer for life. I honestly don't know which side to be on.

A critically thinking listener, B, might respond with one of the following:

> "I don't know either."
> "I don't think you can talk about human life and tax dollars as being equal."
> "I wouldn't mind using my tax dollars to try rehabilitation even though that might not work."
> "I believe killing is wrong, no matter who does it."

But suppose that B, instead of responding to A's remark, heard only part of it and said: "And another thing. They keep giving in to the prisoners; some people are doing better in prison than they'd do on the outside." In this last instance B has heard bits and fragments of what A said. B has picked up "honestly don't know" and has moved from the issue of capital punishment—the abstract moral argument—to a complaint about permissiveness in jails. The literalist goes step by step without seeing the shape of the street.

Literalism also stems from self-preoccupation. Literalists are too busy waiting for their turn to speak, too busy thinking of what they might say to hear what others are saying. Even a transition like "I have nothing to contribute to this discussion. May we turn to another?" gives evidence of a critical mind at work, and is easier to deal with.

Literalists seldom seek a perspective on world events. They are likely to have some interest in national problems, more in state issues, much more in matters relating to the city, and above all, the neighborhood. Characteristic of literalists, once again, is self-centeredness. The closer the problem comes to home, the greater the involvement.

During a conversation, uncritical thinkers will be thinking ahead to what they will say when it is their turn to speak. Perhaps an amusing story will occur to them, a joke they have just heard the day before, which they are anxious to tell to others. They may impose the joke on the group whether the moment is appropriate or not. They are forever changing the subject, not having followed the thread of the conversation to begin with. They are so immersed in their own problems, their own worries and fears, or so anxious to impress others with some good fortune that has befallen them, that often their sole concern is to talk as frequently and as long as possible.

The compulsive need to talk and not listen, however, does not always erupt into overt speech. Another noncritical person can be shy and introverted, so fearful of being rejected by others that he or she does not dare say much of anything. But reticence does not mean one is listening. One may be carrying on an internal dialog.

It is surely ironic that unassertive, unassuming people often give the impression of needing to have their egos built up, while the cool and confident critical thinker is often identified as an egotist. This is precisely what the critical thinker is *not*. People who are unsure of themselves, who are defensive, must always personalize whatever happens, whether they do so openly or not. You cannot become a critical thinker until you learn that impulsive, self-centered responses are not the only ones that can be made. A rule of thumb is to delay reacting.

Personalizing what happens and what others say is usually a cover-up for a lack of perception. We may have become so accustomed to leap without looking or listening that we are easily confused by events. We manipulate them inside our own brains so that they seem not to be confusing: "Oh, I see what that's all about," or, "Nobody can fool me on that one." Another ploy is to force someone else to support our manipulations: "Am I right? Wouldn't you have done the same thing? Sure you would!" Other people, perhaps involved in their own personalizations, may offer positive support just to avoid having to figure out the situation for themselves.

Thought would destroy their paradise.
No more; where ignorance is bliss,
'Tis folly to be wise.

Thomas Gray

For most of us, the roots of imperception lie buried in our childhood. Think back to dinner table talk. Was it full of silly little details, such as "Who spilled the salt?" or "Finish every mouthful of that meat, or you'll get no ice cream"? Or were real subjects discussed?

One must become able to transcend the narrow confines of a self-centered existence and believe that one will make a significant contribution to life—if not right now, then at some future time.

Bruno Bettelheim

Literalism is not always a sign of a nonthinking person. Some very bright people have proved incapable of moving from dead center in any conversation. One reason may very well be a humorless approach to life, a belief that mind play is childish and that all thought and discussion not directly related to action or the making of money should be avoided. Such people are used to working with the concrete realities of each moment and adjust their responsiveness to experience accordingly. Life is detail after detail. They are often not so much blind to general principles as impatient over wasting time. Sometimes they enjoy discrediting those who are not dedicated to "important" matters but spend their time idly chatting about books or world affairs which obviously have nothing to do with making a living.

Recognizing Contexts

No one goes through life completely isolated. We cannot live on an island, never making contact with others. Therefore, everything we say or do occurs in a context—a framework of circumstances and relationships. The *figuratist* perceives context; the literalist seldom does.

Enter a room, and you are in the midst of a context. Who is present? What are they talking about? What precisely is going on? What relationship do you have with each of these people? The figuratist rarely barges into the midst of the conversation or ventures an opinion before forming a perception of the total context. The literalist, in the habit of responding to parts, never wholes, almost always reacts to random stimuli.

Each day can be divided into contexts. We usually awaken to the family setting—to a family context. There is always unfinished business, some ongoing problem, some existing network of relationships. The nature of the context changes consistently, so we must keep tuned in. Family contexts are easily ignored; that is, an issue involving the whole family can immediately be translated into "How am I affected?" How often do we really look at and listen to close family members? How often do we ask, "I wonder if brother (sister, mom, dad) perceives the problem as I do"? We believe that, because of the peculiar nature of the family circle, we are exempt from having to view family matters objectively.

Some contexts happen without warning, and the literalist is caught napping. A chance remark, a quick reply, the exchange of glances between two other people—and a context is set up. Anthropologist Gregory Bateson laments that too many people live in terms of "pieces," but "the pieces of . . . patterns are not the patterns." One example he uses is the prosecution of an offender for alleged "criminality." What, after all, is criminality? It is a type of behavior for which one may be held responsible and made to pay a penalty. But, in Bateson's opinion, the specific behavior in question is only a piece of the pattern, not the entire pattern. Later, when the offender is released from prison, he is determined to "work the pattern with more skill, so as not to get caught. For thousands of years people have tried to punish pieces of the pattern."

Contexts exist whether recognized or not. Almost any remark contains assumptions which provide a hidden contract. For instance, if someone giving a party remarks, "Let's invite Laura for Albert," there is the assumption that couples are better off at parties than individuals; that Albert can't find his own women; that matchmaking is an honorable enterprise; and even that an "unattached" man or woman would somehow be an intrusion for others at the party.

What is the context of the following remarks?

"You'll appreciate your college education more if you find a part-time job."

"When you were in India, what did you learn about the country and the people? No, more important what did you learn about yourself?"

"If God had intended women to be men's equals, He would have made them so."

"You come to my house for dinner this time. I went to your house last time."

Literalists make and hear context-ridden statements without knowing they are doing so. Do you think any of the above remarks were made by figuratists? Can you justify your answer?

Linguistic Tip-offs

Figuratists are so called because their language gives them away. It is colorful and imaginative, nonliteral. Their language declares their independence of the details. Instead of telling you everything that happened, the figuratist sums it all up in a few bold strokes.

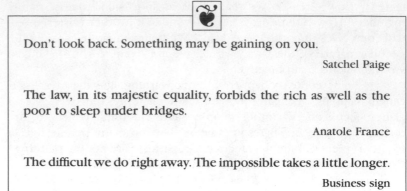

Don't look back. Something may be gaining on you.

Satchel Paige

The law, in its majestic equality, forbids the rich as well as the poor to sleep under bridges.

Anatole France

The difficult we do right away. The impossible takes a little longer.

Business sign

Literalists frequently mix their metaphors. The literalist says, "People walk all over me, but I'm putting my foot down!" (Unaware of whose foot is down.) The figuratist is likely to reply, "If people walk all over you, make sure you have a good strong mattress." And the literalist is likely to add, "I buy almost everything at Sears."

The secret of figuratism is knowing what is appropriate to think and say about a given phenomenon. When the state representative reports to a group of his constituents, all teachers, that his bill for higher educational budget was defeated because "the conservatives literally emasculated me," the figuratist lifts an eyebrow. How well is he handling his job up there in the capital?

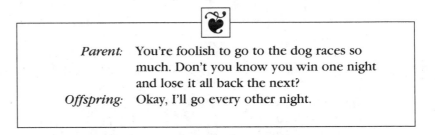

Parent: You're foolish to go to the dog races so much. Don't you know you win one night and lose it all back the next?

Offspring: Okay, I'll go every other night.

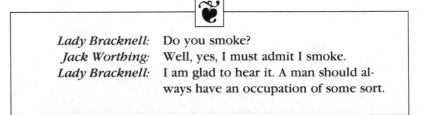

Lady Bracknell: Do you smoke?
Jack Worthing: Well, yes, I must admit I smoke.
Lady Bracknell: I am glad to hear it. A man should always have an occupation of some sort.

When it is appropriate—and it is not always appropriate—figuratists operate from general principles rather than a long string of specific instances. It strikes the figuratist as a waste of time to bore friends with a blow-by-blow description of all the incompetents met during the course of a single day, but the figuratist would rather ignore the matter altogether—on the grounds that everyone is familiar with the existence of incompetence at every turn. The observation "I also did some shopping today and was pleased to see that standards of incompetence are being met in every store" ends the subject.

Literalists relive their days over and over because they never stray very far beyond their own egos. If they do discover a general principle, it is usually that people and events are conspiring against them. They are fearful of being objective, of seeing things as they are, for if they ever do they might not find their way back home!

Figuratists, on the other hand, are free spirits, not easily threatened by situations, not easily cowed by other people. They do not have to talk about themselves all the time, because they are not insecure about their own worth. At the same time, they save themselves from arrogance by the very fact that they do attempt to be objective about all things, including themselves. They make mistakes like anyone else, but do not hide guiltily from them. They may even joke about them. Nobody can be a critical thinker all the time. There are times when only the hard details matter.

> *Mechanic:* The distributor cap is cracked, the points are worn, and the rotor needs replacing. As a matter of fact, the points should be gapped with a gauge; the dwell should be checked with a tach, and the timing needs resetting. The gap should be set at 35, the rpm at 750, and the timing at 6 degrees before top dead center.
>
> *Bewildered:* Why doesn't the car run?

Parents often make the mistake of supposing that children are immature and can thus be dealt with in any way that suggests itself at the moment. Many parents do not bother to prepare their children to follow the rules of responsible, critical adults. If the family watches a television show together, is it talked about afterwards? Or does the following happen? "Turn off the set and march right up to bed." If a bedtime story is read, does the parent show an obvious desire to turn out the light and leave the room, or is the story discussed? It is a sad fact of human experience that little of general, impersonal concern is mentioned within the family circle.

In this world there are only two tragedies. One is not getting what one wants, and the other is getting it.

   Oscar Wilde

Put all your eggs in one basket and—WATCH THAT BASKET.

   Mark Twain

"Business is business."

"Family is family."

"Boys will be boys."

Situation	Impulsive Noncritical	Delayed Critical
People are talking about a book you have not read.	"I think they're show-offs; they probably haven't read it either."	"What is the book basically about?"
You discover that the number of burglaries in your neighborhood has tripled.	"Thank God my house has been spared!"	"Perhaps I should get an estimate on a security system."
You read that two small Third World countries control much of the Earth's supply of energy.	"What's that got to do with me?"	"Why is our country not developing new energy sources? How may I show my concern?"

Most of us grow up, as Paul Goodman put it, "absurd." Most of us grow up any way we can. There is very little we can do about how we grew up. But we can decide it is high time to start thinking, to start examining our remarks and our thoughts for the amount of personalizing and the lack of general awareness we will find. It is possible to make the conscious decision to be otherwise. The very best starting place is silence and a determination to hear and notice more.

The Critical Thinker as Critic

In its more formal aspects, criticism is associated with literature and the arts. A professional critic is someone paid to read, view, or listen and present an informed opinion. Society absolutely needs such people. Critics are to plays and concerts what medical specialists are to desig-

> Once there were two performers opening in new plays on the same night. After the performances both entertained friends and fans in their dressing rooms.
>
> One performer asked: "How was I?"
>
> The other performer asked: "How was it?"

nated parts of the body. Professional critics must discern and evaluate with cool detachment.

But the general public, too, can increase its enjoyment of the arts by practicing some of the skills of the professional critic. Since no one begins with those skills, we achieve competence gradually. With growing experience, and with attentive listening or reading, we begin to discern the various elements of the music or the play; to compare the work with different interpretations in previous performances; to see what the author or composer is driving at. Each new experience is added to the old, so the effect builds. We concentrate on the music or the plot structure. At this stage we require more knowledge: information about musical or literary genre, compositional technique, the sounds of various instruments, methods of acting, and knowledge of the past.

Reviews, program notes, and art catalogs for museum exhibits produced by professional critics are often helpful. Professionals have the trained eyes and ears; they are the guides, until we are ready to pick our *own* way along unfamiliar trails. Since the artist is frequently ahead of—or at least traveling in a different direction from—the public's taste, the critical thinker as critic should withhold judgment until a work has been thought about for a time. It would be totally unacceptable to make up our minds in advance, pretending to like something because the experts do, or ridiculing it because it is unfamiliar. The opportunity to be a critic does not depend entirely on visits to concert halls or museums. There is always television, which we may approach with an equally dispassionate and analytical mind. When a news event is considered important enough to be carried simultaneously by major television networks, the critical viewer thinks: "Is this really that important?" It's an old question, a philosophical one: "What is worth doing?" And if something is government-sponsored, further questions occur: "What should the state encourage? pay for? withdraw support from?"

A well-known entertainer, on in years but still popular, died suddenly and unexpectedly of a heart attack while in Europe. Two of his friends, also famous entertainers, were asked for comments.

One said: "I feel crushed, abandoned. I idolized him. I used him as a model. I would never have become successful had it not been for his encouragement. Life for me will never be the same without him."

The other said: "He changed the entire history of popular songs. He introduced a style of singing that countless have imitated. He was the first performer to use the microphone instead of merely standing behind it. He created a sound that will probably never be forgotten."

After a while, critical thinking becomes an enjoyable part of being a spectator, though there will always be the uncritical friend who insists: "I'd rather not think about what I see. I'd rather enjoy myself." And there's no way to convince that friend it is possible to do both.

Glossary

critical: An adjective referring to one who makes a habit of standing back and surveying a situation as a whole before reaching a conclusion about it.

criticism: Analysis leading to evaluation (*not* used here in the narrower sense of "finding fault with").

figuratist: One who knows what is appropriate to think and say about a given phenomenon; who engages in "mind play" rather than passively existing; who has acquired the good habit of noticing and listening instead of being preoccupied with self; whose language is full of fancy and good humor; and who, above all, practices the art of critical thinking.

literalist: One who sees specific instances rather than general principles; who moves from point *A* to point *B* in a thought sequence without grasping the essential point of a discussion; who seldom identifies contexts, is generally self-centered, and speaks in plodding cliches.

NOTES

1. William Wharton, *Dad* (New York: Avon, 1981), pp. 419–420.

2. From *The Collected Poems of A. E. Housman.* Copyright © 1922 by Holt, Rinehart and Winston, Inc. Copyright 1950 by Barclays Bank Ltd. Reprinted by permission of Holt, Rinehart and Winston, Publishers.

Samuel F. B. Morse, "Gallery of The Louvre," 1831–33
(Courtesy of Terra Museum of American Art, Daniel J. Terra Collection)

9

CRITICAL THINKING AND THE ARTS

OVERVIEW

As the previous chapter has indicated, critical thinking can assist in matters of personal health, business, school, self-concepts, and human relationships. It is the means whereby we observe, analyze, and clarify all elements of living. If we would seek viable examples of critical thinking in action, if we would require role models by which to guide our own efforts to develop this perhaps most treasured of all human skills, where would we look?

Fortunately for us, critical thinking is more than an invisible halo which adorns the heads of some but not others. It is a legitimate category of the humanities in its own right. Its systematic practitioners are, of course, *critics,* some of whom write for daily or weekly publications, some of whom express their views in books that are eagerly awaited by a knowledgeable, if relatively small, circle of admirers. The study of the humanities is incomplete without some consideration of the critics who spend their lives thinking and writing about the arts and who consequently can be seriously regarded as artists themselves.

THE CRITIC AS GUIDE TO TASTE

The actor and the theatre are lovers; the critic is the chaperone.

George Jean Nathan

The invention of criticism is attributed to—who else?—the Greeks, and in particular to Aristotle, who has earned the right to be called the world's first critic. Ever since, many important critics—that is, people who produce a considerable body of writing about the arts, people whose opinions prove valuable and highly sought after—have viewed their function as an Aristotelian one—that of guiding taste. Beginning readers of serious criticism often experience some resistance to this notion.

Do Absolute Standards Exist?

Important critics are seldom considered by their publishers as belonging in a "service" category—as, for example, the travel or restaurant editor might be. For centuries criticism (as opposed to reviewing) has been an institution of higher consciousness in society, and the very best critics often attain a stature equal to that of highly respected philosophers and speculative scientists. If the latter concern themselves with the ultimate truth about things, the former seek *the truth of excellence.*

Critical thinking is a legitimate category of the humanities in its own right; its systematic practitioners are critics.

The true critic is not attempting to recommend this book or that movie. Critical consciousness really has no interest in what entertains us and doesn't care whether we agree with the opinions expressed. It is frequently regarded as snobbish, especially by those who are put on the defensive by an exhibition of broad knowledge and intricate mind patterns. But, like any other thought process, critical consciousness is a role model for those who recognize that the intellect needs exercise as much as does the body.

In a now-classic article written more than two decades ago, Robert Brustein, an eminent theater critic, expressed quite clearly his purpose in writing theater reviews. First, he indicated that he does not regard potential theatergoers as his target audience.

> Dear reader, let me assure you that I do not write to arbitrate your theatregoing activities. I confess to the deepest ignorance about who you are, how much you know, or

> what you consider a good play, so it would be the sheer-
> est impertinence for me to try to guide your taste. . . . I
> imagine you as an ideal spectator, one who responds only
> to the best in the theatre, and who therefore visits it very
> seldom.[1]

He has some pretty high-handed advice for the reader who enjoys
going to the theater for relaxation:

> Perhaps you are a "common" spectator, and for the sake
> of a few hours of relaxation are willing to accept consid-
> erably less than perfection. If so, depart from me, along
> with your brethren the "common" reader and the "com-
> mon" man, and go consult a "common" reviewer. You
> will find him in your newspaper, especially hired to cater
> to your taste, his virtue being that he knows just as little
> as you.[2]

However outrageous one might consider such verbal lashing,
however arrogant and impossible one might personally consider Mr.
Brustein to be, one cannot find fault with his honesty and precise articulation of what he is about. He does not ask that anyone like what he
says, any more than does the philosopher who has no choice but to
think a certain way. Philosophers and philosophical critics are not in
the business of winning popularity contests. They are, in fact, not in
any business. They represent particular kinds of sensibilities, functioning analytically, for they know of no other way of being in this world.

Critical consciousness has no interest in what enter-tains us and doesn't care whether we agree with opin-ions expressed.

Brustein sees criticism as being still as it was when Aristotle
invented it 2500 years ago: something "designed for experts, dedicated to absolute standards, and practiced today by very few." Why
should he, a theater critic, rant and rave ecstatically about plays that
provoke a few chuckles *if* sober reflection indicates that they will be
easily forgotten by the next morning?

This kind of critic deserves the designation philosophical,
because absolute standards—by which he means the truth of excellence—are glimpsed by him. He knows they are there, whether anybody is interested or not, much in the same way that the physician as
philosopher knows we shouldn't drink or smoke. We might add, not so
incidentally, that in our heart of hearts *we* know it too, whether we
follow medical advice or not.

Brustein views his function even as Aristotle himself viewed
his own: to work toward the "correction of taste." The phrase is intended to mean *defining* and *analyzing* matters of taste, setting the
record straight, so to speak—not "redoing" people. If you were to argue that a currently popular rock singer is "just as good" as the leading
tenor at the Metropolitan Opera on grounds that "it's all a matter of

personal taste," the philosophical critic would reply that you are personally entitled to believe whatever you wish about tenors and rock stars. You may even prefer the food at a popular fast-food restaurant to that of Lutèce in New York or Antoine's in New Orleans. Your personal preferences, however, may well be quite different from those of objective critics, in the same way that universal moral principles exist whether a given individual wishes to live by them or not.

If the critic does have a target audience, Brustein adds, it is probably the future itself—or rather, future generations of people who seek the very best in the arts and might look back at what he has written, laughing to themselves if, in the unguarded moment, he once happened to praise something nobody will take seriously anymore. "This laughter is what terrifies us in our sleep, and nudges us forward in the ruthless pursuit of art."

Brustein, like most others in his profession, believes that absolute standards exist by which the classic works are known and aspiring new works are evaluated. If this were not the case, critical consciousness would disappear from society. Surely it would be unnecessary. Critics who spend their lives reading books, seeing plays, going to art shows would not have to express their opinions, since anybody's "gut" reactions would count just as much.

The critic, in the classic sense of the word, does not believe "gut" reactions are valid as standards, though they may be fine for an individual. This critic is saying to us:

> Like what you will; *do* what you will. Enjoy yourself as you please. What I write may have nothing to do with you at all. Standards of excellence are like the crown jewels. Some people have no interest in the fact that they exist and can be viewed. Some people live perfectly wonderful lives without going near them. But surely, we can all agree that they are not the same as costume jewelry from the five-and-dime and that they *do* need to be guarded.

Nonetheless, debate over what constitutes an absolute standard does go on among people who are widely versed in the arts. But disagreement at a certain level of critical awareness is not the same as abandoning the whole idea of standards altogether and saying that *all* taste is completely relative.

Responsible Reviewing

The critic who holds down a 9-to-5 job on a daily paper is often considered to be a middle-brow office worker by critics who express themselves mainly in essays or books. True, the daily "reviewer" of movies or plays (often one person is supposed to be an expert in

Whether I do or do not like the taste of chocolate cake has nothing to do with the inherent value of chocolate cake. It's irrelevant. It's only my whim. It has nothing to do with whether it's a good cake, a well-made cake whose recipe was followed precisely, the end result of which is the total, the sum of all its parts. So is the same thing true of music.

Frank Cooper

Brustein sees criticism as being still as it was when Aristotle invented it 2500 years ago: "designed for experts, dedicated to absolute standards, and practiced today by very few."

either category) or books can become quite harried and must sometimes feel as though trapped in a revolving door: The curtain falls at 10:30, then it's back to the office in a speeding cab to punch out a two-column review in time for the morning edition. There is seldom time for ample reflection and sober analysis.

And true, when one has to worry about the weekly paycheck, there is such a thing as irritating the paying customer and having to answer for it. There was the famous case two decades ago in which Pauline Kael—generally acknowledged as a film critic of considerable taste—was fired from her magazine post after hordes of angry readers protested her unfavorable review of *The Sound of Music.* Ms. Kael survived the indignity, her critical consciousness still intact. But many local reviewers are forced to leave their integrity at home in a closet when they report for "work."

And yes, there have been scandals in the reviewing profession. A major California newspaper recently fired its dance critic after publishing his scathing review of a ballet which had been withdrawn before performance. The beleaguered critic, questioned by reporters, said he had been overworked, had been feeling ill, and did not remember whether he had attended the performance or not.

Nonetheless, those of us who have only so much time (and funds) to spend on leisure will want to consult reviewers and are generally glad they are around. Without expecting a broad, universal critical awareness, we *can* learn how to tell the responsible reviewer from the one who enjoys the buffet at the local dinner theater and doesn't want to see it go out of business for that reason.

The most basic and most obvious way to "use" a reviewer is as an aid in getting good value for your money. In the case of a concert or a play, attending the performance may be a one-time experience, and the price of admission is often high enough to make consumer guidance worthwhile. Films, which cost less and can be viewed at a variety of times, still require a choice between alternative ways to spend leisure time.

Since we will probably not want (or be able) to read every review of a new movie, we need to seek out the one or two reviewers whose opinions we have come to trust. Even reviews by someone who has been disappointing in the past can be useful as a negative guide. Many people use critics in this way, knowing that a highly favorable review, replete with the critic's favorite cliches like "hilarious" and "wholesome family fun," guarantees the film is well worth missing.

A responsible reviewer usually does more than describe what took place on the stage or the screen, or what can be heard on a record. A review of a new record album or videotape, for example, may compare it with previous work by the same performer. "So and So has dropped his previous angry sound and become more mellow. Many of the songs are ballads of love and nostalgia." From responsible

A major California newspaper recently fired its dance critic after publishing his scathing review of a ballet which had not been performed.

critics we come to expect *comparison.* If you liked the previous work of this actor, star, artist, expect more of the same—or be alerted to a major change.

In these review-essays we can also expect the responsible critic to display a breadth of knowledge about the art discipline to which the work under discussion belongs. Such reviews are usually found in magazines and journals and are seldom pounded out hastily under a solitary light bulb at midnight. This critic is a serious philosopher of a particular art and jealousy guards the fortress against unworthy guests.

Not long ago music critic Andrew Porter witnessed a performance of a new opera called *Goya,* which deals with the life and death of that famous Spanish painter. The music was written by Gian-Carlo Menotti, a composer of some significance, whose work always arouses high expectations among sophisticated operagoers. Reading such critics, we recognize that less is forgiven the established artist than might be the case with an exciting newcomer who shows great promise. Porter's evaluation of the final moments bespeaks a knowledge of art as well as music and displays an intellectual competence that assures us we are reading words that can be trusted:

> Finally, around the aged Goya some of his genre scenes, caprichos, war paintings, and black paintings are given animated representation, and his young self arrives to tax the dying man with having cared more about art than about life; against oppression by church and state "you were fighting with a brush." It's a serious theme—that of Hindemith's noble "Mathis der Mahler"—here glibly treated and resolved.[3]

The reason the professional critic is paid to have an opinion is that the opinion is expected to be informed.

The more one knows about other works, Porter's subtext goes, the less satisfied one may be with a given experience. Menotti has a serious theme, but Hindemith's treatment of it was "noble." What, Porter implies, can I be expected to say about a far lesser effort?

One might be tempted to suppose that, because Paul Hindemith's reputation as a major contemporary composer is much more assured than Menotti's, Porter is merely bowing to the might of tradition. The responsible reviewer can seldom stand accused of superficial deference to a great name. That is not how the reputations of the important critics are earned.

For example, theater critic Brendan Gill dares to defy tradition when, in a review of Eugene O'Neill's *A Moon for the Misbegotten* performed in revival, he seizes the occasion to reevaluate the play itself, a work which he says has been overpraised by a dramatist he finds generally second-rate. Almost anyone who takes a course in modern drama is very likely to be told that O'Neill is the greatest of all American playwrights and very probably the greatest twentieth-century dramatist regardless of country. But Gill, as we see, is confident of his own seasoning as a critical observer of the theater and does not depend upon the opinions of others:

> There are those who claim to see in O'Neill's "A Moon for the Misbegotten" a masterpiece; to me, it is a fustian, ill-plotted melodrama, which might have attained some measure of public acceptance in Victorian times, when stage-Irish characters were mistakenly assumed by American audiences to be the real thing, but which, written in the nineteen-forties and set in Connecticut in a period some twenty years earlier, stops just short of travesty. We must remember that O'Neill was, among other things, the son of a wealthy father, and although he often wrote about working-class people, as a Princeton dropout he was always, drunk or sober, a voyeur in their midst, self-consciously aware of them as material for his future literary labors.[4]

Gill appears to have the goods on O'Neill. Gill appears to know whereof he speaks. Certainly the average theatergoer might not be expected to be as conversant with O'Neill's background and its uneasy relationship to his plays.

Critics like Brendan Gill and Andrew Porter offer us perspective; they help keep the record straight, so to speak. Responsible reviewers make for responsible audiences, people who will not be satisfied with less than the finest work they can be shown. Responsible reviewers' contributions to the humanities are considerable. Their perceptions and writings are far more valuable to us than are those of indulgent or uncritical critics, whose columns crowd the pages of daily newspapers. These "reviewers" want to promote everything in sight, in prose that is filled with superlatives not unlike those found in paid advertisements. They sound and write as if it were bad manners to do anything but rave, as if the Chamber of Commerce were paying their salaries. They neither compare nor analyze; they simply admire, and their admiration is not good enough for those of us who are neither members of the Chamber of Commerce nor relatives of someone in the cast.

The acutely critical critic can be just as misleading. Some reviewers have gained reputations based almost exclusively on their acid remarks and much-quoted cleverness. Years ago Dorothy Parker was celebrated for having written the shortest review on record: "*The House Beautiful* is the play lousy." If the playwright had not so unwisely reversed the normal word order, that review would not have been possible. No doubt, friends roared with laughter when they read these words of yet another critic: "I saw the play under regrettable circumstances. The curtain was up." But the state of the art is hardly advanced through such blatant destructiveness.

Often a responsible critic will write a general essay using a recent performance as a springboard for announcing some general esthetic principle, reminding readers of necessary standards. In doing so, the critic performs a great service even for those who cannot experience the work or performance which led to the observation.

For example, in recent years, operas have been restaged in ways very different from their original settings. Puccini's *Madama Butterfly,* with its traditional first act that shows a Japanese garden, a bridge, and a house, depicts the love of a young Japanese woman for the American Naval Officer who marries her. He goes away, she has a child, and then he returns to demand that she surrender the child to be taken back to the United States and raised as an American citizen. If, instead of following tradition, the director of the opera decides to stage *Madama Butterfly* in a modern Tokyo brothel, the critic is expected to take a stand. Was the change an improvement? Did it add new meaning to an old story? Is the opera expected to be a period piece, forever performed as originally written? What about staging a Mozart opera as a comment on the Vietnam experience, or *Rigoletto* set in the New York underworld?

The moral critic continually asks the difficult question: Is anything acceptable?

Critic Donal Henahan (*New York Times*, "Music View," July 27, 1986) argues that operas should be staged in settings and costumes suitable to their original performances. He opposes radical restaging of familiar operas and believes that the greatest damage is done to the less familiar works, because so many in the audience will be seeing them for the first time in a way that he describes as "trashing." The fact that strong arguments can be made on the other side simply adds to the sort of debate which delights lovers of the arts. No one expects a definitive answer to the question of how operas "must" be staged, but everyone enjoys a good fight among those with well-argued, passionate beliefs.

It has become commonplace to expect these well-argued, passionate beliefs among sports fans. Was the fight judged fairly? Would so-and-so have been able to beat an athlete from an earlier generation? Should a pass play be called instead of a kick? Should the rule for designated hitter be changed? And so on. None of these questions admits to final answers, but sports lovers enjoy being Monday Morning Quarterbacks, and the after-the-fact analysis spills out of the stadium to newspaper columns and radio call-in shows. Those who know less about sports learn from those who know more, just as we learn when we listen to any knowledgeable, articulate person.

The responsible critic teaches us to be dissatisfied with the second-rate. The critic warns us not to expect a good concert when a famous tenor sings in a cavernous auditorium requiring microphones.

Those who might have been satisfied just to be near the live performer they have seen so often on television are now instructed about the importance of hearing the natural voice unamplified by electronic equipment. Those in attendance may still think the experience was worth the price of admission, even if the singer could hardly be seen from the back of the second balcony. But the critic has reminded them that they were probably attending an "event," a chance to observe a celebrity, rather than a musical recital performed under the best circumstances.

Critical Perspective

We have certainly indicated that responsible reviewing can and does exist and that it has a legitimate and important place in society. But accustoming ourselves to read such reviews, even when we will probably never see or read a work in question, we begin to develop within ourselves what can be called a *critical perspective.*

In the broadest sense, critical perspective belongs to people who have a "handle" on current works of interest as well as a working knowledge of outstanding human achievements in the past. But it is more than a body of information. It is a skill. It is being able to think critically—something we discussed at some length in the preceding chapter. Staying in the habit of reading responsible criticism helps us to develop the skill.

The writings of John Berger, a contemporary art critic, exemplify a form of criticism which enlightens even as it comments. If we are unfamiliar with his subject when we begin reading, we are sure to know a great deal about it and related subjects before we are through. Writing about the artist Amadeo Modigliani, Berger first describes the artist's widespread appeal, the reproduction of his paintings in countless postcards, the new generations which continue to "discover" him. Then, like a good teacher showing slides in class, he calls attention to particular details, writing this on Modigliani's attachment to curves:

> The curve of an eyebrow, the shoulders, a head, a hip, a knee, the knuckles. And after hours of work, correction, refinement, searching, he hoped to refine, preserve the double function of the curve. He hoped to find curves that simultaneously would be both letter and flesh.[5]

Berger notes Modigliani's use of color and compares it to that of other artists, particularly Titian and Rubens. He speculates on possible influences on the artist, on other critics' beliefs that Modigliani was influenced by Italian primitives, Byzantine art, Ingres, Toulouse-Lautrec, Cézanne, Brancusi, Italian sculpture. But he rejects these critical ideas in favor of his own belief that the artist shows a close affinity with a Russian icon. Berger's article "Amadeo Modigliani's Alphabet of Love" appeared first in *The Village Voice,* which regularly carries serious essays about the arts, sometimes in the form of topical reviews and sometimes as critical essays designed to inform about the arts in general and not tied to a particular museum or gallery show. Like other teachers who develop perspective, the critic as teacher does not transform students overnight, but the best ones are accessible to willing learners on more than one level.

Once having acquired critical perspective, one discovers a whole new world, filled with cross-references, allusions, comparisons and contrasts, and, above all, responsible generalizations. A good deal of what we call education is concerned with being able to infer characteristics of a general class of things from observation and analysis of particulars. The adventure novel has certain characteristics: usually a hero of few words, with the ability to endure pain; action which starts within the first few pages; brief descriptions; quickly sketched characters; surprise; an ending survived by at least the hero, no matter how many others have been killed off. The romantic novel has a certain kind of heroine who is expected to do certain things and not to do others. The man who excites her attention is a little dangerous and mysterious but in the end protective and faithful.

Science fiction, coming-of-age films, lyrics of popular songs— almost any specific work—have relatives, other works of the same *genre.* Genre awareness is a gift which critical perspective offers us. We learn that a mystery thriller is better evaluated in relation to other thrillers than to the slapstick comedy we saw last week. Viewing a film on the Vietnam War, one doesn't walk out angrily because there is no apparent love interest. One doesn't condemn a screwball comedy of the 1930s because the plot doesn't make a lot of sense. A contemporary poem written as the poet's stream-of-consciousness without meter or rhyme cannot be judged as worthless because it has not the elegance and rhythm of a Shakespearean sonnet. Nor does the perceptive person deplore an abstract painting because it doesn't seem to be "about" anything.

Critical perspective is forever enlarging its own awareness. If a new work does not immediately "fit" into a genre, one withholds judgment for a time. One attempts to enter compassionately into the psyche of the piece. Maybe it belongs somewhere else. Or maybe it "adorns Nature with a new thing," as Ralph Waldo Emerson said that all real poets do. The critic Russell Baker reminds us:

> As soon as you define a thing it will show you a piece of itself you failed to notice while working out your definition. Then you either have to redefine it or start weaseling about exceptions that prove the rule.[6]

Take, for example, the following little lyric by Langston Hughes, who has long since won critical acceptance as an important modern poet.

> *I could've died for love—*
> *But for livin' I was born.*
>
> *Though you may hear me holler,*
> *And you may see me cry—*
> *I'll be dogged, sweet baby,*
> *If you gonna see me die.*
>
> *Life is fine!*
> *Fine as wine!*
> *Life is fine!*[7]

Once having discovered critical perspective, one discovers a whole new world, filled with cross-references, allusions, comparisons and contrasts, and, above all, responsible generalizations.

A teacher of literature would be hard pressed to tell us what kind of poem Hughes has written. It is not a sonnet or a Japanese haiku, nor does it have a recognizably conventional rhyme scheme. A perceptive critical reaction might be to relate it to the blues. It is straightforward, honest, filled with what we might call free-wheeling emotion. Above all, it does its job, does it not? Makes its point short and sweet. Even without knowing that the author enjoys an established reputation, we could accept this piece as a small gem that sparkles with its own mysterious fire. Critical perspective knows that all art is mysterious.

Humor can be dissected, as a frog can, but the thing dies in the process and the innards are discouraging to any but the pure scientific mind.

E. B. White

CRITICISM AND MORALITY

As we pointed out at the beginning of this chapter, the Aristotelian tradition of criticism is one in which the wise and knowledgeable critic articulates certain opinions for the guidance of others. If we would read, view, or listen to what the critic recommends, presumably the conduct of our lives would be the better for it. No one could argue against this concept if indeed the wisdom of the critic were beyond question and the motives of the critic were solely to guard the integrity of the arts. In many cases the motives are actually to protect public morality against the harmful effects of art, on the grounds that human behavior can change for the worse because of a book or a play, a painting or a symphony.

The interrelation between art and morality cannot be ignored, because no one has yet proved (or seems ever likely to prove) that antisocial behavior can be or cannot be attributable to the characters or actions in fiction and drama or to inroads into the unconscious made by certain types of paintings or sculptures and certain musical sounds and rhythms. The controversy over whether criticism should legitimately have a morally based orientation is continually fanned by documented incidents in which art works have appeared directly responsible for antisocial acts. At a performance of Ravel's *Bolero*—a familiar musical piece in which one insistent theme is repeated over and over, becoming louder and louder and rhythmically more pronounced—a riot broke out in the audience, as men spilled onto the stage, reportedly in an effort to assault the young lady who was dancing to the music.

The Critic as Censor

It is a short step from observing that an art work may prove publicly harmful to proclaiming that it should be banned from publication, exhibition, or performance. Censorship has always been around. Each age has produced its appointed (or self-appointed) guardians of the general moral good. Sometimes religion is the context within which censorship operates; sometimes censorship claims to be an appeal to reason.

Moral criticism of literature, drama, and films proceeds from the rationale that, since these genres offer characters, situations, and plot resolutions, there are moral attitudes at work behind the scenes which need to be scrupulously examined. *The Godfather* film trilogy of Francis Ford Coppola, back in the 1970s, was hailed as an advance in film art by some and denounced as morally dangerous by others. The issue at stake: whether the films were too sympathetic to the Corleone family, members of the Mafia and perpetrators of violent crimes against society. At the center of the controversy: whether the perception of such sympathy could encourage people in the audience (especially young people) to try their own hands at violence.

During the first four decades of filmmaking, Hollywood exerted strong censorship on the studios. Illicit romance between unmarried partners always had to have disastrous consequences; murderers, however sympathetic, always had to be caught and punished; and people who led morally untarnished lives always had to find happiness at the end. Nonmoralistic critics decried these requirements on the grounds that they were more dangerous than "uncensored" material, because they set up false expectations about life.

Many literary and dramatic works of the past, however, now widely accepted classics, do, in fact, contain a view of a moral universe in which good and evil are clearly separated and are appropriately dealt with. All the novels of Charles Dickens, for example, have happy endings—that is, morally appropriate endings—no matter how intrigued we have been all along by fascinating rogues like Fagin, the sleazy king of young pickpockets in *Oliver Twist,* and no matter how boring have been heroes ("good guys") like David Copperfield. Dickens wrote serially for popular magazines and knew quite well he

The critic who would ignore the moral aspects of an art work might be disposed to downgrade an important new piece solely *because it offers a moral vision.*

could not be published without morally manipulating his plots. Dickens acted as his own censor, but this is a far different matter from having someone *else* control art.

A very famous piece of moralistic criticism came from the pen of Jeremy Collier, a priest of the Anglican Church, who in 1698 wrote *A Short View of the Immorality and Profaneness of the English Stage.* The British theater was shut down in the 1640s after the Puritans seized control of the government, to reopen in the mid-1660s with the restoration of monarchy. Charles II, the new king, was celebrated for his free and easy life-style, and during his reign London theaters were allowed all sorts of liberties. Comedies were most popular, their favorite subjects being seductive flirtations and adultery. There was a play called *The Busy Body,* written by a woman (!) and dealing with just what you might think. There was another called *The Country Wife* with a hero named Horner who pretends to be castrated in order to gain "access" to the married women of the town. An "anything goes" attitude seemed to pervade the scene.

Collier asserted that the institution of marriage was being held up to ridicule and licentious behavior treated as so harmlessly amusing that the public was encouraged to imitate it. (Moralist critics have lodged a similar complaint about the contemporary treatment of alcoholism, as in the film *Arthur,* in which the charm of the hero is partly attributed to his being in a continual drunken stupor.) Collier is clear about the function of drama:

> The Business of *Plays* is to recommend Vertue, and dis-
> countenance Vice; to shew the Uncertainty of Humane
> Greatness, the suddain Turns of Fate, and the Unhappy
> Conclusions of Violence and Injustice.

Since what he considers vice is often triumphant and virtue the attribute of stupid characters; since the witty conversations and amoral actions of the intelligent and aristocratic are held up for admiration, he concludes: "To what purpose is *Vice* thus prefer'd, thus ornamented and caress'd, unless for Imitation?"

If it were ever to be established that those who deal sympathetically (or at least nonjudgmentally) with antisocial behavior were *advocating* it, and worse, were successful in modifying the behavior of the viewer, then there would no doubt be many, many who would support censorship. But the strong argument has always been made by writers that antisocial subject matter is not at all the same as advocating antisociality.

William Congreve (1670–1729), often considered the major playwright of the Restoration era, is taken to task by Collier for some of his alleged excesses. But Congreve, like many of his colleagues, often argued that his mission as a playwright was to *mirror his time.*

The controversy over whether criticism should legitimately have a morally based orientation is continually fanned by documented incidents in which art works have appeared directly responsible for antisocial acts.

What struck him as immoral was to put untruth on the stage for the sake of getting some laughs from the audience:

> Is anything more common than to have a pretended Comedy, stuff'd with such Grotesques, Figures, and Farce Fools? Things, that either are not in Nature, or, if they are, are Monsters and Births of Mischance.

In the same year, 1698, he wrote a reply to Collier, making the point that art is involved with truth, not obscenity for its own sake.

We are living in yet another age of strong censorship advocacy, this time on the part of parents' groups and clergy who denounce films and television programs that offer irreverent treatments of family life and appear to make violence and drug use not only understandable, but glamorous and exciting to boot. School children, they argue, should not be allowed access to works dealing with divorce, teenage pregnancy, or the realistic depictions of biological processes in puberty. America is a violent place, they say, partly because of the violence in the popular media. Writers, directors, and producers counter by saying they must show violence if they are to be honest about modern life.

Is Any Subject Acceptable?

All morally oriented criticism does not advocate censorship, however. Some of it is interested primarily in the process by which certain works are classified as art, *regardless* of their subject matter. Yet are there to be no limits? May any artist inflict any vision whatever upon us?

In his review of an autobiography of the Spanish surrealist artist Salvador Dali, George Orwell (1903–1950) examines the problems of attempting to ignore unacceptable subject matter in the appraisal of art. Dali, by his own account, was attracted to subjects which involved torture, humiliation, sexual perversity, death, and excrement. His account of his own life is filled with episodes of actual or dreamed cruelty, and his pictures have titles like "The Great Masturbator," "Sodomy of a Skull with a Grand Piano," and "Mannequin Rotting in a Taxicab."

Orwell does not rush us into the view that "extreme" subject matter should be automatically shunned by the critic. He would not be numbered among those who condemn the depiction of all objectionable persons and events and "crush every new talent as it appears." This he calls anti-intellectualism and points to such greats as James Joyce, Marcel Proust, D. H. Lawrence, and T. S. Eliot as having been victims of unfair attacks by unthinking moralists:

> Such people are not only unable to admit that what is morally degraded can be esthetically right, but their real

> demand of every artist is that he shall pat them on the
> back and tell them that thought is unnecessary.[8]

At the opposite end of the spectrum is the critic who believes in art for art's sake (sometimes called *artsakism*) to the extent that the very issue of subject matter is totally irrelevant. This critic, according to Orwell, leaps to the defense of any artist who is attacked for going beyond the bounds of esthetic propriety:

> If you say that Dali, though a brilliant draughtsman, is
> a dirty little scoundrel, you are looked upon as a savage.
> If you say that you don't like rotting corpses, and that
> people who do like rotting corpses are mentally diseased,
> it is assumed that you lack the esthetic sense.[9]

What disturbs Orwell is that critical acceptance of antisocial subject matter easily transforms itself into acceptance of intolerable overt behavior, forgiven because the doer is supposedly an artist:

> If Shakespeare returned to the earth tomorrow, and if it
> were found that his favorite recreation was raping little
> girls in railway carriages, we should not tell him to go
> ahead with it on the ground that he might write another
> *King Lear.*[10]

But even if the artist's antisociality is limited to the art itself, we cannot be endlessly forgiving. "By encouraging necrophilic reveries one probably does quite as much harm as by, say, picking pockets at the races."[11]

Orwell, author of *1984* (1948), one of the most stridently antirepression novels of all time, is hardly the one to recommend censorship. But he does believe fervently that great art should uplift the spirit and indeed does so by virtue of *being* great art. What worries him is that the products of "diseased and disgusting" minds so often pass for great art and deceive a great many people.

Whether or not "diseased" subject matter "encourages" abnormal reveries and whether or not such reveries are really dangerous in the long run are issues that will forever be debated without resolution. Those who cite Aristotle as the revered founding father of criticism might do well to look carefully into that master's theory of why tragic theater is psychologically beneficial to the viewer. By exposing ourselves to the catastrophic lives of fictional characters, says Aristotle, by becoming emotionally "wrung out" from the experience, we leave the theater in what we would today call better mental health. And what was the subject matter of many Greek plays? Incest and murder—the murder of a husband by his wife, of a mother by her son, or of children by their mother. Great fun, eh what? Yet audiences have survived for thousands of performances.

Art as Moral Vision

Another trap into which artsakists can fall—those critics who would exclude consideration of subject matter altogether—is to be unable to recommend art that does, in fact, seek to communicate a profound moral vision of life. There is a perfectly respectable school of criticism that believes the duty of art is to provide us with such visions, that *defines* an artist as such a visionary.

During the early part of the eighteenth century in England there occurred a general critical rejection of many novels and plays from the preceding period, the time of the Restoration, which we mentioned earlier in this chapter. If you recall, at issue then was the question of whether dramatic artists should be called immoral when they insisted they were only mirroring life. Despite strong critical defense of the Restoration era, by the next century a consensus arose that the purpose of art was to instruct and to ennoble, not to present filth, no matter how true to life it might be.

Who shall say whether a movie about crime will "inspire others with a desire for imitation?" A classic example is on file at the offices of the movie censors. There one can find a clipping about a youth who murdered his teenage date while they were necking in a car shortly after seeing a movie. The film was Walt Disney's Snow White and the Seven Dwarfs.

Murray Schumach

A cornerstone work dealing with the debate of so-called truth vs. so-called moral ennoblement is *The Battle of the Books* (1704) by Jonathan Swift (1667–1745), known to all the world as the author of *Gulliver's Travels*. At one point Swift recounts the fable of the spider and the bee, the former symbolizing permissive modern art, the latter art of classical purity. The spider points out that he deserves the highest praise for the expert craftsmanship by which he spins an intricate web out of his own self, bringing to the world something that was not there before. The bee, he adds, is a mere vagabond, living off the land, enjoying himself as he flies. He produces honey and wax, true, but he has to use things that are already there; he is not a true creator. The bee, however, is not intimidated. He *knows* his true worth. First, the spider should be wary of boasting that his creations come out of himself, for, after all, they are made of dirt and poison. The bee, on the other hand, visits flowers, collects pollen, but does no injury to them. From this pollen come the honey and the wax which increase the "sweetness and light" in the world. The spider "feeding and engendering on itself, turns all into Excrement and Venom, producing nothing at all but Flybane and a Cobweb."

Eighteenth-century criticism deplored the tunnel vision of writers who, having seen the pig in nature, we might say, insisted that nature must be nothing but a pigpen. Like the eighteenth century, we have our share of the latter, as we all know. Our times are liberal to the point at which almost nothing can be excluded from the possible domain of art, nothing, that is, except possibly what Swift called "sweetness and light" itself. We have few if any champions of arts as ennoblement. The pendulum seems to have swung far in the opposite direction. Where the bee accused the spider of bringing forth dirt and poison, substances of his own depraved imagination, a contemporary moral idealist would be afraid his work would be accused of being silly and unrealistic, a product of his own useless fantasies.

The last century produced what may well have been the last of the great idealists in literature, Count Leo Tolstoy (1828–1910), who was a writer as well as a critic. Author of two great novels, *Anna Karenina* and *War and Peace,* as well as many great short stories, Tolstoy looked with a critical eye upon not only the work of others but his own as well. In later life, having undergone a profound religious transformation, he denounced his earlier writings because, as we would say, they were overly realistic and lacked the vision of what human life *ought* to be. They were entertaining to read, true, but, since the creation of art required so much time and effort, that labor needed to be devoted to an *important* function, namely, *the betterment of life.*

Tolstoy also considered his earlier work as having been too complex and obscurely written to reach the majority—a strong failing, because how might one better human life if one's work were not understood? Great art then had to be important, accessible to the ordinary citizen, and helpful toward achieving human brotherhood under the fatherhood of God.

Tolstoy believed the goal of brotherhood could be achieved directly by works which clearly set forth Christian morality, such as *Les Misérables, A Christmas Carol,* and *Uncle Tom's Cabin,* or indirectly "by dealing with basic human experiences which can be shared by all men, and thereby increasing the emotional area in which men can feel together and increase their sense of human brotherhood." He cited as examples *Don Quixote, David Copperfield,* and the comedies of Molière.

Tolstoy totally rejected the notion that art can be left to individual taste: "Beauty or that which pleases us can in no sense serve as a basis for the definition of art." He dismisses as poor art many masterpieces which failed to meet his criteria. A work by Beethoven may be critically acclaimed but fail because only the educated taste can appreciate it. Art, he insisted, must achieve its purpose through appeal to natural, universally held and *shared* feelings.

Tolstoy was never more idealistic than when, as a critic, he was completely convinced that the common man—and in his time he meant the peasant or farmer—must be the final judge. The assumption was clearly that peasants were not only able but willing to spend time in the company of works that, because of universally held feelings expressed, would improve their world.

No one could question the merit of the desire to achieve a better world. If, however, all art that does not meet Tolstoy's criteria were to be abolished, some might argue that the "better" world would be all the poorer for having its humanistic resources curtailed. Gone would be any stories, no matter how honest, in which the main character did not undergo a change of heart, like Scrooge, and be morally improved. Gone would be works of visual art and music which could be considered too "difficult" for and inaccessible to undeveloped tastes.

Whenever we are faced with the issue of moral idealism in criticism, with the denunciation of art that seems negative or morally unacceptable, then we are also confronting the question of *monitoring* the ideals. That is, how is the critic to be assured that the public will not be affected by attitudes and feelings which do *not* work toward human betterment? Will there be a "party" formed, comprised of moral idealists who will see to it that their standards are enforced? What will happen to those who do not "measure up" but who insist on having their views aired? Will they be fined? Imprisoned? Exiled? Marxist critics of today who regularly denounce work that is negative, elitist, obscure, and politically suspect would concur that strong steps need to be taken for the "betterment" of humankind.

Tolstoy was obviously not thinking of such a society, but there is always a danger when a critical viewpoint—*no matter how morally beneficial it may seem in essence*—achieves a position of power. Perhaps it is better for all of us that in a free society like ours divergent critical views are available and no critics have any power that their readers do not wish them to have. Those who, for example, refuse to see a film that has been panned by Pauline Kael in the *New Yorker* do so out of their own free will. Perhaps it is better for all of us that in a free society like ours our most valuable critics have in fact very little power. They are there for our edification (if it happens) and, like Robert Brustein, whom we considered at the opening of this chapter, would be the first to laugh at the thought that they should have *any* power at all.

Why do we need them? Why do we need a sculpture on the lawn of City Hall? Why do we need a symphony orchestra downtown? Obviously they have much to offer us. *That* is not the same as saying we should be forced to agree with them.

GLOSSARY

artsakism: A traditional view held by some critics that the arts are to be cultivated and enjoyed just because they are the arts, not for any expected personal, moral, or cultural value.

elitism: A traditional view held by some critics that the arts have no obligation to people at large, that they belong to the few who can appreciate and cherish them.

NOTES

1. Robert Brustein, *Seasons of Discontent* (New York: Simon & Schuster, 1965), p. 11.

2. Ibid.

3. *New Yorker,* December 22, 1986, p. 90.

4. *New Yorker,* May 14, 1984, p. 130.

5. *Village Voice,* June 2, 1981, p. 38.

6. *Norton Book of Light Verse,* Russell Baker ed. (New York: Norton, 1986), p. 36.

7. Langston Hughes, "Life Is Fine." Copyright 1948 by Alfred A. Knopf, Inc. Reprinted by permission of the publisher.

8. Melvin Rader, *A Modern Book of Esthetics* (New York: Holt, Rinehart & Winston, 1979), p. 419.

9. Ibid., p. 420.

10. Ibid., p. 422.

11. Ibid., p. 425.

James Ensor, "Masks Confronting Death," 1888
(Courtesy of The Museum of Modern Art, Mrs. Simon Guggenheim Fund)

MYTHS

OVERVIEW

This chapter is not about lies people tend to accept without question. Yet when the word *myth* is introduced, people almost immediately think of "untruth." Unfortunately, we seem to be saddled with one word that can be used in two, very opposite ways.

In popular usage, myth is something erroneous yet widely believed—something to be exposed. Look at any library bookshelf, and you will see titles like *The Myth of the Self; Napoleon—the Man and the Myth; The Myth of Mental Illness;* and so on. The sensation-mongering advertisement screams MYTH OF CALORIES EXPOSED! EAT ALL YOU WANT AND GET THIN! If we are to limit ourselves to this one definition, we should be convinced that wisdom can be attained as soon as we recognize and then exorcise all of our useless myths.

But the best-seller list does not tell us about the story of Gilgamesh, as ancient as any literature and still very much alive; or that of Hercules, the man with incredible strength, and his contemporary incarnation, Superman. It does not tell us why children never seem to tire of Cinderella. Or why one particular kind of story—sometimes called the monomyth—seems to have sprung in some version from nearly every culture on this earth.

The two contrary definitions of myth are truth and untruth. In special instances, myth can also stand somewhere between these poles. That is, the early mythology of many cultures embodies imaginative explanations of natural phenomena not scientifically understood at the time, phenomena like rain, thunder, lightning, earthquakes, and solar eclipses. Sometimes called "prescientific," these ancient stories nonetheless suggest the basic human urge to know—not to remain mystified. All mythology shares this urge.

Even the "untrue" myths, which thinking people should expose, probably stem from the same need for understanding. This mythology has been absorbed into long-standing popular culture and dies hard. Some of it often passes for folk wisdom: *Feed a cold and starve a fever. Beware the ring around the moon. Never walk under a ladder.* Untrue mythology contains vast numbers of unexamined beliefs. But they *are* beliefs. At some stage or other, they passed for knowledge. Thus, we see, humanity is a myth-making species.

In its fundamental form, myth, according to Carl Jung, is deep-rooted psychological truth. Jacquetta Hawkes tells us that

> myth represents an absolute truth, affords insight into the "indescribable realities of the soul," or, as Malinowsky says, "is not in the nature of an invention . . . but living reality." [1]

Jung, further, saw myths as emanating from what he called a universal, or collective, unconscious: stories that have the quality of dreams, but not the private dreams of the individual—rather, the inherited dreams of humanity, embodying, as all dreams do, basic realities. After all, psychological reality is probably more compelling than scientific reality.

Much myth is as true today (psychologically) as it was thousands of years ago.

Through the stories we call myths, human beings have told and continue to tell each other things about themselves and their world. Some of it, as we said, is now outdated. Thunder is *not* the sound made by bowling balls of the gods. But much of it is as true today (psychologically) as it was thousands of years ago.

Reading myths, we learn what we have been, what we are, what we hope to be, what we long for, and what we dread. Some have called mythology in this fundamental sense the cumulative wisdom of the human race. Small wonder that an introduction to humanities should give serious consideration to a tradition that spans the centuries from Gilgamesh to Superman.

MYTH AS EXPLANATION

The need to understand and the urge to explain have always been and remain striking characteristics of human beings. They underlie nearly all of the myths we create. Sometimes, especially among very early peoples, the explanation takes the place of scientific knowledge. But sometimes it is very complex—an attempt to account for human behavior. Psychologists of today would be hard-pressed to categorize and label certain behavioral patterns without the assistance of mythology. If there were no myths, it is safe to say, we should know less about ourselves than we do, no matter how naive some of the old stories may seem.

The Natural World

When early peoples observed their world, they were uncertain about nature: day and night, the change of seasons—violent occasions for wonder, apprehension, and worship. Early myths were designed to explain nature, and early rituals were efforts to control it.

In Scandinavian communities, for example, the fertility deity was Freyr, who was thought to bring rich harvests to the earth. He did so by wooing a maiden, symbolizing the union of earth and sky. Rituals which honored Freyr and the abundance he gave were essential for survival. In almost all early cultures help from the gods was needed if crops should fail or were insufficient, for then the mortals had to turn to the sea, where food could be found if the storm god could be placated.

From Mount Olympus, Apollo, the sun god, drove his chariot across the sky each day, thus accounting to the Homeric Greek world for the rising and setting of the sun, just as Apollo's sister Artemis presided over the moon at night. The king of gods, Zeus, was responsible for hurling thunderbolts, and Poseidon controlled the sea.

But these activities could be altered at the whim of the gods. Thus the sea might be made so calm that no ships could move when Poseidon wished to punish a fleet dependent on favorable winds. A tidal wave might appear in response to the prayer of a mortal owed a favor by a god, as when Theseus requested the destruction of his son Hippolytus.

Early peoples performed "sympathetic magic," acting out ceremonies designed to affect the behavior of the gods. Thus at the time of the winter solstice, the longest night of the year, continued darkness was a terrifying event; people in countries throughout the world attempted to evoke the return of the sun through the lighting of candles, as if the sun—or the powers in charge of light—would imitate the light below.

The division of seasons in Greek mythology was explained through the story of Pluto's abduction of Proserpine and the despair of Proserpine's mother, Ceres, during the dark months of fall and winter. During the spring and summer, Ceres, the earth mother, encouraged the crops to grow, because she was temporarily reunited with Proserpine. But for the other half of the year, the daughter had to return to the underworld, presided over by Pluto.

Trees could be connected to the tales told of gods and their frequent involvement with beautiful mortals. The hyacinth and the narcissus are two blossoming trees which celebrate their namesakes and whose origins we recall from childhood. The beautiful young man or woman dies, sometimes in an effort to elude his or her pursuer, sometimes as the result of an accidental wounding, "and every spring the flower bearing the name of the dead ——— blooms again, to remind us that ——— once lived." But Edith Hamilton found a more ominous note in these stories of blooming trees which commemorate mortals. They are, she speculates, vestiges of ancient human sacrifice rather than of accidental death. Ancient people did offer a select number of handsome young people in sacrificial rituals designed to appease the gods. According to Hamilton, when the Greeks told their myths in later years, they revised the stories to rid themselves of this violent era in their past.

It might happen, if the fields around a village were not fruitful, if the corn did not spring up as it should, that one of the villagers would be killed and his—or her—blood sprinkled over the barren land. . . . What more natural then, if a beautiful boy had thus been killed, than to think when later the ground bloomed with narcissus or hyacinths that the flowers were his very self, changed and yet living again? So they would tell each other it had happened, a lovely miracle which made the cruel death seem less cruel.

Edith Hamilton

In North American Indian mythology, human sacrifice was needed in order to make the heavens work properly. After four worlds which had not worked (the final disaster including a devastating flood), a fifth world was revealed, but it was discovered that the sun and moon could be set in their courses only by the death of a Navajo each day and the death of another each night. Later, when human beings claimed credit for the prosperity of the world, they were punished by plagues and monsters.

In Scandinavian myth, it was a giant whose sacrifice was necessary. Ymir, who was nourished by a cow, was the giant responsible for forming men and women (from his left armpit); eventually he was killed and his body "used by the slayers to form the world—his flesh providing the soil, his bones the mountains and rocks, his blood the sea and his hair the vegetation of the earth." [2]

Mythology as explainer of natural phenomena must have made the natural world an anthropomorphic place for members of *any* culture who believed that a god, goddess, nymph, dryad, or water sprite "resided" in a particular place. It made each act of the weather seem a sign of friendliness or terror. Sailors, hunters, and farmers could recognize a threat and request the desired change from the *particular* deity "in charge of" that department. Such belief proved difficult to exchange for later, scientific views.

Indeed, even as late as the fourth century B.C., when Aristophanes wrote his satirical drama *The Clouds,* the character called Socrates (in a deliberate lampoon of the actual man) was ridiculed for his insistence that rain is caused not by a god of rain but by the natural action of clouds. The school in which Socrates taught is called derisively "The Thinkery," which young Athenians in the play were shown to attend in order to learn what Aristophanes clearly depicted as dangerous mischief. In the Aristophanic version of the Socratic school, young people were taught not only to doubt the obvious relationship between gods and weather but to rehearse clever ways of questioning so that a son might actually outwit his father in an argument. It is said that the play, in depicting a dangerous fictional Socrates, helped to convict the actual Socrates by influencing the jurors, who eventually imposed the sentence of death upon the philosopher for alleged "atheism."

Greek Myths of Human Behavior

The Greeks contributed the word *psychology* (study of the mind) without ever knowing that someday it would be a nearly scientific label. They would also be quite astonished to discover how many of their own myths, evolved through an oral tradition spanning centuries, would form the basis of what we know about a good deal of human behavior. The father of psychoanalysis, Sigmund Freud, borrowed from the Greeks as he sought labels to identify certain syndromes, such as the Oedipal conflict.

Even those of us who lack professional training in psychology probably learned the old stories when we were young. And who knows the extent to which the characters and relationships affected our early

The Greeks would be quite astonished to discover how many of their own myths form the basis of what we now know about a good deal of human behavior.

perceptions of what life was all about? See how many of the following plots you remember.

A. An older brother decides to retire; he asks his younger brother to preside over his kingdom until the rightful king, the older brother's son, shall come of age. When it is time to relinquish his power, the temporary king sends the heir on an extremely dangerous mission.

B. A young woman is warned not to open a certain box. Though she has everything in the world, she cannot resist the temptation to see what is meant to be beyond her reach.

C. A wife whose husband is presumed dead after being away at war for 20 years is urged to choose a new husband from among the many suitors visiting her each day; but her loyalty is so strong that she tricks them into believing she will be ready at a specified time—and continues to delay the deadline.

D. A woman married to an older man falls in love with her handsome stepson. When she tells the youth of her passion, he rejects her. Then, when the husband returns from a journey, she reverses the story, claiming that the *stepson* made sexual advances.

E. A man is killed by his wife and her lover. Years later, the dead man's children decide to avenge their father's death—but to accomplish this, they must kill their mother. They do so, and are haunted by guilt.

Readers of some of the many excellent books on mythology—books by Edith Hamilton, James Frazer, or Thomas Bulfinch are among the best known—will recognize the main characters in the examples given above. In A, the young man is Jason, the treacherous uncle is Lycomanus; in B, the girl is Pandora; in C, Penelope is the loyal wife of the wandering Odysseus; in D, Phaedra is married to Theseus and attracted to Hippolytus; in E, Agamemnon's death is avenged by his son, Orestes, and his daughter, Electra.

The myths tell "the common experience of mankind," based on psychological truth, acknowledged by Sigmund Freud himself when he said, "The poets have preceded us." Modern psychology would recognize in Phaedra's accusation against her stepson the defense mechanism of "projection," by which someone attributes to others the deed he or she is personally considering. When the Greeks told about Phaedra, they made her the victim of a fight between two goddesses, Artemis and Aphrodite. Hippolytus is the victim of Aphrodite's anger at his desire to hunt rather than to make love to women. Today we would say he showed arrested sexual development.

The same myth was the basis for a powerful seventeenth-century play by Jean Racine, *Phèdre.* Concentrating on the obsessive emotions of the love-struck queen, Racine devised one of the strongest roles ever written for an actress. Driven to the point at which she cannot bear the touch of even the lightest veil on her skin, the queen finally surrenders to the need to declare her love—and is horrified when she is rejected, in this case because the young man prefers the love of a woman his own age. Racine's impeccable characterization of the catastrophic effects of unrequited love owes everything to the myth which preceded him by thousands of years.

The characters in the stories outlined here behave like real people with recognizably human emotions. This is not surprising. It was, after all, the myths that provided the great Athenian playwrights with plot and character for their tragedies, especially the astonishingly real confrontations between members of the same family at odds over the right course of action—tightly focused scenes of angry denunciation (Creon demanding to know whether his son prefers him or Antigone) and filial agony (Electra prodding her brother, Orestes, into the murder of the mother he adores).

Even when the myths deal with gods and goddesses, they reveal familiar emotion. We recognize, as if they were squabbling sisters, the mortal vanity of three goddesses in a well-known myth. When Hera, Athena, and Aphrodite fought over who should possess the apple labeled "for the fairest," Zeus refused to decide on the winner but rather sent for a shepherd named Paris. The goddesses offered various prizes, even as members of a family compete for the interest of a favorite nephew. But in this case the stakes were high indeed, and, when Paris selected Aphrodite's offer of the most beautiful woman in the world, he failed to note that "strings were attached," that the woman was already married. The elopement of Paris and Helen to Troy led to the famous mythical war, stories of which in themselves could fill a basic course in psychology.

The Family in Greek Mythology

The family seems to have counted very heavily in the Greek view of human existence, a view which, as we know, was not usually a happy one. Judging from the mythology, we can tell that the Greeks attributed much of life's bitterness to family ties, family obligations, and, especially, the continuing impact of ancient, ancestral sins. Without Greek family myths, world literature and our understanding of human behavior would be greatly diminished. Of all the legendary families, that of the House of Atreus is foremost.

The patriarch Atreus committed an original family sin by killing his brother's sons, dismembering them and then serving them as food to their own father. For these atrocities, Atreus and all of his progeny were cursed. The two sons of Atreus were Agamemnon and Menelaus. The latter, of course, suffered when his wife, Helen, ran off to Troy with Paris. The former, having fought for his brother's honor, met with his own disaster upon his return from the Trojan War.

When Agamemnon returned from Troy, he faced a deceptively hospitable wife. Clytemnestra the queen concealed her hatred as she welcomed her husband, under whose leadership the Greek forces had, after ten years, finally conquered Troy. Her hatred was understandable. Agamemnon had been responsible for the death of their daughter Iphigenia when he ordered her sacrifice in order to satisfy the gods, without whose help his ships would not have been able to proceed toward Troy at the beginning of the war. In sending for the girl, Agamemnon had lied, saying that he had arranged for her marriage to Achilles.

Though we are far from Greek mythological concerns like winds and sacrifice, we are close to the drama of family tension. Agamemnon was clearly in what we would call a "no-win" situation. If he had placed his family feeling before his duty as a general and a leader, his troops would have lost the war before it began. Like many others after him, Agamemnon chose the public good over his personal happiness, a choice his wife could not approve.

In a Homeric version of a contemporary divorce trial, Clytemnestra's attorney would have given clear evidence that the bereaved mother had much cause for resentment. However, Greek mythology had too piercing an insight to let matters go as simply as that. Despite the additional grievance Clytemnestra might have cited, her husband's returning from battle with his concubine, the Trojan princess Cassandra, there was the fact of her own infidelity—an affair with Agamemnon's cousin Aegisthus.

Pretending to a revenge motive, Clytemnestra and Aegisthus slay Agamemnon to assure their own future together. But they do not anticipate the impact of the crime on the children of Agamemnon: Orestes and Electra. Caught in a bind that has fascinated no fewer than four tragedians, Orestes ultimately allows his need to avenge his father's honor to override his love for his mother, and so murders her and her lover.

Living in an age dominated by the thought and psychology of Sigmund Freud, Eugene O'Neill came forth with his own version of the House of Atreus. The astonishing fact about *Mourning Becomes Electra* (1931) is not how cleverly the playwright has transplanted the events of the plot from ancient Greece to Civil War New England, but how little the inner lives of the characters had to be changed in order for the work to accommodate modern psychology.

The major change in O'Neill's tragedy is the emphasis he places on the daughter, Lavinia, the Electra of the original myth. As the title suggests, she is the central figure. O'Neill views the character as someone hopelessly caught in an insoluble family dilemma. With a knowledge of Freudian psychology not shared by his Greek predecessors, the American dramatist shows us a daughter who is still bound by unconscious sexual ties to her father and, consequently, repressed hostility toward her mother. When that father is murdered by the object of her unconscious malevolence, Lavinia has an even stronger motive than her Greek counterpart to persuade her brother to avenge the crime.

But what of the brother, Orin? On his part, he is bound by a still unresolved Oedipal conflict—his unconscious sexual attraction toward his mother. At the same time, the object of that attraction has violated the family honor. With a third pressure weighing on him—an unconscious, totally unexpressed attraction to his sister—Orin is finally driven to kill his mother and her lover, a deed that proves more than he can handle. O'Neill's hero takes his own life, as Electra shuts herself up in the old house, there to mourn and suffer the psychological consequences of past guilt for as long as she lives.

Some critics have dismissed *Mourning Becomes Electra* as heavy-handed, as a dramatized Introduction to Psychology 101, as an amateur's guidebook to Freud. Certainly the science of psychoanalysis has come far since its Freudian beginnings, and no one pretends that O'Neill's tragedy is timeless in its applicability. But the enduring impact of Greek family mythology is undeniable. Family ties *do* motivate many of our actions; most families have skeletons in their closets from past misdeeds, which continue to haunt, which cast a pall over the lives of generations not responsible but forced to atone for buried sins. Nor is O'Neill by himself in his fascination for the old myths. Many of the novels of William Faulkner would not exist without Greek family myths. After all, names and nationalities have changed, but the family endures. So does the web of guilt.

MYTHS AND ARCHETYPES

The philosophers Aristotle and Kant, separated by thousands of years, both explained the human ability to organize and interpret experience in terms of innate structures within the mind. Kant, for example, maintained that the sense of space could not be acquired from experience, since experience would not be possible without an awareness of space which all of us bring to it. Other philosophers have argued that each of us is a total blank at birth, but no one has proved it.

The linguist Noam Chomsky believes that a knowledge of grammatical syntax is inborn, otherwise we should not be able to learn to communicate as rapidly as we do. No one has proved *this* point either. The important thing is that we do not appear to have

Jung believed we are born with a knowledge of archetypes, models by which we comprehend experience, models derived from ancient myths.

"outgrown" the need to assert that human beings come into this world with some—or many—resources already in hand.

> The ultimate meaning of these stories is psychological rather than concrete, and the stories themselves serve only as metaphors for the myth, expressing something that is deeply felt but not easily said. Myth in this sense has been compared to music—both involve a form of communication that transcends articulated language.
>
> David Leeming

The philosopher/psychologist Carl Jung (1875–1961) believed we are born with a knowledge of *archetypes,* models by which we comprehend our experience, models derived from ancient myths shared by all of the cultures of the world—mythological symbols and buried assumptions transmitted genetically from one generation to another through what Jung described as the collective unconscious:

> From the unconscious there emanate determining influences which, independently of tradition, guarantee in every single individual a similarity and even a sameness of experience, and also of the way it is represented imaginatively. One of the main proofs of this is the almost universal parallelism between mythological motifs.[3]

Jung's collective unconscious is not accepted by all psychologists or scholars of myths. Without the theory, however, we have a hard time accounting for the reappearance of myths throughout the world: the same accounts of a terrible flood and the salvation of one good man with special advance information; dangerous journeys into the underworld; and above all, identical major points in the life of a singular, partly human, partly divine product of universal imagination known as the *hero.*

One scientific theory favors diffusion, according to which specific myths originated in specific places and then were transported as people warred upon, intermarried with, and otherwise became acquainted with each other. This theory explains how we can find the same myths among people whose migrations we can trace. But Jung was thinking of cultures separated by time and vast distances that nonethcless describe the origins of life and the nature of existence in remarkably similar ways. In particular, the archetype of the hero appeared to him to be universal and not explained through geographical or other natural phenomena.

The World Myth, or Monomyth

Called by some anthropologists the world myth, and labeled the *monomyth* by the Irish novelist James Joyce, the life and circumstances of the hero form Jung's dominant archetype. As early as 1909, a disciple of Freud, Otto Rank, had discovered the characteristics which many mythic heroes share:

> The hero is the son of parents of the highest station. His conception takes place under difficulty. There is a portent in a dream or oracle connected with the child's birth. The child is then sent away, or exposed to extreme danger. He is rescued by people of humble station, or by humble animals, and reared by them. When grown, he discovers his noble parentage after many adventures, and, overcoming all obstacles in his path, becomes at last recognized as the hero and attains fame and greatness.[4]

Freud, a pioneer in the psychological interpretation of ancient mythology, maintained that the two families in the monomyth represented the child's parents as they appeared at different stages of the child's development. But Jung went beyond this interpretation, arguing that the components or motifs of this pervasive myth were primordial images, "or—as I have named them—archetypes."

Whatever the specific interpretations given, the world hero appears to represent humanity in an idealized form: special, nearly godlike, destined for better things, but beset by incredible obstacles. The world hero, unlike the wish-fulfillment figures of early childhood mythology (like Superman), is not morally perfect and does not always triumph. The monomyth is an adult story and does not falsify life.

From a synthesis of major scholars of world mythology, we can derive the following milestones in the life of the hero.

Birth.   In the monomyth the hero's birth occurs under wondrous circumstances: bowing trees; a shower of gold penetrating the ceiling of a room in which a young girl has been confined; the visit of a god in the guise of some other creature, animal or human; and mysterious prophecies. In most cases the hero is sired by a supernatural being, or chooses to believe that he is. Among the Greek mythic heroes whose conception and birth were extraordinary we number Perseus, Hercules, Theseus, and Oedipus.

From the beginning of human awareness, the phenomenon of birth has preoccupied human curiosity. Eventually people came to

THE MYTHIC HERO . . .

is born miraculously

has a strange destiny

is recognized through the performance of some extraordinary feat

reaches a pinnacle of fame through some youthful success

becomes a powerful ruler for a time.

THEN HIS FORTUNES GO DOWNHILL.

know the causal sequence which led to reproduction. But even then, they must have marveled over that sequence, that such a miracle should be possible!

As a way of organizing human experience, the hero myth becomes a counterpart of the way the rest of us "ordinary" mortals are perceived by our progenitors. Each person who comes into the world through the miracle of birth is special in some way. The universe does not roll idly by, indifferent to each birth. The newborn child is a unique individual who matters, not just an entry in the Bureau of Vital Statistics, and the date of birth is not just another day on the calendar. One's birthday remains special for life.

As a human extension of the wondrous prophecy which attends the birth of the hero, the parents of the newborn child are given "best wishes," and the newly arrived hero or heroine is always thought destined for a wonderful future. The congratulatory greeting card perpetuates the prophecy of love and success. In invoking these hopes, we are urging providence to take note of the hero.

Many grow into adulthood believing they have been earmarked for all good things; and if the glorious future does not exactly materialize, they may consider themselves somehow "cursed by fate."

Early Recognition.   The hero must be recognized early in life as one who has been destined for greatness. Such recognition often comes about after the accomplishment of a spectacular physical deed—such as the young Arthur's removal of the sword Excalibur from the stone which has possessively held it until the rightful owner should come along. Recognition of Theseus as a king's lost son came when he proved to be the only one capable of lifting a heavy stone which covered a golden sword and sandals. (One version of the myth credits him not so much with strength as ingenuity in lifting the stone through devising a lever.) Sometimes recognition comes through the fulfillment of a prophecy, as when Jason arrives in the kingdom wearing only one sandal.

In displaying early recognition, myth identifies a universal need for acceptance. In the painful stages of early adolescence, we first ask, "Who am I?" and are fearful that the answer will be, "You're nobody." Children are so small in relation to the adults around them that it is no wonder they develop a sense of unworth.

Many later admit that in early childhood they harbored fantasies of being "secret" princes or princesses stolen from their cradles by gypsies or given away by their true parents. This unknown identity allows the extraordinary child to live with such average people and perform dreary domestic tasks unsuited for royal beings. One day, the child-turned-adolescent knows, the recognition of special status will surely arrive.

The Great Deed.   The vital part of every monomyth is the hero's performance of a magnificent feat, always in young adulthood, at a time when the hero has left home, separating himself from his parents—a mythical version of the universal rite of passage: the attainment of adult status at puberty.

Almost every early culture has required the accomplishment of an arduous task to signify an end to childhood: enduring bitter cold, surviving the wilderness, conquering a predatory beast. Theseus destroyed the Minotaur of Crete, a creature with the head of a bull and the body of a man, a creature which had demanded regular sacrifice of the finest Athenian youths and maidens. In order to kill the Minotaur—an extraordinary feat in itself—Theseus first had to find him by making his way through the labyrinth, an involved series of deceptive passages, which Freud-oriented myth commentators have viewed as the journey through the maze of childhood sexual stages. The ultimate discovery of the Minotaur becomes symbolic of the newly arrived adult male's sexual potency.

Many of the great deeds in world mythology are physical, but others, notably in Greek mythology, are intellectual. Oedipus, for example, had to solve the riddle of the frightening Sphinx: "What creature walks on four legs in the morning, two in the afternoon, and three at night, and moves most slowly when it has the most feet?" Correctly responding, "Man," Oedipus celebrated the human progression from crawling (when we move most slowly) through unsupported strength to the need for a cane in old age; in so doing, he won what appeared to be a prize: rule over the kingdom of Thebes and marriage to the widowed queen, who was in reality his natural mother.

Freud's use of the Oedipus myth is widely known. In accomplishing his great deed, Oedipus won his mother's love and affection, something Freud tells us all young boys seek. The desire for the mother is, of course, an unconscious one—a stage through which the emerging male must pass. Eventually a conflict ensues between the conscious demands of adult rationality and the suppressed love for the mother, a conflict which is not always successfully resolved.

King Arthur's spectacular deed was social: the creation of policy making within an absolutely noble state governed by kindness and good will. A key feature of this utopian society was chivalry, the special protection of and reverence for women.

The empathic celebration of a hero's successful and wondrous feat is a need that stays with us long after our first exposure to myths. We mark the milestone achievements, and they are ways of structuring our personal calendars: Inauguration Day, the Academy Award ceremonies (". . . the envelope, please!"), the placing of the ribboned gold medal around the neck of the Olympic champion. The heroes of these achievements are unable to go anywhere as private citizens. Autograph seekers mob them; screaming fans press forward in an effort to touch them. They possess magic, which the fans think will rub off on those aspiring to equal fame.

Loss of Power. Myths as imaginative presentations of the human story do not end at the top of the hill. (Fairy tales do. When the Prince marries Cinderella, we never hear a word beyond "They lived happily ever after." Perhaps children are too young to hear complete stories.) In myth, the heroes inevitably fall from greatness.

Theseus, for example, soon runs into trouble at home. His wife persuades him that his son by a previous marriage has made improper advances toward her. In a rage, Theseus invokes Poseidon, the god of the sea, to destroy the young man. And there is no miraculous rescue in the nick of time. Hippolytus is destroyed; only then does the wretched father discover that the advances were those of his wife, not the son. But a tragic personal doom also awaits him, as he is treacherously pushed from a high precipice by a supposed friend of his father.

Nor is it enough that Oedipus finally learns the shocking truth of his parentage and incestuous marriage. Refusing to blame fate for his misfortune, the hero blinds himself and goes forth in exile and shame, to wander homelessly for the rest of his life. "I am the unclean one who has defiled this land," are his words to the citizens of Thebes. But why? A prophecy has apparently established all of the circumstances of the hero's entire life. What could be easier than to exonerate himself from all guilt? But in accepting full responsibility for the unmentionable crime of incest, in passing judgment on himself, Oedipus retains his noble status. In Sophocles's overwhelming dramatization of the myth, the doomed hero staggers forth from the city, but *he is not bowed.* The grieving citizens make a path for him. A vast presence is departing, and he will be mourned for many years to come.

The loss-of-power motif in the monomyth can be at once a courageous confrontation with the universal fact of failure and a strategy for coping with failure by a heroic model of the self-determining and unique individual.

Fickleness of Society. Not every myth hero accepts responsibility, nor is every version of the Oedipus myth exactly the same. What Sophocles did was utilize the subject in a way that suited him. But the potential was there in the myth.

Another strategy for coping with failure, also present in the monomyth, is the attribution of loss of power to public rejection. The previously loyal subjects of Theseus did not stand by him. Blaming him for the Spartan invasion of Athens at a time when Theseus was gone from the kingdom, the people drove out their ruler, forcing him to seek the hospitality of the king who eventually destroyed him. Significantly, however, the citizens later realize the mistake they have made and,

Myths often demonstrate the fickleness of society, which first accepts and then rejects the hero, only to glorify him in death.

When the best leader's work is done, the people say, "We did it ourselves."

Lao Tzu

remorseful over the hero's death, erect an enormous tomb to honor his memory. Thus failure is transformed into eternal reputation.

The human need for public recognition and lasting memory seems hardly limited to early mythology, though it may be predominantly Western in character. The history of Western civilization has recorded many instances of heroes rejected or highly controversial during their lifetimes but revered after death: Joan of Arc, Gandhi, John F. Kennedy, Martin Luther King—to name a few. The archetype of heroic failure incorporates the attainment of glory, giving all of us a resource with which to bear significant loss.

In the monomyth the hero's failure is transformed into eternal reputation.

MYTH THEMES AND SYMBOLS

In addition to the extraordinary universality of the monomyth, the student of myth will find a number of recurrent themes and symbols which either lend structure to a story or serve as significant plot elements. Some are readily understandable in terms of real life. Others are like the motifs that recur in our dreams: running toward or away from someone not immediately identifiable, for example, or falling from a high place into an abyss; or opening one's mouth to scream and having no sound emanate. We shall attempt to identify the ongoing relevance of certain omnipresent themes. That some are dreamlike should not be surprising. Joseph Campbell, an expert in the interpretation of myth, has said that dreams are private myths, while myths are public dreams.

Gilgamesh

Yet another hero. Once there was a creature, *part god* and *part mortal man,* who overcame a *giant* and resisted the love of a goddess. She was so angry she asked still another giant to send a *magic animal,* with the mission of releasing the dead from the *underworld* to consume the living. But the hero killed and *dismembered* the animal, then went to *visit the underworld* in a *search* of eternal life. While he was there he met a former king and his wife, who had eternal life and warned him not to seek it; they told him that humans were not made for immortality. Still he persisted but failed in his attempt when he was unable to stay awake for a week. He did, however, obtain a *plant* of *rejuvenation.*

The story is that of Gilgamesh. It is outlined here to suggest the universality of myth from many cultures (in this case Babylonian), as well as the dreamlike quality and symbolic nature of myth. Giants, magic, animals, and plants are but a few of the universal symbols which

Dreams are private myths. Myths are public dreams.

Joseph Campbell

are regarded as of such importance that scholars of myth have devoted their lives to the study of them.

Magic

Magic is almost always present in myths—magic rings, magic weapons, monsters. One would *need* magic against some of the mythic opponents—a sword at least, or the assistance of a clever witch to make things disappear or to cause enemies to fall asleep or to lead one out of a complex trap. (Remember your dreams? Running as fast as you can, losing ground, being lost . . .) One interpretation of magic may be the human need to believe that the resources for coping with life are, like the sword, literally at hand. Another is that only *certain* people can do the big tasks. If you don't have the sword, don't take on the dragon! The magicians, like Merlin, reassure us that someone is there to do the impossible.

"Mystique" is probably a contemporary version of the magic archetype. While we all desperately believed in magic as children, we grow up to discover that reality is not quite so wondrous after all—an awakening unforgettably captured in James Joyce's short story *Araby* (1926), in which a young boy returns to a bazaar after it has closed for the night and becomes disillusioned at seeing the two-dimensionality of all the marvelous exhibits. But although *we* gradually yield to the demands of realistic thinking, we exempt certain others: an idolized teacher; the dazzling uncle who lives far away and visits occasionally, carrying a magical and bottomless bag of gifts; the new president, who has promised an end to hard times and then is immediately criticized for not waving a wand and summoning forth the god of prosperity.

Words

Language itself is a recurrent mythic symbol. "In the beginning was the Word," we are told; and also, "It is written." One interpretation of word significance is male jealousy over female reproductive powers. In early cultures, when birth was itself considered a magic act, men may well have sought ways to match or even surpass this phenomenon in which they seemed to play no part. So in myth, the power of the uttered word could be supreme. Men *could* talk!

The words "Open Sesame!" provided wonders for Ali Baba, even as *Sesame Street* serves as a modern archetype—the thoroughfare which takes children from ignorance to knowledge through the magic of letters and numbers and the fantasy creatures which attend them. In the fairy tale "Rumpelstiltskin," the young queen is in danger of losing her first child unless she can guess the name of the magical elf. Unless you are told "Simon says," you may *not* imitate the leader; unless you ask, "May I?" you do *not* advance in the game Take a Giant Step.

One interpretation of word significance is male jealousy over female reproductive powers. In myth, the power of the uttered word could be supreme. Men could *talk!*

For thousands of years the world of human (usually male) affairs has counted on the reliability of someone's word, as when a pact is made over a handshake and the inevitable "I give you my word." In this age of high technology we have yet to dismiss the crucial significance of giving one's word or to minimize the disappointment when people have broken their word. (*Break* is an interesting verb to use in conjunction with *word,* is it not? To break a word is tantamount to breaking a wand.)

Numbers

Magic words in myths must often be repeated a specific number of times. Humanity soon discovered numerical units, as if numbers, like words, were basic to the design of the universe. In *The Divine Comedy,* Dante makes spectacular use of the number 3, in honor of the Trinity: 3 major parts; 33 cantos in each part (for Christ's age at his death); plus an extra canto to bring the total to what was considered the perfect number, 100.

People still have mystic feelings about numbers and sequences, expecting that news of two deaths will lead inevitably to news of another—often that of a famous person. A person doing 99 push-ups would probably do one more "to round it out." Tests tend not to have 14 or 19 questions, not just because scoring would be difficult but because the unusual numbers would hang inconclusively. Numbers help to provide the appearance of order. Nearly everyone has a "lucky" number that will guarantee winning the door prize or the weekend cruise. If the universe is orderly, it also contains magic. Luck is archetypically incorporated within that order.

The Command Not Kept

Even with supernatural elements in abundance, the myth often confronts failure. Why should it not? If no other catastrophe ever happens to us, there is still the inevitability of age, pain, and death. Mythology has always dealt heavily in these grim events, but, as we should expect, not objectively, not clinically, not with the matter-of-fact recognition that they exist. A common motif in mythology is an explanation of pain and death in terms of an underlying cause—hence the suggestion that, were it not for a particular occurrence, the dreadful ending of life could have been avoided.

The supreme example of the motif, at least for Western culture, is the story of Adam and Eve and the loss of Eden. The forbidden fruit, traditionally depicted as an apple (though apples are not commonly grown in the Middle East, where the myth originated), contains the knowledge of good and evil. But Adam and Eve were instructed not to eat that fruit; that is, not to avail themselves of this knowledge.

Before breaking the command, the first couple were happy in their simplicity and ignorance—another mythical motif, incidentally, which has stayed with us through the centuries. (Ignorance is bliss.) The aftermath of the first sin was, of course, the introduction to the world of pain, age, and death.

The story is clear enough in its original intentions. However, one of the great characteristics of myth is its flexibility and adaptability. Using the Eden theme, subsequent writers and philosophers have shaped the archetype to express their own views, often quite hopeful. In addition to death, for example, Adam and Eve gained wisdom. Intimacy with each other, unknown before the fall, brought the phenomenon of reproduction. In Milton's epic *Paradise Lost* (1667) the sin is called the "fortunate fall," for without it humankind would never have known Christ and his philosophy of love; humankind would have been denied the glorious possibility of redemption. Without sin how can there be forgiveness? We might even extend this line of questioning and ask: Without so great a loss, how would people have understood the full meaning of Eden?

The Greeks had their own versions of the story. Pandora was commanded not to open a certain mysterious box. Unable to resist the impulse, she finally disobeyed and thus let loose upon the world all of its evils. Realizing what she had done, she slammed the box shut, not knowing that one ghostly entity remained within: *hope.*

Then there was Orpheus, whose songs could melt the heart of a confirmed cynic. Orpheus loved the beautiful Eurydice, lost her to death, and followed her down into the land of darkness. There he worked his musical magic upon the king of the underworld and was given the opportunity to return to life with his beloved. The condition: Orpheus must walk straight up the path to the world of the living, without once turning his head to see whether Eurydice was following. The pact was almost kept, but at the very last, the hero, unable to bear the suspense, turned around for the barest glimpse of the maiden. The command broken, Eurydice was reclaimed forever by the powers of darkness.

The Biblical story of Lot's wife contains similar circumstances. Able to escape the destruction of Sodom and Gomorrah, Lot and his family were given the one condition—that they not turn around to see what was happening. Lot's wife (in this case the woman, we note) could not resist the temptation, did indeed look at the dying cities, and was immediately turned into a pillar of salt.

The broken command as an explanation for human misery— as an alternative to the suggestion that humankind is innately corrupt—has proved widely useful, especially for generations of men able to point to Pandora or Eve as the source of their troubles. But the myth has had less blatantly sexist uses as well—in fact, uses that are not tragic at all. If Eden has been lost, the garden (or age) of innocence

Space-age myths are filled with Eden-revisited themes: colonizing remote planets where war, moral corruption, and environmental pollution are unknown.

is still there, waiting for the pure in heart to find it. Where else did Oz, Shangri-la, or Bali Ha'i come from?

Space-age myths are filled with Eden-revisited themes. Classic science-fiction novels and films have for decades harped on the idea of colonizing remote planets, where war, moral corruption, and environmental pollution are unknown. Eden is an archetype by which we may continually measure what might have been—or what may still be.

The Circle and the Journey

There are two symbolic elements in myths so pervasive and universal that they deserve special consideration. One is the circle as an ever-present geometric shape. It is found as a shield, a ring, a pendant, the sun, the moon, and markings on cave walls or stones. Its importance to the myth-makers is paralleled by countless examples of circular structures throughout the world which have survived from early times: temples, stone circles, and, of course, that most intriguing of all round monuments to ancient humanity, Stonehenge.

The universal form of this myth symbol is the *mandala,* found in the art of almost any period. It is an enclosed circle, often with an intricate design representing the organization of the universe and the various deities which control it. The exact nature of the design is perhaps less significant than the implications of the circular shape. It tells us that the universe is an entity—*one* thing, as indeed our very word for it suggests. It tells us that if it could be viewed from an alternate universe, it would be a round object, something like a gigantic crystal ball, self-contained and distinguishable from anything else hovering in space.

The circle, or mandala, told the myth-makers that the universe was manageable, within human comprehension.

Eastern and Western minds apparently came to similar conclusions about the universe. Both decided on the circular, hence perfect, shape, which made the universe seem somehow *manageable*—that is, within the scope of human *comprehension,* if not control. Contemporary scientific theories, which imply that the universe is misnamed, believe it to be not one thing but an infinite series of galactic systems. Such scientific views push that dreamed-of comprehension of the universe so far into the future that it seems reasonable that we may never be able to understand it. Yet we have Einstein's belief that space is both infinite and *curved;* curved because the principle of gravity is such that an object attempting to move in a straight line forever would be pushed by gravity into a circular orbit, making it eventually return to its place of origin.

Einstein's universe is circular: Space is at once infinite and curved.

Carl Jung saw in the mandala a universal symbol of not only cosmic but psychic organization. He believed that, just as humanity from the beginning appeared unwilling to exist within a shapeless, infinite universe, humanity resisted disorder in human existence, that it rejected discontinuous sensations, made up of a hodgepodge of sen-

For Jung, the circles in myths are projections of an inner need to identify a coherent self.

sory reports, emotions, and thoughts ever bobbing around inside us. The circular shapes in myths, according to Jung, are projections of an inner need to identify a coherent *self,* a shaped self, one that can be thought about and discussed.

Just when human beings began to think self-consciously about themselves is hard to say. We do not find Plato or Aristotle talking about themselves in this way. The notion of an inner ego or self seems absent from their work. One recent study concludes that in Plato's time people still believed their inner thoughts were voices from the gods and that the self did not originate until people stopped believing in such supernatural phenomenon. In any case, if Jung is right, the continual appearance of round objects in myths is an indication that early people were instinctively visualizing the human psyche as a shaped entity.

Like the circle, the journey is integral to the majority of myths—perhaps because human existence so obviously proceeds from one stage to another. Change is fundamental to existence, so why have stories in which people stay just as they are? On the other hand, there are numerous fairy tales—which are myths that do not *quite* tell the whole human story—about arrested development, so to speak. Sleeping Beauty and her parents come to mind immediately.

The journey of life is accomplished by the passing of one milestone after another—usually in the form of a severe test, such as the spectacular deed we were talking about. This is a mythic form of the rite of passage, known to every anthropologist and social scientist. Without the ceremony of commencement, would you really have graduated? Weren't the caps and gowns a way of making the event official? Couldn't the awards have been sent through the mail instead of being announced from the stage of the school auditorium? Wouldn't a marriage be just as legal without the slow march up the aisle? Ceremonies remain important to us, as we continue to picture life as a passage. Society has taken the journey from early myths and transformed it into the means by which the course of anyone's life is defined and measured.

The journey is one of the secret influences of myth. It organizes our lives into goals, destinations, and milestones.

The mythical journey may be slowed by disastrous circumstances. Characters momentarily lose their way in dense forests. Magical potions force slumber and prevent motion. But sooner or later, the journey continues. Our expectations thus formed by myth, we look for progress in our own lives and those of others. When the expectations are thwarted, we say, "He is behaving like an adolescent," or "She's still at the same old job!"

The mythical journey has a goal and is therefore a *quest.* The hero searches for his homeland, a buried treasure, a beautiful princess held captive. The attainment of the goal gives shape and purpose to the linear journey, as though to say that, even though life is marked by continual change it *does* come to something after all.

The twentieth-century philosopher Albert Camus once gave this capsule description of human life: "Man is born, suffers, then dies." In myth these things are also true, but there is more to the story. People are born with a significant destiny; they suffer because of their important quest; and they die only after they have accomplished something.

In myth, the circle and the journey ultimately intertwine. Recurrent motifs mark the course of the quest, and, when the goal is attained (even though death may soon follow), we can say that life has come "full circle." In myth the end is not thousands of miles from the beginning. In myth tomorrow is not just another day. It is eventually that long-awaited tomorrow which was foretold, which *must* happen, or else life is incomplete.

In a hundred different ways we are profoundly affected by these two vast symbols. The "incomplete" life is unacceptable—or tragic. "She died before her time" is a meaningful—and mythic—observation. So is "Here he is, 35 years old, and what does he have to show for it?" Myth keeps us from looking at life as simply "one thing after another."

We are profoundly affected by the two vast symbols: the circle and the journey. The incomplete life is unacceptable.

SHAPING OUR WORLD

We do not want to walk away from this chapter believing that (1) all mythology happened a long time ago, or (2) myths are curious phenomena people use when they don't know any better. Mythology is fundamental to the ongoing process of being human, and it is just as much alive today as it was for the ancient Greeks. Myths are not fairy tales. They are psychological realities which help us shape our expectations and our way of interpreting the world. We absorb mythology in the act of growing up: from the culture surrounding us, from our family, from education and religion. All of these forces supply us with the symbols, themes, and archetypes which constitute what Carl Jung has called the collective unconscious. Without our myths we would not be the species we are.

Mythology and Science

We have said that one form of myth is spawned by the need to explain. It is *pre*scientific rather than *non*scientific. Example: the old Greek explanation of lightning as being deadly spears hurled down upon the Earth by Jove, king of the gods. Nobody believes that anymore. At one time it was a legitimate myth because it gave sense to an occurrence that would otherwise have left people confused and chaotic—and very frightened.

Prescientific beliefs are still around and contribute to the shaping of some people's ideas of the world. Astrology, for example, has fierce loyalty from believers. At a recent conference bringing together highly trained counselors, zodiac signs were used to divide participants into groups, on the professed assumption that those born under the same sign would automatically share common interests. The return of Halley's comet every 75 years is usually preceded by speculations about possible catastrophic or wondrous events that might occur. Mark Twain (1835–1910), it has been noted, was born in a year of Halley's appearance and died 75 years later "with" its reappearance. We can be certain that many believed Twain's life was directly tied in with this celestial supershow.

In earlier decades, when alarms were being sounded over what industrial pollution and nuclear testing were doing to the atmosphere, Hollywood obliged by creating a superficial mythology of its own, in which nature returned the favor by plaguing humanity with one disaster after another: devastating fires, killer earthquakes, volcanic eruptions, radioactive insects and rodents grown to mammoth proportions. In some respects this mythology was not very far removed from Greek myths depicting the wrath of the goddess Nemesis, who lived on Mount Olympus and whose job it was to punish the sin of pride.

Even outside of environmental concerns the myth of Nemesis stays with us. We cling to the fervent belief that those who live evil lives will not escape retribution—even when there are no religious grounds for such a belief. Retribution is somehow built into the scheme of things. When a speeding car cuts us off, nearly causing an accident, we hope to find it eventually apprehended and stopped on the side of the road by a scolding sheriff. On the reverse side, we expect that a good deed will somehow be rewarded. Surely there must be many scientists with such expectations, people who otherwise maintain a detached, purely objective view of the world.

The return of Halley's comet every 75 years is usually preceded by speculations about possible catastrophic or wondrous events that might occur.

Widespread also is the myth of science itself, the conviction that somehow science—a solid entity, an Olympian god, rather than a vast, often disconnected series of hypotheses, experiments, and products—will know what is now unknown, will solve what is now unsolvable, will find what is presently hidden. We speak of finding the cure for a certain disease as if the cure were an elusive forest elf jumping from one tree to another.

The myth can also be harmful. Thus one says to oneself, "I can keep on smoking, because by the time I'm old enough to be in danger, 'they' will have discovered the cure for lung cancer," or, "Of course, I occasionally think about the hole in the ozone layer that keeps growing every year, but after all, it's not my problem; somebody else is taking care of it."

Equipped with a vague and undefined phantom concept of science, or impatient with its slowness to find a cure, many fall into the hands of certain practitioners who promise that people can control their own fates by thinking positively, that concentrating on "wellness," for example, will cause the reduction or total disappearance of tumors. We seek cures through meditation, diet, being touched by those with miraculous hands. Rightly or wrongly, this mythology underlies the expectations of a great many people and is often the cause of deep depression when expectations are not realized.

The myth of science also includes the complacent attitude of educated and sophisticated modern people who talk about mythology as the superstition of our ancestors, who couldn't possibly have known what we know now. Thus is the phantom science given a sibling name, "progress": each generation better off than the last; each new discovery destroying a former scourge; each new truth obliterating a former falsehood—a steady, inevitable march toward the time when . . . when what?

Widespread also is the myth of science itself, the conviction that somehow Science—an Olympian god, rather than a vast, often disconnected series of hypotheses, experiments, and products—will know what is now unknown, will solve what is now unsolvable.

The progress myth also has its opposite, which perhaps we can call the "downhill" myth: Time is running out. Each generation is worse off than the last. Our forebears never realized "how good they had it." Oh, why could I not have been born into a more innocent bygone age before automobiles, before computers, when people were genteel, civilized, caring; when crime was unknown?

The Garden

A close kin to the downhill way of shaping experience is primitivism, an eighteenth-century but still surviving philosophy we discussed more fully in Chapter 3. *Primitivism* is the belief in a reality we can call the "state of nature"—a condition in which one lives close to the earth, eats only the food of the earth (vegetables, fruits, nuts, grains), lives in the simplest of habitats without "artificial" luxuries like electricity, stoves, air-conditioning, and supermarkets. In such a state one is healthy, happy, and safe. No crime exists. There is no competition, for the earth, left to itself without human scientific interference, will always produce enough for all.

The businesswoman, returning to her apartment after an exhausting day of intense, closed-door meetings, switching off the lights, and resting her head for a few minutes, may well derive a fleeting bit of comfort in the dream of drifting in a tiny houseboat on a lazy river. All of us share the dream at one time or another. Suburbia itself is part of it. We must get out of the city. Let's go camping on our vacation. Crime is always more abundant in the city. People in small towns are happier and nicer than people in the city.

In the eighteenth century, when places like London and New York were becoming ugly, dirty, and overpopulated, the "unspoiled" countryside beckoned to everyone, and the mythic figure of the noble, happy savage made a hugely popular appearance on the stage and in fiction. Primitivism gave birth to the story of Robinson Crusoe and his benevolent, faithful Friday, a magnificent and benevolent savage who is what he is because civilization has never been close to him. The desert island, in fact, has never left the writer's or the world's stockpile of myth. Who has not got—tucked away in a remote corner of the semiconscious—the impressionist image of a secret retreat, a place where one cannot be reached, cannot answer the phone, cannot be held responsible for a single action?

The "discovery" of America in 1492—with the Indians standing by watching it happen—gave rise to a new version of the Garden archetype: the idea of the New World.

Mark Twain—he of the comet birth—gave us Huck Finn and his wonderful raft, not to mention the limitless horizons of the eternal Mississippi River, a perpetual escape from civilization, its moral codes, its social demands, and its unhappy inhabitants. Sir James M. Barrie gave us Peter Pan, who eludes the aging process and lives an irresponsible boy's existence in Never-Never Land. More recently, Steven Spielberg gave us E.T., the Extraterrestrial, an adorable, unspoiled child from outer space who manages to escape the clutches of humanity, generally—except for a tender and understanding little boy—unworthy of his purity, and waits somewhere "up there" for a true believer who can find a way out of the mess we humans have made of this once-beautiful earth.

Many scholars of myth believe that the archetype of the country (as opposed to the city) or the desert island (as opposed to civilization) is a variation of the original and overwhelmingly powerful archetype of the Garden. The Bible is only one ancient source of the Garden symbol: the original, the pure, the natural place people enjoyed before something happened to change everything—and not for the better.

In the Bible there occurs, however, a countermyth with a countersymbol: If Adam and Eve were expelled from the Garden of Eden for their sin, there will be the Land of Canaan, promised to the descendants of Abraham. Though these descendants were originally understood to be the Hebrews alone, other cultures have developed their own versions of the Promised Land. In gospel songs and spirituals, blacks sing of crossing the Jordan and finding salvation. Hindus and Buddhists long for nirvana, which is not, philosophically speaking, a place, but which nonetheless holds out the promise of a better life. Our Native Americans thought about the Happy Hunting Grounds.

The "discovery" of America in 1492—with the Indians standing by watching it happen—gave rise to a new version of the Garden archetype, the lustre of which has never diminished: the idea of the New World. First came the explorers proudly planting their nations' flags on the "virgin" soil. Then came fragile boatloads of pilgrims seeking a new start in life, seeking freedom. Then by the thousands came the immigrants seeking prosperity in streets paved with gold. As the eastern half of the United States became densely populated and the dream of prosperity became a bit gray around the temples, the archetype of the Garden was transformed into the frontier, the wide-open West, the lush green fields of California. Whatever disillusionment may have been suffered by however many millions, the symbol of the New World is still there, as new dreamers arrive by the boatloads or as artists-on-tour defect from repressive governments.

When they come to the Promised Land, these modern immigrants bring with them a strong archetype, that of the Family and the customs, traditions, beliefs, and rituals which hold the Family together. They transplant these rituals to the new land. Sometimes they are received with enthusiasm by "the natives," and sometimes, regrettably, they are rejected, scorned, derided. Often, members of the younger generation drift away, become part of the new culture. The elders sometimes intensify the traditional rituals, hold even more tightly to the Old World customs, close themselves in for fear of losing identity, self-respect, dignity. Disenchanted by the New World, they lie in bed at night and remember the "old country," where things were better, people were nicer, the streets were safer. Like Dorothy in the Land of Oz, they discover that maybe Kansas wasn't so bad after all. The Garden seems always to be somewhere else. But if this archetype can cause depression, it is also the source of much-needed hope.

The Hero Today

We keep alive the archetype of the Hero. We still have demigods, if not as the literal result of the union between a deity and a mortal, as in olden days, then in the form of celebrities whose exploits we follow in magazines, gossip columns, and television interviews; people who set the trends in clothes, hairdos, language.

We revere the athletes who still have Herculean tasks to accomplish—and do, and so we celebrate the record-breaking home run, the world's fastest mile, the first woman to walk the length of Tibet on foot. A few decades ago came the first astronauts to admire and marvel at. Our artists are less likely to be granted heroic stature, less likely to be models, unless a few of them happen to strike it rich and become admired for their success. But the self-made person who climbs to the top of the corporate ladder and turns the business completely around—then writes a best-seller about the feat—is alive and well and very much in our thinking.

One reason intellectuals, teachers, and laboratory scientists almost never make the Hero charts may be not our celebrated lack of intelligence, but our unconscious perpetuation of the rest of the Hero myth: namely, the Hero's downfall. We tend to care less about those who work steadily and diligently at their jobs, than those who will sooner or later topple from the heights. We secretly know the view from the bottom is ultimately safer than the view from the top. Nobody's up there forever. Eventually there will be a scandal we love to read about—public exposure, humiliation, loss of prestige, loss of riches. Like the Greek tragic chorus waiting for the king to tear out his

We keep looking for the Promised Leader: that special Someone who is not here yet, but should be, and could solve our problems for us.

eyes in atonement for his sins, we know our heroes will be joining us at ground zero.

On the other hand, we keep looking for the Promised Leader: that special Someone who is not here yet, but should be, and could solve our problems for us; that wonderful presidential candidate with precisely the right qualifications who will walk quietly and unnoticed into Iowa and be instantly recognized as the new political messiah. One archetype we cannot seem to tolerate is the ordinary human being, the merely mortal person, who announces candidacy for office and then is found to be as prone to error as the rest of us.

We are living at a time when Woman as Hero is no longer an impossibility, though she has some ground yet to make up. In the sci-fi movies we have had spacewomen who are allowed to exist on equal terms with men, who destroy monsters with the best of them. But a television series about a female president is bound to be listed as "sit-com" and be accompanied by a laugh track. The notion of Woman the Mysterious stays with us. In advertisements for luxury items, recurring words are "tempting" and "seductive," and "witchcraft." Models in perfume ads are made to look like descendants of the sirens who lured Odysseus. If woman is no longer the root of all evil, as in many an ancient myth, she is still portrayed as holding forth the promise of forbidden fruit. Some few honored and revered personalities—usually older actors—advertise stock brokerage firms or collections of popular light-classical music, but they are never women.

EPILOG

I've always preferred mythology to history. History is truth that becomes an illusion; mythology is an illusion that becomes reality.

Jean Cocteau

Myth, originating in the depths of the unconscious and in the primordial prehistory of our species, can be an aid to clear thinking if we could learn how to see which myths are shaping our experience and could sit back and select those we find beneficial and cast aside those which hinder critical thought. But myth tends to remain outside the critical realm. One cannot editorialize and suggest what myth ought to be or ought not to do.

Surely we know in our lucid moments that no myth contains the full truth. But perhaps this knowledge is less important than the mystery and magic at the root of our nature from which mythology springs. By studying myth objectively, we can see ourselves a little better; yet this does not mean we can change what we are—at least not entirely. Some mythology interferes with our judgment, and some is downright superstition. But then there are those haunting mazes and those magic rings and the wonderful Stranger we keep expecting to arrive. We need a little mist in our gardens.

GLOSSARY

archetype: The model or original of something (e.g., the hero; our first parents) which, according to Jung, exists innately in the collective unconscious and can be found in mythology, and by means of which we organize our thinking about the universe and human life.

hero: Probably the most universal of all archetypes: The man or woman whose deeds and destiny automatically involve the listener, simply because he or she possesses the attributes most prized by the culture. We usually take heroes for granted, without analyzing what they mean to us.

mandala: A universal (archetypal) myth symbol: an enclosed circle often containing a design that represents the organization of the universe. The mandala is always circular, suggesting that in Western culture at least, the universe is one thing, as opposed to many unrelated things. The mandala also symbolizes the inner world, and in this function suggests that many prefer to believe in a coherent self as opposed to an inner life comprised of a series of momentary sensations.

monomyth: Also known as the *world myth* and the *hero myth*. The universal tale, occurring from culture to culture and from age to age, with surprisingly similar characteristics. The story of Theseus is an example.

myths: Tales, transmitted from generation to generation, which project underlying psychological truths of the human race. There is a great deal of uniformity in mythic themes and symbols throughout all cultures and ethnic groups.

NOTES

1. Veronica Ions, *The World's Mythology in Colour* (London: Hamlyn, 1974), p. 224.
2. Ibid., p. 160.
3. Cited in June Singer, *Boundaries of the Soul: The Practice of Jung's Psychology* (New York: Doubleday, 1972), p. 79.
4. Cited in ibid.

Daumier, "Family Scene"

11

LOVE

OVERVIEW

We can scarcely overestimate the importance of love to most of us. Even the successive marriages of the frequently divorced give evidence that people believe so strongly in love they keep looking for it. It is not too much to say that the search for love dominates the consciousness of people from early adolescence even up to advanced age. To have "lost out on love" is certain to make many believe their lives were wasted. The theme of many poems, novels, plays, operas, and works of visual art is love, in all of its guises—love as pleasure, love as pain. If love cannot be described scientifically; if it has no objective existence, as some have insisted; if it is indeed solely the invention of human imagination, none of us could easily forge a life in which love is not an object of concern.

Not surprisingly, artists are often the most cynical in their denunciation of love or the most aggressive in labeling it a lie and a delusion. Perhaps the reason is that creative people have wanted to believe in love so desperately, have expected so much from it. But there are knowledgeable observers who view love as an authentic experience. The psychological theories of Erich Fromm and Eric Berne, for example, include the belief that love exists, however different it may be from its depiction in the arts.

This chapter does not pretend to offer a definitive resolution to the issue, only an analysis of ways in which through both art and life we are likely to be affected by the myth or the mystery of love. Recognizing this all-important obsession and its impact on our beliefs is crucial to the art of being human.

A Time for Love

Love is . . .

For Dante: *A macrocosmic force that moves the sun and other stars.*

For Samuel Johnson: *Of no great influence upon the sum of life.*

For H. L. Mencken: *A state of perpetual anesthesia.*

For Morton M. Hunt: *Any and every form of relationship between human beings when used in conjunction with the phrase "falling in love" or "being in love."*

Despite the sentiments in poems and songs that love is timeless, that true love lasts forever, one is better off facing the truth that, if it is to have any meaning as a concept or as a major force in human life, love has to be considered in the context of history. *Love* has meant different things at different times and particular places, and it is a safe bet that there are millions of people in the world today for whom the word is hollow and unrelated to the tough realities of their lives.

The appealing use of the term—and perhaps we mean the idealization of a relationship between two or among more than two persons—comes to us very strongly from the humanities, as do so-called words of wisdom like "Love is blind" and "Love is the answer, but what is the question?" We gain a very definite and possibly helpful perspective by examining specific cases from art, literature, and philosophy of bygone days (which in our analysis is limited to Western humanities, though an investigation into expression in other cultures would probably yield results that are just as interesting).

The Classical Definition: Lust

Men have died from time to time and worms have eaten them, but not for love.

Shakespeare

It has been said that love is an invention rather than a natural instinct or need, and the fact that such societies as ancient Greece and Rome appear to have gotten along without it proves the contention. Of course, people had sexual relationships. People married and raised families. But the theory goes that they did so for practical, survival reasons, not because they "fell in love." Some would go so far as to insist on calling lust a universal instinct, while love—when defined as something superior to lust—is a humanistic creation similar to the classical, unrealistic depiction of the human body. We know that the ancient Greeks and Romans also married for reasons of money and land—motivations which are still prevalent. But lust was the subject of their interest.

In Greek and Roman mythology we find much idealization of lust, of physical passion, together with a favorite theme: the sickness which comes from sexual desire. There is the Roman story of Venus and Adonis, for example, in which the goddess of Love (a condition which can only be considered affliction) is herself overcome after being wounded by an arrow shot by her mischievous son Cupid. As is the case whenever such wounding occurs, the victim desires the first man she looks upon; this time it happens to be Adonis, a young mortal. Noting that he enjoys hunting, she pleads with him not to go in search of dangerous game but to be "brave towards the timid." Such advice being distinctly anti-Roman, the hero of the myth understandably ignores it and promptly is killed by a wild boar. To perpetuate his memory, Venus transforms his blood into a dark red flower called anemone. But like passion itself, the anemone is short-lived, for "the wind blows the blossoms open, and afterwards blows the petals away."

Though both Greeks and Romans were not averse to the pleasures of the flesh, their myths show these pleasures to be the source of both human and godly misery. In fact, the story of Venus and Adonis is one of many in which a deity is revealed as less than perfect, and often lust is the flaw. In classical mythology and literature nothing good ever comes from love, which is almost always depicted as a wrenching emotion which topples reason and renders a person unproductive and unfulfilled. The classical world almost never saw love as an admirable goal of human existence.

The notable exception which comes to mind is what has come to be termed *Platonic love*, usually misrepresented as a relationship without sex. Plato's is one of the few voices from the classical world to accept love as a valid human need and to consider it as something other than a source of unhappiness.

Plato's Definition: A Longing for the Ideal

In his dialog *The Symposium,* one of the world's richest veins of complex thought, Plato states that love is clearly the secret to living, but we must first understand that love exists on several levels. Fundamental to us all is the physical desire of one person for another. Since desire is a human instinct, it cannot be deprecated or regarded as a sickness. It is not a deterioration of the rational faculties but is its own separate and unique event in human consciousness.

In Plato's philosophy, however, physical union with another and the pleasures of the body can never be the highest possible good.

In classical mythology and literature nothing good ever comes from love, which is almost always depicted as a wrenching emotion that topples reason and renders a person unproductive and unfulfilled.

And this energy is always on-going, whether or not it is seen through the confused filter of ego. It cannot be destroyed or interrupted at all. It is like the ever-burning sun.

Chögyam Trungpa

The beauties of the body are as nothing to the beauties of the soul, so that wherever one meets with spiritual loveliness, even in the husk of an unlovely body, he will find it beautiful enough to fall in love with and to cherish.

Plato

He believes each of us is born with a soul, which is the rational capacity for comprehending all of the eternal truths, and that the soul soon recognizes it is imprisoned in a body. The body is subject to deterioration, pain, and death, whereas the soul is immortal. Upon the death of one's body the soul finds a new home in a new body, and the same cycle is repeated. The constant longing of the soul is therefore to escape from the body.

A human being's attraction to another, even on the lowest or physical level, is at least a step in the right direction. It represents a preoccupation with something beyond the self. The goal of this attraction is reproduction, the generation of another life; and generation is closer to immortality than being trapped in the trivial, everyday "details of the self." It offers us a glimpse of the eternal, for we have substituted a new life for an older, decaying existence. In Plato's words:

> For here again, and on the same principle too, the mortal nature is seeking as far as possible to be everlasting and immortal: and this is only to be attained by generation, because generation always leaves a new existence in place of the old.[1]

One can only assume that Plato would cast a disapproving eye toward casual sex that seeks only momentary gratification of the senses. Physical love can be construed as a good only when it is an expression of the need for contact with what is not the self.

How does one know the difference? How does one know one's motives? The answer is that, if we are truly on the right track, sooner or later we glimpse the higher visions. We long for experiences that satisfy the soul itself, not just the senses. And what is it the soul wants? To be at one with the world it leaves when it enters the prison of the body, the world of eternity in which resides the truth of all things. The soul desires the contemplation of this world—a condition of peace, serenity, and ultimate knowledge. In such a state one is free of the trivial details of self, free of the pain caused by bodily deterioration. Sometimes Plato calls this the state of contemplating *ideal beauty.* Ultimate knowledge and ideal beauty are the same thing. The attainment of full understanding has no end except itself and is thus an experience of the beautiful. There is nothing *to do* with beauty except to have it.

Think, if you will, of the mathematician's bliss when a complex and seemingly impossible problem has been solved. The answer is there in letters and symbols and has no reference whatever to the familiar world of everyday reality. The recognition that the solution "works" is a vision of perfection. The mathematician has reached a truth that will stand for all time. The equation is thus both true and beautiful; and the mathematician also feels love for it.

Love has meant different things at different times and particular places, and it is a safe bet that there are millions of people in the world today for whom the word is hollow and unrelated to the tough realities of their lives.

Thus, one can be in love—Platonically—with a painting, a sculpture, a symphony, with phenomena which are characterized by the approach to perfection of the parts. It is such love for which the soul longs, and it can be experienced in the presence of another person or a thing or a place—anything, in short, which seems to come close to the perfection which exists in its full majesty only in the ideal world beyond the senses. This is the reason the physical desire for another person exists for Plato only at the bottom rung of the ladder, a ladder that leads us past physical pleasure, past self-gratification, and upward toward experiences that cannot be expressed in words, but only felt by the soul:

> He who from these ascending under the influence of true love, begins to perceive that beauty, is not far from the end. And the true order of going, or being led by another, to things of love, is to begin from the beauties of earth and mount upwards for the sake of other beauty, using these as steps only, and from one going on to two, and from two to all fair forms, and from fair forms to fair practices, and from fair practices to fair notions, until from fair notions he arrives at the notion of absolute beauty, and at last knows what the essence of beauty is.[2]

Biblical Love

The French satirist and social reformer Voltaire (1694–1778) once defined the family as a "group of people who cannot stand the sight of each other but are forced to live under the same roof." The American poet Robert Frost (1875–1963) in his narrative poem *Death of the Hired Man* has one character observe, "Home is the place where, when you have to go there, They have to take you in."[3] Whether home and family prove burdensome depends upon one's maturity level, emotional stability, and willingness to work on the difficulties which arise from close relationships. Most would agree, however, that there are few households which glide serenely along on a perpetually even keel.

The majority of us are born into a family circle and take for granted having parents, siblings, cousins, and aunts—a host of close kin who sign letters and postcards "With love," who hug and kiss us at family gatherings, and who expect loyalties and favors from us—even as we expect such in return—without having to analyze reasons; and all of it under the rubric of the seldom-defined word *love*.

Nonetheless, even family love has roots in historical time and geographical location. Anthropologists studying the social structures of remote groups have found groups in which tight family circles do

A mathematician's love of a perfect equation is an example of Platonic love: a reaching out for the ideal.

In the Old Testament one can trace the evolution of the concept of universal love that goes beyond the family and the tribe.

not exist. One such group is the Ik, an isolated tribe in Africa in which children are nurtured by their mothers until the age of five and then are cast out to fend for themselves. In ancient Greece men ate separately from the women and children, sometimes even had separate living quarters. In Plato's Republic, a supposedly ideal community, children, the philosopher suggests, should be taken from their parents and raised by the state.

The ancient Hebrews may possibly have given the world its first idea of the family as more than a convenient survival mechanism. In developing the father-children relationship between God and humanity, Judaism created a model for earthly existence. First came the tribe, the larger group comprised of interrelated families and governed by a patriarch, an older and presumably wiser man who exercised great powers of judgment over all members. Abraham and Moses are prominent Biblical patriarchs. One can easily see how such an arrangement was logically paralleled by the idea of God the father with the same power over His human children. Some historians, in fact, see the Jewish religion as having developed as a mythical parallel to an already established tribal-patriarchal structure needed for Hebrew survival. Anthropological studies of religious origins have disclosed that in very ancient times Hebrew and Arab tribes were all one people, the Semites, divided into smaller units the more readily to cope with the severities of nomadic desert existence, and that each had an earthly as well as heavenly patriarch.

How many gods there may have been is still a matter of speculation, though Biblical historians have uncovered a number of them. The tribes and families which traced their ancestry to Moses and Abraham are the people we now designate as Hebrews, and their earliest known god was Yahweh.[4] As first described in Genesis this god possessed distinctly human traits, among which were anger, a sense of possessiveness toward those who served him, and a warlike animosity toward their enemies. Early Biblical writings contain passionate exhortations that Yahweh show enemies no mercy but smite them according to an "eye for an eye" code of vengeance.

Within such a value system and because of the difficulties of surviving, the family circle inevitably became sanctified. It became imperative for the family to stay together, otherwise the larger unit, the tribe, would be endangered. Love for Yahweh, which meant fear of and respect for him, was also demanded for the father of the earthly family, who, like the tribal patriarch, had powers of life and death. Without obedience there was no order, and without fear there could be no obedience. Fear of God, fear of one's father—both were ways, the only ways, of showing love.

If Biblical historians are accurate, a group of Hebrew elders got together hundreds of years after the historical events we read about in the earliest portions of the Bible; gathered up all known written accounts of Hebrew history and cultural practices; and embarked upon the astonishing project of setting everything down in what they considered proper order. The Bible grew and flourished over many centuries, the work not of a few prophets which tradition has associated with the books bearing their names, but of a no-doubt prodigious number of poets, philosophers, and deeply religious people.

Many of the concepts belonging to ancient tribal customs are still in the Bible, but one also finds much that has come to belong to the entire human race. Hebrew scholars, in tracing their history back to the creation of the world, also revised and enlarged their vision of the deity. The God who created the heavens and the earth is clearly no longer the warlike Yahweh. This God is obviously the father of all people, since He is seen as omnipotent.

Even though the Biblical story of Abraham and the promise made to him by God is there as part of human history, the fact that others live in this world is not overlooked. Though the children of Abraham are God's Chosen, Biblical teachings are still heeded by all other religious denominations which accept the work as a valid history of the human race. Thus the Ten Commandments are perceived as binding on all, not merely those in the lineage of Abraham and Moses; and one of the Commandments—*Honor thy father and mother*—is a restatement and an enlargement of early tribal requirements. Both parents now are supreme authorities within the family circle. Fear of authority is not stressed so much as the gentler, more civilized "honor."

In fact, a close study of the Bible reveals radical changes occurring in the Hebrew vision of love. The "eye for an eye" attitude is not the only one we find. The famous Twenty-third Psalm, which begins, "The Lord is my shepherd," bears witness not to anger and hysterical entreaties for God to strike out and destroy the singer's enemies, but to a peaceful, mystical sense of union with a kind and caring God.

Many of the stories in the Hebrew Bible contain moral messages which do not differ very much from those of the parables in the so-called New Testament. The story of Susanna and the Elders, for example, has little to do with narrowly Hebrew concerns and everything to do with what is clearly a universal plea for honesty and charity toward others. Susanna, the beautiful wife of Joachim, is the secret object of two old men's lust. The men also happen to hold positions of honor and respect in the tribe and serve as judges in legal matters. One day they demand physical favors from her, threatening that, if she denies them, they will lie in court and say they witnessed Susanna's committing adultery with a young man. Susanna calls their bluff, only to find herself on trial for her life. The tale would have ended tragically but for the cleverness of the young defense lawyer who asks each of the elders separately to name the tree under which Susanna and her alleged suitor were making love. Naturally the stories conflict, and so it is the elders, not Susanna, who are put to death. The story imparts the definite warning that there is a universal God who punishes the wicked.

In the books of the Prophets we also find a widening of the concepts of both God and love. In Jeremiah, for example, the message is that the suffering of the Hebrews is not the result of unfair treatment by enemies, but is the judgment of God upon them for their own wickedness. Jeremiah is more interested in teaching his people to behave ethically toward each other and toward others than he is in having them retain their tribal identity through the observance of certain laws and customs.

In Isaiah we discover a curious split personality. On the one hand, the prophet echoes many of the familiar warnings to enemies of Israel in the form of prophecies about the future and the inevitable downfall of hostile nations. On the other hand, the prophet also speaks in gentler tones, as if offering comfort to an oppressed people who will one day achieve bliss and serenity. Most Biblical scholars agree that the Book of Isaiah is, in fact, the work of two different prophets, the second offering words of hope and the promise of a Messiah—not the son but a servant of God—who will come bearing a new kind of message to the world. This unknown prophet writes down the words of the Lord:

> *Here is my servant, whom I uphold,*
> *my chosen one in whom I delight;*
> *I will put my Spirit on him*
> *and he will bring justice to the nations.*
> *He will not shout or cry out,*
> *or raise his voice in the streets.*
> *A bruised reed he will not break,*
> *and a smoldering wick he will not snuff out.*
> *In faithfulness he will bring forth justice;*
> *he will not falter or be discouraged*
> *till he establishes justice on earth*
> *In his law the islands will put their hope.*[5]

This prophet is speaking of justice for all people. He is speaking of a universal code of ethics and, in so doing, is very much suggesting the idea of the universal family of humanity. To Israel the Lord lays down this mandate:

> *It is too small a thing for you to be my servant*
> *to restore the tribes of Jacob*
> *and bring back those of Israel I have kept.*

I will also make you a light for the Gentiles,
that you may bring my salvation to the ends
of the earth.[6]

The prophet also sees a vision in which the Servant who is to be sent
to the earth will be reviled, will suffer from the sins of the people, and
be "assigned a grave with the wicked."

The New Testament, believed to be the history of the promised Messiah, who is Jesus, the son rather than servant, offers in the
teachings of Jesus a further articulation of the doctrine of universal
love. Emphasis is placed on humility; meekness rather than aggressiveness; loving one's neighbor more than oneself; loving one's enemies
because you recognize that they are your brothers and sisters; gentle-
ness, tenderness, and mercy. All of these concepts can properly be said
to have evolved throughout the long history of Biblical literature and
philosophy and should not be considered to have arisen from one Testament rather than another. Taken all in all, they have created a model
of human behavior, a standard for the world that is beautiful to contemplate, if not easy to achieve. The difficulty makes the vision no less
precious, and the pursuit of the goal more desperately needed than
ever before.

ROMANTIC LOVE

As you can see, love in both the classical and Judeo-Christian worlds
was not confined to the relationship between a man and a woman.
Such relationships, when dealt with in art and literature, are physical,
often tragic (as in many of the Greek plays), or practical, as when the
patriarch Abraham spurns his barren wife Sarah and turns instead to
Hagar in order to produce offspring. We are not intended to believe
that this was a love "triangle," that Hagar was the "other woman" in
the soap-opera sense understood today. The preoccupation with emotional ups and downs of male-female involvement did not happen until
much later and proves once again that love cannot even be defined
without specific reference to history and geography.

Romantic love has its roots
in the medieval idealization
of sexual attraction that
cannot go any further, often
because one or the other is
married to someone else.

Mariolatry

The Christianized world of western Europe evolved from feudal settle-
ments—centering on castle-fortresses and the isolated lives of the
land barons, their families, servants, and armies—into a collection of
nations, principally France, Spain, and England, each with urban centers, cathedrals, and highly cultivated monasteries containing libraries
with carefully copied and illustrated manuscripts, treasures of the past

preserved for all time. By the "high" Middle Ages—the eleventh and twelfth centuries—the Christianized world of western Europe had given rise to the sophisticated philosophy known as Scholasticism, through which the revealed truths of religion were proved logically; and to an artistic tradition that had never been known in the world before.

This new artistic tradition is sometimes given the name *Mariolatry,* a coined word meant to suggest idolatry of the Virgin Mary, mother of Jesus. In point of fact, the writings of the New Testament do not say very much about Mary; at least the references are scarce when one considers the centrality of Mary in a good deal of Christian art and literature. After the account of the death of Jesus on the cross there is almost no mention of his mother, except a passing reminder that on earth Jesus had been "born of woman." What happened to her is indeed a mystery, and certainly one might think it strange that a figure who has inspired countless artists, poets, and composers should have been given so little prominence in the New Testament.

Yet, like the idea of love itself, the idea of Mary is rooted in history. During the Middle Ages, as the Christian religion spread, was taught and argued about; as Christian artistic tradition grew, the subject of the mother became increasingly important and often charismatic. The simple words spoken by the angel Gabriel that are contained in the gospel of Luke, words to "a virgin pledged to be married to a man named Joseph," that she would be visited by the Holy Ghost whose power would overshadow her, leaped forth from the pages of the Gospel into many creative minds. Thus was born the cult of Mary, whose members were men impelled to canvas and poetry by the power of one supreme idea: the specialness of this one woman, the purity of one woman honored among all others to be the mother of God's own son—an honor without human parallel. This honor was to elevate not only the idea of Mary, but—at least for a time—that of all women.

Everyone is familiar with medieval and Renaissance paintings of the Madonna and Child, a subject which was never exhausted. To complement these works came poem after poem extolling the glory of Mary as a holy and undefiled vessel, and, by natural association, the spiritual beauty of chaste women. References we still make to placing women on a pedestal may well spring from the cult of Mary.

The idealization of women in Mariolatry was also found in popular literature. There the earthly love of a man for a woman was presented in spiritual terms, even if lust was involved as well. In this literature was born the ideal of romantic love, of serenading the fair lady under her balcony, of sending love poems tied around rosebuds; the ideal of a love in which spirit, not body, was the subject—at least the alleged subject—of desire. Platonic love would readily have been understood to be the pursuit of an ideal, pure, chaste, and true love, undefiled by lust—the love of man and woman that lasts through time and cannot be destroyed even in the grave.

Romance

The word *romance* has never left our cultural vocabulary since its introduction in the very period we are discussing. In the beginning, however, it did not mean what we generally understand by the term: a courtship filled with moonlight and roses and talk of "sweet nothings." During the eleventh and twelfth centuries the French word *roman,* meaning "long fictional narrative" (today, "novel"), was absorbed into English as the word *romance,* but with the same meaning.

Since there was no printing press, stories circulated through recitation. One can imagine how popular the most exciting tales were—not to mention how many invitations the good storytellers must have received! The romances were not just about love. Some did not even contain plots concerning man-woman relationships; instead they were filled with breathtaking adventures. The Crusades were still within cultural memory. How enthralled listeners must have been to hear about distant, Eastern lands and the dangers lying in wait for noble Christian knights. Many of the best-loved romances were the stories about King Arthur, Camelot, and the Knights of the Round Table.

Out of the traditions of knighthood came the term *chivalry,* which now refers to genteel behavior toward women: opening doors, pulling out chairs, walking on the curb side of the lady so she will not be splattered with mud from careening vehicles, and so on. Like the word *romance, chivalry* has gone through many changes. Stemming from the French *cheval,* meaning "horse," the word long ago referred to courageous feats performed by knights, who of course were often on horseback. Then the term acquired the specialized meaning of the particular qualities a knight was expected to possess. Respect for women was one such quality.

Many of the romances therefore *did* contain stories about the relationship of a brave knight with one particular lady in whose name he would perform valorous feats. The lady was not expected to reward her champion with anything except the honor of allowing him to do brave and daring things for her. In the jousting tournaments, for example, the lady would place her scarf around the knight's lance as a symbol of the honor she was bestowing. He would ride into actual battle holding his lady's scarf on high, prepared to die for her.

Relationships in the romances were nonphysical, even if the couple secretly (or openly) lusted for one another, because sex outside of marriage was sinful and few indeed would have allowed a storyteller to repeat a tale of lust and adultery. The "purity" of relationships

Romantic love is among the most enduring of ideals. Despite widespread cynicism about the younger generation, one suspects that our young people still look for tender love and considerate behavior from the "right" person.

in the romances is similar to the nonphysical relationships in the films of the 1930s and 1940s, when audiences never seemed to tire of the plot in which a woman must stand forever in the shadows because the man she loves is married, usually to a cruel and unfeeling wife who shouts gleefully that she will never give him a divorce. Or else the wife is an invalid, and he is too noble to desert her.

Often in the romances one or the other *is* married, and the love is doomed never to be consummated. These were Christian times, however; and Christianity considered human beings sinful, easily tempted creatures. Sometimes the lovers yield to temptation, and there is a tragic ending. Among the most enduring of the tragedies has been the story of Guinevere, Arthur's queen, and her love for Lancelot, which she tries so hard but unsuccessfully to resist. Another is the story of Eloise, a novice, and Abelard, a priest, who have fallen in love before either enters holy orders and who meet again when consummation is forbidden.

Why did the romances not give rise to stories of happy and unending love within the sacred bonds of marriage? Probably for the same reason that nobody today wants to read a book or see a film about happy people without problems. The romances were the escapist literature of the Middle Ages, counterparts of whatever escapist literature is currently in fashion, and with the identical purpose of offering the listener or reader something quite different from daily life. Another reason is medieval marriage itself, which for the most part was a humdrum, businesslike venture joining two people for money and property. Love in what we have come to call the romantic sense of the term had little to do with the matter. It was there, if at all, strictly by accident. And in reality, men and women probably longed in secret for other partners whom they could either never love in the flesh or do so sinfully, risking the pain of a guilty conscience. Neither option was a very happy one. Small wonder that the theme of tragic but pure and honest love was dear to many hearts.

Whether physical gratification ever took place or not, the assumption must always have been that the love denied was better and purer and nobler than the marriage realized. Since the theme occurs in so many romances, we long ago took into the cultural vocabulary the term *romantic love,* which usually exists outside marriage, which may or may not have a physical side to it, but which in any case is *always* comprised of genuine, tender, noble emotions felt by two persons of honor and altruism who bear malice toward no one in the world and who, in our estimation, deserve only happiness.

In more recent times romantic love has sometimes been shown as the motivation for marriage in story or film, with the rest of the plot depicting the unhappy ebbing away of an ideal relationship. Sometimes the lovers simply "live together," but the formula is always the same. People come to discover that ideal love has either withered or never existed to begin with.

An interesting contemporary twist to the theme is the story about the once-happy couple who divorce and later come back together again, this time with more realistic expectations. One suspects that, despite the widespread cynicism about the "younger generation" and its supposed lack of strong values, romantic idealism remains very strong and expectations continue to include tender love and considerate, compassionate behavior from the "right" person. The near-miss divorce plot is escapist fantasy, perhaps concealing our latent fears that the family unit, once the indestructible backbone of society, is being blown apart. The root of the problem may still be disenchantment, and the cause of disenchantment is very likely an ideal that refuses to die.

Proof of our idealism can be found in our euphemisms. The word *romance* has all but disappeared from conversational idiom, films, novels, and songs, while *affair* has taken its place. The latter term contains sexual implications that the former term did not always have, but we note that it is still a relatively civilized way to describe a relationship. An affair, like a medieval romance, exists outside of marriage, and is almost always considered a flame that burns brightly for a short time, only to die away. Moreover, unless used derogatively by an estranged and furious spouse, *affair* often suggests idealistic expectations. Perhaps we believe we have become far too sophisticated to be caught hoping for romance, when all the while the affair someone is having amounts to pretty much the same thing—or one hopes it does! In much popular film and literature a character may embark upon an affair with pretended casualness, only to be deeply hurt and hope it doesn't show.

We have not lost the ability to be hurt by love. What better indication that the myth—if that is what romantic love should be called—is one that continues to haunt, and plague, our most sensitive selves? Seldom do we hear of frank admissions that sex is all there is, that sex is unrelated to deeper feelings. There may now be more direct and much faster physical contact than in the medieval romances, but who is to say that for young and old alike sex is devoid of spiritual meaning?

THE ROLES WE PLAY

Perhaps we have learned to be somewhat more tentative when we tell ourselves or others that we have fallen in love. Are we pursuing the ideal of love itself, Platonic-style? Are we in love with an idea of perfection in another person? Is it fundamentally physical lust we experience masquerading in the guise of romantic love? If we believe we are in love romantically, have we truly examined our expectations? And are they realistic?

To add to the complexity of these and similar questions, we now must consider the startling fact that, whatever answer we choose, *love* is not just a state of being in which *one* person exists. There is a definite relationship which regrettably is not always implied in the use of the verb. For example, one man tells his close friend, "I am in love with the most beautiful woman." Nothing is said about the woman's feelings. If questioned, the man may reply, "I think she loves me too," or "She has said she loves me." These are at least honest answers, which do not imply a relationship that may not be there. We do not, however, always remember how we described our situation at the outset. In the aftermath of breaking up there can be outraged accusations: "You made me think you loved me!" or "You deliberately led me on!" A statement from the other party does not always guarantee that each means the same thing by *love.* The accused woman may well rejoin, "I didn't know then what I was getting into," or "I never knew what you expected from me."

Unless one falls in love with the ideal beauty of another's face and never expects the other to have a voice or a personality—unless, in short, one can be in love in the privacy of one's own feelings, the declaration of love to another person implies that a relationship is to exist. The intelligent follow-up to hearing the same declaration from the other is for each to demand to know *what the rules are,* in much the same way that one does not play contract bridge with a new partner without first asking which bidding system the partner intends to use.

Since love is generally a relationship, each partner has a *role.* In times past, the roles were limited in number and very clearly defined. Today they are not. Today it is easy to accept a certain role at the outset, only to begin playing a different role later on without announcing the switch. Confusion, heartbreak, anger, sometimes violence are the unhappy results.

Throughout history love has been a game with changing sets of rules.

Courtly Love

"How to handle a woman," muses King Arthur in the 1959 musical play *Camelot.* The hero decides after some analysis that the way to handle a woman is "to love her, love her, love her." The king had forgotten that his queen Guinevere is, indeed, someone with whom he can discuss affairs of state and complex legal matters, but only up to a point. In any case, we are not to forget that she is obsessed with the need to be adored and that this obsession is a basic right belonging to her role.

The Arthurian times were mythical, but they reflect what was actually the case in the courts of England, France, and Spain in the late Middle Ages. In this era of romantic love, which, as we have seen, usually existed outside of marriage (and in which Guinevere herself was engaged without Arthur's knowledge), the man was expected to be chivalrous, brave, and always considerate of the woman, never, *never* forcing his attentions upon her or asking—let alone pleading—for more than she was prepared to give. The woman, on her part, could yield to his desire if she chose (as Guinevere ultimately did with Lancelot) or let him stand under her balcony wafting sweet nothings upward to her unimpressed, unchanging face with never so much as a promise. In short, as romantic love became popular, it turned into a game with codified rules. It also, we might add, raised the status of women enormously, since they were given *carte blanche* to treat their would-be lovers in just about any manner they wanted, even if it were a momentary whim.

Readers may know Cervantes' epic satire *Don Quixote* (1605) or have seen the contemporary musical adaptation *Man of La Mancha,* in both of which the hero, an old man who lost his mind from devouring too many romances, believes himself to be a knight wandering forever in the service of the Lady Dulcinea, a lady he never expects to meet or at least to thank him in any way. The code of *courtly love*— the medieval game in which the male was supposed to endure any hardship for the lady—is nowhere better illustrated than in this letter from Don Quixote in which the old man writes to his beloved:

> SOVEREIGN LADY,—The wounded by the point of absence, and the hurt by the darts of thy heart, sweetest Dulcinea of Toboso! doth send thee that health which he wanteth himself. If thy beauty disdain me, if thy valour turn not to my benefit, if thy disdains convert themselves to my harm, maugre all my patience, I shall be ill able to sustain this care; which, besides that it is violent, is also too durable. My good squire Sancho will give thee certain relation, O beautiful ingrate, and my dearest beloved enemy! of the state wherein I remain for thy sake. If thou please to favour me, I am thine; and if not, do what thou likest: for, by ending of my life, I shall both satisfy thy cruelty and my desires.—Thine until death,
> 'THE KNIGHT OF THE ILL-FAVORED FACE.'[7]

In his amusing and informative *The Natural History of Love* (1959), Morton M. Hunt suggests that the model for Cervantes' great work may have been a relatively obscure book of the thirteenth century called *Frauendienst* (The Service of Woman) by a real knight-errant Ulrich von Lichtenstein. The book contains 30,000 lines of narrative verse, all claiming to be the autobiography of a man who literally sacrificed his entire existence for a princess who for years did not know he existed.

When he was 12, Ulrich, knowing that, if he were to become a knight, he must adopt the role of the courtly lover, chose to serve the lady, become a page in her court, and forced himself to feel tenderly toward her. He secretly followed her everywhere.

> When he saw her hands touch the petals of flowers he had secretly placed where she would see them, he was all but in a faint. And when she washed her hands before dinner, young Ulrich would sometimes filch the basin, smuggle it off to his room, and there reverently drink the dirty water.[8]

After risking his life in tournament after tournament and developing a reputation as the strongest and bravest knight around, he at last made so bold as to send his niece to visit the princess and tell her of his all-consuming obsession. Scornfully, the princess sent back word that he was too ugly to be even a distant admirer, whereupon Ulrich underwent dangerous surgery to correct a harelip.

Even this failed to please the lady, though she went so far as to allow him to send notes to her. Her answers were usually filled with derision and heartless rebuffs. "But this," the author comments, "was exactly what was expected of her."[9] To show the extent of his devotion Ulrich then proceeded to cut off a finger and send it to her. Pleased at this sign of "her power over him," the princess sent back word that she would keep the finger if that would make him happy.

After a number of years, the princess finally agreed to allow the lovesick and suffering man to visit her, but insisted he come as a leper in the company of other lepers. After spending a long, rainy night outside in a ditch, he was allowed into the lady's chamber, only to find a hundred candles burning and eight maids standing by the bedside. He entertained a fleeting hope that all of his suffering was but an elaborate prelude to a long-awaited night of joy. But true to her role as the cruel mistress, the lady told him to join the Crusades, earn a big reputation for valor, and then maybe she would see. Fifteen years later Ulrich was still hoping for his reward, but all he can tell the reader is that she "wounded him in some fashion so cruel that he could not bring himself to name it."[10] Ulrich's book does contain some cynical observations about women—rare for the time, but understandable in his case. Nonetheless, he was undeterred from finding another object of adoration in whose service he spent the rest of his life, and with a somewhat happier outcome.

The term *courtly love* presumably derives from actual mock-court proceedings, held in the royal halls, in which women judges decided whether this or that suitor had acquitted himself according to the proper rules and should be granted the favors he so eagerly sought. Most of the time such favors were *not* allowed, an outcome which in no way was supposed to diminish the plaintiff's ardor. Hunt's research has led him to the conclusion that these courts of love had their origin in the twelfth century with Eleanor of Aquitaine, mother of Richard the Lion-Hearted.

Eventually the "rulings" in the courts of love were set down in writing as guides to the proper conduct of an "affair of the heart." The rules lasted for several centuries, well into the Renaissance, where we find them absorbed into a lively little book called *The Courtier* (1507) by Baldassare Castiglione, an Italian military hero and later ambassador.

In *The Courtier* we see the influence of Renaissance worldliness and sophistication. Nobody chops off fingers for love anymore, and ladies are no longer expected to be cruel and forever unreachable. High-bred ladies are now allowed to have a degree of education, intended to give them wit and polish and equip them for their role in life: to be a delightful, scintillating partner in the game of love.

Since among other things the Renaissance represented a new interest in classical art, literature, and philosophy, who should turn up in this updated version of courtly love but Plato himself? In *The Courtier,*

> the fundamental theme is that love is the source of all sweetness and moral virtue, since it leads men to concentrate on beauty, and beauty leads the mind toward the contemplation of divinity.[11]

This being the case, the lady could see and talk with the gentleman but was not expected to cheapen the relationship by allowing so much as a hint that she might be interested in a physical encounter.

Renaissance poetry, including much of Shakespeare's, is filled with the theme of unrequited love, of the man's figurative "death" while the lady rewards him only with wit and a smile. Shakespeare's comedy *Much Ado About Nothing* contains the stylish pair of lovers Beatrice and Benedick, who play the game in almost balletlike fashion. Shakespeare's *Taming of the Shrew,* on the other hand, is a delightful farce in which Petruchio in the name of suffering manhood reverses the traditional Renaissance sex roles, putting the scornful Kate in her place, even if he has to beat her into submission. The feminist movement of today decries the fact that Kate buckles under Petruchio's will, but there have been productions in which the shrew delivers her famous final speech to the ladies in the audience, a speech in which she entreats them to be sweet and demure as a woman should be, but with a decided wink in her eye.

During the latter half of the seventeenth century, the period known in England as that of the Restoration (when in 1661 monarchy was restored to the English throne after 20 years of Puritan rule), sex roles reached an equality never before known. Charles II was famous for his amorous exploits and extravagant parties; his court was continually aglitter with banquets, dancing, and civilized conversation. Sexual mores changed considerably. Where the emphasis before had been on charm without fulfillment, the lady was now permitted a wide range of options. Physical encounters outside of marriage were scandalous only if the cheating were blatant and without finesse. The game of love became the game of seduction, and the rules became more rigorous than ever.

In this period women were expected to achieve a high degree of social and cultural grace. With the rise in status of the merchant class, people could be ladies and gentlemen without necessarily having titles, and such liberalization helped the spread of the civilized arts now encompassed under the term *urbanity*.

The theater also underwent drastic changes. Women were allowed to become actresses as well as playwrights, and thus a more genuinely feminine viewpoint could be heard. Those who study the history of women's rights (or the lack of same) often point to the English Restoration as a period in which women took giant steps forward—before the nineteenth century was to set them back.

William Congreve's *The Way of the World* (1700), a giant among the plays of the time, sums up the rules of the game as played by two of the most civilized partners ever devised: Mirabell, the hero, is widely known for his attractiveness to women, but though the code of the time permits faithlessness so long as one's social behavior remains carefully polished, he truly loves Millamant, also widely known for being the object of many men's desires. If the code were not so demanding, either one would probably forget the rules and declare genuine feelings to the other. They cannot, however, and manage to conceal their true selves behind the surface banter of which the author definitely approves.

In the famous marriage contract scene in Act Four, the would-be lovers meet to discuss their upcoming nuptials. Each lays down requirements for the other. First, Millamant demands that, even after the wedding, he must respectfully *request* sexual favors from her, not considering them as rights automatically owed to the husband. She will also sleep as late as she wishes in the morning without obligation to administer to his every fancy. Nor will she permit him to call her names, such as "wife, spouse, my dear, joy, jewel, love, sweetheart, and the rest of that nauseous cant." In fact, they are not even to exchange kisses in public, nor "visit together, nor go to a play together." She will carry on her own private correspondences without having to explain anything to him and insists she must

During the Restoration period there occurred a move toward unprecedented sexual equality.

> have no obligation upon me to converse with wits that I
> don't like, because they are your acquaintance; or to be
> intimate with fools, because they may be your relations.
> Come to dinner when I please, dine in my dressing-room
> when I'm out of humour, without giving a reason. . . . And
> lastly, wherever I am, you shall always knock at the door
> before you come in. These articles subscribed, if I con-
> tinue to endure you a little longer, I may by degrees
> dwindle into a wife.

Mirabell is agreeable to such "trivial" conditions, but adds a
few of his own: She must like her own face as long as he does and "en-
deavour not to new-coin it." She must totally shun the use of lying cos-
metics, and when she becomes pregnant ("Ah, name it not," she inter-
rupts) she is not to squeeze her body into corsets and so pretend the
blessed event is never going to happen. She and her friends may have
their idle-minded feminine conversations at tea but may *not* sit
around and drink in the fashion of men. "These *provisos* admitted," he
concludes, "I may prove a tractable and complying husband." Her
reply: "I hate your odious *provisos.*" He answers with a smile: "Then
we're agreed."

If Congreve's portrait of his society is accurate—and we have
no reason to believe otherwise—sex roles were such that neither man
nor woman could claim the upper hand, and the marriage of Mirabell
and Millamant will be about as solid and lasting a union as any writer
has ever imagined.

The Victorian Model

We mentioned earlier the rise of the merchant class during the seventeenth century. For the next two centuries that trend continued, and it
brought about much social alteration on both sides of the Atlantic.
During the period we tend to call *Victorian,* which roughly spanned
the years of Victoria's reign (1837–1901), the increasingly prosperous middle class in Europe and America changed the rules of male-
female relationships, a change that continues to affect us all.

Still very much with us is this *Victorian model* of how relationships are conducted—and, in particular, how marriage works. As
fortunes became less and less matters of inheritance or arranged marriage, as the idea of working for one's living and getting ahead by honest means (often called the Protestant work ethic) became increasingly honorable, the role of the husband tended to become that of the
provider, and the role of the wife—because she was the "weaker sex"
and not expected to be able to compete in the ruthless world of business—tended to become that of home-manager and child-raiser. The
slogan "A woman's place is in the home" typifies the Victorian attitude.

At the same time that the husband was decisive in running his business or profession, he was usually quite boyish at home, where he could lose his temper, become concerned about minor illnesses, and be demanding about his food and comfort. The wife's competence in the home would be demonstrated by her meeting his demands, carefully avoiding confrontations, meticulously preparing his favorite foods, and soothingly ministering cold compresses and headache powders as necessary. But she would not have liked to be reminded of her "competence," for the term sounded masculine. In quite public ways she was definitely to seem incompetent. She needed clear directions for finding addresses, for example. She was not expected to deal in any but the most trivial ways with tradespeople, or to make important decisions about vacations, the education of the children, or any other matter requiring long-range planning and organization. Such things needed the sure, guiding hand of a husband.

A product of her times, but hardly in sympathy with them, was the poet Emily Dickinson (1830–1886), who describes the misgivings of a young woman contemplating marriage:

> *She rose to His Requirement—dropt*
> *The Playthings of Her Life*
> *To take the honorable Work*
> *Of Woman, and of Wife*

Commenting on this poem, critic Paul J. Ferlazzo remarks:

> The husband . . . is here depicted not as lover, companion, or friend, but as a standardbearer of excellence. . . . Dickinson is clearly contemptuous of the enforced inferiority of women and of the fact that their value and individuality are recognized only in terms of the men they marry.[12]

Attacks on the Victorian model have come from a variety of sources, but one of the earliest occurred during the Victorian era itself. In 1879, the Norwegian playwright Henrik Ibsen examined the ideal marriage of his time and found it to be fraudulent. Nora, heroine of his play *A Doll's House,* appears at first to be the perfect wife and mother to represent the period. Her husband is rich and responsible, her children healthy. There is plenty of domestic assistance to run the house. Nora's main task, it would seem, is to supervise the tasks assigned to women of the time—details of clothing and food—and to be an impulsive, flirtatious wife who follows her husband's orders.

But Ibsen exposes the lie of the contented "doll" when Nora's husband Torvald denies her a most vital part of a husband's supposed strength in such arrangements: protection against a menace from the past. The plot is melodramatic, complete with the blackmailer who threatens to ruin the family's reputation if he doesn't get a position in the bank managed by Torvald. He holds a promissory note with her father's signature forged by Nora years before, in a desperate attempt to borrow money to take her ill husband to Italy for the winter. Now that Torvald, completely recovered, is in a position of power, the man holding the note prepares to strike. When she can conceal her deed no longer, Nora, the proper Victorian wife, tries the standard wifely method of communication of that time: tears, explanations, and promises, believing that her husband will assume *his* proper role, too: that of stern protector. Instead, he denounces her, orders her kept from their children; she is to be locked in her room, a prisoner in her—or rather his—house.

When at the eleventh hour the blackmailer returns the note and the threat is over, Torvald awaits a return to the idyllic past: "Nora, I'm saved." "I?" she replies. "I thought it was *we*." In a denunciation scene before walking out (scandalous for a drama in those days), Nora tells him that she must be first a human being before she can be a wife. She rejects his promise to change, hands him her wedding ring, and closes the door firmly on her way out. Nora was one of the first fictional women to awaken and reject her assigned role in life.

A Doll's House is often given credit for having altered the direction of the theater from a preoccupation with romantic melodrama to a direct confrontation with social issues. But though Ibsen was controversial and in some quarters scandalous, social codes did not change abruptly. Neither World War I, which brought to a violent end many Victorian traditions, nor the 1920s, in which striped blazers and flapper dresses were seen whizzing by in horseless carriages and both sexes smoked and drank, could topple the conservative middle-class family from its secure position in the social hierarchy. Flappers with cigarette holders were exciting fantasies for the average housewife, but they were not to dictate her assigned role.

Life with Father, the Broadway hit play of the 1930s, which for a long time held the record for most successive performances on Broadway, running for around eight years, is a play which confirmed the validity of "old-fashioned" values. In it, playwright Clarence Day, Jr., fondly remembers his parents' marriage arrangements: Father is irascible, opinionated, and completely dominant—he thinks. But in one scene after another, Mother is shown getting her own way, never by direct statement or confrontation, but always by devious means. Sometimes she pretends not to understand, sometimes she plots with others, and sometimes she talks in such a disorganized manner that Father backs down after giving vent to one more roar of anger. Since the play is a comedy, nothing is a matter of life and death, but, as the son lovingly recalls the Victorian marriage, Mother wins the "right" to entertain visitors, spend more than her budget, and see to her husband's baptism, all through what modern feminists would call "slave" tactics. This Victorian wife secretly ran the house. In our time, this version of the Victorian model is still in favor with many women, who shun liberationism on the grounds that they already enjoy unlimited power and might lose it if their true feelings were made public.

Victorian marriage provides the repressive background for D. H. Lawrence's *Lady Chatterley's Lover* (1928), which shocked people even more than Ibsen's *A Doll's House*. The novel, so sensational that at the time it was first published it was deemed worthy of expurgation and banning, recounts the sexual attraction of an upper-class Englishwoman for the gameskeeper on the estate where she and her husband live. Her husband is crippled and impotent. Lady Chatterley is drawn to the gameskeeper, Oliver Mellors, in a completely erotic way, which Lawrence describes in a style more than explicit for its time. The scenes in the gamesman's cottage are mostly wordless, except for an occasional tribute to the overwhelming beauty of sexuality, identified by Lawrence with the gameskeeper's outdoor life rather than with refined urban offices and drawing rooms. Lawrence saw Victorian morality as "a denial of the purity of love," now not poetic and romantic, but natural and basic to the species.

In the British courtroom trial testing whether *Lady Chatterley's Lover* was either great literature or pornography, one witness, a professor of literature, testified that the novel was well written, true to life, and deserving of a place on any library shelf. But the judge pointed out that the book included a number of "carnal acts of wanton intercourse" before either Lady Chatterley or Mellors mentioned love: indeed, they hardly spoke. "Yes," replied the witness, "that's the way it is sometimes, my lord."

Attacks on Victorian repressiveness written in an entirely different style came from a witty American author of the 1920s, Dorothy Parker, who expertly surveyed the marriage scene and depicted many cases of evasion and concealment. Parker was herself a clever, intellectual woman at a time when women were expected to be less literate than and subordinate to successful men from whose achievements they would gain reflected glory. Hers is the rueful comment:

> *Men seldom make passes*
> *At girls who wear glasses.*

In one of Parker's short stories, italics tell the thoughts of a girl dancing with a boorish partner while the conventional typeface records her flattering lies. In another story, a honeymoon couple, both sexually inexperienced, try to make conversation and encounter constant embarrassment as one phrase or another shows what each is trying not to mention.

Still-surviving Victorian conventions doom Parker's married couples, partly because the husbands' worldly, wise, and knowledge-

It is this little imp of raw sensuality which he set out to canonize, to celebrate. Of course the intention was dogmatic—for he was something of a puritan himself. He was out to cure, to mend; and the weapons he selected for this act of therapy were the four-letter words about which so long and idiotic a battle has raged.

Lawrence Durrell on D. H. Lawrence

able ways contrast so with the naive pettiness of their wives, none of whom ever works for a living. In "Glory in the Daytime," a wife is excited by the opportunity to visit a famous stage actress, someone she has admired from afar. The husband, amused by his wife's enthusiasm, warns her about the rich and famous. Sure enough, the wife's admiration becomes disgust when the actress turns out to be coarse, drunken, and overly interested both in her own female companion and in the details of her visitor's sex life. In a burst of renewed affection for her husband, the heroine goes to a gourmet grocery and purchases his favorite foods. But when the husband resumes his aggressive teasing, the wife sees their relationship in a new light and quietly puts the groceries back on the shelf.

Love and Liberation

Dorothy Parker was a little before her time. Her jibes at the Victorian model were only "quietly" appreciated. She might have been more appreciated had she written during the peak years of feminist literature, which appear to have been the late 1960s and the 1970s. During this period a succession of novels appeared about women who marry early, then find themselves trapped, living only to fulfill the expectations of society (still branded as Victorian), to please a man, to be the lesser half of the couple, and to subordinate her separate and true identity to the honorable title "Mrs." The best-known of these works denouncing traditional sex roles are *Up the Sandbox, Fear of Flying, Diary of a Mad Housewife,* and *The Women's Room.*

Marilyn French's *The Women's Room,* which appeared in 1977 and is one of the bitterest anti-Victorian statements of our time, describes the dramatic awakening of a wife and mother who has been nearly devoid of personality and interest in anything save her husband's professional career. But the awakening, which includes a love affair with a man she believes to be sensitive and understanding—everything her husband is not—turns out to be an illusion. Her lover finally plays his hand. He expects the heroine to marry him and move to Africa, where he will be doing research, even though the trip will interfere with her own newly found academic interests. The conclusion of the novel, like that of many others, finds the heroine strong, self-sufficient, and alone. French and her colleagues have surveyed the modern battlefield in the war between the sexes and found that compromise is seldom possible, and won't be until both men and women are freed from stereotypical sex roles.

In all the above-mentioned novels of women's liberation there is little doubt as to the authors' positions, even if at times they are communicated along a single track. But the popularity in the media of liberation themes has brought to light some of the contradictions still inherent in our thinking. Sometimes we find a liberationist message tensely undermined by a fear—conscious or otherwise—of

Everything up until the time you walk down the aisle has been polite, guarded and a little superficial. Returning from the altar is a different feeling altogether. You have not contracted for a temporary position, this is a permanent career. You have just bet all your chips on the biggest crapshoot of your life.

Erma Bombeck

abandoning the model that has "worked" for so long. Modern films like *Kramer vs. Kramer* (1979) and a succession of made-for-TV movies have exploited the theme of liberation and changing sex roles with varying degrees of honesty, but seldom without confusion. *Kramer vs. Kramer* shows us a liberation-seeking mother walking out on her family—much like Ibsen's Nora—in order to establish her true identity, then returning to reclaim her son when she feels she is ready to be an honest mother. But in her absence the husband has assumed the mother's role and has done it very well. After a fierce legal battle the court decides the child belongs with the natural mother, but the latter, observing the close bond between father and child, heroically leaves again. *Kramer vs. Kramer* represents a reaffirmation of the family unit. Sex roles have not been redefined—merely reversed.

Decades ago, the films of Spencer Tracy and Katharine Hepburn began raising consciousness in some areas, but with whimsy and without the bitter ironies of recent novels and films which examine the issue less benignly. *Woman of the Year* (1942) has long been considered a classic, though not by dedicated feminists of both sexes. The film illustrates how much Hollywood has done (and in many instances is still doing) to keep subtly alive the Victorian model. The heroine—rich, successful, brilliant, witty (all characteristics sublimely possessed by Hepburn)—finally renounces her husbandless life after discovering she is unable to cook breakfast.

In 1949 this great acting team followed with *Adam's Rib,* which promised to be stridently antisexist. This time Tracy and Hepburn played married attorneys on opposite sides in a case of attempted murder, ultimately won by the wife. The conflict of the trial has put such a strain on the marriage that divorce becomes inevitable. Just before the divorce decree is to be made final, the protagonists appear at an accountant's office to discuss tax deductions. Upon learning that the last payment has been made on their country house, the husband puts his head in his hands and cries. The wife, overcome by sympathy, changes her mind about the divorce, whereupon the hero reveals that women are not the only sex able to use tears to get what it wants. The dominant male reasserts himself; the once-liberated female relents and obviously accepts his dominance; and the sanctity of marriage, the Victorian fortress, is preserved.

Where Are We Now?

The 1940s were not quite ready to go all the way with liberation themes. During the '50s, the issue was underground but ready to explode. During the '60s, men and women demanded to be themselves, whatever that might be. Both gay and heterosexual love were granted equal respectability, though not very much by the middle class. Cultural and sexual revolutions were erupting mainly in youthful circles.

People demanded the right to equate love with physical passion and to consider passion both spiritual and beautiful. People were urged to "Do your own thing." If you wanted marriage, okay. If you wanted a one-night stand, okay. "Do your own thing as long as you don't hurt anyone" was a pervasive motto. Above all, there were sometimes eloquent pleas to accept people as they were, to do away with the myth of the strong, protective male and the "feminine" female who wanted a husband more than anything else.

During the '70s, in addition to liberationist novels and films, there developed an almost boundless permissiveness about sexual matters on stage and screen. The right to use any sort of language and to show both graphic sex and violence was quickly seized upon. Anyone who might have dropped in from outer space would have assumed from popular entertainment that ours was a society in which the only thing held sacred was being oneself. Love consisted of one sexual encounter after another and was not expected to endure. Marriage was usually the source of misery and almost never the solution to the problem of loneliness. *An Unmarried Woman* and *Starting Over,* two films of the late '70s, both begin with a divorce and purport to deal honestly with the problems faced by newly single people at or nearing middle age. Whom do they date? What commitments do they dare make? A favorite line goes something like: "I don't want to be hurt anymore." The answer these films offered is that no answer exists, that marriage is a myth surviving from a previous age and is no longer believable, that maybe human beings were never intended to share life together, even though there is nothing better to take its place.

The '80s are beginning to look, in retrospect, like a decade of backlash. First, we have experienced a turning away from the prescriptive nonfiction works of the '70s (the so-called "Me" decade, in which men and women were encouraged to "find" themselves, to assert themselves at whatever expense, and to exorcise the harmful myths people used to live by). These self-help "how-to" books sold in the millions: *How to Be Happy Without a Wife; How to Become a Corporate Woman; How to Stop Playing Games with Other People.* During the '80s, nonfiction best-sellers covered a wide range of subject matter, but do-it-yourself psychology was on the decline. Some predicted we were headed back to traditional values, with deemphasis on self.

Factors affecting this retreat to tradition include the spread of drug addiction among teenagers, the rise of teenage pregnancies (causing many to blow the whistle on the sexual revolution), and the sobering effect of the AIDS epidemic in all corners of society (there is overwhelming evidence that the original spread of AIDS was mainly the result of sexual promiscuity).

The dissolution of the family as the foundation of society is being blamed for both drug use and sexual freedom run wild. Tele-

Was anyone in love before we had the word love? I imagine so. . . . But all the complexities that make love so blissful, so exasperating, so tenuous, would have been impossible. Love was not love until the first woman said, "You never say 'I love you' any more."

Jack Smith

We may be living in a period of backlash against the permissive sexual attitudes of past decades. In popular culture there seems to be a resurgence of the family.

vision evangelists have become harbingers of doom and continue to underscore the need for a quick return to the wholesome stability of family life that our predecessors once knew. There has emerged no new definition of love. Instead, one gets the distinct impression that love, an indissoluble partnership, and responsible parenting all mean pretty much the same thing.

The family—a group of people who cannot stand each other . . . forced to live under the same roof.

Voltaire

On television the family sitcom has made a tremendous comeback after a two-decade vacation. And prime-time soap operas about rich, morally bankrupt families—such as *Dallas, Dynasty,* and *Falcon Crest*—have remained popular, perhaps as strictly escapist fare; and perhaps they have always appealed to families who watch television together and never truly reflect on their values. Notably in decline, however, are shows which glorify drug smugglers and Mafia bosses.

Significantly, *The Godfather* film trilogy of the '60s has its 1987 counterpart in *The Untouchables.* In the former, the criminals are the sympathetic focal point; in the latter, the hero is the FBI agent who manages to conquer Al Capone, the prince of all gangsters.

One box-office smash of the late '80s, *Fatal Attraction,* is a film about the tragic consequences of a casual sexual encounter enjoyed by a respectable husband and father during his family's absence. The other woman continues to harass and torment the man long after he has announced that he regrets what he did, has no interest in an adulterous relationship, and demands that she leave him in peace. Ultimately the unsuspecting wife finds out. The other woman attempts to kill her, and is herself finally murdered by the shattered husband. The moral was quite plain: stray from the safe harbor of family life, and disaster will follow.

A Perspective

If love is a myth, how is it that we have not lost the ability to be hurt by it?

Looking back over nearly the entire century, one can hardly say that views of love have been subject to massive fluctuations; rather, one suspects that both Victorian and romantic ideas have remained deep inside the consciousness of average people everywhere. Romantic love, in particular, seems to remain a strong ideal, whether always admitted or not. So-called sexual freedom may well be sexual confusion—as people of all ages take advantage of the opportunity to seek something permanent and beautiful that may, of course, not be waiting around the next corner. One doubts that the majority look *only* for temporary pleasure. America's widespread alcoholism may reflect heart-broken disenchantment as much as it does moral dissolution.

In recent years the size of the "Personals" ads in publications like the *Village Voice* and the *New York Review of Books* seems to have shrunk. The threat of sexually transmitted disease is, of course, one factor. But there is also the strong possibility that those who used to advertise their loneliness have grown a little jaded from so many disappointments.

We may be on the brink of a truly far-reaching change in consciousness. If the romantic ideal was indeed a product of history, we have had it now for nearly a thousand years. We still revive Shakespeare's *Romeo and Juliet* and we still listen to Tchaikovsky; but the effects of recent trends cannot be totally dismissed. We may have to start whittling away at our secret idealism and become more realistic in our expectations without at the same time running to the extremes of the recent sexual revolution. Some battles seem clearly to have been won: Men have earned the right to cry, and women have become skilled in the martial arts. Such changes do not necessarily mean that romance no longer exists.

Whatever the future of marriage and divorce statistics, the fact remains that women have joined the labor force in impressive numbers, and in more than a few marriages role responsibilities have changed hands without endangering the bond. A 1983 study of sex ratios disclosed that women now outnumber men; therefore women can be more aggressive about calling the shots. That is, since fewer women now find husbands and decide on alternative futures, sex-role reevaluation is now possible for all women. In times past, when the scales were tipped in favor of males, women were a scant resource who were viewed in Victorian terms: as weak, fragile creatures who needed to be protected. Since women had fewer opportunities for marriage, they could ill afford to waste any by behaving in an unorthodox fashion.

The sex-ratio factor may be all-important. When women were in short supply and men were setting the rules, the romantic ideal may have been less involved. With women in abundant supply—as now seems to be the case—the element of choice is greater; and the choice of a career rather than marriage may be lowering the surplus of women, forcing men to take a long, hard look at their own expectations. "What do you look for in a woman?" may be a prehistoric question, even as many woman have long since stopped asking that question about men.

Nevertheless, and having said all that, we may have to conclude that there is no final answer, no final definition, no true perspective. (Finding out that much is also part of being human.) We can, if we choose, solve all problems in human love relationships with the question "What did you expect?" But who is ever going to enter into a relationship expecting absolutely nothing and therefore avoiding disappointments? Maybe the truth is quite simple after all, and, as this contemporary poet tells us, each of us has a deep intuition to pay no attention to all the cynics and philosophers and those who collect data.

There is nothing we learned about each other in bed that we could not have learned—had not already begun to learn—in conversation; for that matter, by going to basketball games together. Sex is just a metaphor, isn't it, a way of focusing, intensifying, otherwise inchoate feelings.

Richard Schickel

The most unlikely people may fall in love with each other; their friends, amazed, look for the reason. This is useless; there is no reason.

Muriel Spark

Signature

If I sing because I must
being made of singing dust,

and I cry because of need
being born of watered seed,

and I grow like twisted tree
having neither symmetry

nor the structure to avert
the falling axe, the minor hurt,

yet of one thing I am sure
that this bears my signature,

that I knew love when it came
and I called it by its name.[13]

Hannah Kahn

GLOSSARY

courtly love: An artificial and codified set of rules governing the behavior of the sexes which prevailed during the late Middle Ages and early Renaissance. Principal among these rules was the right of the lady to make any demands she wished to test the loyalty and devotion of her suitor.

Mariolatry: Idealization of the Virgin Mary as practiced by a late medieval cult of poets and painters. Not only did it ennoble the life and characteristics of the mother of Jesus, but it tended to elevate the status of women.

Platonic love: Popularly considered to be any nonphysical relationship. In philosophy, however, it is a spiritual, intellectual relationship with others achieved after one has gone through lower (i.e., exclusively physical) kinds of attachment.

romance: A narrative tale popular during the Middle Ages centering on the dashing adventures of a knightly hero and his idealized passion for a (usually) beautiful young lady.

romantic love: An idealized relationship (either vaguely physical or not physical at all) between two people. Full of tenderness, devotion, sensitivity, understanding, and altruism, it continues to thrive in movies, television, and popular fiction and to affect the expectations of people, probably more than most would admit.

sex role: A characterization of self grounded in traditional and social expectations of behavior appropriate for men and for women.

Victorian model: The prototype of the male-female relationship borrowed from the Victorians and still very much with us. It includes definite sex roles, in which the male is the dominant bread-winning force in the home, and the female is the submissive bread-maker, generally uninformed and requiring the protection of her lord and master. While the liberation movement has done much to undermine the Victorian model, one needs to be aware of the extent to which *both* sexes find little to quarrel with in its basic values.

NOTES

1. Plato, *The Symposium,* trans. Benjamin Jowett.

2. Ibid.

3. "The Death of the Hired Man," *The Poetry of Robert Frost,* ed. Edward Connery Lathem (New York: Holt, Rinehart & Winston, 1969).

4. The name *Yahweh* probably derives from *Yahu,* an old Canaanite thunder god.

5. Isaiah, 42:1–4.

6. Isaiah, 49:6.

7. Miguel de Cervantes, *The First Part of the Delightful History of the Most Ingenious Knight Don Quixote of the Mancha,* trans. Thomas Shelton (New York: Harvard Classics ed., Collier), p. 222.

8. (New York: Grove Press, A Black Cat Book, 1959), pp. 134–135.

9. Ibid., p. 136.

10. Ibid., p. 139.

11. Ibid., p. 181.

12. *Emily Dickinson* (Boston: Twayne, 1976), p. 74.

13. Hannah Kahn, "Signature." Copyright by Hannah Kahn. Reprinted by permission of the author.

Edward Hopper, "Nighthawks," 1942
(© 1988 The Art Institute of Chicago, Friends of American Art Collection. All rights reserved.)

HAPPINESS

OVERVIEW

Since this book is concerned primarily with themes in the humanities, an inquiry into the nature of happiness is inevitable. Consider how many novels and plays have dealt with unhappy people and either ended sadly, all happiness denied, or somehow managed to find the format for a "happy ending." Think of how many poems have expressed the intricacies of joy or despair. Some of the world's greatest art works capture human faces in moments made significant by the presence or absence of happiness.

Small wonder that a major branch of philosophy, ethics, devotes itself to exhaustive analysis of this apparently elusive state which most of us would say is more important than anything else. When we

Happiness may be better experienced by its absence than any conscious state of present bliss.

think of ethics, our natural inclination is to think of morality. And rightly so. But in its broadest sense, *ethics* is an inquiry into the nature of the good: not only what is good as distinct from bad or evil in human affairs, but what it is that makes *life* good. Inevitably the question arises of what constitutes happiness. Yet most people, if asked what they meant or understood by happiness, would offer a very wide range of answers.

One difficulty is that people often become acutely aware of happiness only when it appears to be absent from their lives. There is a sense of something missing, something lost, and then comes the desperate search for the correct definition, at least one that will *work.* People go to psychiatrists; they write or read any number of books on the subject of being happy. Bookstore cash registers jingle from the rocketing sale of hundreds of "how to make yourself happy" manuals. Those who dart from one author's prescription to another often wind up confused and frustrated.

This chapter does not necessarily have how-to implications. What it does is pull together some of the major viewpoints on happiness and then subject each one to fair analysis and possible evaluations. Although the final answer will probably remain as obscure as most final answers are, *some* answers are available.

HEDONISM: HAPPINESS AS PLEASURE

The Greek philosopher Aristippus (435−356 B.C.) declared happiness to be the *sum total of pleasures experienced during one's lifetime.* Pleasure he defined in purely physical terms: taste, sexual excitement, touch, and so on. People, he said, are selfish animals, concerned solely with their own comforts. The idea behind living is to seek out the most gratifying comforts, avoiding situations which yield few or none at all. Thus, if Aristippus is right, people prefer not to work, but they do so only because what they earn will provide them with pleasure. There is no satisfaction in work for its own sake. As a matter of fact, Aristippus believed there was no true satisfaction in the memory or anticipation of pleasure. Nothing counted except what could be experienced *at the moment. Hedonism* is the name given to this philosophy that happiness is pleasure.

Many people today are proud to call themselves hedonists. They openly boast of their income and possessions. They assert that with only one chance to live they should deny themselves nothing and try to "have it all." Other, more idealistic philosophies are disappointments to such contemporary hedonists, who maintain that only pleasure can be known with any certainty.

Others resist applying the term *hedonism* to themselves. While a good many admit that they seek comfort and avoid discomfort, they do not accept selfishness as their primary motive. High on their list of pleasures are love (in more than a physical sense), the raising of a family, finding a useful and satisfying occupation, having the chance to get ahead in the world, having security, the pursuit of intellectual stimulation, and the opportunity to express themselves creatively. Aristippus would contend that such persons are secret hedonists but are afraid to admit that they are and that they *ought* to be selfish. They seek pleasure, but deny themselves too much. They save their money for a rainy day, and there is a drought. They sacrifice everything for their children, only to be confronted later with a thankless "What did you ever do for me?" They live frugally so that their retirement years will be truly golden, and die just before their pension comes due.

Hedonist Assumptions

Hedonists generally feel cheated. There never seem to be enough pleasurable moments in life. There seems to be so much undeserved pain. "Why me?" is a frequent question silently asked. "Did I deserve to be the sole support of my parents when my brothers and sisters flatly refused to help? When am I going to get *my* chance to be happy?"

So assumption number one of the hedonist is that *everyone deserves as much pleasure as possible.* A variant of this assumption is that *people never really get as much pleasure as they deserve.* Other people always appear to have more. Other hedonists communicate (even exaggerate) their pleasures, especially unexpected bonuses, which point out how truly deserving they really are. To share unpleasant experiences is to advertise unworthiness, and nobody wants to do this. Hence the perpetuation of the myth that other people are "getting more from life."

A second assumption, vitally related to the first, is that *pleasure is automatically good.* During the Great Depression of the 1930s, when so many Americans were barely eating enough to get by, those who were able to eat anything they wanted were undoubtedly objects of envy. Who thought to feel sorry for the affluent people who might overeat and overdrink?

Hedonists recognize that people cannot possibly have pleasure every moment of their lives, but this does not stop them from thinking they should. A third assumption, therefore, is that *no amount of pleasure is ever too much.* There may be a submerged feeling of guilt about gorging oneself in an "All U Can Eat" restaurant or downing one drink after another at somebody else's open house, but the typical hedonist response is, "There will be time enough to cut down; don't bother me now." Besides, overindulgence in moments of plenty supposedly means "making up" for past disappointments.

Another hedonist assumption is that *the absence of pleasure is a misfortune for which compensation is due.* The son or daughter

Hedonism in Oscar Wilde

I can resist everything except temptation.

    Lady Windemere's Fan

How are you, my dear Ernest? What brings you up to town?

Oh, pleasure, pleasure. What else should bring one anywhere?

    The Importance of Being Earnest

who sits with baby four nights during the week is bound to claim the weekend as a long-lost right. Many who have been arrested while attempting robbery have believed they were only getting even with society. If you carry the hedonist viewpoint through life, you find yourself plotting continually: "Just wait until *I* have the upper hand!" Since moments without definite feelings of pleasure are an abomination, one entertains oneself by thinking of the moment when rightful pleasures are finally gained.

This particular mindset stems from the *big-earnings theory.* An earning is considered the pleasure owed to a deserving person. The oldest child in a large family, for example, may have gone to work to help out and to assure younger brothers and sisters of proper clothing, education, and so on. In the ledger many hedonists carry inside themselves, there is a strict accounting of pleasures owed them; eventually a vast number may accumulate. Unless something happens to change his or her philosophy of happiness, the hedonist may become obsessed with thinking about pleasures due. If they are paid off, life is good; if not, life is bad. Life is evaluated strictly in terms of total payments received. A supergood life is one in which no good deed is left unrewarded.

Hedonism Reconsidered

Since it is one of the oldest-known theories of happiness, hedonism has been subjected to ongoing critical appraisal by philosophers and cultural historians alike. Hedonism seems to have inspired two major critical questions: first, whether this philosophy is based on an accurate view of human nature; and second, whether people are pleasure-loving at all times and in all places.

That we are living in a pleasure-oriented society is difficult to deny. Implicit in TV commercials, popular songs, and the casual talk of celebrities on interview programs is a general concern over what one is "getting out of life," and surely what people mean is pleasure. How is the new romance coming along? Do you like the new house and swimming pool in Bel Air? The ad for the sports car implies, "If you have to ask the cost, you can't afford it." Hair must be shampooed to a silky sheen for the pleasurable touch. Both sexes must wear delicate fragrances to gratify the olfactory sense. Even the quasi-serious, somewhat intellectual magazines, directed toward "thinking" people, run page after page of liquor advertisements. Nearly every song that blares from a juke box or throbs inside the earphones clamped tightly to the head celebrates the glory of physical lovemaking.

The Greek society in which Aristippus lived and wrote was hardly shy when it came to pleasures of the flesh. But it is one thing to justify hedonism on the grounds that we would rather do what the others are doing, and quite another to say that hedonism alone is in

"You deserve a break today."

"If I have one life to live, let me live it as a blond."

"You only live once!"

tune with human nature. Plato's famous analysis of the stages of love (see Chapter 11) does not discredit the pleasures of a physical relationship, but recognizes and then elevates the nonphysical.

The crux of the argument may be how limited or unlimited is our definition of *pleasure*. Fundamental hedonism is clear: Pleasure is experienced through the five senses. People who spend time in thought—that is, on the mental plane—are denying themselves that much pleasure and, we assume, that much happiness. People who spend their lives working in a clinic a thousand miles from civilization, who expose themselves daily to the risk of disease and never achieve outside recognition for what the hedonist would surely call a "sacrifice," are supposedly doing without pleasure. But how can we assume that such people—and there are many of them—are deliberately perverting their own natures to follow a calling which requires them to labor in the interest of others?

Buddhist monks sitting alone in silent meditation for hours and days at a time lose contact with a "self" in ways that the hedonist could never understand. Are they robbing themselves of the pleasure that their natures crave? Are the analysts accurate when they tell us that the spirituality of the celibate Catholic priest is a "sublimation" of normal sexual passions? Or is human nature such that it cannot be narrowly defined? Might *sensory* pleasures be all-sufficing for some and less fulfilling to others? Are we to suggest that the social worker, the rabbi, the minister, and the hospital volunteer worker are wasting their time or denying themselves pleasure? Or is perhaps limiting the quantity and duration of personal pleasure for some the way happiness is attained?

If, as the existentialist maintains, no such thing as human nature exists at all and humanity is indeed a self-defining, self-determining species, then there is ample room for alternate ways of defining pleasure and even for relegating physical pleasure to a low position on our priority list.

Another argument against hedonist assumptions is based on a historical overview. The theory is sometimes advanced that the prevalence of hedonism indicates the *declining*, not the normal, stage of a civilization. In other words, human societies are seen as moving in cycles. During the disintegrating phase, when a civilization is falling apart at the seams, it becomes affluent, greedy, fat, pleasure-oriented, and vulnerable. The cultural historian and sociologist Pitirim Sorokin (1889–1968) believed that growing societies experience a *religious* phase, in which concentration is non-self-centered; then a *political* phase, when they are oriented toward the development of great art and great institutions of learning and government; and then a *sensate* phase, when, overly secure after their place in the sun has been established, they gratify the senses and neglect their intellectual and spiritual needs. Sorokin, like Oswald Spengler (1880–1936) before him,

Gather ye rose-buds while ye may,
  Old time is still a flying;
And this same flower that smiles today,
  Tomorrow will be dying.

          Robert Herrick

saw Western civilization as being in the twilight of its greatness, mainly because of its selfish preoccupation with the senses.

Whether or not the cyclical view of history offers too neat a package, we can at least say that it presents us with choices. Sorokin's three phases *can* be applied to individuals and to societies, at least in part. Why should we be constrained by the need to single out only the last and say that *it* constitutes the norm? May not one possibility be that the sensate is the most immediate and therefore the quickest—but not necessarily the lasting—way to be happy?

EPICUREANISM: AVOID PAIN

The sudden cessation of a toothache is not directly pleasurable in itself, but it does *bring happiness, the happiness of not being in pain.*

In a musical comedy some years back, the heroine, trying to explain to the audience in song why she loved the hero, compares her love to a number of familiar pleasures. She includes the smell of bread baking and the feeling she has when a tooth stops hurting. In the first instance, she is a hedonist, directly sensuous in her values. In the second, however, she turns to a different philosophy of happiness: *Epicureanism*. The sudden cessation of a toothache is not directly pleasurable in itself, but it *does* bring happiness, the happiness of not being in pain.

Epicureanism is named for the Greek thinker Epicurus, who first formulated its precepts. Aware of Aristippus and his beliefs, Epicurus was highly critical of a philosophy he believed weak in logic and, more than that, impossible to follow.

Epicurean Assumptions

Epicurus indirectly accepted the initial premise of hedonism: that pleasure is a great good. But he refused to say with the hedonists that the more pleasure we have, the happier we shall be:

> And since pleasure is the first good and natural to us, for this very reason we do not choose every pleasure, but sometimes we pass over many pleasures, when greater discomfort accrues to us as a result of them.

Epicurus was particularly critical of recommending pleasures in excess, for these, he knew, would always be followed by both physical and moral pain:

> For from prudence are sprung all the other virtues, and it teaches us that it is not possible to live pleasantly without living prudently and honourably and justly.

For Epicurus, hedonism was a time-conscious, death-ridden philosophy. If happiness increased with the quantity of physical pleasures, then logically no life could ever be long enough. Death is never bearable, never coming at an acceptable time. But, surely, we are here for an uncertain amount of time, all of us subject to the gradual infirmities that come with age—if indeed we do not burn ourselves out before age ever becomes a problem. Therefore hedonists are fundamentally insecure and unhappy, unable to accept the inevitability of age and death, always worried about the loss of pleasure. So the major assumption of Epicureanism is that nothing lasts forever and we must accept the fact cheerfully.

Another Epicurean assumption is that no one can sustain pleasure over prolonged periods of time. How long can we gorge ourselves on delicious food? Indulge in sex? Stay drunk? Why, then, saddle ourselves with a philosophy of life that is so limiting from the very outset?

Unable to satisfy our pleasure-seeking instincts perpetually, we do the next best thing: seek material possessions or notoriety, both of which symbolize happiness without bringing happiness. Money and vanity are constantly in the hedonist's thoughts. They are the compensations for what may be passing us by: the tangible embodiments of a successful hedonistic life. But Epicurus recognized that the pursuit of the physical pleasure for which wealth often substitutes was self-defeating, futile. The same is true of fame as a substitute. The wealthy or the famous person feels insecure and distrustful of others, certain that others are envious and scheming.

Why, asked Epicurus, burden ourselves with a philosophy with built-in disappointments, frustrations, and inevitable pain? Why not, rather, change the *requirements* for happiness? Epicurus was influenced by the materialistic philosophy that had been popularized by Democritus, a formulator of the first atomic theory (see Chapter 5). But Epicurus did not carry materialism as far as some would later do, that is, into a thoroughgoing determinism (see Chapter 15) which reduces human behavior to a matter of cause and effect and denies the role of human will. Epicurus assumed the person of reason had free will and could control his or her pleasures and therefore reduce the amount of pain to be endured. The Epicurean is highly selective.

Epicureanism is therefore not so much an all-out attack upon as a modification of hedonism. It assumes unpleasantness is part of life and plans strategies to ward it off as much as possible rather than march forward in the blind hope that things are going to be fine. The worst that can happen when you anticipate pain is that you will not be disappointed. But clearly, you have a good chance of doing something about much of life's pain before it occurs *if* you apply yourself conscientiously to the task.

The taste of exquisite food is high on the list of hedonists' priorities. So it is for the Epicureans. The difference is that the latter, anticipating the pain of overindulgence, stop themselves before reaching their limit. They will drink, but never to the point of drunkenness, and not at all if they are certain their health cannot stand it.

A character in one of Hemingway's short stories marries a beautiful but flirtatious woman considerably younger than he. He goes off to war, is injured, and during his stay at a rehabilitation center learns that his wife has run off with another man. His response is typically Epicurean: Instead of being angry or feeling sorry for himself, he admits to having made a mistake. A man, he comments, should never place himself in a position to lose so much.

The Epicureans pursue physical pleasures in moderation, realizing that any excess is likely to lead to pain. But they also seek out nonphysical pleasures. They are generally lovers of the arts, the theater, books, and music. Intellectual and esthetic pleasures can be experienced in abundance without the fear of pain. Epicureans are also wary of becoming overly dependent upon such stimuli, for then they run the risk of being unable to compromise. You cannot spend all of your time reading or thinking; there are other necessary tasks that need to be done.

Epicureans tend to be highly disciplined. They are generally lean and trim, exercising their bodies to keep in the best possible shape. They are mentally agile and aware of the latest developments in many fields. They are good workers, and the one who finds a marital partner with a similar outlook is likely to build a reasonably happy home.

Pure hedonists, however, warn Epicureans that they sell themselves too short and may often settle for less than they have a right to expect from life. The hedonist maintains that unless you work aggressively at being happy, you will give up too easily, spending too much time in a void.

Epicureanism Reconsidered

One objection that can be raised to Epicureanism is that it is rooted as firmly in self-interest as the philosophy from which it departs. We may question how profound or lasting would be the peace of mind which comes from the careful control of one's own life if such were achieved at the cost of worrying about the pain of others.

While many people live as though pure hedonism were their creed, Epicureans have enjoyed considerably more prominence in philosophy through the centuries. Accepting a materialistic view of existence, not considering the possibility of a divine hand at work behind the universe, they continue to espouse a theory of happiness which is based on controlling one's attitudes and desires. "No one can make you happy but yourself," they say. The Epicurean alternative to the endless quest for pleasure is very tempting, and deserves a closer, critical scrutiny.

One objection that can be raised to Epicureanism is that it is as firmly rooted in self-interest as the philosophy from which it departs. We may question how profound or lasting would be the peace of mind which comes from the careful control of one's own life if such were achieved at the cost of worrying about the pain of others. Granted, classical theories of happiness focus on the individual, as though happiness *by definition* were a matter of how one's *own* life is faring. Social consciousness was not predominant in classical thinking. We could even argue that concern for the neighbor, stressed in Judaism and early Christianity were in contrast to the emphasis of Epicurus. Religious leaders have said that personal happiness was less important than caring for others, and not that the means to personal happiness was that very caring.

We cannot rule out the possibility that happiness can be and is often achieved only by working to combat pain wherever it is found, and sometimes the battle incurs personal suffering, which is accepted as the high price of success. After all, there are people, seldom mentioned in history books, who voluntarily spend their shortened lives nursing the sick in leper colonies. What of the thousands who have forfeited the comforts of a good standard of living and gone off with the Peace Corps to remote villages, where adequate food and medical care would not be available to them?

Now, social consciousness *might* be an extension of a principle already stated by Epicurus: "The just man is most free from trouble." That is, happiness consists of an undisturbed conscience; so if you want tranquility, you must sometimes labor in the interest of others. After all, can you sit down to relish a gourmet meal with three ragged and starving children pressing their noses against the restaurant window? But it seems unfair to assume that all apparently selfless work is ultimately rooted in the effort to reach inner peace.

Another possible objection to the Epicurean way of life is purely economic. To pick and choose carefully among the available pleasures of life can be costly. The well-rounded Epicurean likes to read and listen to music, of course, but not all the time. Expensive food, drink, and travel are also desirable if one is to avoid the pain of unfulfilled longings.

Yet even with a hefty budget and an abundance of leisure, the Epicurean is likely to be a passive spectator and enjoyer rather than an actor in the drama of living. Epicurus stresses the suppression of want, deciding beforehand that the struggle to obtain something may well not be worth the pain of failing:

Even with a hefty budget and an abundance of leisure, the Epicurean is likely to be a passive spectator rather than an actor in the drama of living.

> He who has learned the limits of life knows that that which removes the pain due to want and makes the whole of life complete is easy to obtain; so that there is no need of actions which involve competition.

But the countersuggestion can be made that not risking much in a challenge means there is less chance for a significant victory.

STOICISM: STRATEGIES FOR SURVIVING

There is a famous poster showing a cat holding tightly to a knotted end of a rope and just hanging there in empty black space. The caption reads, *When You Come to the End of Your Rope, Tie a Knot and Hang On.* This, in capsule form, is the philosophy of *Stoicism.* It operates under even fewer illusions about life than does Epicureanism. It tells us neither to plan ahead for a lifetime of unlimited pleasure nor to expect to avoid pain through discipline and moderation. Stoicism asserts pain is intrinsic to living. Even the most dedicated Epicureans will feel a certain amount of frustration when their disciplined approach to living goes awry and the ceiling caves in on them. The best possible course is to be prepared for the worst and to develop a technique for coping with it, a mental technique.

The Epicurean

Moderate eating and drinking, the pursuit of intellectual pleasures,

> *and*

an awareness of the impossibility of permanent pleasure.

Working On the Mind

Stoicism is still a popular philosophy of happiness, for many still a viable approach to the business of living, despite the fact that it was born over 2000 years ago. Like hedonism and hedonism's modified offspring, Epicureanism, it is the product of Greek intellect; but unlike the others, it lays heavy stress on human reason, on the belief that humankind is a superior form of animal life. Zeno, its first major advocate (?–264? B.C.), is therefore closer in spirit to Plato and Aristotle than to either Aristippus or Epicurus.

The name of the philosophy derives from the fact that the school founded by Zeno was located in a columned portico area called the *Stoa.* Central to Stoicism is that true happiness is not a matter of circumstance, of good fortune, nor a matter of what happens to us, but rather a matter of *how we respond to what happens.* Happiness, like sorrow, is an idea, not an object, not an event. If no people exist to welcome the first day of spring, how can it be said that spring is a time of hope and joy? If in some remote civilization with peculiar customs and mores the birth of a child were considered a dreadful curse, then the inability to produce offspring might be regarded as a happy stroke of luck.

In other words, Stoicism teaches that, to find the roots of unhappiness, one must look inward. Nothing is under our control except the way we think about things. Natural disasters, social upheavals, wars, revolutions, outbreaks of disease, rising crime rates—all happen as a result of either accidental or highly complicated causes. Our happiness should not depend upon their *not* taking place. We cannot alter external circumstances, but we *can* decide not to feel negatively toward them.

"How do you expect me to feel?" is a common response when we are asked why we are so glum about a certain outcome—say, not being promoted to a higher position. Stoics cite habit as the guilty culprit. That is, they contend people are conditioned by the values their society puts on what happens to or around them: This is acceptable; that is not. This is cause for joy; that is cause for tears. Reactions become automatic after awhile. People come to *think* they are unhappy; hence they are unhappy. But typical responses can be altered. We can refuse to be affected in customary ways or as others tend to be affected.

One of the best-known Stoic teachers was a Greek named Epictetus (A.D. 60?–120?), who became a Roman slave. His genius was finally recognized and he was allowed to conduct classes. But prior to that, Epictetus was tortured and oppressed in his captivity. On one occasion his leg was broken on a whim of his master's. During this period of extreme trial and suffering, Epictetus was faced with the choice of surrendering to despair or finding some means of enduring. He chose the latter course, recognizing that nothing, not even torture, was unbearable unless one wished to find it so. After his "liberation," he dedicated his life to spreading the Stoic creed which had preserved his spirit intact for so many years.

Stoicism found ready acceptance among the Romans and eventually became a sort of "official" state philosophy. Its emphasis on reason and the control of negative emotions accorded well with the Roman ideal of humanity. Besides, Rome was an empire-building civilization, requiring a superbly disciplined military machine to carry out its conquests. It therefore found a meaningful application of Stoic teachings. The rigors of military training as well as the hardships of war itself must never depress the human spirit. Good soldiers must have feelings so well under their command that they become indifferent to suffering.

When Christianity began to spread through the Roman Empire, many of the converts had, naturally enough, already been exposed to Stoic beliefs. The by-then ancient and honorable philosophy accorded well with the outlook and needs of the Christians. After all, they had to face untold sufferings—continual persecution, torture, flight, starvation, separation from loved ones. The Stoic doctrine of inner control blended perfectly with the Christian belief that only the soul, not the body, mattered. One could endure all manner of pain and stay inwardly serene. Christians supposedly sang while waiting for the lions to devour them in the Circus Maximus.

What more dramatic model of the Stoic being could there have been than Christ himself? Had Christ not allowed himself to be mocked, taunted, whipped? Had he not carried his own cross to Calvary and then refused to come down from that same cross when the challenge was given? Had he not forgiven his tormentors?

If you are told that such an one speaks ill of you, make no defense against what was said, but answer, He surely knew not my other faults, else he would not have mentioned these only!

Epictetus

Live rationally, and part with life cheerfully.

Marcus Aurelius

But I say to you, do not resist one who is evil. But if any one strikes you on the right cheek, turn to him the other also.

Matt. 5:38

Stoicism remains as pervasive as ever and offers to many a genuine alternative to hedonism. In a period of ever-accelerating rates of change, of densely packed urban centers in which violence has become a way of life, of depression in farm belts and neurosis in high-rent districts, it is small wonder that many are asking less for pleasure than for inner peace. While weekly pilgrimages to analysts continue, we wonder whether some principles of Stoicism are not at work here also. After all, self-knowledge is vital to psychoanalysis. It is the analyst's contention that, once people understand what is making them depressed, they will be able to transcend negative feelings. Happiness is really within our own power to create and preserve.

God grant me the serenity to accept things I cannot change, the strength to change the things I can, and the wisdom to know the difference.

Alcoholics Anonymous creed

Stoicism Reconsidered

Stoicism in modern dress is for many a viable theory of happiness. Often unworkable without a little help from Valium, its basic assumption remains much the same as always: Tranquility is worth any price. Stoicism has something to offer the chronically poor and dispossessed, who also suffer from low self-esteem and cannot see that they deserve any better fate. Even the most zealous social worker might agree that in some cases a stoic attitude is better than false hope for a better tomorrow.

An obvious negative aspect of Stoicism would then be its convenience. If you're down and out, abandoned by family and friends, with no prospects that things will turn around for you, why not become a Stoic? Surely the distance is short from "Things are pretty bleak" to "There is no reason to believe things should be otherwise."

Suppose, however, that the ad hoc Stoic—the person who adopts this philosophy out of sheer desperation—suddenly experiences an unexpected reversal of fortune. Winning $5 million in the state lottery or, more modestly, a kindly social worker chances by and provides a paying job. Suppose, as actually happened in the wake of a TV newscaster's human-interest documentary about the homeless people who sleep in New York doorways, a couple randomly singled out for an interview found themselves swamped with offers of money, jobs, shelter—even a film contract! What happens to Stoic doctrines then? Can a legitimate theory of happiness be Stoic one day and hedonistic the next?

If your answer to this question was "Why not?" let us analyze the response. If adversity can be endured because the rational control of emotion makes endurance possible, then dropping Stoicism when convenient negates the importance placed on reason to begin with. Indeed, that same reason which justified the initial adoption of the

Stoic philosophy requires us to believe that good fortune is not likely to be permanent.

There is an old fable about a tyrannical king who, finding himself plagued by bad fortune, kept asking various wise men to give him grounds for hope. If they could not, their heads were chopped off. Finally, one clever sage gave him a plaque to hang on his bedroom wall: THESE THINGS SHALL PASS. The king, deriving much comfort from the plaque, rewarded the sage handsomely, until it came to pass that the king's fortunes turned good. The maxim, which had once buoyed up his spirits, now angered him, and he beheaded the once-favored philosopher.

Suppose that the ad hoc Stoic—the person who adopts this philosophy out of sheer desperation—suddenly experiences a reversal of fortune.

Another frequently raised objection to Stoicism is that Stoics secretly want everyone else to be as miserable as they are. Adversity is more bearable when no one around you is having a run of good luck. Loving the company of the miserable may be a fundamental human trait. Enjoying nothing so much as the sad tales of other people's disasters may be as universal as secretly resenting the prosperity of others or supposing they must be lying about it. But sharing human characteristics is not the same as having a consistent theory of happiness.

But why should our idea of happiness have to be rational, or arrived at through logical means? The answer is, of course, that it doesn't have to be. We need not even entertain *any* belief about happiness. But Stoicism is based on the rational control of the emotions and so assumes the validity of the rational process. We could say, then, that yet another basis for criticizing Stoicism is that the Stoic is guided by something that appears to be reason, but actually is not.

Very often what passes for reason should really be called rationalizing, a process by which we find workable rather than logical reasons for believing something. The possibility exists that control for the Stoic actually means manipulating thoughts so that reality becomes bearable. When loved ones stop calling, do we endure the absence by admitting the possibility that they have transferred their affections or have ceased to be interested in us for this or that reason? Or do we find acceptable reasons such as a sudden trip out of town because of a relative's illness? The trip may well turn out to be the actual reason, but the manipulator picks and chooses among comfortable versions of reality, bearing unpleasantness so long as it seems under his or her control. In this way, what masquerades as stoic resignation is secretly a way of gaining control over reality itself.

Classical Stoicism emerged from two cultures, the Greek and the Roman, which were fate-oriented. The universe was run by all-powerful deities who could and did intervene in human affairs whenever they chose. The gods and goddesses were capricious, but human reason could counteract heavenly whimsy by expecting ill times before they occurred. In other words, the universe of the Greeks and

Expecting to fail has kept many a potential winner from even getting started.

Romans was predictably full of disaster. But perhaps the universe really does not make even that much sense. Perhaps disasters are no less certain than continual success. A very strong criticism of Stoicism is, thus, a recognition of the debilitating passivity which it can inspire. Expecting to fail has kept many a potential winner from even getting started.

ARISTOTLE: HAPPINESS IS NOT PLEASURE

For Aristotle (384–322 B.C.), Plato's famous pupil and founder of the Lyceum, an early version of the liberal arts college, happiness was a major concern, central to his curriculum—almost, we could say, the most important object of study. In analyzing this most complex of phenomena, Aristotle concluded that happiness is not a state to be experienced but a concept to be comprehended—crucial to education, since it is the very goal for which we live.

Pleasure, a Limited Goal; Happiness, a Complete Goal

Aristotle's great work on the conduct of living is called *The Nicomachean Ethics*. In analyzing the things which can be said to make life good, Aristotle was led to his famous theory of happiness. Since the pleasure creed was very much in the air, Aristotle gave it a fair share of reflection. He agreed that pleasure must be counted as something which makes life good. Obviously nobody hates having it. Nobody refuses to experience it when the occasion arises. But, he added, if pleasure is to be considered life's *highest* good, it must be our ultimate goal. It must be worth having for its own sake, and, once achieved, it cannot cause us to desire anything beyond it.

The hedonists, of course, claimed that there *was* no good greater than pleasure. As if to give them their due, Aristotle agreed that "any good thing . . . is made more desirable by the addition of pleasure." When you add pleasure to something good, the result is something even better. Can anyone deny this? We can imagine ancient hedonists shaking their head no. Then the master logician strikes!

In modern-day terms, let us suppose that a person, popular with her office colleagues, is promoted to management. She likes her work, has traded off family ties for a business career, at which she has been eminently successful. The promotion reinforces her view that both present and future are going her way. Under such circumstances, could anyone believe the promotion to be anything but a great good?

If pleasure makes us happy, then it is a means, not an end.

"Every good thing is sought in order that, by possessing it, one may become happy."

Aristotle

To celebrate the happy occasion, the woman's colleagues, who like her very much and want to express their feelings, invite her out for fellowship and several rounds of toasts. No one drinks to excess. There is simply the slow and mellow "attitude adjustment" which often accompanies so happy an occasion, one which even the most ardent cynic would have to admit deserves the label "pleasure." In terms of Aristotle's analysis, "if pleasure combined with something else is better than pleasure alone, it follows that pleasure cannot in itself be the supreme good." That is, if we allow that the promotion is certainly a very high order of good, we can see how the pleasure of companionship and mellowness, added to the promotion, creates something better than the promotion would be by itself. But—and here is the crux—the pleasure by itself is also not as great a good as the two things combined.

To carry the analysis further, let us isolate attitude adjustment as a pleasure, as indeed it must be, since so many thousands seek it out. But indulging in a "happy hour" by oneself is for most people less desirable than having company in either joy or misery. Hence we see again that pleasure can be made more enjoyable by the addition of other goods.

Since logic tells us that pleasure cannot be the highest good, does it not fall into the same category of means to that end, which is happiness? People seek pleasure to be made happy by having it; otherwise there would be no point in it. By the same token, pleasure *can* lead to misery, as when we allow our attitudes to be overadjusted, or when the joy of being in love with another creates an overdependency, then leads to an obsession and the anguish of jealousy, wondering where the loved one is at all times and with whom, and so on. At such times, many would agree, the pleasure did not produce what it should have: happiness!

What all of this meant for Aristotle was that, in trying to determine the highest of all goods, we could easily imagine something better than pleasure. Could we not do the same for, say, health, which some people might suggest as the highest good? Indeed, yes. What could be better than health? The answer is: the thing for the sake of which we wish to be healthy—in other words, happiness. No one would wish for health if health brought misery. When we are healthy, we have a definite sense of well-being; when we don't have that sense of well-being, then we fail to be healthy to that extent. (Nowadays this includes mental as well as physical health.)

What of other possible contenders? Wealth, for example—or, in any event, "sufficient means"? Can we deny that the need to have financial security, for the poor especially, must rank close to the top in priority? But that person would have to be mentally sick indeed who became obsessed with the acquisition of wealth solely for itself. The American novelist Frank Norris used this obsession to characterize a

It is theoretically possible to be living a happy life and never receive any material rewards.

dangerously sick woman in his novel *McTeague* (1899). The hero's wife, wanting not only to have money, but to possess it physically, keeps her money in gold coins:

> She would lock the door, open her trunk, and pile all her little hoard on her table. By now it was four hundred and seven dollars and fifty cents. Trina would play with this money by the hour, piling it and repiling it. . . . She polished the gold pieces with a mixture of soap and ashes until they shone. . . . Or again, she would draw the heap lovingly toward her and bury her face in it, delighted at the smell of it and the feel of the smooth, cool metal on her cheeks. She even put the smaller gold pieces in her mouth and jingled them there.[1]

For the average person, wealth, like health, can be separated from a greater good for the sake of which it is desirable: something, that is, *better* than wealth. This something is, again, happiness. Why have financial security if we are made miserable because of it?

For Aristotle, the means to happiness are virtue, wisdom, health, sufficient means, and friendship, with the first two the most important.

Other goods we seek in order to be made happy include friendship, virtue, and wisdom. The last two Aristotle places in a special category because they are so very close to happiness itself that they could *almost* be said to be equivalents. Once having attained an upstanding moral character and developed the mind to the fullest of its potential, we cannot fail to be happy. Surely these two goods never lead to anything *but* happiness. The perfectly virtuous and learned person may lack all of life's other goods without being one whit less happy. A high moral character guarantees that all relationships will be good ones, and reason will control any negativity which other wants could inspire.

The result of Aristotle's analysis is the recognition that happiness is indeed the highest good—and therefore the goal for which we live—because, having attained it, we can desire nothing else. Can we advance any reason for wishing to be happy? No, and we cannot even imagine having to do so. The question "Now that I'm perfectly happy, what is next?" cannot be made by the rational person. To no other good in life can we attribute total self-sufficiency.

While two and a half thousand years have rolled by since this theory was set forth, we must still regard it with awe and respect. People are *still* confusing happiness with the things they need to make them happy—and wondering why they are not yet satisfied. Obviously the new car in the driveway is not the goal itself. Aristotle's analysis also explains why the car may make us happy for a time, but not indefinitely. Only happiness in its pure essence endures through time. What we can say is that we change, but it doesn't. We glimpse it if we are lucky, peeking at us from behind the clouds.

How to Reevaluate Your Life in Aristotelian Terms

Revisiting the past in order to become familiar with a significant Greek philosophical achievement is more than paying tribute to lasting genius. Aristotle's theory continues to have many implications for us. One of the most striking, if unexpected, of these is the realization that *happiness in itself is not directly experienced.* We know we are happy by having in our hands the means to that end.

Another statement by Aristotle may help us to grasp this all-important point: Happiness is the quality of a life that has been made good by the presence of good things. A life that in retrospect is seen to have included health, wealth, pleasure, friendship, and especially virtue and wisdom can be said to have been a happy one. But the things that carry us to the quality are what we experience along the way. By the same token, the temporary absence of some of those things deludes us into believing we are unhappy.

We can compare happiness to the ordinary air we breathe. Constantly around us, it becomes a factor when we cannot get enough of it, when, for example, a blockage of some sort exists. Hospital attendants then place a tube inside us, which permits air to pass into the lungs. We say we feel "relief," and are very likely to give thanks to the tube rather than the air itself. We may even claim that the tube has saved our life. But that same tube, resting pointlessly on a hospital shelf, is not a life-saving instrument. Merely to hold the tube in our hands during times of normal breathing is not even sensible.

Unhappiness can be identified with the temporary absence of happiness-bringing instruments in the same way that patient discomfort can be identified with the temporary absence of an air-supplying tube. We can lack for air for a time without dying. We can lack for health, wealth, and so on and feel miserable *without having to say that our life is an unhappy one.* Logic does not require that a happy life be defined as one in which the things that bring happiness are always present or present in equal amounts.

Consider this remarkable passage by Austrian psychiatrist Viktor Frankl, who was held prisoner at Auschwitz and, though continually in fear of imminent death, managed to be happy:

> The size of human suffering is absolutely relative. . . . It also follows that a very trifling thing can cause the greatest of joys. Take as an example something that happened on our journey from Auschwitz to the camp affiliated with Dachau. We had all been afraid that our transport was heading for the Mauthausen camp. We became more and more tense as we approached a certain bridge over the Danube which the train would have to cross in order to

How about the pleasure of having someone dear sitting next to you and holding your hand? Is this too much to ask?

reach Mauthausen. . . . Those who have never seen anything similar cannot possibly imagine the dance of joy performed in the carriage by the prisoners when they saw that our transport was not crossing the bridge and was instead heading "only" for Dachau.[2]

In addition to the immediate realization that the prisoners were not going to the camp which meant certain extinction, Frankl, as we learn, retained his wisdom (including a life-saving sense of humor) and his moral character, which were for Aristotle the two major happiness-bringing conditions. Having these, Frankl would, in Aristotle's view, have possessed all he needed.

Many would argue—and not without some justification—that merely knowing our life will be assessed as a happy one after we have died is insufficient compensation for the lack of tangible evidence along the way. How about just a drop more wealth here and an occasional visit by a close friend there? How about the pleasure of having someone dear sitting next to you and holding your hand? Is this too much to ask?

Since virtue and wisdom are the closest of life's goods to actual happiness itself, we *can* experience the knowledge that ours is a happy life by deliberately practicing the improvement of our minds, using every means possible, and by always making choices that are in accord with rational codes of conduct among civilized people.

Having proceeded this far in his analysis, Aristotle knew that he had made a portentous discovery, not just about happiness, but about the very reason for which we live. Virtue and wisdom were the sentinels of happiness, the *bodyguards,* if you will. And nothing could provide more compelling justifications for existing than those states and the actions which manifest them. In other words, happiness was the complete goal of life, and those who displayed virtue and wisdom in their deeds gave clearest indication of having come close to it.

Aristotle went further. Having deduced the purpose of living as becoming happy, and practicing virtue and wisdom as the sure means of getting there, he wrote that human society and its institutions must exist for no reason other than to promote that end and those means. The political state could not logically exist to promote only the well-being of those in power, for, in so doing, it would be working against the goal of everyone else.

But law and order in the well-regulated state are necessary to help people realize their ultimate purpose. People must be protected against their own baser natures so that their higher potential may be realized. State-supported education, we can say, exists in order that the mind can grow and the rational powers become stronger. (How different from some modern assumptions about the direct and exclusive relationship between education and jobs!)

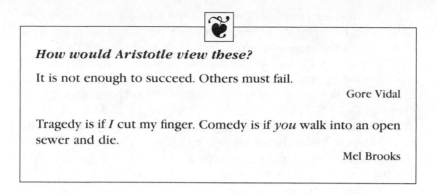

How would Aristotle view these?

It is not enough to succeed. Others must fail.

Gore Vidal

Tragedy is if *I* cut my finger. Comedy is if *you* walk into an open sewer and die.

Mel Brooks

The reason Aristotle, like Plato before him, did not favor democracy, which he identified as irrational mob rule, is that he did not believe enough people had sufficiently developed rational powers to make decisions for their own good, let alone for that of others. He did not believe that the majority could be trusted to act in every instance with moral integrity. Hence rulers were necessary, but rulers must never forget that their job is to use their intellect to bring about the happiness of their charges. Presumably our elected leaders understand the identical mandate.

We assume that in the backs of their minds, present-day leaders of state, both in the Western world and elsewhere, agree with Aristotle in principle. The only question we might raise is whether their view of happiness is always the same as the people's. More than likely, *both* can be confused about what happiness truly means and how it may be attained. Happiness is not luxury; but while, as Viktor Frankl demonstrates, it can be achieved despite appalling conditions, the state should guarantee that all reasonable measures are taken to remove the barriers which can make the practice of virtue and wisdom difficult indeed: barriers like hunger, illiteracy, and discrimination. What other reason can government have for existing?

Possible Limitations of Aristotle's View

As often happens when we follow the impeccable, almost surgical, clarity of a great thinker like Aristotle, we nod, say, "Yes, how logical," then go back to the everyday world, which seems as confusing as ever. For example, a seldom-mentioned fringe benefit of the sheltered academic life is the scholar's ability to spend time in the company of great minds without their ever making the least bit of difference beyond the hallowed pages which preserve them. In the case of happiness, however, the appropriate definition ought to be one that *does* make a difference for all of us.

An alternative to the Aristotelian analysis of happiness is the personal example of people who have provided role models of the happy life and therefore deserve a place in the history of philosophy.

A possible limitation of Aristotle's theory is its assumption that the personal achievement of the good life is all that matters.

There are people to consider like Gandhi and Martin Luther King. Both of them advocated nonviolent resistance to oppression and, in so doing, triggered hostile reactions even among those they were trying to help. Both of them knew very well how dangerous it was to stand by uncompromising principles in the name of a cause higher than their own well-being. Both of them finally paid the supreme price for their cause. Can we say that Gandhi and King willingly sacrificed their happiness for a higher good? Or can we say that Gandhi and King were indeed happy men, even when most beset by danger?

A possible limitation of Aristotle's theory is its assumption that happiness is ultimately the characteristic of a *person's* life, that person being any of us—in other words, that the personal achievement of the good life is all that matters. But take away the martyrdom of Gandhi and King, take away the universal significance of their deaths and the impact of their beliefs on millions of people they never met—and have you not lessened the degree to which their lives can be said to have been good? Now suppose that both men had preferred to practice virtue in a modest, everyday fashion, without martyrdom, and to allow a calm rationality to govern every decision. Surely their lives would still deserve to be called good, but perhaps not *as* good. Involvement in a cause which transcends one's personal happiness may bring *greater* happiness. In short, the Aristotelian analysis would seem not to discriminate among levels of good, though we could still argue that the world in Aristotle's time was not as overcrowded as it is in our century; or that there existed no role model of humanitarianism; or that, if we make allowances for social and cultural differences from one era to another, today's person of unimpeachable reason and virtue would inevitably be led to the larger causes of injustice and deprivation.

How much time he gains who does not look to see what his neighbor says or does or thinks, but only at what he does himself, to make it just and holy.

Marcus Aurelius

But there is also the case of the many thousands who do not or cannot take the extreme steps of Gandhi or King, who do not in fact alter the consciousness of an entire age, but who nonetheless care deeply about, say, the environment—especially the harm being done to the nation's water supplies, the wasting of dwindling resources, the annual killing of baby seals and blue whales, and, more recently, the awesome perils of building more nuclear power plants. These people find they cannot be personally happy in the midst of so much that is clearly wrong. They join the ranks of people who, though reasonably comfortable in their standard of living, think about hungry children in Asia or street people in New York—people for whom complete happiness requires a very different kind of world, particularly one in which responsible leaders do not even *think* about "winning" a nuclear war. The cynic might argue that those made chronically unhappy by the state of the world are secret hedonists who worry about their own loss of pleasure in these dangerous and corrupt times. But the chronically unhappy might argue right back that the cynics are taking the path of least resistance and finding quick and easy happiness regardless of the cost.

In any event, one good that Aristotle does not place near the top of his list is love, a fact which might strike some readers as surprising. That many prize love above all other goods tells us we cannot leave it out of consideration. On the other hand, Aristotle might well argue that, unlike virtue and wisdom, love depends upon how others feel and what they do: that is, not on the exercise of a person's own rational powers and self-discipline. Making happiness equivalent to or dependent upon feelings of love might be to build extreme limitations before we even begin the quest.

The unhappiness brought about by the absence of love is, however, so universally recognized and shared that even the very hope of one day finding an ideal love is enough to reverse that condition for many people. Popular songs, magazine stories, and countless motion pictures have for years conveyed the same message: What good is having money, fame, even health, if one is unlucky in love? Here the myth—if indeed that's what ideal love can be called—is so powerful that the continual quest may itself be happiness. While many fall in love with love, they fall *out* of love with John or Sue. Lost love is certainly not a myth for millions of us, and thus the poets' and songmakers' expectation of finding the "new love" can also be very real. The glorification of the unending search for love is telling us something.

As people grow older, they tend to substitute words like *companionship* and *understanding* for *love.* May we then say that the requirements for happiness can change with age? Some of the good things on Aristotle's list may be in this category. Those who are 65 and don't have *sufficient* means, but just barely get by, may well settle for barely getting by and not be unhappy. So too with health. You may reach an age at which you neither feel well continually nor expect to, but find happiness during times of relatively less infirmity. Or perhaps you can make a substitution for health altogether. Aristotle, of course, would contend that the two major requirements for happiness— virtue and wisdom—change with age only in the respect that they can and should shine more brightly.

Still, viewing the subject of happiness from the perspective of aging presents us with yet a final possibility: *work.* There are two senses in which we can understand the relationship between work and happiness. In the first, we achieve happiness by day-to-day activities that are meaningful, and we define *meaningful* in the way most appropriate for the circumstances of our life. The Manhattan executive, for whom a typical workday includes breathlessly catching a cab, holding twelve conferences, firing an employee, skipping lunch, and finally sinking into the leatherette peace of a stately hotel bar, may be less than satisfied by trading places with an Iowa farmer. The latter, on the other hand, might find the frenetic New York tempo absurd and pointless. Assembly-line workers who have never had a personal relationship with any final product may still miss their jobs after retirement and may *not* look back with sadness upon a life which Thoreau might have characterized as one of "quiet desperation." The author of a financially successful best-seller, envied by hundreds of unpublished garret dwellers, may secretly be ashamed of the "trash" he or she has written and ardently long for a burst of true inspiration.

In another sense, however, we achieve happiness only after doing work of universal meaningfulness, work that others recognize and applaud. Bertrand Russell, who lived into his nineties and stopped writing only at the very end, once said in an interview that nothing quite equals the satisfaction of having completed a really significant piece of work. For him this meant the publication of a provocative contribution to human thought which would be hailed by people of letters throughout the world. For the average person, "really significant" work is anything that requires the realization of an inner potential. Assembly-line workers may miss the job because they have never known anything else, but still be vaguely aware of talents never developed, doors never opened, words of praise never heard. Socrates is famous for having told the court: "The unexamined life is not worth living." Perhaps we can add: "And the unaccomplished life is not worth having been lived."

On the other hand, what shall we say of those who walk with leaden steps through life, dissatisfaction written all over their faces? Those who say with King Lear, "I will do such things . . ." and have no idea of what they are? Those who have not accomplished anything because they "know" they have potential but not what they can in reality *do?* While the poet Browning made himself famous by advising that a man's reach should exceed his grasp, he was not implying, as some no doubt believe, that no possibility of achievement need ever exist. Perhaps the trick is to assess our resources fully, be stern and uncompromising with ourselves, and *then* create realistic expectations.

A clear-headed attitude toward the appropriateness of the work we choose to do is, therefore, a major consideration. Epictetus advised: "Desire that things be as they are." We can borrow that advice without necessarily becoming a complete Stoic, for Stoicism *can* make us relax a bit too soon, pull back with the finish line in sight, because "I probably wouldn't win anyway."

Literature is filled with admiration for the unrealistic striver. Cervantes created Don Quixote as a way of making fun of silly old romances, but appears instead to have given us the mad but wonderful gentleman who makes us weep as well as laugh when he undertakes the impossible task of restoring the Golden Age of Chivalry. The appar-

Much madness is divinest sense—To a discerning eye.

　　　　Emily Dickinson

ently indestructible quixotism of the impossible dream is summed up in this poem by Stephen Crane:

> *I saw a man pursuing the horizon;*
> *Round and round they sped.*
> *I was disturbed at this;*
> *I accosted the man.*
> *"It is futile," I said,*
> *"You can never—"*
> *"You lie," he cried,*
> *And ran on.*

In another corner sits the cynical but self-styled "realist," who advises us to become reconciled to boring routines on the grounds that nothing is worth trying anyway. In yet another, we have what amounts to the folk wisdom of our time and society: "Winning isn't everything; it's the *only* thing." While some tell us it's how we play the game that matters, the peppery manager of the old Brooklyn Dodgers left his mark on our national consciousness with an incisive and curt "Nice guys finish last."

What work can mean and how "successful" it must be in order to make us happy has yet to be given definitive expression. Aristotle, as we have said, didn't mention it, perhaps because the nature and purpose of an individual's life did not in his time and place revolve around work, as they seem to do from *our* vantage point. The least that can be said is that a modern theory of happiness should include a vision of work and its relative importance to the totality of our lives.

GLOSSARY

Epicureanism: A philosophy of happiness developed and taught by Epicurus in third century B.C. Athens. It takes exception to hedonism in particular, arguing that what makes life good is not the amount of pleasure experienced, but the absence of pain. It urges moderation in all things, for pain usually results from excess.

hedonism: A philosophy, advanced in fifth-century B.C. Athens by Aristippus and his followers, which holds that the happy life is one characterized by an abundance of physical pleasures. It is rooted in the as-sumption that human beings are selfish animals, dedicated—and rightly so—to their own enjoyments.

Stoicism: A philosophy, developed originally by Zeno, a Cypriot, in the third century B.C. and raised almost to the level of a national belief system by the Romans, which strongly influenced early Christian ideology. Its basic premise is that if one cannot control painful external events, one can control one's response and thus become relatively immune to pain.

NOTES

1. Frank Norris, *McTeague* (Cambridge, Mass.: Robert Bentley, Inc., 1971), p. 238.

2. Viktor Frankl, *Man's Search for Meaning: An Introduction to Logotherapy* (New York: Pocket Books, 1971), p. 70.

Vincent van Gogh, "Hospital Corridor at Saint Rémy," 1889
(Courtesy of The Museum of Modern Art, Abby Aldrich Rockefeller Bequest)

13

COPING WITH DEATH

OVERVIEW

For many, the fact of death is something not to be thought about until it cannot be avoided. Such people believe that death is a "morbid" subject, and that only sick minds would dwell on it. To them the very word conjures up subliminal flashes of dark tombs, hollow corridors, skeletons, ghosts, solemn organ chords, gray caskets, cemeteries (always at night), the odor of flowers, tapered candles, a quiet guest book on a fragile stand, whispers in a side room.

In one sense humanity has invented the very death it traditionally shuns. Throughout the history of the arts, people have painted

*And all our yesterdays have
lighted fools
The way to dusty death.*

                        Shakespeare

this death, sung about it, spoken in trembling or resolute voice about that which no one knows for certain. Such images of death swirl around inside us, and small wonder that sometimes we want to close them off, push them into the subconscious—until the "proper" time, which is the hated time, the unfair time. Everything else about living— even the rough times—can be faced, dealt with. But why must we die? How do we deal with *that?*

The arts—especially what we sometimes call the popular arts—are perennial sources of negative death images. Ever since the middle of the eighteenth century, readers have gorged themselves on what used to be called "penny dreadfuls," set in haunted houses, dreary castles, remote inns—all with sliding panels, quick knife thrusts in the dark, bodies hanging on closet hooks, distant shrieks of terror. Nowadays the penny dreadfuls cost $20 or so and reward their authors with lucrative screen contracts. No celluloid image of gore can, apparently, be too horrible for us popcorn-eaters. Audiences are particularly fond of watching teenagers being slaughtered in all manner of clever ways during a summer camp vacation. Or watching other teenagers turn into vampires and werewolves all the better to wipe out an entire town. Is it perhaps that we enjoy torturing ourselves with a superabundance of the very thing we hate to think about? Is it that we fear death less if we camp the whole subject up? Maybe there's no real death if we try to keep it on the pages of fiction or in the movies. Or maybe we like to see others die in the popular arts because it takes our minds off what must in reality eventually happen to us.

All the same, the frightening images of death remain. No matter what our underlying purpose may be in reading or watching the dreadfuls, we haven't really faced the issue, have we? The phone ringing in the middle of the night is something we are never prepared to answer.

We have also looked to the popular arts for escape. There will always be the improbable happy ending: The diagnosis was wrong after all; or the real murderer confesses so that the sympathetic hero needn't go to the electric chair; or the runaway child is found safe. The mythology of denial has always been around. No one is arguing that it doesn't help some of the time. Sooner or later, however, the intelligent move is to face up to reality. If we are to be strong and skillful in being human, we must not tuck death away in the back of the closet. As in the rest of the animal kingdom, death has its rightful place in the cycle of human things.

In looking at the subject directly, we find that—far from being successful in never thinking about death—many of us die a thousand times before we have to. Surely a crucial aspect of the art of being human is to find a sane and sensible way to live with the stable awareness that we do not go on forever.

MEANINGS OF DEATH

Many of our writers, poets, and philosophers have told us that death is what gives life meaning, that death defines life, puts brackets around it, makes us see the possibilities in it. Using the same chain of reasoning, we are justified in observing that it is life which gives meaning to death—particularly when life is valued highly, viewed as a treasure or blessing. Frequently we speak of the *gift* of life, and when we do we never think at the same time of death as a gift. If life is a wondrous, often unearned, present bestowed upon us, then death automatically becomes the taking away of that present. We are like little children on New Year's Day, watching tearfully as the beautiful Christmas tree is suddenly tossed out.

Presumably we are not helped if someone—say, a scientist— were to point out that death has no meaning whatever except as a physical phenomenon to be described in objective laboratory terms which have no relation to personality, human greatness, or the devastation in the family circle. We are not helped if we realize that doctors and nurses in overcrowded hospitals—or just because they must detach themselves from involvement—may refer to "the carcinoma in Room 302" rather than Mr. Summerfield or Ms. Whitney.

We can be sure that death *has* meaning for the medical staff as well as the family. It has acquired meaning gradually but persistently as the human race has developed, has become what we like to call civilized. The price of civilization has been for many a specialized view of time: We never have enough. The price has also been for many (and there are notable exceptions) a specialized attitude toward being a person, a person as a singular, unprecedented phenomenon which will never happen in precisely the same way again.

*Five times five years I lived
a virgin's life;
Nine times five years I lived
a virtuous wife;
Wearied of this mortal life,
I rest.*

*Inscription on tombstone,
1888, Plainfield, Vermont*

Death as Personal Enemy

Starting with the most pervasive image of death, we see "him" as the dark-robed phantom that either pursues us or waits in silence around the next corner. He pounces upon us without warning. Or with infinite cunning he lifts his razor-sharp scythe, poised for the final blow.

The idea that death is a struggle against odds that will finally overwhelm us, however unfair the inevitable outcome, probably stems from a dominant myth of Western civilization (see Chapter 10) in which a nearly superhuman hero fights bravely against powerful foes. Sometimes the heroes win all battles and we hear no more about them—a version of the story that makes us all the more unprepared to accept the finality of death. Sometimes they win all battles but one. The greater the hero, the more irreplaceable the hero is shown to be and the more unacceptable is the hero's death.

A cherished myth changes the realm of death into a mysterious place to which brave heroes go when they have accomplished all they can, accomplished more than ordinary mortals. Since we cannot bear to think they have physically died and are no more, we can believe they have, like King Arthur, sailed to Avalon, or to the Grey Havens, like Frodo, hero of the popular trilogy *Lord of the Rings* (1955):

> And the ship went out into the High Sea and passed on into the West, until at last on a night of rain Frodo smelled a sweet fragrance on the air and heard the sound of singing that came over the water. . . . [A]nd he beheld white shores and beyond them a far green country under a swift sunrise.[1]

The Grey Havens is not, we must understand, a literary version of heaven, the Christian abode of the blessed after death. Neither Arthur nor Frodo is ever shown undergoing the physical act of dying. Never do they experience the cruel pain which Christ and Peter suffered on the cross or Joan of Arc at the stake. The pain-free death of Arthur and Frodo borrows the Greek vision of the Elysian Fields, a special land of immortality for warriors felled in battle who are whisked away before the stroke of death. Perhaps such myths are the source of our euphemistic verb "pass away," which seems to circumvent the physical reality.

These stories, as well as the image of death as the *Grim Reaper,* indicate that the actual *moment* is deeply feared in our civilization, intensifying the belief in death as personal enemy. Perhaps for this reason we tend to be thankful when we hear that someone has indeed "passed away" during sleep. If the Grim Reaper *must* come, the least he can do is not let us know about it.

While the pain of death is naturally a source of great fear, there is also a strong correlation between fearing death and placing a huge and usually unquestioned value on the sheer act of *being.* We seldom put the word "die" in a sentence involving us. The furthest we want to go in talking about a future in which we are not around is perhaps to start a sentence with "If, God forbid, anything should happen to me . . ." (Note how we still allow a tiny margin for luck.) Even when we are businesslike and make out a will or purchase a cemetery plot well in advance, we have a difficult time thinking realistically about not being—in particular, not being *ourselves.*

The terror of ceasing to be ourselves will never stop tormenting us so long as our culture indulges in the worship of singularity. Unless one is born into a large rural family in which everyone has to work as soon as possible for the survival of the group and no one has time to lavish attention on a particular family member, one is usually

In the midst of the current technological emphasis on the success story of healing, the patient whose disease cannot be cured, the human being who is dying is inexorably perceived to be a failure to the health professions.

Elisabeth Kübler-Ross

raised to be self-centered. One is encouraged to aspire to great heights and vicariously identify with those who succeed. In this context death is viewed as the great failure, hence a great injustice, for, unless one dies at 95, having "lived to a ripe old age," one should always, of course, be alive and striving.

Believing in the injustice of the personal enemy is secretly an inward act of adoration. Well, you say, so be it. Is it not the nature of humankind to be self-centered? The answer is: perhaps not.

When Self Is Not Central

It may come as a distinct surprise to some readers, but the slogan "Look out for Number One" is *not* as old as the hills. Nor is it universally accepted today. When the activity is more important than the actor, the myth of death as personal enemy is less influential as a molder of values. Think, if you will, of a research specialist who, having been told that she has a terminal illness, replies: "But the work will nonetheless proceed."

Socrates, the father of philosophy, must have had selfhood, but there is no evidence that he was preoccupied with self*ness*. In all the accounts of Socrates which Plato has given us, the mentor seems out of touch with himself in our sense of what "himself" means. Found guilty of alleged crimes against the state, Socrates was given a choice: death by poison, or a life in exile without the right to engage in free inquiry or philosophical discussion. Socrates chose death. Why? The answer, it seems, is that the activity of philosophy meant more to him than life. Without the activity there would be no point in living. The importance or preservation of personal identity does not appear to have been the issue:

> Someone will say: Yes, Socrates, but cannot you hold your tongue, and then you may go into a foreign city, and no one will interfere with you? Now I have great difficulty in making you understand my answer to this. For if I tell you . . . that I cannot hold my tongue, you will not believe that I am serious; and if I say again that daily to discourse about virtue, and of those other things about which you hear me examining myself and others, is the greatest good of man, and that the unexamined life is not worth living, you are still less likely to believe me.

Assuming that Plato's portrait of Socrates is accurate, that Socrates was generally concerned with the mental act of reaching an understanding of certain absolutes like justice, virtue, and beauty, we do not detect any indication that Socrates was ever defensive or artificial. He always seems to have been genuinely interested in seeking

In many a village in Mexico I have seen what happens when social security arrives. For a generation people continue in their traditional beliefs; they know how to deal with death, dying, and grief. The new nurse and the doctor . . . teach them about a Pantheon of evil clinical deaths, each one of which can be banned, at a price.

Ivan Illich

Those of us who think that death is an evil are in error.

Plato

wisdom and not at all interested in making people feel sorry for him or afraid of him. On his final day, when he drinks the poison, surrounded by the young intellectuals who adore him, Socrates shows a singular absence of self-consciousness. He sounds willing to let go of his hold on his own identity. He does not say, "Remember always what I have taught you" or "Promise to keep going what I have begun."

Thus when Phaedo, one of the followers, observes that the master has drunk the poison "cheerfully," we have no reason to believe that Socrates was struggling to put on a brave act in front of his friends. And then there occurs a most telling statement:

> And hitherto most of us had been able to control our sorrow; but now when we saw him drinking, and saw too that he had finished the draught, we could no longer forbear, and in spite of myself my own tears were flowing fast; so that I covered my face and wept, not for him, but at the thought of my own calamity in having to part from such a friend.

Phaedo's weeping for himself rather than for Socrates reminds us that the inability to cope with the death of another is more personal than we often realize. Is it perhaps a resentment that the personal enemy has struck rather too close to home? Is it an unwillingness to alter the daily course of one's own life to accommodate the disappearance of a component of that life?

Imagine two very dear friends who share pleasure in the same things. Perhaps they enjoy art, politics, sports, religion. They like to attend concerts, ball games, and the latest films. They enjoy trying new dishes at different restaurants. Neither suffers from an oversized ego or a neurotic inner sense of inferiority, so that neither one needs the other's self as complement or reinforcement to his or her own. Each enjoys the other as a phenomenon, an important source of delight in a world of other delights, on the order of, but to a greater or lesser degree than, magnificent music. It is possible to suppose that the death of one can be accepted by the other without its having a shattering effect, without its leaving a void in a life that can never be filled. There is a certain rhythm to the existence of the mourner. There will be some grief—a normal and probably universal emotional response to death. But the stride will not break. Life will make the necessary adjustment—and move on. The reason is that the one who is still alive is strong enough not to need a reinforcement of identity. As with Socrates, the activities rather than the concentration on self have been central in life, and will continue to be.

Insecure lovers sometimes test each other with questions like "If I should die, would you ever get over it?" or "If I should die, would you ever love anyone else?" The expectation is usually "No—I'd be miserable forever, if I didn't have you!" A reply like "Surely you would

---

To the question "If I should die, would you ever love anyone else?" the reply "Surely you would want me to find someone else" would not be understood, or there would not have been a question to begin with.

So, when our mortal frame
*   shall be disjoin'd,*
The lifeless lump uncoupled
*   from the mind,*
From sense of grief and
*   pain we shall be free;*
We shall not feel, because
*   we shall not be.*

Lucretius

want me to find someone else" would not be understood, or there would not have been a question to begin with.

Death the Leveler

We have said that death lends meaning to life, but sometimes it does so negatively. For some people the inevitable fact of death makes life mean precisely *nothing.* The fact of death causes a total reversal of the dominant life plan in our society: Grow up, become something; be successful at what you have become; surround yourself with the visible trappings of that success; think, as you age, of leaving behind a legacy for the future, some tangible embodiment of your having lived. Instead, one decides in advance that the struggle makes no sense when one will not be around long enough to enjoy the spoils.

During the Renaissance the fact of death came to be viewed in a manner far different from the medieval Christian outlook. In the Middle Ages the true believer had no choice but to think of death as a happy exit from this vale of tears. Life was pain; death was release. Death was a passage to a better, an eternal existence in paradise. This attitude can still be found in some parts of the Christian world: in Puerto Rico, for example, where the death of an innocent young child is a cause for joyous celebration.

The Renaissance, of course, assigned a higher value to both human life and the world in which it took place. People were less certain that there *was* a world beyond this one, or, if there were, that it was necessarily a better world. Renaissance poets sang the glories of love and other youthful sports that were here to be enjoyed, but as often as not ended by brooding over their inevitable passing. Yes, Renaissance art and architecture surrounded those who were alive with rich and sensuous color; Renaissance literature resounded with the clear tolling bells of passionate communication. But underneath the pomp and the glitter ran a deep vein of melancholy. We are born. Some of us move on to greatness. The power of a signature can change the destiny of thousands. Yet in the end all comes to nothing.

Shakespeare's works are obsessed with images of decomposition and a sometimes tragic, sometimes bitterly comic awareness of the final indignity that awaits us all. *Hamlet,* perhaps the greatest of all plays, is many things surely, one of them a vast and complex meditation on death, the common destiny that renders worldly grandeur and ambition laughable. Hamlet says:

> What a piece of work is a man! how noble in reason! how
> infinite in faculty! in form and moving how express and
> admirable! in action how like an angel! in apprehension
> how like a god! the beauty of the world! the paragon of
> animals! And yet, to me, what is this quintessence of
> dust?[2]

Without death there would scarcely have been poets on earth.

Thomas Mann

The famous graveyard scene could almost be removed from the intricate context of the tragedy and played on its own as perhaps the most disquieting literary work of the futility of life ever penned. At the opening of the scene Hamlet comes upon two clowns digging a grave for what Hamlet does not yet know is the remains of Ophelia, the girl he has loved but who has gone mad and drowned herself. There is much joking between the gravediggers over the fact that the drowned woman is to be given a Christian burial, though they are certain this would not be the case had she been a commoner. Their irreverent banter sets the tone for the rest of the scene. Christian burial or not, commoners and gentlepeople all wind up rotting in the earth.

Hamlet and his closest friend, Horatio, come upon the macabre proceedings. Fascinated by the place, Hamlet pokes about in the dirt and finds the skull of the late court jester, a man he remembers from his childhood as having been full of life and joy. Hamlet says:

> Alas, poor Yorick! I knew him, Horatio: a fellow of infinite jest, of most excellent fancy: he hath borne me on his back a thousand times; and now, how abhorred in my imagination it is! my gorge rises at it. Here hung those lips that I have kissed I know not how oft. Where be your gibes now? your gambols? your songs? your flashes of merriment that were wont to set the table on a roar? Not one now, to mock your own grinning? quite chap-fallen? Now get you to my lady's chamber, and tell her, let her paint an inch thick, to this favour she must come; make her laugh at that.[3]

So appalling is the fact of death, so powerful is this scene of decay that a mournful response is beside the point. All one can do—if one has any human feelings at all—is tragically to laugh. Then Hamlet decides that the greater the person, the more amusing death becomes: "To what base uses we may return, Horatio! Why may not imagination trace the noble dust of Alexander, till he find it stopping a bung-hole?"[4]

Earlier in the play, Hamlet, continually obsessed with the idea of life's futility, has contemplated suicide—an option which is for many both sane and rational and which we shall be discussing in a later section. But though "to be or not to be" is for Hamlet the only valid question, there is no simpler answer. Death may be the common end, but who is to say what it is? If it were merely an endless sleep, an absence of consciousness, all well and good. But suppose it is something even worse than life? What then? Death is an "undiscover'd country from whose bourn/ No traveller returns." No one can tell us what may wait beyond the grave. The only course to follow is to play out the game of life until it is finally over.

If we do not know for certain what death is like, our artists generally have expressed, like Hamlet, the strong suspicion that it is nothing if not democratic. Thus does the poet Shelley in "Ozymandias" remind us of what worldly ambition amounts to:

> *I met a traveler from an antique land*
> *Who said: Two vast and trunkless legs of stone*
> *Stand in the desert. Near them, on the sand,*
> *Half sunk, a shattered visage lies, whose frown,*
> *And wrinkled lip, and sneer of cold command,*
> *Tell that its sculptor well those passions read*
> *Which yet survive, stamped on these lifeless things,*
> *The hand that mocked them and the heart that fed;*
> *And on the pedestal these words appear:*
> *"My name is Ozymandias, king of kings:*
> *Look on my works, ye Mighty, and despair!"*
> *Nothing beside remains. Round the decay*
> *Of that colossal wreck, boundless and bare*
> *The lone and level sands stretch far away.*

Looking upon death as a leveler, an equalizer, is not necessarily an unhealthy practice if it manages to buoy up one's sense of self-worth and impart the belief that one's goals are as valid as anybody else's. Like many of his early-nineteenth-century contemporaries, Shelley was a champion of the poor and the oppressed, an opponent of unearned privilege, one who believed in causes, especially those which contributed to the betterment of human life. This attitude says that everybody has to die and most of us may well be forgotten, but what matters is not to waste the energies and intellectual gifts one may possess. Life alone is real, and it is precious, though we must never lose sight of the destiny which unites us in brother- and sisterhood and makes despotic power unendurable.

This democratic view of death can therefore lead to either of two overall philosophies of living. One is Hamlet's: cynical, often wryly humorous, but so filled with shadows that endeavor seems hardly worth contemplating, much less pursuing. The other is life-affirming.

A more recent example of Hamlet's view can be found in the writing of Ambrose Bierce (1842–1914), an American journalist whose obsession not only with death but with the belief that everything in life turns out as horribly as possible gave him the nickname "bitter Bierce." Collections of his cynical stories can be found under such engaging titles as *Cobwebs from an Empty Skull.* Though his most famous collection is *In the Midst of Life,* be not tempted to believe the author is arguing for life-affirmation; in fact, the title sentence concludes with the words "we are surrounded by death." One of Bierce's most well-known pieces is "Occurrence at Owl Creek Bridge," in which a Confederate prisoner of war waiting for the hangman to spring the trap imagines that he escapes and makes his way back to the arms of his beloved. So real is the fantasy that we find ourselves believing it, and the ending, in which the trap is actually sprung, seems doubly horrifying.

The other philosophy of living can be called life-affirming. Having said that a common destiny awaits us, having made the decision—conscious or otherwise—to continue living, then we have no reason for wry cynicism and a despairing unwillingness to become involved in meaningful projects. A contemporary of Bierce's was the poet Edwin Arlington Robinson (1869–1935), whose masterpiece "The Man against the Sky" involves an analysis of possible approaches to living. Observing the silhouette of an unknown man walking along the crest of a hill, the poet finds himself wondering who the stranger might be and where he might be going. Of only one thing is he certain: Each of us is walking alone to a mysterious destination; and each of us, alone, must determine whether the journey or the destination is meaningful.

Robinson's personal choice is an affirmation not only of life but of faith. If the end of life is veiled in mist, who is to say that what lies inside that mist is oblivion? Furthermore, if life is meaningless, why do we instinctively struggle each day, often against impossible odds, to achieve something?

> *Why pay we such a price, and one we give*
> *So clamoringly, for each racked empty day*
> *That leads one more last human hope away,*
> *As quiet friends would lead past our crazed eyes*
> *Our children to an unseen sacrifice?*
> *If all that we have lived and thought,*
> *All comes to Nought,—*
> *If there be nothing after Now,*
> *And we be nothing anyhow,*
> *And we know that,—why live?*[5]

Setting aside for the moment Robinson's professed belief that an afterlife is at least a possibility, we find an extraordinary timeliness about these lines. Their sentiments are finding new expression from younger artists, who have never known a world in which the prospect of not only personal extinction but the death of human civilization has not been intrinsic to daily consciousness. True, we have had our share of the obvious responses: apocalyptic visions of nuclear devastation like Neville Shute's 1957 novel *On the Beach* about Australians, the last survivors, stoically awaiting the arrival of the mushroom cloud; Stanley Kubrick's 1963 film *Dr. Strangelove,* which culminates with a tragically comic, psychotically overjoyed "commie"-hater gleefully playing kamikaze as he rides the Big Bomb straight toward Moscow; and recent television "specials" like *Testament* and *The Morning*

After, which attempt to make us fully appreciate what the nuclear Armageddon would be like.

Nonetheless, whether or not one believes in Robinson's "after Now," consciousness of the possible death of humanity on Earth creates in many the need to engage in serious life-affirming activities that transcend a self-centered fear of extinction: activities like joining the Peace Corps; taking part in peaceful demonstrations that make a statement about nuclear power plants and the need to stop the nuclear arms race; walking for miles to collect money for world famine relief. The history of the humanities may well look back at our time and listen once more—and with admiration—to the songs of peace and world unity which abound despite the opportunity that is plainly there for thinking to oneself: "Well, it's all going to be over soon enough, so why should I not indulge my every whim?"

The image at the end of the film version of *On the Beach* comes to mind. Earlier in the film we have seen a fanatic religious cult that, anticipating the imminent end of the world, marches about trying to convert those for whom time is running out. They carry a sign which reads THERE IS STILL TIME, BROTHER. The very last shot is of this same sign, blowing along a street in a deserted town from which all human life has vanished. This was the statement the film was making.

Since *On the Beach* was produced nearly 30 years ago, nuclear weapons have reached a level of "sophistication" (what a strange Fifth Avenue kind of word the military generals use!) which could not have been anticipated by the artistic minds of the '50s. Yet the message on that sign still applies. One wonders how the art of being human can be practiced without heeding it.

Fatalism

A popular poster takes some lines from Rudyard Kipling and gives them a darkly humorous twist:

> *If you can keep your head*
> *While all about you are losing theirs*
> *YOU SIMPLY DO NOT UNDERSTAND THE SITUATION*

One way of coping with the possible collapse of everything, including the entire human enterprise, is to joke about it. The poster implies, however, that somebody is planning to do something. Another—and very widespread—response is fatalism, the belief that all events, including the death of civilization, are predetermined, or at least that things sort of just *happen* whether we want them to or not and there isn't much that anyone can do. Fatalism has been around for thousands of years, and it probably stems from very ancient fears of dreadful events like death that nobody understood and therefore couldn't control.

Much fatalism is directly tied in with a religion. If events are not within human power to control, they must therefore be caused (or at least governed) by the gods or by God. Fatalism has taken the guesswork out of death and, where there is also a belief in an afterlife, out of salvation.

John Calvin (1509–1564), an extreme Protestant reformer upon whose views was founded the Puritan religion of the first American settlers, believed emphatically in predestination. Nothing else, for him, was compatible with God's omnipotence. A perfect being could not leave matters to chance and allow those He created to carve out their own destinies. The doctrine of predestination also extended to the afterlife. There was a heaven and there was a hell—everyone knew that. But only God knew the names of those destined for salvation and those destined for damnation. Calvin rejected the Catholic position— that humankind has free will to choose between right and wrong and thus has some control over reward or punishment in the next life. Historians of Puritanism sometimes wonder why any Puritan ever went to church at all, since according to their beliefs nothing anyone did in this life could alter one's eventual destiny.

The Bible affords us many images of an all-controlling God who does as He will with human destiny. Perhaps the classic statement of God's omnipotence and humanity's limitations is given to us in that extraordinary work, the Book of Job, which begins with an encounter between God and Satan. With some justifiable pride, God points to Job as a very model of the pious, humble, good man. With his characteristic cynicism, Satan reminds God that Job is good because God has showered him with a loving wife, with children, and with vast property holdings. Take it all away, Satan challenges, and see how pious Job will be. Accordingly, God allows Satan to inflict any sort of suffering on Job, short of allowing him to die.

Suddenly the good man is visited by a series of disasters: His children are killed. He loses his livestock. His land becomes barren. Terrible boils break out on his body. Various friends come to see him, to offer him comfort, but all they can tell him is that he must in some way have offended God. His wife urges him to complain bitterly to God about the apparent injustice. But though he curses the conditions of his life, he maintains his famous patience for a very long while. Just as Job can stand his existence no longer, just as his patience is about to crack, God's voice comes thundering out of the whirlwind. Job is told in no uncertain terms that it is not his, nor any person's, right to question the workings of God. Since human beings did not create the Earth, since they have no ultimate power, they must accept divine wisdom, no matter what happens to them. Though in one version of the story Job's possessions and his happiness are restored, that happy ending in

All is, if I have grace to
use it so,
As ever in my great
Task-Master's eye.

John Milton

Then shall the dust return to
the earth as it was:
And the spirit shall return
unto God who gave it.

Ecclesiastes

no way alters the fatalism of the work. God gives and God takes away, and humanity must accept either action without complaint.

There also exists a popular brand of fatalism with nebulous roots in religion. Many who believe they are religious and profess a faith in the doctrine of free will, not predestination, are also prone to fatalistic attitudes, which come and go, as convenient. A person can, for example, be a fatalist and still refuse to take unnecessary risks, such as joining a parachute-jumping club or riding a roller coaster standing up or entering the Indianapolis 500. An individual might refuse to undergo a delicate operation with a 50/50 survival rate on the grounds that the odds are not favorable enough. But the same people who refuse risks for themselves can say of the death of another, "His time came," or use that unpleasant metaphor, "Her number was up."

Fatalistic beliefs continue to be put on and taken off like topcoats. Death is explained to children in fatalistic terms by people who may otherwise find fatalism confining: "God so loved your mother that He wanted her to be with Him always, and so He took her up to heaven." How many adult anxieties have been caused by such a statement, which may seem comforting at the time, but which can lead to highly ambivalent feelings toward a God who could be so cruel?

The child who understands the abstraction of time is ready to cope with the idea of death.

Of course, we may well ask, "How *can* children be made to understand?" The answer is that they cannot, if they are very young. If, however, they are old enough to comprehend the abstraction of *time,* then some *simple* efforts can be made to explain the natural progression of age which everyone must experience. Throwing in fatalism as a means of getting the explainer off the hook is definitely *not* an answer.

Fatalism in its purest sense—as in the doctrine of predestination—represents a full commitment. It is not always bleak, not always an affirmation of Murphy's law that, if anything can possibly go wrong, it certainly will, and at the worst possible moment. But one cannot embrace fatalism and retain the belief in freedom of the will, as well as the right to blame others for what happens. Possibly the most hypocritical of all quasi-fatalistic positions is that which absolves the self of any responsibility for an action but is quick to attribute guilt to others for "wrongs" *they* commit.

Death as a New Beginning

Like the poet Robinson, many reconcile themselves to death in varying degrees because of the belief that this present life is merely a preparation for one that will be perfect and eternal in some form or dimension that cannot be comprehended by the mortal mind. The major religions of Western civilization appear to the majority as authoritative sources for this belief.

In point of fact, however, Christian Testament does not talk about an afterlife in specific, substantive terms. Christ on the cross is reported to have told one of the thieves being crucified alongside him that he would that day be in paradise, and Christians, of course, believe that Christ, after rising from the grave, did indeed ascend bodily into what many now call heaven. But it is not clear that this other world, this paradise, is an actual place with a geography of its own.

The Hebrew Testament is very much reality-oriented. The Book of Job demands faith in God no matter what an individual may suffer, and no material reward is supposed to be an issue. No eternity of bliss is ever promised Job. What is promised in the earliest books is that the Hebrews, the Chosen People, will eventually possess Canaan, the land of milk and honey; but this was and still is a very real place, a highly desirable fertile tract of land at the eastern edge of the Mediterranean Sea where water is available and crops can be raised, a land that people continue to cherish, long for, die for.

Still, for countless others the prospect of an afterlife is what makes both life and death bearable. The simplistic interpretation is that one will survive death and continue living in a different form *but with the same identity.* Romantic literature, such as Emily Brontë's wildly mystical novel *Wuthering Heights* (1848), helped popularize the dream. In the novel the dead Catherine stays very close to her mortal lover Heathcliff until he perishes in a storm and presumably joins her for an eternity of something like human love. Movies of the 1930s and 1940s frequently showed lovers reunited in the next world, looking exactly as they did in this world, except that their bodies were transparent. Films like *Portrait of Jennie* and, more recently, *Somewhere in Time* have kept alive the myth that those who fail to find their true loves in this life will have a second chance, that somehow death steps aside to accommodate love. One notes a little fatalism showing up here which reinforces, if not a serious philosophy of transmigration (such as Plato's), then at least the continuing faith that people have in eventually meeting Mr. or Miss Right.

Millions have insisted on the view that death only means their personal continuation. In some evangelical, but hardly major, religions, realistic afterlives are guaranteed. One bumper sticker, for example, employs the language of real estate: HEAVEN IS A REAL PLACE—HAVE YOU RESERVED YOUR SPOT? During a tent revival meeting, the preacher told the congregation that heaven is exactly like Earth, only better. But, he continued, one still needs a house, and that will take money. Fortunately, he said, God is the president of the Bank of Heaven, and the money you place in the basket today will be deposited in your account with lots of interest so that you can buy your dream house when the time arrives.

The judgmental aspect of the afterlife is often stressed in major religions, even if the geography is left obscure. The good are to be rewarded in an eternity of bliss, however ill-defined, while the bad are to be punished. The concept of hell is invoked time and again, though one suspects that religious thinkers of the past have been more psychological than literal in references to hell. Stamped in the human imagination as Dante's "Inferno," a seven-tiered subterranean land of endless torment, hell continues to mean raging fires, except that one wonders how one can experience physical pain there without a body.

Thornton Wilder's play *Our Town* (1940) offers in the final scene a view of the next life which probably does not please those who for private reasons need the belief, but which makes good sense, assuming there is such a life to begin with. The dead of Grover's Corners are seated on one side of the stage, without expression, in straight-backed chairs. At the opposite side the funeral of Emily, the heroine, is in progress. When Emily, as a soul, joins the other dead, the girl is told that very soon she will begin to think less and less of her life on earth and after awhile will become totally indifferent to it. If one cannot bear such a thought, then there is a strong possibility that one needs to reassess one's motives in believing.

Self-Inflicted Death

A very different meaning is given to death by a vast number of people—probably far more than make themselves known—who believe that coping with *life,* not death, is the challenge. For them death and personal extinction—suicide—offer a more attractive goal than trying to come to terms with what is happening to them.

We really have no way of knowing exactly how many Egyptians, Mesopotamians, Greeks, Romans, Hebrews, and Christians of the past either contemplated or actually committed suicide. Studies *have* been made from historical records and religious writings, especially the literature of earlier societies. For example, Linnea Parsons, a Unitarian minister, in a provocative work called *Separate Paths,* finds that the Greeks and Romans generally condoned suicide for four reasons: "to show bereavement, to preserve honor, to avoid pain and shame, and for the benefit of the state."[6] Aristotle called suicide a "crime against the state," while Socrates, the spokesman for Plato's philosophy in the dialogs, warned that human beings were the "property" of the gods and therefore not at liberty to dispose of their bodies as they willed.

From the beginning, Jewish law forbade suicide. But we find that early Christians, oppressed by hostile forces and made to suffer appallingly, frequently took their own lives. Christianity has since expressly forbidden the act, but Parsons raises the interesting question of whether martyrdom, accepted in certain instances by the Christian Church, should not be considered suicide, even whether Christ's death on the cross does not belong in this category.

Parsons' raising even the possibility that martyrdom and suicide might be equated has probably scandalized a good many readers,

Death is not the worst evil, but rather, when we wish to die and cannot.

Sophocles

*Parsons has made an in-
depth study of the circumstances which led to the suicides of Marilyn Monroe
and Ernest Hemingway and
is convinced that these acts
were the conscious choices
of people who should be respected for what they did,
not pitied as once-successful
individuals whose lives
ended in bitter tragedy.*

but her contention that suicide is a rational act more often than the result of mental illness deserves our consideration. The common attitude may have developed from a widespread unwillingness—or inability—to view death as anything but an unthinkable, outrageous intrusion upon life; and difficult as it may seem, we ought to be able to open our minds to an alternate attitude: namely, that looking upon death with horror may itself be somewhat less than rational. If such is the case, at least some of the time, then may a rational person make a rational decision that he no longer wishes to be in this world?

In Christian tradition there have been four requirements for a death to be considered martyrdom:

1. Rationality behind the act.
2. Certainty that the act has been willed by God.
3. The intent of sacrifice behind the act.
4. Commitment to a cause larger than self.[7]

Much Christian belief also requires an acceptance of free will, otherwise there is no such thing as sin. If martyrs, then, are free to choose their own deaths, should their deaths *not* count as suicides? The opposite view—that only God, but not the martyrs themselves, willed the deaths—diminishes the honor accorded them by succeeding generations.

Within such parameters a case could also be made for regarding as suicides the deaths of Becket, Joan of Arc, even Bernadette of Lourdes. In the case of Bernadette, failure to report that she was suffering from a terminal disease made medical intervention hopeless. And what of the thousands of soldiers who "gave" (as we prefer to say, rather than "took") their lives to save others?

The whole issue is very complex. Surely we are not justified in accepting martyrdom as a "special" kind of suicide but denouncing other kinds as manifestations of mental illness. Parsons has made an in-depth study of the circumstances which led to the suicides of Marilyn Monroe and Ernest Hemingway and is convinced that these acts were the conscious choices of people who should be respected for what they did, not pitied as once-successful individuals whose lives ended in bitter tragedy. True, self-inflicted death is usually the result of an unhappy state of mind, but who would dare equate unhappiness with mental illness?

In Europe there are suicide clinics, whose purpose is not to recommend suicide but to offer sympathetic counsel to those who see no other way out. In England there is a society which distributes pamphlets to its members, discussing the latest and most effective means of putting an end to one's life.

Of late, we have had numerous cases, often given wide media coverage, involving people with incurable illnesses who took their lives with their families' permission. Parsons chronicles the suicide pact of an elderly couple who, with the permission of friends, took an overdose of pills rather than face debilitating years in a nursing home.

Though Buddhism as a religion does not condone suicide, many Buddhist monks and nuns turned themselves into flaming torches to protest the war in Vietnam. Can we say that every one of them was mentally disturbed? Or that the act was somehow "wrong" and "immoral"? In what sense? Can we even say it was foolish? How many otherwise-indifferent minds may have been made painfully aware of a war that others in their own way were also protesting?

Since a study of the humanities invites growth first and foremost, to have a closed mind on the subject may be to resist growth. The world today is a very different place from that of our suicide-abhorring grandparents. A major French philosopher, the existentialist Albert Camus, opened one of his most famous writings with this statement: "There is but one truly serious philosophical problem, and that is suicide."[8] Camus did not recommend self-inflicted death, but he *was* saying that the dilemma of whether to remain in existence or not is a rational one.

> *There is but one truly serious philosophical problem, and that is suicide.*
>
> *Albert Camus*

SYMBOLIC FORMS OF DEATH

Death is an integral part of life in the sense that no one can evade it. There is even the possibility that self-inflicted death can be an integral part of life for certain people under certain circumstances, that is, those who came to suicide by rational choice after leading productive, meaningful lives up *until* the choice was made. Perhaps far more tragic are those people who forget they have but one death to die. They cannot go on with the business of living because the shadow of death is continually blocking their paths. Consciously and unconsciously such people are filled with death attitudes, or symbolic forms of death.

Many of us die symbolically many times, even in the course of a single year. Feeling a sense of unworth, we kill ourselves in a number of ways: We hang back from taking growth-producing risks. We worry continually about what others are saying, though most of the time chances are they have more to do than gossip about us. We convince ourselves we shall fail before we ever make an attempt. Because of unresolved guilt in the past, we yield to failure because we secretly believe we deserve it. Growing older, we allow ourselves only certain acceptable forms of behavior, out of fear of not "acting our age."

Death attitudes can even influence our physiology. We can will ourselves into extinction. A recent case, which became celebrated among the medical faculty of a prominent university, involved a woman admitted to a hospital for treatment of what was thought to be

Death Attitudes

"I'm too old to do that."

"What will they think of me?"

"Nothing ever turns out right."

a harmless leg infection. She remained there for six months, growing progressively weaker, losing 85 pounds though no signs of malignancy could be detected anywhere in her body. A psychiatric examination, administered while the woman was still relatively well, revealed a profound depression, induced by feelings of unworth, that became so massive her entire system absorbed the message and began to destroy itself.

The outcome of this case must not be confused with the possibility of rational suicide. This woman's choices were not under rational control. True, we can say that she eventually "found peace," but perhaps had her eyes been opened in time, she might have found other roads to peace and, along the way, have richly contributed to the lives of others.

Unworth and Symbolic Suicide

On the symbolic level, suicide is far and away the leading cause of "death." Negative self-concept saps the energy not only of the victim, but of others as well. Like the woman in the case cited above, *symbolic suicides* do not find peace in living.

Self-inflicted martyrdom is a form of symbolic suicide. There are people who will immediately volunteer for any task which appears distasteful or time-consuming or requiring of personal sacrifice. While others try to evade being asked, the martyr seizes almost gleefully upon the chance to overdo once more and draw from others the inevitable "Oh, you poor thing." Unfortunately, the circle is a vicious one. Martyrs, seeking acceptance in this destructive way, are doomed, for their feelings of unworth run too deep. Not able to believe what others say of them, self-appointed martyrs wait desperately for the next opportunity to hold up the world, Atlas-like, on their own stooped shoulders.

In the opinion of many psychologists, compulsive gambling is another version of symbolic suicide. Those who continually wager large amounts on almost any chance happening—from the Kentucky Derby to the exact number of votes a candidate may earn—are said not to be people who desperately need money or who enjoy pitting their own intellect or intuition against reality, but who secretly hope they will lose the bet. Their sense of unworth drives them to play for high stakes, knowing deep down that statistics run high against them, ensuring they will lose.

Winning, for compulsive gamblers, is a source of momentary joy, because they experience a sudden flash of worth. They have successfully outwitted a system that is supposed to be unbeatable. But what do they do? Take their profit and leave? The answer is almost always that they bet again, usually risking even more money. Like the martyr, compulsive gamblers do not believe the signs that they are

Many of us die symbolically many times even in the course of a single year. Feeling a sense of unworth, we kill ourselves in a number of ways. We hang back from taking growth-producing risks. We worry continually about what others are saying.

I'm not afraid of dying. I just don't want to be there when it happens.

Woody Allen

worthy of their success. The only recourse is to try once again—to lose. Should they be successful in losing, they may experience a sense of depression, but this generally takes the form of self-castigation: "Why did I bet so much? Why didn't I quit while I was ahead?" The symbolic beating administered by the self to the self is just treatment for a being which, in its own opinion, can never amount to anything, consequently deserves nothing but hatred.

Other forms of symbolic suicide include the obvious taking of unnecessary risks, such as driving at breakneck speed, stunt flying, and the like. People who engage in such delightful pastimes are sometimes called "thrill-seekers," but often such "thrills" mean the enjoyment of being punished as the terrible creatures they know themselves to be. The world may be fooled, but the self-punishers are not.

Gambling is usually a self-destructive activity. The compulsive gambler is secretly hoping to lose.

Yet another vicious circle is created by professional gloom-gatherers, people followed by a private black cloud which rains only on them. So depressing is the company of such individuals that few people request it. Gloom-gatherers receive few invitations. Sensitive to a slight, but recognizing deep inside how justified the slight really is, they may seize the chance for self-punishment even more by confronting the source of rejection in hopes of being rejected once more: "I didn't mean to call at this time of night, especially when I know you're having a party, but I had to ask you about . . ." The flustered party host at the other end of the line can stammer out a few apologies about "mislaid" invitations or coolly ignore the hints. Either response is enough to constitute the right upper hook the gloom-gatherer is asking for.

Unworth and Symbolic Murder

There are two ways of dealing with one's feelings of unworth: destruction of self or of others. At almost any moment self-haters may turn their venom away from the self, projecting it upon an unsuspecting world. If unable to punish themselves because the threat of mirror-facing is too great, they may easily find unworth outside the self. Other people may become symbolic versions of the self, but "their" unworth is easier to face.

Symbolic Murders

"Go home. I don't mind staying late and missing dinner again."

"Hello. This is your mother. Remember me?"

"Darling, I loved your performance. I argued with everyone."

Gossip about others is probably the most universal form of symbolic murder. The number of people who engage in it gives some indication of how widespread feelings of unworth really are. And the most prevalent form of gossip is, of course, the spreading of information, however accurate, about somebody else's scandal or misfortune—anything, really, that seems to guarantee a disaster for somebody else. Since everyone has some feelings of unworth, everyone is capable of some gossip, but the degree to which one is passionately devoted to the sport offers some indication as to the seriousness of one's self-hatred.

Gossip is a form of *active* symbolic murder. (The passive kind is waiting in secret excitement for others to experience setbacks.) In its more extreme manifestations the active variety occupies itself with the stealthy manipulation of people and events in order to bring about an envied person's hoped-for misfortune. Letters signed "From a friend" are sent to appropriately inappropriate parties. In a work setting, twisted remarks are made to a boss or supervisor about someone in line for the promotion one had been expecting.

While reasonably well-adjusted people may stop short of wreaking actual destruction upon others, almost no one is exempt from wishing and hoping that bad things will happen to those whose fortunes are perceived as being better. Often the helping hand is extended, but only those with a strong sense of self-worth are in a true position to fulfill the needs of others altruistically, that is, with no ulterior motive. We might be surprised at how many times we *think* we are coming to the aid of a friend in distress only to aggravate the situation by constantly reviewing the disasters that have occurred, giving lip service to a sympathy which deep down affords us a perverse kind of pleasure.

In cases of symbolic murder, the victims in the long run may suffer less than the murderers. The victims may be so caught up in their troubles that they fail to note the secret intentions of the comforter. The victims may even emerge all the stronger for having endured hardship. But the murderers, acting out of hidden feelings of unworth, are not and may never be in control of their life.

We need to catch ourselves in the act of slipping in the symbolic dagger and laugh inwardly at our own absurdity. If we cannot do this, if we take ourselves far too seriously, if we always see the problem as the other person's—*that* person's failures and misfortunes and stupidity, never *our* envy and insecurity—then we can become symbolically dead without ever knowing it.

Burnout

Burnout has no doubt always existed among people in important, powerful roles, but its diagnosis is relatively recent. It is a slow atrophy or indifference that sets in after one has reached what one had earlier believed to be "the heights," only to discover that even the most creative position can become dull and unchallenging after a time. It is also a symbolic kind of chronic illness that, like its physical counterparts, can be incurable.

Burnout occurs more frequently among professional males, though the reason probably has less to do with gender than with the fact that women have assumed dominant power positions only recently. The professional woman, often feeling herself on trial, cannot afford to allow the job to become routine, cannot afford to find its potential too limiting. A man who has had the easier time of reaching the top is more likely to be bored when he gets there.

We include burnout in this chapter because we believe it to be a form of symbolic death. Does this mean burnout is ultimately linked to feelings of unworth? The answer is a definite maybe. The problem is a complex one and has yet to be fully studied over a long period of time. But the symptoms of burnout seem to point to such a conclusion.

Burnout appears to take place when a challenge is perceived—consciously or otherwise—to be less than one's output of energy. One reaches a point at which the need to do *more* than is required is no longer intense, when one feels, correctly or not, that things are well in hand and one can begin to sit back and begin to enjoy the fruits of one's efforts. It is possible to become overly organized at this point, to recognize that one has created a well-oiled machine that virtually runs on its own.

There may be a transitionary period we can call *the phase of dangerous pride,* a symbolic counterpart of that time in the development of a serious disease when we ignore little warning signs: the headaches—not severe, probably just eye-strain; the slight weight loss—why be upset about achieving what others work at so intensely?; the fatigue—I'm at the office very late and naturally I'm tired a lot. During this symbolic phase we begin to close our minds to new possibilities on the grounds that we have worked out a system that is too efficient to disturb. Why read up on the latest theories? Why call in people who might know more than we do about our own business? Above all, why request feedback from the staff about the way we operate? Why elicit suggestions from people who couldn't possibly be as skilled as we are?

The most dangerous aspect of the phase of dangerous pride is the reputation one may have gained from the previous phase, when one's responses were always in excess of the minimum requirements. One's reputation having become secured, one has every right—or so one believes—to start "taking it easy." There are long lunches to be savored, business trips of increasing frequency and length, phone conversations that may not be necessary but take the place of getting down to serious work on needed changes.

Candidates for burnout have not, you understand, reached their position because they lack creativity and vision. Therefore, because these still exist inside them, they begin to know secretly that something is wrong, even as the person with the beginnings of a serious illness knows that all is not well, though, of course, there is no need for a doctor just yet. They have not changed their method of operation in 15 years because—well, why fix something that isn't broken? Still, their creative conscience begins to trouble them. They may feel a twinge of guilt, which may take the form of paranoia. People are talking about them. There is a new member on the board who . . .

Burnout happens in every profession that rewards creative persons with status, a high salary, the security (however false) imparted by a reputation *which is no longer current.* A sure symptom is that people close themselves in, separating themselves from others, especially to avoid real conversation, as opposed to talk about restaurants, hotels, and airline schedules. Burnout happens, we might say, when the position has devoured the human being.

Fortunately, burnout does not happen to everyone. Here are some prevalent signs of continuing creative health:

1. Continuing to take chances; trying new things even though the old system appears to be working well.
2. Developing a structure and a set of rules as *guidelines* only.
3. Not becoming smothered by wall charts, printed schedules, memos, and meetings.
4. Not being locked into a hyperawareness of hierarchy to the point at which one does not allow oneself to associate with "inferiors."
5. Exhibiting a willingness to hear criticism from peers and even those not considered peers.
6. Not seeking escape from one's fears through alcohol or chemical substances.
7. Maintaining a sense of humor, even a degree of playfulness.

The ability to play is something many of us begin to lose with age, as if it were proper only for the young to enjoy nonsense. But playfulness acts as a time-release capsule, immunizing us against the slow rigor mortis that comes with the bureaucratic syndrome. Not by sheer accident do we speak of the humorless boss as being *dead* serious.

Fear of Aging

In view of the utmost relevance of death, the avoidance and denial of the problems related to this area are truly astounding. Aging, fatal disease, and dying are not seen as a part of the life process but as the ultimate defeat and a painful reminder of the limits of our ability to master nature.

Stanislav Grof

Our society is in the throes of the greatest antiaging campaign in human history. Fitness is not only a fad but a multibillion-dollar industry. Almost any new diet makes the best-seller list. Cosmeticians and plastic surgeons rake in unbelievable fees. Television commercials exhibit product after product guaranteeing that the user will retain the appearance of youth as modeled by beautiful, vibrant, sexually attractive men and women. Older people are shown, if at all, playing golf on the grounds of their Florida condominium or, looking trim and fit, doing high kicks at the clubhouse in rehearsal for a musical event. No one ever advertises the "quieter" pleasures of age. No one ever says that the lovely retirement village contains an extraordinary library. We are conditioned to believe that to resist age, not to accept the biological and sociological changes which age inevitably brings, is life-affirming, the sign of a healthy society.

To enjoy looking dapper for one's age, to exercise and maintain a sensible diet, to avoid excessive use of life-shortening pastimes like drinking and smoking . . . these *can* be called life-affirming and can be the signs of a creative approach to one's existence. Having attained the age of, say, 75, one is not automatically required to consider oneself *old* or to obey the rule our society has adopted for its "senior citizens": look young and act young for as long as possible and then have the decency not to bother us anymore.

If we had a truly realistic appreciation of age, we would make a clear separation in our minds between staying healthy and vigorous because one knows how to live and *looking* young and vigorous because society dislikes being reminded of the physical (*and* sexual) deterioration that are part of nature's cycle. Because of our deep-rooted fear of death we are too often hedonistic—pleasure-seeking—driven by the philosophy that time is running out on us, engaging in activities that are distinctly life-denying, then only later becoming fad-conscious in a desperate effort to hold time at bay.

Fear of aging is also related to our success orientation. One looks in the mirror, notes the deepening wrinkles, the shadows, and the crow's-feet, and thinks: "Already here, and what have you got to show for it?" People who in their opinion have not "won," have not been promoted to that longed-for post, have not possessed the symbols of power and success, see the signs of age as visible confirmation of their deteriorating self-image.

Whatever the reason we fear the aging process, there is no question that for thousands the fear is a slow death long before their time. Physiological changes, including the gradual waning of sexual desire, are hard to accept when one has never learned to understand the different rhythms of life. Though difficult to accept, the changes do come, and faster for some than for others. Premature baldness, loss of teeth, or excessive weight gain can make middle age hard to disguise. For some the changes are so overwhelming they throw up their hands in despair, convinced they have already been rejected, so why bother? The result can be a surge of life-denying behavior considered appropriate only for old folks, and a total withdrawal from participating in activities society considers inappropriate.

One good reason for the media success of youth-oriented products is that the ad campaigns are built on the solid foundation of the traditional rules of age. The subtext is: You're not supposed to be able to get out on the dance floor at your age, but if you take our vitamin supplement, you'll astonish the children. Presumably over 40 we do not contort our bodies in a spirit of fun. Surfing and water-skiing are beach activities permissible for the young. The old are supposed to wade.

Fear of aging is related to our success orientation. One looks in the mirror, notes the deepening wrinkles, the shadows, and the crow's-feet, and thinks: "Already here, and what have you got to show for it?"

The ability to play is something many of us begin to lose with age, as if it were proper only for the young to enjoy nonsense. But playfulness acts as a time-release capsule, immunizing us against the slow rigor mortis that comes with the bureaucratic syndrome. Not by sheer accident do we speak of the humorless boss as being dead serious.

If cultural age barriers did not exist, the need to maintain a youthful appearance might not be so great. As activities and locations one by one become "inappropriate," as "membership cards" in certain age groups expire, together with all of the rights and privileges, it becomes for some people a little like watching the lights go out in the stadium after the game is over.

No matter how glamorous the ads for retirement villages and so-called adult congregate-living facilities, we like to isolate older people as much as possible. We tell them they are better off with people of their own age who have common interests, such as, perhaps, comparing symptoms. We are continually reading about the "problem of the elderly," and the problem, simply stated, is that in the minds of the young, old people hang around too long. They are a drain on the national economy. They have to be cared for at some point. Sadder still is the fact that many are expressing to their children the hope that they will never be a "burden" to them. The notion that one is a burden when one needs assistance in walking is a death attitude. Death is obligatory. Death attitudes can be refused if we let ourselves say no.

MODELS OF LIFE AFFIRMATION

If negative attitudes and negative internal imagery act to dampen people's lives and cause them to "die" many times over before the actual and unique moment of true physical death, then it should follow—and it does—that positive attitudes and positive images are possible. No one is talking here of shallow optimism, of spur-of-the-moment good feelings. The issue here is the profound realization that the potential for a productive, exciting life belongs to each of us. *We* control our attitudes—that is, we can if we allow ourselves to. Of course, others—society and the media—will influence those attitudes if we allow *them* to.

Life affirmation, as opposed to death attitudes, is recognizing that real death happens only once and, in a sense, does not "happen" to us at all. We are no longer feeling sensation at the exact moment; for most people conscious sensation has terminated considerably before the stroke of death. Even in cases involving sudden death—a plane crash or an automobile accident—it is likely that everything happens too fast for a rational analysis of the situation, the kind we harbor catastrophic fantasies about, when we think to ourselves, "I am going to . . ." We have much testimony from people who have come very close to death and who retain the memory of what they experienced. There are few reports of terror and many reports of a sense of calm and well-being, and even of disappointment at being "brought back."

The Phoenix

An ancient and enduring symbol of life affirmation is that of the Phoenix, a mythological bird of rare and exotic plumage and supernatural powers. The Greek historian Herodotus reported that the Phoenix actually existed and was known to have visited the Egyptians every 500 years. The Roman belief was that each era bears witness to the birth of one and only one Phoenix bird, that it lives for a very long time, and that, at the moment of its death, it generates a worm which becomes the Phoenix for the next age.

Yet another version of the legend is that the Phoenix is a bird from India which lives for 500 years and then flies to a secret temple, where it is burned to ashes upon the altar, only to rise from the ashes three days later, young and resplendent.

In folklore, poetry, and song, in fiction, drama, and epic, the Phoenix has endured through time as a symbol of rebirth, new growth, regeneration, and redemption. Religions have counterpart symbols: gods who die or descend into the underworld, there to remain for a time, and then to rise, reborn and renewed.

The Phoenix has given structure to many masterworks, such as Dante's *Divine Comedy*, in which the poet, seeking a vision of God in Paradise, must first travel through the very depths of hell before his wish is granted. The Phoenix has suggested to many people certain ways of thinking about events. Thus does "I've been through hell" often preface an account of some happier turn of events, or at least invite the listener to effect a happy change for the sufferer through lavish sympathy or some other sign of affection. People say, "I'm going to pull myself out of this." Even the popular exhortation "Lift yourself up by your own bootstraps" has underlying suggestions of the Phoenix myth, for there exists within the bird the creative thrust to soar from its own ashes.

Nor is the Phoenix merely an empty symbol, a literary convention with no basis in reality. If we stop to think of it, the whole phenomenon of existence is Phoenix-oriented, not death-oriented.

Natural Cycles

In human negative thinking, death is final, the end, KAPUT! No such finality exists in the real world. Whether planned this way by a rational deity or evolved this way through some inner sense of order or simply by accident (though many of the greatest philosophers *and* scientists have a hard time believing so), the natural world seems "dedicated" to perpetuation and continuity. There seem to be cycles everywhere: the seasons, the ecosystem, the rhythm and balance of birth and death.

In one sense many things "die." Animal and human life ceases to exist *in a particular form.* But like plants, other living things revert

A Death Model

I've already taken the qualifying exam for the third time. Now I'm out for good. I'll never amount to anything."

A Phoenix Model

"I'm obviously not suited for that kind of work. Let me see . . ."

to the natural world and are caught up in the nitrogen cycle. If people were willing to allow the bodies of loved ones to be placed beneath the ground without embalming and without caskets, the chemical process, not of disintegration but *re*integration, would begin to take place immediately.

It is alarming to realize how one-way-oriented humanity has become. All of nature appears to offer the cycle model, and yet we humans have created as many noncycles as we can think of. Individual and personal consciousness has been given such central importance in many cultures of the world that the loss of private awareness seems a disaster for which the physical facts of nature cannot compensate. In addition, with breathtaking ingenuity we have created nonbiodegradable products (plastic milk cartons, for example). Instead of foreseeing a time when energy derived from fossil fuel must be exhausted, we embarked years ago upon a reckless depletion of the earth's fuel resources. So now we are facing the eventual *death of energy,* a condition not metaphoric but tragically real. It almost seems as though we have decided that, since we must perish as individuals, we may as well take everything with us.

Life-Affirming Attitudes

Armed with legendary and scientific models, not to mention religious Phoenix symbols like "born-again baptism" or confession and absolution, we can set about making personal applications and developing "Phoenix strategies" which can combat the idea of premature death.

We can, for example, replace pyramids with circles as dominant inner images. In pyramid imagery, we visualize ourselves as rising through the ranks (of life, on the job, etc.), reaching a peak or crest, and then being "over the hill." In circle imagery, life can be like a ferris wheel, rising, reaching a crest, going back down, and *then* starting up all over again.

You can consider you "lost" a job, or you can consider you are changing one phase of life, only to begin another. You can experience the end of love (the *death* of romance) or you can reach a new beginning, looking forward with excitement to the next love, which will inevitably come along. The great baseball catcher Yogi Berra once said, "It ain't over 'til it's over," a hopeful reminder for more than the last-inning scoreboard.

There are recycling, Phoenix-oriented ways of living each day, such as:

Rearranging the furniture.
Changing routes going to or coming from.
Deciding to do everything during one day in a totally different manner.

Changing a hair style.
Buying a new outfit.
Writing a long-delayed letter.
Telephoning someone out of town.
Walking out on a distasteful obligation.

The sheer act of will involved, the realization that we are in control of our internal imagery, can be the beginning of a whole new way of living: living *without dying.*

But probably most important is the *forgiveness ritual,* which we can and should indulge in every so often. This ritual involves sitting quietly in a corner, concentrating very hard on all of the guilt we have accumulated, gathering up all of the negative thoughts we can possibly muster and compressing them into a tight ball, and then—calmly and deliberately—hurling the ball straight up toward the sky. It is possible to do this, to let the ball of guilt go where it may. It is even possible to imagine the ball of guilt suddenly transformed into a bird winging its way over a cloud, becoming lost in an obscure blue paradise, and never being heard from again. Then there will be time to live.

Cosmic Thoughts

One can do nothing more life-affirming than to think beyond oneself. The moment we grasp the profound truth that our single selves are not crucial phenomena in the life of the universe, we can begin to relax, to be free forever of the desperate obsession with being who we are. To stand outside at night and look up at the awesome reaches of space is to give the idea of personal importance a very different perspective.

Personal death can seem dwarfed by the thought that the universe has generated a magnificent process of immortality.

The poet John Keats (1795–1821), who never reached his twenty-sixth birthday, expresses many thoughts about death in the all-too-brief legacy he has given us. Though he may well have experienced premonitions of his own early passing, he does not refer to death in sorrowful tones. In one sonnet "After dark vapours have oppress'd our plains" he describes the beautiful thoughts that come to him on the first day of spring, culminating with the most beautiful of all: "a poet's death." Critics have praised the "startling" climax, but perhaps it was for Keats fitting rather than startling.

In one of his greatest sonnets, the poet both confronts and transcends the thought of personal death, even if this is to happen before he has experienced love and fame:

> *When I have fears that I may cease to be*
> *Before my pen has glean'd my teeming brain,*
> *Before high-piled books, in charact'ry,*
> *Hold like rich garners the full-ripen'd grain;*

When I behold, upon the night's starr'd face,
  Huge cloudy symbols of a high romance,
And think that I may never live to trace
  Their shadows, with the magic hand of chance;
And when I feel, fair creature of an hour!
  That I shall never look upon thee more,
Never have relish in the faery power
  Of unreflecting love! then on the shore
Of the wide world I stand alone, and think
  Till love and fame to nothingness do sink.

The model which Keats has given us is one in which we cope with what we might call our "cosmic insignificance" while we are still current, while we are still living and striving to accomplish. In doing so, we have nothing to lose. Intelligence, creativity, talent—whatever distinguishing characteristics go to make a person THAT person and no other, will still be there, no worse for the dimming of the spotlight. The depression that comes with aging or the proximity to personal death can become minimal. If it ceases to matter *terribly* that one special existence is not assured indefinitely, then death as a terrifying idea begins to fade.

Contemporary physics has become an ally of life affirmation and the Phoenix model. First there came the law of conservation: Energy can neither be created nor destroyed. Then there came the now widely accepted theory that what we call the universe is cosmic debris expanding outwards from a gigantic explosion (the Big Bang) which took place billions of years ago. But can the expansion go on infinitely? Or will universal gravity finally catch up with expanding matter and bring everything back into a mass of such density that it would look like a black hole in space? If such a phenomenon occurs, will the seething subatomic activity within the black hole cause another Big Bang as the cycle of expansion and contraction begins once more? Many of our foremost scientific minds say this is exactly what must and will happen. They have given us, in short, a scientific vision of eternity that might well cause each of us to feel as Keats did when he gazed up at the "huge cloudy symbols of a high romance." Personal death can seem dwarfed by the thought that the universe has generated a magnificent process of immortality.

GLOSSARY

Elysian Fields: In Greek mythology, a special land of immortality for warriors, whose spirits go there without having to suffer the pain of death.

fatalism: The belief that all events, including one's death, have been predetermined.

Grim Reaper: Figure of death in myth and art, usually depicted as wearing a shroud and carrying a scythe to cut down the person appointed to die.

Job: Biblical character who lost almost everything as a test from God and who questioned why he, a man who had led a nearly blameless life, should suffer when others no better than he were free of pain. Having taken his agonized questions to God, he was reminded that humanity must not presume to make demands on a power beyond human comprehension.

life affirmation: An outlook toward a specific event or contemplated action which sees it as a form of growth and is therefore supportive of it.

Medieval view of death: Death is a release from this painful world (or vale of tears),

with hoped-for passage to an eternal and better life.

romantic view of death: In nineteenth-century Romantic art and literature, the belief that lovers cruelly separated on Earth will be reunited in an afterlife; a familiar theme found in the theater of the time, particularly opera.

symbolic murder: Negative actions toward others springing from suppressed hatred or jealousy, often the result of a poor attitude toward the self.

symbolic suicide: Negative actions aimed at the self because of poor self-image. Compulsive gambling and excessive drinking are examples.

NOTES

1. J. R. R. Tolkien, *The Return of the King* (New York: Ballantine Books, 1966), p. 384.

2. *Hamlet,* Act II, Sc. 2.

3. Ibid., Act V, Sc. 1.

4. Ibid.

5. Edwin Arlington Robinson, "The Man Against the Sky," from *Collected Poems* of Edwin Arlington Robinson. Copyright 1916 by Edwin Arlington Robinson, renewed 1944 by Ruth Nivison.

6. Linnea Parsons, *Separate Paths* (New York: Harper & Row, 1977), p. 48.

7. Ibid., p. 128.

8. Albert Camus, "An Absurd Reasoning," in *The Myth of Sisyphus and Other Essays,* trans. Justin O'Brien (New York: Random House, Vintage, 1952), p. 3.

Fragonard, "Satyr Squeezing Grapes, with Tiger"
(© 1988 The Art Institute of Chicago, gift of Mr. and Mrs. Robert Hamman. All rights reserved.)

14

APOLLO
AND DIONYSUS

OVERVIEW

The heroine of a recent comic novel[1] has been telling her male companion that she must leave. She is attending a conference on world problems, and the main speaker is scheduled to go on. Still, she is attracted to the young man, who tells her:

> "Good. Do that. But if you're interested in experiencing the world as a better place, then stay here with me."
> "Oh yeah? That'd be fine—maybe for you and me, but how about the rest of humanity?"
> "A better world has gotta start somewhere. Why not with you and me?"

Their conversation illustrates two approaches to life which were named by a nineteenth-century German philosopher. The emphasis on emotional experience and pleasure was part of what Friedrich Nietzsche called the *Dionysian* element in our personality. The desire to deal with humanity in the abstract, purposefully working toward planned, logical improvements, he called *Apollonian.* The labels come from the names of two major Greek gods: Dionysus, the god of wine, passion, and spontaneity; sometimes of excess and lack of control but also of creativity; and Apollo, the god of the sun, exemplifying reason, order, clarity, purpose, and indirect experience through art.

Art and music mentioned in this text:

Apollonian	*Dionysian*
Greek tragedy as instruction	*Greek tragedy as emotional experience*
Structure of Gothic cathedrals	*Kierholz'* Still Live—1974
Michelangelo's David	*Goya's* The Family of Charles IV
A Haydn symphony	*Tchaikovsky's* 1812 Overture
Mondrian, Composition with Blue and Yellow	
Disciplined framework in jazz	*Rock*

These *polarities* were first described by Nietzsche in an analysis of tragedy. Strong drama, he argued, has its impact not from a conscious desire to learn from the example of a worthy hero, but in the dark recesses of the unconscious, in dreamlike, unexamined emotions. In short, great drama is Dionysian, not Apollonian.

These same opposing forces are found in people, too, as well as in government, education, and other institutions. In general, the Apollonian spirit is scientific; by emphasizing reason, it offers assurance that the universe can be understood by the human mind. The Apollonian person delights in connections which can make sense out of apparently unrelated phenomena. Those philosophers who have extolled reason, from Aristotle to Kant, can be described as Apollonian.

The Dionysian state is nonrational, trusting that indulgence, even to excess, will reveal the true nature of life. When Freud made his discoveries about the unconscious, he was exposing the Dionysian self to Apollonian awareness. Existentialism, a dominant contemporary philosophy, is Dionysian in its rejection of values imposed by others and its insistence on subjectivity rather than on universal, objective truth.

This chapter deals with the Apollonian and the Dionysian as we find them in the individual, in the arts, in law, religion, and education. While no one is completely Apollonian or Dionysian, there are tendencies toward one pole or the other, as well as occasional reversals of customary behavior in institutions as well as people. To be prepared is to be less surprised, as for instance, when people who have been cautious all their lives uncharacteristically spend money on something frivolous instead of wisely investing; or when the policy-making group recognizes that authority from on high may *not* be able to put forth principles which the public can accept.

This book, like most books, is Apollonian. If it were not, it would stress instinct, intuition, even frenzy and hallucinatory visions, or at least some way of acting upon profound feelings. Being a book, it can only present both sides, sympathetically, using Apollonian tools, in the hope that conscious recognition will lead to the perfect balance long believed to represent the ideal mode of living.

Apollo

reason
order
clarity
moderation
analysis
control

Dionysus

passion
spontaneity
instinct
frenzy
faith
excess

PERSONAL TEMPERAMENT

Scholars, almost invariably Apollonian, make classifications. This period in history was the "Age of Reason," that of "Romance," one age paving the way for a dominant idea in the next. Yet, within each "age," characterized in Apollonian course outlines, people continue to live their own lives, within families, with little regard for intellectual pronouncements. As children develop, their parents observe that one child seems to become upset often (even within an Age of Reason, people did); another child needs a lot of support and assurance about exactly what the results of a proposed action will be. One is neat, another untidy; one aggressive, the other timid; and so forth. These temperamental differences are apparent to anyone who knows the children, without regard to historical period. The toys change—wood, plastic, or electronic—but the responses of the children who play with them and the variety of individual temperaments do not always follow the historical designation of a period.

Labels give a false picture of uniformity. The majority of Athenian contemporaries of Socrates did not engage in dialogs exploring ultimate principles, and in the time when poets proclaimed their willingness to die for love, prosaic tasks such as floor-sweeping and bill-paying continued to be performed. Historical periods, in the eyes of historians, are stable units of time. Real life is not so easily categorized.

But historical labels address the human need for order, for the assurance that "history" is very real, that the "onward" course of humanity is interpretable. We can use the labels so long as we keep reminding ourselves that they can be misleading and are often legitimately subject to debate. Just when did the Renaissance start? At the stroke of midnight in the year 1400? Were there not thousands of human beings who never even *knew* that they were living through a Renaissance?

Nonetheless, as the gulf in time widens between us and the death of Nietzsche, we look back with growing admiration at those remarkable labels which the philosopher has given us, for if people are not always "modern" in the historian's sense, they *do* appear to oscillate between the extremes of order and disorder. They can even be said to gravitate closer to one or the other pole, making very broad personality distinctions meaningful.

Ways of Observing

Walking in a forest, the Apollonian would derive pleasure from recognition of the kinds of plants growing there, not just naming them but comparing the shapes and textures of their parts. It would be a delight to observe that a tiny fragment of a fern had the structure of a giant plant seemingly unrelated to it. Such recognition reassures the Apollonian of the order in a planned universe. Botanical information would be available to the scientist, who is Apollonian. But even the casual Apollonian walker, unaware of species or genus, can and does notice, group, and compare. The Apollonian walk is a way of seeing and thinking with care and reflection.

Walking in a forest, the Dionysian would feel the cool air, touch leaves, smell fragrances, sit, run, or climb, without the need to analyze sensations and feelings. The experience would be worthwhile for its own sake. With no need to discover order, real or assumed, the Dionysian accepts what comes. There is no need to debate with the Apollonian (who tends to win debates, as well as succeed in other language-related activities). The Dionysian becomes part of nature in a way envied by Apollonians (who may rush back to their desks and compose poems about fortunate savages they claim to admire).

The simple act of walking in a forest may change according to different sensibilities. The two described do not, of course, exhaust the possibilities. We have seen that the Apollonian remains aware, while the Dionysian simply experiences without thinking about it. The Dionysian moving through the forest derives as much delight from this venture as the more controlled Apollonian gains from keeping an alert mind throughout the walk.

With no need to discover order, the Dionysian accepts what comes.

Using the distinctions Nietzsche has provided, we can identify the consciousness which falls exactly in the middle, the person who moves so routinely that there is no memory of having been in a forest at all. This is also the consciousness—shared at *some* point by all of us—which becomes accustomed to taking a certain path in a daily trip from one point to another. *All* trips seem to be the same, with no sense of novelty, hence no need to notice or to mentally record the scene, no desire to open one's senses—to hear unfamiliar sounds, touch unusual surfaces, and look at what the filter of overlapping leaves does to sunlight. The routine walk leaves the individual unaware of either sensibility, unable to enjoy life from either the Apollonian or the Dionysian perspective.

Expectations

In *Zorba the Greek,* a novel by Nikos Kazantzakis, later made into a film (1964) starring Anthony Quinn, the Apollonian and Dionysian approaches to life are represented by two men. One, the Englishman, is studious and quiet, dispassionately observing the primitive people in the little village on Crete. The other, the Greek, is Zorba, who understands what is not written in books: compassion for the weak and lonely, acceptance of those elements in other people which cannot be changed, recognition of the eventual futility of long-range plans and scientific efforts.

Working together, the men attempt a profit-making scheme for transporting wood from the top of a mountain. After the failure of a device invented by the Dionysian Zorba, Zorba teaches his companion to bear the pain, just as he has tried to teach him to follow his instincts and take chances in encounters with people on the island, instead of fearing his impulses and depending so much on written authorities. The uninhibited Zorba and the reserved Englishman stand on the shore at the water's edge, where the Englishman suddenly and uncharacteristically says, "Teach me to dance."

Beginning slowly, then with increasing energy, Zorba begins the steps of the ancient dance, as music fills the theater. With hypnotic repetition, the music continues, inviting viewers to a Dionysian response as the two men give themselves over to movement of increasing abandon.

Of course that was fiction. In real life, the Apollonian may react differently, not willing to learn from the Dionysian. Bankrupt, he would blame himself—or others—and be determined to begin still another enterprise. And the Dionysian might not be as charming and wise as Zorba. His childlike exuberance and inability to work without distraction on an important assignment might be regarded as signs of unfitness for adult life rather than as admirable manifestations of earthiness and folk wisdom. Perhaps, however, the Apollonian workaholic can learn from the Dionysian a more relaxed approach to what is, after all, a temporary stay on the planet.

The truth was felt by instinct here,—Process which saves a world of trouble and time.

Robert Browning

Leisure

The Sabbath has been a major contribution to human development. Observing the commandment "Remember the Sabbath to keep it holy," the early Hebrews decreed that no work should be done on a day set aside for rest and study. So important was the Sabbath that nothing, not even a recent death in the family, was allowed to interfere with the "keeping" of the special day. Whether tied to religion or not, the practice serves to change the rhythm of the week and prevents work from completely dominating us.

In recent years, emphasis has been on the *Dionysian* weekend, a time for eating, drinking, loud music, "getting away from it all." With a slight hint of the Puritan work ethic and its ancient prescription that fun has to be earned, advertisements encourage pleasure and weekend abandon, accompanied by a deliberate rejection of thought and control. A popular jingle would have us always remember that we "deserve a break today," though no reason is given.

Advertisements may encourage Dionysian activities, but not all responses are purely Dionysian responses. The Apollonian at play remains in control, knowing when to quit, willing to spend the weekend mowing the lawn and doing household repairs before retiring to an evening of television watching or reading. The Apollonian is always aware of the consequences and is thus unwilling to risk a hangover and the regret which might follow spontaneous outbursts. The "pure" Dionysian at play is, of course, a descendant of the original followers of Dionysus—or Bacchus—in his guise as the god of wine, devotion to whom required drunken revelry and riotous orgy. Drink loosens the tongue, making us say and enjoy hearing remarks which the "daytime self" would find foolish. Dionysian drinking is a group activity, democratic in its rejection of rank, title, or ceremony, as has been demonstrated by many an office Christmas party. When junior clerk faces chief executive officer the following Apollonian week, both, now sober, may be frantically trying to recall how much the refreshments contributed to regrettable intimacy: "Did I really say that?" "Will somebody hold me to that promise?"

The Apollonian at play remains in control, knowing when to quit, willing to spend the weekend mowing the lawn and doing household repairs.

Food

The Dionysian approach to food has nothing to do with diet, health, or moderation. Those who cook the food may require Apollonian skills painstakingly acquired. But those who eat it can indulge in gastronomical pleasures without concern, permitting no prohibitions of any kind. "Go on, you only live once," says the Dionysian host urging a friend to eat forbidden fat or sugar. In eating to excess and indulging in pent-up food fantasies, the weekend Dionysian is likely to reject all rules of nutrition. A deliberate lawbreaker, the Dionysian gives in to

There is a Dionysian delight in the deliberate flaunting of medical science and the many other kinds of restraints which insist we do only what is good for us.

madness which may bring eventual regret, but which, for now, is believed worthwhile. This breaking of diet represents more than the weakness of someone who would like to obey but lacks the will to do so. It is also a challenging of Apollonian medical authorities, a desire for the suspension of rules. When we read about a celebration of the 100th birthday of someone who brags about having outlived the doctor who put him on a restricted diet, we have met a worshipper of the god of good luck, another Dionysian deity. There is a Dionysian delight in the deliberate disregarding of physicians' nutritionists, and the other advisors who insist we do only what is good for us.

Sex

As a fundamental event, sexual encounter is Dionysian. Sex, in the natural sense of attraction and fulfillment, frequently is uncontrolled and inevitable, without plans, appointments, or vows. Songs and stories celebrate the unaccountable attraction of one person for another. The words describing passion are strong, natural, without control: thrill, surrender, a heart which stood still, a roller coaster ride, an enchanted evening. (Evenings which are enchanted have more to do with witchcraft than with science or careful, rational marriage counseling.)

The key word is, of course, *natural.* One enduring belief in our society is that unschooled primitives enjoy sex in a way undreamed of by city dwellers, who are so repressed by their Apollonian restraints on desires that they must seek assistance from guide books and counselors to attain their birthright. Since the Apollonian must plan all other activities—education, a career, the use of time—in order to achieve a goal worth waiting for, can there be a planned, Apollonian approach to passion? The words sound contradictory, conjuring up an image of a sober, unromantic would-be lover surrounded by charts, working hard at being swept away. Does the Apollonian truly plan the age at which, other items out of the way, "falling" in love *should* occur? Doesn't the habit of being aware and alert to obligations interfere with uncontrollable feelings— when, for instance, in the midst of an embrace, one lover or the other remarks that a bill must be paid or a household article repaired?

A serious accusation against the Dionysian is sounded by columnist George Will, who maintains that there is a double standard, that those (Dionysians) who proclaim themselves above the law are willing to invoke it when it suits their (Apollonian) purposes. He cites two examples: the woman who demands a large sum of money from a man who did not tell the truth about being infected with herpes; and the woman who sues under the "palimony" law to receive money due her by someone with whom she has lived without being legally married. In both cases, people want freedom from conventional sexual restrictions and then want (rational) restitution when dissatisfied with consequences of that freedom. The law, says Will,

> sanctioned the idea that persons who reject the legal responsibilities of marriage can nonetheless use the law to impose responsibilities on others when that becomes convenient. One does wish that today's free spirits, who are too emancipated to conform to the law's codification of social values regarding marriage, would at least have the consistency not to come running to court seeking the help of a society whose codified values they reject.

Those who refuse excess are made to feel unwelcome, in a jeering appeal to the conformity of the nonconformist.

Well, that is beginning to sound like Apollonian disapproval. But there is Dionysian disapproval too, a sort of tyranny imposed by those wishing to use their own rules to "free" others from sexual inhibitions. One example might involve the sudden appearance of a low-keyed, conservative guest at a nude beach. Urged to strip, a bathing-suit-clad visitor could well resist. "Take your clothes off. Have *fun!*" is not only the exhortation, but the commandment. Those who refuse excess in whatever form are made to feel unwelcome, in a jeering appeal to the conformity of the nonconformist.

A Way of Understanding the Humanities

Apollonian and Dionysian outlooks may be seen in diverse elements of human life. They are also apparent in their impact on the arts. The basic difference, according to Nietzsche, was in the extent to which morality was imposed on artistic purpose and in the effect on audiences. Living during the Victorian era, Nietzsche was particularly sensitive to the predominant moral approach, which emphasized the *good* a work of art should accomplish in terms of edifying subject matter, with lessons designed to improve the values and ideals of audience and reader. This section will examine the possibility that the humanities can be, at will, either Apollonian or Dionysian.

Poetry

Dionysian literature would seem to be a contradiction in terms. After all, even the most chaotic-appearing novel and the most disorganized poem are *about* an experience, and words are required to communicate it. We comprehend the emotions, but an artist is recording them, thus placing the reader at one remove from the event itself. Apollo-

nianism in literature was cited by Nietzsche as an orderly expression
of distanced emotion, which, no matter how well done, is no substitute for the actual experience of living.

Still, even within literature, the two forces appear to exist,
with order, morality, and submission to authority on one side, disorder
and revolt against authority on the other. Two poems help to illustrate:
John Milton's "On His Blindness" and A. E. Housman's "The Laws of
God, the Laws of Man." Both originate in despair and a Dionysian urge
to rebel. Milton says:

> *When I consider how my light is spent*
> *Ere half my days, in this dark world and wide,*
> *And that one talent which is death to hide,*
> *Lodged with me useless, though my soul more bent*
> *To serve therewith my Maker, and present*
> *My true account, lest he returning chide:*
> *"Doth God exact day-labor, light denied?"*
> *I fondly ask; but Patience, to prevent*
> *That murmur, soon replies, "God doth not need*
> *Either man's work or his own gifts; who best*
> *Bear his mild yoke, they serve him best. His state*
> *Is kingly. Thousands at his bidding speed*
> *And post o'er land and ocean without rest:*
> *They also serve who only stand and wait."*

The first seven and a half lines of the poem reveal an impatience to
accomplish, but it is the Apollonian need to leave a mark, certain that
human achievement will have lasting results. This is a theme found in
much literature. Theme itself is an Apollonian element, and the
humble obedience to God, urged in the final line, is also Apollonian,
though it might seem not to be. Milton's sense of a creative void is not
antireason in its calm assertion that there is a tangible purpose in
waiting.

It can even be argued that no poem adhering to the formal
requirements of meter and rhyme can be Dionysian. But—and here is
the paradox—we must accept the possibility of there being a totally
Dionysian *idea* sitting (sometimes uneasily) within an ordered context. The result is poetic tension: the calm of poetic form in subtle
conflict with an emotional explosion longing to take place. The experience of that tension is essentially Dionysian, as this poem by A. E.
Housman (1859–1936) illustrates. Though the poet does not explode, he is clearly not content with the Apollonian:

> *The laws of God, the laws of man,*
> *He may keep that will and can;*
> *Not I: let God and man decree*

Laws for themselves and not for me;
And if my ways are not as theirs
Let them mind their own affairs.
Their deeds I judge and much condemn,
Yet when did I make laws for them?
Please yourselves, say I, and they
Need only look the other way.
But no, they will not; they must still
Wrest their neighbour to their will,
And make me dance as they desire
With jail and gallows and hell-fire.
And how am I to face the odds
Of man's bedevilment and God's?
I, a stranger and afraid
In a world I never made.
They will be master, right or wrong;
Though both are foolish, both are strong.
And since, my soul, we cannot fly
To Saturn nor to Mercury,
Keep we must, if keep we can,
These foreign laws of God and man.[2]

Much poetry can be described as Apollonian for holding in check Dionysic emotions.

What so often happens is that the artist, like Housman, hearing the subterranean whispers of unbridled Dionysian passions, seeks in Apollonian form—here, the regularity of the rhythmic and rhyme patterns—a way of controlling his emotions. Otherwise, if he is completely carried away by them, by what right does he claim to be an artist to begin with? Is there not something fundamentally Apollonian in the very *idea* of a work's aspiring to the status of art and the artist to a place in human memory? Can such a place be reserved for the millions of us who *do* give free rein to our emotions, often regretting the fact the next day and surely very seldom leaving something of note behind?

The question we have raised leads in turn (which is an Apollonian thought progression, of course) to the larger issue of how Dionysian a work can become in form as well as content and still deserve the designation of art. Were Housman to be completely Dionysian in approach, he would have splattered the words all over the page, even as many modern artists splatter their paint, introducing nonsense terms and utilizing an irrational syntax that disorients the reader.

Music

On the one hand, we could argue that music by its very nature is essentially Dionysian. Its appeal is to the emotions, not the intellect. On the other, music, like poetry, has formal characteristics which act as potential restraints on uncontrolled passion. It too has underlying rhythm and frequently a principle of repetition which, like rhyme, keeps the artist from becoming lost in the labyrinth of the unconscious. With music, we face the same question posed in relation to poetry: How Dionysian can we become without saying we have left the domain of art?

Designations in music must be tentative, at best, since much music that is now considered highly formal and highly traditional, such as the symphonies of Beethoven, were in their time often viewed with a certain amount of distrust. The dissonant seventh chords introduced by Beethoven would surely have been called Dionysian by early-nineteenth-century critics, but they are now comfortably ensconced within the archives of classicism. Time and tradition often lend an air of Apollonian respectability to what was once outrageous and shocking.

Serious, or concert, music of all periods except our own may generally and safely be termed Apollonian. Even the drawn-out emotionalism of Tchaikovsky and the extreme Romanticism of Richard Strauss do not violate the principles of musical form. By the time of Tchaikovsky and Strauss, from the latter half of the nineteenth century to the early years of the twentieth, music was expected to have a more direct assault upon the emotions without losing all perspective. Orchestral poems like *Manfred* and *Don Quixote* allow the composer more freedom in developing his themes than did earlier forms, but we can note the use of repeated themes, which keep the experience turning back upon itself, giving it shape and direction.

Often we mistake a Dionysian "message" for pure Dionysianism in music. A case in point is Ravel's popular *Bolero* (1928), originally written as a ballet and the source of a near riot upon the occasion of its first performance. The insistent theme, endlessly repeated with increasingly pronounced rhythmic underpinnings, seems to be encouraging the listener to throw aside all restraint and surrender to an orgiastic, completely irrational state. No doubt the visual impact of a distinctly un-Victorian dance had something to do with the riot at the premiere. But nothing more Apollonian can be imagined than a piece of music which is a continual restatement of, not even a variation on, just one theme and which has a boldly identifiable rhythm. A real-life Dionysian orgy is characterized by totally innovative—nonrepeated—behavior and an absence of regular rhythm, an absence of things which remind the Apollonian self to take care.

We are living at a time of near-extreme Dionysianism in behavior, hence one in which the arts are filled with adventurous experiments in rule-breaking. We would suppose that certain uncontrolled forms of rock can be considered Dionysian, if only because they continue to set new records in decibels, loudness usually interfering with our ability to put experience into any kind of perspective. Perhaps, by

Ravel's Bolero, *which seems at first to be Dionysian, is basically Apollonian in form and structure. The music of the Beatles also turns out to be highly structured.*

supporting the rock movement, we are really saying we are afraid to think, afraid to face some unpleasant realities about ourselves and our times.

But the music of the Beatles, which, like that of Beethoven, shocked a good many purists in the beginning, now begins to take on the glow of high respectability. Many of their songs, at first sounding ear-splitting and totally nonsensical, have shown themselves to be highly structured pieces, built firmly on recognized musical principles. Many traditionalists in music education use "Eleanor Rigby" as an almost classic example of syncopation, the principle by which the main theme plays against, not with, the underlying rhythm.

Conservative adults tend to believe that all rock music is a dangerous lure, debasing the minds of both listeners and dancers. At one time, even jazz was considered detrimental, partly because its origins were outside the mainstream of white-dominated power and partly because its appeal, like liquor, aimed at passions considered base. Today, jazz has become an art form, an accepted Apollonian art form, which has achieved the respectability of being a part of university curricula, listed in the catalog and studied for credit. Jazz has recognized and teachable styles and patterns, as well as a place in history.

By the same token, there has developed a musicology of rock, a tradition with influences and styles which are being analyzed seriously by music students. We may have even reached the point at which the apparent abandon of so-called "punk" rock is a sociological, not an artistic, event, a point at which we can tell the difference between the two yet regard "punk" with Apollonian seriousness.

Drama

So we find ourselves, in critically Apollonian fashion, returning to the same question: How Dionysian may a work of art be in form as well as in spirit? This issue is paramount in the drama, an ancient art form, which seems absolutely to depend on repeated and recognizable characters, portents of things to come, and an obligatory climax in which conflicting forces inevitably collide and some resolution is reached.

But Nietzsche's original designation of the Apollonian and the Dionysian grew out of a discussion of the drama: specifically, Greek tragedy. Aware that the birth of tragedy lay in primordial rituals (such as that of human sacrifice), which were anything but Apollonian, Nietzsche argued that, by emphasizing the moral lessons to be learned from tragedy, early critics like Aristotle had taken the form out of its primitive—and, for Nietzsche, far more exciting—context. By concentrating on what was to be *learned* from tragedy, later critics ignored the excitement of the play in favor of schematic patterns which ultimately instructed audiences in the proper way to behave. In their eyes, so Nietzsche believed, tragedy became a pale replica of basic human passions.

Oedipus Rex, often considered the perfectly structured and therefore representatively Apollonian tragedy, can be viewed in two contrasting ways. In addition to its geometrically designed plot, which brings the hero ever closer to the truth of his birth and incestuous marriage (see Chapter 3 for a fuller discussion), the play can be seen as having a decidedly Apollonian moral theme: *Mortals should not try to outwit fate.*

But we must not forget that Freud and his disciples saw in *Oedipus* a drama of the titanic struggle between the forces of organized society and the unconscious Oedipal desire of the male for his mother. Freud saw primitive myth, and so did Nietzsche, who, like the first of the psychoanalysts, was responding to the restraining effects of Victorian morality.

For Nietzsche it was decidedly wrong to be concerned with morality to an extent which made no allowance for the strong emotions a tragedy unleashes. These emotions, which we mentioned in Chapter 3, were considered dangerous by Aristotle. Over the centuries dramatic criticism has stressed the importance of the calming effect which takes place in tragedy following the catastrophe. In both Greek and Shakespearean tragedy, moral order reasserts itself after emotion has run its course. If the fallen hero is the king or queen, a new and rational ruler comes upon the scene. We leave the theater satisfied, our Apollonian selves assured that chaos does not reign.

But can we say that every Greek tragedian looked to the Aristotelian norms for guidance? Or that Shakespeare left his theatrical kingdoms in reestablished order for any reason beside political ones? (Shakespeare wrote for the company which was supported by the royal house itself!) May not Nietzsche have a point when he says that drama is essentially Dionysian in that it constitutes a living, direct experience, as opposed to the secondary experience of literature?

Significantly enough, many contemporary dramatists have resisted the efforts of critics to interpret and explain their work and to criticize it on intellectual and moral grounds. Both Eugene O'Neill and Tennessee Williams (1912–1983), two of the most formidable forces in American theater, were seldom capable of rational discourse about their plays. They appear to have relied on instincts far below the rational surface.

Williams, in particular, was obsessed with the very theme of Apollo versus Dionysus. Coming as he did from a background of Old South (Apollonian) gentility, he enjoyed creating plays about the destructive effects of suppressed passion. While we could argue that his themes were actually Apollonian *statements* and that his strongest plays—*Streetcar Named Desire* (1947) and *Cat on a Hot Tin Roof*

Both Eugene O'Neill and Tennessee Williams were seldom capable of rational discourse about their plays. They appear to have relied on instincts far below the rational surface.

(1955)—owe their audience success to an unerring sense of structure that is Greek-like in its mounting intensity, we can also not fail to see that Williams's most powerful scenes, such as Stanley Kowalski's rape of the heroine in *Streetcar,* unleash white-hot emotion that sears the viewer.

Unlike poetry, drama contains the additional element of an actor's living presence. Even in highly symbolic plays, the living actor will duplicate real-life emotion. Anger is anger, whether it occurs in a highly realistic play like *Cat on a Hot Tin Roof* or a German expressionistic work in which both set and characters represent ideas. Engulfed by the emotions pouring forth from the stage, audiences seldom ask themselves, "What is the playwright trying to tell us?" Or, if they do, they may sense that something is missing from the experience.

On the other hand, much contemporary theater may be perceived as going "too far"; at least, it does to the Apollonian inside us. Like some modern art and music which seems to be working from highly obscure formal principles, modern theater sometimes goes out of its way to be unusual to the point of being unidentifiable. There has even been a performance at which the audience was blind-folded and forced to sit in terror while bodies and other objects tumbled over it and deafening music drowned out any screams that might have been uttered. Dionysianism is always there to support the interests of those who wish to rebel against all authority, even that of art itself.

Tolerance for the unfamiliar in art has been a persistent theme in this book. But we must not rule out the possibility that the nonfamiliar, having been given its say, may still be dismissed as nonart. Some formal principle, however eccentric, appears to be necessary. This, of course, may subsequently be discovered, as has been the case with the music of the Beatles. But think how confusing it will be for future humanities teachers to say to their classes: "The world of art contains art itself and its own opposite, that which lacks art." How unanswerable might be the question: "Then are we to consider *everything* as belonging to the world of art?" To measure the artistry of some recent events calling themselves drama, we might suppose a high admission price to be a "logical" yardstick for the critic to use.

Think how confusing it will be to say to a class: "The world of art contains art itself and its own opposite, that which lacks art."

The Arts as Revolutionary Forces

In the late 1960s the most popular show on Broadway was the musical *Hair,* which was proudly passed off as a show without a book. Almost—but, we hasten to add, *not completely*—devoid of plot and transitions from song to song, *Hair* managed to bubble along just below the conscious level, its lyrics often not quite making rational sense. But its music was loud and insistent, and at the end of the evening, the audience was invited to come up onto the stage and join the cast in wild dancing. The show was a huge financial success, meaning that its high-priced appeal went far beyond the audience of young revolutionaries, whose movement was the original inspiration. Respectable executives and their spouses, often dressed to the teeth, let themselves go in the final dance. It began to look as if the Apollonian Establishment were quite ready to let down its own hair and get back to Dionysian basics.

Whether the off-center effects of *Hair* were coldly calculated and its destiny as a monumental money-making enterprise carefully sculpted, the case has been made many times for the arts as being properly revolutionary in nature and purpose. Both Karl Marx and Chairman Mao were advocates of this view. So was, much earlier, Jean-Jacques Rousseau (1712–1778), who, in commenting on the function of drama, insisted that, to obtain committed revolutionaries, it was necessary to inflame them, to show a wrong, and to leave it unresolved, thus allowing audiences to stream out of a theater and into the streets with the determination to do something in real life rather than be tranquilized by the leveling-off of emotions onstage. The ending would be played out in physical action, in the rallies and riots which would put into play the Dionysian elements deliberately ignored by scholars and critics such as Aristotle.

We can see other people's behavior, but not their experience.

R. D. Laing

For Rousseau the purpose of art was to provoke rather than soothe, to show an injustice, draw the audience to the side of one clear victim and then reach an abrupt, unsatisfying ending. If the wrongdoer were not brought to justice, audiences would remain indignant. They would not be allowed the calming luxury of sighs and tears in witnessing a victim's death and release from suffering, nor be calmed by a philosophical acceptance of disappointment as a part of living. They would simply be aroused and left at a peak of emotion.

The contemporary labor organizer Cesar Chavez successfully employed this technique in his presentation of plays about the hardships suffered by Mexican migrant workers. In his Teatro Campesino, Chavez typically showed a poor man brutally deceived, first by those he paid to guide him across the border, then by the foremen under whom he worked long and arduous hours for almost no compensation. The plays at the Teatro Campesino never had resolved endings. Instead, they encouraged an aroused audience, usually on its feet, to demand immediate social action.

Rousseau believed the purpose of art was to provoke rather than soothe, to show an injustice and then reach an abrupt, unsatisfying ending.

Teachers of the humanities have tended to resist the revolutionary aspect of the arts, carefully separating artistic works from those considered propagandistic or blatantly didactic. The controversy continues. We may be assured that people will always use the arts as a means of expressing revolutionary ideas. If they are successful, as was Clifford Odets when his 1930s play *Waiting for Lefty* was the direct cause of a massive taxi-driver strike, who are we to say that their intention has not been Apollonian; that they have not had the formal purpose of effecting social change through an artistic medium, not street violence; and that, being successful, their work does not deserve to be recognized *as* art?

Religion

Religion seems to be just Apollonian, requiring a regular routine of worship, obedience to authority, distrust of emotion, and often consciousness of a stern, demanding God. But religion can be Dionysian, too, in its appeal to untutored feeling, in worship services appealing to the senses, in defiance of morality. It was this Dionysian impulse which Nietzsche praised when he contrasted the Apollonian Judeo-Christian beliefs of his own time with the pagan beliefs of the past. The Greek god Prometheus, he pointed out, stole fire from Zeus and gave it to humanity because he believed Zeus to be unfair in trying to prevent this wonderful resource from reaching Earth. The myth encourages sympathy with humanity against the tyranny of Zeus. But the disobedience of Adam and Eve in gaining knowledge of good and evil is, in Hebrew scriptures, regarded as worthy of punishment. It is time, said Nietzsche, to give credit to the Dionysian side of human life and to stop the emphasis on human sin and God's mercy.

The Apollonian approach to religion has been found in a variety of forms: in commandments and restrictions; in rules for clothing and diet, as well as ritual observances; in the orderly rhythm of celebrations; in the quiet design of simple places for worship, as well as in gigantic cathedrals; in sermons emphasizing social conscience; and in prescribed, planned responses from the congregation. But Apollonian religion, like Apollonian government, can become repressive.

Hawthorne's The Scarlet Letter *shows us the stern repressiveness of extreme Apollonianism in religion.*

In Nathaniel Hawthorne's *The Scarlet Letter* (1850), the heroine, Hester Prynne, was required by the community to wear the letter *A,* which proclaimed her an adultress. The Puritan community of New England regarded the application of God's laws to be of public concern rather than a matter for the private conscience of each person. Social condemnation was a means of requiring adherence to law. In his novel, Hawthorne portrays the disgrace of the sinner, who has borne a child by a man other than her husband, and the unrelenting inner agony of the adulterer, who is the town minister himself, able to hide the sin from everyone except God. In Puritanism, God *and* community are unyielding, avenging forces.

New England Puritanism was a branch of Protestantism, which began in the Reformation out of protest against Catholic ritual, denounced as excessive and sensual—hence, we would say, Dionysian. Protestant worship was based on the Bible as a holy book read by each congregant, rather than on the authority of priests and other interpreters of God's law. Worship was held in plain, undecorated churches without incense, images, or processions of church dignitaries. Nor were there parades and street dancing to celebrate a holiday or honor a martyred saint. Puritans abolished Christmas decorations as pagan practice. Secular activities on the Sabbath were strictly forbidden, a practice still found today in "blue laws" restricting business enterprises from operating on Sundays in predominantly Protestant communities or on Saturdays in the State of Israel, evidence that Puritan values are not restricted to any one religion.

Apollonian religion can have positive impact as well. Religious rituals, experienced from week to week, have a steadying effect. They reestablish the broken rhythms of our lives. Whether we always accept every belief espoused by a given sect, the process itself of attending a church, of hearing old rules repeated—good rules to guide the lives of reasonable human beings, set forth by many wise individuals—cannot be lightly dismissed. Hawthorne's world of grim, austere Puritans is one extreme. It is found, we must remember, on the pages of a novel. We should not make the mistake of regarding the community aspect of every religion as being potentially repressive, a denial of human rights.

The Apollonian approach to religion includes morality, an insistence on distinguishing between right and wrong. Often the distinction is hard and fast—and unalterable. Nietzsche was opposed to the imposition of moral values from a central religious authority. For him, rigid morality weakens a society, preventing strong energies from seeking a healthy outlet. Apollonians in religion frequently cite extreme Dionysian examples to support their disapproval. True, over the years Dionysian worship has involved uninterrupted, often orgiastic dancing, repeated chants, the removal of sin through animal sacrifice, and the ritualistic use of hallucinatory drugs.

But Dionysian religious practice also includes ceremonies that spring from feeling and instinct, not reason. It includes the emphasis on fellowship rather than moral instruction, on the giving of love more than the categorization of sins. The mystical elements within the Judeo-Christian mainstream tradition can be termed Dionysian, and so can the traditional stories and songs which demonstrate simple, humble faith, as opposed to the intellectual grasp of large realities. Even the most dedicated Apollonian is likely to find warmth and comfort in the popular carol of "The Little Drummer Boy," who could give the baby Jesus only the "rum-a-tum-tum" rather than the costly gifts of royal visitors.

A similar tale exists in Jewish tradition. The story is of a boy who was not learned in letters and who was unable to read prayers; nevertheless his father took him to pray on Yom Kippur, the holiest day of the year. The boy took his flute out of his pocket and played it during the concluding prayers. Everyone heard it. The father was ashamed, but the pious leader, the Baal Shem Tov, said, "This child's flute has lifted up all our prayers. Through the strength of his yearning he played his heart's note perfectly. This was very dear to God, and all our prayers were accepted for his sake."

Some Dionysian elements in religion: the simplicity of "The Little Drummer Boy"; Mardi Gras; Easter Sunday.

Ritual is often Dionysian in its appeal to the senses and the emotions, in its dramatic rather than literary representation of a basic element of belief. Consider the phases of the Easter story. First comes the revelry of Mardi Gras as the last fling before the restrictions of Lent. *Carnival* (a word derived from the Latin words for "farewell to meat") offers unrestrained merriment, costumes, pageantry, parades. Then come the somber days of restriction, symbolically purifying the believer for the celebration which is to come. In many churches, Good Friday finds a dark place of worship, all sources of beauty shrouded, windows covered. Then, on Easter Sunday, light streams through stained glass windows; the church is at its most resplendent, and members of the congregation sit in brightly colored new clothes, listening to joyous hymns and sonorous, overwhelming chords from the organ. Countless people flock to the churches at such festive times, seeking, if nothing else, an emotional uplift.

The Apollonian/Dionysian conflict often comes about through efforts to change practice and belief from within. Attempts at modification of old, established religious customs can be met with bitter resistance, as recently happened with the introduction of jazz masses and the singing of folk-rock hymns on once-hallowed altars.

Rebellion against orthodoxy is also found in the practice of "Santeria," a religion which originated some time ago in Africa and came to the United States via the islands of the Caribbean. Outwardly practicing Catholicism, the religion of their masters, slaves working in Cuba combined, or "syncretized," elements of polytheism with the saints of their new religion. In the synthesis, certain gods were "assigned" to cure certain parts of the body, and medicine men assisted in the rituals associated with the cures. Along with therapy, this blend of religions offered freedom from moral restrictions. The lovesick sufferer, lusting for someone already married, could seek help in the form of love potions and magic words, the Santerian gods not being guardians of traditional virtue.

For Nietzsche, this departure from morality would have provided a necessary counterbalance. We have already spoken of the contrast between the Greek and Hebrew approaches to human defiance of deity. The Greek myth encourages sympathy for Prometheus, benefactor of humanity. In Genesis, the disobedience of Adam and Eve is punished by banishment from Eden, and eventually death. Both Jews and Christians are *instructed* to regret this fall from Paradise and to wait— in different ways—for deliverance from human suffering. The Promethean act of defiance was thus heroic, grand, emotionally stirring; that of Adam and Eve, a shameful lesson. Nietzsche feared that the Apollonian emphasis on sin would mean the triumph of all that was tame, cerebral, and passive in our nature.

APOLLO AND DIONYSUS IN EDUCATION

Almost nowhere in the personal experience of the average person are Apollonian and Dionysian factors likely to be as evident as they are in schools and colleges, for education itself as a process is always destined to be a showdown between the two forces. On one hand, education aims at the growth and unfolding of the individual, which can be Dionysian matters. If students were allowed to fully explore their creative potential, to develop in any chosen direction, without regard for the requirements of the teacher, the local school board, parents, and society, they would be following a purely Dionysian course. But even before the creative potential of the kindergarten pupil or the first-grader is ever perceived—in fact, often before the child has entered school—certain Apollonian expectations have been impressed upon the pupil. For example:

> The pupil must learn to behave.
> The pupil must remain confined for long hours.
> The pupil must show the results of certain teaching methods.
> The pupil must therefore learn things which he or she may not want to learn.
> Others know better than the pupil what is worth doing.

The ideal condition would be, I admit, that men should be right by instinct; but since we are all likely to go astray, the reasonable thing is to learn from those who can teach.

Sophocles

The Lower Grades

Many problems arising in earlier years of education can be attributed to the imbalance between Apollo and Dionysus. Whether the problems were understood in precisely these terms or not, about half a century ago, sweeping changes began to be made. Educators recognized the need to allow pupils more Dionysian freedom to learn who they were and what they wanted to become. Experimental schools sprang up everywhere, many of which developed reputations for over-permissiveness and abandonment of the three R's in favor of chaos. Typical of these early Dionysian classrooms would be sessions in which pupils banged objects together in a "rhythm band," got together in little groups to act out plays (which were really unconscious fantasies in disguise), and engaged in finger painting, much to the detriment of their clothes, the other children, and the classroom floor.

Most elementary schools, however, have sought to maintain a balance between excessive order and unbridled freedom. Educational theory, which is basically Apollonian, demands organization, planning, the writing of objectives, and the development of ways to measure a pupil's growth. Some teachers are overly Apollonian, insisting upon the lesson plan to the exclusion of all else, even when a given lesson appears not to be working. Others allow for Dionysian free spirits, with the result that they always seem to be running to catch up with their own objectives.

Schools tend to be top-heavy with administration, which is a very Apollonian entity. The teacher is answerable to the principal, the local school board, the PTA, county overseers—ultimately to the state department of education. The extreme Dionysian has a hard time bringing pupils into line and getting them ready for the battery of tests which come along frequently, not to mention for classroom observers.

Schools are Apollonian in their insistence upon ordered rituals, from flag salutes to the straight-line march along the corridors to the cafeteria or the playground. Even where permissiveness reigns in a particular classroom, the schools themselves are often run like army training camps. Pupils must have a pass if they are found walking through the halls. They may not be many minutes late, if at all. They usually may not rise from their seats at will or talk to their classmates.

Since children are too young to comprehend the why's behind the subjects they study, they must do a great deal of rote learning, which is Apollonian, too. They must memorize the spelling and meaning of words as well as the multiplication tables. They must learn the capitals of every state and country and what crops are grown in the "black earth region."

Critics of excessive Apollonianism in education cite the fact that pupils become memorization machines at too early an age to defend themselves. After a time, pupils become exasperated with meaningless rote learning and start rebelling. The rebellious stage, say the critics, begins in the junior high school. It soon becomes obvious to the student that, even though requirements are many, it is not necessary to shine in order to get by.

It also becomes obvious that as students "put out" less and less, the Apollonian demands, while still there, do not have to be taken seriously. Some tests cry for cheating. The classroom has become so artificial, say the critics, that few teachers are able to convince students to apply themselves. The content of most classes is irrelevant to the student's own life.

The charge is also made that schools in Western society are dominated by a *white*, middle-class Apollonian system. The value system of the dominant culture determines what is to be studied, and how. Grammar workbooks may ask the student to analyze sentences like the following:

If this pupil happens to be of so wayward a disposition that he would rather listen to a fictitious tale than to the narrative of some fine voyager or a wise conversation, . . . I see no other remedy but that his governor should . . . bind him prentice to a pastry-cook in some good town, though he were the son of a duke.

Montaigne

> Mother and Jeff have gone to the shopping center to buy
> vinyl upholstery cleaner, and Jeff will polish the station
> wagon in the afternoon.
> After returning from a 14-day Caribbean cruise, Grand-
> mother felt completely rejuvenated and no longer re-
> quired the services of her psychiatrist.
> Father came home from the office looking very tired after
> a full day of business conferences and was in no mood
> whatever to learn that Eddie had been swimming in the
> deep end of the pool without permission.

Apollonian critics, on their part, charge that efforts to make the lower grades "relevant" usually end in disaster. They contend that changing grammar workbooks to make them reflect a multiethnic social base does not motivate students to learn how to spell, write, and speak any more effectively than they did before. Often, they say, their hands are tied. The pressures are Dionysian rather than Apollonian. Parents are becoming less and less concerned, having already given up. School administrators are afraid of having so many students fail that the newspapers will do an exposé; hence the better part of valor is to pretend that standards are important but let students get away with anything.

High Schools and Colleges

In the secondary schools and in institutions of higher learning, the Apollonian/Dionysian conflict becomes acute. High school teachers often inherit students who, having become alienated from school long ago, are barely literate. The recourses are few:

> Remedial programs with long hours of drill and rote
> learning.
> Abandoning classical educational ideals, and taking students
> "wherever they are."
> Attempt to rekindle interest in school through innovative
> strategies like games and self-paced studies.

Those who cling to the Apollonian hope of raising the literacy of their students often sacrifice real interest in the subject in favor of having a "tight ship" in which the students perform decently on objective tests. Those who want to make education a profound and meaningful experience often sacrifice literacy and the student's ability to perform well on tests in favor of excitement in the classroom.

The degree to which a college leans toward Apollo or toward Dionysus depends upon the prestige of the institution. The pillars of education—Ivy League colleges in the United States and the distinguished institutions of Europe and Latin America—are likely to be strongly Apollonian, requiring long hours of study and the passing of rigorous examinations. Colleges and universities of more recent vintage—especially the community colleges—are likely to be more experimental and allow for Dionysian exploration. At the same time, some teachers in these institutions, deeply feeling the stigma attached to an "upstart" college with no reputation, can become ruthlessly Apollonian in their demands.

In schools given over to the free exercise of either Apollonian or Dionysian educational principles, understandable confusion reigns. Students come from a calculus class in which there is no room for personal expression to an experimental English class in which finger painting is an acceptable substitute for a theme. Some teachers within a given department acquire a reputation for being "tough" (hence Apollonian), while others are known for grading on a generous curve, accepting substitutions for last night's assignment, allowing students to steer a discussion away from the homework so that the teacher never finds out who was prepared and who was not. While a student might want to learn something substantial, the temptation to enroll in the Dionysian class may be irresistible because, since no clear objectives have been stated, most people receive high grades.

No easy solution presents itself. The Apollonian college with its traditions and high standards may be paying little attention to the real needs of the student as human being. The Dionysian teacher with a "like me, like me at any cost!" approach may be paying little attention to the real needs of a human being as student.

Apollonian Rules and Dionysian Feelings

Theory is Apollonian; practice is Dionysian. The rules are Apollonian, whether for calculus, a bridge game, or living in organized society. Every classroom must have its rules of operation. Not even a Dionysian creative unfolding can take place in a totally disorganized atmosphere.

But the flow of life is itself Dionysian, as is the willingness to adapt to new and unfamiliar circumstances. Education must allow time for experimentation, exploration, and the discovery of possibilities that may lie dormant within the student.

A rigid objective test is Apollonian all the way, particularly when answers are either true or false. But a critical essay about a poem, a novel, or a painting is also Apollonian when the teacher insists that the writer actually deal with the work in question and not respond to it on a purely personal level.

Apollonian discussions relate to theme, color, use of language, historical effect, similarity in the works of two artists, growth from one period to another in the work of the same artist, the use of a particular

I knew then that "w-a-t-e-r" meant the wonderful cool something that was flowing over my hand. That living word awakened my soul, gave it light, hope, joy, set it free!

Helen Keller

technique of fiction, symbolism, and the influence of certain key events in an author's life on his work. Apollonian analysis is critically detached, objective, maintaining perspective at all times. It is fundamental to the Western tradition, which venerates rationality and clear-sightedness.

We may argue that becoming objective and clear-sighted is a fundamental right. If students are encouraged to express themselves haphazardly at too early a stage in their growth, they are likely to have less and less to say later. For expression to be full there must be a command of words and practice in putting one word after another in some kind of meaningful sequence. Otherwise, scattered, impressionistic discourse becomes the only means of communication. ("How I Feel About the French Revolution" as a theme topic is surely more personal than historical!)

At the same time, educators of the Apollonian perspective point out, the Dionysian promise can be misleading and ultimately cruel. If students are granted excessive subjective license, if the statement "Shakespeare has nothing to offer as far as I'm concerned" is allowed to stand unchallenged, students may be sent into the world unprepared for reality, for society never has been and never will be dominated by Dionysus. What does it profit a student to go through many years of school receiving high grades for undocumented, undefended opinions based on feelings, only to discover that in the Apollonian world such feelings are irrelevant to others?

But the truth of the matter probably is that the purely Dionysian teacher does not exist. Authority is authority, when all is said and done, and often those teachers who claim to be facilitating student learning by keeping quiet have developed subtle tricks to bring about certain predetermined results. Not to share these techniques with students—allowing students to imagine that they are developing freely and according to their own true natures—can be fostering a very dangerous delusion.

There seems no genuine alternative but to provide students with both Apollonian and Dionysian approaches in the classroom. Such influences will thus enable and motivate students to take responsibility for what happens to them in higher education. The awareness that disciplined Apollonian approaches to learning are important for success in life should motivate the student to seek out the most demanding and challenging courses and teachers available. Yet as students meet these challenges, they will recognize the value of Dionysian warmth, good humor, and flexibility in their teachers. Students and teachers alike should recognize that the classroom need not imitate the world, but neither is the world going to be a very meaningful place without some principles to take into it.

GLOSSARY

Apollonian: Derived from Nietzsche's symbolic use of the name of the Greek god of light and truth, Apollo, to describe a psychological condition, the term can be either a noun—meaning "one who must have order and discipline in his life"—or an adjective, referring to the orderly, rational component in a person, a society, or a work of art.

carnival: [From the Latin *carne vale* ("farewell to the flesh")] Originally a medieval festival before Lent, highlighted by all manner of Dionysian excess. Its most notable present-day counterpart is Mardi Gras.

Dionysian: Derived from Nietzsche's symbolic use of the name of the Greek god of wine and vegetation, Dionysus, to describe a psychological condition, the term as a noun means "one who enjoys excess in pleasurable activities" or "one for whom intuition and spontaneity predominate," and as an adjective refers to the spontaneous or creative components in a person, a society, or a work of art.

polarities: Derived from the idea of natural poles (North and South; positive and negative), these are explanations for principles of alternation which appear to pervade the universe. Cyclical theories of history (e.g., Marxism) are based on certain types of polarities. In this chapter they are the Apollonian and Dionysian components, which apparently keep succeeding each other within a given personality, culture, or period of time.

NOTES

1. Tom Robbins, *Still Life with Woodpecker* (New York: Bantam Books, 1980).

2. From *The Collected Poems of A. E. Housman.* Copyright 1922 by Holt, Rinehart and Winston, Inc. Copyright 1950 by Barclays Bank Ltd. Reprinted by permission of Holt, Rinehart and Winston, Inc.

Geroge Inness, "The Lackawanna Valley," 1855
(Courtesy of the National Gallery of Art, gift of Mrs. Huttleston Rogers)

15

THE MECHANICAL MYSTIQUE: THE RELATIONSHIP BETWEEN MACHINES AND HUMAN WORTH

OVERVIEW

Though the urge to create machinery must be as old as the urge to create art, these two siblings have been raised in separate households and have grown up not understanding one another. Rousseau in the eighteenth century and Thoreau in the nineteenth both saw human salvation as the return to a "state of nature" in which one lived a non-urbanized, nonmechanical life. Doing for oneself—working with one's own hands and by the sweat of one's brow—was for them fully human and therefore more desirable than benefiting from what machines could do. Only here and there have humanists viewed machines themselves as expressions of human need, human ingenuity, human art. Today we have a roaring conflict in the humanist camp over the true value of machinery.

We are living at a time when many people fear that machines are "taking over the world." A parallel fear is that in the universities the sciences are too dominant, getting all the grant money, luring all the students away from the humanities. Many in the humanities speak of the mechanization of our world and view it as disaster. Novels like *Brave New World* (1932) and *1984* (1948) as well as movies like *Brazil* (1985) and *2001: A Space Odyssey* (1968) depict the world of tomorrow as one entirely run by machines, or by people who have lost their humanness and have come to look and think like machines.

But why need we bother with attitude toward machines which come to us from mythology, literature, philosophy, drama, the visual arts, and, yes, even music? What possible difference will it make to the conduct of our lives if we know that Leonardo in the fifteenth century appears to have made no distinction between inventing the hydrometer and painting the *Mona Lisa,* but that Mary Shelley's *Frankenstein,* published in 1818, sounded an early warning about the destruction which awaits those who tamper mechanically with nature?

The answer is very simple: As with any other crucial issue, the humanities give us *perspective.* Our artists, writers, and philosophers are people who see things many of us ignore. This chapter will not cause anyone's life to be more mechanical or less mechanical, but it will, one hopes, remind the concerned reader that there are more effective and less effective ways of relating to machines. Computers may have been modeled after the human mind at its most logical, but that mind is, after all, not a machine. Neither is the body. If we take our machines for granted, let us not take ourselves for granted.

Mechanical Models in the Ancient World

The modern world is thought of as having "begun" during that period, several centuries in duration, which witnessed the growth of cities as we know them, the founding of universities where one could study something other than theology, and, above all, a renewed respect for the power of humanity—the period traditionally called the Renaissance. The beginnings of the Renaissance can be traced with a fair degree of accuracy to stirrings among the Florentine artists of the fourteenth century, an insistence on their part that they be allowed to depict the human body *as it is* in all its naked glory. Naturally the

Computers may have been modeled after the human mind at its most logical, but that mind is, after all, not a machine.

movement caused dismay among traditionalists, including, especially, those in the Church; and it soon led to pleas for political and social reform. For the sake of convenience we shall label the times before this long transition the "ancient world." The terms *ancient* and *modern* have neither positive nor negative connotations.

Looking casually over the past, one tends to think of the ancient world as a place in which nobody enjoyed the "luxury" of machines. But in the broadest sense, a machine is anything that performs tasks by a design not given it by nature. The dam built by the beaver is a machine by our definition. So too are the tools and weapons used by primitive peoples. Some of these were probably animal bones and thus at some point were organic parts of nature, but they became machines the moment they performed designed tasks. Eventually, nature itself came to be regarded as a machine, but that was humanity using a metaphor derived from its own traditions.

The discovery of fire may be taken as a milestone in the evolution of the machine, for, though fire in one sense does exist naturally, its widespread use as a supplier of energy for human needs is a mechanical one. The wheel, of course, is a clear-cut example of the mechanical instinct at work: Early people had a need for transportation, and so they made something that would do the job.

Yet we must be cautious about describing the history of human "progress" as that of the human genius for technology. Our history is not a cause-and-effect, straight, ascending line, with each plateau marked by a technological response to an existing need. There might well have been more technology a whole lot sooner if something had not interfered. That something may have been the way people thought about machines.

A machine is anything that performs tasks by a design not given it by nature

GREEKS AND GADGETS

Before the civilization established by the Greeks, which reached its high point during the fifth century before Christ, there were wheels, weapons, and tools. There were the people at Stonehenge predicting the seasons by using their enormous stone computer. There were certain animals doing work which humanity, not nature, designed. One finds references to horsepower even before the Egyptians. The plough also existed in early agrarian societies. In fact, almost all of the mechanical additions to human life were connected with agriculture, with the means of performing work which would have been backbreaking if people had to do it by themselves.

The problem in early societies, however, so far as we know, was that there inevitably arose a sharp distinction between the haves and the have-nots, between those who found a way to rule and those who were ruled, between masters and slaves. Contemporary thinker

Fernand Braudel, now hard at work on a monumental series called *Civilization and Capitalism,* has found that mechanical progress did not occur when there were far more slaves than masters, when the cost of human labor was extremely cheap. The Pharoahs had little need to worry about more efficient methods of hauling the stones to build the pyramids when they had thousands of slaves at their command.

> The precondition for progress was probably a reasonable balance between human labour and other sources of power. The advantage was illusory when man competed with machines inordinately, as in the ancient world and China, where mechanization was ultimately blocked by cheap labour. There were slaves in Greece and Rome, and too many highly efficient coolies in China. . . . When man has a certain cost price as a source of energy, then it is necessary to think about aiding him or, better still, replacing him.[1]

It is difficult to imagine that the Greeks, to whom we credit the serious beginnings of so many other ideas, did not give us wondrous machines in addition to mathematics, art, philosophy, drama, and at least a model for democratic government. They did, however, invent the water mill—perhaps not so surprising when we remind ourselves how great a part water played in all phases of Greek art and thought. But the Greek water mill was a horizontal one, as it would be in China, Japan, and the Scandinavian countries, because, apparently, of the abundance of cheap labor to make the waterwheel turn. It is the vertical mill wheel that harnesses the energy of rapidly moving water to such an extent that fewer hands are involved.

Aristotle, the most distinguished student at the Academy, founded by Plato in perpetuation of the intellectual tradition established by *his* mentor Socrates, devised the broad outlines of scientific methodology and even introduced lab science into the curriculum of his own school, the Lyceum. But these were radical innovations. The Greeks were generally not big on science. In fact, both Socrates and Plato had much antipathy toward the speculations of some of their predecessors into the physical nature of the world. Socrates did not even enjoy taking long walks in the countryside, because these took him away from the precious time he could spend in intellectual exchanges with his students. Such machines as existed are never mentioned by Plato; assuredly they did not strike him as an index of human greatness.

In their mythology the Greeks view mechanical artifacts as playthings of the gods. Apollo, god of light and truth, drove a winged

The Greeks were not big on science. Such machines as existed are never mentioned by Plato; assuredly they did not strike him as an index of human greatness.

chariot, but the mythical first human aviator, Daedalus, tried to emulate the gods by inventing his own flying machine. Attaching waxen wings to themselves, he and his son Icarus soared into the heavens. Icarus, however, ignored his father's warning not to fly too close to the sun and became instead the first casualty in the history of flight.

A well-known classical example of advanced technology is the *deus ex machina*—literally, "god from a machine"—a device employed by the fourth-century B.C. tragic dramatist Euripides as a convenient, sometimes the only, way to end his plays. In order to untangle the affairs of unhappy mortals, a character portraying a god from Mount Olympus would descend by pulley-operated crane to stage level in a contraption probably resembling a chariot without wheels (or perhaps, we could say, a cable car). As an immortal deity, the personage could resolve the play's events any way at all, even by resurrecting the dead. No other element in Greek theater has had such a long life or exerted such a widespread influence. To this day plays and movies are given happy endings through a convenient, if illogical, twist of plot; and very much as in Euripides, the illogical event (no longer a god out of a machine, of course) has nothing to do with the characterizations that have been created. We still use the phrase *deus ex machina* to describe such sudden endings, as when the outraged wife decides to forgive her errant husband in order to bring down the curtain on sweetness and light.

Greek mythology by and large reveals a titanic struggle between gods and mortals. The machine-using gods are often shown to be jealous, scheming plotters against their inferiors, who even in defeat acquit themselves heroically, glorious in their ruin. By the time of Socrates, Plato, and Aristotle there was little serious religious belief among artists and philosophers; instead there was an obsession with the possibilities of human greatness. And there was more interest in what a *person* could do than in what a *machine* might do.

The Human Mind as Perfect Machine

Everything about Greek civilization, in full flower during the late fifth century B.C., was humanity-oriented. The nerve center of this extraordinary outburst of genius was, of course, Athens; and it is safe to say that no culture before or since has been as confident of the human potential. Under the leadership of Pericles, citizens of Athens were convinced that they were rivals of the ancient Olympian gods. Two Persian invasions—the first under Darius in 480 B.C., the second led by his son Xerxes in 440 B.C.—had been repulsed, even though the Persians greatly outnumbered the Athenians and were widely renowned for their military expertise. These successes, however, did not impress the Athenians with the need for organizing and mechanizing a civilian standing army. They wanted instead to enjoy the fruits of civilized living—sports, fine dining, theater, and intellectual discourse. While they were enjoying these pleasures, the military-minded Spartans were equiping themselves for a knockout blow against Athens, and were eventually successful. But that is another story.

In philosophy the Greek ideal was a human mind rendered perfect by rigorous study and continual exercise: in short, the closest thing possible to a true machine, except that humanity alone would deserve the credit. Aristotle created a system out of the philosophical discourse in which he and his fellow students had engaged while studying under the tutelage of Plato, and called it *logic.* Aristotle believed steadfastly that the human mind, unassisted by any force beyond itself, was capable of arriving at absolute, objective truth. For Aristotle the mind was everything that many today believe the computer to be: foolproof, error-free, even maintenance-free!

The Greek ideal was a human mind rendered perfect by rigorous study and continual exercise: in short, the closest thing possible to a true machine, except that humanity alone would deserve the credit.

At the heart of the Aristotelian logic is the *syllogism,* a relatively simple three-step thought process which guarantees that, if the first two steps are valid, the third, or conclusion, follows unavoidably and unarguably. Today, tiny silicon chips inside computers are capable of performing syllogisms, but Aristotle would insist he had thought of the steps a very long time before. To use the syllogism, one must work with a major premise and a minor premise which share a common, or middle, term. Here is the classic example used by Aristotle himself:

MAJOR PREMISE: All men are mortal.
MINOR PREMISE: Socrates is a man.
CONCLUSION: Socrates is mortal.

The middle term, *men,* guarantees an inevitable relationship between the other two terms, *mortal* and *Socrates.* Another way of putting the matter is to say: If a statement about an entire class of things is true, then a statement about a member of that class must also be true.

Other logicians were also reveling in the possibilities of the mind. Some were especially fond of devising logical paradoxes, conclusions which have to be accepted as true even if they can't *possibly* be true! Here's one famous syllogistic paradox:

MAJOR PREMISE: All Cretans are liars.
MINOR PREMISE: I am a Cretan.
CONCLUSION: (Obvious, eh what?)

What makes this syllogism so tantalizing is that we have to admit this much: *If* the premises are true—and who is to say that they are not?— then the conclusion, which also has to be true, is automatically false at the same time. The Greeks loved paradoxes because they suggest that the human mind is somehow "superior" to natural reality itself.

Rome and Technology

The traditional historical perspective might lead us to the conclusion that Rome took up where Sparta left off. The Spartans were military geniuses, not humanists, and conquered the Athenians, cultivators of peacetime arts. But the Romans, who eventually conquered the whole works, proved to be the most technologically advanced people the world had yet known. In addition to creating an awesome military machine, the Romans were tremendous engineers, road-builders, and architects of grandeur. They are also depicted in film and popular literature as fat, often cruel hedonists—the very antithesis of all that is human and good.

Despite the bad press suffered by ancient Rome, despite blood-curdling tales of gladiatorial combats unto the death, lions devouring Christians, mass crucifixions, not to mention those famous orgies, a truly great civilization did exist there, eventually undone by its excesses, true, but leaving behind far more than viaducts and roads. The Romans enslaved the Greeks but also recognized their artistic and philosophical greatness. Instead of wishing to wipe out all trace of their enemy's past, Roman patricians saw to it that the most educated slaves were assigned to their own households as tutors.

Rome endeavored to recreate if not surpass Greek theater, philosophy, poetry, mathematics, and, most particularly, the Greek art of debating. In Rome the word was as mighty a weapon as the spear, and the Roman mind, which could put words together in new and exciting ways, was thought to be the torch of humanity. Roman imperialism was, in theory at least, humanistic. By the same token, Roman machinery was not there to replace cheap labor but to proclaim the glory of civilized humanity. If Rome was destined to enlighten the earth, it needed technology to do it.

There is in Roman literature a very famous antitechnological incident, one that represents a switch in traditional views, because in this incident the Greeks are shown to be both mechanical and inhumane, while the ancestors of the Romans are depicted as noble *and* innocent of technological skill.

Virgil's *Aeneid,* the epic of Rome, traces the history of the empire back to Aeneas, a Trojan prince, who escapes destruction at the hands of the conquering Greeks and then goes on to establish the Roman state. Everybody now knows that the Greeks masterminded the fall of Troy by offering to the Trojans a "gift" of a gigantic wooden horse which secretly contained armed Greek warriors waiting to spring out under cover of darkness and massacre the whole city. (The account of the massacre is understandably *not* found in Homer's *Iliad,* the epic poem of Greece.) Instead of depicting the Trojans as naive or stupid (imagine accepting a gift taller than the highest temple), Virgil gives us a tragic picture of noble, honorable men totally unprepared

The conquest of Troy by the Greek army concealed inside a huge artificial horse is an example of anti-technological sentiments in Roman literature.

for the mechanization of warfare. No nation had ever before found the means of smuggling an entire army into the enemy camp.

Stripped of the right to defend his country in man-to-man combat, Aeneas says:

> *To arm was my first maddened impulse—not*
> *That any one had a fighting chance in arms;*
> *Only I burned to gather up some force*
> *For combat, and to man some high redoubt.*
> *So fury drove me, and it came to me*
> *That meeting death was beautiful in arms.*[2]

To die as a human being, fulfilled by meeting one's destiny in the service of one's country, is infinitely better than to be on the winning side, to be spared death, but to do so *technologically!*

God and the Machine

During the Middle Ages the Christian church, which dominated most of Western civilization, taught that neither humanity nor its technological potential was worthy of the term *perfectible.* Except for the Pope, no human being could come close to the intellectual and moral perfection found only in heavenly beings. Humankind, fallen and sinful from birth, was redeemable only through God's mercy; consequently, the church demanded of its flock total dedication to the task of doing penance for sin and striving for communion with God through continual prayer. Who would have dared pursue an interest in technology? Who would have been encouraged to waste precious time trying to invent an easier plough to pull when God required the show of humility and when humility could best be evidenced through hard labor? Besides, technological innovation meant science, and science meant using the mind for something other than striving for salvation.

These considerations notwithstanding, interest in machines began to surface in ways not necessarily technological as such. The printing press would be invented in the late fifteenth century, but long before that, there were pious monks called scribes who labored long hours by flickering candlelight to reproduce the great books of humankind—especially, of course, the Bible. Their task was to copy old manuscripts carefully, letter by letter, decorating each page with paints derived from brilliantly colored dyes and the juices of rare plants. The product of this labor was the illuminated manuscript, glorious samples of which survive and are on proud display in great libraries and museums of the world. The greatest effort was extended to conceal the fact that human hands had wrought such marvels.

By far the most extraordinary scientific achievement of the Middle Ages was the feat of engineering genius known as the Gothic cathedral. Throughout the thirteenth and fourteenth centuries there were built throughout Europe huge stone edifices with spires soaring heavenward, meant to honor the Virgin Mary and to create a mystic atmosphere within which the sinner could kneel and communicate with God, surrounded by light. With walls externally buttressed these buildings were taller than anything before known on earth, encompassing huge, open interiors that suggest the airy weightlessness of deep, infinite space. The cathedrals of Notre Dame in Paris and of Chartres are perhaps the ultimate representations of this architectural form, which, in its striving to be an earthly symbol of heavenly perfection, was devised with such mathematical precision that the stones, it is said, could stand even if there were no mortar to bind them. They remain standing, as glorious as ever.

The medieval world developed so elaborate a social system within both the monasteries and the castles of knights and their ladies fair that purely necessary machines like clocks and tools came inevitably to be invented. Even if religion decreed that work was godly, there were plenty of people who secretly believed it was also tiring, or at least that God might not object to being prayed to on knees that were not prematurely arthritic from labor.

The Name of the Rose (1980), a novel by the medievalist Umberto Eco, creates a highly detailed and believable picture of monastic life in the period, as well as of the hero, Brother William, a profound scholar of complex theology, but also a citizen (intellectually) of a world that is to come. Among his curious possessions are clocks, astrolabes, magnets, and reading glasses, which his youthful scribe Adso regards in the beginning as certain signs of witchcraft until his master tells him:

> Roger Bacon,[3] whom I venerate as my master, teaches that the divine plan will one day encompass the science of machines, which is natural and healthy magic. And one day it will be possible, by exploiting the power of nature, to create instruments of navigation by which ships will proceed . . . far more rapid than those propelled by sails or oars; and there will be self-propelled wagons . . . of such form that a man seated in them, by turning a device, can flap artificial wings. . . . And tiny instruments will lift huge weights and vehicles will allow travel on the bottom of the sea.[4]

This passage is intended, of course, to establish Brother William as something of a radical, one who incurs the distrust of older members of the order; but Eco is not spinning a mere fantasy. Sentiments like these were indeed possible during the waning years of the Middle Ages. The idea of *progress* on Earth, which is always there when the

Science and technology were not stressed during the Christian Middle Ages, because life on earth was to proceed according to God's will, not human inventiveness.

mechanical mystique is recognized for what it is, would become less and less heretical. What we call the modern world would not have been possible without this idea.

In one sense, the concept of human progress was lurking there in the scriptures from the very outset, though not stated as such; that is, of course, if we assume that "exploiting the power of nature" underlies technology and technology underlies at least a certain kind of measurable progress. Both Hebrews and Christians are taught by the Bible that God not only created humanity but made the earth as its dwelling place *and* gave it *dominion* (mastery) over that earth. Both Hebrews and Christians are taught to accept the doctrine of *creatio ex nihilo*—creation from nothing—which clearly separates the substance that is God from matter, of which Earth is composed. Though God thus rules the Earth, God is not the same as the Earth. Material substance is not divine; hence it is inferior to divine substance. But humankind, created "a little lower than the angels," is also superior to matter, for, while the body *is* material, humans also possess an immaterial soul, which entitles them to exert dominion over Earth.

An integral part of such dominion, according to Eco's Brother William, is the right to study the inner workings of nature and to *imitate* them by inventing machines. Brother William advises Adso not to "worry if they do not yet exist, because that does not mean they will not exist later. And I say to you that God wishes them to be."[5]

If pious medieval Christians had heard the myth of Daedalus and Icarus, many would have observed: "If God had intended humans to fly, He would have given them wings." A major reason for the absence of material progress on this Earth during the Middle Ages was the deep-rooted belief that everything that happened did so according to God's will. If people were going to delve seriously into science and technology, the implication had to be that God's will was just not enough, that it was all right for *human* will to exert itself, to make the Earth a better, more comfortable, and happier place.

The devastation of the four-teenth-century Black Death very probably changed the thinking of many concerning the need for medical research.

A pivotal occurrence, one that helped to hasten both the demise of medievalism and the emergence of the modern world, was the so-called Black Death, the bubonic plague which carried off a large part of the known world's population from 1348 to 1350. This tragic event was perhaps unmatched for its impact on humanity, at least until the bombing of Hiroshima in 1945. In both cases the life of every human being on Earth changed irreversibly. But whereas the latter occurrence has touched off a fear of nuclear technology, which still holds us in its grip, the former planted a seed from which would grow the realization that, if humanity were going to survive, it must substantially deepen its understanding of the Earth and what happens on it. Contemporary historian Barbara Tuchman comments on the lack of scientific inquiry which might have helped:

> Ignorance of the cause augmented the sense of horror. Of
> the real carriers, rats and fleas, the 14th century had no
> suspicion, perhaps because they were so unfamiliar. Fleas,
> though a common household nuisance, are not once men-
> tioned in contemporary plague writings, and rats only in-
> cidentally. . . . The actual plague bacillus, *Pasturella
> pestis,* remained undiscovered for another 500 years.[6]

In 1348 the medical faculty at the University of Paris, probably the
leading institution of higher learning in all the world at the time, made
a careful "scientific" analysis of the plague, which was to kill half the
city, and "ascribed it to a triple conjunction of Saturn, Jupiter, and
Mars in the 40th degree of Aquarius said to have occurred on March
20, 1345."[7]

The church allowed the practice of medicine but not the
study and development of it. This would have required the dissection
of corpses—very much against church law. Doctors ministering to the
sick and dying used spells, potions, and, as we have seen, the signs of
the zodiac.

Two obvious consequences inevitably followed. Since the
heretofore cheap labor force was decimated, the market value of
people began to rise, a precondition for the development of machines.
Such development would take a long time. It would be four centuries
before the full dawn of the Industrial Revolution. But the impetus was
there. People were interested in machines. Galileo would invent the
telescope and discover the moons of Jupiter three centuries after the
Black Death.

A second consequence was a profound, philosophical one. It
had to do with God's will. If the plague had indeed been sent by
God—or, at least, if He had done nothing to prevent it or *could* have
done nothing, then should humanity sit back passively and simply *accept* whatever happened? More than any other single belief, the idea
that humankind could and would control its own destiny is what really
brought the dawning of the modern world.

By a curious irony the intellectual conditions for the modern
world's love affair with machinery were already there—like an underground spring looking for an outlet. Without being aware of the implications for a future in which faith in the machine would be as dominant as faith in a divine force had been, the medieval church gave the
world a belief in mechanical perfection, except a perfection that had
been wrought by God, not people. As presented by the church, the
universe was indeed a marvelous machine. It was formed in the perfect shape—the circle—with the Earth at dead center and the moon,
the five planets (Mercury, Venus, Mars, Jupiter, and Saturn), the sun
and all the stars (sometimes referred to as the lanterns of heaven) re-

volving around it on circular wheels that made sublime music as they turned. This perfect cosmos appeared to guarantee that human technology would be delayed indefinitely, if not forever. No machine invented by humanity could match the celestial orbits or the regularity of the seasons. Despite Brother William's prophecy, the statement was clear: God was master of both mortals and machines.

THE CHANGING MYSTIQUE

In the Renaissance the machine came to be viewed as an extension of human power. Leonardo was an inventor as much as he was an artist.

Today we take for granted the relationship between the machine and us. That is, we know we invented machinery because of the human needs it could serve. We know (sort of) how important the machine is to our lives, how different, how strange, how utterly unrecognizable life would be if all machinery were suddenly to vanish. Despite the recognition, our artists, as we have said, are not especially pro-technology. They continually warn us that becoming too complacent and dependent on machinery is not good for the human soul.

At the time of the Renaissance, however, this attitude was not prevalent. The idea of the machine seemed to support the noble view of humanity which was beginning to emerge, for the machine was humanity's *own* discovery. There were not that many machines or even that many fantasies of machines, but the genius of one particular man gives us a supreme example of Renaissance technological thinking: Leonardo da Vinci.

Leonardo

The pioneer groundwork for a mechanized world can be found in the fantastic imaginings of Leonardo da Vinci (1452–1519), whose career epitomizes everything we have come to label "Renaissance." Philosopher, poet, artist, futurist, Leonardo has been accorded by history that rarest of titles *Homo universale*. Leonardo is widely celebrated as a great artist (perhaps the greatest?) of the Renaissance. If he had never conceived of his amazing machines, his reputation would not suffer one iota. Yet one can also say that, had he never painted "The Last Supper" or the "Mona Lisa," he could rightfully claim his share of space in history books on the strength of his technological imagination alone. How can one man have achieved so much? Is there any relationship between artist and inventor? The answer is a decided yes.

Leonardo was a person of limitless energy, of boundless curiosity, and of a stubborn determination to do everything, especially that which was considered impossible. This characteristic he shared not only with his fellow artist Michelangelo but with generations of scientists to come.

The extent of his scientific zeal has been fully grasped only in comparatively recent times. His visions were scrawled and entered into huge, almost unreadable notebooks, but the painstaking study of centuries has revealed a range of interests unmatched in science today, except perhaps by Albert Einstein. Leonardo's concern for the realistic portrayal of the human body led him to an obsession with anatomy, to inquiries into the circulation of the blood; and the artist's delight in the phenomenon of seeing led him to the scientific investigation of optics. He was a meteorologist as well as geologist centuries before people seriously began to question the age of the Earth. Scientists today acknowledge that his fanciful flying machines came whirling out of an imagination that nonetheless understood aerodynamics. Like a true son of his Roman ancestors, Leonardo was fascinated by hydraulics, the study of the mechanical properties of water (he invented the hydrometer, a machine that measures the specific gravity of liquids).

There was no such devastating event as the bubonic plague in Leonardo's lifetime—not one that wiped out so much of the world—but there appears to have been in northern Italy a storm of such incredible fury that the artist was impelled to write to a friend:

> At first the Winds attacked us ferociously with all their might and made war upon us. They were joined by toppling mountains of snow, which filled all our valleys and destroyed a great part of our town. Not content with this, a sudden flood of water deluged the low-lying parts of the city. In addition, there came a sudden rain, or rather a ruinous hurricane, carrying water, sand, mud and stones in its path, entangled with roots, branches, broken trees, and all this, rushing through the air, fell upon us. . . .
>
> You can thus imagine our condition; yet all these sufferings are as naught compared with those said to be in store for us.[8]

There are theories that none of this ever really happened, that Leonardo, especially in his later life, was obsessed with the Apocalypse, with the ending of the world through a series of disasters. But even if the theories are valid, we must also add that Leonardo does not appear to have found a solution in paying greater homage to God. Nonetheless, solutions he *did* seek, and they were in the human domain. He longed to see, for example, a world in which humanity would unite against the ills that might be visited upon it:

> Men shall speak one to another from the most countries and shall give answer *by writing letters from one country to another.*

> Men shall speak one to another, and shall touch and em-
> brace one another, though they stand in different hemi-
> spheres, and they shall understand each other's language.[9]

Though he did not realize it, Leonardo was invoking future machines which would make possible rapid forms of communication (television, satellites, computers, telex relays)—humanity using machines to improve its lot.

Leonardo was also a military genius, invoking science rather than God as had been the case with the so-called Holy Wars of the Middle Ages. In a letter he wrote:

> If during a siege the engines cannot be effectively used on
> account of the height or strength of the town wall, I have
> means to destroy every tower or fortification. . . . I know
> of a kind of siege-machine which is very light and easy to
> move and which can be used to hurl firebombs. . . . I
> know how to construct subterranean caves and winding
> passages which can be made without any noise. . . . I can
> make sound, indestructible armoured vehicles. . . . Where
> cannons cannot be used I shall construct stone-throwing
> machines, catapults, slings and other instruments, amazing
> and hereto completely unknown.[10]

That the otherwise astonishing modernity of this idea is clearly of another age, however, is indicated by the absence of any sign that the writer is acting under orders from a superior officer, a surrender of autonomy quite characteristic of our present-day machine-dominated consciousness. Leonardo as a man of the Renaissance clearly sees himself as master, the machine as slave.

A Fascination with Clocks

Not only the Black Death but another event, intellectually if not physically devastating, contributed to the demise of medievalism. This was the theory advanced by the Polish astronomer Nicolaus Copernicus (1473–1543), using the most primitive telescopic instruments, that the Earth actually moves about the Sun, not vice versa. Since the medieval church taught as a matter of strictest doctrine that God had created the universe with the Earth at its center, one can imagine the blow struck by the Copernican theory. Was the Earth indeed just one of several planets that rotated about the Sun? Moving the Earth away from its former position at dead center was tantamount to divesting it *and* human life of importance. The idea that the circle was the perfect geometric shape was deeply ingrained in medieval thinking, and the center of the circle was obviously the only place for a God-created humanity.

Though the Copernican view was a long way from being scientifically proved (and would not be actually proved until the nineteenth century), the theory itself was enough to set inquiring minds in motion. The primary impact, however, was not the loss of the idea that this was a perfect universe; in the centuries following Copernicus what lost ground was the idea that the teachings of the church were infallible. The church found itself in a most precarious position, having to defend a belief which fewer and fewer scientists would support.

Perhaps the most dramatic confrontation occurred during the seventeenth century, when Galileo (1564–1642) invented the telescope and saw many more wonders in the heavens than Copernicus had suspected or that the church had information about, including the moons of Jupiter. This revelation suggested that Earth's little moon was not a major heavenly body designed by God to revolve about our planet, but that it, like the Earth itself, was simply one item in perhaps a vast store of cosmic entities, whirling, Galileo was convinced, about the Sun. Galileo would, of course, ultimately retract his heretical theories, but the retraction could not reverse the tide of new thinking.

As the Renaissance gained momentum, moving from Italy to France and Spain, and then northward into England and Germany, interest in science also increased. Very likely Spain, with its long standing ties to Islamic culture, contributed much scientific fervor, for, while the otherworld orientation of the Christian Middle Ages was showing little interest in a technology for *this* world, the Arab world was refining the scientific methodology that Aristotle had devised. Christian faith did not diminish so much as learn to live side by side with the new scientific zeal for discovering everything about the Earth and the universe. The major view which emerged from the new consciousness was that, even *without* being earth-centered, the universe was a perfect and—as Isaac Newton would reveal—a mechanical marvel.

Isaac Newton (1642–1727) was another *Homo universale*, like Leonardo, except that most of his intellectual energies and tremendous insights were focused on physical science. Whether or not the apple story is true, Newton formulated the law of universal gravitation when he was only 24, working out the complex mathematical proof when he was in his mid-forties. He formulated the three basic laws of motion, which were generally accepted until the early twentieth century, when they were replaced by Einstein's theories of relativity. The Newtonian universe, a product of seventeenth-century physics and mathematics, was also one of perfect order, in which the planets and the stars revolved around the sun but were held in their orbits by *the eternal force of gravity*. It was a spectacle that was seen to continue on into infinity.

One of history's most intriguing coincidences is the emergence of sophisticated clock mechanics during the same era which saw the birth of the Newtonian worldview. Clocks themselves, of one

The Newtonian universe of the seventeenth century was a grand machine, created, some believed, by God but left to operate on its own according to mechanical, unchanging laws. This view lent even more glory to machines.

sort or another, had been in existence ever since the third century before Christ with the invention of the sundial. Even before that, people had a sense of time's passing and a desire to measure it, to use time as a means of structuring the consciousness of reality. Thousands of years ago the Chinese measured time by watching a flame traveling from knot to knot along a rope. Other ancient people used notched candles or hourglasses. During the Middle Ages the bell towers of the cathedrals tolled the passage of each 60 minutes, though we cannot be sure how accurately. Late in the sixteenth century Galileo experimented with a pendulum and discovered that the time it took the pendulum to swing from one side to another was constant. This discovery led to the first regulated clock machines—the first "tick-tock."

Since Newton's universe operated with order and precision, like a well-crafted pendulum clock, an analogy was made between the two. The clock analogy, as a matter of fact, was the first extensively employed argument advanced to prove God's existence without disturbing the course of scientific thought. Newton himself called the universe a clock, and God the inevitable clock-maker.

Reconciling religion with the new science became for many an obsession. One of the most popular works of the post-Newton period was *Natural Theology, or Evidence of the Existence and Attributes of the Deity,* by the British clergyman and philosopher William Paley (1743–1805), which uses the clock analogy to prove that (1) the universe is a nearly perfect mechanism that demonstrates careful planning and design and (2) one cannot conceive of a design without accepting the existence of a designer. Paley extended the analogy to account for the apparent evils which beset the world. Do not clocks sometimes go awry? Does this fact make us lose faith in them? For Paley it "is not necessary that a machine be perfect, in order to show with what design it was made."

Nature as Grand Machine

The attempt to prove God's existence by pointing to creation as a mechanical marvel led to a new kind of religion which captivated minds in Europe and America during the eighteenth century. Given a generic name—*deism*—it was founded on the belief that order and design cannot just create themselves. The mechanical universe was the creation of a rational superbeing, God, who then "went away" and left it to run by itself, as any good machine should be able to do.

One of the strongest exponents of deism was Thomas Paine (1771–1809), the American author of *Common Sense,* the pamphlet that spread the gospel of the American Revolution throughout the world. Paine was a professional radical who could not tolerate either a government or a traditional religion that held its power by suppressing the rights of human beings to question and to dissent. After the

American Revolution was won, he involved himself with the struggle of the French citizens against *their* king, and finally, in *The Age of Reason,* he attacked Christianity from a scientific point of view. The apostle Thomas, he declared, could not believe in the resurrection of Christ because he had not seen it for himself, and *"neither will I."*

For Paine, as for all the deists, the word of God is not to be found in any mythological "revelation," but "is the creation we behold." Refusing to believe anything that does not make "common sense," Paine says reason requires us to believe that this creation we behold did not happen by itself. God is thus a *first cause*—the same term employed by Aristotle. In fact, Paine is all for discarding the Christian writings of many centuries and going straight back to the insights of the Greeks. Yet God's having made the universe, Paine argues, is no reason to be bound by the rules and regulations of the church. Theology "is the study of human opinions and of human fancies *concerning* God . . . not the study of God himself in the works that he has made."

So the deists in effect used God to account for what would otherwise be unexplainable, but they dispensed with prayer, sin, church-going, redemption, and all the other elements of a religion founded on the idea of a humanized God the Father who continually watches over his errant children. Their writings had a devastating impact on the society of their time, attracting followers among those who believed in human rights and in the integrity of the individual regardless of social rank or ethnic background.

Little by little the focus of eighteenth-century thought came to be nature itself, not the issue of who was responsible for creating this wonderful machine. By the latter part of the eighteenth century the worship of nature as the source of life was a major trend among artists and philosophers on both sides of the Atlantic. The strong belief in "natural" things led to a focus on "natural" rights. Democracy, as we understand the term today, had its beginnings in the late-eighteenth-century nature movement. Both the Declaration of Independence and the Constitution were the work primarily of deists, who argued that oligarchy (power invested in a privileged few) and monarchy were human fabrications, not institutions derived from natural law. In the natural state all people were equal and, if left alone to be guided by their own conscience, honest and trustworthy. Nature was not only a perfectly operating machine, but a moral one. We should therefore not be surprised to learn that among writers and philosophers there were few champions of the Industrial Revolution, which by the late eighteenth century was already starting to attract enemies.

Humanists became depressed over what was happening to cities on both sides of the Atlantic. In the early part of the eighteenth century, industry tended to be located in rural areas, close to the major source of energy, which was then wood. But the replacement of

wood with coal and improved road systems that made the transportation of coal readily possible led inevitably to the growth of the town
factories and, of course, the migration of the work force from the country to the city. The aristocracy fled beyond the city limits (the beginning of today's suburban culture), leaving the cities to the lower
classes, some members of which, because of rising wages and the demand for labor, soon became the middle class. The latter in turn created lucrative markets for domestically produced goods, particularly
clothing made from cotton.

Humanists took note of what life was like for the poor in the
crowded, garbage-strewn streets of the city, where ancient professions
like thievery and prostitution flourished once more. "London," by the
nature-oriented poet William Blake (1757–1827), just about sums up
the situation:

> *I wander thro' each charter'd street,*
> *Near where the charter'd Thames does flow,*
> *And mark in every face I meet*
> *Marks of weakness, marks of woe.*
>
> *In every cry of every Man,*
> *In every Infant's cry of fear,*
> *In every voice, in every ban,*
> *The mind-forg'd manacles I hear.*
>
> *How the chimney-sweeper's cry*
> *Every black'ning church appalls;*
> *And the hapless Soldier's sigh*
> *Runs in blood down Palace walls.*
>
> *But most thro' midnight streets I hear*
> *How the Youthful Harlot's curse*
> *Blasts the new-born Infant's tear,*
> *And blights with plagues the Marriage hearse.*

The poem's most famous turn of phrase "mind-forg'd manacles" is a
reference to the loss of freedom people suffer when their natural
selves are perverted by rational activity, including the establishment of
institutions governed by rational, logical, but soulless purposes. The
effect of the eighteenth-century factory system, one such institution, is
summed up by one historian:

> But in the factory the regimentation enforced by the ma-
> chine system changed people's attitude to work. Now
> there was no longer personal freedom to work or stop as
> you chose. The new discipline aroused animosity and a
> sense of servitude.[11]

In literature, philosophy, art, and music the late eighteenth century sent forth a vigorous outcry against industrialization. This widespread movement is called Romanticism, and it is marked by strong idealistic feelings for nature, the idealization of the simple life, an antiintellectual strain—the belief that intelligence is responsible for the evils of modern civilization, that human reason and nature are at odds with each other—and, very particularly, a strong push for human rights, for a renewed assertion of human dignity, so often trampled upon in the capitalistic countries denounced as exploiting masses of people for profit. Both the United States and England were very much into the slave trade, we must remember. Even a staunch exponent of democracy like Thomas Jefferson held slaves without, apparently, seeing any contradiction whatever between the practice of slavery and the cause of independence. The economic well-being of nations in both hemispheres depended on cheap labor in India, Africa, and the Caribbean. In prosperous countries the poor did not fare much better than imported slaves or exploited natives. They lived in squalor, working long hours in coal mines or cotton factories. Though unionism did not yet exist, though the down-trodden had no political leverage, the Romantic writers were there early as prophets of social unrest on behalf of minorities.

With machines came urbanization, and with urbanization came, in the opinion of many poets and novelists, the degradation of the human being.

Central to Romanticism was the plea for strong, often unbridled, individualism, for breaking stiff social barriers, even shocking those who would uphold traditional mores at all costs—not unlike the "do your own thing" bent of the 1960s. One of the more strident antisocial voices was that of George Gordon, Lord Byron (1788–1824), whose life and work embody the extreme characteristics of the Romantic mind; even apart from his powerful poetry, the Byronic outlook on life, the Byronic *behavior,* has much in common with a way of being that favors the individual against the tyranny of established authority.

The Romantic movement in literature during the early nineteenth century was in part an attack on the machine and on science, and an invitation to return to nature.

Byron's words, written almost 200 years ago, sound very modern. In fact many very current ideas had their roots in the Romantic movement.

> *I have not loved the World, nor the World me;*
> *I have not flattered its rank breath, nor bowed*
> *To its idolatries a patient knee,*
> *Nor coined my cheek to smiles,—nor cried aloud*
> *In worship of an echo . . .*

Byron's heroes are all feeling, all passion. They act upon impulse and are always right, even though they continually fly in the face of convention and morality. Like many others in the Romantic movement, Byron is antireason, viewing human logic as a deliberate and tragic deviation from nature. If we lived as nature intended, we would be spontaneous and deliciously happy. The Industrial Revolution in many respects supported not spontaneity but a mechanical, imposed discipline.

If Byron had lived in the 1960s, he would have led protest marches, eaten only natural foods, made love on the slopes of muddy Woodstock, been in and out of jail innumerable times, and without a doubt indulged in certain substances forbidden by law but believed by their exponents to put to sleep the rational self in order to release the deeper, truer, hence *natural,* self. He would assuredly have been against the machines that corrupt the natural environment.

If he had lived in the 1960s, he might also, however, have been less conspicuous than he was in the House of Lords in 1819; and perhaps something of what he stood for was needed at the time. Few artists have earned an epitaph like the one given him by the German poet Goethe: "[He was] a personality in eminence such as never had been and is not likely to come again; a fiery mass of living valor hurling itself on life." That life was a short one. Byron died at age 36 fighting for Greek independence. The gun fired in a human cause was the one machine he found useful.

Frankenstein: An Early Prophecy

In 1818 there appeared a novel, in three slender volumes, the work of a 20-year-old girl, that would provide one of the cornerstone antimachine myths of all time. It was *Frankenstein, or The Modern Prometheus;* its author, Mary Shelley, wife of the famous poet and daughter of the radical political philosopher William Godwin. Victor Frankenstein, the central character, is not the mad scientist of the well-known movie adaptation. Rather, he is a sensitive, gentle person intrigued from childhood by science (then called "natural philosophy") and eager to grow up and learn everything that could possibly be learned so that he might help to make life happier for all people. As he matures, he finds himself particularly concerned with the way the body functions:

> Wealth was an inferior object; but what glory would attend the discovery, if I could but banish disease from the human frame, and render man invulnerable to any but a violent death![12]

But how is he to find the secret of immortality unless he first learns where life comes from?

For Mary Godwin, friend of Romantic writers, married to Percy Bysshe Shelley at the age of 16, the miracle of nature was an all-consuming passion. She and her husband loved especially the grandeur of lakes and mountains. Switzerland, the locale of the novel, was her favorite spot on Earth. Nature was to be admired, adored, worshipped, not analyzed; and certainly no mere human being had the right to a comprehension of its mysteries. The tragic flaw of Victor Frankenstein is that he is a man who aspires to become greater than his nature will allow. Not content with understanding how the spark of life enters lifeless matter—from electricity, he is convinced—he must go one step further: He must assemble parts of cadavers into an eight-foot superman who will represent the perfection of the species and, of course, live forever.

The outcome of his experiments is, physically, as everyone knows, not what he anticipated:

> I had selected his features as beautiful. Beautiful!—Great God! His yellow skin scarcely covered the work of muscles; and arteries beneath; his hair was of a lustrous black, and flowing; his teeth of a pearly whiteness; but these luxuriances only formed a more horrid contrast with his watery eyes, and seemed almost of the same colour as the dun white sockets in which they were set, his shrivelled complexion, and straight black lips.[13]

Yet the "daemon," as the author calls him, since he has no other name, is not naturally evil. Having received the spark of life from the lightning bolt, he is, like his creator, a child of nature and therefore basically kind and gentle. Along with her fellow Romantics, Mary Shelley believed implicitly that nature, undisturbed, is good at heart.

What happens, what causes the "daemon" to become a wanton, vicious killer, is that he is rejected by society. "Misery," he explains after he has murdered his first victim, Frankenstein's younger brother, "made me a fiend." The spark of life has given him, hideous and misshapen though he may be, the noblest of feelings. He is a vegetarian, believing it immoral to consume animal flesh. Overhearing an account of the discoveries of America, he finds himself weeping at the fate of the "original inhabitants." Hiding out in a farmhouse, he even stops stealing food when he observes members of the family sharing what little they have with each other. When at last he reveals himself to the farm family, expecting to be received joyously into their circle, he is attacked and brutally driven from the house. His natural sense of love perverted, he seeks revenge against society by destroying innocence: the hero's brother, his closest friend, and finally his bride on the wedding night.

For Mary Shelley, evil springs from the institutions of humankind, including the family circle, which becomes a perversion of love when it turns vicious in the act of protecting itself. Social order, which reason sees as indispensable to existence, also goes awry when it becomes pure form—that is, a machine in itself operating relentlessly without concern for the individuals it may destroy in order to survive. Human institutions are thus like Frankenstein's monster, created for good reasons, but becoming twisted and dangerous out of self-interest. The law, for example, has been established to protect society as a whole and to prevent wanton acts of destruction. Yet in the novel, an innocent woman is hanged for the murder of Frankenstein's brother because the law demands a culprit and she happened to be at the scene of the crime.

The most bitter irony of the novel, however, is not the effect human reason has on social institutions, but rather what Frankenstein's intellectual brilliance does to *him*. Here is the man of science—and science is supposed to be cool, objective, concerned only for the truth of things—the man who once wanted to be the savior of the earth, now obsessed with the destruction of his own creation. Victor Frankenstein becomes more irrationally murderous than the creature. In an extraordinary finale, anticipating Melville's *Moby-Dick* by over 30 years, Frankenstein pursues his demon relentlessly to the very ends of the earth, insanely believing that, once the monster is destroyed, all the world's evils will automatically disappear.

In the end it is Frankenstein, not the demon, who dies—from cold and disease. Our final glimpse of the monster is that of a wretched creature, no longer larger than life, but dwarfed by glass mountains as he sails on a raft of ice into a mist, there to meet who knows what destiny; and we feel the monster belongs nowhere else but in a primordial limbo which exists outside of time and deep within which lie the true secrets of life, unleashed but never comprehended or controlled by Victor Frankenstein.

There are parallels to this ending in other works of art, especially in music, which is the understandable medium for an expression of mystic feelings about nature, feelings that reach beyond the domain of language. The reader is advised to listen, for example, to *Symphony Number Seven* by the British composer Ralph Vaughn-Williams, appropriately subtitled the "Antarctic Symphony." Making strings sound like echoes from an untraveled land and using human voices in ways that hypnotize the listener, the composer seems to be reaching into the very heart of existence: where it began, a secret that in the music keeps receding from us, like Mary Shelley's demon "borne away by the waves, and lost in darkness and distance."

The language of *Frankenstein* may strike the modern reader as ornate and artificial and the characters as more than slightly unbelievable, accustomed as we are to psychological realism in fiction. But there is nothing dated about Mary Shelley's attitude toward nature and the tragic results of human tampering with it. Are there not definite parallels between Victor Frankenstein's well-intentioned efforts to release the secret "stuff" of life and similar contemporary efforts to release and then control nuclear energy for the supposed betterment of humanity? Frankenstein's laboratory may seem a bit old-fashioned, but it is closer to Chernobyl than the author could have known.

SWITCH ON, TUNE OUT

Despite Mary Shelley's grim prophecies, the natural world of 1818 was quite accessible—a pleasant carriage drive from the dirtiest street in London. Since her day, however, the Industrial Revolution has proved a clear victory for the mechanizing forces of the human world, and now, at the doorstep of the twenty-first century, many humanists tell us we are faced with only two possible questions: "How may we best relate to machines without becoming their slaves?" and "Is the damage we have done to the natural world irreversible?"

The aim of this chapter has not been to argue with or even question the validity of mechanization. People drive their cars in comfort to visit the ruins of the hut in which Thoreau roughed it at Walden Pond, appalled at discovering a hot dog stand complete with the same kind of microwave oven they have in their kitchens. The pond—a local swimming hole for most of this century—is dangerously on the brink of pollution, although water-treatment technology can perhaps save it. Thousands of tourists stop each year to visit the retreat of St. Kevin the hermit at beautiful Glendalough in Ireland, but to our knowledge nobody tries to move in. Who could think of living for very long without a TV, a VCR, a blender, or even a simple gadget like a can opener? No one reading this book could survive in what the Romantics used to call a "state of nature."

Yet this *is* a book about the humanities as a technique for living, and humanists generally stress freedom of choice. They continue to tell us that our heritage is our human potential—our creativity, our imagination, our ability to conduct rational discourse and to see possibilities where none apparently existed before. For this reason they warn against an *overdependence* on machinery. Used with restraint and critical intelligence, machines can add significantly to the quality of our lives. Used as a substitute for human creativity, they could turn out to be the ultimate enemy of humankind.

As he grew accustomed to the great gallery of machines, he began to feel the forty-foot dynamos as a moral force, much as the early Christians felt the Cross.

Henry Adams

Ownership

People like to own machines the way they used to like to own animals, territories, and other people. Often the purpose served by the machine is less important than the fact of ownership itself, that it represents upward mobility. Every new machine that can be purchased is a sign that the owner is advancing financially. Consider the following machines or mechanical gadgets for their relative importance to our basic needs:

washer/dryer
garage door opener
home computer
riding lawn mower
home and auto alarm
    systems
vacuum cleaner and
    attachments
Walkman headset

central air-conditioning
dishwasher
electric car windows
compact disc player
videocassette recorder
automobile telephone
telephone answering
    machine

Unquestionably some of these mechanical marvels perform tasks which were once laborious and time-consuming. Who wants to go back to washing clothes in a nearby stream? Who would give up air-conditioning if financial constraints did not require the sacrifice? Writers often wonder how they ever got along without word processors, which greatly simplify the once-arduous task of editing a manuscript.

The need to own machines is one of the cornerstones of contemporary economic systems. As "new and improved" models appear, those who rush to get them are surely providing jobs for many people. Market research discloses that many who can barely afford minimum shelter and nutrition insist on having cable television even if this means doing without some basic necessities. Nor must one shake a head at the "foolishness" of such a choice. In a technologically oriented society, not having cable television can create a very real sense of privation, much greater than the longing for higher-quality foods. Making a blanket assertion that technology is automatically dehumanizing is both arrogant and unrealistic.

Today we have no choice but to live with machines. The question is: Do we forget about the creative imagination which belongs to us as human beings and allow machines to both think and create for us?

Motorcycles and Other Choices

An argument can easily be made for the decision not to get a remote control for one's television or acquire a new car every year for the sole purpose of demonstrating to the neighbors that one is doing very well. There are people who have made a conscious, calculated choice to declare their lack of dependence on excessive machinery, who in fact see machinery as a barrier against reality.

Ever since the 1960s, that era which raised the social dropout to the status of new American hero, the motorcycle has been for some a great symbol of independence and a means of coming closer to reality. Machine though it may be, the "bike" is far easier to maintain and operate than large automobiles or complex sports cars with their overhead twin cams, their 5.0 fuel-injected turbos and dual-exhaust systems, their digital instrument panels, not to mention the multiple fog lights which many drivers keep burning even in clear weather, allowing their auto "extras" to make a statement about the owner's economic status.

True, the motorcycle easily makes a statement of its own, particularly about the driver's alleged sexual prowess. But there are any number of bikers who find motorcycle driving a meaningful escape from the tangled complexities of modern life, back to a simpler way of life which the nomadic American cowboy once enjoyed.

Zen and the Art of Motorcycle Maintenance (1974) is Robert M. Pirsig's autobiographical account of how he left the sheltered, safe, but sterile confines of a university campus to take to the open road on a bike. He contrasts riding a motorcycle with driving a gadget-packed automobile, noting the closeness to the road and vivid consciousness of things to be seen and experienced along the road as opposed to the sealed-in journey of the car driver, doors and windows electrically locked, air-conditioning and radio turned up. An automobile journey is one that passes through time; a motorcycle journey passes through space:

> You're completely *in* the scene, not just watching it any more, and the sense of presence is overwhelming. That concrete whizzing by five inches below your foot is the real thing . . . and the whole thing, the whole experience, is never removed from immediate consciousness.[14]

Furthermore, bike owners generally become much more knowledgeable about the inner workings of their simple machines than car owners, who live in dread of unexpected and strange noises and in total dependence upon factory-trained experts who know how to order and replace expensive electronic components:

> I check the engine temperature with my hand. It's reassuringly cool. I put in the clutch and let it coast for a second in order to hear it idling. Something sounds funny and I do it again. It takes a while to figure out that it's not the engine at all. There's an echo from the bluff ahead that lingers after the throttle is closed. Funny.[15]

Pirsig's work rudely confronts us with a truth we may not have had the time to think about: Machines may "do the work" for us, but *they also alienate us from the very thing they are supposed to replace.* If the automobile is meant to make easier a trip from A to B, it not only erases the sense of what it means to go from A to B, but it conceals from us the fact that *it* is a traveler. When, for example, you make a journey on foot, you may well grow tired. You become aware

Often a move to smaller quarters makes us suddenly realize how many gadgets we can do without.

of what is happening inside your body as a result of the demands of the hike. The automobile, on the other hand, is expected to be what ambitious advertisements often proclaim: ALMOST MAINTENANCE-FREE! Perhaps we should envy those who live on tight incomes and are forced to become intimate friends with their old clunkers.

Pirsig could have afforded "better" things, but chose not to have them. One of the heartening developments of our time is that many are rejecting mechanical comforts because of the environmental price they may have to pay for them. Think how many of our machines are run by fuel—either petroleum products or electricity, which frequently also depends upon oil. Many today find they can do without electric irons and instead wear clothes which are either wrinkle-free or are stylishly wrinkled to begin with. Where climate permits, people are turning away from air-conditioning or elaborate heating systems.

Often a move to smaller quarters makes us suddenly realize how many gadgets we can do without. When family size is reduced and father and mother decide to live in a trailer or on a boat, they find out what has been truly important in their lives and what was purchased on a whim. Even the "indispensable" VCR, which won't fit in the new quarters, can be found to have been a foolish investment. How many programs, recorded because the automatic apparatus was there for the use, remain vital? How many could easily have been missed? How many great opportunities would *really* have been lost had there been no answering machine? Do we *really* need to take all seven cameras? How many photographs of trips do we ever *really* look at years (or even days) later? Is a picture as memorable as a conversation? Even the photographic likeness of a departed loved one . . . does it *really* capture the essence of the person? Don't memories do that better?

Whether Hal could actually think was a question which had been settled by the British mathematician Alan Turing back in the 1940s. Turing had pointed out that, if one could carry out a prolonged conversation with a machine—whether by typewriter or microphone was immaterial—without being able to distinguish between its replies and those a man might give, then the machine was thinking, by any sensible definition of the word.

Arthur C. Clarke, 2001

Mechanical Thinking

What has a lot of writers and philosophers most worried is that the machine is not just replacing conversation, but is replacing *thought itself.* How ironic that the superior intellectual faculties which caused us to create technology may be destroyed *by* it!

Gary Benson, director of Business Management Programs at the University of Wyoming, Casper, has determined that although high-tech (computer) industries may lure the best and the brightest of business school grads, in the end they deaden the very skills they claim to have required.

> The result is jobs and work environments where people do not have to use their minds—an environment where computers, robots and other forms of high technology do the "thinking" and people are only appendages to the pro-

cess. Such an environment produces drug and alcohol abuse and an epidemic of job theft and work-related accidents.[16]

Back in the 1960s, Marshall McLuhan was discovering the importance of media in shaping our consciousness and making us aware of how deeply we are affected by television: the size of the screen, the breaking up of reality into units followed by commercials, and so on. We have yet to develop a full sensitivity to the long-range effects of computerization and its offshoots. Why waste time trying to figure out one's financial future when the home computer can do it? (Do we ever really determine what we do with the time thus saved?) Why have conversations when there are computer games to fill the void?

Humanistic concerns about an increasingly "computerized" world are perhaps helpful as reminders that we must stay active in our thinking and not be the willing slaves of computer software that continually commands us to "Press Enter" and leads us methodically through a series of programmed steps. The joy of carrying out the commands and being rewarded with a new screen image is still relatively new to us, and we may be forgiven if we, the lowly consumers, take a certain measure of pride when we figure out the instructions and keep the machine contentedly moving ahead. But there is also the reverse, the humiliation which comes when the screen informs us that our instructions are unintelligible.

On the other hand, if we *do* remain active in our thinking and aggressive in our use of the computer, we may remember that it is one of *us* who invented the dad-blamed thing, that *we* developed the programs which so astound us when we get them working. Writers who have incorporated the theme of computers into plays, films, and fiction still tend to see them as the very termination of human creativity; but the time may not be too far off when we will have a "user-friendly" computer that is a warm, sympathetic ally in a human cause — not a dread *thing* without feeling. That the human mind could have conceived of and perfected such a machine is, after all, as worthy of the humanist's attention as a great work of art. Science fiction has made much of computers which operate entirely on their own, oblivious to human needs. But no one has yet met a computer that does not require a human finger to turn it on.

What is troublesome, however, is that many of us for much of the day do think mechanically without realizing it. Perhaps this helps to explain the strong antimechanical bent among humanists. Take, for example, our day-to-day vocabulary, including the casual idioms which spring to our lips without conscious pre-thought: How many of us talk about "losing it" as a reference to the disruption of ordinary behavioral patterns? The phrase is also, we note, a reference to a machine's failure to work properly, as in "The car is losing its zip" or "The

A telltale sign of our dependence on machines is the number of mechanical terms we use unconsciously: "How goes it?" "I'm losing it." "I'm getting it together."

Everybody will have realized from personal experience how closely we are integrated psychologically with the instruments that serve us. When a car bumps into an obstacle, we wince more through an actual referral of pain than through a sudden premonition of the sour and skeptical face of an insurance assessor. When the car is running badly and labors up hills, we ourselves feel rather poorly.

Sir Peter Medawar

TV picture is losing its sharpness." If we "lose it" for too long, we suffer a "breakdown" and perhaps go to a "shrink" to be restored to a good mental "condition".

Like the mind, the body is unconsciously compared to a machine that is expected to give faithful service for many years. Just as we count on mechanics to "fix" strange noises in the car engine, we abuse our bodies—or rather, do to them what we like without believing our actions constitute abuse—because doctors exist solely to "fix" whatever might go wrong. Ours has become a medicalized society, and medical science is a giant machine that will send forth just the right cure at the right time.

Not only do we continually "lose *it,*" but we use the pronoun *it* mechanically. We greet each other, in a variety of tongues, with "How goes it?" When a relationship begins to fall apart (even as a car falls apart), we say to each other "It's not working"—with perhaps a little unconscious wistfulness; maybe we can get a refund. If our life in general isn't working or just isn't "going right," we shrug our shoulders and add yet one more mechanical metaphor: "It's one of those *things.*"

By far the most mechanical of our myths is *luck.* A succession of unhappy events earns the label *bad luck.* We use it to explain away our failures as well as the success of our friends. When others do well, we suppose that life is like a slot machine: They came along at the right time, while we just happened to pull the handle at the wrong time. (Right and wrong in the luck metaphor are mechanical, not ethical, distinctions.) Of course, we pull out of our mechanical thinking ruts when we encounter good fortune. Then we somehow find a way to look back proudly on our own ingenuity, our careful planning, our personal charisma.

The Arts and the Machine

Many of today's artists use machines and parts of machines for their own creative ends.

Visual artists, however, have been among the first humanists to accept the machine not only as an exciting addition to the human environment, but as a potential object of beauty in itself. It has been said that poets and philosophers are antimachine because the machine represents the negation of language (talking computers notwithstanding). Nonverbal artists have less trouble in this respect.

Michelangelo spent long, arduous hours chipping away at the block of Carrara marble that would become the *David.* Had the technology been available to him, he might have donned a protective face mask, like many sculptors today, and, blow torch in hand, set himself to the task of fashioning heavy metal according to his will. Who knows? He might have tried to outdo the massive sculptures in the Soviet Union and in most American metropolitan centers, which are not only machine-produced but actually *resemble* huge machines.

Machine-inspired art had its true beginnings back in the 1920s, that decade when sophisticated people on both sides of the Atlantic were proclaiming themselves both modern and liberated. The Great War of 1914–1918 had, as wars often do, put an end to the era which preceded it. In this case it had been an era of moral and political conservatism as well as of a strong humanism, which was basically pessimistic, seeing on all sides the demise of human importance.

The 1920s lifted ladies' skirts to the knees as one sign that human beings were free spirits capable of doing anything they wanted. The machine became a mighty symbol of humanity's potential, and the automobile was the machine at its most fashionable. In close order came the telephone, the radio, and all-electric devices, including the washing machine, which was already in use in great homes like that of the Vanderbilts in Asheville as early as 1895!

Why should our visual artists not have responded positively to the machine?

> These new mechanical forms and forces offered themselves as inspiring symbols of unprecedented human well-being, signaling a new epoch in communications, transportation and the mass production of consumer goods. It was not unusual, especially during the 1920's, for intellectuals and artists to speak of the machine as a religious force, a "new divinity."[17]

The rush to purchase mechanical goods led artists to think in terms of using design to make functional items esthetically pleasing. Automobile design, which remains one of the strongest areas of art-in-everyday-life, gave jobs to hundreds of artists. A ringing declaration by art critics and historians was: *Form follows function.* There was a widespread revolt against the purely decorative use of art of decades past: statues, fountains, and architectural "gingerbread" on the exterior of houses . . . all for the apparent sake of showing off wealth.

The 1930s, otherwise known as the Great Depression, was not marked by a declining interest in the machine. Rather, the so-called Art Deco of the time—very much in revival today—reflects the tremendous impact of machinery. If technology were going to transform society and bring it into the modern era—and there was the continual prophecy that the world would pull itself out of the Depression, with technology leading the way—art was going to change the *look* of that society. Everybody—the poor as well as the rich—wanted to gaze at the rounded corners, the shimmering glass brick, and the glowing neon which characterized Art Deco.

Visual art has never lost its love affair with the machine. Mechanical parts, like mufflers and tailpipes, are as common in today's sculptures as marble used to be. Claes Oldenburg's *Giant Ice Bag*, cre-

Purists and traditionalists of all denominations— rockabilly, classical music, rhythm-and-blues, jazz— inveigh against sounds that are electronically triggered rather than bowed or blown or fingered. Professional musicians worry about whether they wasted their Wonder years perfecting nuances of vibrato or octave-leaping dexterity. College radio stations play grunge-guitar bands for hours on end; critics carp about high-gloss productions. The villain, all agree, is computer-driven tunes, and they want to smash those dark, satanic music mills.

Jon Pareles

*I like to see it lap the miles,
And lick the valleys up,
And stop to feed itself at
   tanks;
And then, prodigious, step*

*Around a pile of
   mountains,
And, supercilious, peer
In shanties by the sides of
   roads;
And then a quarry pare*

*To fit its sides, and crawl
   between,
Complaining all the while
In horrid, hooting stanza;
Then chase itself down hill*

*And neigh like Boanerges;
Then, punctual as a star,
Stop—docile and impo-
   tent—
At its own stable door.*

Emily Dickinson

ated for the Osaka World's Fair of 1970, fully exists only when the bag is mechanically inflating and deflating. It is not art reflecting the machine, but art *as* machine.

Music has not been far behind and may in fact now be leading the way in "technological esthetics." The pulsating rhythms and harmonic dissonance of much contemporary concert as well as popular music probably owes a great deal to factory noises, the droning of airplane engines, and the sound of cars whizzing along on freeways. George Gershwin introduced automobile horns as an integral part of the orchestration for his tone poem *An American in Paris* (1928), though Tchaikovsky had much earlier used "live" cannons exploding for the spectacular finale to his *1812 Overture* (1880).

Russian composers throughout this century, in fact, have been profoundly influenced by machinery. Both Sergei Prokofiev (1891–1953) and Dimitri Shostakovich (1906–1975) were drawn to heavily percussive effects as well as clashing dissonance in their orchestral works. At times, one is tempted to believe that they are sounding dire warnings through their music, warnings against mechanization—in particular, the loss of individualism which industrial mechanization brings about. Both composers were often criticized by Communist party officials for improper political sentiments in their music. On the other hand, they were just as frequently praised. The reverberating thunder of their tympani can easily be interpreted as a proud statement of a new order and the emergence of a mighty, industrialized society. They make much use of ringing brass also in stirring passages that could well accompany a slide show of the huge Soviet sculptures.

At the same time, the reader who takes time out for listening is encouraged to experience the many moods of Shostakovich's *Symphony Number Four* (1935). The opening movement is unmistakably Russian contemporary with its dominating percussion, brass, and woodwinds, and its march themes suggestive of regimentation and well-disciplined assembly lines. The orchestration is rich and full, but as the symphony continues the composer introduces a great many themes for solo instruments as well as romantic violin passages which sound more like late-nineteenth-century German than modern Russian. The final moments of the work, however, are among the most moving ever composed. Unlike the traditional symphonic finale, which is loud and stirring and has the entire orchestra playing, this is breathlessly quiet, dominated by a muted trumpet and a celesta (a very small keyboard instrument producing clear but fragile and bell-like tones). Caught as he was in a political bind, fighting to preserve his individuality, is the composer there *himself* in these sounds, an absolutely *clear* human voice fading off into the distance, soft and subdued but not dwarfed by a monumental society?

While Shostakovich was working on his symphony, he commented in a press interview, "I am not afraid of difficulties. It is per-

Shopping Mall

No sunsets fall,
no moons arise
in the shopping mall.
The weather lies
outside it all.

The still air hovers
in the corridors
for manikin lovers
in summer stores
under winter covers.

Glitter and clash
of merchandise
from class to trash
at a new low price
for credit or cash

is all designed
to lure the hunger
and blur the mind
of older and younger
looking to find

some living air,
some meaning space,
but unaware
that the last place
to look is there.[18]

Richard Lyons

haps easier, and certainly safer, to follow a beaten path, but it is also dull, uninteresting and futile." Shortly afterward Shostakovich was denounced by *Pravda* for his dissonant and "nonconformist" music. The premiere of the Fourth Symphony was cancelled. The composer then subtitled his Fifth Symphony "A Soviet Artist's Reply to Just Criticism."

The Antimechanical Strain

If Shostakovich can be subtly antitechnological (or at least a critic of a rigorously mechanized society), other artists of today are more stridently holding their ground against mechanical encroachments. True, we have electronic synthesizers, which may well revolutionize music to a point of no return. State-of-the-art machines can now reproduce the full acoustical spectrum of a large jazz band or a symphony orchestra. In pop music and jazz there are "groups" which exist in name only, being in reality one or two people pulling hundreds of switches, really "into" the "trip" of bringing forth sounds never heard before. Undeniably the positive endorsement continues. But for every lover of manufactured sounds, there is someone else to ask, "Is it art?" On all sides there are strong feelings of hostility toward anything's aspiring to art that is not the result of someone's slow and painful labor.

Many artists, composers, writers, and poets of today resist the *predictability* of machines. Yes, they say, you can build a computer that can beat you at chess, but the stuff of true creativity is the unexpected, the off-center, the mysterious. Computers are too logical. Just see how far we have come from the days when Aristotle created a system of logic that only the human mind could make work. With computers to be logical for us, we can, say many artists, we *should* explore the remote corners of the mind and create art that defies logical analysis. We should not, therefore, be surprised to hear at a concert music that is not orderly, that does not have a beginning, a middle, and an end, that just sort of starts and stops. Or to read a poem that, when you turn the magazine page and find an ad, you realize is over before you had the vaguest notion of what it was all about. Or to see a huge canvas in an art gallery that is composed of blotches of color and jagged lines which seem to say nothing to you at all, and, even worse, to have the artist right there saying she has no idea what it *means* and doesn't think the question is very important.

In schools and universities, however, we see another trend developing that is, surprisingly, not in conflict with the antilogic movement. Courses in critical thinking are being added to curricula, perhaps as one way to stop young minds from a lazy dependence on machines to do their thinking, calculators to manipulate figures, TV commentators to give them opinions; perhaps in urgent response to the information overload that can sink us all unless we learn how to process carefully the data which fly at us from all directions. There are

In the back of my thoughts about computers taking over is my fear that we are not capable—as human beings—of taking care of ourselves. We are just going mad. I don't think we can remain humane very much longer.

George Williams

This new phenomenon and a work force whose composite educational achievement level is higher than ever combine to produce the newest and potentially most devastating dimension of technological alienation mindlessness.

Training and Development Journal

still those who care about that fragile entity—the mind; who know that, unlike machines, a mind that won't start from not being used cannot be replaced by next year's model.

GLOSSARY

creatio ex nihilo: In both the Hebrew and Christian religious traditions, the act of God by which the material world came into being from no previously existing substance.

deism: A popular eighteenth-century philosophy which held that the universe was created by but is not supervised by God. Among other things, it did away with religious justification for social classes. Many deists were deeply involved with the common-man revolution.

deus ex machina: Literally, "god out of a machine"; a device often used by the Greek tragic playwright Euripides (and probably others as well) whereby an Olympian deity would be introduced suddenly at the end of the play by means of a crane to resolve the plot and, particularly, to give the play a happy ending; phrase employed nowadays to mean the manipulation of plot to have a work end as it *should*, not as in reality it *would.*

doctrine: In this chapter, a reference to certain beliefs, such as belief in the Virgin birth and in the Trinity, which are held to be absolute truths despite the absence of rational proof.

faith: The ability to believe in God and doctrine without *requiring* proof; said to be a gift bestowed by God upon the devout.

romanticism: A movement in the arts, as well as a philosophy that had its roots in the late-eighteenth-century rediscovery of nature; generally antitechnological, anti-reason, and, politically, very much against power vested in the privileged few.

syllogism: A fundamental component of Aristotelian logic; composed of a three-step process: (1) a major premise which states what is true of an entire class, (2) a minor premise which states what is true of one unit of that class, and (3) an inescapable conclusion which states a truth about that individual unit.

technology: Perhaps the key term in this chapter; a broad reference to the entire science and use of machinery; the underlying condition of modern life, except in some Third World nations, which are just beginning to replace human labor with mechanized energy.

NOTES

1. Fernand Braudel, *The Structure of Everyday Life* (Vol. I of *Civilization and Capitalism*) (New York: Harper & Row, 1979), p. 339.

2. *The Aeneid of Virgil,* trans. Robert Fitzgerald (New York: Random House, 1983), Book II, 11.312.317.

3. 1214–1294, a British philosopher and a very early advocate of the scientific method.

4. English translation by William Weaver

(San Diego: Harcourt Brace Jovanovich, 1983),
p. 7.

5. Ibid.

6. Barbara W. Tuchman, *A Distant Mirror*
(New York: Alfred A. Knopf, 1978), p. 101.

7. Ibid.

8. *Letters of the Great Artists, from Ghiberti
to Gainsborough,* ed. Richard Friedenthal
(New York: Random House, 1963), p. 32.

9. Ibid., p. 34.

10. Ibid., p. 37.

11. James Burke, *The Day the Universe
Changed* (Boston: Little, Brown, 1984), p. 193.

12. Mary Shelley, *Frankenstein, or The Modern Prometheus* (Berkeley: University of California Press, 1984), p. 24.

13. Ibid., p. 51.

14. Robert M. Pirsig, *Zen and the Art of
Motorcycle Maintenance* (New York: William
Morrow & Co., 1974), p. 12.

15. Ibid., p. 56.

16. *Training and Development Journal,* September 1985.

17. Alan Trachtenberg, "The Art and Design of
the Machine Age." *The New York Times Magazine,* September 21, 1986, p. 62.

18. Richard Lyons, "Shopping Mall." Harvard
Magazine (July/August, 1986). Reprinted by
permission of the author.

Henri Matisse, "Piano Lesson," 1916
(Courtesy of The Museum of Modern Art, Mrs. Simon Guggenheim Fund)

16

FREEDOM

OVERVIEW

Though it might seem that, given a choice, everyone would prefer to be free, there is something convenient about a belief that we are not. Without freedom, one can explain lack of success, happiness, and clear thinking in one's life. Without freedom, the individual is not in control; rather, "things happen" from the outside.

Those who believe that freedom is *not* a human attribute share the assumptions of a great many philosophers, sociologists, economists, and psychologists. More important than freedom, say these commentators, are the accidents of birth: the genetic code which determines physical characteristics and perhaps intellectual ones as well;

family class and income, which can set limits on opportunity; parental success in nurturing children, which can determine whether offspring receive damaging bruises or encouragement to fulfill their potential; and even time itself. The accident of having been born in one year rather than another is clearly a factor beyond one's control. Yet, say those who question the concept of freedom, the attributes admired and needed by one generation may be worthless in another. In a sense, one may claim that luck or fate are more important than freedom.

An assumption of the humanist is that freedom is vital to the art of being human, which has been described as the art of making free and intelligent choices among significant options. Traditionally, the study of the humanities has shared this assumption, insisting that the freedom to create and the freedom to enjoy what has been created are natural rights everyone should have.

Where these rights are denied, poets cry out in defiance; artists paint their anger in bold colors; composers sound their trumpets—or would if they could. No great art has been created explicitly to defend enslavement or to justify oppression. The poet William Blake expressed the matter simply and incisively:

> *A robin redbreast in a cage*
> *Puts all Heaven in a rage.*

Man is free. This is at once a heady luxury and also the source of his discontent.

Carlton Beck

On the other hand, even those who claimed to believe in freedom were often unwilling to grant it to everyone. The Greeks invented the word and concept of *democracy* and passed on as their legacy the model of the democratic state in which every citizen was "free" to think, to question, to speak out. But citizens comprised only five percent of the population. The rest were slaves and women, neither of whom were expected to be rational, responsible human beings. In other words, the Greeks believed that only those should be free who could handle freedom. Even at that, Socrates, surely as rational as a person could have been, was deprived first of freedom, then of life.

That freedom is, or should be, the basic human condition is implicit in our own Bill of Rights, the remarkable first ten constitutional amendments, ratified in 1791. Guaranteed, among others, are the rights to speak out freely, to assemble in groups, to have one's dwelling protected against forcible entry without a warrant, and, of course, not to have to testify against oneself. In our own time the United Nations has passed the Universal Declaration of Human Rights, reaffirming what much of the world already knew but perhaps took for granted.

From a humanistic perspective, the issue is greater than that of liberties denied, or the bitter history of cruel inhumanities inflicted upon the innocent—appalling as those issues surely are. What saddens the hearts of those who have seen loved ones tortured and slain, who have dedicated themselves to a continuing, desperate fight for freedom, is the undeniable fact that *freedom is still being rejected by those who do not recognize its worth,* like so many sparkling diamonds carelessly thrown from the window of a speeding car.

But before we decide that freedom is ours if we would only reach out for it, we must consider arguments for and against its very existence.

In all this he always acts according to necessary laws, from which he has no means of emancipating himself.

Baron d'Holbach

EXPLOITERS AND EXPLOITED: THE VIEW THAT HUMANS ARE LIMITED IN THEIR CHOICES

A number of philosophies dispute the idea that freedom for all people is a natural human condition: philosophies that draw parallels between the human kingdom and the animal kingdom, pointing to the fierce and bitter struggle for survival which takes place in both. In nature, they say, no creature is free except to follow *its* nature, which is to be either the exploiter or the exploited.

Rousseau's Man with the Stick

One of the staunchest advocates of the philosophy of total and unlimited freedom for all was Jean-Jacques Rousseau (1712–1778), considered by many as the conscious architect of the French Revolution, by some as the indirect architect of modern society, and by at least one French historian as the individual most responsible for all of the *evils* in that society.

In fanning the revolutionary flames beginning to sweep through a France becoming increasingly outraged at the decadence of the aristocracy and the gross injustices suffered by the common people, Rousseau constructed a mythical account of the origin of the species, to prove that freedom was both a natural condition and a natural right. Called *A Discourse on the Origins of Inequality,* the myth draws a romantic picture of a lost Age of Innocence, when early people lived in peace and harmony, sharing the fruits of the abundant earth through a common realization that nature provided equal bounty for everyone. At this time no laws or government existed, because, obviously, law and government are not necessary when everyone is happy and there is no crime.

Then one day came the Man with the Stick, the first person to take it into his head to grab off more than his natural share of things,

If there is no natural condition as freedom, then the humanist ideal is open to serious question.

the first person to *abuse* nature's gift of freedom by putting it to his own advantage. With his stick he carved out a private piece of territory for himself.

> The first man, who, after enclosing a piece of ground, took it into his head to say, "This is mine," and found people simple enough to believe him, was the true founder of civil society.

The Man with the Stick was the founder of society because, by creating the model of the exploiter, by establishing for all time the inhuman alternative to natural freedom, he and his followers became an ever-present threat to the rights of the others and therefore had to be suppressed by the gradual development of law, government, and all other institutions dedicated to the curtailment, or the limitation, of all rights. But these "safeguards of liberty," once in place, become despotic in themselves.

Rousseau's position is clearly a revolutionary one. Revolution, even if violent, is a genuine alternative to exploitation and may often be the only means by which to deal with it. The first revolution against the Man with the Stick, would, however, have been a peaceful one had there arisen a daring enough activist

> who, pulling up the stakes or filling up the ditches, should have cried to his fellows: Be sure not to listen to this imposter; you are lost if you forget that the fruits of the earth belong equally to us all, and the earth itself to nobody!

If Rousseau not only explains but justifies revolution in the name of natural rights belonging to all, he does *not* in his myth account for the *origin* of the Man with the Stick. What made this one man decide to become possessive, when the others were joyously bobbing for golden apples in an age of sun and fun? Or was he merely the first to manifest himself? Did the potential for exploitation lie deep within *every* member of that "innocent" society? If so, why are institutional safeguards *not* needed?

Rousseau's anti-institutional bias is based on the assumption that in the "state of nature" (a phrase hotly debated then and since) humankind is decent, tame, moral, and benevolent. Only when held in check, only when threatened with punishment for disobedient acts, do people become hateful, aggressive, and violent—except for periods of rebelling in a just cause. But what Rousseau did not know, because he died a decade before the Revolution he predicted, was that Napoleon Bonaparte would rise from the ashes of France and, sword in

Lo, the poor Indian!
  whose untutored mind
Sees God in clouds, or
  hears Him in the
  wind;
His soul, proud science
  never taught to stray
Far as the solar walk or
  milky way.

        Alexander Pope

hand, lead forth a new age of exploitation, perhaps even more oppressive than the one it was to supplant.

How shall we ever put Rousseau's assumption to the test? How shall we ever know whether most people, left on their own without law or government, would remain peaceful and willing to share the fruits of the earth with each other, or whether the Men with Sticks would come along and start once again the cycle of exploitation and revolution? What *does* appear certain is that no revolution within human memory has been without its exploiters. We think of Jonestown and its loyal population, led to a remote wilderness in the name of communal love and decency, only to yield up life itself in the name of that very loyalty.

Nietzsche: Masters and Slaves

Friedrich Nietzsche, who is discussed in Chapter 14 in connection with the Apollo/Dionysus polarity, was more than concerned—he was *obsessed*—with the problem of the exploiter. For Nietzsche, no god imposed a definite meaning or purpose on life. Existence therefore belonged to the person who could define it and persuade others to follow. All values were relative, and the person who could convince everyone else of certain "truths" would prevail. Whether the truths were "true" or not did not matter, so long as people were willing to accept them.

Nietzsche thus divided society into two classes of people: masters and slaves. The masters were those who assumed they could prevail, and, in the absence of serious opposition, *did* prevail. The slaves were those who allowed it to happen, who were willing to be exploited—would, in fact, *rather* be exploited than live in confusion, without guidelines or direction.

Nietzsche coined the label *übermensch,* or superman, to refer to the master who proved eminently successful in imposing his own vision of reality, his own value system, upon others. In his view, Jesus Christ was the very model of the superman. Nietzsche never believed that Jesus was a supernatural being, but he marveled at Jesus's ability to sway a crowd. Nietzsche saw that Jesus was able to convince millions that he was the son of God, sent down to earth by his father to redeem humankind. What concerned Nietzsche was not the authenticity of the claim but the model that Jesus represented. It could be possible for someone equally visionary to rise up, step forward, and claim to be the vehicle of the Divine Voice.

Nietzsche also believed that people born into a "slave" background—that is, belonging to a group of people having the slave mentality—would develop their parents' self-negation. People would not claim a right to freedom if all they ever heard in the home was that no

*I am as free as Nature
first made man,
Ere the base laws of
servitude began,
When wild in woods the
noble savage ran*

John Dryden

one in the family deserved much of anything, and should be grateful for whatever charity those "better" than they (i.e., the "masters") wished to grant. For Nietzsche, the slave outlook valued virtues such as charity, love, altruism, caring, but the master outlook valued power, strength, cleverness, manipulation, and all of the characteristics which gave authority to the human enterprise. The "Master" honored traits that could restrain the impulses of the slave mentality.

Nietzsche believed no one was necessarily intended to be either a slave or a master. That is, human nature did not automatically place a person in one category or the other. But human nature *did* tend to narrow itself down to two alternatives. Nietzsche believed the choice was a matter of laziness versus aggressiveness. Some people had sluggish metabolisms perhaps, while others were hell-bent on bettering themselves no matter at whose expense. Whether or not the division is as natural as Nietzsche believed, it seems clear that the urge for freedom is not shared by all. Some people are far happier allowing themselves to be led.

Karl Marx: The Determinism of Money

Not humanity, not nature, but money calls the turn—so believed Karl Marx (1818–1883), the economist and philosopher who, in the opinion of many intellectual historians, brought forth ideas that permanently altered the destiny of the human race. As an economist, he developed a theory which explained the behavior of all members of society: the haves, the in-betweens, and the have-nots. As a philosopher, he created a blueprint for a utopian, classless society in which the haves and have-nots would disappear, and, in the words of Rousseau, the fruits of the earth would belong to all. The ideas contained in *The Communist Manifesto,* published in 1843 and co-authored by Marx and his colleague Friedrich Engels (1820–1895), changed the world, though both would have said it is economics that does the changing and all they did was report the facts.

As a young intellectual Karl Marx fell under the strong influence of an earlier German philosopher, Georg Wilhelm Friedrich Hegel (1770–1831), who had developed two massive theories pertaining to the workings of (1) the human mind and (2) history. Both theories were absorbed and then reinterpreted by Marx.

Hegel developed a logical method of thinking, called a *dialectic,* based on his view of how the mind operates. Like everything else in nature, Hegel believed, the mind oscillates back and forth between poles and strives for a balance between them. First we begin with a *thesis,* the conviction that something is true. Soon the thesis is countered by its own opposite, which Hegel called the *antithesis,* for, in testing the validity of a proposed truth, we must determine whether its negation can also be entertained. If the antithesis and thesis can be held with equal conviction but *each negates the other,* then the mind has no choice but to seek a point midway between the two, a point called the *synthesis.*

What interested Marx particularly was the application of the dialectic to the theory of history which Hegel also worked out. In the dialectical method, both poles—the thesis and the antithesis—are limited by what they contain. If the thesis statement is positive—for instance, *He is an only child* (assuming, of course, that we do not *know* whether he is, only that we can entertain such an idea)—we can say that the statement is limited by not including its negation, *He is not an only child,* which, lacking the facts, we can also believe. But the antithesis is also limited by not including its positive form. The synthesis statement, *He is or is not an only child,* is, of course, not limited, since it includes both the positive and the negative versions. Hegel saw human history as an alternation of political and social systems, all in some way limiting the freedom of human beings, as thesis and antithesis were limited. He envisioned a future "synthesis" world in which people were totally free of all limitations—the philosophical model for the Marxian classless society.

Marx saw Hegel's dialectic working through history in economic form; hence the name *dialectical materialism,* by which the Marxian theory of history is better known. For Marx, the future would bring freedom from want, from the one important negative factor in the life of ordinary working-class citizens: the lack of enough money to meet their needs and those of their families. His future world developed an *economic synthesis,* in which the balance of power was held not by the affluent (society's positive thesis statement—in short, the haves), nor by the poor (the antithesis—or have-nots), but by all. *Communism* would be a social structure in which all property was publicly owned.

Dialectical materialism has, of course, an underlying assumption: namely, that economic survival and the meeting of their economic needs are what drives human beings, what alone accounts for human behavior. Everything we do has an economic aim, whether we know it or not. If we are rich, we act so as to become richer or at least to preserve what we have. If we are an in-between, everything we do is in the interest of climbing upward. If we are poor, we love, hate, reward, and punish according to the way these actions are likely to affect our pocketbooks.

That Money Is the Root of All Action

The fear prevailing in the free world today over the creeping spread of Communism is impelled by the threat of lost liberty. The violent revolutions of the haves against the have-nots in Russia and elsewhere have resulted not in workers' utopias but in totalitarian states in which capi-

Marx applied Hegel's logical method, called the dialectic, *to the economic progressions of history, and came to the conclusion that an economic synthesis was logical and inevitable.*

The freedom and independence of the worker during the labor process do not exist.

Marx

When the state exists, there is no freedom. When there is freedom, there will be no state.

Lenin

The inherent vice of capitalism is the unequal sharing of blessings; the inherent virtue of socialism is the equal sharing of miseries.

Winston Churchill

Dialectical materialism assumes that economic survival and the meeting of economic needs are what accounts for human behavior.

When I once asked a Russian economist why men will work when all food, clothing, and housing are free, he replied with a confident smile, "for the common good," but that is by no means certain.

B. F. Skinner

We should have had socialism already, but for the socialists.

George Bernard Shaw

Those who make peaceful revolution impossible will make violent revolution inevitable.

John F. Kennedy

Marry somebody rich—and then be pure.

John Ciardi

talism, which is private ownership of property, is held in check by stiff regulations and secret police. In other words, where the classless society exists at all, though never perfectly, it does so by the machinations not of history but of human beings in power. We note a shift in determining forces.

But for many, *not* to endorse the workers' paradise is to negate the idea that money motivates our actions. Humanists, in particular, have traditionally held themselves aloof from money as a primary goal of life. They have tended to attribute free will to those who allow reason to be their guide and to deplore those who, lacking reason, surrender themselves to a lust for money. A questionable separation has been established: Rationality equals free will equals antimaterialism; materialism equals irrationality equals determinism. One cannot therefore make a free choice to devote one's life exclusively to the pursuit of money. If one is "into" money, one has given up all chance to be a free human being, according to this traditional view.

The philosophy behind capitalism is the viewpoint that drives our economy, and it *is* based on the assumption that people are both rational and free. Rational human beings are out for themselves (and for those genetically or amorously close to them), and economic well-being is always central to their thoughts. If people do not want money for the things money can buy, a free economy cannot survive. In capitalist thinking, people are free to want, to make, and to spend money. One can be economically determined in this sense without being a slave of history, or of dark, underground, aggressive drives.

Traditional humanists often find it degrading to suppose that money should be a paramount concern. After all, philosophy, literature, and music are supposed to be *alternatives* to the accumulation of wealth, are they not? Still, finding pleasure in other than material resources is one thing; denying that economic motivation drives enlightened people is quite another.

The art of being human does not entail making a choice between the humanities and money. It *does* require that we observe ourselves in action. If economic motives are not the sole reasons why we do what we do, they *are* sometimes the major ones. Common sense tells us that the poorer we are, the more we look for opportunities to advance. The chronically poor, those who barely survive on the fringes of society, whose former means of livelihood may have been displaced by technology, derive values from their economic plight. They may resent the life which passes around them. They probably admire charity and a helping hand. But even creative artists, once romantically thought to be "above" the vulgarity of seeking money, retain agents, negotiate contracts, charge high fees for television interviews and college lectures, and go on autographing tours to boost the sales of their latest publication.

We never know when economics will suddenly assume the dominant role in our lives. Thirty years with the same company, and now we are being phased out! Where do we turn? Who hires people in their fifties? Or: After all I've done for this company, they bring in someone from the outside and make her the general manager. Not fair! But I'll show them. Just see how much loyalty they'll get from me!

While all of our choices may not be economically determined, there are times in everyone's life when money is the root of action.

Humanism has been on the side of free will, but free will is not a constant state. Certainly it isn't a commodity. It can be defined as a condition in which, when the opportunity for choice arises, a number of options can be seen to exist, any one of which we may select. Moreover, for totally free will to exist, the options need to be sufficiently dissimilar. We are constrained by economics when the only options are selling the summer cottage in Maine, fixing it up for the convenience of our clients, or moving there from Boston even if it means a cut in salary.

To be economically determined is not the same as being a Marxist or a crass materialist. The important thing is at all times to recognize the roots of our behavior (a utopian state of consciousness seldom achieved). We are chronically unfree the more we remain blind to the reality when it confronts us. We take a step on the path to freedom when we begin to see the things which limit us—or when we impose the limitations on ourselves.

We do not want to be like the woman of 50-plus years who joined an intense encounter group, openly confessing to the others that what she wanted was a higher opinion of herself. After two weeks of soul-searching, "letting it all hang out," and receiving brutally honest "feedback" from her now-surrogate family, the woman finally announced that she had arrived at a moment of self-realization, adding:

> When I was young, my mother instilled in me a terrible fear of what people would say. If I dressed improperly, I had to worry about what they would say about me. If I stayed out too late at night, I imagined the neighbors peeking through their curtains and tongues wagging incessantly about my wantonness. But now I see that I no longer have to worry about what they're saying. After all, who am I that they should be talking about me?

How Free Is a Free Society?

Those who risk everything, including often their very lives, to reach our shores always do so in the name of freedom. They mean freedom to vote for whom they please without outside pressures; freedom to work in any capacity that seems appropriate and for anyone who will hire them; freedom to earn as much as possible and to spend or not spend as they desire. For many who are born and bred on these shores, the new arrival's view of freedom is severely limited, is not, as a matter of fact, freedom at all. Even without a repressive government, even with the right to change governments every four years, we still have our choices determined by the people in Washington.

Some use the Great Depression of the 1930s as the "great divide" between a time when people had freedom to pursue the American Dream as far as they were able and the present era, when government restrictions impede us at every turn. During this period the British economist John Maynard Keynes (see Chapter 6) proposed that in times when national income was very low and unemployment very high, government could step in, derive revenue from those for whom high taxes were not a burden, and revive the economy by spending money on social programs. The views of Keynes greatly influenced the economic policies of Franklin D. Roosevelt and lay behind much of the New Deal legislation. Followers of the New Deal contend that these policies saved the nation; others say that big government, once an invited guest, has stayed around too long, and, worse, has taken over the house.

Political conservatives, traditional nonsupporters of Keynesian economics, decry excessive government intervention in the name of what they consider a vanished America of frontier spunk and rugged individualism, when the entrepreneur, like the cowboy of old, could move in any direction desired. Traditional liberals, of course, support government intervention on the grounds that the "cowboys" of big business would end up exploiting the less fortunate, and we would end up with Nietzsche's master-or-slave option, with the majority falling into the latter category.

But the split between liberal and conservative is, by now, a historical one. Government spending—regardless of which party is in power—is now so huge that no economic philosophy appears capable of changing the pattern. Starting with social security, the government spends billions on social programs and even more on defense. We are taxed at every turn. Taxation, in the opinion of many, diminishes the incentive to work creatively and industriously to get ahead. It is easily possible now for a person to make too much money.

The size of both the government's budget deficit and its indebtedness, incurred by its continuing, desperate need to raise revenue, affects interest rates, which in turn limit the choices available to citizens. The young, in particular, often rely on interest rates to determine whether they should get married or even become "serious" with one another. Interest rates also affect the strength of the American dollar abroad. Currency exchange helps determine where and when we can travel.

Worse still, in the opinion of many concerned about the erosion of human freedom, is the feeling of dependency which government engenders in us all. With the government's having picked up so many tabs during the last half-century, members of the work force reach a point where they simply *assume* they have no power to improve their lives, that they do not particularly want power. What they want is for their lives to be improved *for* them. Thus we hear: "It's high time they (i.e., the people in Washington) did something about the economy." Or: "The recession can't last much longer. The economy is bound to bottom out pretty soon." In truth, there is nothing inaccurate about thinking that, between the legislature's power over our pocketbooks through taxation and the Federal Reserve Board's power over the money supply and the interest rates we pay for loans and mortgages, there is often little most of us can do about our standard of living. The number of free options available to us is often very small indeed.

The federal bureaucracy, not originally designed to curb the rights of citizens, cannot function at the same time in the best interest of everyone. Still, instead of bemoaning our insignificance, we might remind ourselves that government is not willfully anti-individual and that the individual retains some powers not always used, including the power of the ballot and the power of the mail. Elected officials respond more directly than we might think to the voices of their constituents. The origin of many actions which affect us mightily need not *always* be traced to smoke-filled rooms in the hotels along the Potomac. For some it may lie partially in their indifference.

OTHER LIMITATIONS ON THE IDEA OF ABSOLUTE FREEDOM

There are millions upon this earth who exist under severely repressive governments. The conditions under which every action is dictated, if not by direct government regulation, then by the omnipresence of want or hunger, are real and define what human life is like in all too many places. But the opposite—a state in which one's actions are solely the result of a free choice one has made—may exist only in theory—a theory widely questioned at that. The philosophy that challenges this theory is called *determinism*. It holds that all actions are the results of prior causes.

Character Consistency

Enduring characters in memorable works of fiction—Don Quixote, Becky Sharp, Huckleberry Finn, Scarlett O'Hara, for example—stay in our minds not because they are amorphous, fluid, and unpredictable,

A frequently advanced determinist argument is that only the insane are always and completely "free."

The federal bureaucracy, not originally designed to curb the rights of citizens, cannot function at the same time in the best interest of everyone.

but because they have specific character traits that can be summarized and that readily explain what they do in the novels. Indeed, what they do is usually obvious before they act. If they were real people, the determinist would say they lack free will, that they are bound by the very traits which make them come alive to us. A determinist argument often advanced is this: *Only the insane are always and completely "free."*

For example, one person stops another in the street and strikes that person in the face. Imagine a panel of experts on human behavior being told this story and asked to predict what the response of the stricken person would be. Their predictions would surely be based on some cause-and-effect view of human interaction which they would call "rational behavior." But what does this mean? Does it not mean that the stricken person is expected to respond within clear limitations that are accepted and shared by all rational persons? Thus, the assaulted person may be projected as (1) striking back out of righteous anger; (2) not striking back, because of pacifist beliefs, but attempting to leave without undergoing further harm; (3) deciding against the use of force on his or her own, preferring to call a police officer; (4) turning the other cheek, because of a strong Biblical upbringing; or perhaps (5) simply staring in disbelief at the assailant, not quite knowing what to do under the circumstances.

But now suppose the victim does not respond in any of these admittedly rational ways but, instead, were suddenly to produce a sword and bid the attacker kneel down and be knighted. There is a good chance that not the assailant but the assailed would be hauled away for observation. Such a response would not fall within any *meaningful* category of behavior. The determinist is likely to argue that of the actions considered, the "King Arthur" action is the only one rightfully to be labeled "free." Under these circumstances, who would wish to live in a "free" world?

Of course, if we were bent on finding support for the *libertarian,* or free will, point of view, we could argue back that we are free or unfree according to the terminology we use to think about these states. Advocates of libertarianism are talking about unfettered choices among *rational* options. Certainly, in a rational universe each effect has an antecedent cause, but it is usually one of many that *might* be the cause before the action is performed. The fact that possible causes can be discarded, that a thought or feeling can be entertained and then become a noncause, supports the libertarian position, or so the libertarians insist.

On the other hand, there are libertarians who not only criticize the character-consistency argument but who urge us not to be bound by the character traits instilled in us during the so-called acculturation process. They tell us we can be rational without being continuously predictable. If such were not the case, how could we explain the creative and the imaginative, the divergent thinkers whose oddball notions have in one way or another altered the shape of human experience? Were all of them insane? And, come to think of it, does any of us want to acquire a hard-and-fast reputation for being always and tiresomely the same?

Sigmund Freud

The study of the mind, which has come to be called *psychology,* is over a century old. It has not traditionally been as concerned with the question of free will as has been classical philosophy, but much psychology has been based on the premise of a modified determinism: the contention that whatever we think or do is impelled by a previous cause, *which is not of our own choosing.* Psychotherapy, on the other hand, seeks to free people.

The aim of psychotherapy is to help people integrate their behavior by learning the causes of deviant, antisocial, or uncharacteristic actions. The theory generally is that, once the cause is discovered, the subterranean forces driving one's actions can be fully or at least partially controlled. In other words, people go into therapy because they don't like what they appear to be or what they do. Therapy holds out the hope that through understanding and proper guidance, people can change and become less "determined" than they were before.

Though many of his theories have been seriously questioned, the pioneer work of Sigmund Freud (1856–1939) cannot be underestimated. His ideas have profoundly influenced not only the humanities but, whether the average person knows it or not, twentieth-century consciousness. Philosophy has been especially cognizant of Freud, not always positively, in its efforts to deliberate the ancient question of free will.

Famous for his "discovery" of the unconscious mind, that mental "place" in which unpleasant memories and unfinished business are hidden, Freud would later replace his earlier concept of the dual self with what is now called the *structural* model of the mind. According to this model, the inner being is comprised of three layers, or levels. There is the *id,* that part of us which is to some extent a remnant from the animalistic, less civilized past, which contains all of our drives, including the sex drive. In terms of the metaphor we presented in Chapter 14, the id is our Dionysian self, operating as it will, without control by reason.

Passing over the middle self for the moment, we come to the topmost level of our inner being, the *superego,* where are stored the moral values instilled within us during the acculturation process. The superego is like the tablets Moses carried down from Mount Sinai: It represents our consciousness of THE LAW. The superego is a universal presence within each of us, something very like *conscience,* except that its source is not God but the accumulated moral traditions of human society.

Midway between the Dionysian id and the Apollonian superego stands the *ego* itself, the conscious, rational, adult, functioning mind which each of us develops, though hardly in equal amounts, as we mature. The Freudian view of the typical human being is that of a generally unhappy, neurotic creature struggling to achieve an internal equilibrium.

Why is the inner self unbalanced? The answer is that the id and the superego are in conflict with each other. The id is amoral, consisting of appetites and needs which exist only to be satisfied, never controlled or modified. When we are, for example, physically attracted to another and desire intimacy, it is the superego, never the id, which bids us to back away and *not* seek fulfillment. Left to its own devices, the id would always get its way, because it knows only the law of its nature, in the same way that a rapacious wolf cannot be expected to hold itself in check. The wolf stalking its prey is stopped only by the force of superior power: another, stronger wolf or a human being with a gun. The superego holds the rifle against the rapacious id.

The conflict between the higher and lower selves of a human being begins long before conscious memory, and it centers on the erogenous zones. During the earliest phase of human development, the infant derives erotic pleasure from sucking at its mother's breast. Later it is the anus which is the source of erotic feelings; still later, the sexual organs themselves. As our brains mature, we are made to "learn" that eroticism must be held in check, cannot be given free rein. The superego begins its powerful efforts to control our natural tendencies.

The problem is, however, that few persons manage to go through phase after phase of the conflict with understanding. The result is that, when we attain so-called adult intellect, we function *only partially.* A bit of us is rational, but, like the giant iceberg that lies hidden under the icy sea, most of the self remains submerged. Why? Unfulfilled erotically at the oral, anal, or genital stage of development, the id slinks underground, like an overgrown, monstrous animal retreating to its lair, afraid of the superego, that tall hunter with the high-powered rifle. It understands enough to realize that whatever it has desired is bad, but not being rational, it cannot question or otherwise resolve its anguish. In other words, the principal weapon used by the superego to curb the "disgusting" wants of the id is *guilt.* In Freud's view, humanity is a wretched, guilt-ridden species, trembling with anxiety as the underground monster thrashes against the walls of its cave.

A major example—and probably the most famous theory developed by Freud—is that of the hostility each of us experiences toward the parent of the same sex, a hostility engendered by a forbidden attraction toward the other parent. All male children, Freud said, develop an *Oedipus complex,* named for the Greek tragic hero (see

The id slinks underground, like an animal retreating to its lair, afraid of the superego, that tall hunter with the high-powered rifle.

Chapter 10) who killed his father and married his mother; while female children develop an *Electra complex,* named for the Greek tragic
heroine who plotted her mother's death to avenge the murder of her
father. The attraction/hostility conflict is suppressed along with the
guilt it creates. Most people, it is hoped, outgrow both conflict and
guilt before they mature, marry, and have children of their own. But
Freud did not dare postulate that the majority of us could ever free
ourselves totally from our past feelings, buried deep within us because
of the stern moralism of the superego.

 Psychoanalysis is the therapy invented by Freud to assist
people toward mental health. It is based on the assumption that, because of the suppressed past, many of us have bizarre dreams, make
odd statements which seem to make no sense, and perform actions we
cannot comprehend. In other words, our lives are determined by prior
causes unknown to us: sometimes by guilt-ridden emotions we have
refused to deal with; often by responses of the id, that irrational, primitive self human beings possessed long before they developed the rational ego. The aim of the therapist was, and still is, to analyze the patient's dreams, characteristic use of language, and free associations; to
uncover the hidden self responsible for neurotic behavior; and to lead
the patient to a happier life dominated by the ego. Presumably the successfully psychoanalyzed patient comes to possess freedom of the will,
having been released from the determining phantoms of the past. Will
resides in the ego.

 Nonetheless, Freud's vision of the world is a pessimistic one.
He saw a vast population of neurotic and sometimes psychotic people,
many of whom exhibited extremely deviant behavior, the causes of
which might elude detection forever. Freudians believe that almost
nobody is truly happy, and, as a result, the basic animal instinct for
survival is overcome by a death wish.

 Despite the criticism directed against Freud during the last
two decades, psychoanalysis continues to be popular. Thousands see
their analysts far more frequently than they do their family doctor or
dentist. But Freudian analysts warn that the motivation for these visits
may be the desire to find in the analyst a substitute parent and thus
to retard self-awareness even further. Such a substitution may be useful in early analysis, when patients are encouraged to reveal more of
themselves if the trust level is high.

 From statistics alone—the sheer quantity of office visits to
analysts each year—we could infer that Freud may have been on the
right track. Whether all of his theories hold up or not, there seem to be
a number of people who consider themselves disturbed and who seek
someone to help them through the fog of their unsure identities.

 In the decades since Freud's death, the number of therapists
has grown to proportions Freud himself could not have imagined. So
has the expense of being brought to a rational sanity. The "identity

crisis" may now be a neurotic status symbol for the affluent, and the price of a conscious ego may be beyond the reach of the ordinary worker.

Skinner: Freedom Is a Word

Freud made people aware that what they did was seldom a direct result of conscious thought or desire. If Freud showed that most people were not in control of their destinies, B. F. Skinner (b. 1904) has sought to radically alter the way people think about freedom. In effect, Freud said, "You can't be free until your conscious mind, ego, understands the source of your neurosis." Skinner, who calls himself an operant psychologist, says, "Let's reconsider what we think we are talking about when we say we want to be free."

Skinner's beliefs are rooted in a science barely getting under way in Freud's day: *behaviorism.* The central point of behaviorism is that human beings are behaving creatures. To understand people better and work to improve their lot, it is necessary to begin with what people actually *do,* not what they think, feel, or say.

Skinner has denied that the language of feeling or thought has a direct relationship to any observable reality. To say, "I feel cheated" or "I want to be free" or, in the words of the popular song, "I want to be me" means nothing without accompanying action. What matters is not what people say about inner states, but what they do in response to an external stimulus. Thus, if the shackled prisoner is suffering the pain and discomfort of solitary confinement and is threatened by the guard with a nightstick, the prisoner may out of sheer desperation shout obscenities in the guard's direction. This, says Skinner, is concrete behavior, not the feeling "I want to be free." By the same token, if the shackled prisoner is promised that he will be removed from solitary confinement and "allowed" to work on the rock pile so long as he refrains from future obscenities, he is very likely to accept the terms and avoid four-letter words. The "privilege" of working on the rock pile, in contrast to being in the dark and dingy cell, may well constitute an activity closer to "freedom" than the word or the so-called feeling.

Skinner calls freedom the effort to escape from the unpleasant consequences of certain actions. We slap at a mosquito that's about to attack, to avoid the annoying itching which will follow. A child who has thrown a tantrum and been sent to bed without supper may cry loudly to escape hunger pangs. To have freedom there must be a condition acting as a stimulus to a response. No such thing as pure and absolute freedom exists or can be defined.

People, Skinner goes on, often identify the state of absolute freedom as one in which "aversive control" is absent; that is, if there is no apparent oppression, then people imagine themselves to be free. The literature of freedom, such as Rousseau's writings, which helped

What matters is not what people say about inner states, but what they do in response to an external stimulus.

According to proponents of behaviorism, if humanity can be said to have a nature it lies in the capacity to be conditioned.

and

According to the opponents, conditioning reduces human dignity and diminishes the contributions of great artists, writers, and philosophers.

inspire the French Revolution, has always urged people to act against aversive control, against obvious forms of oppression. It either beckons followers, who have the false hope of believing society might be better organized but without controls, or else it fails to point out that there can be controls which appear less threatening but which nevertheless also condition people's behavior.

The fact is, Skinner tells us, there is no way to escape all forms of control. If humanity can be said to have a nature, it lies in *the capacity to be conditioned.* Everything we do is the result of a reinforcement of behavior. Those actions which are followed by pleasant consequences tend to be repeated; those followed by unpleasant or painful consequences tend to be avoided.

Even aggression and exploitation, which Marx implied were basic to human nature, are forms of behavior induced by external circumstances. Aggression is one way of escaping negative reinforcement (an unpleasant consequence). If we act first, we escape being acted *upon.* We may exploit others as long as possible to escape controls we have experienced in the past but do not want to see in the present. Aggressors or exploiters may imagine themselves to be free, but they have simply not understood the forces that are conditioning their particular behavior.

Victims of aggression or those who are exploited are better off than those being conditioned by nonaversive, nonthreatening controls, says Skinner. The obvious victims are either rescued eventually by some freedom movement, or they themselves rise up and rebel. (Or else they prefer to be victims.) The ones who are really in bad shape are the "happy slaves"—people who are molded by hidden controls and don't know it; people who believe themselves to be free. In Skinner's words: "The literature of freedom has been designed to make men 'conscious' of aversive control, but in its choice of methods it has failed to rescue the happy slave."[1]

Skinner is aware that his outlook is often rejected by humanists, for whom (as was pointed out in the Overview to this chapter) the question of freedom is likely to be the most important single issue, the thing that clearly distinguishes human beings from other animals. Skinner says the desire to hold fast to this ancient and honorable abstraction "freedom" is tied in with the belief that human dignity is lost if it is shown that humanity is not nor ever can be considered free. For what happens to the great artists, writers, and philosophers if they were only products of conditioning forces? "We are not inclined to give a person credit for achievements which are in fact due to forces over which he has no control."[2]

But, argues Skinner, "dignity" has no meaning as an absolute abstraction. People do not vibrantly experience an inner something called "dignity" at the thought of being free. Like every other human condition, dignity is a very specific response to a particular kind of stimulus: It is the positive reinforcement given to one who has behaved properly or who has performed some achievement deemed notable. Dignity = praise. Dignity = recognition. Robbing people of their dignity is taking away recognition they believe is rightfully theirs.

Praise and recognition represent very positive reinforcements and, as such, are among the most pervasive of conditioning forces. Moreover, we may push Skinner's idea even further and point out that, to win praise and recognition, some people would do just about anything required of them. Many have forgiven their own lapses of artistic or intellectual integrity because the stakes were high enough. How many writers and composers have said a fond farewell to the novel in the closet or the sonata in the piano bench in exchange for fame and fortune in films or television?

Now, a case could be made for the contention that dignity is personal integrity and that those who hold fast to their dignity, in this sense of the word, are indeed free. We could cite the example of Vincent van Gogh, an artist who received during his lifetime virtually no praise or attention for any of his work, except from his brother, Theo. Far from doing everything in his power to win recognition, van Gogh continued to paint exactly as he wished. There never was any doubt in his mind concerning his mission as an artist. He wanted to move people, to touch them in a very special kind of way. He was often discouraged by his obscurity, but it is probable that he never lost faith in the way he painted. Some might say that van Gogh possessed both artistic dignity and creative freedom.

A Skinnerian might counter by pointing out that van Gogh's genius was nurtured by the very absence of recognition, the lack of positive reinforcement. Can anybody say for certain that the artist's style was not in some sense a response to critical indifference, not in some sense the result of a decision to paint as eccentrically (for his time) as possible? The "freedom" of artistic expression which some might claim for van Gogh may have been, in reality, a positive response to negative conditions. Can anybody say for certain that a critically acclaimed van Gogh would have remained the same person, felt the same emotions, and continued to express himself on canvas in the same style?

Hence Skinner's title for his most comprehensive work: *Beyond Freedom and Dignity* (1971). We need, says Skinner, to take broad terms that mean very little in themselves and redefine them in strictly behavioral language. We need to concentrate on creating what Skinner calls a "technology of behavior." Since people are going to be conditioned anyway, the focus should be on the good controls that *can* exist: "The problem is to free men, not from control, but from certain kinds of control, and it can be solved only if our analysis takes all consequences into account." [3]

Skinner is also a kind of modern utopian thinker, believing that eventually an ideal society can be designed in which people develop to the maximum of their abilities through carefully preplanned reinforcements. In such a society there would be no crime, no aggression, no exploitation. If it could ever come about, this society could well be closer to the humanist's dream than any that has yet existed. But *can it come about?*

Humanists do not question Skinner's motives, but they do show some concern for methods. A "technology of behavior" sounds too precise, too clinical for most humanists, who keep asking about the behavioral technicians, the engineers of this utopia. When these people realize how much power they have, what will stop them from using those very aversive techniques which Skinner wants to eliminate?

Then too, the humanist does not cherish the thought of giving up the "human mystery"—the haziness about creativity, genius, and human potential which keeps us from knowing too much about what we are doing. Do we wish, asks the humanist, to avoid doing those very things which lead to human milestones? After all, what if van Gogh had lived in Skinner's behaviorally engineered society? He might have filed a petition against public indifference, been given a stipend by the Minister of Culture, and perhaps never painted again. Is this what we want?

Genetics

Genetics, the science of heredity, studies the role played by innate biological factors in determining reproduction in plants, animals, and human beings. It has not yet become a branch of philosophy or psychology, but its pervasiveness in our culture indicates that theories of existence or human behavior are now almost required to consider the relationship between genetics and character, genetics and actions, genetics and the possibilities for freedom of the will.

In the social sciences there has long been a debate about heredity versus environment. This is also known as the nature/nurture dispute. Does biology condition us, or do we owe our personalities and behavioral patterns to the influence of family, peers, education, and the social structure around us? Both sides of the argument imply determinism, you will note.

Of late heredity has been receiving most of the attention. One reason is surely our increasing knowledge about the DNA molecule and the crucial role it plays *before* the fetus begins to develop inside the womb. We now understand that, when the male sperm fertilizes the female egg, a molecular binding of the two cells takes place which has been named the DNA (deoxyribonucleic acid) molecule and which contains genetic information from both parents. This information

All of us alive today are not products of laboratory precision. We are safe from attempts to induce biological and mental strengths, but are left with the "satisfaction" of having genetic weaknesses. Would we have been better off in a time of genetic engineering?

serves as a code to determine thousands of characteristics, including the color of the child's eyes and hair, the optimum height he or she will reach, the capacity for learning (if not the actual intelligence level the child will attain), perhaps even the inclination toward science or the creative arts.

No one can say for sure just how *much* of what we become is already there in the DNA molecule and to what extent other factors, including environmental influences and the exercise of one's own will, can operate to alter one's genetic destiny. Nevertheless, enough is known for genetic science to press forward in often breathtaking experiments with plant and animal life. Knowledge of how to isolate and then open the DNA molecule is increasing almost every day, as is the ability to read genetic codes, to rearrange genetic patterns, to alter the very nature of the molecule *in order to bring about a prearranged result.* The alteration process is called "genetic engineering," and it already boasts of brighter, longer-lived orchids, for example, and insects that exhibit no undesirable characteristics.

Naturally, there is fear in some quarters that genetic engineering is leading up to an eventual control over the human population. How far off is the day when the genetic coding of human offspring will be hooked up to a computer that has been told what kind of child the parents have requested? If the father's genetic contribution, for example, is deficient in a certain area, one "merely" goes to the storehouse of carefully labeled genes and selects those which will produce the child that is wanted.

Since artificial insemination and test-tube babies are already laboratory realities, the apparently logical next step is DNA interference, a prospect which has many humanists shaking their heads fearfully. Are we closer to the sort of preplanned society of which we were warned in novels like Aldous Huxley's *Brave New World* and George Orwell's *1984*?

But *without* genetic engineering, can we realistically say we are better off? If genetic factors are as powerful as they appear to be, the argument for determinism would seem to be all but won. All of us alive today are not products of laboratory precision, but rather, it seems, of molecular interaction over which we had no control and from the impact of which we may never be able to free ourselves. In other words, we are safe from attempts to induce biological and mental strengths but are left with the "satisfaction" of having genetic weaknesses.

A new social science called *sociobiology* assumes the absence of free will and studies people in terms of the behavior which genetics makes inevitable. For example, we are destined to favor family members in our dealings because of genetic ties, not out of some spiritual something we might call love. We are less likely to sell a junk car to a brother or sister than to someone outside the family circle. People fall in love to ensure genetic propagation. "I am not ready to get married" translates into "I am not prepared to make a genetic investment." Altruism is stripped of traditional humane values and becomes an extension of genetic self-interest. A mother sacrifices for her children, but only because they represent the continuing life of her own genes. She would face death to save her child, but not that of another—*except* for cases in which she identifies strongly with the mother. A soldier might die to save his battalion, but only after this has become a substitute family.

Why, asks the sociobiologist, do so many persons become depressed when they realize they are both childless and the last of their line? Why do so many childless couples seek to adopt children? Is it not that, lacking real genetic survival, people despair and are willing to settle for what they can get?

Ironically, the widespread use of birth control devices as well as the liberalization of abortion laws may be all we have left that even resembles freedom of will. Those who uphold the "right to life" would, however, argue that the achievement of freedom in this manner is itself a force which prevents a potential human being from having the most basic freedom of all: life.

POSSIBILITIES FOR FREEDOM

The literature and philosophy of determinism have always seemed to be greater in quantity and intensity than their libertarian counterparts. Is it easier to tell why we are not free than to find logical support for a belief that we are? The reader will discover that this chapter has also devoted most of its space to the determinists. One reason is that their arguments are powerful and must be reckoned with. Another is that, when the summing up is made, we shall find that much of what they say does indeed apply to many, if not all, people. The state of being a free person is perhaps not equally shared. Perhaps the art of being human includes the art of being free, and like any art, freedom needs to be very delicately and carefully fashioned and preserved.

Without assuming free will, we would not be able to venerate our great artists.

Will

The issue of freedom has much to do with the *will.* For centuries philosophers asked, "Is the will free?" More recently they have asked, "Is there such a thing as the will?" B. F. Skinner, for example, argues that the will cannot be detected, cannot be felt. We cannot say, "I have free will" with reference to a specific sensation or emotion. The will, whether free or not, may be only a word.

The unfree choice is to be either an exploiter or the one exploited by nature, a conditioner or the one conditioned by circumstance.

Arthur Schopenhauer (1788–1860), a German philosopher of the last century, was concerned with the problem of whether the will existed. After much deliberation he came to a most interesting conclusion. Stand, he said, in front of a mirror. Observe yourself. Then think that you would like to raise your left arm. Decide that you *want* to raise the arm. Then do it. There is no doubt that anyone who followed those instructions would see the left arm being raised (assuming no physical impediment, of course). The final observation is that of *the will objectified.* One instant the desire to raise the arm is locked inside the mind, the consciousness. The next instant, it is visibly present in the action perceived in the mirror.

Schopenhauer's simple experiment can be repeated in thousands of different ways, and in each case we experience the will. At this very moment the reader may decide to stand up or not, turn on the television set or not, hum a few bars of a song or not. We can experience a direct sense that what we are *not* doing is a deliberate act of omission.

When Skinner tells us we cannot feel the will, he *may* mean that most people do not bother to focus their thoughts on the will. At any given moment they cannot say whether they are doing what they have willed to do or are not doing what they have willed not to do.

Classroom students told to close their books in preparation for a surprise quiz may groan and feel at that instant like slaves or prisoners. They may feel they would rather be at the beach, at the movies, driving a car. Instead of groaning, however, they have the option of saying to themselves: "I do not will that I must take a test this morning." If the proposition sounds reasonable—that is, not absurd—they have confirmed the existence of their will. They are withholding their will. If the will were merely an illusion, they could have no rational opinion about the test. It could not be an unpleasantness, an imposition upon them, unless there were other occasions upon which they could say, also quite reasonably: "I will that I am doing this . . ."

Direct consciousness of will, such as in Schopenhauer's suggested exercise in front of a mirror, can have the effect of halting a chain of mechanical actions. That is, if we focus on the very next step, the immediate reality of the next moment—regardless of the circumstances that have brought us to this pass—the possibilities of free choice seem to be there, especially in the split-second flutter of the "afterchoice," when we cry, "Oh, but I meant to do *that!*"

Perhaps some behaviorists are not making sufficient allowance for the play of acute intelligence. Perhaps people can slow down their rate of response to a prior cause and choose not to become robots obediently following the command implicit in that cause. Another exercise is to sit down and make a list of the cause-and-effect chain that has brought you to the exercise; determine what you *probably* would do; and then coolly and calmly do something clearly not programmed. Not a bad exercise in these days of computers and video games, when the programmed response is accepted as the way of all beings, both mechanical and human!

Regret and Relief

The American philosopher William James (1842–1910) reviewed the case for pure determinism as set forth by European philosophers and concluded they were wrong. In fact, James developed a theory he pointedly called *indeterminism,* which presents the world as a random collection of chance happenings. Determinism, for James, was too coldly logical. Cause *A* leads to Effect *A.* Determinism made people seem like well-run, well-oiled machines. James said, on the contrary, people were indecisive, unpredictable, exactly the opposite of machines.

People are able to think back over a hundred choices they wish they had not made.

Regret, he added, was a universal phenomenon. At any given moment people are able to think back over a hundred choices they wish they had not made. But at the same time, regret could not be meaningfully experienced unless there existed an opposite—satisfaction—which gave regret its identity. In other words, within the random collection of happenings, people sometimes make what they consider the right move and many times make what they consider the wrong move. If everything were predetermined—that is, if the will were not free—looking backward could not reveal missed chances, roads not taken, opportunities wasted. We could not see them unless they had existed, though we may have been blind to them at the moment of choice. How often might murderers think back and realize that they did not *have* to carry a pistol for confronting their enemy? For James, hindsight was proof that genuine alternatives always exist.

If we were to extend the philosophy of indeterminism, we could say that another revealing exercise (similar to the arm in the mirror) is to sit back and think of all of the terrible things we might have done last week but refrained from doing, such as:

That we can say we have made many mistakes is an admission that we know ourselves to be free agents.

> *Having a confrontation with a friend that could have threatened the relationship.*
> *Lying about something that would have involved a whole series of other lies.*
> *Dropping a course in an impulsive moment, a course that is required for graduation.*
> *Taking a chance and driving the old car with two bald tires.*

There is yet another opposite of regret, and that is *relief.* Again it is a matter of intelligence, of focusing the attention on the vital matters. We are not aware of relief unless we survey the wrong moves that might have been made but were not.

Our lives are probably split down the middle, with good moves on one side and bad moves on the other. That we can say we have made many mistakes is an admission that we know ourselves to be free agents. That we have sometimes chosen wisely seems to back up the claim.

The Need to Challenge Determinism

One strong possibility is that we are free at close range—from the perspective of our consciousness of ourselves—and determined at long range—from the perspectives of both philosophy and science.

A college professor lecturing on the subject of freedom and its importance to humanity once observed that "freedom is something St. Augustine invented to get God off the hook." As we saw in Chapter 5, Augustine's logic led him to the inescapable conclusion that, since God is all-powerful, He must also be all-knowing. There is no way that the result of our next choice could be hidden from God until we actually make it. Thus we have to say that the option is predetermined. Does this mean we lack the freedom to choose? No, was Augustine's answer. If we deny ourselves the freedom, we also deny responsibility; consequently, we have negated the whole idea of sin—clearly against God's teaching. We must therefore conclude that God gives us the gift of free will as well as of responsibility, though we cannot rationally understand how we can be *both* free and predetermined.

Ever since Augustine, the issue of free will has been of great importance to writers and philosophers, even outside a religious context. The possession of a free will has over the centuries—for many great thinkers—been the one constant that defines humanity as something distinct from the rest of the animal kingdom. The works of Shakespeare, some of which were discussed in Chapter 3, illustrate the Renaissance passionate belief in freedom. Most of his tragic heroes die by their own hand after pronouncing judgment upon themselves. But as far back as the Greek plays, we find the human resistance to pure fatalism. Oedipus, born under a curse that dooms him, wrenches out his eyes but cries out to his children:

> *Apollo. Apollo. Dear*
> *Children, the god was Apollo.*
> *He brought my sick fate upon me.*
> *But the blinding hand was my own!*[4]

Humanism—the study of human worth as expressed in the creative arts and philosophy—has insisted on freedom as the underlying human condition for literally thousands of years. Since the present book is an addition to humanistic studies, we may assume that it contains a bias toward at least the *possibility* of free will, though, consistent with a humanistic approach, we have attempted to explore many sides of the issue.

The question is: Why insist upon the declaration that humanity in its proper, its *optimum,* state is free to weave its own destiny? The pragmatic philosopher might ask: Does free will really make that much difference? The law in our society assumes free will. Why not let the matter go at that? If one is a thoroughgoing determinist, one cannot evade a court sentence by applying the label. Outside of legal matters, does the question warrant the passionate arguments which have been advanced to "keep" humanity free?

One answer, often overlooked, is that humanism is more than a study—it is a *veneration* of human achievements. Those who develop a taste for greatness, who spend their lives with Chaucer, Shakespeare, Bach, and van Gogh, cannot remain indifferent to the artists while enjoying their art. That is, it is very difficult indeed to sit back and *deny credit* where credit seems very much due. Few would buy the argument, if advanced, that the genius of Michelangelo was "simply" the result of genetic and environmental factors, not to mention his eating habits, digestive system, and the fact that he was probably not proud of his face and physique. We still have a hard time entertaining the possibility that genius can be explained away easily, that genius can be broken down into component factors like a chemical equation. Humanism tends to preserve the mystery of humanness, if only that we may think well of ourselves. After all, without some degree of pride, what would we accomplish with our free will, just in case we really have such a thing?

One strong possibility is that we are free at close range—from the perspective of our consciousness of ourselves—and determined at long range—from the perspectives of both philosophy and science. Whether or not cause and effect explain the entire workings of the universe, as believed in the days of Newton, the pervasive presence of causality seems hard to deny. So it is entirely possible that the decision you just made—to go to bed, for example—*can* be traced all the way back to a genetic disposition toward fatigue. But when one thinks about all those people who lived before Newton developed the idea of nature as a closed, mechanical system, one would be hard put to ask: "Were they *all* deceived?" If somebody had set Shakespeare straight, Othello could have appealed his conviction in court on the grounds that he was temporarily insane and unaware of what he was doing. Somehow that might have taken some of the majesty away.

SELF-IMPOSED LIMITATIONS

It seems fitting to close this book with a theory—and it is just that—by means of which we can apply the word "free" to ourselves in some meaningful sense. First, let's narrow the focus and define freedom in a very specialized way by taking into consideration the determinist argument of causality: If every effect has a cause, there must be many effects *which are caused by oneself.* In strict determinism, one derives the impression that one is always the effect of a previous cause. But surely one can be the causer. One can derive a definite sense of being a free agent by saying: "I—and nothing else—have brought this to pass." The price of obtaining freedom in this way is limitation.

If I claim responsibility for an action, I limit the number of possible causes to one. To put the matter in reverse: I limit the number of effects my decision will have. I am late for an appointment. I am driving at night without the glasses I need to see well. Furthermore, I am driving in the rain. As my vehicle careens wildly from one side of the road to the other, I *could* think to myself, "How exhilarating. Anything might happen," or, placing a limitation on possibilities, "I am driving irresponsibly. I have no choice but to pull over and stop." Control may be where freedom starts.

I know of no more encouraging fact than the unquestionable ability of man to elevate his life by a conscious endeavor.

Thoreau

The Stoic teacher Epictetus once advised his students to sit and not eat the next time they attended a banquet. Such advice was part of Stoic training, for the Stoic philosophy is built on the idea that we can be happy, can cope with life's horrors by controlling our attitudes. An opinion about what happens is unnecessary; events cease to be either good or evil. To refrain from eating at a banquet, therefore, means that we were in control of appetite. If something so basic as appetite were within our power to manage, why not everything else? To convert hunger into an attitude and to refuse to hold the attitude—that is, to refuse to allow hunger to enter the consciousness—is true liberation.

The Stoic teachings are among the most enduring influences on the humanist's methods of achieving a clear sense of freedom. We do exactly the reverse of what we might think "freedom" entails. Instead of running about wildly doing whatever comes into the head, we willfully set up certain parameters—which include limitations—within which to operate. These, of course, are changed as the situation demands.

People who jog know all about the relationship between freedom and limits. They will tell you about a consciousness of freedom in running, pushing against the wind, and feeling their arms and legs equal to the demands made by the will, for runners, in contrast to what Skinner has said, *do* feel their will. When there is a sharp incline, runners must draw upon reserve strength. On the downward slope, runners know that power may once more be conserved. If they are running against others in a race and there is a need to win, they accelerate; if there is only the need to complete the course, they adopt a more leisurely pace.

The vivid experience of will does not happen all of a sudden. In the beginning, jogging is a distinct effort accompanied by pain and soreness. There is the inevitable shortening of breath, the pulling of muscles, the labored breathing, the tendency to overheat rapidly. In the beginning joggers stop running for the slightest excuse. After a time they set a goal: to the end of the road and then back. If they are developing into runners, the self-imposed limit is crucial. Gradually the "required" distance is lengthened. Nothing on Earth, including wind and rain, will deter most runners from completing their course. The ultimate sense of liberation—the experience of floating on a cloud that all runners know about—occurs only when and if the runner has been faithful to the limitations imposed by the inner self.

Consider a different sort of example—that of a wife and mother who is also the producer of a public service television program. The local studio has determined that, if viewership does not increase, the program may be canceled or moved to an undesirable time slot. But cheer up! The producer has lined up a world-class interview for this week's program. Her host will be talking with a Soviet chess champion who has just defected. The station manager is delirious with anticipation.

Man's actions are best understood as determined when a person *objectively* observes his own functioning or when he attempts to observe other individuals and seeks reasons for their behavior. On the other hand, belief in freedom is both necessary and possible . . . when a person *subjectively* experiences himself or empathetically experiences another person.

Bruce Shertzer and Shelly C. Stone

On the day of the telecast the woman's son is in the hospital for minor surgery. No matter. She need not be at the studio. Everything has been carefully arranged. But who promised anyone a logical universe? The unthinkable happens. The host also has to be rushed to the hospital. No one else is available to do the interview, *except the producer herself.*

Time was (and not too long ago) when the limitation of possibilities worked against freedom for the producer. Her motherly sense of duty would have required that she stay with her child, the chess champion notwithstanding. Even now, the Skinnerian psychologist would probably bet money on the woman's "inevitable" choice of her son's security instead of an interview with a stranger for the sake of her job (a job, which, by the way, she *wants* but does not *need*). No doubt many women would do the predictable thing, faced with the same conflict of options.

But it is not impossible for a human being to do the *un*predictable thing by a self-imposed limitation of will. It is not impossible for the producer to decide, for once in her life perhaps, that she will think of herself—that she will be *selfish,* if husband and son decide to give her action that label. The issue is not family morality here. The issue is freedom, for, surely, if the producer forgoes her own desire in the "higher" interest of her family, we can view her as being constrained, her decision determined perhaps by the entire history of marriage.

Now, assuming that the history of this particular marriage has been one in which the woman's wifely and motherly actions have always received what Skinner calls positive reinforcement, so that the producer has been thoroughly conditioned to perform both roles cheerfully and to give her own job lower priorities, the deliberate absence from the son's hospital room could well be called uncharacteristic by the behaviorists. Most likely she had better be wary of her husband's displeasure! But who is to say that, knowing all of this in advance, the woman may not decide to endure the negative reinforcement rather than surrender too easily?

The friend who advises, "Talk to your husband and son; make them understand" is only reinforcing the old, determined pattern. So would the producer herself should she back down at the last minute, cancel the interview, and go to the hospital, her marriage protected against crisis. Many of our actions (or omitted actions) are performed because the easy way out avoids the confrontation and guilt that can follow. One possibility of avoiding the hassle is, of course, to know that we have *freely chosen determinism.*

Yet the choice of doing what the woman *really* wants to do represents the free choice of being a free agent. It is a different kind of limitation, one that is imposed by the woman herself, not her family, not society, not tradition. To argue that few women would do such a thing—or that no woman *should*—is to make no real point about freedom. The choice we have suggested is one that could be made. There is nothing in the cosmic scheme of things to prevent it, if that is what this woman is bent on doing.

So we have another possibility: to do what one does not *have* to do may be where freedom begins. Whatever repercussions may follow the producer's decision to go with the interview, the opportunity is there for her to experience a true sense of having broken a rigid pattern of behavior. The number of people who even *want* to be free in this sense may well be limited. Not everyone likes football either. Or Bach.

Skinner is probably right, up to a point. But then, William James may also be right, up to a point. Freudian therapy may be highly accurate for some kinds of problems. We can, however, derive a measure of satisfaction from the knowledge that no one has yet been shown to have said the final word for every person on this Earth. This knowledge in itself constitutes one road to freedom.

EPILOG

The message we would like you to carry away from this book is that you, the reader, as a human being possess something the determinists cannot take from you: *the right to see many roads.* All of the art and all of the beliefs we have presented are forms created by our species, but what it all comes down to is that the universal spotlight is on you and *your* forms.

It is your birthright to reach up and mentally redo the Sistine Chapel ceiling if you don't happen to like it. It is your birthright to let go of the past, to reach into the darkness and from it pull forth a new lantern, however unfamiliar the shape, however irregular the beam of light. Not the DNA molecule, not prison doors can deny you the right if you choose to have it.

People very rarely realize the real happening in the arts comes out of the most enormous discipline, because when you've disciplined yourself thoroughly, you know what is possible. That's when you let your imagination move, because you know that by discipline and study and thought you've created the limits.

Isaac Stern

GLOSSARY

behaviorism: A school of psychology which believes that people are what they do and that what they do is determined by the way past actions have been reinforced (either positively or negatively). Philosophers who accept a deterministic view of life frequently cite behaviorism for support. Humanists are traditionally antithetical to behaviorism, arguing that one need not be conditioned entirely by external forces.

Communism: A system of social organization in which all property and businesses are publicly owned. Marx envisioned such a system as the end result of the collision between capitalism and labor, but communism in a pure form exists nowhere in the world.

determinism: The philosophy that holds that free will does not exist.

dialectic: A method of logical thought, developed by Hegel, in which one considers an idea (thesis), its opposite (antithesis), then achieves a synthesis of the two.

dialectical materialism: Marx's application of Hegel's logical method to what Marx believed were the actual facts of his-

tory; a way of interpreting history as an economic struggle between social classes, culminating in a social synthesis, or the classless society.

genetics: The science of heredity, which believes that physical traits and even more are determined by codes which nature places inside genes, infinitesimally small parts of plant, animal, and human cells. In the latest and most controversial phase of this science, experiments are being conducted by which genetic codes are altered, thus giving science potentially powerful control over reproduction.

indeterminism: A philosophy held by William James which says that free will is a real possibility, otherwise regret over choices not taken would be meaningless. Insofar as in looking back we can wish we had acted differently, we must assume the existence of freedom.

libertarian: One who adopts the view that freedom of choice is possible.

psychoanalysis: A method developed by Freud and his followers of helping patients to a rational awareness of the neurotic basis of antisocial behavior. Freud gambled on the fact that, once patients understand clearly why they behave in certain ways, once able to "talk it out," they will be liberated. Much psychoanalysis depends upon interpreting patients' dreams.

sociobiology: A relatively new science/philosophy which maintains that the preservation and reproduction of the genes form the basis of all human behavior and value systems.

übermensch (superman): In Nietzschean philosophy, the inevitable product of a human species whose intellect has developed to no avail except to create a subjective fantasy it considers reality. The übermensch is the visionary with so powerful a fantasy that he succeeds in getting others to accept it as the truth. In a negative sense, the übermensch constitutes a danger to the rest of us. In a positive sense, he represents the glory of an otherwise absurd existence.

will: A major term in philosophy, referring to the individual's inward consent that a certain event take place. The crucial argument in this chapter revolves around the issue of whether that consent is self-conceived, or whether it occurs because of a long history of causes, making it inevitable.

NOTES

1. B. F. Skinner, *Beyond Freedom and Dignity* (New York: Bantam/Vintage, 1972), p. 37.
2. Ibid., p. 41
3. Ibid., p. 39.

4. *Oedipus Rex,* trans. Dudley Fitts and Robert Fitzgerald, Copyright 1949 by Harcourt, Brace, and World Inc. Reprinted by permission of Harcourt, Brace, Jovanovich.

INDEX